Other works illustrated, annotated and formatted by
John W. Cirignani include:

My Life on the Plains

by George A. Custer

Boots and Saddles

by Elizabeth B. Custer

www.HistoryInWordsAndPictures.com

FOREWORD

The *History in Words and Pictures Series* is a collection of books written at the time the history occurred, by the people who made it. We often "learn" our history from one author's interpretation, which then becomes an interpretation of an interpretation, then morphs several more times over generations until the interpretations are accepted as fact.

I found this especially true when researching General George Armstrong Custer. I had been developing a screenplay for a major Hollywood movie producer, the topic which included Custer. After reading his own words in *My Life on the Plains*, I started to come to the conclusion Custer was not the man typically depicted in various books and movies. Further research confirmed my suspicions. The Custer stereotype is so different from the actual man that I began to wonder how this phenomenon began.

The answer is that we tend to rely on interpretations of authors who, whatever their intentions, see history through their own contemporary biased lens. What makes us rely on this material? The answer is simple; the interpretation is packaged in a format that we are used to.

The primary problem in reading historical works is the antiquated reading experience. Single paragraphs often stretch over several pages. Punctuation is different. Photographs and illustrations are rare.

Therefore, rather than rewrite history, I've reformatted the text to modern standards. I added annotated illustrations and photography, contemporary when possible, of the people and places included in the story. The result is a visual characteristic absent from most works published in the 19th century and prior. The book is then packaged into a series that will continue so long as I find interesting material.

A COMPLETE LIFE OF GENERAL GEORGE A. CUSTER is the sixth book of the series, written by Custer's official biographer, Frederick

Whittaker. Like the first five books, it encompasses the life and career of Custer. This is no accident. Custer's life spanned the lead up to the Civil War, the war itself, the occupation of Texas, the origination of the Ku Klux Klan, the Indian Wars in Kansas, westward emigration and settlement and the Indian wars in the Dakotas. His story embodies what the series is all about; reading our vibrant history through the words of those who made it!

My wish is that the *History in Words and Pictures Series* will help ignite a new interest in the past that doesn't exist among our younger generations. There is so much fascinating material, and so much to be learned from it. How it is interpreted is still up to the individual, but at least they're getting it from "the horse's mouth."

John W. Cirignani

TABLE OF CONTENTS

PRELIMINARY REMARKS	9
EARLY LIFE	11
PLEBE CUSTER	27
CADET CUSTER	37
LIEUTENANT CUSTER, SECOND CAVALRY	63
THE BATTLE OF BULL RUN	77
ORGANIZING AN ARMY	97
THE PENINSULAR CAMPAIGN	115
WINNING THE BARS	127
FROM RICHMOND TO MALVERN HILL	143
McCLELLAN'S REMOVAL	151
THE CAVALRY CORPS	169
WINNING HIS STAR	183
THE GETTYSBURG CAMPAIGN	197
AFTER GETTYSBURG	215
TO THE RAPIDAN AND BACK	227
THE WILDERNESS AND THE VALLEY	255
WINCHESTER	269
WOODSTOCK RACES	285
CEDAR CREEK	301
THE LAST RAID	309
FIVE FORKS	319
APPOMATTOX	335
THE GREAT PARADE	349
THE VOLUNTEERS IN TEXAS	357
THE REGULAR ARMY	369
THE SEVENTH CAVALRY	381
THE HANCOCK EXPEDITION	395
THE FIRST SCOUT	411
THE WAGON TRAIN	422
THE KIDDER MASSACRE	433
THE COURT MARTIAL	447
THE WINTER CAMPAIGN	465
BATTLE OF THE WASHITA	479
CLOSING OPERATIONS	509
LOUISVILLE TO THE YELLOWSTONE	529
THE BLACK HILLS	561
RAIN-IN-THE-FACE	577

SITTING BULL	593
CRAZY HORSE	603
CUSTER AND GRANT	613
THE GREAT EXPEDITION	631
THE LAST BATTLE	641
CUSTER, THE SOLDIER	679
CUSTER, THE INDIAN FIGHTER	685
CUSTER, THE MAN	695
PERSONAL RECOLLECTIONS OF GENERAL CUSTER BY LAWRENCE BARRETT, THE GREAT TRAGEDIAN CONTRIBUTED AT THE JOINT REQUEST OF MRS. CUSTER, THE AUTHOR, AND THE PUBLISHERS	699
ILLUSTRATION CREDITS	715

PRELIMINARY REMARKS

THIS book aims to give to the world the life of a great man, one of the few really great men that America has produced. Beginning at the foot of the social ladder, with no advantages beyond those physical and mental given to him by the God who made him, he rose to the top. His upward career was so rapid and phenomenal in its success as to deceive the world in general as to the means by which he rose, and none more completely for a time than the present writer of his biography.

Much of Custer's success has been attributed to good fortune, while it was really the result of a wonderful capacity for hard and energetic work, and a rapidity of intuition which is seldom found apart from military genius of the highest order. It is only after a careful and complete examination of the character of the man, and the perusal of a mass of private correspondence, beginning in his days of obscurity, after the unconscious revelation by himself of his inmost thoughts and aspirations, that the author has learned aright to appreciate the personality of the subject of this biography.

Few men had more enemies than Custer, and no man deserved them less. The world has never known half the real nobility of his life nor a tithe of the difficulties under which he struggled. It will be the author's endeavor to remedy this want of knowledge. To paint in sober earnest colors the truthful portrait of such a knight of romance as has not honored the world with his presence since the days of Bayard.

This may sound exaggerated praise to some. A few short weeks ago, it would have sounded so to the writer. He only asks the world to accept it today, as the honest conviction and sober testimony, arrived at after very thorough and careful examination of one who entered on the task with very different impressions.

The current idea on the subject, largely due to the expression set

PRELIMINARY REMARKS

afloat by Custer himself, has been embodied in the words, "Custer's Luck," but never has there been a more mistaken impression. To remove that impression, to show to the world the dead as he really was - not as an ideal hero - is the object of these pages, which seek to show the truth, the whole truth and nothing but the truth, limited only by such knowledge of facts as may be accessible at the time of writing. The author earnestly hopes his efforts may be successful.

EARLY LIFE

GEORGE ARMSTRONG CUSTER was born in New Rumley, Ohio, December 5, 1839. New Rumley is a group of houses, an old established settlement in Harrison County on the border of Pennsylvania, and peopled from thence early in the last century. It is a small place, not set down on any but very large scale maps, and most of the population of the township is scattered in farm houses about the country. The family history, gleaned from the family bible, is plain and simple. It is that of an honest group of hard workers, not ashamed of work, and it shows that the stock of which the future general came was good, such as made frontiersmen and pioneers in the last century.

Emmanuel H. Custer, father of the general, was born in Cryssoptown, Alleghany County, Maryland, December 10th, 1806. Today, a hale hearty old man of seventy, somewhat bowed but well as ever to all seeming, he stands a living instance of the strong physique and keen wits of the determined men who made the wild forests of Ohio to bloom like the rose. He was brought up as a smith and worked at his trade for many years, until he had saved enough money to buy a farm, when he became a cultivator. All he knows, he taught himself, but he gave his children the best education that could be obtained in those early days in Ohio.

When quite a young man, he left Maryland and settled in New Rumley, being the only smith for many miles. He prospered so well that he was able to get married when twenty-two years of age. He married Matilda Viers, August 7th, 1828, and their marriage lasted six years, during which time three children were born of whom only one, Brice W. Custer,

of Columbus, Ohio, is now living. He is bridge inspector on one of the railroads leading from that place. The first Mrs. Custer died July

EARLY LIFE

18th, 1834.

The maiden name of the second Mrs. Custer, mother of the general, was Maria Ward. She was born in Burgettstown, Pennsylvania, May 31st, 1807, and was first married when only a girl of sixteen to Mr. Israel R. Kirkpatrick. Her husband died in 1835, a year after the death of the first Mrs. Custer. The widow Kirkpatrick had then three children, whereof two are now alive. David Kirkpatrick lives in Wood County, Ohio, some forty miles south from Toledo. Lydia A. Kirkpatrick married Mr. David Reed of Monroe, Michigan, and in after she became more than a sister - a second mother, to the subject of our biography.

Custer's birth house in New Rumley, Ohio. Today, a bronze statue of a sword carrying Custer stands next to the outline of the long gone home.

After two years widowhood, Mrs. Kirkpatrick married Emmanuel Custer, April 14th, 1837, and became the mother of the general two years later, as the second Mrs. Custer. She is still, at the present date of writing, living, but in very feeble health. The children of this second marriage were born as follows:.

1. George Armstrong Custer, December 5, 1839
2. Nevin J. Custer, July 29, 1842
3. Thomas W. Custer, March 15, 1845
4. Boston Custer, October 31, 1848
5. Margaret Emma Custer, January 5, 1852

FREDERICK WHITTAKER

All were born in Harrison County, in or near New Rumley. Nevin and Margaret alone now survive, the latter the widow of Lieutenant Calhoun, who was killed on the field of battle with his three brothers-in-law, June 25th, 1876. Nevin Custer now lives on a farm near Monroe, Michigan. During the late war, he enlisted as a private soldier, but was thrown out for physical disability in spite of his anxiety to serve his country. He had all the spirit of the Custers, but lacked the good physique of the other members of the family.

Nevin Custer. Years after George A. Custer's death, Nevin Custer said, "I didn't intend to say it, an' I won't say much, but I'll tell yuh this, if it hadn't been for U.S. Grant, George Custer would a been alive today."

I have been thus particular in giving the family record, because little is known to the world on that subject. It is the record of a plain yeoman family, such as constitutes the bone and sinew of the country. The name of Custer was originally Kuster, and the grandfather of Emmanuel Custer came from Germany; but Emmanuel's father was born in America.

The grandfather was one of those same Hessian officers over whom the colonists wasted so many curses in the Revolutionary war, and who were yet so innocent of harm and such patient, faithful soldiers. After Burgoyne's surrender in 1778, many of the paroled

EARLY LIFE

Hessians seized the opportunity to settle in the country they came to conquer; and amongst these the grandfather of Emmanuel Custer, captivated by the bright eyes of a frontier damsel, captivated her in turn with his flaxen hair and sturdy Saxon figure, and settled down in Pennsylvania; afterwards moving to Maryland.

It is something romantic and pleasing after all, that stubborn George Guelph, in striving to conquer the colonies, should have given them the ancestor of George Custer, who was to become one of their greatest glories.

Of this family, the boy George Armstrong was born, and grew up a sturdy, flaxen-headed youngster, full of life and frolic, always in mischief and yet strange to say, of the gentlest and most lovable disposition. The closest inquiry fails to reveal a single instance of ill temper during Custer's boyhood. All his playmates speak of him as the most mischievous and frolicsome of boys, but never as quarrelsome. There is actually not a single record of a fight in all his school life, though the practical jokes are without number.

He was very early however, imbued with a passion for soldiering; how early he could not tell himself. In those days, Emmanuel Custer, like most countrymen, was in the militia, and very fond of his uniform and his little son. When "Armstrong" or "Autie," as the boy was always called, was only about four years old, a miniature military suit,[*] was made for him. Whenever father Custer went to training, Autie went with him and marched after the soldiers as well as he could, his small legs doing their best to make big strides. After drill, it was a favorite pastime of the "New Rumley Invincibles" to see little Autie go through the old Scott *Manual of Arms* with a toy musket, and thus the boy became imbued from his earliest years with the soldier spirit.

As Autie grew older, like all the Custer boys, he was sent to school - district school - where he learned in the good old fashioned way how to read, write and cipher. The winter schooling over, in the summer he worked on the farm, like all the Custer boys; ploughing, mowing, chopping wood, doing chores and developing into a strong hearty boy.

---

[*] This tiny soldier suit still exists, in the keeping of General Custer's mother.

FREDERICK WHITTAKER

It was this early farm life, the constant and vigorous exercise that he underwent, that laid the foundation of that iron constitution which he afterwards possessed, and gave him that capacity for bearing fatigue, which made him such a tremendous marcher in days to come.

He could handle an axe when he was a general officer as well as any pioneer, and has been known on more than one occasion to set to work to help the fatigue parties when clearing a way over fallen timber in the forests of Virginia and the coppices that fringe the Black Hills.

When Armstrong was about ten years old, an event happened in the family which changed the current of his life to an extent which no one at the time expected would happen. His half-sister Lydia was married to Mr. Reed, a young man who came from Monroe, Michigan, and after her marriage departed to live at Monroe. Now, in those days Monroe was a long way off from New Rumley. There were very few railroads in the United States, and none between the two towns. The state of Michigan was then sparsely settled. The act admitting it into the Union was only passed the year in which young Custer was born.

The site of Lansing, the present capital of the state, was in 1846, only a few years before Mrs. Reed's marriage, occupied by a single log cabin, and the population of the state was not quite four hundred thousand people. The only old settled places were Detroit and Monroe. The former dated from the days of the fur posts before the Revolution, and it was very near Monroe (then called Frenchtown) that the massacre of 1813, known as the battle of Raisin River, took place, in which the British General Proctor and Tecumseh with his Indians annihilated eight hundred mounted riflemen of Kentucky.

Mrs. Reed felt that she was going away among strangers, with none of her own kin near her, and she begged that Armstrong might go with her to her new home. The boy, like all boys, was only too glad to see new scenes, and went to Monroe with his sister and her husband, remaining there for two years. Newly settled as was the state of Michigan in those days, it was already becoming noted for its excellent educational advantages, which have since expanded into one of the best school systems in the Union. When young Custer went there, he was at once put to school in Stebbins Academy, where he remained until about

EARLY LIFE

twelve years old.

Of those early days, the records and reminiscences are many and amusing, and we shall quote a few of them. Custer's chum at school, the boy who sat at the same desk with him, was named Bulkley, and the friendship that then began has since continued through life. In the case of Mr. Bulkley, who still lives in Monroe, it survives in the form of an ardent love and appreciation of his quondam desk mate.

Many years after, when the old Stebbins Academy was broken up and the property sold at auction, Mr. Bulkley found the same old desk at which he and Custer used to sit, with their names carved on it in school boy fashion. He bought it in, and it now stands in his store, the receptacle of the various papers connected with the "Custer Monument Fund Society" of which Bulkley is the Secretary, General Sheridan being President. How little those two boys thought, a quarter of a century ago, what would be the ultimate fate of that old desk as they furtively whittled away at its corners.

Young Custer was a smart lad with very quick appreciation, a remarkably rapid student, but one who hated study. He seldom or never looked at a lesson out of school, trusting to the short period before recitation to skim over his task, and yet rarely failing to have a creditable lesson. He was always smuggling novels into school and reading them furtively, and his old comrade cannot help, even at this late date, a chuckle of lawless satisfaction as he recalls the way in which he and Custer used to cheat the old schoolmaster in "geography hour."

Custer used to have his geography wide open, while beneath it lay "*Charles O'Malley*," also wide open. With a pencil in his hand, he would be earnestly tracing the course of a river on the map when old Stebbins came round behind him, it being the habit of that worthy man to wear list slippers and to be on the watch at all times for surreptitious amusements among the boys. Sly as he was however, Custer was slyer. His senses were as sharp as those of an Indian even then, and Stebbins never found him otherwise than busy and studying intently, to the worthy pedagogue's great satisfaction.

As he passed, he would pat the boy's head and pronounce him a credit to the school, a compliment received by the youngster with an edifying air of virtuous humility. No sooner was Stebbins gone however, than the end of the geography was lifted while Armstrong returned to the perusal of the humors of Mr. Michael Free and the gallant charges of the Fourteenth Light Dragoons with renewed zest.

His passion was reading military novels, his chief ambition to be a soldier. Even then, he had made up his mind to go to West Point when he got old enough. One thing that tended to inflame his martial spirit in those days was the Mexican War, just then closed. The heroes of that war were almost all West Pointers, and the little regular army made a very considerable figure therein. However that may be, he had formed the firm resolve to go to West Point when old enough.

Out of school, he was always in the midst of rough horseplay with the other boys, fond of practical jokes, a great wrestler and runner, and the strongest lad of his age in the place. He became an acknowledged leader in all the athletic sports of the day, the only thing in which he did not excel being swimming. Curiously enough, he never liked the water much, to the day of his death, and though he could swim, seldom did so. Boating was also one of his dislikes. He would do anything on land, but had no aspirations as a sailor.

At home, he was chiefly distinguished, according to the account of Mrs. Reed, by his extreme gentleness and kindness of heart. To her, he was the most docile of boys, obeying her slightest wish the moment it was expressed. He was exceedingly tender hearted also; so much so that he never could bear even to see a chicken killed; and the sight of suffering of any kind completely unnerved him. He was very fond of nursing Mrs. Reed's children as they successively arrived, and was especially proud of her first boy who - was named Armstrong, after himself. Poor little Autie Reed; he died on the same field with Custer, together with Custer's youngest brother, on that last fated expedition.

A strange compound of qualities was this lad in those days, gentle and brave, with an overflowing sense of humor, hating his books, and yet working to the head of his class by fits and starts when he took a notion, obstinate under harsh treatment, opposing the constituted authorities at school with all ingenious evasions, meeting the wily tricks of his pedagogue with tricks still wilier, but ruled by his gentle sister

EARLY LIFE

with an absolute sway. He reminds us of one of Thackeray's schoolboys, full of vague poetical yearnings, tempered by the savage freedom of overflowing physical strength and health, a boy all over, a boy to the backbone, with the promise and potency of…"Who knows what?" of manhood.

The ruling traits of his character, as they struck his family, were those of great goodness, of duty performed, of kindness, love and devotion. To this day, they seem to think of him not as the brilliant warrior, but as the exemplary son and brother who never omitted a duty, never abated in his love. Inside of all the rough play of the champion wrestler of the school lay this hidden kernel of surpassing gentleness and love that was to snake the foundation of the future knight. And yet he was a plain American boy who knew little or nothing of mediaeval lore, and less of European History, as was the necessary consequence of the habitual American education. He was then, and remained to the last, a thorough American, a Western boy at that.

After spending two years at Stebbins Academy, he returned to New Rumley and passed some time there on his father's farm. When about fourteen, he was again sent to Monroe, this time to the "Seminary," the principal school of that place, then and now kept by the Reverend Mr. Boyd. The Seminary is a fine old brick mansion, large and irregular, stretching out its wings in the midst of shady grounds, a pleasant and picturesque home. Here, Custer finished his education in the English branches, remaining there two years. It was a far better school than the old Academy, Mr. Boyd being a man of much greater refinement and taste than was then common in the west, and young Custer worked under him to more advantage. He left school at the age of sixteen and went back to New Rumley.

It was however, while at the Seminary, that a little incident occurred which subsequently influenced his whole life, as Mrs. Reed's marriage had done when he was a child. The incident is so small and trifling that it seems nothing, and yet on such trifles hang human lives. Coming from school one day to Mrs. Reed's, the rough, flaxen-headed, freckled-faced boy was pertly accosted by a little girl with black eyes.

FREDERICK WHITTAKER

She was a pretty little creature, rounded and plump, her father's pet, an only child and naturally spoiled. Like most little children, she was proud to show all she knew, and she knew that Custer was a stranger. She said archly as she swung on the gate, her pretty face dimpling with smiles, "Hello, you Custer boy!" then frightened at her own temerity, turned and fled into the house.

Young Ladies' Seminary of Monroe, at Monroe, Michigan

A trifle, you will say, not worth recording; yet it was the beginning of Custer's first and last love. The sweet arch face of that little girl was the first revelation to the wild young savage whose whole idea of life was that of physical exercise, war, and the chase of something else, of another side to life. It was to him love at first sight, and he then and there recorded an inward vow, that some day that little girl should be his wife. He kept the vow through many obstacles.

This little girl was Libbie Bacon, only child of Judge Daniel S. Bacon, one of the oldest settlers of Monroe. The Judge had come there long before Emmanuel Custer's first marriage, and fifteen years before Armstrong was born. Beginning as a school teacher, he had become a lawyer, a member of the Territorial Legislature before Michigan was yet erected into a state, Judge of Probate, President of the Monroe Bank,

EARLY LIFE

director of the first Michigan Railroad; in short he was one of the first men of the little town, and the centre of its "upper ten." To young Custer, poor and obscure, it might have then seemed as if a great gulf divided him from the little girl whose arch beauty flashed on him for the first time. It was characteristic of the determination which afterwards marked his whole career that he should make such a vow and keep it. To this, we shall afterwards return.

Custer had now lived at Monroe, off and on, for four years. His return to Ohio must have seemed to him an exile, for he ever after seems to have looked on Monroe as his home. He went back to New Rumley, and soon after obtained a place as teacher at Hopedale, Ohio, not far from his native place. Here, he earned his first money - not much - to our notions now, but a little fortune to him in those days. Twenty-six dollars a month and his board were the terms, and he brought the whole of his first month's salary and poured it into his mother's lap.

Hopedale Normal College, Hopedale, Ohio. George Armstrong Custer graduated and earned his teacher's certificate here.

In after years, he often referred to the joy he then experienced as being the greatest he had ever known, as being his first opportunity to repay in a measure the love of his parents, for whom he ever cherished the fondest affection. That affection was well deserved. Hitherto, we have spoken but little of Custer's father and mother, but when we reflect on the fact that out of the savings of a small farm, and burdened with the support of a large family, they had managed to pay for the best education then to be found in the Western country for their eldest son, we can understand much of the spring of that son's energy and goodness of character.

Long years after, when Custer was distinguished among men, an eminent warrior, courted and petted by all, he wrote his father and mother a letter, which is worthy of being printed in letters of gold. It shows what parents and what a son combined to make the perfect knight that Custer became. We quote but a fragment, in answer to one of their letters, in which the modest parents have disclaimed any merit of their own in the success of their brilliant son. Custer writes:

> You do yourself injustice when you say you did but little for me. You may forget it, but I never can. There is not a day but I think with deep gratitude of the many sacrifices, the love and devotion you and mother have constantly bestowed upon me. You could not have done more for me than you have. A fortune would be nothing to me with what I am indebted to you for. I never wanted for anything necessary, and if you did not give me a fortune in money, you did what was infinitely better. You and mother instilled into my mind correct principles of industry, honesty, self-reliance; I was taught the distinction between wrong and right; I was taught the value of temperate habits; and I now look back to my childhood and the days spent under the home roof as a period of the purest happiness; and I feel thankful for such noble parents.
>
> I know but few if any boys are so blessed as I have been by having such kind, self-sacrificing parents to train and guide them as I have had. I know I might heap millions of dollars at your feet, and still the debt of gratitude on my part would be undiminished.

All honor to parents and son. In that letter lies much of the secret of Custer's success. At Hopedale, young Custer remained for a year, teaching; but he was not the man to stagnate into a pedagogue. Teaching was to him, as to many another men in the United States, a mere stepping-stone to better things, a temporary means of support. He had determined to go to West Point; the question remained, how was he to get there? Father Custer was a staunch old Jacksonian

EARLY LIFE

Democrat, double-dyed and twisted in the wool; the member for the district was an equally staunch Republican. It was now the year 1856, the time when Fremonters began to be enthusiastic and aggressive, when the burden of the campaign songs was "Free speech, free press, free soil, free men, Fremont and Victory!"

The member for the district was an enthusiastic Republican; what chance was there that he would use his influence to advance the son of an equally enthusiastic Democrat? So Emmanuel Custer thought when his son pressed him to try and get Mr. Bingham to nominate him to West Point. He said frankly that it was no use trying, that the young fellow might try if he wished, but he could not help him. He had no influence, and none but humble friends.

But Armstrong would not give up. He would try for himself, and trust to his own efforts alone. He had one advantage; habits of study and facility in using his knowledge. Teaching had given him that, as it has many others. No way to master a science so good as to undertake to teach it. One must know it then. So he sat down and wrote the following letter:

HOPEDALE, OHIO, MAY 27th, 1856
TO THE HONORABLE JOHN A. BINGHAM

SIR: Wishing to learn something in relation to the matter of appointment of cadets to the West Point Military Academy, I have taken the liberty of addressing you on the subject. My only apology for thus intruding on your notice is that I cannot obtain such information here. And as the matter is to be finally settled in Washington, I have thought better to make application at headquarters from the beginning. If in the multiplicity of your duties, which I know you must have on hand, you can find time to inform me as to the necessary qualifications for admission, and if our congressional district is unrepresented there or not, or at least when there will be a vacancy, you will confer a great favor on me.

I am desirous of going to West Point, and I think my age and tastes would be in accordance with its requirements. But I must forbear on that point for the present. I am now in attendance at the McNeely Normal School in Hopedale, and could obtain from the principal, if necessary, testimonials of moral character. I would also say that I have the consent of my parents in the course which I have in view.

FREDERICK WHITTAKER

>Wishing to hear from you as soon as convenient,
>I remain,
>Yours respectfully,
>
>>G. A. CUSTER

It will be seen from this letter that Custer had at the time ceased teaching for awhile to further perfect his education. The handwriting is very strongly contrasted with that of his later years, which is rather light and pointed, resembling a lady's hand in many respects. In the Bingham letter, it is that of a particularly careful schoolboy of the old time, with down-strokes of portentous weight and blackness, with fine hair lines for upstrokes. The letter brought forth a reply from Bingham, in which the requisite information was given, and it appeared that others were after the place. In answer to this, Custer wrote again. He would not be denied, if persistency would effect his purpose. There was another young man after the place, but he wrote as follows:

>MCNEELY NORMAL SCHOOL, Thursday, June 11, 1856
>HONORABLE JOHN A. BINGHAM
>
>DEAR SIR: Yours of the fourth was duly received and I feel myself compelled to write again to express my sincere thanks for your prompt attention, explicit information as to qualifications, etc. I will also add that in all the points specified, I would come under the requirements set forth in your communication, being about seventeen years of age, above the medium height and of remarkably strong constitution and vigorous frame. If that young man from Jefferson County of whom you spoke does not push the matter, or if you bear of any other vacancy, I should be glad to hear from you.
>>Yours with great respect,
>>
>>>G. A. CUSTER

Nothing came of it that year, however. The young man from Jefferson County got the place, but there was still time during the next year. That summer, Mr. Bingham came home at the close of the session of Congress, and young Custer went to see him. The result of the interview was that Bingham, pleased with the frank face of the boy, his modest determination and something in his looks that told that he

EARLY LIFE

would yet be a credit to his nominator, promised that he would give him the next year's vacancy, and Custer went home happy.

The rest of the year 1856 was passed by him partly at the Normal School, partly teaching, partly on his father's farm. At last came the eventful day when he received his commission and was ordered to report at West Point. The die was cast. He had longed to be a soldier. From henceforth to the day of his death, he was a soldier to the core.

Congressman John A. Bingham was the principal framer of the 14th Amendment to the United States Constitution which guaranteed to African Americans citizenship and all its privileges. Over the next century and a half, the 14th Amendment has vastly expanded civil rights protections.

This period of Custer's life may be regarded as that of his first awakening to the consciousness of his own powers and of the deficiencies of his early education. One evidence of this is the fact of his attendance at the Normal School and his selection of teaching for an occupation. He had already received more than enough education to fit him for such a life as his father or any of his relatives led, and the fact of his voluntarily entering the Normal School to avail himself of its further advantages shows that he was already looking forward to a change in his prospects before he applied to Mr. Bingham.

The latter had told him of all the difficulties besetting an applicant for a cadetship, and especially of the preliminary examination, and Custer occupied all the rest of the year in fitting himself therefore. The result was that, when he went to West Point, he had already mastered as much mathematics as any one of the one year cadets, and was so far ahead of his class that he found all his subsequent studies as easy as he had his earlier labors at Stebbins' Academy. Of the other troubles of a cadet, lessons apart, he was now to gain his first experience. He found his troubles there, much the same as at school, in the irksomeness of discipline, not the severity of study. Such as he was, a headlong, impulsive, generous lad, full of life and spirits he entered West Point. Would there were hundreds more today there, like him.

PLEBE CUSTER

A TALL, slender lad of seventeen with frank, handsome face and fair hair landed on the wharf at West Point in the summer of 1857. A certain free, careless air told of the Western man, so different in his surroundings, and bearing from the town-bred citizen of the East. It was our young hero, fresh from the independent merry life of the West, and plunged all alone into the peculiar life of West Point; a Plebe, with all his sorrows to come.

A great change for the careless young fellow, overflowing with the fun and frolic that comes of magnificent physical organization and keen intellect. There is something in the atmosphere of Western life that seems to rebel against rules and restrictions and everything narrow. It goes straight to its purpose, whatever it be by direct common sense methods, original in their simplicity, but appears awkward and rough when contrasted with Eastern polish.

With all his differences of race and education, coming from the most perfectly Republican part of the Union, young Custer was dropped into the midst of one of the most absolute despotisms on earth; the Military Academy at West Point. What the change is for a young fellow fresh from home life, and especially from country home life, it is difficult to picture without a knowledge of that curious microcosm, the "Point."

There is something in the Military Academy so totally different from the usual life of America, that it has fixed a great gulf between West Pointers and the outside world, none the less real because impalpable. It shows itself in the reception accorded to the "Plebe" when he first enters the Academy, so different from that accorded to a freshman at college, the nearest person to a Plebe in condition. The poor Plebe comes from the world of freedom and enters another world,

PLEBE CUSTER

where implicit obedience is the unflinching rule. Instantly, everyone seems to set on him to make his life miserable.

From time immemorial, it seems to have been the tradition at the Academy that every new-comer should be made to suffer all the discomforts possible during his first months, without a possibility of escape. His ordinary treatment has been embalmed in some very truthful, though undeniably doggerel verses, in the "*West Point Scrap Book*," entitled "*West Point Life*." The composition from which they are taken was written for the Dialectic Society of West Point in 1859, and therefore may be said to portray very accurately the state of society at the Point when Custer was a cadet. The minstrel, describing the Plebe, breaks out:

> When landed at the Point, you ask a man where you report,
>   And ten to one you get from him a withering retort.
>   He'll say, "Subordination, Plebe's, of discipline the root;
>   When you address an old Cadet, forget not to salute."
> He sends you to a room and says, "Report and then come back."
>   You enter and discover there only the old boot-black.
>   You wander like Telemachus; at last you find the place
> And see the dread INSTRUCTOR yes, and meet him face to face.
> He shouts out, "Stand attention, sir! Hands close upon your pants,
>   And stand erect. Hold up your head! There-steady I don't advance;
>   Turn out your toes still further, look straight toward the front,
> Draw in your chin! Throw out your chest! Now steady! Don't you grunt."
> Says the Instructor, "Where's my pen? This old one doesn't suit me."
> "There it is, sir." "You hold your tongue! How dare you talk on duty?
>   I'm not surprised to see you quail and flutter like a partridge,
>   But soldiers' months must only open when they tear a cartridge."
> He wants to know all things you've brought, your clothes of every kind;
>   (You think the gentleman's endowed with an enquiring mind)
>   You get a broom, some matches, and a bed made up of patches,
> Though little do you think such schools could ever have their matches.
>   A comforter you also get, a thing that most you need,
>   A comforter! It's one of Job's, a sorry one indeed!
>
> "On your return, report yourself," they earnestly exhort you.
>   Report yourself!!! When twenty men are eager to report you!
>   You're now assigned to quarters - there deposit bed and broom,

FREDERICK WHITTAKER

And though in want of shelter, wish for you there was no room.
Are these the luxuries on which our Senators agree?
You do not fancy this "hot-bed of aristocracy."
The drill drum beats, so does your heart, and down the stairs you scud,
You slip before you reach the ranks, fall full length in the mud;
How strange you think it when next night reported you have been,
In spite of all your efforts, for neglecting to "fall in."

When reading in your room, absorbed in prison discipline,
You suddenly hear someone knock; jump up, and cry "Come in!"
You find the dread INSTRUCTOR already in the door,
He says "Did you give that command to your SUPERIOR?"
You ask to be forgiven, say you'll never do't no more,
You didn't yet know all the rules and articles of war.
Next day they march you into camp. How pretty it does look!
That you may fare the better, you have brought a cookery book.
You get in camp, an old cadet cries, "Come put up this tent."
And with the aid he renders you, you're very well content.
You thank him, take possession; when you find that all is done,
He coolly tells you "Plebe, that's mine; go, get another one.
What you have done is only play; Plebes always make mistakes."
Foul play you think it is, when you have put down all the stakes,
You possibly are six feet high; some officer you dread
Arrests you at the break of day, for lying long in bed.

July the Fourth at last arrives; you think it rather hard,
When on this day of liberty, the Plebes must go on guard.
You go on post, the night arrives, you scarcely are alive,
But still a lonely watch you keep, way down on "No. 5"
At first you like the lonely post, the path's so nicely leveled,
But soon you share the fate of ham - that is, you're nicely "devilled"
Bodies vast of men approach, and sound their rude alarms-
From divers punches you receive, you find they all have arms -
Baggage wagons, ropes, and ghosts, upon your post appear -
Teeth begin to chatter - though, of course, it's not through fear,
A spirit white you seize upon, and hold it on your post,
Until the corporal arrives, when you give up the ghost.
When in a wheel-barrow you fall, that's moving up behind,
To rapidly desert your post, you're forcibly inclined.
Then you swear that you'll resign, the climate is too damp,
But once within the tented field, you find you can't decamp.
Resolving then to be content, there's no more hesitation,

PLEBE CUSTER

You find more satisfaction in this kind of resignation.
Spartan like, you stay until encampment has an end,
And when that time is closing up, your times begin to mend.

The woes of the poor Plebe on first joining, as recited in the above pathetic ballad, are by no means over-strained. An old graduate says of the new comers very feelingly;

"We cannot but feel an involuntary pity for the new cadet who is just landing at the old wharf, where a sentinel is waiting to conduct him to the adjutant's office, there to record his entrance on - he knows not what small and great tribulations. The poor fellow has just left the endearments of home, and by a rapid transition has become a stranger among the mighty hills. But worst of all, instead of receiving kindly hospitality, he becomes, for a time, one of an inferior caste toward whom, too often, the finger of derision is pointed, and over whom the Fourth Class drill master flourishes, with too snobbish zeal, his new-born authority. Then too, to be called a "conditional thing," a "thing" and a "plebe" in slow promotion; to be crowded five in a room, with the floor and a blanket for a bed; to be drummed up, drummed to meals, and drummed to bed, all with arithmetic for chief diversion; this is indeed a severe ordeal for a young man who is not blessed with good nature and good sense; but with these excellent endowments, it soon and smoothly glides on into a harmless memory.

People are found who contend that West Point is a hotbed of aristocracy, where caste and titles rule. It would be pleasing to exhibit to such and one, the un-uniformed new class, presenting a line of about one hundred young men of all types, at least in externals. Side by side are seen the flabby Kentucky jeans, and the substantial homespun, the ancient long-tailed, high-collared coat of the farmer's boy, and the exquisite fit of the fashionable New York tailor. We have known two presidents' sons, two protégés of General Jackson, several sons of secretaries, and other high functionaries, found deficient for the simple reason that they were deficient. Before us lies a little volume, by a Vermont farmer's son, who successfully competed for the headship of his class, with a talented son of Henry Clay."

FREDERICK WHITTAKER

Into the midst of West Point dropped young Custer. As far as temperament went, he was just the one to get on among his comrades and be happy; and we find accordingly that he was soon a general favorite. The hardships of Plebe life passed over him lightly. He had the advantage of being a tall, strong young fellow, not easily browbeaten or physically oppressed, and his good nature and jolly ways saved him from the more annoying kinds of small persecution.

West Point South Wharf. General George Washington personally selected Thaddeus Kosciuszko, one of the heroes of Saratoga, to design the fortifications for West Point in 1778. Washington transferred his headquarters to West Point in 1779. It is the oldest continuously occupied military post in America.

The first week's squad drills and the preliminary examination being safely passed, young George Custer at last received his full appointment, was permitted to don the uniform, and became a full-fledged cadet. The happy day arrived when he, with the other Plebes, shed the badges of their servitude, and all the black coats vanished from the cadet battalion. Then, at the close of June, the barracks were abandoned and Cadet Custer, along with his comrades, marched out for the annual encampment.

West Point Barracks. The garrison at West Point originally centered around Fort Clinton and the defenses built upon Constitution Island. Many of the Revolutionary War fortifications still stand on the more remote landscapes of the academy grounds. Some are fully restored while others have been partially restored.

This takes place every year at the same time after graduation. The first class of 1857 was examined and graduated while the Plebes were joining, the second class became the first, the fourth became the third and went on furlough for the summer; and the "June Plebes" blossomed out into the fourth class. Then, at dress parade, the order was read out to go into camp, the barracks being vacated. The young cadets turned into May-Day car men, without any carts. Not even a wheel-barrow was to be obtained. Mattresses, tables, chairs, trunks, every article had to be cleared out, the furniture placed in the empty recitation rooms, leaving only iron bedsteads in the dormitories, which were to be thoroughly cleaned by the workmen. The camp ground on the northeast of the plain was laid out and the tents all pitched before breakfast; then at the exact hour indicated in the order, the companies formed on the parade ground and marched out to the camp with band playing.

The cadets at West Point are divided into four companies. During the June examinations, the Plebes, being an additional class, had been of course stinted for space in the barracks, but in camp there was plenty of room. There were eight rows of tents, two opening on each street, company officers in a row at the end of the streets of their companies, commandant's marquee opposite the centre of the camp, which was the same as that of a small battalion of infantry. The guard tents, six in number, were at the other end of the streets, and there were six sentries on duty round the camp. Each walked his beat two hours, being then relieved for four hours, after which he went on again, his tour of duty being six hours out of twenty-four, the guard having three "reliefs," or eighteen cadets, besides a corporal to each relief, a sergeant, and an officer of the guard.

During the encampment, the duties of the cadets were wholly military. It was a relief from the long course of hard mathematical studies which they had pursued when in barracks, served to maintain their health, and especially to accustom them to the daily routine of soldier's life. During the time the camp lasted, from the end of June to the end of August, the drills were constant and un-intermitting, in infantry evolutions, with artillery drill for the upper classes.

The result was a most wonderful perfection of mechanical movement from which even the newly joined Plebes were not exempt, the nearest approach to which is today seen in the street parades and drills, on grand occasions, of the celebrated New York Seventh Regiment when put on its mettle. During the summer encampment, the vicinity of West Point is always crowded with visitors, and as the members of the upper classes are allowed considerable liberty at this time, it becomes to them a season of comparative enjoyment.

At last came the close of August. The barracks were awaiting their occupants, and the time of serious work for the Fourth Class had come. On the 29th, the cadets carried off their blankets and clothing to the rooms soon to be occupied for the fall, leaving in camp only their muskets and full dress uniforms. The order for breaking camp had been read on dress parade the previous evening, and at the fixed hour the drums were heard beating "the general," the signal to pack up and be off.

Then came one of the most imposing sights in military life; and one which always impresses the civilian spectator with a certain feeling of desolation when it is over. Before us stands the populous little town, that for two months has been the scene of such picturesque activity, with all the "pride, pomp and circumstance of glorious war." The cadets fly to their tents at the beating of the "general" and await three taps of the drum amid breathless silence. "Tap!" comes the first, and the whole camp is alive in a moment, the men flinging themselves on the stakes, which are pulled up, leaving the tents supported only by the four corners. Then comes another breathless hush, every one waiting. "Tap!" comes the second signal and up come the corner pegs, while the canvas is swept into the centre and a man stands at each pole, all the tents still up and hiding the view. Another hush and then, "Tap!"

In a moment, ere the sound has time to die away, down goes every tent with a single clap, and the lately populous town has vanished, leaving behind it nothing but a bare plain while the men, like a swarm of bees, fling themselves on the prostrate tents, withdraw the poles and roll up the canvas in long rolls which are piled in heaps for the quartermaster's people to take away. Then comes the "Assembly," and the companies take their stacked arms, while the battalion is formed and marched to the barracks.

Cadet Custer had seen his first camp, and it was over. This West Point camp is one of the very best features of academic life. It serves as a wholesome relaxation to the cadets, who are necessarily working at books all the rest of the year; and it tends to remind them of what they might otherwise easily forget; that they are soldiers, not schoolboys.

The influence of academic life at other times on both officers and students is very injurious to breadth of mind. To the officers, it is indescribably narrowing. They generally become, after a long residence at the "Point," more like school masters than soldiers; fond of espionage, with sympathies and tastes confined to the small circle of a classroom, as contracted in their views of life as so many school teachers, besides being strongly inclined to petty tyranny. The camp comes to remind them that there is a whole world outside of West Point, and that the end of the academic course is to make officers, not pedants.

To the incoming cadets, it serves as a good introduction to what follows and gives them courage to attack their winter studies, which commence as soon as the encampment is over. So it was now with Cadet Custer. His work was beginning.

CADET CUSTER

THE Fourth Class, to which Cadet Custer belonged, was now safely ensconced in the barracks, and entering on the unvarying routine of cadet life. What that routine is, has become pictured by more than one old graduate in that same storehouse of information from which we have already quoted, and it will serve, in addition to the personal reminiscences of his classmates, to complete the picture of Cadet Custer's life at West Point.

Let us commence at early dawn, when the faint grey light first steals over the heavens. The rounded tops of the encircling mountains are cut clearly against the bright sky, old Cro'nest brooding protectingly over the little settlement. The sentry by the gate looks northward over the plain and hears through the silence the distant thunder of paddies, as the Albany night boat comes sweeping down the river on her way to the city below. There is a gay twittering of birds, growing louder and louder, from the woods that clothe the mountains from base to summit.

The river in the distance gleams white in the dawn and the lights of the steamer, not yet extinguished, glide slowly along. The edge of the plateau cuts the view; and it would hardly seem possible that the same river sweeps almost beneath our feet, black and glistening in little eddies, surrounded by the bold Highlands that form the bay at West Point. Nestled at the foot of those Highlands, on the opposite side of the river, are the white cottages of Cold Spring, and the distant murmur of Buttermilk Falls can be heard through the stillness.

Now, the faint white light of dawn grows stronger, and a crimson flush is on the east, while the little floating clouds overhead are speckled with gold and rose color. Louder grows the sweet clamor of the birds in the early morning, and the barking of dogs from the village below announces the increasing stir of life. Anon the crimson flushes into

CADET CUSTER

scarlet, the scarlet flames into gold, and a bright shaft of light bathes the top of old Cro'nest and comes creeping down the mountain side.

Boom!!!

A bright flash and a volume of snow white smoke, as the morning gun awakens the echoes. The smoke goes drifting away on the breeze towards the water, and the sharp boom of the gun reverberates from hill to hill all around the bay, ending in a dull grumble far up the river. Simultaneously, the long roll of the drum-corps, mingled with the sweet notes of the fifes, softened by the distance into a strain of perfect sweetness, comes gaily out on the morning air as the drummers beat the long reveille.

Cadet Custer and his roommate are sleeping the sound sleep of the tired plebe, in their little room in the North Barrack, when the loud boom of the gun comes through the open window. Up they spring, for the two months of camp life have already inured both to the soldier's habit of coming broad awake in a moment. No rubbing of eyes, stretching or yawning. Outside, the reveille is beating and the fifes are piping sweetly forth the first tune of the three that constitute the morning call. Each tune lasts about two minutes, and at the end of six minutes, every cadet knows that the orderly sergeant will be standing on the company parade ground, book in hand, ready to call the roll.

Into their clothes as hastily as possible, little time for toilet comforts, and down the barrack staircase scud Custer and Parker. As the rollicking notes of the last quickstep are in full progress, they dart to their places, and a moment later reveille ceases. There are the four companies, each on its own ground, the stiff orderly sergeant in front, book in hand, the cadet captain behind him, while the officer of the day, arms folded, solemnly surveys the scene from his distant post. The cadets are standing at "parade rest," the weight resting on the right leg, hands crossed in front. Hardly has the last strain of the fife, the final roll of the drum died away, when we hear the sharp voices of the First Class men, who act as sergeants, all together, "Attention, company!"

In an instant, every cadet has stiffened into a statue, in "position of a soldier," eyes staring straight to the front with that vacant glare which marks the modern soldier in ranks. Out come the books and each sergeant rattles off the names of his men in alphabetical order; having the list by heart.He knows every voice in his company, and is as sharp as a needle. Not a late man can slink into his place but the sergeant notices him and checks a mark against him in that inexorable roll-book.

If a head turns, or a whisper mars the perfect stillness, the sergeant can pick out the guilty one in a moment; even the shelter of the rear rank is no protection for the offender, for the Second and Third Class sergeants and corporals are ready to report him, in terror lest that lynx-eyed sergeant should report them for neglect of duty.

The roll call is rattled off in a minute and a half, and the sergeant faces around, stiff as a stake, salutes and says to the captain, "Sir, all are present or accounted for," or "Sir, so many absent." The young captain touches his hat and proceeds forthwith to the cadet adjutant, where the same formality of report takes place for each company, the adjutant standing book in hand to receive the reports. Finally, the adjutant in his turn proceeds to the officer of the day and reports the result of the whole battalion roll call to that mighty official whose place it is to report the absentees at the end of his tour of duty.

The sergeants then warn the cadets detailed for guard on that day and ranks are broken. Now Cadets Custer and Parker are to be seen hastening to their little barrack room, having time to wash and comb and clean up their room. Reveille during summer is at five, and by half past five, every room must be in perfect order for the captain and lieutenants of each company come around for morning inspection.

From this time until seven o'clock, the two cadets are hard at work at their books, studying for the morning recitations. At half past six, they can hear the drummers beating the "sick call," when all the sick, lame and lazy troop to the surgeon to be excused from duty or dosed as the case may be. Custer and Parker are healthy young fellows and the life of "The Point" leaves little excuse for sickness. Besides, both are yet Plebes, and have not learned so thoroughly as they will someday, how to play "old soldier."

Very amusing stories are told of the efforts of older cadets to appear terribly sick all of a sudden, when the day's lessons promise to be uncommonly hard. The Academy surgeon is no exception to army medical officers in time of peace; half of his time is wasted in detecting fraudulent cases of sickness feigned to evade duty. One very ingenious trick by which a surgeon was completely deceived was once played by a cadet who was out all night, and whose pulse was consequently feverish and irregular. He put a piece of chalk in his mouth which he chewed, and when his turn came to go to the doctor, complained of having a sunstroke. The pulse indicated not much the matter, and the doctor was about to put him off with a dose, when his forlorn aspect induced the functionary to ask to see his tongue. Its white and furry aspect alarmed the doctor, who pronounced it a clear case of high fever, and Cadet Foxey was excused from duty.

These and similar mean tricks were entirely uncongenial to the frank nature of Custer. His pranks at the Academy were those of a high-spirited boy anxious to escape from restraint, but he was always ready to take the consequences. The sick call this morning passes away, and he and Parker are hard at work on geometry and algebra, tactics and French, fortification and gunnery, until the welcome notes of *"Peas upon the Trencher"* echo through the quadrangle, calling to breakfast.

West Point Mess Hall. The "Old Cadet Mess Hall" was built on the site of the current Grant Hall in 1852. It served as the dining hall for the Corps of Cadets until it was replaced by Washington Hall. It was demolished in 1930 to make way for the current Grant Hall.

FREDERICK WHITTAKER

Now another roll call, and the companies are marched to the mess hall; from thence until eight o'clock there is leisure to study or look around one and watch guard mount. At eight, old Rentz, the Academy bugler for thirty years, calls the cadets to quarters and now, for five mortal hours, the routine of study and recitation is unvarying. Now, another roll call. The classes that recite are marched to the recitation rooms by the section marchers and reported to the instructor. The first half of the corps works until half past nine when the second half relieves them, while the fencing classes are called up.

At one o'clock, dinner call is beaten; and for this and recreation an hour is allowed. From two until four, more recitations, after which afternoon drill for an hour and a half; then liberty until sunset.

Sunset is the signal for dress parade of the battalion, when there are more roll calls, and retreat is beaten by the drum corps while the band plays, and everything puts on its most imposing and martial aspect. As the band paces up and down the front of the motionless line of cadets, the setting sun gleaming on the fixed bayonets, officers at parade rest, the solitary figure of the commandant standing with folded arms in front of the centre, the scene attracts multitudes of spectators, and the effect on the imagination is romantic and warlike in the highest degree.

The band wheels into its place, the gorgeous drum major flings up his staff, and as the melancholy notes of "retreat" echo on the evening air they are interrupted by the sudden boom of the evening gun. Down comes the great standard, fluttering on its way from the summit of the lofty flagstaff. As the last roll of "retreat" ceases, the line springs into sudden life at the sharp voice of the adjutant and the brief formality of dress parade proceeds on its way. A few moments later, the companies are marching away to the sweet strains of the famous West Point band, and the day's work is over.

Now comes supper and half an hour's time for recreation, when the bugle is heard once more, calling "to quarters." Every cadet must be in his room and studying, or at least quiet and orderly, until tattoo at half past nine when the beds are spread. At ten o'clock, the quadrangle is nearly silent, the subdued murmur of conversation dying away, the light in the different rooms twinkling like stars.

CADET CUSTER

Tap!

A couple of drummers proceed slowly along around the barracks, and at every hundred steps or so, each gives a single tap. As if by magic, the twinkling lights disappear and the Academy is silent as the grave, buried in sleep.

The duties of the guards during barrack time are much less onerous than when in camp. They walk post only at meal times, during drills, at dress parade and during evening study hours. Each sentinel is responsible for the rooms on his post, which he is required to inspect. He must report all absentees as well as suppress all noise and disturbances. Of course, this part of his duty is the most onerous and delicate he can have during the day, as the strict restraints of discipline, irksome at any time to young men, are doubly so when night and darkness give them an opportunity to escape surveillance.

This is the time when cadets fall into most of their scrapes, by getting out of quarters, either during study hours, or more commonly after taps. In the case of Cadets Custer and Parker, these escapades and frolics were born of that irrepressible spirit of fun so common in the West, for Parker was a Missourian. There seems to be something peculiarly enticing to a high-spirited cadet in the idea of getting out of bounds, and when to that is added the attractions of "Benny Havens," the temptatious to the bold spirits were much greater than the cadets could resist.

Benny Havens has been for many years a famous character at the Point. Long before the Mexican War, he was established within the lines and under the guise of an honest seller of coffee and cakes, was wont to administer surreptitious egg-flip, when no officers were around, to the thirsty cadets. Expelled for this cause, he established himself about a mile from the Point in a little cabin under a cliff, which has ever since been the rendezvous of innumerable pilgrims from the barracks.

The attractions of Benny Havens' cabin did not seem, then nor now, to lie so much in the fact of his selling liquor. In the case of young Custer, who very seldom, except as hereinafter referred to, used spirits or tobacco, this could have been no temptation. But Benny has been so long at the Point, and seen so many generations of cadets, that he has become a perfect store-house of interesting legends, and these constitute the charm which draws so many to his little cabin from far away.

Benny Havens. Benny Havens tavern had to eventually be relocated to make way for the West Shore Railroad. It was disassembled and re-erected by Long Pond Mountain five miles away. The original transplanted tavern then became a victim of fire. A reincarnation still exists on Main Street in Highlands Falls today.

Grey-headed general officers, distinguished in active service, come today to the Point to revisit the scenes of their youth, and always pay a visit to Benny, and the old man knows them all, and can tell stories of the days when they were cadets. No wonder the cadets of all time have been fond of slipping out of quarters after taps to visit Benny, to sit around his fire, to listen to stories of the day when Grant, Sherman, and Thomas were wild boys at the Point, to dream as they listen of the days when they perhaps may rival the fame of those great leaders.

Meantime, they eat Benny's buckwheat cakes for which he is famous, and drink his old wine, while at intervals they join in the time-honored song of *"Benny Havens, oh!"* This is one of the regular institutions at Benny's. The song was written by Lieutenant O'Brien of the 8th Infantry, assisted by others, many years ago, and set to the tune of *"Wearing of the Green."*

When O'Brien afterward died in Florida, stanzas were added to commemorate his death. A very few verses will give an idea of the song, which is quite long. Imagine a group of young cadets, who have stolen away after taps, gathered in Benny's little parlor, awaiting the coming of the celebrated buckwheats. One stands up and cries:

> "Come, fellows, fill your glasses and-
> (All join in.)
> Stand up in a row.
> For sentimental drinking, we're going for to go,
> In the army there's sobriety, promotion's very slow,
> So we'll cheer our hearts with choruses at Benny Havens, oh!
> Benny Havens, oh! Oh! Benny Havens, oh!
> We'll sing our reminiscences of Benny Havens, oh!"

Then the song proceeds to describe the features of army life in various verses, until the chief breaks out rapturously:

> "To the ladies of our army, our cups shall ever flow,
> Companions of our exile, and our shield against all woe,
> May they see their husbands generals, with double pay also,
> And join us in our choruses at Benny Havens, oh!
> Benny Havens, oh! etc.

> May the army be augmented, promotion be less slow,
> May our country in her hour of need, be ready for the foe,
> May we find a soldier's resting place beneath a soldier's blow,
> With space enough beside our graves for Benny Havens, oh!
> Benny Havens, oh! etc."

Year by year, as new generations of cadets have passed through the Academy and former graduates attain fame, their names are embalmed in successive verses. In Custer's day, the only heroes were Taylor and Scott, for the regular army that within a few years was to produce so many distinguished names, was then sunk in the rust of peace with little chance of distinction before it. It seems to us now, looking back at that indefinite period "before the war," as if a whole century had passed since then. The state of the army, its names and traditions, its' very dress and appearance, are so different now, that in a few years all memory of that old army will have faded.

Quietly glided away the days and nights at West Point, in the monotonous round of duties that came to Cadet Custer and his roommate while in the fourth class; and the dreaded January examination came when, if not successful, the Plebe would be "found deficient" and sent back to civil life. It was safely passed however, and the spring wore on, bringing nearer and nearer the memorable June day that opened to Cadet Custer "third class encampment," when he ceased to be a Plebe and became at one bound an "old cadet," no longer on probation, but only liable to be put back a class if he failed in studies.

Now came the real pleasures of camp, when visitors were present in crowds, when the evening balls were crowded with cadets on leave, when the new Plebes were to be drilled and the old torments inflicted on a new generation. To join in these, young Custer was too good-natured and jovial, but at the balls he was in his element. His remarkably handsome face and figure were wonderfully effective among the ladies, as they continued to be all his life and attracted no little of the envy of his brother cadets.

In those days, before the heavy blonde moustache had come to lend an air of sternness to his features, his bright locks gave him a girlish appearance which, coupled with the remarkable fact of his strictly temperate habits, procured him the nickname of "Fanny." Boys always have good names for each other, indicative of character or personal appearance, and the name "Fanny" stuck to Custer through his academic life and long after, when he met his former classmates as enemies in the field. "That's just like Fanny," said one of them when he received a note from Custer, left at a farm house, informing him politely that he had just whipped such an one (a former classmate) handsomely and was coming next day to repeat the operation on the recipient of the letter.

Camp wore its way out and the Third Class went into barracks once again for the same routine, the studies being advanced and much more severe than before, the principal recreation being mounted drill in the riding hall. Here it was that Cadet Custer developed that perfection in horsemanship which distinguished him afterward, with the more ease

CADET CUSTER

as every Western boy knows something of riding early in life.

To those who do not, the riding school of West Point is a hard one, but very effective. The Third Class men take up riding in November and are exercised by platoons of about twenty at a time, the same old troop horses being used from year to year in the riding hall. The floor is strewn with tanbark several inches in depth, so that there is no danger to life or limb in a fall and the animals are caparisoned in full army rig at the close of the course. Usually, the class commences on blankets alone, without stirrups, and when this is the case the lesson is comparatively easy; but sometimes the riding master orders on saddles and gives the command to the cadets "Cross-Stirrups!"

Those who have ever tried to ride in a large McClellan saddle without stirrups, on a hard trotting horse, can imagine the torments of the poor boys on strange animals. In the army, a man gets used to his own steed and inured to his paces, but where rider and horse are frequently changed, as at West Point, it is a very different thing. The constant alterations spoil the horses' tempers, and most of them get to be hard-mouthed, unruly brutes, full of bad tricks and always on the watch for a chance to unseat a rider.

Put a lot of green riders on such animals and make them cross stirrups, then let the platoon start at a walk, and all is well, but when the command is given "Trot-March!" what a jolting and pounding ensues, the unlucky cadets trying to hold on with knees and thighs to a saddle flap that seems as slippery as glass! And yet two-thirds of the practice in the riding hall is done at the same trot, and the unfeeling riding master sits on his horse in the centre, cool as a cucumber. His stirrups are not crossed, you may be sure, or he could not smile so sweetly over the miseries of the poor pupils, bumping about.

One of the late cadets, a young fellow too, promoted from the ranks of the army during the war, and who had served in battle with the volunteer cavalry before he came to West Point, says; "It is one of the most cruel things that can be thought of, to be obliged to ride without stirrups for the first time on such perfect devils as some of these horses are. There were upwards of thirty in my class who were thrown, though only three or four of them were injured - none severely. One had his foot stepped on in a playful manner by one of the incarnate fiends, mashing his big toe to a jelly; but that was not of much consequence, as it has now recovered. Many were severely bruised, but in ninety-nine cases out of a hundred it is impossible for a cadet to be hurt badly by being thrown in the riding hall. The only way is to ride right through and take the pounding and bruises, and get used to it. The remedy is a rough one, but the only one effectual."

Through all the troubles of the riding hall passed Cadet Custer, as blithe and debonair as ever. His length of limb gave him great advantage, his rough Western life still more. A tall, wiry built man has greater ease in riding than a shorter aspirant; and it was not long before "Fanny" was known as one of the best riders at the Point, emulating the fame that belonged in bygone times to Cadet Grant, whose famous leap on "Old York" is traditional to this day.

The winter passed away and another spring, and then the airs of June were felt once more, blowing over "Second Class Camp" and - blessed news - furlough to see home for the first time in two years. Furlough lasts till the Second Class goes to works again in barracks, and there is no need to say how it was enjoyed by Cadet Custer at his home, nor how many of his buttons he exchanged for locks of hair and vows of affection. In this, he was not peculiar. All cadets have done it from time immemorial, and Cadet Custer, nearly twenty, handsome as Apollo, was by no means behind the fashion. How he enjoyed his furlough, how he hated to go back, how his work during the winter seemed duller and harder than ever, all these things are understood. The daily routine of his further life was a repetition of the past.

But the time was coming, as Custer approached First Class and graduation, when a change passed over the spirit of West Point such as it had never seen before and is never likely to see again. This it was which rendered the experiences of Custer's classmates unique in the annals of the Academy, and from henceforth it is fitting that Custer himself should take up the story, as he has done in the opening chapters of his War Memoirs, wherein he rapidly summarizes his Academic career in the following fashion:

CADET CUSTER

The first official notification received by me of my appointment to the Military Academy bore the signature of Jefferson Davis, then Secretary of War in the cabinet of President James Buchanan. Colonel Richard Delafield, one of the ablest and most accomplished officers of the Engineer Corps, occupied the position of superintendent of the Academy, and Lieutenant-Colonel William J. Hardee, of the cavalry, afterward lieutenant-general in the Confederate army, was the commandant of the Corps of Cadets.

Among the noticeable feature of cadet life as then impressed upon me, and still present in my memory, were the sectional lines voluntarily established by the cadets themselves; at first barely distinguishable, but in the later years immediately preceding the war as clearly defined and strongly drawn as were the lines separating the extremes of the various sections in the national Congress. Nor was this fact a strange or remarkable one. As each Congressional district and territory of the United States had a representative in Congress, so each had its representatives at the Military Academy.

In looking back over the few months and years passed at West Point immediately preceding the war, some strange incidents recur to my mind. When the various state conventions were called by the different states of the South with a view to the adoption of the ordinance of secession, it became only a question of time as to the attempted withdrawal of the seceding states. And while there were those representing both sections in Congress who professed to believe that war would not necessarily or probably follow, this opinion was not shared in even by persons as young and inexperienced as the cadets.

War was anticipated by them at that time, and discussed and looked forward to as an event of the future, with as much certainty as if speaking of an approaching season. The cadets from the South were in constant receipt of letters from their friends at home, keeping them fully advised of the real situation and promising them suitable positions in the military force yet to be organized to defend the ordinance of secession. All this was a topic of daily if not hourly conversation. Particularly was this true when we assembled together at meal time when, grouped in squads of half-a-dozen or more, each usually found himself in the midst of his personal friends.

I remember a conversation held at the table at which I sat during the winter of '60-'61. I was seated next to Cadet P.M.B. Young, a gallant young fellow from Georgia, a classmate of mine, then and since the war an intimate and valued friend - a major-general in the Confederate forces during the war and a member of Congress from his native state at a later date. The approaching war was as usual the subject of conversation in which all participated, and in the freest and most friendly manner; the lads from the North discoursing earnestly upon the power and rectitude of the National Government, the impulsive Southron holding up pictures of invaded rights and future independence.

Finally, in a half jocular, half earnest manner, Young turned to me and delivered himself as follows; "Custer, my boy, we're going to have war. It's no use talking; I see it coming. All the Crittenden compromises that can be patched up won't avert it. Now let me prophesy what will happen to you and me. You will go home, and your abolition Governor will probably make you colonel of a cavalry regiment. I will go down to Georgia, and ask Governor Brown to give me a cavalry regiment. And who knows but we may move against each other during the war. You will probably get the advantage of us in the first few engagements, as your side will be rich and powerful, while we will be poor and weak. Your regiment will be armed with the best of weapons, the sharpest of sabres; mine will have only shotguns and scythe blades; but for all that we'll get the best of the fight in the end, because we will fight for a principle, a cause, while you will fight only to perpetuate the abuse of power."

Lightly as we both regarded this boyish prediction, it was destined to be fulfilled in a remarkable degree. Early in the war I did apply, not to the abolition Governor of my native state, but to that of Michigan, for a cavalry regiment. I was refused, but afterward obtained the regiment I desired as a part of my command. Young was chosen to lead one of the Georgia cavalry regiments. Both of us rose to higher commands, and confronted each other on the battlefield.

On December 20, 1860, South Carolina formally led the way by adopting the ordinance of secession; an example which was followed within the next few weeks by Mississippi, Alabama, Florida, Georgia, Louisiana, and Texas, in the order named. As soon as it became evident that these states were determined to attempt secession, the cadets appointed there, from imitating the action of their Senators and representatives in Congress and influenced by the appeals of friends at home, tendered their resignations, eager to return to their homes and take part in the organization of the volunteer forces which the increasing difficulties and dangers of the situation rendered necessary. Besides, as the Confederate Congress was called to meet for the first time at Montgomery, Alabama, February 6, 1861, and would undoubtedly authorize the appointment of a large number of officers in the formation of the Confederate armies, it was important that applicants for positions of this kind should be on the ground to properly present their claims.

One by one, the places occupied by the cadets from the seceding states became vacant; it cost many a bitter pang to disrupt the intimate relations existing between the hot-blooded Southron and his more phlegmatic schoolmate from the North. No school girls could have been more demonstrative in their affectionate regard for each other than were some of the cadets about to separate for the last time, and under circumstances which made it painful to contemplate a future coming together. Those leaving for the South were impatient, enthusiastic, and hopeful. Visions filled their minds of a grand and glorious Confederacy, glittering with the pomp and pageantry which usually characterizes imperial power, and supported and surrounded by a mighty army, the officers of which would constitute a special aristocracy.

Their comrades from the North, whom they were leaving behind, were reserved almost to sullenness; were grave almost to stoicism. The representatives of the two sections had each resolved upon their course of action; and each in a manner characteristic of their widely different temperaments, as different as the latitudes from which they hailed. Among the first of the cadets to leave West Point and hasten to enroll themselves under the banner of the seceding states, were two of my classmates, Kelley and Ball, of Alabama. Kelley became prominent in the war, and was killed in battle. Ball also attained a high rank, and is now a prominent official in one of the most extensive business enterprises in this country. They took their departure from the Academy on Saturday.

West Point Chapel. General Custer's funeral took place here on October 10, 1877. His saber and hat were placed on his coffin, which was surrounded by flowers. At the foot of the coffin was a wreath that read "Seventh Cavalry" entwined with an American flag. A blue silk battle flag hung on the wall behind which in gold letters spelled out "God and Our Country."

I remember the date the more readily as I was engaged in to adopt the cadet term "walking an extra," which consisted in performing the tiresome duties of a sentinel during the unemployed hours of Saturday, hours usually given to recreation. On this occasion, I was pacing back and forth on my post, which for the time being extended along the path leading from the cadets' chapel toward the academic building, when I saw a party of from fifteen to twenty cadets emerge from the open space between the mess hall and the academic building, and direct their steps toward the steamboat landing below. That which particularly attracted my attention was the bearing aloft upon the shoulders of their comrades of my two classmates Ball and Kelley, as they were being carried in triumph from the doors of the Academy to the steamboat landing. Too far off to exchange verbal adieus, even if military discipline had permitted it, they caught sight of me as, step by step, I reluctantly paid the penalty of offended regulations, and raised their hats in token of farewell, to which, first casting my eyes about to see that no watchful superior was in view, I responded by bringing my musket to a "present."

The comrades who escorted them were Southerners like themselves, and only awaiting the formal action of their respective states on the adoption of the secession ordinance to follow their example. It was but a few weeks until there was scarcely a cadet remaining at the Academy from the Southern States. Many resigned from the border states without waiting to see whether their state would follow in the attempt at secession or not; some resigned who had been appointed from states which never voted to leave the Union; while an insignificant few, who had resolved to join the Confederate forces but desired to obtain their diplomas from the academic faculty, remained until the date of their graduation. Some remained until the declaration and commencement of hostilities; then, allowing the government to transport them to Washington, tendered their resignations and were dismissed for doing so in the face of the enemy. Happily, the number that pursued this questionable course did not exceed half a dozen.

At no point in the loyal States were the exciting events of the spring of 1861 watched with more intense interest than at West Point. And after the departure of the Southern cadets, the hearts of the people of no community, state, town or village beat with more patriotic impulse than did those of the young cadets at West Point. Casting aside all questions of personal ambition or promotion; realizing only that the government which they had sworn to defend, the principles they had been taught from childhood were in danger and threatened by armed enemies, they would gladly have marched to battle as private soldiers rather than remain idle spectators in the great conflict.

As the time for the inauguration of Mr. Lincoln approached,

rumors prevailed, and obtained wide belief to the effect that a plot was on foot by which the inauguration of Mr. Lincoln was to be made the occasion on the part of the enemies of the government, of whom great numbers were known to be in Washington, for seizing or making away with the executive officers of the nation and taking possession of the people's capital. Whether or not such a scheme was ever seriously contemplated, it was deemed prudent to provide against it.

The available military resources of the government amounted to but little at that period. Lieutenant-General Scott, then Commander-in-Chief of the army, issued orders for the assembling at Washington of as large a military force as circumstances would permit. Under this order it became necessary to make a demand upon the regular military forces then employed at West Point. A battery of artillery was hastily organized from the war material kept at the Academy for the purpose of instruction to the cadets. The horses were supplied by taking those used by the cadets in their cavalry and artillery drills. The force thus organized hastened to Washington where, under the command of Captain Griffin - afterward Major-General Griffin - it took part in the inaugural ceremonies. Then followed the firing upon Sumter; the intelligence of which waked the slumbering echoes of loyalty and patriotism in every home and hamlet throughout the North.

It is doubtful if the people of the North were ever, or will ever be again, so united in thought and impulse as when the attack on Sumter was flashed upon them. Opponents in politics became friends in patriotism; all differences of opinion vanished or were laid aside, and a single purpose filled and animated the breast of the people as of one man - a purpose unflinching and unrestrained - to rush to the rescue of the government, to beat down its opposers, come from whence they may. In addition to sharing the common interest and anxiety of the public in the attack upon Sumter, the cadets felt a special concern, from the fact that among the little band of officers shut up in that fortress were two, Lieutenants Snyder and Hall, who had been our comrades as cadets only a few months before.

As already stated, the time of study and instruction at West Point at that period was five years, in the determination and fixing of which no one had exercised greater influence than Jefferson Davis - first as Secretary of War, afterward as United States Senator, and member of a special congressional committee to consider the question as to whether the course should extend to five years or only include four.

In the general demand in 1861, not only from the National Government, but from States, for competent and educated officers to instruct and command the new levies of troops then being raised in response to the call of the President to oppose the rebellion, it was decided by the authorities at Washington to abandon the five years' course of instruction at the Military Academy, and reestablish that of four years. The effect of this was to give to the service in that year, two classes of graduates for officers, instead of but one.

By this change the class of which I was a member graduated, under the four years' system, in June, while the preceding class was graduated, under the five years' rule, only a couple of months in advance of us. The members of both classes, with but few exceptions, were at once ordered to Washington, where they were employed either in drilling raw volunteers, or serving on the staffs of general officers, engaged in organizing the new regiments into brigades and divisions. I was one of the exceptions referred to, and the causes which led file in a different direction may be worthy of mention.

My career as a cadet had but little to commend it to the study of those who came after me; unless as an example to be carefully avoided. The requirements of the academic regulations, a copy of which was placed in my hand the morning of my arrival at West Point, were not observed by me in such manner as at all times to commend me to the approval and good opinions of my instructors and superior officers. My offences against law and order were not great in enormity, but what they lacked in magnitude they made up in number. The forbidden locality of Benny Havens possessed stronger attractions than the study and demonstration of a problem in Euclid, or the prosy discussion of some abstract proposition of moral science. My class numbered, upon entering the Academy, about one hundred and twenty-five. Of this number, only thirty-four graduated, and of these, thirty-three graduated above me. The resignation and departure of the Southern cadets took away from the Academy a few individuals who, had they remained, would probably have contested with me the debatable honor of bringing up the rear of the class.

We had passed our last examination as cadets, had exchanged barrack for camp life, and were awaiting the receipt of orders from Washington assigning us to the particular branches of the service for which we had been individually recommended by the academic faculty. The month of June had come, and we were full of impatience to hasten to the capital and join the forces preparing for the coming campaign. It is customary, or was then, to allow each cadet, prior to his graduation, to perform at least one tour of duty as an officer of the guard instead of the ordinary duties of a private soldier on guard.

I had not only had the usual experience in the latter capacity, extending over a period of four years, but in addition had been compelled as punishment for violations of the academic regulations to perform extra tours of guard duty on Saturdays - times which otherwise I should have been allowed for pleasure and recreation. If my memory serves me right, I devoted sixty-six Saturdays to this method of vindicating outraged military law during my cadetship of four years.

It so happened that it fell to my detail to perform the duties of officer of the guard in camp at a time when the arrival of the order from Washington, officially transforming us from cadets to officers, was daily expected. I began my tour at the usual hour in the morning, and everything passed off satisfactorily in connection with the discharge of my new responsibilities until, just at dusk, I heard a commotion near the guard tents. Upon hastening to the scene of the disturbance, which by the way was at a considerable distance from the main camp, I found two cadets engaged in a personal dispute which threatened to result in blows.

Quite a group of cadets, as friends and spectators, had formed about the two bellicose disputants. I had hardly time to take in the situation when the two principals of the group engaged in a regular set-to, and began belaboring each other vigorously with their fists. Some of their more prudent friends rushed forward and attempted to separate the two contestants. My duty as officer of the guard was plain and

CADET CUSTER

simple; I should have arrested the two combatants and sent them to the guard tents for violating the peace and the regulations of the Academy. But the instincts of the boy prevailed over the obligation of the officer of the guard. I pushed my way through the surrounding line of cadets, dashed back those who were interfering in the struggle, and called out loudly, "Stand back, boys; let's have a fair fight."

I had occasion to remember, if not regret, the employment of these words. Scarcely had I uttered them when the crowd about me dispersed hurriedly and fled to the concealment of their tents. Casting about me to ascertain the cause of this sudden dispersion, I beheld, approaching at a short distance, two officers of the army, Lieutenants Hazen and Merrill (now Major-General Hazen and Colonel Merrill of the Engineer Corps). I sought the tent of the officer of the guards promptly, but the mischief had been done. Lieutenant Hazen happened to be officer of the day on that particular day, whose duty it was to take cognizance of violations of the regulations.

General Hazen often clashed with Custer, as he did with many other officers and superiors, culminating with the narrative; "Some Corrections of Life on the Plains," by W.B. Hazen in 1874, which criticized Custer's version of events preceding and during the Battle of Washita.

Summoning me to his presence, near the scene of the unfortunate disturbance, he asked me in stern tones if I was not the officer of the guard; to which I of course responded in the affirmative. He then overwhelmed me by inquiring in the same unrelenting voice, "Why did you not suppress the riot which occurred here a few minutes ago?" Now, it had never been suggested to me that the settlement of the personal difficulty between two boys, even by the administering of blows, could be considered or described as a riot. The following morning I was required to report at the tent of the commandant (Lieutenant-Colonel John F. Reynolds, afterward General Reynolds, killed at Gettysburg). Of course, no explanation could satisfy the requirements of military justice. I was ordered to return to my tent in arrest. The facts in the case were reported to Washington, on formal charges and specifications, and a court-martial asked for to determine the degree of my punishment.

General Reynolds death spot. The image shows McPherson Woods where Reynolds fell on the first day of the battle. The sign was erected in the 1880's.

Within a few hours of my arrest the long expected order came, relieving my class from further duty at West Point, and directing the members of it to proceed to Washington and report to the Adjutant-General of the army for further orders. My name however, did not appear in this list. I was to be detained, to await the application of the commandant for a court-martial to sit on my case.

The application received approval at the War Department, and the court was assembled at West Point, composed principally of officers who had recently arrived from Texas where they served under General Twiggs until his surrender to the Confederate forces. The judge advocate of the court was Lieutenant Benet, now Brigadier-General and Chief of the Ordnance Corps. I was arraigned with all the solemnity and gravity which might be looked for in a trial for high treason, the specification setting forth in stereotyped phraseology that "He, the said cadet Custer, did fail to suppress a riot or disturbance near the guard tent, and did fail to separate, etc., but, on the contrary, did cry out in a loud tone of voice, 'Stand back, boys; let's have a fair fight,' or words to that effect."

To which accusations the accused pleaded "Guilty" as a matter of course, introducing as witnesses, by way of mitigation, the two cadets, the cause of my difficulty, to prove that neither was seriously injured in the fray. One of them is now a promising young captain in the Engineer Corps. The trial was brief, scarcely occupying more time than did the primary difficulty. I dreaded the long detention which I feared I must undergo while awaiting not only the verdict, but the subsequent action of the authorities at Washington to whom the case must by law be submitted.

My classmates who had preceded me to Washington interested themselves earnestly in my behalf to secure my release from further arrest at West Point, and an order for me to join them at the national capital. Fortunately, some of them had influential friends there, and it was but a few days after my trial that the superintendent of the Academy received a telegraphic order from Washington, directing him to release me at once and order me to report to the Adjutant-General of the army for duty.

This order practically rendered the action and proceedings of the court-martial in my case nugatory. The record, I presume, was forwarded to the War Department, where it probably lies safely stowed away in some pigeon-hole. What the proceeding of the court or their decision was, I have never learned.

George A. Custer

Thus ends the record of Cadet Custer's life at West Point as traced by his own hand. It shows him as he was, but as usual with the author, tells far less of himself than we should like to know. We see the generous impulsive boy before us, always doing the first thing that came to his hand, and never recking of the consequences. There is something in this wild free character that seems utterly unsuited to the pedantic martinetry and restraint of the Point. "Let's have a fair fight" smacks of the old days of chivalry. It was to be the watchword of the young cadet's future career.

It seems plain, although Custer did not say so, that in his heart he had long chafed against the arrogant superciliousness of the Southern members of his class, who in those days thought to monopolize all the chivalry in America. As his first recorded escapade tells of the chivalrous spirit, so his early career was to be the very incarnation of chivalry, and he was fairly to eclipse the most romantic heroes of the South in brilliancy and dash.

But after all, this was only one phase of his character, overlying the sterling sense at the bottom of it, as will appear in its place. During his career at West Point, Custer kept up a strict correspondence with his sister Mrs. Reed, and spent a large part of all his furloughs at her house in Monroe. He seems to have become much enamored of this sleepy little country town, with its broad streets planted with handsome trees, the brawling little river that runs through its midst, its old houses, and general air of quiet respectability.

So fond was he of the place that he even persuaded his parents to move there, which they did, remaining for about a year. Not liking the place, they concluded to return to New Rumley, but afterwards compromised the matter by moving to the vicinity of Toledo, taking a

CADET CUSTER

farm in Wood County near that of Mr. David Kirkpatrick, Mr. Custer's step-son. From his first entrance to Monroe, young Custer seems to have identified himself with it, to have been a "Monroe boy," to have loved all the "Monroe boys." Years after, we find his staff full of Monroe boys, and right well they fought, too.

What was the magnet that drew him to Monroe? The place never did him any material good. He owed his cadetship to Ohio, and his parents lived there. Everything seemed to point his way to his native state. Yet there was a little thing, a mere trifle in the world's eye, a secret vision locked in his own breast, which even his sister, who was his closest confidant in all else, never suspected; that was the magnet that drew him to Monroe.

Elizabeth Bacon Custer was the daughter of wealthy, influential Judge Daniel Stanton Bacon and Eleanor Sophia Page. Beautiful, 5' 4" tall, chestnut-brown hair and blue-grey eyes Elizabeth met her future husband at a Thanksgiving Day social in 1862 in the midst of the Civil War.

The vision of a little dark eyed maiden of only eight summers, swinging on a gate and flinging him a careless salutation in very want of thought, then shyly fleeing into the house when she met his eye, and realized something strange and undefined in its glance. It was four, five, six, seven, eight years later, as he came home on his several vacations, that he saw the little maid shooting up into a shy, modest young lady, guarded around so closely by parental care that he could rarely catch a glimpse of her.

No more salutations for him; she no longer recognized him. The innocent freedom of the child had been changed into the reserve and dignity of the young lady. She was either at home with her father, or at school in the Seminary (by this time a young lady's school), of which she was one of the most promising and painstaking scholars. The gulf that divided the Judge's heiress from the penniless cadet seemed to grow wider and wider, and more impossible to leap, for as yet he had not even been introduced to the young lady.

All the same, Custer bided his time in silence. He felt that time was coming, and meantime his "vision" was out of danger from anyone else, hedged round with every safeguard. To pass away the time, a candid biographer is compelled to admit that he flirted with other girls considerably, even what strict church members would call outrageously, but it was all only skin-deep. He was still, after all, only a boy. When we next come to him, it will be as a man among men.

LIEUTENANT CUSTER, SECOND CAVALRY

THE introduction of the young officer to military life can hardly be told by anyone so well as he has described it himself. It is unique. Probably no cadet ever experienced such a quick transition from school to active duty. Hear him:

I left West Point on the 18th of July, 1861, for Washington, delaying a few hours that afternoon on my arrival in New York to enable me to purchase, of the well known military firm of Horstmanns, my lieutenant's outfit of sabre, revolver, sash, spurs, etc. Taking the evening train for Washington, I found the cars crowded with troops, officers and men, hastening to the capital.

At each station we passed on the road at which a halt was made, crowds of citizens were assembled, provided bountifully with refreshments which they distributed in the most lavish manner among the troops. Their enthusiasm knew no bounds; they received us with cheers and cheered us in parting. It was no unusual sight, on leaving a station surrounded by these loyal people, to see matrons and maidens embracing and kissing with patriotic fervor the men, entire strangers to them, whom they saw hastening to the defense of the nation.

Arriving at Washington soon after daylight, Saturday morning, the 20th of July, I made my way to the Ebbitt House, where I expected to find some of my classmates domiciled. Among others whom I found there was Parker, appointed from Missouri, who had been my room and tent mate at West Point for years. He was one of the few members of my class who, while sympathizing with the South, had remained at the Academy long enough to graduate and secure a diploma.

Proceeding to his room without going through the formality of announcing my arrival by sending up a card, I found him at that early hour still in bed. Briefly he responded to my anxious inquiry for news, that McDowell's army was confronting Beauregard's, and a general engagement was expected hourly. My next inquiry was as to his future plans and intentions, remembering his Southern sympathies. To this he replied by asking me to take from a table nearby and read an official order to which he pointed.

Ebbitt House, a hotel and restaurant, was located at the southeast corner of F Street NW and 14th Street NW in Washington DC. Ebbitt House and other area structures were demolished in 1872 to make room for a new, a six-story, 300-room hotel (also called Ebbitt House) erected on the same spot.

Upon opening the document referred to, I found it to be an order from the War Department dismissing from the rolls of the army Second Lieutenant James P. Parker, for having tendered his resignation in the face of the enemy. The names of two others of my classmates appeared in the same order. Both the latter have since sought and obtained commissions in the Egyptian army under the Khedive. After an hour or more spent in discussing the dark probabilities of the future as particularly affected by the clouds of impending war, I bade a fond farewell to my former friend and classmate, with whom I had lived on terms of closer intimacy and companionship than with any other being.

We had eaten day by day at the same table, had struggled together in the effort to master the same problems of study; we had marched by each other's side year after year, elbow to elbow, when engaged in the duties of drill, parade, etc., and had shared our blankets with each other when learning the requirements of camp life. Henceforth this was all to be thrust from our memory as far as possible, and our paths and aims in life were to run counter to each other in the future.

James P. Parker was a West Point roommate of Custer. He joined the Confederate First Mississippi Artillery and was captured at Port Hudson, Louisiana, in 1863.

We separated; he to make his way, as he did immediately, to the seat of the Confederate Government, and accept a commission under a flag raised in rebellion against the Government that had educated him, and that he had sworn to defend; I to proceed to the office of the Adjutant-General of the army and report for such duty as might be assigned me in the great work which was then dearest and uppermost in the mind of every loyal citizen of the country.

It was not until after two o'clock in the morning that I obtained an audience with the Adjutant-General of the army, and reported to him formally for orders as my instructions directed me to do. I was greatly impressed by the number of officials I saw, and the numerous messengers to be seen flitting from room to room, bearing immense numbers of huge looking envelopes. The entire department had an air of busy occupation which, taken in connection with the important military events then daily transpiring and hourly expected, and contrasted with the humdrum life I had but lately led as a cadet, added to the bewilderment I naturally felt.

Presenting my order of instructions to the officer who seemed to be in charge of the office, he glanced at it, and was about to give some directions to a subordinate nearby to write out an order assigning me to some duty when, turning to me, he said, "Perhaps you would like to be presented to "General Scott, Mr. Custer?" I joyfully assented. I had often beheld the towering form of the venerable chieftain during his summer visits to West Point, but that was the extent of my personal acquaintance with him. So strict was the discipline at the Academy that the gulf which separated cadets from commissioned officers seemed greater in practice than that which separated enlisted men from them. Hence it was rare indeed that a cadet ever had an opportunity to address or be addressed by officers, and it was still more rare to be brought into personal conversation with an officer above the grade of lieutenant or captain; if we except the superintendent of the Academy and the commandant of the corps of cadets.

The sight of a general officer, let alone the privilege of speaking to one, was an event to be recounted to one's friend. In those days, the title of general was not so familiar as to be encountered on every hotel register. Besides, the renown of a long lifetime gallantly spent in his country's service had gradually but justly placed General Scott far above all contemporary chieftains, in the admiration and hero worship of his fellow countrymen; and in the youthful minds of the West Point cadets of those days, Scott was looked up to as a leader whose military abilities were scarcely second to those of a Napoleon, and whose patriotism rivaled that of Washington.

Following the lead of the officer to whom I had reported, I was conducted to the room in which General Scott received his official visitors. I found him seated at a table over which were spread maps and other documents, which plainly showed their military character. In the room, and seated near the table were several members of Congress, of whom I remember Senator Grimes, of Iowa. The topic of conversation was the approaching battle in which General McDowell's forces were about to engage. General Scott seemed to be explaining to the Congressmen the position, as shown by the map, of the contending armies.

General Winfield Scott and staff. When Scott was tasked with assembling the Union Army to defeat the Confederacy, he initially offered command to Robert E. Lee, his former comrade. Lee declined, and subsequently led the opposing Confederate Army.

The Adjutant-General called General Scott's attention to me by saying, "General, this is Lieutenant Custer of the Second Cavalry; he has just reported from West Point, and I did not know but that you might have some special orders to give him." Looking at me a moment, the General shook me cordially by the hand, saying, "Well, my young friend, I am glad to welcome you to the service at this critical time. Our country has need of the strong arms of all her loyal sons in this emergency." Then, turning to the Adjutant-General, he inquired to what company I had been assigned. "To Company G, Second Cavalry, now under Major Innes Palmer, with General McDowell," was the reply. Then, addressing me, the General said, "We have had the assistance of quite a number of you young men from the Academy, drilling volunteers, etc. Now, what can I do for you? Would you prefer to be ordered to report to General Mansfield to aid in this work, or is your desire for something more active?"

Major Inns Palmer

Although overwhelmed by such condescension on the part of one so far superior in rank to any officer with whom I had been brought in immediate contact, I ventured to stammer out that I earnestly desired to be ordered to at once join my company, then with General McDowell, as I was anxious to see active service. "A very commendable resolution, young man," was the reply, then turning to the Adjutant-General, he added, "Make out Lieutenant Custer's orders directing him to proceed to his company at once;" then, as if a different project had presented itself, he inquired of me if I had been able to provide myself with a mount for the field. I replied that I had not, but would set myself about doing so at once. "I fear you have a difficult task before you, because, if rumor is correct, every serviceable horse in the city has been bought, borrowed or begged by citizens who have gone or are going as spectators to witness the battle. I only hope Beauregard may capture some of them and teach them a lesson.

However, what I desire to say to you is, go and provide yourself with a horse if possible, and call here at seven o'clock this evening. I desire to send some dispatches to General McDowell, and you can be the bearer of them. You are not afraid of a night ride, are you?" Exchanging salutations, I left the presence of the General-in-Chief, delighted at the prospect of being at once thrown into active service, perhaps participating in the great battle which everyone there knew was on the eve of occurring; but more than this my pride as a soldier was not a little heightened by the fact that almost upon my first entering the service, I was to be the bearer of important official dispatches from the General-in-Chief to the General commanding the principal army in the field.

I had yet a difficult task before me, in procuring a mount. I visited all the prominent livery stables, but received almost the same answer from each, the substance of which was that I was too late; all the disposable horses had been let or engaged. I was almost in despair at the idea that I was not to be able to take advantage of the splendid opportunity for distinction opened before me, and was at a loss what to do, or to whom to apply for advice, when I met on Pennsylvania Avenue a soldier in uniform, whom I at once recognized as one of the detachment formerly stationed at West Point, who left with those ordered suddenly to the defense of Washington at the time of Mr. Lincoln's inauguration, when it was feared that an attempt would be made to assassinate the President elect.

Glad to encounter any one I had ever seen before, I approached and asked him what he was doing in Washington. He answered that he belonged to Griffin's battery, which was then with McDowell's forces at the front, and had returned to Washington by Captain Griffin's order to obtain and take back with him an extra horse left by the battery on its departure from the capital. Here then was my opportunity, and I at once availed myself of it. It was the intention of this man to set out on his return at once; but at my earnest solicitation he consented to defer his departure until after seven o'clock, agreeing also to have the extra horse saddled and in readiness for me.

Promptly at seven o'clock, I reported at the Adjutant-General's office, obtained my dispatches, and with no baggage or extra clothing to weight down my horse, save what I carried on my person, I repaired to the point at which I was to find my horse and companion for the night. Upon arriving there, I was both surprised and delighted to discover that the horse which accidently seemed to have provided for me was a favorite one ridden by me often when learning the cavalry exercises at West Point. Those who were cadets just before the war will probably recall him to mind when I give the name, "Wellington," by which he was then known.

Washington DC Livery. This was John C. Howard's stable on G Street between 6th and 7th. John Surratt, a Lincoln assassination conspirator, kept horses here before skipping town on April 1st, 1865.

Crossing Long Bridge about nightfall, and taking the Fairfax C.H. Road for Centreville, the hours of night flew quickly past, engrossed as my mind was with the excitement and serious novelty of the occasion, as well as occasionally diverted by the conversation of my companion. I was particularly interested with his description, given as we rode in the silent darkness, of a skirmish which had taken place only two days before at Blackburn's Ford between the forces of the enemy stationed there, and a reconnoitring detachment sent from General McDowell's army; especially when I learned that my company had borne an honorable part in the affair.

Long Bridge. With the South's secession from the Union, Long Bridge took on an added importance. Alexandria was quickly occupied by the Union Army and the bridge's north and south shores were guarded by Federal troops vigilant for spies, contraband and invasion. The White House, Capitol and Federal Legislature were less than three miles away.

It was between two and three o'clock in the morning when we reached the army near Centreville. The men had already breakfasted, and many of the regiments had been formed in column in the roads ready to resume the march; but owing to delays in starting, most of the men were lying on the ground, endeavoring to catch a few minutes more of sleep; others were sitting or standing in small groups, smoking and chatting. So filled did I find the road with soldiers that it was with difficulty my horse could pick his way among the sleeping bodies without disturbing them. But for my companion, I should have had considerable difficulty in finding my way to headquarters; but he seemed familiar with the localities even in the darkness, and soon conducted me to a group of tents near which a large log fire was blazing, throwing a bright light over the entire scene for some distance around.

As I approached, the sound of my horse's hoofs brought an officer from one of the tents nearest to where I halted. Advancing toward me, he inquired who I wished to see. I informed him that I was bearer of dispatches from General Scott to General McDowell. "I will relieve you of them," was his reply; but seeing me hesitate to deliver them, he added, "I am Major Wadsworth of General McDowell's staff." While I had hoped from ambitious pride to have an opportunity to deliver the dispatches in person to General McDowell, I could not decline longer, so placed the documents in Major Wadsworth's hands, who took them to a tent a few paces distant where through its half-open folds, I saw him hand them to a large, portly officer, whom I at once rightly conceived to be General McDowell. Then, returning to where I still sat on my horse, Major Wadsworth (afterward General Wadsworth) asked of me the latest news in the capital, and when I replied that every person at Washington was looking to the army for news, he added, "Well, I guess they will not have to wait much longer. The entire army is under arms, and moving to attack the enemy today."

Major James Wadsworth

After inquiring at what hour I left Washington, and remarking that I must be tired, Major Wadsworth asked me to dismount and have some breakfast, as it would be difficult to say when another opportunity would occur. I was very hungry, and rest would not have been unacceptable, but in my inexperience I partly imagined, particularly while in the presence of the white-haired officer who gave the invitation, that hunger and fatigue were conditions of feeling which a soldier, especially a young one, should not acknowledge. Therefore, with an appetite almost craving, I declined the kind proffer of the Major. But when he suggested that I dismount and allow my horse to be fed, I gladly assented.

While Major Wadsworth was kindly interesting himself in the welfare of my horse, I had the good fortune to discover in an officer at headquarters, one of my recent West Point friends, Lieutenant Kingsbury, aide-de-camp to General McDowell. He repeated the invitation just given by Major Wadsworth in regard to breakfast, and I did not have the perseverance to again refuse. Near the log fire already mentioned were some servants busily engaged in removing the remains of breakfast. A word from Kingsbury, and they soon prepared for me a cup of coffee, a steak and some Virginia corn bread, to which I did ample justice. Had I known however, that I was not to have an opportunity to taste food during the next thirty hours, I should have appreciated the opportunity I then enjoyed even more highly.

As I sat on the ground sipping my coffee and heartily enjoying my first breakfast in the field, Kingsbury (afterward Colonel Kingsbury, killed at the battle of Antietam) informed me of the general movement then begun by the army, and of the attack which was to be made on Beauregard's forces that day. Three days before, I had quitted school at West Point. I was about to witness the first grand struggle in open battle between the Union and secession armies; a struggle in which, fortunately for the nation, the Union forces were to suffer defeat, while the cause for which they fought was to derive from it renewed strength and encouragement.

So closes the record of the young officer's first tour of duty. As long as we can, let us follow him, for no one else can tell his story so well as himself. In the whole of his story of this period, there is great freshness, and its only fault in the eyes of the general public is that it tells so little of Lieutenant Custer, the real point of interest. In this, as all through his published memoirs, noticeably so in his *"My Life on the Plains,"* written at a later period of his life when he was a public character, Custer always exhibits this modesty of self-reference, a characteristic of the true knightly soldier.

Whenever he mentions Custer, it is only to make the story realistic, and never to boast of his own deeds. He never seems to have got over the fear that a personal story must be a bore to the general public. In a general sense, he was quite right, for personal stories of adventure from commonplace people are very apt to be uninteresting. In the case of men like Custer, centres of popular favor and of whom little is certainly known, the more particulars given us the better, and the more complete our knowledge of them, the more we are satisfied.

Very luckily for the success of his biographer, young Custer soon after became quite a constant and voluminous correspondent with his family at home, and did not make the same mistake with them. There, he was quite sure where the interest lay. The gentle loving women at home did not care a pin for details of battles and campaigns which they hardly comprehended, but they did care very much for what Lieutenant Custer, or rather their dear boy Armstrong was doing, and in his letters he tells them this freely, without any mock modesty. At a little later period, we shall see a good deal of these letters; for the present it is thought better to go no further in our researches than Custer himself has indicated that he wishes us to go. We shall therefore follow him to Bull Run and to the Peninsula, taking up the parable ourselves only when he stops.

The personal interest of these letters is great, and their reading is much more racy than the published narratives of Custer himself. They reveal the real natural Custer, full of life and spirits, generous and ardent, so clearly, that it is like talking with a famous actor off the stage, far more interesting than seeing him act. Unlike most actors however, Custer is better company off the stage than on it, and we hope that these letters, when they come, will aid in undeceiving the world as to his character and free him from one very unjust charge, that of vanity.

FREDERICK WHITTAKER
From this vice, no man was freer, and his most private letters show as much real modesty as his most studied published memoirs.

THE BATTLE OF BULL RUN

THE Battle of Bull Run has been often discussed, and was once the occasion of the fiercest controversies. At the time it was fought and for at least a year thereafter, it was almost impossible to form a clear idea of anything, except for a general impression that a great panic had taken place, that Mr. Russell, of the London Times, had abused the great Yankee nation in the most outrageous way, and that someone was to blame - it was hard to say who. McDowell and Scott went down at once under the popular storm, and the former has perhaps never entirely recovered from the hasty verdict then passed on him.

The preliminary reflections of General Custer on this remarkable battle, the first in which he was engaged, are so opposite that they well deserve quotation. He says truly that no battle of the war startled and convulsed the entire country, North and South, as did the first Battle of Bull Run, although in any succeeding it, both in the East and in the West, were more notable from the fact that greatly superior numbers were engaged, more prominent or experienced chieftains arrayed upon either side and greater results obtained upon the battlefield. Nor is this difficult to explain.

The country, after the enjoyment of long years of peace and prosperity, was unused to the conditions and chances of war. The people of neither section had fully realized as yet the huge proportions of the struggle into which they had been plunged. This is shown not only by the opinions of the people as shadowed forth in the press, but by the authoritative acts and utterances of the highest officials of the land; for example, the proclamation of President Lincoln as late as April 15, 1861, after Fort Sumter had been fired upon and had been surrendered.

In this proclamation, calling for 75,000 troops, or rather in the call sent to the loyal Governors of the States, the period of service was limited to three months. To this can be added Mr. Seward's well known "ninety days" prediction, all tending to incline the people to believe the war was destined to be brief, perhaps to be terminated by a single engagement. Then again, war was not regarded by the masses as a dreadful alternative, to be avoided to the last, but rather as an enterprise offering some pleasure and some excitement, with perhaps a little danger and suffering.

Last of all, the people of the two contending sections had, through the false teachings of their leaders, formed such unjust and incorrect notions in regard to the military prowess and resolution of their opponents that it required the wager of actual battle to dispel these erroneous ideas.

How true these sayings of Custer are, we can remember. The awakening from delusion was marked by much of the same unpractical extravagance of feeling which dictated the previous blind confidence. It was the childish and passionate resentment of those who knew nothing of war save from unprofessional books. The United States had seen no real serious war from its foundation, the influence of the brief invasion of 1812-14 being so partial and slight that the distresses of campaigning were practically unknown. The Mexican War wasn't but a brilliant memory of a holiday excursion to the vast masses of the country, and its veterans were even then fast dropping off the list into superannuation.

In the first flush of bitter mortification and anger at the unexpected reverse, the general run of northern people were as feverishly unreasonable as the French Republicans of the year '93, and every man turned at once into a volunteer spy on his neighbor if the latter were suspected of sympathy for the victorious South.

A somewhat ludicrous instance of this occurred within the knowledge of the writer, having been witnessed by a personal friend. It will give a very fair idea of the state of gloom and acrimony of feeling engendered in the North by the news of Bull Run. It took place, moreover, close to New York City, then and thereafter the place in the whole Union where Southern sympathizers were most common and outspoken, a place not to be compared in ardor of sectional feeling to the country towns.

Crossing on the Brooklyn ferry boat the day after the news of Bull Run had electrified the country, the passengers seemed gloomy and preoccupied. A single exception was found in a foreign gentleman who was conversing with a friend, and who finally broke into a loud laugh where he sat. Instantly a man on the other side of the cabin, who had been regarding him with great disfavor since his entrance, rose, stalked over to him and struck him a violent blow on the face crying, "How dare you laugh, sir, when the country is in danger?"

It seems hardly credible now and yet the fact is undoubted, and it appears that the action attracted no sympathy for the sufferer who had run counter to the intensity of popular feeling. At that time, it must be remembered that the sympathy of most foreigners was, actively or passively, for the South; and the news of the Southern victory determined many waverers against the General Government. Looking back now, after the practical test of actual warfare in which success depends so little on ardor of feeling, so much on dogged determination, these outbursts of feeling appear in their true light as childish ebullitions, unworthy of earnest men conscious of their strength. The real trouble then was that the people were not conscious of their strength, but exaggerated their temporary weakness as they had their primary resources.

Such as it was, the Battle of Bull Run had several curious points about it, which we will endeavor to elucidate for the general reader, assisted partly by General Custer himself and partly by the narrative of the Confederate commander, General Joseph E. Johnston.

The Confederate forces were thus disposed, according to the first; "Beauregard's headquarters were at or near Manassas, distant from Centreville, where General McDowell was located in the midst of his army, about seven miles. The stream which gave its name to the battle runs in a southeast direction between Centreville and Manassas, somewhat nearer to the former place than to the latter. The Confederate army was posted in position along the right bank of Bull Run, their right resting near Union Mill, the point at which the Orange and Alexandria railroad crosses the stream, their centre at Blackburn's Ford, while their left was opposite the Stone Bridge, or crossing of the Warrenton Pike, at the same time holding a small ford about one mile above the Stone Bridge."

Located near Popes Head Creek, Union Mills Station was one of the original stops on the Orange and Alexandria Railroad line. By the summer of 1862, the sprawling depot covered nearly a square mile with sidings for more than 100 cars and its warehouses crammed with military supplies. After the war ended, it faded from the maps, its civilian functions absorbed primarily by the new station at Clifton.

It consisted, according to the order of General Beauregard prescribing the march to the battlefield, (quoted in full in the Appendix to Johnston's Narrative) of seven brigades of the Army of the Potomac, Beauregard's force proper, with forty-two guns and twelve companies of cavalry. These brigades were those of Ewell, D. R. Jones, Longstreet and Bonham in the first line, stretching in the order named from Union Mills on the right to Mitchell's Ford on the left, facing northeast.

Supporting them in the second line were those of Holmes and Early. The last brigade, Colonel Cocke's, was four miles further to the left, guarding the fords. The cavalry was split up into squadrons of two companies, one to each of the first four divisions, which were composed of two brigades each or one with some additional forces. They were commanded respectively by Ewell, Jones, Longstreet and Bonham. Jackson's brigade, of the Army of the Shenandoah, with two regiments of another brigade, were also present from Johnston's forces in the valley, and later in the day, Elzey's brigade of that army arrived just in time to turn defeat into victory. The two extra regiments from the valley were hastily consolidated with two others of Beauregard's army early in the day and constituted Bee's brigade, which suffered worst of all. All the troops from the valley came from the left, and were put in on the left.

The Battle of Blackburn's Ford took place on July 18, 1861, as part of the First Manassas Campaign of the Civil War. During the war, the North generally named a battle after the closest river, stream or creek. The South tended to name battles after towns or railroad junctions.

It had been Beauregard's intention before Johnston arrived, to strengthen his right and attack the Federal left, so as to turn it and push it towards the valley into the clutches of Johnston, who would take it in rear. This disposition was changed by the arrival of Johnston, about noon. It was then found that McDowell's plan was exactly the reverse of Beauregard's. He intended to attack with his right, under the impression that Johnston would be detained in the valley. If he succeeded, he would drive Beauregard into the sea, but his plan was entirely predicated on the absence of Johnston. If the latter came in during the battle, he was certain to strike the Federal right wing square in the rear. As it happened, that is just what Johnston's last brigade did.

McDowell's forces were otherwise disposed. They were organized into four divisions, led by Brigadier-General Tyler, (Connecticut Volunteers) and Colonels Hunter, Heintzelman and Miles of the Regular Army. Tyler's division was to threaten Cocke's brigade on the Confederate left, while Hunter and Heintzelman were to move still further up and cross the stream above so as to turn the Confederates. Miles was to be in reserve near Centreville to frustrate any attempt made by Beauregard to attack on that side. One of Tyler's brigades was to assist Miles and keep the enemy amused by cannonading his centre at Blackburn's Ford. McDowell had a fifth division, Runyon's, back on the Orange and Alexandria Railroad, guarding communications. It was not engaged.

Thus it will be seen that Hunter's and Heintzelman's divisions were to do all the fighting. Tyler and Miles were to keep the enemy amused. The only fault of the disposition, outside of the Johnston possibility, was that Bull Run separated half the army from the other half. From henceforth, let us permit the story to be taken up by Custer himself. It is so freshly, graphically and clearly told by him that it cannot be improved. He takes up the description from where we left him, eating his hasty breakfast at McDowell's headquarters in the grey morning, and continues:

In the preceding chapter, I described my night ride from Washington to the camp of General McDowell's army, at and about Centreville. After delivering my dispatches and concluding my business at headquarters, I remounted my horse, and having been directed in the darkness the way to the ground occupied by Palmer's seven companies of cavalry, I set out to find my company for the first time and report to the commanding officer for duty before the column should begin the march to the battleground.

As previously informed by a staff officer at headquarters, I found it only necessary to ride a few hundred yards, when suddenly I came upon a column of cavalry already mounted and in readiness to move. It was still so dark that I could see but a few lengths of my horse in any direction. I accosted one of the troopers nearest to me and inquired, "What cavalry is this?" "Major Palmer's," was the brief reply. I followed up many interrogations by asking, "Can you tell me where Company G, Second Cavalry, is?" the company to which I had been assigned, but as yet had not seen. "At the head of the column," came in response.

Making my way along the column in the darkness, I soon reached the head, where I found several horsemen seated upon their horses but not formed regularly in the column. There was not sufficient light to distinguish emblems of rank, or to recognize the officer from the private soldier. With some hesitation, I addressed the group, numbering perhaps, a half dozen or more individuals, and asked if the commanding officer of my company, giving its designation by letter and regiment, was present. "Here he is," promptly answered a voice, as one of the mounted figures rode toward me, expecting no doubt I was a staff officer, bearing orders requiring his attention.

I introduced myself by saying, "I am Lieutenant Custer, and in accordance with orders from the War Department, I report for duty with my company, sir." "Ah, glad to meet you, Mr. Custer. We have been expecting you, as we saw in the list of assignments of the graduating class from West Point, that you had been marked down to us. I am Lieutenant Drummond. Allow me to introduce you to some of your brother officers."

Then, turning his horse toward the group of officers, he added, "Gentlemen, permit me to introduce to you Lieutenant Custer, who has just reported for duty with his company." We bowed to each other, although we could see but little more than the dim outlines of horses and riders as we chatted and awaited the order to move "forward." This was my introduction to service, and my first greeting from officers and comrades with whom the future fortune of war was to cast me.

LIEUTENANT CUSTER, SECOND CAVALRY

Lieutenant Drummond, afterward captain, to whom I had just made myself known, fell mortally wounded and died gallantly on the field at the battle of Five Forks, nearly four years afterward.

The cavalry on the Federal side, consisting of only seven companies of regulars under Major Palmer, were not employed to any considerable extent during the battle, except as supports to batteries of artillery. One charge was made in the early part of the battle, near the Warrenton Turnpike, by Colburn's squadron. In advancing to the attack in the morning, Palmer's companies accompanied Hunter's division in the long and tedious movement through an immense forest by which Bull Run was crossed at one of the upper fords, and the left flank of the Confederates successfully turned.

After arriving at Sudley Springs, the cavalry halted for half an hour or more. We could hear the battle raging a short distance in our front. Soon, a staff officer of General McDowell's came galloping down to where the cavalry was waiting, saying that the General desired us to move across the stream and up the ridge beyond, where we were to support a battery. The order was promptly obeyed and as we ascended the crest, I saw Griffin with his battery galloping into position. The enemy had discovered him, and their artillery had opened fire upon him, but the shots were aimed so high the balls passed overhead.

Following the battery, we also marched within plain hearing of each shot as it passed over Griffin's men. I remember well the strange hissing and exceedingly vicious sound of the first cannon shot I heard as it whirled through the air. Of course, I had often heard the sound made by cannon balls while passing through the air during my artillery practice at West Point, but a man listens with changed interest when the direction of the balls is toward instead of away from him.

They seemed to utter a different language when fired in angry battle from that put forth in the tamer practice of drill. The battery whose support we were, having reached its position on an advanced crest near the right of the line, the cavalry was massed near the foot of the crest and sheltered by it from the enemy's fire. Once the report came that the enemy was moving to the attack of the battery which we were specially sent to guard, the order was at once given for the cavalry to advance from the base to the crest of the hill and repel the enemy's assault. We were formed in column of companies, and were given to understand that upon reaching the crest of the hill we would probably be ordered to charge the enemy.

Structures in the Sudley Springs area were used to shelter the wounded at the Battle of Bull Run. Sudley Church served as a field hospital.

When it is remembered that but three days before I had quitted West Point as a schoolboy, and as yet had never ridden at anything more dangerous or terrible than a three-foot hurdle, or tried my sabre upon anything more animated or combative than a leather-head staffed with tan bark, it may be imagined that my mind was more or less given to anxious thoughts as we ascended the slope of the hill in front of us. At the same time, I realized that I was in front of a company of old and experienced soldiers, all of whom would have an eye upon their new lieutenant to see how he comported himself when under fire.

My pride received an additional incentive from the fact that while I was on duty with troops for the first time in my life, and was the junior officer of all present with the cavalry, there was temporarily assigned to duty with my company another officer of the same rank, who was senior to me by a few days and who, having been appointed from civil life, was totally without military experience except such as he had acquired during the past few days.

My brief acquaintance with him showed me that he was disposed to attach no little importance to the fact that I was fresh from West Point and supposed to know all that was valuable or worth knowing in regard to the art of war. In this common delusion, I was not disposed to disturb him. I soon found that he was inclined to defer to me in opinion, and I recall now, as I have often done when in his company during later years of the war, the difficulty we had in deciding exactly what weapon we would use in the charge to which we believed ourselves advancing. As we rode forward from the foot of the hill, he in front of his platoon and I abreast of him in front of mine, Walker (afterward captain) inquired in the most solemn tones, "Custer, what weapon are you going to use in the charge?"

From my earliest notions of the true cavalryman, I had always pictured him in the charge bearing aloft his curved sabre, and cleaving the skulls of all with whom he came in contact. We had but two weapons to choose from; each of us carried a sabre and one revolver in our belt. I promptly replied, "The sabre;" and suiting the action to the word, I flashed my bright new blade from its scabbard and rode forward as if totally unconcerned. Walker, yielding no doubt to what he believed was "the way we do it at West Point," imitated my motion, and forth came his sabre.

I may have seemed to him unconcerned, because I aimed at this, but I was far from enjoying that feeling. As we rode at a deliberate walk up the hill, I began arguing in my own mind as to the comparative merits of the sabre and revolver as a weapon of attack. If I remember correctly, I reasoned pro and con about as follows; "Now the sabre is a beautiful weapon; it produces an ugly wound; the term 'sabre charge' sounds well; and above all the sabre is sure; it never misses fire. It has this drawback, however; in order to be made effective, it is indispensable that you approach very close to your adversary... so close that if you do not unhorse or disable him, he will most likely render that service to you.

FREDERICK WHITTAKER

So much for the sabre. Now as to the revolver, it has this advantage over the sabre; one is not compelled to range himself alongside his adversary before beginning his attack, but may select his own time and distance. To be sure one may miss his aim, but there are six chambers to empty, and if one, two, or three miss, there are still three shots left to fire at close quarters. As this is my first battle, had I not better defer the use of the sabre until after I have acquired a little more experience."

The result was that I returned my sabre to its scabbard and without uttering a word drew my revolver and poised it opposite my shoulder. Walker, as if following me in my mental discussion, no sooner observed my change of weapon than he did likewise. With my revolver in my hand, I put it upon trial mentally. First, I realized that in the rush and excitement of the charge it would be difficult to take anything like accurate aim. Then might not every shot be fired, and without result? By which time in all probability, we would be in the midst of our enemies and slashing right and left at each other; in which case a sabre would be of much greater value and service than an empty revolver.

This seemed convincing; so much so that my revolver found its way again to its holster, and the sabre was again at my shoulder. Again did Walker, as if in pantomime, follow my example. How often these changes of purpose and weapons might have been made I know not, had the cavalry not reached the crest meanwhile, and after being exposed to red hot artillery fire, and finding that no direct attack upon our battery was meditated by the enemy, returned to a sheltered piece of ground.

A little incident occurred as we were about to move forward to the expected charge, which is perhaps worth recording. Next to the company with which I was serving was one which I noticed as being in most excellent order and equipment. The officer in command of it was of striking appearance, tall, well formed and handsome, and possessing withal a most soldierly air. I did not then know his name; but being so near to him and to his command, I could not but observe him. When the order came for us to move forward up the hill, and to be prepared to charge the moment the crest was reached, I saw the officer referred to ride gallantly in front of his command, and just as the signal forward was given, I heard him say, "Now men, do your duty." I was attracted by his soldierly words and bearing; and yet within a few days after the battle he tendered his resignation, and in a short time was serving under the Confederate flag as a general officer.

With the exception of a little tardiness in execution, something to be expected perhaps in raw troops, the plan of battle marked out by General McDowell was carried out with remarkable precision up till about half past three p.m. The Confederate left wing had been gradually forced back from Bull Run until the Federals gained entire possession of the Warrenton Turnpike leading from the Stone Bridge.

Warrenton Pike. During the first Battle of Bull Run, Confederate positions stretched from Stone Bridge, where the Warrenton Pike crossed Bull Run, to Union Mills Ford in the south, covering five major fords on Bull Run.

It is known now that Beauregard's army had become broken and routed, and that both himself and General Johnston felt called upon to place themselves at the head of their defeated commands, including their last reserves, in their effort to restore confidence and order; General Johnston at one critical moment charging to the front with the colors of the Fourth Alabama.

Had the fate of the battle been left to the decision of those who were present and fought up until half past three in the afternoon, the Union troops would have been entitled to score a victory with scarcely a serious reverse. But at this critical moment, with their enemies in front giving way in disorder and flight, a new and to the Federals an unexpected force appeared suddenly upon the scene. From a piece of timber almost directly in rear of McDowell's right, a column of several thousand fresh troops of the enemy burst almost upon the backs of the half victorious Federals.

I was standing with a friend and classmate at that moment on a high ridge near our advancing line. We were congratulating ourselves upon the glorious victory which already seemed to have been won, as the Confederates were everywhere giving way, when our attention was attracted by a long line of troops suddenly appearing behind us upon the edge of the timber already mentioned. It never occurred to either of us that the troops we then saw could be any but some of our reinforcements making their way to the front. Before doubts could arise, we saw the Confederate flag floating over a portion of the line just emerging from the timber; the next moment the entire line leveled their muskets and poured a volley into the backs of our advancing regiments on the right.

At the same time, a battery which had also arrived unseen opened fire and with a cry of "We're flanked, we're flanked!" passed from rank to rank, the Union lines, but a moment before so successful and triumphant, threw down their arms, were seized by a panic and began a most disordered flight. All this occurred almost in an instant of time. No pen or description can give anything like a correct idea of the rout and demoralization that followed. Officers and men joined in one vast crowd, abandoning, except in isolated instances, all attempts to preserve their organizations.

A moderate force of good cavalry at that moment could have secured to the Confederates nearly every man and gun that crossed Bull Run in the early morning. Fortunately, the Confederate army was so badly demoralized by its earlier reverses that it was in no mood or condition to make pursuit and reap the full fruits of victory. The troops that had arrived upon the battlefield so unexpectedly to the Federals, and which had wrought such disaster upon the Union arms, were Elzey's brigade of infantry and Beckham's battery of artillery, the whole under command of Brigadier-General E. Kirby Smith, being a detachment belonging to Johnston's Army of the Shenandoah, just arrived from the valley. Had this command reached the battlefield a few minutes later, the rout of Beauregard's army would have been assured, as his forces seemed powerless to check the advance of the Union troops.

General McDowell and his staff, as did many of the higher officers, exerted themselves to the utmost to stay the retreating Federals, but all appeals to the courage and patriotism of the latter fell as upon dumb animals. One who has never witnessed the conduct of large numbers of men when seized by a panic such as that was, cannot realize how utterly senseless and without apparent reason men will act. And yet the same men may have exhibited great gallantry and intelligence but a moment before.

The value of discipline was clearly shown in this crisis by observing the manner of the few regular troops, as contrasted with the raw and undisciplined three months' men. The regular soldiers never for a moment ceased to look to their officers for orders and instructions, and in retiring from the field even amid the greatest disorder and confusion of the organizations near them; they preserved their formation and marched only as they were directed to do.

The long lines of Union soldiery, which a few minutes before had been bravely confronting and driving the enemy, suddenly lost their cohesion and became one immense mass of fleeing, frightened creatures. Artillery horses were cut from their traces and it was no unusual sight to see three men, perhaps belonging to different regiments, riding the same horse and making their way to the rear as fast as the dense mass of men moving with them would permit.

The direction of the retreat was toward Centreville, by way of the Stone Bridge crossing and other fords above that point. An occasional shot from the enemy's artillery, or the cry that the Black Horse Cavalry, so dreaded in the first months of the war in Virginia, were coming, kept the fleeing crowd of soldiers at their best speed. Arms were thrown away as being no longer of service in warding off the enemy. Here and there the state colors of a regiment, or perhaps the national standard, would be seen lying on the ground along the line of retreat, no one venturing to reclaim or preserve them, while more than one full set of band instruments could be observed, dropped under the shade of some tree in rear of the line of battle, and where their late owners had probably been resting from the fatigues of the fight when the panic seized them and forced them to join their comrades in flight.

Stone Bridge crosses Bull Run at the east entrance of the Manassas National Battlefield Park. The original bridge was destroyed during the first Battle of Bull Run on July 21, 1861. A new bridge, similar to the original design, was built in 1884 on the site of the old bridge.

One good steady regiment composed of such sterling material as made up the regiments of either side at the termination of the war could have checked the pursuit before reaching Bull Run, and could have saved much of the artillery and many of the prisoners that as it was fell into the enemy's hands simply for want of owners. The rout continued until Centreville was reached; then the reserves posted under Mills gave some little confidence to the retreating masses, and after the latter had passed the reserves, comparative order began in a slight degree to be restored.

General McDowell at first decided to halt and make a stand on the heights near Centreville, but this was soon discovered to be unadvisable if not impracticable, so large a portion of the army having continued their flight toward Washington. Orders were then given the various commanders to conduct their forces back to their former camps near Arlington, opposite Washington, where they arrived the following day.

When the retreat began, my company and one other of cavalry, and a section of artillery commanded by Captain Arnold, came under the personal direction and control of Colonel Heintzleman, with whom we moved toward Centreville. Colonel Heintzleman, although suffering from a painful wound, continued to exercise command and maintained his seat in the saddle. The two companies of cavalry and the section of Arnold's battery moved off the battlefield in good order, and were the last organized bodies of Union troops to retire across Bull Run.

When within about two miles of Centreville, at the bridge across Cub Run, the crossing was found to be completely blocked up by broken wagons and ambulances. There being no other crossing available, and the enemy having opened with artillery from a position a short distance below the bridge, and commanding the latter, Captain Arnold was forced to abandon his guns. The cavalry found a passable ford for their purpose and from this point no further molestation was encountered from the enemy. After halting a few hours in some old camps near Centreville, it now being dark, the march was resumed, and kept up until Arlington was reached during the forenoon of the 22nd.

I little imagined when making my night ride from Washington to Centreville the night of the 20th that the following night would find me returning with a defeated and demoralized army. It was with the greatest difficulty that many of the regiments could be halted on the Arlington side of Long Bridge, so determined were they to seek safety and rest under the very walls of the capitol. Some of the regiments lost more men after the battle and retreat had ended than had been killed, wounded and captured by the enemy. Three-fourths of one regiment, known as the Zonaves, disappeared in this way. Many of the soldiers continued their flight until they reached New York.

Centreville was of significant strategic value due to its proximity to several important roads and its position atop a ridge, which provided a commanding view of the surrounding areas. It was also a frequent base of operations for Confederate Colonel John S. Mosby's partisans.

Here ends the vivid personal narrative of the young officer, placed so suddenly in the midst of the first great battle of the war. The reader will have noticed ere this, the frank and candid naiveté of his style, and the real modesty which pervades the account, the way in which he tells a story against himself, as to his first charge, and the perfect greenness to which he confesses, in spite of his West Point education. The reflections with which he closes his story of Bull Run are as just and sober, as the narrative is fresh and picturesque, and equally worthy of quotation. Besides this, they have the further advantage of being true to the letter. He says:

While the result of the Battle of Bull Run startled and aroused the entire country from the St. Lawrence to the Rio Grande, the effect upon the people of the North, and that upon those of the revolted states was widely different. The press and people of the South accepted the result of the battle as forecasting if not already assuring the ultimate success of their cause and marking, as they expressed it, the birth of a nation; and while this temporary advantage may have excited and inspired their enthusiasm, and increased their faith as well as their numbers by drawing or driving into their ranks the lukewarm, and those inclined to remain loyal, yet it was a source of weakness as well, from the fact that the people of the South were in a measure confirmed in the very prevalent belief which had long existed in the Southern states regarding the great superiority in battle of the Southron over his fellow countryman of colder climes.

This impression maintained its hold upon the minds of the people of the South, and upon the Southern soldiery, until eradicated by months and years of determined battle. The loyal North accepted its defeat in the most commendable manner, and this remark is true, whether applied to the high officials of the States and General Government or to the people at large. There was no indulging in vain or idle regrets; there was no flinching from the support and defense of the Union; there was least of all hesitation as to the proper course to pursue.

If the idea of compromise had been vainly cherished by any portion of the people, it had vanished, and but one sentiment, one purpose actuated the men of the North, as if acting under a single will. Men were hurried forward from all the loyal States; more offered their services than the government was prepared to accept. The defeat of the Union arms forced the North to coolly calculate the immense task before it in attempting to overthrow the military strength of the insurgent states.

Had Bull Ran resulted otherwise than it did, had the North instead of the South been the victor, there would have been danger of a feeling of false security pervading the minds of the people of the North. Their patriotism would not have been awakened by success as it was by disaster; they would not have felt called upon to abandon the farm, the workshop, the counting room and the pulpit in order to save a government tottering almost upon the brink of destruction.

It only remains to follow the soldier-author in his analysis of the subsequent careers of the officers present on both sides in this famous fight, and the story of Bull Run will be complete. It is interesting, says Custer, to note the names of officers of both contending armies who were present at the Battle of Bull Run, and who afterward achieved more or less distinction, and exercised important commands in later years of the war.

On the Union side there were McDowell, Hunter, Heintzelman, Burnside, Howard, Keyes, Franklin, Schenck, Wilcox, Gorman, Blenker, Ward, Richardson, Andrew Porter, Terry, Slocum, Wadsworth, Sykes, Barry, Hunt, Fry, Averill, Innes, Palmer, Wheaton, Barnard, Abbot, Webb, Griffin, Ricketts, Ayres, Baird, Wright, Whipple and Richard Arnold.

Of those officers who were present at the Battle of Bull Run, McDowell was the only one who held a rank above that of field officer, he being a brigadier-general. Sixteen held the rank of colonel, one that of lieutenant-colonel, six that of major, five that of captain, and eight the rank of lieutenant. Nearly all were advanced in time to the rank of major-general; more than half the number were appointed subsequently to the command of armies, corps or departments, while but few held positions below that of division commander.

Among the colonels of regiments at Bull Run was W.T. Sherman, now General of the Army of the United States. Of the present three major-generals of the regular army, one was the commander of the Union forces on that day; and of the six brigadier-generals now in the line of the regular army, two, Howard and Terry, were colonels of volunteer regiments at the battle of July 21.

Upon the side of the Confederates there was Johnston, Beauregard, Jackson (who obtained at this battle the *sobriquet* of Stonewall), E. Kirby Smith, Longstreet, J.E.B. Stuart, Hampton, D.R Jones, A.P. Hill, Ewell, Early, Kershaw, Elzey, Echolls, Hunton, Cooke, Pendleton, Holmes, S. Jones, Barksdale, Jordan and Evans. The great majority of these became prominent generals, and as commanders of armies or of large bodies of troops in several of the decisive battles and campaigns of the

LIEUTENANT CUSTER, SECOND CAVALRY

war, displayed great ability and gallantry, and won lasting renown by their prowess and military skill.

ORGANIZING AN ARMY

FOLLOWING our original design, we shall utilize, in describing the period immediately following the Battle of Bull Run, the scanty memoirs left by General Custer wherever they relate to personal adventures. We are convinced that they possess an interest and value to the public, especially since the early death of their author, to which a more elaborate narrative from another hand could not aspire.

The matter most to be deplored is that they are so very short that we shall soon be compelled to drop them, and that the last part was written in such exceeding haste, in the midst of camp life and even on the march against the Indians, as not fairly to represent the author. Had General Custer been spared another year, enjoying the advantages of leisure under which he wrote his *"My Life on the Plains,"* his contributions to the early history of the war must have proved of exceeding value. As it is, let us continue with him on his journey as far as he goes with us.

In selecting from his memoirs, we consider it due to the public however, to omit those purely personal estimates of the character of the various officers who at an early period of the war fell, justly or unjustly, under popular or political censure, with which the early chapters of the memoirs abound. The proper place for such estimates is to be found in the future history of the war so often dreamed about, and some day possibly to be written.

In the personal history of a single officer, other than that of the commander-in-chief, such estimates are only provocative of controversy, and needless for the elucidation of truth. Where they affect only the private character of the illustrious dead whose peculiarities are matter of public interest as in the case of Kearny, we quote them in full, especially where they illustrate the keen eye for character possessed by Custer himself. Accordingly, we will let him take up the narrative of events immediately following the Battle of Bull Run in his own language:

When McDowell saw the victory which he had planned so ably to achieve swept from his grasp almost at the moment when he deemed it secure, and beheld his forces, which but a moment before were driving their adversaries in disorder before them, now turn and abandon the field they had fought so gallantly to win, his first idea was to retire his army behind its reserves at Centreville, reform the disordered regiments, and renew the advance from that point. But when he reached Centreville, he saw that all efforts to stop or rally the flying Federals must prove unavailing, many of the regiments having without instructions continued their flight in the direction of Washington.

Orders were therefore given for the entire army to fall back to its old camps near Arlington, opposite the capital. The retreat was continued all night, and by noon of the following day the Federal army could be said to be safely back in its old camps near the capital. While the losses in the battle had been severe, they would have been almost unprecedented had all the absentees from the Union regiments, upon the arrival of the latter at Arlington, been chargeable to the legitimate losses of battle. The truth was that hundreds of men belonging to some of the regiments had not pretended to halt at their old camps, but had rushed across the Long Bridge over the Potomac, which separated their camps from the capital, and continuing their flight, made no halt until they had placed hundreds of miles between themselves and the scene of their late disaster.

Hundreds of these fugitives, including among their numbers a few officers, were seen in the streets of New York within forty-eight hours after the arrival of the routed army at Arlington. One regiment, the Second New York militia, reported one hundred and forty men missing after the battle, yet the regiment had not crossed Bull Run during the engagement.

The company of cavalry to which I belonged, and one other, with a section of Arnold's battery as already stated, were the last organized bodies of troops to leave the battlefield, which they did under the immediate command of Colonel Heintzelman. The guns had to be abandoned upon our arrival at Cub Run, owing to the passageway becoming blocked with broken vehicles. I had ridden nearly all the night preceding the battle to enable me to join the army and participate in the struggle. When the battle reached its disastrous termination, and night spread its mantle over our defeated and demoralized troops, I found myself hastening with the fleeing, frightened soldiery back toward that capital which I had left but a few hours before. To add to the discomforts and delays of the retreat, the rain fell in torrents, rendering the road almost impassable.

When the bridge at Cub Run (above) was destroyed at the Battle of Bull Run, cutting off the Union's major route of retreat, the retreat became a rout. The narrow roads and fords were clogged by carts and wagons full of people who had driven out from Washington, D.C. to see the spectacle, further hampering the withdrawal of the Union Army.

Reaching Arlington Heights early in the forenoon, I scarcely waited for my company to be assigned to its camp before I was stretched at full length under a tree where from fatigue, hunger and exhaustion I soon fell asleep, despite the rain and mud, and slept for hours without awakening. When I finally awoke and attempted to take a retrospect of my late introduction to actual service, I could find but little to console or flatter me, and still less to encourage a hopeful view of the success of the Union cause in the future; and yet while I do not now recall, even among the many dark and trying days passed through at later periods of the war, any event which brought with it more despondency and discouragement than the defeat at Bull Run, neither then nor at any subsequent period did I ever lose or lessen my faith, my firm belief and conviction, that the cause of the Union was destined in the end to triumphant over all obstacles and opposition.

General McDowell at once set himself to the immense work of restoring order and establishing discipline among his badly shattered columns. The President himself drove in an open carriage through the camps of the volunteers, occasionally halting and addressing a few words of comfort and encouragement to the groups of dispirited soldiery as the latter formed about his carriage. But something more substantial than speech making was speedily resolved upon. As the firing upon Sumter had been immediately followed by a call from the President for 75,000 men to serve for a period of three months, so was the disaster at Bull Run made the occasion for issuing a second call for a much greater number of men to serve for three years, or during the war.

The harsh and unjust criticisms which were showered from all parts of the land upon General McDowell for the unfortunate termination of the Battle of Bull Run, decided the government to call to the active command of the forces then assembled and about to assemble at Washington, a new chief. In making the selection for this important position, the opinion of the government officials charged with this duty, and that of the people as indicated by the public press, seemed to centre upon a single personage as the one best fitted to restore confidence to the troops, and to inspire the country with hopes of success in the future.

General McClellan, on the breaking out of the war, had been appointed by Governor Dennison of Ohio, to the grade of major-general of the state troops, and charged with the duty of organizing and equipping the immense force of volunteers furnished by that State, under the call for three months' men. Afterward assigned to the command of the military department of West Virginia, containing at that time a considerable number of troops in the field, opposed to which was a Confederate army under command of educated leaders, McClellan devised and put in execution a plan of operation which, after a series of rapid and most brilliant victories, resulted in the capture or overthrow of all the forces of the enemy operating in his, department.

Major General George B. McClellan and staff. From left: Lt. Williams, Surg. Walters, General Morell, Lt. Colonel Colburn, McClellan, Lt. Colonel Switzer, Prince de Joinville, Compte de Paris.

So decisive and gratifying were these victories, coming as they did almost simultaneously with the disaster and disappointment of Bull Run, and the operations of the Shenandoah, that all eyes had singled out the youthful victor in the West Virginia battles as the one destined to lead the armies of the republic to future victory.

On the 25th of July, four days after the defeat at Bull Run, McClellan, having turned over his command in West Virginia to

General Rosecrans, the next in rank, was assigned to the command of a geographical division which included the departments of Washington and Northeastern Virginia, with headquarters at Washington. No appointment to high command during the war received higher commendation or more universal approval from the people and the army, not even excepting that of General Grant in 1864.

It can also be truthfully said that no officer of either side ever developed or gave evidence of the possession of that high order of military ability which at that peculiar and particular time was so greatly demanded in the Federal commander, and which General McClellan brought to the discharge of his duties as the reorganizer and commander of a defeated and demoralized force, and to the formation of a new army composed almost entirely of new levies fresh from the counting house, the farm and the workshop.

Subsequent events and results of the war did much to detract from and cover up the real merit and worth of McClellan's achievements in this respect, but to him alone belongs the credit of that system of organization, discipline and supply by which the Army of the Potomac was created, and owing to which that army was unlike as well as superior to any other army of the republic, in all the acquired elements which tend to make a powerful and efficient force.

After some personal estimates of the causes of McClellan's failure, Custer proceeds:

After remaining at Arlington a few days, the company to which I belonged was ordered to Alexandria, at which point it only remained a brief period, being moved still further to the front, thus twice going beyond the Alexandria Seminary, where we were destined to remain some weeks. While at this point, General Philip Kearny, who had just been appointed Brigadier-general U.S. Volunteers, arrived and assumed command of a brigade of volunteers composed of four regiments of New Jersey troops, afterward known and distinguished as the Jersey Brigade.

To this brigade my company was temporarily attached, thus

bringing us under the command of Kearny. When he arrived from Washington with his commission as Brigadier-general, and with orders to organize the Jersey Brigade, he was not provided with a single staff officer, and being unacquainted with the younger officers of the brigade, was unable to select the necessary officers for his staff. In this dilemma he asked the officer commanding my company (Lieutenant Drummond) if, having three officers present for duty, he could not dispense with my services, I being the junior, to enable me to do duty upon the brigade staff.

To this proposition Drummond assented; whereupon Kearny, by a formal order, detailed me first as aide-de-camp, afterward as assistant adjutant-general, I being the first staff officer detailed by Kearny. I found the change from subaltern in a company to a responsible position on the staff of a most active and enterprising officer both agreeable and beneficial.

Kearny was a very peculiar, withal a very gallant leader. Formerly an officer of the regular service, he had enjoyed rare and unusual opportunities for perfecting his knowledge and experience in all matters relating to the military profession. He had while an officer of the army been detailed by the government as one of three officers to be sent to Europe, particularly to France, to study the military art and customs of service as prevailing in that country.

While abroad on this mission, he had opportunities to see the French army in actual service; and as results of his observation made some interesting and valuable reports to the government at Washington. He participated in our war with Mexico as a cavalry officer, losing an arm while leading a charge of cavalry which was characterized by its great boldness, if not by its success. After the war with Mexico, Kearny resigned his commission in the regular army, and being possessed of great wealth and a love for foreign travel and adventure, he spent several years abroad, during a portion of which he entered the French service under Napoleon III, and by his gallantry and conspicuous conduct won the marked commendation of the French military authorities.

He returned to his native country as soon as he learned of the

ORGANIZING AN ARMY

threatened outbreak between the North and South, and promptly sought to obtain a command which would enable him to fight in defense of the Union. In this, he was at first unsuccessful, and was forced to see other and inferior men appointed to commands which he would gladly have accepted. Finally successful in obtaining a commission, he at once formed his brigade and began devoting himself to the discipline and organization of that splendid body of men afterward destined to become so famous as Kearny's or the Jersey Brigade.

General Philip Kearny fought with Napoleon III's Imperial Guard at the Battle of Solferino, where he charged with cavalry under *Général* Louis-Michel Morris, braking the Austrian defenses. For this, Kearny was awarded the French *Légion d'honneur*, becoming the first U.S. citizen to thus be honored.

Of the many officers of high rank with whom I have served, Kearny was the strictest disciplinarian. So strict was he in this respect that were it not for the grander qualities he subsequently displayed, he might well have been considered as simply a military martinet. His severity of discipline was usually visited upon the higher officers, the colonels and field-officers rather than upon the subaltern and enlisted men. Once aroused by some departure, however slight, from the established regulation or order, and the unfortunate victim of Kearny's displeasure became the object and recipient of such a torrent of violent invectives, such varied and expressive epithets, that the limit of language seemed for once to have been reached; and luckless offenders have more than once tendered their resignations rather than subject themselves a second time to such an ordeal.

Kearny was a man of violent passions, quick and determined impulses, haughty demeanor, largely the result of his military training and life, brave as the bravest of men can be, possessed of unusually great activity, both mental and physical, patriotic as well as ambitious, impatient under all delay, extremely sensitive in regard to the claims of his command as well as his own. Distrustful of all those who differed with him in opinion or action, capable as a leader of men, and possessed of that necessary attribute which endeared him to his followers despite his severity, he presented a combination which is rarely encountered.

He constantly chafed under the restraint and inactivity of camp life, and was never so contented and happy as when moving to the attack. And whether it was the attack of a picket post or the storming of the enemy's breastworks, Kearny was always to be found where the danger was greatest. Notwithstanding the fame he achieved as an infantry commander, he never felt that he was in his proper place, but always longed to command immense bodies of cavalry, believing that with that arm he would find service more in keeping with his restless, impulsive temperament. Brave in battle, imperious in command, and at times domineering toward those beneath him, no one could wear a more courtly manner than Kearny, unless he willed to do otherwise.

During my brief but agreeable tour of duty with Kearny as a staff officer, I found him ever engaged in some scheme either looking to the improvement of his command or the discomfiture of his enemy. The pickets of the Confederates were stationed along a line but four or five miles distant from Kearny's headquarters. He determined, with the approval of higher authority, to organize a small expedition and effect the capture of what was believed to be one of the principal picket posts

ORGANIZING AN ARMY

of the Confederates. In fact, it was believed that on a particular night there were to be assembled at the house near which the picket reserve was located several Confederate officers of importance, who were reported to be reconnoitering the ground between the two hostile forces.

Kearny fixed the night in question as the one upon which the attempt to effect the capture should be made. Three hundred picked men from the Jersey Brigade were named for this duty. Lieutenant-Colonel Buck was assigned to the command. Kearny directed me to accompany the expedition as a representative from headquarters. It must be remembered that officers and men were at that time totally lacking in the actual experience of war. Those who fought at Bull Run had been discharged; and raw, inexperienced regiments had taken their places.

The night chosen for the undertaking proved to be a lovely moonlight one. The troops assembled near Kearny's headquarters about nine o'clock in the evening, and leaving all impediments in the way of blankets, overcoats, and unnecessary accoutrements behind, we soon began our silent march to the front.

It was known that the Confederate pickets were posted four or five miles in advance, but before marching half that distance a halt was ordered, and additional precautions adopted to preserve secrecy in our movements. From that point, we pursued our way as quietly as possible, no one being allowed to speak above a whisper. Sometimes, instead of following the road, we made our way through paths in the forest, feeling our way as cautiously as if masked batteries, then the *bête noire* of the average volunteer, were bristling from beyond every bush. The cracking of a twig in the distance, or the stumbling of one of the leading files over a concealed log, was sufficient to cause the entire column to halt, and with bated breath peer into the darkness of the forest in vain endeavor to discover a foe whose presence at that particular time and place was not desired.

In this manner we continued our course, at each step the tension on our nerves, to describe it by no other name, becoming greater and greater until we resembled in enlarged form some ludicrous stage picture in which the alarmed family, aroused from their beds by noise of imaginary burglars, come stealthily, timidly into the room, staring in all directions to discover the disturber of the household, and ready to drop all weapons of defense and seek safety in flight at the first real cause of alarm.

So it was with us. Inexperienced, magnifying the strength and terrible character of our unseen foes, dreading surprise, we had worked ourselves up to so excitable a condition, that all that was necessary to terminate our anxiety as well as the expedition, was to confront us with an undoubted enemy. We were not to undergo much longer delay. The house about which the picket was posted, and which was to be the object of our attack - a surprise if possible - was located at one end of a long lane, at the foot of which we now found ourselves. A brief halt was made, final instructions from our leaders were whispered from ear to ear, and again we moved forward.

Owing to clouds, we could only receive partial benefit from the moon; sufficient however, to discern in the distance at the head of the lane a clump of trees within which the house was said to be located. As we silently made our way up the lane, moving in column of fours, with not a skirmisher or advance guard thrown to the front, every isolated tree or even the farmer's herd grazing in the fields nearby were sufficient to make us halt and determine whether or not we were being flanked. Frequent discoveries of our errors in this respect might have inspired us with some little confidence, but at that moment we surely heard human voices up the lane in the vicinity of the house. Of course, we halted.

It did not impress me that we were engaged in a military undertaking; on the contrary, it struck me as resembling upon a large scale some boyhood scheme involving a movement upon a neighboring orchard or a melon patch, and the time had arrived just before crossing the fence, when the impression prevails that the owner of the orchard and his dog are on the lookout. Halting to listen and distinguish the voices again, a few moments silence ensued during which the clouds cleared away, permitting the moon to shine forth and light up the whole scene, and enabling the enemy's pickets to take in at a glance who and what we were.

'Who comes there?' rang out on the still night air, and without waiting for an answer, bang, bang, bang, went three muskets. It was a sorrowful waste of ammunition to fire three muskets when one would have answered as well. I am sure that while we may all have been facing toward the house when the first shot was fired, we were not only facing but moving in the opposite direction before the sound of the last one reached our ears. I presume too that the fellows who fired the shots ran in the opposite direction faster than we did; that is, if they were disposed to be active. But all chance to effect a surprise having been lost, our party did not propose to expend either time or ammunition in furtherance of the object of the expedition.

We beat a hasty if not precipitate retreat and returned to our camp in less than half the time it had required to march from there. The same officers and men who participated in this little affair, if charged with the same duty one year later, at a time when they had become more familiar with the operations of war, would have in all probability succeeded in capturing and bringing away as prisoners the entire picket guard and its immediate reserves.

I remained on Kearny's staff as aide until an order was issued prohibiting officers of the regular army from serving on the staffs of officers holding commissions as volunteers. Early in the fall of 1861, the principal portion of the cavalry, both regular and volunteer, was formed into one organization and collected near Washington under the command of Brigadier-General Philip St. George Cooke, an officer who had rendered valuable service as a cavalry officer on the plains, and who had more recently attracted attention in military circles as the author of a system of cavalry tactics based upon the single rank formation, the principles of which, under another name, have been largely adopted by the government for all arms of its service.

Brigadier-General Stoneman, another cavalry officer, was announced as chief of cavalry on the staff of General McClellan. To Stoneman was assigned the task of organizing and equipping the cavalry forces which were to operate in the field with the Army of the Potomac. The concentration of the cavalry near Washington transferred my company from its camp with Kearny's Brigade below Alexandria to Cliffburn, about two miles east of the capital. The fall and winter were passed in perfecting, as far as possible, the preparations for the spring campaign.

George A. Custer

During the fall of 1861, Lieutenant Custer was ordered home on sick leave in October, and remained there until February, 1862, when he rejoined the Army of the Potomac, being assigned to the Fifth Cavalry.

This period of leave brings us to a time in Custer's career which witnessed the final formation of his moral character, and changed him in many respects from a wild and reckless boy into a self-respecting man. In regarding his character as testified to by others, we have hitherto found everything to admire and little to censure, his uncommon goodness in youth being remarkable. This, his first army leave, was distinguished by his solitary lapse from exemplary life, but it was marked also by his sudden and permanent reform and awakening to principle.

We have said in an early chapter that Custer never at any time drank intoxicating liquors, nor smoked. This statement must now be qualified. In his early life and while at West Point, he never did. The influence of a pure and virtuous home life, of a family of exemplary piety, saved him from all such dangers. It was not until he entered the army and lived around Washington that he learned what temptation was, and then it came on him with resistless force.

It must be remembered that at that time the Army of the Potomac had gathered to itself, along with many good men, many worthless, dissipated scamps, even among the highest officers. The amount of hard drinking that was done by all, from general to lieutenant, was frightful, and the language in common use was of the vilest description. While all this at first made a pure-minded country boy disgusted and ashamed, he found, like all others, that familiarity blunted his senses, and finally he yielded to the prevailing habits.

Poor lad, how could he help it! He saw his general Kearny, whom

ORGANIZING AN ARMY

he admired and respected as a model soldier, given over to both, swearing with an elaboration of blasphemy that shocked him at first, amused him later, and finally almost compelled his imitation, from unconscious habit. Everyone drank deep, and there seemed to be no escape from the habit.

Briefly, this period was the one little spot in Custer's career, the one fault in a perfect life. He fell in with the prevailing habits, drank as deep and swore as hard as any man in the army. With these habits, he went home and paid a long visit to Monroe. While there, he at once became somewhat of a pet. In those days, every soldier was a favorite, and Lieutenant Custer "of the Regular Army" was a very different person from the schoolboy "Armstrong," who used to wrestle with the boys and run the streets in old times. He was becoming a man of mark, and was one of those who were "making history."

Judge Daniel S. Bacon, Mrs. Eleanor Bacon and Elizabeth Clift Bacon. Daniel and Eleanor had three other children - 2 girls died in infancy and a boy died at the age of 8 of a childhood disease.

The public characters of the little town began to notice him, and among others Judge Bacon recognized him publicly and praised his conduct. The Judge was an original Old Line Whig, and therefore almost of necessity an ardent Republican and firm supporter of the Union under Lincoln. He was an enthusiastic admirer of the soldiers, and during the early part of the war lived much in public, frequently addressed Union meetings, and used all of his great influence to forward the cause he loved.

It was quite natural therefore that he should look on the rising young officer; who had been on Kearny's staff, with great favor, and he did so. The Judge however, was one of those men of firm and unbending rectitude and fastidious social sense, who make a great distinction between public and private life. While his acquaintance with young Custer in public life was quite cordial, he never (at that time) offered to introduce him into his private family. There was a certain gulf still existing between the chief personage of Monroe and the young officer which might have been overlooked elsewhere, but not in a place where the distinctions of circles are so marked as in a small country town like Monroe.

Still, the Judge was much interested in young Custer and frequently spoke of him to his daughter, now a young lady of sixteen and approaching her graduation at the Seminary. But with the natural perversity of the female sex, the more the Judge spoke in praise of the young man, the less did the daughter seem inclined to like him. She remembered him as one of a crowd of "boys," and like almost every young girl brought up at home and under strict religious teachings, she looked on "boys" as a sort of wild beasts with whom she could have no feelings in common.

Affairs were in this state, young Custer on a long visit to Mrs. Reed, when he fell in one day with a number of old school cronies and started on a grand spree. Custer had always been of a peculiarly nervous and excitable temperament, and liquor made him a perfect maniac, no matter how little he took. The result was that towards sunset, the young officer and one of his old schoolmates were seen coming up Monroe Street past the Judge's house, going towards Mrs. Reed's, and Custer was taking the whole sidewalk to himself in a peculiarly free and easy state.

ORGANIZING AN ARMY

Bacon House. Elizabeth Clift Bacon lived here with her father, Judge Daniel S. Bacon, until her marriage in 1863. The house also served as a home for the Custers in early 1868, and Libbie again lived there for a time after Custer's death in 1876.

As luck would have it, the Judge's daughter was at the window; she saw him, and her dislike was intensified at once. Custer went home to Mrs. Reed's, and there too his sister saw him, for the first time in his life as far as she knew, plainly under the influence of liquor, if not decidedly drunk. That night was the turning point of young Custer's life, and the country is today indebted for all the beauty and nobility of his subsequent career to the earnest will, love and piety of one of the best Christian women that ever breathed.

Mrs. Reed saw him. Surprised, shocked and grieved as she was, that good creature never hesitated. She went straight to him, wild as he was in looks, and told him she wished to speak to him alone. His companion left, feeling somewhat ashamed of himself, Custer throwing him a gay promise to meet him downtown. Then as the door closed, Lieutenant Custer of the army found himself undergoing a strange transformation back to quiet docile Armstrong before the grieved and steady gaze of his sister.

She led him to her room in silence, locked the door on both, and then asked him "what he had been doing." The proud young soldier sobered in a moment, crimsoned like a girl, and felt horribly ashamed of himself.

Downtown Monroe, Michigan, 1865

What passed at that interview between the anxious loving sister and the impulsive erring boy, already repenting of his degradation and error, will never be fully known until the last day. Far be it from us to strive to lift the veil. It was a season of tears, prayers and earnest pleading on one side, overcoming all resistance on the other. The result was that George Armstrong Custer then and there, in the presence of God, gave his sister a solemn pledge that never henceforth to the day of his death should a drop of intoxicating liquor pass his lips. That pledge he kept in letter and spirit to the last. His first excess in Monroe was his last anywhere, and henceforth he was a free man.

It may be asked perhaps why we have related this incident of Custer's career, the only painful one that mars an otherwise perfect life. We have done so because it was really the turning point for Custer, and for the purpose of reimpressing on the world the nature of those home influences, so sweet and pure, which ended in moulding a character of perfect knighthood. Mother, sister and finally wife, three noble women aided to mould that character. True, the material was noble and plastic, but at that early period how easy it would have been to have made thereof a fierce type of destroying power, devoid of moral beauty. From all the errors of such a sombre figure of valor and unhappiness, Custer was saved by the influence of a Christian sister. Honor to her for it!

His punishment for the brief lapse was yet to come, but it found him prepared with strength of purpose and principle to live down the past and conquer his future. His error was public, and the one woman of all others whose opinion he valued had seen him degraded. How should he ever now attain her love? The gulf widened to an almost immeasurable distance at once. To most men, it would have seemed hopelessly wide. Was it to him? We shall see further on. For the present let us turn from his private to his public life.

THE PENINSULAR CAMPAIGN

WHEN Custer returned to his post in February, he found that a marvelous transformation of affairs had taken place. Washington was securely girdled with fortifications and, what was of more importance; the Army of the Potomac was created. The question of the best method of advance was even then in progress of hot discussion between McClellan and the President; and this discussion consumed most of the month. Into the merits of the controversy, it is not the purpose of General Custer's biographer to enter, further than to state its nature and chronicle its result.

The President wished McClellan to advance on the Confederate forces at Manassas and fight a second Battle of Bull Run. McClellan wished to transfer the army by water to the Peninsula and operate on Richmond from thence. The difference of opinion caused a long correspondence between the two, which ended in McClellan gaining his point; and the transports were accordingly gathered in the Chesapeake to transfer the army to Fortress Monroe.

General Custer, in his last published papers, enters warmly into the controversy in favor of McClellan, for whom he entertained a most sincere admiration. Without following him into the vexed region, we shall again quote from him in all that pertains to the record of facts affecting himself. On the eighth of March, 1862, the President issued his "War Order No. 2," dividing the Army of the Potomac into four corps under Generals McDowell, Sumner, Heintzelman and Keyes:

On the 9th of March, continues Custer, McClellan received information that the enemy was evacuating his position at Manassas, a move, as was afterward ascertained, decided upon when an idea was gained upon the part of the enemy in regard to the transfer of the Army of the Potomac to a new base. This was the effect foreseen by

THE PENINSULAR CAMPAIGN

McClellan, but the bad condition of the roads between Washington and Manassas prevented him from embarrassing the enemy in his retirement.

Fairfax Court House. When Confederate troops withdrew from Fairfax Court House in the fall of 1861, George Washington's will was secretly removed from the building by the court clerk, Alfred Moss, and taken to Richmond, Virginia. There, it was placed for safekeeping with the Secretary of the Commonwealth of Virginia. At the end of the war, it was returned to Fairfax.

As the transports could not be ready for some time to move the army to its new base, McClellan decided to march it to Manassas and back in order to give the troops some preliminary experience in marching and the rigors of actual service. Orders were issued during the 9th for a general movement of the army the next morning toward Centreville and Manassas. At noon on the 10th, the cavalry advanced under Averill, reached the enemy's lines at Centreville, and found them abandoned, the enemy having burned a considerable amount of military stores and other valuable property.

On the 13th of March, McClellan called a council of war at his headquarters in the field of Fairfax Court House, the council consisting of the four corps commanders, McDowell, Sumner, Keyes, and Heintzelman, at which it was decided that the enemy, having retreated from Manassas to Gordonsville, behind the Rappahannock and Rapidan, it is the opinion of generals commanding corps that the operations to be carried on will be best undertaken from Old Point Comfort, between the York and James Rivers.

Operating against Richmond from Fortress Monroe as a base, it would be desirable to use both the James and York Rivers as lines of communication and supply; but the appearance on the 8th of March of the Confederate iron-clad Merrimac off Fortress Monroe, and the havoc created in the Federal fleet, imperiled the adoption of the peninsular plan of campaign; but on the 9th of March, the Monitor, as invented by Ericsson, engaged the Merrimac near Fortress Monroe, and so clearly established its superiority over the latter, as to remove considerable of the apprehension entertained in regard to the Merrimac's ability to embarrass operations. Even if the James River remained closed, the line of the York and its tributaries was open.

While the army was being marched toward Manassas, I obtained my first experience with cavalry advance guards. General Stoneman, chief of cavalry, was directed to push a large force of cavalry along the line of the Orange and Alexandria railroad to determine the position of the enemy, and if possible drive him across the Rappahannock. Upon arriving at Catlett's Station, near Cedar Run, the enemy's pickets were discerned in considerable force on a hill about one mile in our front. The Fifth United States Cavalry, to which I then belonged, was in advance. Upon discerning the pickets, a halt was ordered, and intelligence of the enemy's presence sent to General Stoneman.

An order was soon received from that officer directing that the pickets of the enemy be driven back across Cedar Run. When this order reached us, the officers of the regiment were generally assembled in a group at the head of the column, Major Charles J. Whiting in command. I at once asked permission to take my company, the command of which I accidentally held owing to the absence of the captain and first lieutenant, and perform the duty of driving in the pickets. Permission being accorded, I marched the company to the front, formed line and advanced toward the pickets, then plainly in view, and interested observers of our movements.

Catlett's Station. The battle at Catlett's Station was the scene of the first "charge" commanded by Custer, taking place on March 14th, 1862.

Advancing without opposition to the base of the hill upon which the pickets were posted, when within convenient distance I gave the command 'Charge' for the first time. My company responded gallantly and away we went. Our adversaries did not wait to receive us, but retreated hurriedly and crossed the bridge over Cedar Run, setting fire to it immediately after.

We pursued them to the bank of the run, and then exchanged several shots with the enemy, now safely posted on the opposite side. Being unable to advance across the stream and exposed to a serious fire from small arms, I ordered my command to retire, which it did in excellent order, but not until one man, private John W. Bryaud, had been shot in the head, fortunately not seriously, and one horse wounded.

Battles and skirmishes at that time were unfamiliar events to the men composing the Army of the Potomac, and the little episode just recorded furnished a topic for general discussion and comment. The company that had been engaged in the affair was praised by its companions, while it was a question whether private Bryaud suffered most from his wound or the numerous and inquiring visits of the enterprising representatives of the press, each anxious and determined to gather and record for his particular journal, all the details connected with the shedding of the first blood by the Army of the Potomac.

Federal Battery at Cedar Run. The Battle of Cedar Run, also known as Slaughter's Mountain or Cedar Mountain, took place on August 9, 1862. The battle was the first combat of the Northern Virginia Campaign.

Such was the first introduction of the young officer to actual fighting, for at Bull Run he must be considered merely as a spectator. When the great enterprise and moral force of the rebel cavalry at that time is considered, it is interesting to note how, even then, they always shrunk from the cold steel of a charge. The only American cavalry at that date capable of a mounted charge in real earnest was the small force of regulars, and the superiority of that method of fighting cavalry over the "shooting business," indulged in by the enemy, was first illustrated in Virginia by Custer - it was symptomatic of the future of the young officer, for almost all his subsequent successes were obtained

THE PENINSULAR CAMPAIGN

in the same manner, by rapid mounted charges.

Continuing his narrative of facts, we quote now from the last paper ever furnished by Custer to his publishers. It was written while on his march toward the foe that slew him and was not received until some days after the news of his death.

In endeavoring, says Custer, to quiet the anxious fears of President Lincoln in regard to a movement of the Confederate army at Manassas against Washington after the transfer to the Peninsula of the Army of the Potomac, McClellan assured him that the latter movement would of itself be the surest and quickest method as well as the one involving the least loss of life by which the enemy would be forced to abandon his fortified positions at Centreville and Manassas, and thus free Washington from the menace of attack.

This opinion was promptly verified by the course adopted by the Confederate leader, General Joseph E. Johnston. No sooner did he learn of the contemplated transfer of the Army of the Potomac to the Lower Chesapeake than he evacuated every fortified position in front of Washington and retired toward Richmond; and McClellan truly remarked afterward that at no former period was southern Virginia so completely in our possession, and the vicinity of Washington free from the presence of the enemy. The ground so gained was not lost, nor Washington again put in danger until the enemy learned that orders had been sent to the Army of the Potomac to evacuate the Peninsula, and thus leave them free to move directly toward Washington, which they did at once, and again seriously menaced the national capital.

Fort Monroe having been selected as the base of operations of the Army of the Potomac by the council of war assembled March 13th, and that selection having been acquiesced in by the President, the next step was to transfer the Army of the Potomac from Washington to the Peninsula.

The first plan for the transfer of the army to its new base involved the embarkation of McDowell's corps first; the intention being to land it either at a point termed the Sandbox on the right bank of York River, about four miles below Yorktown, and thus turn the works of the enemy supposed to be at Ship Point, Howard's Bridge, and Big Bethel, or to land it on the Gloucester side of York River, and move from there to West Point.

This plan was subsequently changed, and the most convenient divisions were embarked first, and moved direct to Fortress Monroe. McDowell's corps, by the new arrangement, was to embark last, and as an entire corps moved to such point on York River as might afterward be decided upon. The first division to embark was that of General Hamilton of Heintzelman's corps, which left Alexandria March 17th. On the 22nd of March, Fitz John Porter's division of the same corps embarked from the same point accompanied by General Heintzelman, the corps commander. McClellan, with his entire headquarters, embarked on the steamer Commodore on the 1st of April, the day after he had been informed by the President that Blenker's division, ten thousand strong, was to be taken from his command.

He arrived at Fortress Monroe the afternoon of the following day, and at once began giving his personal attention to the disposition of his troops as they arrived and disembarked. When the enemy's batteries controlled or threatened the navigation of the Potomac, it had been arranged to embark the troops from Annapolis, Maryland, but upon the abandonment of these batteries by the enemy, it was no longer convenient or desirable to embark from Annapolis. Alexandria, Virginia, was therefore chosen as the point of embarkation, and orders given for the chartering and assembling of the necessary water transportation.

Omitting the details of what in itself was a stupendous undertaking, the transfer to a new and distant base of an immense army with all its material and accompaniments, it will be sufficient at present simply to record that in thirty-seven days from the time the order was given to secure the transportation necessary for so extensive a movement, the transfer of the Army of the Potomac was effected from Washington to Fort Monroe. This transfer involved the shipment of 121,500 men, 14,592 animals, 1,150 wagons, 44 batteries, 74 ambulances, besides pontoon bridges, materials for telegraph lines and other miscellaneous matter. No accident or loss occurred to mar the success of this achievement, save the loss of less than a score of mules.

THE PENINSULAR CAMPAIGN

Fort Monroe Sally Port. Fort Monroe was one of the few forts in the South that remained in Union hands for the duration of the war. It limited the significance of the Confederate naval yard at Norfolk and served as a staging point for attacks on Richmond, the Confederate capital.

The vessels required to effect this transfer were as follows: One hundred and thirteen steamers, at two hundred and fifteen dollars and ten cents per day. One hundred and eighteen schooners, at twenty-four dollars and forty-five cents per day. Eighty-eight barges, at one thousand four hundred and twenty-seven dollars per day.

"Nine of the latter drifted ashore during a severe gale, but their cargoes were saved. The troops were ordered to take up the line of march from Fortress Monroe up the Peninsula, the second day succeeding McClellan's arrival. This was the 4th. The troops moved in two columns; that on the right under Heintzelman by the Big Bethel and Yorktown road, that on the left under Keyes by the James River and Warwick Court House road."

"On the afternoon of the 5th, both columns were brought to a halt. Heintzelman's on the right, found itself in front of the enemy's earthworks at Yorktown, that of Keyes, consisting of Baldy Smith's division, came unexpectedly upon a heavy force of the enemy entrenched near Lee's Mills, at the crossing of Warwick River. The enemy opened upon Smith's troops with artillery and musketry."

"The Warwick River is a diminutive stream, undeserving the name of river, and in itself does not constitute a military obstacle, but the Confederates, by a series of dams, constructed at convenient points the latter, protected by batteries and rifle pits, had enlarged Warwick River until it had become an almost impassable barrier to the advance of troops unless the fire from the protecting batteries and rifle pits could be silenced."

"So formidable were the defensive arrangements of the enemy that General Keyes found it impracticable to execute the order which McClellan had given him, which was to carry the enemy's position by assault. By this system of dams, with their protecting batteries and rifle pits, the Warwick River which heads within rifle shot of Yorktown and flows across the narrow peninsula to the James, became an excellent line of defense for the enemy, and a most serious obstruction to the advance of the Union forces."

"On the 16th of April however, it was determined to push a strong reconnaissance against what was supposed to be the weakest point in the enemy's line, intending if successful to support the movement and make it general. The point selected was a short distance above Lee's Mills, and opposite that portion of the Federal line held by Smith's division. General Smith directed the attack, the brunt of which was borne by the Vermont brigade. The attacking party reached the first line of the enemy's works after wading to the arm pits across the marshy Warwick, but only to find their position commanded by other lines of entrenchments. The movement was a failure, except so far as it developed the strength of the enemy's position. The Union troops were driven back with heavy loss."

"The slow operations of the siege continued. Batteries of heavy guns were brought up and placed in position. Each day marked a step toward the completion of the preliminary preparations. It was about this time that I received an order which greatly changed the character of my duties. I had left Alexandria, Virginia, with my company of the Fifth U.S. Cavalry as second lieutenant of the company, and was among the first to arrive at Fortress Monroe. I served with my company

THE PENINSULAR CAMPAIGN

during the march from Fortress Monroe to the Warwick. When it was decided to commence a siege, there was a demand for young officers competent to serve as subordinates to the engineer officers in superintending working parties engaged in making fascines and gabions and in laying out and erecting field works, a practical knowledge of which was supposed to belong to all recent graduates."

Bridge over Chickahominy River. During the war, the upper reaches became a major obstacle to Union General George B. McClellan's Peninsula Campaign. Docile and narrow dry weather, after periods of rain, it grows across flood plains with swamps as far as a mile across.

"It was my good fortune to be one of the young officers selected for this duty, and I was ordered to report as assistant to Lieutenant Nicholas Bowen of the Topographical Engineers, at that time Chief Engineer on the staff of General W.F. Smith (Baldy). I served in this capacity - obtaining a most invaluable experience - until the army found its advance to Richmond obstructed by the treacherous and tortuous windings of the Chickahominy River, a stream which, however chargeable with some of the misfortunes of the Army of the Potomac, was almost literally a stepping stone for my personal advancement."

Here ends the record of Custer's military life as written by his own hand, and the closing sentence brings us to the first important event of his career, whereby he was brought to the notice of the commander of the army, and earned his promotion to the grade of a captain.

Confederate fortifications at the Siege of Yorktown. At Yorktown, Confederate General Magruder staged an elaborate ruse to fool Union General McClellan. He ordered logs painted black, called "Quaker Guns," placed in redoubts to give the appearance of many artillery pieces. Magruder marched his men to and from to enhance the illusion. The ruse worked, as McClellan became convinced he could not make a frontal assault.

NOTE: Since the publication of his last article, written while on his last expedition, and forwarded from his last camp, and since the writing of the above paragraph, another manuscript has come to light among General Ouster's papers, which covers this period of his life up to the close of the battle of Williamsburg. This manuscript was written after a triumphant Indian campaign and was one of the general's first efforts at authorship. It begins almost the same as his Galaxy "*War Memoirs*," and traverses the same ground, with similar peculiarities of style, but with much superior freshness and raciness of detail. At the end of the battle of Williamsburg it stops abruptly, the author having been discouraged from its continuance by a notion that it was unequal to the subject and feeling, more keenly than the world gives him credit for, his own deficiencies in that mechanical education of a writer on which so much stress is laid now-a-days. This last article was published in the Galaxy for November, 1876, but its contents do not add any very important

THE PENINSULAR CAMPAIGN

information as to the life of Lieutenant Custer at the time, save those details which are always of interest as concerning him.

From this paper, it appears that Custer, while at the siege of Yorktown, was engaged with a working party in throwing up by night a line of rifle pits, the nearest to the enemy of any pushed out during the siege, so near that the working party was compelled to shovel the sandy soil in stealthy silence, while they could hear all the conversation of their enemies within a very short distance.

Besides this duty, Custer was also detailed for a large part of the time on balloon reconnaissance, and he gives a graphic description of his first ascent, and of his subsequent observations of the enemy's line at different periods. He was one of the first, while up in the balloon, to detect the fact of Johnston's evacuation, and hastened to General "Baldy" Smith's headquarters to report the fact. He was met there by the same information, come in from two different headquarters; one of them a Negro who had escaped through the lines; and so the credit of being the first to announce the evacuation was evenly divided.

This paper also makes it clear how Custer came to be at the rifle pit, and afterwards at the battle of Williamsburg with Hancock's brigade. The rifle pit was in front of General "Baldy" Smith's command, to which Custer was attached as assistant engineer, and Hancock's brigade was part of the same division. Custer therefore had a sort of roving commission to go anywhere he could to acquire information, that would aid him in his maps and sketches, and his idea of the duties of an engineer officer as laid down in that paper are exacting enough to fill the role of a general officer. There were not many such engineers as Custer.

WINNING THE BARS

ON the 3rd of May, 1862, General Joseph E. Johnston, who had been appointed to the command of the Confederate forces in the Peninsula; found that his position before Yorktown was no longer tenable. McClellan had pushed his siege works close to Yorktown, his army was all landed and his breaching batteries were ready to open. The Federal gunboats in the York River were moreover ready to move up the river as soon as the fire of Yorktown should be overcome; and that place once passed, there was nothing to prevent the landing of a heavy force in Johnston's rear.

Federal gunboat Mendota. The gunboat was a naval craft designed for the primary purpose of bombarding coastal targets.

WINNING THE BARS

His army, as we learn from the 'Narrative,' then amounted to 53,000 men, while McClellan's forces, as stated by his own morning report, were 112,000 men. By the aid of heavy works, Johnston had held him back so far, just as Lee subsequently did to Grant at Petersburg, but there was this important difference in McClellan's favor against Johnston, that the latter's flanks were only covered by water, and that Federal gunboats controlled that water. It was inevitable that Yorktown should be evacuated as soon as it was seriously attacked. Johnston had done all that could be hoped for when he detailed McClellan a whole month in front of his works.

On the night of Saturday, the Confederates stole away from the lines of Yorktown in the darkness and moved up the Peninsula towards Richmond. Johnston's army consisted of four strong divisions of infantry, those of Magruder, Longstreet, D.H. Hill and G.W. Smith. Magruder and Smith took the lead; then came the baggage, and Longstreet amid D.H. Hill followed, Longstreet forming the infantry rear guard. Stuart's cavalry brigade, then inconsiderable in numbers, stayed at Yorktown to the last and followed the infantry leisurely.

At 2 a.m. May 4th, McClellan's army discovered the fact of the evacuation and began preparations for a move. The small cavalry force of the Army of the Potomac, with a battery, started out in the morning and followed Stuart with excessive caution, under command of General Stoneman. They struck Stuart about 4 p.m. near Williamsburg, drove him in and penetrated to a redoubt called Fort Magruder, one of the works prepared by the providence of the first Confederate commander, as a good point to stay the advance of the enemy.

Longstreet sent back Kershaw's and Semmes's brigades of foot to Stuart's help, drove off Stoneman and took one of his guns, which was found abandoned. That night, Longstreet's division halted near Williamsburg and his rear guard occupied Fort Magruder and six redoubts on a line with it. It began to rain before morning and the mud was soon very heavy, a fore-taste of future Virginia campaigning.

Next day, the Federal advance, consisting of Hooker's division, struck Fort Magruder and fought all the morning, so hard that Hill's division of Confederates had to be sent back to Longstreet's help. On the Federal side, four more divisions came up, but did not join Hooker, who was left to fight his battle almost alone until later in the day, when the pressure of the enemy compelled Peck's brigade and some of "Baldy" Smith's division to be put in. Finally, Kearney's division, in the same corps as Hooker's, came up from the rear, having been the last to leave Yorktown, and went in beside Hooker, who had suffered severely.

The assistance however, did not come in time to prevent the loss of seventeen hundred men in killed, wounded and missing from Hooker's division, with ten colors taken and five guns carried off, besides five more injured and abandoned. In the mean time however, Hancock's brigade on the Federal side had crossed a little run to the right of Fort Magruder and occupied two of the chain of redoubts on the line of the fort, thus turning Longstreet's left.

With this brigade, Lieutenant Custer made his appearance, and behaved with his usual dash and vigor. He does not seem to have had any particular business to call him there, but his restless nature took him always to the extreme advance where there was any duty to be done, and he seems early to have discovered that with Hancock's command was about as good a place as could be found for that sort of service.

George Armstrong Custer

WINNING THE BARS

Very frequently afterwards during the campaign, he found himself with the same brigade. It is noticeable too that at Williamsburg, his military eye led him to prefer Hancock's position to Hooker's. There was much harder fighting in front of Hooker, but it was early evident that it was a perfectly hopeless struggle for that single division to attempt to carry the Confederate works in front. It was a mere useless slaughter of brave men. In Hancock's direction, a success promised something. It turned Longstreet's flank; and had it been supported by other of the numerous troops that lay idly looking on, might easily have resulted in the capture of the greater part of Johnston's rear guard.

As it was, Hancock's single brigade caused Longstreet the only serious alarm he suffered during the day, according to the admissions made in "Johnston's Narrative." It did all that so small a force could be expected to do, occupied the redoubts, driving out the enemy's skirmishers, held its own all day; and when Early's brigade towards evening advanced to dislodge it, went in on the charge and thrashed Early's brigade most handsomely, the only decided success of the day. The part taken by Custer in the affair is characteristic, and is thus mentioned in Hancock's report:

"I now placed the artillery in battery on the crest of the hill in front of the enemy's work at short range, deployed skirmishers on the right and left of the road, and sent the Fifth Wisconsin, preceded by skirmishers under command of Major Larrabee and followed by the Sixth Maine in column of assault across the dam and into the work, Lieutenant Custer, Fifth Regular Cavalry, volunteering and leading the way on horseback."

The little run mentioned had been turned into a millpond in former times, and the troops crossed on the dam. A queer figure Custer then was, according to the accounts of eyewitnesses. One officer took him for a dashing newspaper correspondent, out to see the fun. He wore an old slouch hat and a cavalry jacket, with no marks of rank, the jacket flying open, while his muddy boots did not look worth more than a dollar. His hair was beginning to grow long and aided his careless dress to give him a slouchy appearance, but even then there was something peculiar about him that made people ask, "Who is that young fellow?" It was not for more than a year after, that he came out as a dandy.

In the charge on Early's brigade, which cost Early four hundred men, this careless looking young officer was around as usual, waving his shocking bad hat and cheering on the men in the style afterwards so famous. Few knew him, but his cheery ways and the habit he had of laughing and joking in action helped on the green troops as nothing else would.

In a first fight, the best drilled soldiers are always nervous. When they come on an enemy and deliver their own volley they are alright, but when the counter volley strikes them, and they see their friends cut down all along the line, the faint hearted begin to drop out with the peculiar suddenness that distinguishes the "skulker."

Then the bravest feel discouraged, as if they were being left all alone, and they too are ready to fall back. If at that moment up comes a mounted officer, laughing and cheery with his "Stand fast, boys, we'll beat them! Give 'em another volley now!" it is wonderful how those men will cheer up and load and fire. It comes to a test of who can take most punishment and at Williamsburg, Hancock's brigade showed they could, and ended by sweeping Early from the field.

At the close of the Battle of Williamsburg, Johnston withdrew during the night, and the next month was occupied by McClellan's slow advance up the Peninsula, feeling his way to West Point, whence he turned to the left and bore down on Richmond from the northeast, following the line of the railroad into Richmond. How slow and cautious was his advance may be judged from the fact that it was not until the 22nd of May, seventeen days after the Battle of Williamsburg, that his advance reached the Chickahominy River.

In order to understand the subsequent movements and what is called the "Seven Days Fight," a short account of the Virginia Peninsula and the localities around Richmond is here necessary for those readers not familiar with the ground.

The City of Richmond, the objective point of the campaign of 1862, lies at the very head of the Peninsula, on the north bank of the James River, a large, navigable stream there and below it. About sixteen miles north of Richmond runs the Pamunkey River, a deep black stream nearly parallel with the James. It is crossed by the West Point Railroad at Whitehouse Landing, where it is deep enough for gunboats and schooners. The railroad then goes on and takes a curve to the east, avoiding the seven bends which the Pamunkey there takes, inside of ten miles, and terminates at West Point on the other bank of the Pamunlkey.

Williamsburg. The building is Allen's Farm, headquarters to Union General Fitz John Porter. Troops are camped in the background.

Here, the river receives a tributary from the north and becomes an estuary two miles wide, called the York River. Between the Pamunkey and James Rivers lies the Peninsula. It stretches out to sea for some seventy miles to Fortress Monroe. Yorktown is on the north side, more than halfway down. Williamsburg is in the middle of the Peninsula, some ten miles from Yorktown.

All of the lower part was unoccupied by either side after Williamsburg. The subsequent fighting was up in the very neck of the Peninsula, to the north of Richmond. Here arises a collection of little streams which join together and constitute the Chickahominy. It splits the Peninsula in half. The whole Peninsula is low ground formed by the accumulated mud of the two rivers, stopped and deposited for ages by the ocean tides. The Chickahominy steals along through swamps, and it is hard to tell which is river and which is swamp.

On the 22nd of May, McClellan's army had arrived at the banks of the Chickahominy, only six or eight miles north of Richmond. The different corps came on various roads or across country on each side the West Point Railroad, and stopped on the north side of the stream. It lay in the bottom, fringed with timber and swamp. On each side was a very gentle open slope about a mile wide, the crest covered with timber.

The Federal pickets were on the north side, the enemy on the opposite crest. No one knew anything of the depth of the river. Two country roads crossed it by bridges. One was a mile below the railroad; it was called Bottom Bridge; the other was about eight miles above the railroad; it was called New Bridge. Meadow Bridge was two miles further up still. All these were broken down and left with the bare piles sticking up.

Grant's headquarters at Coal Harbor

On the 22nd May, McClellan established his headquarters at Coal Harbor, about a mile from the Chickahominy; and General Barnard, the chief engineer of the army, at once started off to reconnoitre. The previous day, he had been down to Bottom Bridge, eight miles below, and found no enemy there, while the stream was fordable on horseback. Barnard judged that it must be even shallower in all probability higher up, and if it could be crossed there the position would be better to cover the railroad to West Point, by which the army drew its supplies from the seacoast.

Custer, being on staff duty, happened to be around, and Barnard beckoned him to come with him, not knowing who he was at the time. Both passed through the picket line and went down to the river. The Federal outside pickets were in the clear ground, perhaps two hundred yards from the edge of the swampy bank. The general and the lieutenant went on past the pickets but were warned not to enter the timber, as it was full of the enemy's pickets.

General Barnard heard them, but as no picket shooting had taken place from them, and as his own experience at Bottom's Bridge made him doubt it, he passed on with Custer, reached the swamp, penetrated it and finally the two found themselves alone on the margin of the stream, the dark flow of which gave no revelation of its depths nor of the nature of its bottom. Turning to his young subordinate, General Barnard said, "jump in."

There might have been a passing look of surprise, but the order was instantly obeyed and Custer forded the stream (finding firm bottom) and ascended the opposite bank. The young officer waded the stream in the momentary expectation of being fired at by the enemy's pickets on the other bank. All around him was quite unknown.

There was every reason to suppose that riflemen were in the bushes beyond, and Custer was in the open river, perfectly exposed. He had drawn his revolver and held it up above the water, which rose to his armpits in the middle of the stream; and his feet sunk several inches into the soft, sticky, black mud of the bottom. General Barnard, in his report, calls it "firm bottom," but it will be noticed that the general did not wade it himself, and therefore his ideas of the bottom must be regarded as slightly formal and technical. However, it was not a quicksand.

Arrived at the other side, Custer peered through the bushes and cautiously ascended the bank, being rewarded for his explorations by a distinct view of the enemy's picket fires some distance off, and by the sight of their nearest sentry, lazily pacing his post, quite unconscious of the proximity of any foe. By this time, Barnard was becoming a little nervous for Custer's and his own safety, and began to make silent signals to him to come back, but the young fellow never heeded them until he had carefully examined the whole of the enemy's position, and had found that their main picket post was so situated in the midst of a bend of the river that it might be easily cut off by a bold dash from a point either higher up or lower down.

Not until he had settled this in his mind did Custer return. Then, he waded his way back to Barnard, and briefly reported the stream as being "fordable." The old engineer was not much given to compliments, but even he expressed a certain grim approval of the deed, and told Custer to follow him back to General McClellan.

At that time, army headquarters were some half a mile from the river, on the other side of the northern ridge of the valley at the Widow Gaines' house. The general and his young subordinate mounted and rode up to the house, where they found McClellan about to ride out with his staff to visit the different positions. Here, Custer fell back while Barnard went on. In these army matters, the reader must remember the credit assigned to an officer or soldier is almost always in proportion to his rank. The soldiers fight the battle, and the officer gets the credit.

In this case, Custer had made the risky reconnaissance, but as Barnard was the chief engineer, it would all go to Barnard's credit. So the boy thought, at least. He was yet only a humble second lieutenant, and the riotous life he had led at Washington the previous winter, with the sudden shock of revelation and repentance produced by his sister's solemn warnings and prayers had tended to sober and subdue him greatly.

There are evidences at this time in his private correspondence that he felt at times depressed in mind to some extent, and thought that he had led an unusually wicked life. This tenderness of conscience was natural to him. Moreover, he had spent most of his money, was hard up, shabby in his dress and at that moment was all covered with the black mud of the Chickahominy. He felt very keenly the contrast between his own forlorn appearance and that of the neat and handsome staff of McClellan, where every officer was well brushed and shaved and glittering with bright buttons.

In short, Custer hung back out of sight, and dropped to the rear of the staff as they rode on. General Barnard rode by McClellan's side on the way to the other positions and made his report of the state of the river, so many feet of water, such a bottom, etc. The commander listened, asked a few questions and finally it came out that the general had not gone himself, but had sent in some young officer, really could not say who - had seen him lounging near headquarters - guessed he was somewhere near - would the general like to see him?

Certainly, the general would like to see him - wanted to see him at once - very important - where was he? Word was passed that "General McClellan wanted to see the officer who had been down to the river with General Barnard." It passed from a stately chief of staff, covered with buttons, through a still more gorgeous aide-de camp, thence to another and another until it reached the smart orderlies, and everybody wanted to know where was "the officer that went with General Barnard."

At last he was found and brought up, dirty and muddy, with unkempt hair, coat not brushed, but all creased from being slept in, trousers far from guiltless of rags (fruit of hard riding), boots more russet than black, with red reflections, cap once blue, now purple from many rains and suns. Such was the figure that presented itself before McClellan - general, as always, neat as a pin - boy's face as red as fire with shame at his own carelessness.

But McClellan knew how to conquer *mauvaise honte* as few other men could. He pretended not to notice Custer's confusion, told the lad to ride with him, that he "wanted to hear all about this crossing of the river and what was on the other side."

By a few brief questions, he set the boy at his ease, drew him on to talk, and once talking, Custer was always a remarkably vivid and correct narrator. Before he knew how it happened, he found himself telling all about the position of the enemy's pickets and how easily they might be attacked, forgetting all mention of himself and treating his own exploit as nothing worthy of notice. The tables were turned now. Custer was doing all the talking; McClellan listening. Suddenly the young officer recollected himself again, grew silent and bashful, touched his cap stiffly and said, "That's all, sir."

Then it was that McClellan broke the silence abruptly. "Do you know, you're just the young man I've been looking for, Mr. Custer. How would you like to come on my staff?" Custer made no answer. For a moment, he could make none. He paled and flushed, perfectly overcome. He could not believe his good fortune. "You don't – really – mean it – general?" was all he could stammer out. "I do," said the general, kindly. "How say you? Will you accept?" "How did you feel when the general spoke to you?" asked a friend of Custer's long, long after. His reply was brief, as his eyes filled with tears. "I felt I could have died for him."

That was the commencement, for Custer, of a lifelong adoration of McClellan, which nothing after ever served to weaken. McClellan was the first man whom he found to lend him a helping hand in his course through life, and he never forgot the fact. Hitherto he had been alone, helpless and friendless, all his gallant deeds apparently wasted. It was to no purpose that he had led the first charge in the Army of the Potomac and piloted the way to victory for Hancock's brigade at Williamsburg. He was still a mere second lieutenant of cavalry, while other subalterns of the regular army all round him were entering the volunteer service as captains, majors, colonels, according to the strength of their friends and influence.

He had no friends but humble ones, no influence at all. Now on a sudden, to find himself offered a conspicuous position, which almost certainly promised further advancement, seemed to the young officer like a gift from heaven, and he fell down and worshipped the giver forthwith. The feeling with which Custer then and after regarded McClellan was such as he never gave to any subsequent general, not even Sheridan. It was a compound of respect, gratitude and love amounting to adoration, which remained with him to the last.

While his cooler military sense must have recognized, later in life,

WINNING THE BARS

the undoubted faults of McClellan as a commander, he never would admit them, even to himself. He seemed to feel it a point of honor with him to defend his old commander and first friend against all assaults. When he commenced his War Memoirs in the Galaxy, fourteen years after the events in which he then took a part, McClellan's reputation was regarded as settled by the fact of his ill success, and his apologists occupied a decidedly weak position as well as an unpopular one.

Army of the Potomac at Cumberland Landing, Virginia 1862

It is a characteristic of Custer's loyalty of heart and gratitude for benefits received, that he should have deliberately embraced the unpopular side of McClellan's defense, and have worked so hard and faithfully as he did. He never forgot his early friend, and no one else ever held the same place in his heart.

Custer, having gratefully accepted the offer, took leave of the general and returned to his quarters, where he soon received the following missive:

FREDERICK WHITTAKER

WAR DEPARTMENT, Washington, June 5th, 1862

SIR - You are hereby informed that the President of the United States has appointed you additional aide-de-camp on the staff of Major-General George B. McClellan, with the rank of captain in the service of the United States, to rank as such from the fifth day of June, 1862.

Immediately on receipt hereof, please to communicate to this department, through the Adjutant-General's Office, your acceptance or non-acceptance of said appointment; and with your letter of acceptance, return to the Adjutant-General of the Army the oath herewith enclosed, properly filled up, subscribed and attested, reporting at the same time your age, residence, when appointed, and the State in which you were born.

Should you accept, you will at once report in person, for orders, to Major-General George B. McClellan, U.S. Volunteers. This appointment to continue in force during the pleasure of the President of the United States.

EDWIN M. STANTON, Secretary of War
CAPTAIN GEORGE A. CUSTER, Additional Aide-de-Camp

It is needless to say that the young officer filled out the oath and sent it back post haste, while he reported at McClellan's headquarters. The appointment he sent by mail to his sister Mrs. Reed for safe keeping, and she retains it today.

Even before this appointment came however, Custer had justified McClellan's faith in his dash and energy. He had begged to be permitted to take over some troops and capture the picket post on the other side of the river. McClellan consented, and a detail was ordered to report to "Captain Custer," (as he was already called before his appointment) for detached service.

The detail consisted of two companies of cavalry and one of infantry, and the attack was to be made at dawn. In the meantime, Custer had taken the pains to wade the middle of the river, for nearly a mile up and down, finding it favorable everywhere. At the appointed time, in the grey of the morning, he found his detail waiting and rode down to the river. The cavalry was to follow the infantry as a support, in the wrong headed fashion of those days.

The young officer was absorbed in thought and anxiety about this, his first serious expedition, and consequently did not take much notice of the troops with him until they came to the ford. Then, as the light was growing stronger, he heard a voice say "I want to know! If that ain't Armstrong!" Custer started and looked at the dingy blue-grey crowd of soldiers, and was greeted in a moment by animated cries. "Why, it's Armstrong." "How are ye, Armstrong." "Give us your fist, Armstrong."

He had, by a strange chance, fallen into the midst of Company A, Fourth Michigan Infantry, a company raised in Monroe and composed almost entirely of his old school friends and playmates. With the peculiarly refreshing republicanism of the western and all American country volunteers, the boys recognized no barrier of rank between them and their old playmate. Here, Custer's tact and knowledge of human nature enabled him to maintain discipline where another might have failed.

Instead of putting on cold and distant airs, he hastily grasped the proffered hands nearest, laughing, and said, "Well, boys, I'm glad to see you, you don't know how glad; but I tell you I'm very busy now, too busy to talk, except to say this; All Monroe boys, follow me; stick to me, and I'll stick to you! Come!" And he rode into the water followed by cries of "That's us, Armstrong." "You bet we'll follow."

And they did. To make a long story short, they forded the river and came down in rear of the enemy's pickets entirely unperceived, exactly as Custer had planned. Just before sunrise, they opened fire on the surprised post of the enemy, part of the Louisiana Tigers, shot several and stampeded the rest, driving them down toward the river and taking arms, prisoners and one color, the first ever taken by the Army of the Potomac, captured by Custer himself. Well had he justified the choice of his chief.

In this fight, Custer was associated with Lieutenant Bowen, who was still his nominal chief. Had they been supported by the cavalry that was with them, they intended to have charged much further. Custer came raging back to the river bank, waving a rebel sabre which he had captured and urging, entreating, storming at the cavalry commander to come over, that a grand chance awaited them. The officer refused to be persuaded. He could see that the firing had drawn out a whole brigade of the enemy, and that if he went over a general engagement must follow. For this, the army was not then prepared, so that Custer, alone and unsupported with his Monroe boys, had the undivided credit of this affair.

NOTE: From information received since the above was written, it appears that the whole of the Fourth Michigan regiment wags detailed for this service, but that the greater part was kept in reserve with the cavalry, so that the brunt of the fighting fell on Custer. One great reason for the hesitation of the commander was the black and formidable looking stream, which he hesitated to cross for fear of entangling his horses in some hidden quicksand. His conduct was decidedly prudent, but it must be remembered that in those early days of the war, dash was frowned down and prudence extolled. The Bull Run disaster had ended in exaggerating the caution natural to all beginners, and everyone seemed to be afraid to do anything dashing for fear of an ambush or a masked battery.

FROM RICHMOND TO MALVERN HILL

CUSTER'S new won rank was not yet fairly settled when the prestige of McClellan received a sudden check. After lying behind the Chickahominy for nearly a week, he had pushed out his left wing far in advance of the rest, Casey's division being at Fair Oaks Station on the railroad, while the rest of the army was nearly four miles away. Casey was in full view of Richmond, and his troops were the nearest of any force of infantry that reached there for three long years after.

More than half of McClellan's army remained on the other bank of the Chickahominy, and Johnston saw that he had a good chance to annihilate that part which was so imprudently advanced. By this time, he had accumulated 76,000 men, and felt able to move. He made his plans to strike Casey on the 31st June, and was much assisted by the fact that a heavy rain on the 30th had so swelled the Chickahominy that it became for the moment un-fordable.

On the 31st, Johnston struck Casey, nearly surrounded him, and drove him in confusion, beat back Kearny who came to his support, and completely defeated that wing of the Federal Army. It was only saved from ruin by the coming of Sumner's corps over the trestle bridges that had been placed on the Chickahominy; Sumner partially restored the fight, but McClellan's advance was checked.

He experienced however, a slight benefit of fortune in spite of the defeat. Johnston was so severely wounded as to be taken from the field, and this circumstance paralyzed the attack at nightfall. Next day, G.W. Smith, who was next in Confederate command, proved totally unable to carry on the battle and a lull ensued for some weeks until Lee was appointed General-in-Chief. The lull was a deceitful one for McClellan. It encouraged him in the belief that he could take Richmond by a regular siege, and he progressed slowly, just as he had

FROM RICHMOND TO MALVERN HILL

done at Yorktown.

At last, just as he was ready to begin the bombardment and had telegraphed the President to that effect, Lee, who had gathered together from all quarters an army of about 110,000 men, attacked him in flank and rear, on the side opposite to that which marked Johnston's attack, and at once broke his communications with West Point.

Then followed the terrible slaughter of the "Seven Days Fight." The Army of the Potomac was driven from the railroad and the north side of the Peninsula and compelled to take refuge on the south side, with a new base at Harrison's Landing on the James River, covered by gunboats.

Supplies at James River Landing

In all these battles, Custer and Bowen, who seem to have been inseparable, were seen together, carrying orders from one part of the field to another, cheerful in spite of the disaster. One of the most remarkable features indeed of all the seven days' fight was this wonderful constancy of the whole army under misfortune.

The first day's battle at Gaines' Mills, on the north bank of the Chickahominy, was a blow that would have paralyzed almost any army.

FREDERICK WHITTAKER

Thirty-five thousand men, separated from their comrades by a river, were attacked by Lee with at least seventy thousand, surrounded, crushed, almost annihilated, the whole army found itself driven from its base, out-generaled and flanked; and yet fought on day by day, in fractions, covering the retreat of the rest and repulsing every subsequent assault with terrible loss.

Ruins of Gaines Mill. The Battle of Gaines's Mill was intense, the largest of the Seven Days and the only out-right Confederate tactical victory of the Peninsula Campaign.

The last battle at Malvern Hill, near Harrison's Landing, was the fiercest of all, and ended in the complete overthrow of Lee's army, which was mowed down by thousands as it urged its desperate assaults against a superior force of artillery, splendidly posted. A Confederate officer who afterwards wrote an account of the battle for the Cologne Gazette, which attracted great attention all over Europe, notices the fact that in the last battles, the Union troops advanced to meet them, attacked in their turn, and uttered loud cries of "On to Richmond!"

Most of the corps and division commanders were indeed eager, after Malvern Hill, to advance once more on Richmond; but McClellan refused to move. He was too thoroughly convinced of the dangers of the way, and resolved to await reinforcements as the safest, if not the most brilliant method of procedure.

It was at Malvern Hill that Custer and Bowen once more came to the front in one of their gallant dashes. Always in the advance and reconnoitring, the pair of friends, accompanied by two orderlies, took a gallop outside of the lines that morning to explore a certain thicket in plain view of the army.

Just as they came up to it, out dashed six or seven of the enemy's cavalry and charged for them with loud yells and pistol shots. For a few moments, the two officers were demoralized and fled towards their own army. Then, seeing by how few they were followed, for their pursuers had strung out considerably, Bowen called to their orderlies, who were regulars, turned and charged the over impetuous foe, taking each man almost alone, and actually compelling the surrender of the whole party.

Globe Tavern at Malvern Hill. The Battle of Malvern Hill was the sixth and last of the Seven Days' Battles. After his victory, Union General McClellan withdrew to Harrison's Landing on James River, where his army was protected by gunboats.

The advancing enemy's lines were however so near that they could not bring back their prisoners, but they compelled them to give up their arms, and a great shout of laughter greeted the two mad-caps as they returned, each carrying an armful of sabres, revolvers, carbines and belts, captured in fair sight of both armies. It was a foretaste of the future career of one of them.

Not very long after Malvern Hill, Custer alone enjoyed another dash of exceptional brilliancy into the enemy's lines. In those days as a young officer, he was not so reticent about himself in his letters home as he afterward became, and he thus tells the story of his adventure in a letter to his sister, Mrs. Reed, who was then his chief confidant:

HEADQUARTERS ARMY OF THE POTOMAC,
Aug. 8th, 1862

DEAR BROTHER AND SISTER: I received your letter of the 30th in due time, and found it quite interesting. I received it in the evening about dark, and would have answered it at once, but my horse was saddled and standing in front of my tent ready for me to mount. I had returned the preceding day from a successful expedition across the river, and was about to start upon another.

My regiment formed a part of the troops that were to go. As we were to start at two o'clock in the morning, I deemed it best to join the regiment in the evening and be ready to accompany them in the morning. Our force was not a large one, consisting of about three hundred cavalry and four guns (horse artillery) under the command of Colonel Averill. Our object was to go about twenty miles to "White Oak Swamp" and surprise a regiment of cavalry stationed there.

We arrived in sight of the enemy about eleven o'clock. I was the first to discover them. Our cavalry at once prepared to charge them and away we went, whooping and yelling with all our might. The rebels broke and scattered in all directions, we following as fast as our horses could go. As soon as we came close enough, we began firing at them with our revolvers. Quite a number of them surrendered when they saw that their escape was cut off; others who had good horses were not of this way of thinking, but continued the race.

I was mounted on my "black," who seemed to enjoy the sport as well as his master. During the chase, I became separated from all the command except a bugler boy of my company who was at a short distance front me, but concealed from my view by bushes. I heard him call out "Captain! Captain!" I could not see him, but called to him, asking what was the matter. He replied, "*here are two secesh after me.*" I put spurs to my horse and started in the direction of his voice. I found him with his carbine in his hand, trying to keep off two secesh cavalry who were trying to capture or kill him.

FROM RICHMOND TO MALVERN HILL

I drew my revolver and dashed at one of them, telling the bugler to manage the other. They both clapped spurs to their horses as soon as they saw me. I followed one, the bugler the other, and away we went down the hill. My horse was the fastest. I kept gaining on him until I was within ten steps, when I called out for him to surrender. He paid no attention to me, so I fired twice at him with my revolver. This brought him to a halt. I again pointed my revolver at him, and told him if he did not "surrender at once, I would kill him."

He had a short rifle in his hand, and hesitated a moment whether to surrender or fire at me. He chose the former, and handed me his gun. I then made him ride in front of me until I placed him in charge of a guard. Lieutenant Byrnes, of my regiment, myself and about ten men, then started out again. We had not gone far until we saw an officer and fifteen or twenty men riding toward us with the intention of cutting their way through and joining their main body. When they saw us coming toward them however, they wheeled suddenly to the left, and attempted to gallop around us.

Byrnes called out, "Custer, you take the right hand and I'll take the left," which we did, and then followed the most exciting sport I ever engaged in. My pistol was fresh loaded. I recognized the rebel officer by his uniform. He rode in front of his men and was mounted on a splendid horse. I selected him as my game, and gave my black the spur and rein. If I had been compelled to follow behind him, I could never have overtaken him, but instead of doing so, I turned off with the intention of heading him.

By this means, I came very close to him. I could have fired at him then, but seeing a stout rail fence in front of him, I concluded to try him at it. I reasoned that he might attempt to leap it and be thrown, or if he could clear it so could I. The chase was now exciting in the extreme. I saw as he neared the fence that he was preparing for a leap, and what was more, I soon saw that the confidence he had in his horse was not misplaced, for he cleared the fence handsomely.

Now came my turn. I saw him look around just as I reached the fence, but he certainly derived no satisfaction by so doing, as my black seemed determined not to be outdone by a rebel and cleared the fence as well as I could wish. By avoiding some soft ground which I saw was retarding him, I was enabled to get close upon him when I called to him to surrender, or I would shoot him. He paid no attention and I fired, taking as good aim as was possible on horseback. If I struck him, he gave no indication of it, but pushed on.

I again called to him to surrender, but received no reply. I took deliberate aim at his body and fired. He sat for a moment in his saddle, reeled and fell to the ground, his horse ran on and mine also. I stopped as soon as possible, but by this time Byrnes and his party were around me firing right and left. I joined with them and captured another rebel who had leaped from his horse and endeavored to escape in the woods. We were now some distance from the main body; the colonel became alarmed for our safety, and caused the bugler to sound the "rally" when we were all compelled to join the main body.

Before the "rally" was sounded however, I saw the horse of the officer I had shot, but a short distance from me. I recognized him by a red morocco breast strap which I had noticed during the chase. Four other riderless horses were with him. I rode up to them and selecting him from the rest, led him off, while the others were taken possession of by others of the party. He is a blooded horse, as is evident by his appearance. I have him yet and intend to keep him.

The saddle, which I also retain, is a splendid one, covered with black morocco and ornamented with silver nails. The sword of the officer was fastened to the saddle so that altogether it was a splendid trophy. Owing to the confusion and excitement of such an occurrence, I was not able to see the officer after he fell from his horse, but Lieutenant Byrnes told me that he saw him after he fell, and that he rose to his feet, turned around, threw up his hands and fell to the ground with a stream of blood gushing from his mouth. I had either shot him in the neck or body; in either case the wound must have been mortal. It was his own fault; I told him twice to surrender, but was compelled to shoot him.

Our party then started to return home, as we were twenty miles from camp, and liable to be attacked at any moment. We did not lose a man of the party; two horses were killed by the rebels; we took about thirty prisoners and killed and wounded quite a number besides. My horse is a perfect beauty, a bright bay and as fleet as a deer. I also captured a splendid double barreled shotgun, with which quite a number of the rebels are armed. I intend to send the shotgun home to Bos.* You may expect to hear something from me before long, perhaps we will move our headquarters. Write soon.

Your affectionate Brother,

ARMSTRONG

---

* His brother, Boston Custer, then a young boy, afterwards killed along with Custer, at the Big Horn.

McCLELLAN'S REMOVAL

THE disasters of the Seven Days Fight were followed by a long period of repose, McClellan lying within his circle of entrenchments at Harrison's Landing, and Lee refitting his exhausted army for fresh work. At last, Mr. Lincoln thought fit to recall the Army of the Potomac to Washington, and Lee started off across the interior of Virginia, found Banks and Pope, and beat them one after the other, the Army of the Potomac getting to the scene of action just in time to share in the defeat of the second Manassas.

Harper's Ferry, Maryland Heights. Because the surrounding terrain made Harper's Ferry difficult to defend, it changed hands fourteen times during the Civil War.

Thence Lee pushed off toward Harper's Ferry, took it, and raided into Maryland. McClellan, who had been suspended from command pending Pope's battle, was reinstated after the latter's defeat and commenced the Maryland campaign, ending in Antietam. During this campaign, as during the Seven Days, Captain Custer officiated as personal aide to McClellan, accompanying him wherever he went and being dispatched to the front, whenever the advance struck the enemy.

There was not much work for him to do. It seems that he had an especially pleasant time, judging from what he wrote home about it. The letter was, as usual in those days, written to his old confidant, Mrs. Reed, and we quote it fully:

GENERAL MCCLELLAN'S HEADQUARTERS
Sharpsburg, Maryland, Sunday, Sept. 21st, 1862

MY DARLING SISTER: YOU are perhaps in doubt whether I am still among the living or numbered with the dead. These few lines will show you that I belong to the former. I am well aware that I deserve severe punishment for my long silence and neglect in writing. I have really no excuse, although I have been unusually busy since I last wrote to you, yet I could have found time to drop you a few lines. I will candidly acknowledge my offence and ask your pardon. I was certainly not partial, as I have written to no one since I left Harrison's Landing, except two letters which I wrote to a person in Washington since the first of the month.

I have so many things to write about that I am at a loss to know where to begin. I left Harrison's Landing with General McClellan and travelled by easy marches to Williamsburg. The General remained at this place one day and two nights. You remember that it was at the battle of Williamsburg that my classmate, L., was wounded and taken prisoner by our forces. I had heard that he had been allowed to go from Fortress Monroe to Williamsburg to visit some friends, he giving his parole of honor not to escape.

As soon as we reached Williamsburg on our return, I began making inquiries of the citizens concerning L. I soon learned that he was in town, staying at the houses of a friend. I immediately visited him and was rejoiced to find him almost recovered from the effects of his wound. He was surprised and glad to meet me. I was covered with dust from travelling, but he insisted upon my entering the house of his friend and being introduced to his friends. I did so and met a cordial reception, although the entire family were strong "secesh."

After a few hours pleasantly spent in conversation, I left them to return to camp, but not until I had promised to return and spend the night at their house. I returned to camp, received permission from the General to be absent, changed my dress and again visited L. After partaking of a good supper, we withdrew to the parlor where we listened to some very fine music (secesh).

There were two beautiful young ladies in the house who I supposed were sisters. I soon learned that I was mistaken. L called me to one side and in an undertone asked me what I thought of the two young ladies who were then sitting upon a sofa to the opposite side of the room. I remarked that they were very beautiful to say the least. He then informed me that he was engaged to the elder of the two and that they were to be married the coming week. I congratulated him on the wisdom of his choice and wished him every imaginable success.

He was anxious that I should be present at his marriage; I replied that I would like to do so but feared I could not remain so long; after consulting all the parties concerned, it was decided that the ceremony should be performed the next evening in order that I might be present. No strangers were to be there but myself. The other young lady, who I at first thought was a sister but who proved to be a cousin from Richmond, was selected as bridesmaid, and I was to have the honor of "standing up" with her.

George Armstrong Custer, 1864

I passed the night and most of the next day with L., going to camp just long enough to dress for the wedding, which was to take place at nine o'clock in the evening. I was at the residence of the bride long before the

McCLELLAN'S REMOVAL

appointed time. Both were dressed in pure white, with a simple wreath of flowers upon their heads. I never saw two prettier girls. L. was dressed in a bright new (rebel) uniform, which he had had made for the occasion. It was made of fine grey cloth trimmed with gold lace. I wore my full uniform of blue.

It was a strange wedding. I certainly never heard of one like it. L. and I had met under strange circumstances after the battle of Williamsburg, he an officer in one army, and I in an opposing one. We had been warm friends at West Point, and now he was about to be married and I was to be present at the ceremony. We were both struck by the strange fortune which had thrown us together again, and under such remarkable circumstances.

His marriage from beginning to end was certainly a romantic one. He was, as you know, badly wounded at the battle of Williamsburg. I had taken all the care I could of him while we remained near that place, but upon leaving, he and hundreds of others were left in barns and other out-houses.

He had never met his destined wife until after the battle. She with her mother went one day in their carriage to carry nourishment to the wounded of both armies. In visiting the different places containing the wounded, they for the first time met L. She had him carried to her home, took care of him, etc., etc., and he fell in love with her, courted and married her. I never heard nor even read of a wedding so romantic throughout. The appointed hour was nearly at hand; the young ladies were in their own room, L. and I were in the parlor. He seemed perfectly happy and resigned to his fate.

The minister soon arrived, and at nine precisely we took our places upon the floor. The ceremony was performed according to the Episcopal form. L. made the responses in a clear and distinct tone. The bride made no response whatever except to the first question. She was evidently confused and excited, though she afterward said (laughing) that she neglected to respond purposely, so as to be free from any obligation.

As soon as the ceremony was over, we all wished them happiness, etc. I was the first person to address the bride by her new title of Mrs. L. Everyone seemed happy except the young lady who had been my partner on the floor. She kissed the bride and sat down crying. L. observed this and said, "Why, Cousin Maggie, what are you crying for; there is nothing to cry about. Oh, I know. You are crying because you are not married; well, here is the minister and here is Captain Custer, who I know would be glad to carry off such a pretty bride from the Southern Confederacy."

She managed to reply, "Captain L. you are just as mean as you can be." After congratulations had all ceased, supper was announced. Mrs. L. took her husband's arm, while I had the pleasure of escorting "Cousin Maggie." I told her that I could not see how so strong a secessionist as she could consent to take the arm of a Union officer. She replied "you ought to be in our army." I asked her what she would give me if I would resign in the Northern army and join the Southern. She said, "You are not in earnest, are you?"

The supper was excellent and passed off very pleasantly. The next morning, I returned to camp, but found that the general had started for Yorktown. I afterwards sent a telegram to him and obtained permission to remain in Williamsburg as long as I chose. I remained with L. or rather at his father-in-law's house for nearly two weeks. I would have stayed even longer but the near approach of the rebels to Williamsburg and the departure of our own army rendered a longer stay dangerous (in more senses than one).

I never had so pleasant a visit among strangers. L.'s friends did all in their power to render my visit pleasant. "Cousin Maggie" would regale me by singing and playing on the piano, *"My Maryland,"* *"Dixie,"* (Southern) *"For Southern Rights Hurrah"* or *"Bonnie Blue Flag"* etc., etc.

Every evening was spent in the parlor. We were all fond of cards and took great interest in playing. *"Muggins"* and *"Independence"* were the usual games, sometimes euchre. We would play for the Southern Confederacy. When doing so, L. and I were the only players, while the ladies were spectators. He won every time when playing for the Confederacy, he representing the South, I the North.

L. has been exchanged, and is now in the rebel army, fighting for what he supposes is his right. I left Williamsburg for Yorktown at dark and arrived at the latter place about one o'clock p.m. General McClellan was then at Alexandria. I took a boat from Yorktown for Fortress Monroe, at which place I spent one day. I then took a boat for Baltimore, having with me "Rose," (his dog. ED.) my two horses and servant.

From Baltimore, I went to Washington by railroad. Here, I learned that General McClellan would establish his headquarters in Washington in three or four days, and concluded to await his arrival rather than to meet him at Alexandria. After staying in Washington about two weeks, we set out upon the present campaign, which has lasted about fifteen days, during which time more has been accomplished than during any previous period of the same length.

We have fought three battles, one of which was the greatest battle ever fought on this continent, and in all were victorious. General McClellan, after quietly submitting to the cowardly attacks of his enemies, has by his last campaign in Maryland, placed it beyond the power of his lying enemies to injure him, but what is remarkable, his enemies are all to be found among those who from lack of patriotism, or from cowardice, and in some cases from both causes combined, have remained at home instead of coming forward and fighting for their country.

McCLELLAN'S REMOVAL

Baltimore B & O Railroad Station. The Baltimore & Ohio Railroad (B&O) was the first common carrier railroad, the first to offer scheduled freight and passenger service to the public, and the first intercity railroad in the United States.

The New York ------ is among the most prominent of the vile sheets that have assailed General McClellan. His enemies dwindle down in importance until they reach such insignificant and lying personages as the editor of the Monroe ------.* I do not at present remember his name, but I think he could devote the columns of his paper to a more worthy purpose than by defaming and basely slandering those of his fellow countrymen who have gone forth to battle in defense of a common country while he, like a mean, cowardly liar as he is, remains at home. If I could meet him, I would horsewhip him.

Your Affectionate Brother,

ARMSTRONG

It will be observed that Custer mentions no more fighting adventures in this campaign, for which indeed there was little opportunity. Pope's misfortune had proved McClellan's benefit, enabling him to have his own way at last and giving him command of an enormous army by the junction of his own to the forces of Pope,

---

* We could not resist inserting this letter entire, not to hurt the feelings of the brethren of the paste-pot and scissors, but because it shows the generous, hot-headed boy so perfectly, as he wrote in a white heat of indignation, in defense of his beloved general. Both editors mentioned have gone to their long home years ago.

Banks and McDowell. The numerical superiority of the Federals was indeed so great as to render the campaign really the most brilliant and successful that Lee ever fought, escaping annihilation as he did.

After the battle of Antietam, when McClellan had allowed his enemy to cross the river and get away safely, a long period of inaction followed which was varied by Stuart's daring raid on Chambersburg, the Confederate cavalier marching all round his cautious foe and getting off safely. The small Union cavalry force under Pleasonton started after Stuart just an hour too late, and had the pleasure of coming to the Potomac at the end of the chase, just the same time behind him.

Near Antietam, September-October 1862. Left to right: Col. Delos B. Sacket, I.G., Capt. George Monteith, Lt. Col. Nelson B. Sweitzer, Gen. George W. Morell, Col. Alexander S. Webb, Chief of Staff, 5th Corps, Gen. George B. McClellan, Scout Adams, Dr. Jonathan Letterman, Army Medical Director, Unknown, President Lincoln, Gen. Henry J. Hunt, Gen. Fitz-John Porter, Unknown, Col. Frederick T. Locke, A.A.G., Gen. Andrew A. Humphreys, Capt. George Armstrong Custer.

At last, under the pressure of positive orders, the Union General started from Harper's Ferry, and taking the route east of the Blue Ridge, marched across country for Richmond onto more, this time via

McCLELLAN'S REMOVAL

Warrenton. On his way there, while at Warrenton, he was suddenly dismissed from his command and General Burnside placed in his stead, November 7th, 1862.

Very few measures during the war provoked such strong controversy at the time, both at home and in the army, as the removal of McClellan. No commander who ever subsequently handled it was able to acquire to so great a degree its love and affection, and the amount of ill-feeling and luke-warmness produced among the higher officers of the army by the removal of their beloved chief, afterward produced many disasters.

Under McClellan, the corps commanders always worked cheerfully and generally did more than they were ordered. The only malcontents were the restless and ambitious ones who thought their chief too slow. After McClellan's removal, all this was changed. Corps commanders not only did not exceed their orders, but got into the habit of disputing them, and from highest to lowest the army was full of grumblers. The evil effects did not wear away until the Battle of Gettysburg, after which more harmony was perceptible, but even then the habit of criticizing orders continued, until the accession of the iron-willed Grant and Sheridan to the reins of practical power.

Without entering into the question of the rights and wrongs of the McClellan matter, there is no question that the moral effect of the removal, at the time it was made, was perfectly disastrous to the Army of the Potomac, and very nearly excited a mutiny. Nothing but the real and sober patriotism of the great mass of rank and file, who in their hearts acknowledged that the law must be obeyed, right or wrong, saved the country at that moment from such a violent military revolution as used to take place in the later days of the Roman Republic, when the conquering generals dictated to the senate, and finally created out of the simple name "Imperator,"* a title that has been since held to be superior to that of king.

The tumult at army headquarters was especially great, for of course the first to hear the news were the officers of McClellan's staff. They

---

* General or Commander

were almost, without exception, furiously excited. Had McClellan been removed at Harrison's Landing, while the army was in the first despondency of defeat, it is probable that little would have been said against the chance.

An unfortunate general seldom has friends. But since that time, Pope had suffered an equally crushing disaster, one accompanied by more humiliations, and the government had been compelled to place McClellan in command. Under his orders which were cheerfully obeyed, everything had gone on smoothly up to the battle of Antietam, and at that battle the Federal forces had fought well. While actually a drawn battle, Lee's subsequent retreat had given it the prestige of a Union victory, and no serious disaster had since taken place.

During the long period of idleness that elapsed after Antietam, the contest between McClellan and the government as to further movements had endeared the General to his army. Reveled in all the newspapers, he appeared in the light of a wise, humane chief, standing up for the interests of his men, who needed clothes and shoes, against a clique of a ignorant civilians, who wished him to march on regardless of the sufferings of his army.

Everything had tended to make him the soldier's idol, and more than anything their own real inexperience. In the Peninsula up to the Seven Days, the Federals had only seen the soft side of war such as prevailed in the days of Louis the Fourteenth of France, a system of slow movements, brilliant little picket fights, enormous armaments, imposing preparations, plenty of food and forage and little danger. The brief fury of the Seven Days was now forgotten, or lingered only as a memory of tremendous and glorious fights in which the army had finally beaten off its foes.

The Maryland campaign had been pleasantly exciting, with the same characteristics of scientific warfare which distinguished the Peninsular operations. After a month's pleasant picnic life around Harper's Ferry, in glorious fall weather, when military life wore its brightest aspect, the march to the Rappahannock had commenced by easy stages; and now, in the midst of this movement; when everyone was hoping for a triumph, McClellan was suddenly removed.

McCLELLAN'S REMOVAL

It was no wonder that the army was excited and still less that the officers of McClellan's staff were furious. They especially idolized their chief for his kindness of heart, and verily believed that all the military knowledge of the army was gathered in his head. Under his command, a future full of glory was opened to their delighted imaginations, and now they found themselves suddenly discrowned and sent back to rust in peace. No wonder they were excited. Especially was this the case with the personal and volunteer aides, of whom McClellan possessed such a number, amongst them - young Custer.

An eyewitness who was present at headquarters on that night of sorrow describes the excitement as intense. Some of the officers raved, and wanted McClellan to march to Washington, dispossess the government, proclaim himself dictator and then return and beat the enemy. There was plenty of wild talk going on; and Custer, young and rash as he was, only a boy of twenty-two, adoring the commander who had given him such early distinction, joined in with the rest.

Boy-like, he was wild with indignation. The presence of whiskey in large quantities accounted for much of the excitement of those around him, but in his case it was nothing but the natural, generous impetuosity of his character that put him off his balance, for he never smoked or drank. In the midst of all the turmoil, the deposed general walked out of his tent, and a hush fell on the scene.

There was the group of young officers, inflamed with passion and bad whiskey, grouped around Custer, whose fair curls were tossed back, his eyes bright with anger at the injustice his chief had suffered. McClellan's appearance produced immediate silence, and the narrator proceeds to describe how the fallen general began to speak to his unruly staff.

In a low and sad tone, he commenced. He told them how surprised and grieved he was to hear such sentiments from men who had served with the Army of the Potomac. He reminded them that he and they were soldiers, alike with the private in the ranks, and bound to obey the nation they served, whatever its orders might be. He pointed out in a few words what would be the terrible consequence of such a course as they counseled in the midst of a rebellion which threatened the nation's life; how it would result in certain anarchy; how every army and state would feel at liberty to repeat the operation; and how then indeed secession must triumph. He spoke to them, as described by this eyewitness, as a sensible and patriotic man should, and silenced them all. It is the last glimpse that we have during the war of the quiet figure of the unfortunate McClellan, and it is in keeping with his whole career.

Excellent and competent for almost any subordinate position, he had failed in the highest of all commands, partly from the lack of experience and partly from the want of energy, induced in a naturally cautious nature by the slow methods of his early training and his long practice as an engineer. A safe and cautious commander generally, his only serious mistake was made in the exposure of his right flank at Richmond, which cost him the Seven Days Fight.

He departed into private life amid the regrets of his whole army; and with him went Custer. It seemed perhaps to the boy captain as if his work was done, and he permanently laid on the shelf beside his commander. The personal staff of McClellan, by which is understood only his aide-de-camps, departed with their general. Their appointments were not commissions, and only lasted during "the pleasure of the President."

McClellan was put on "waiting orders" and as the status of his aides depended on him, they also went home on "waiting orders." In the case of Custer, his commander's recommendation had procured him a more substantial benefit than the mere temporary appointment, in the shape of a promotion to First Lieutenant in the Fifth U.S. Cavalry. At the time of his commission, all the cavalry regiments were raised to twelve companies, and Custer was assigned to an original vacancy in Company M of the Fifth. This was a substantial commission, and reached him one month later than his appointment as an aide, namely, in July, 1862.

Until the staff appointment was revoked however, Custer had no work to do. He might go home, or stay with his general, who was ordered to Trenton, New Jersey, his own home. McClellan told him to go to Monroe and see his people, and accordingly, to Monroe went Custer. It was to him a sad return, and he felt very much embittered.

The act of his father being a staunch old Democrat, and he himself the same by imitation, prejudice and affection, added to the measure of his bitterness against the President, who belonged to the opposite party, who had humiliated his beloved general and thrown him, Custer, to all appearance, out of the path of success.

He was, as far as his military career went, thoroughly miserable that winter. He felt like a fish out of water, and longed to be back sharing the dangers of his comrades in the army. A certain gloomy satisfaction of the "I told you so" kind assailed him, as it did all the strong "McClellan men," at the successive disasters of Burnside. In those days, they did not wait to examine how much of those disasters were attributable to grumbling and mutinous corps commanders, but all joined in the chorus of the popular song, "Give us back our old commander;" none so earnestly as Custer.

While his military life was so bitter during this winter, he yet enjoyed plenty of opportunity for fun in a civil capacity. Partly to drive away care, and partly from the natural physical buoyancy of youth that would not be denied, he plunged into all the mild little dissipations of Monroe society with great zest that winter, sleigh riding, flirting, dancing, enjoying all the pleasures of a holiday during November and December, 1862 and part of January, 1863.

One more step in social life had been granted him, with many misgivings and much grudging, by the "upper ten" of Monroe. Cadet Custer had been a step above young "Armstrong;" Lieutenant Custer "of the Regulars" had been a little higher still; but that last unfortunate spree, so small really, had been magnified by scandal into habitual orgies of alarming frequency, and Mrs. Grundy held up her hands in holy horror over the "dissipations of that young man, my dear."

But Captain Custer "of General McClellans staff," was a very different personage - the habitual associate on duty of two real live French princes, who were - on the same staff. Mrs. Grundy smoothed the ruffled plumes of indignant virtue, and welcomed the rising sun, especially with a view to hearing something definite about "those princes." Really, Monroe was beginning to think there was "something in that young Custer after all, although we must allow, my dear, that his antecedents are not quite the thing, you know."

Monroe, Michigan. Today, Monroe is the location of the George Armstrong Custer Equestrian Monument, also known as *Sighting the Enemy*. The statue was unveiled June 4, 1910, was designated a Michigan Historic Site on June 15, 1992 and listed on the National Register of Historic Places on December 9, 1994.

The said "antecedents" were that he had worked for his education, that his father before him had worked for his, that he had been compelled to climb the ladder from the bottom step, alone and unassisted. The world has always found the union of honesty and labor very hard to tolerate, but nothing succeeds with it like two or three successes. Monroe was beginning to forgive Captain Custer for not being born with a silver spoon in his mouth.

This winter witnessed the throwing of a single bridge, narrow and insecure, but still a tangible bridge, over a very wide gulf, which had hitherto parted Custer from one great object of his life. The little maid of his vision, she with the arch dark eyes and merry smile, had shot up into a full-fledged young lady of seventeen, ready to "graduate," full of all sorts of knowledge, beginning to go into "society," and he met her at last that winter.

Yes, it was actually so, he was introduced to her, formally and fully at last, by her most particular friend, a young lady who afterwards became the close confidant of the pair of lovers during the whole of a long and romantic courtship. It was in this courtship that Custer first plainly showed the possession of that quality of invincible determination which was the real cause of all the success of his afterlife.

Hitherto, this had not shone out so conspicuously as it afterwards did. He had worked hard and faithfully, but had not been compelled so far to face active and obstinate opposition. Here, for the first time he found it, found it in the most dangerous quarter, the young lady herself. She was not disposed to like him; his war record went for nothing with her. Brought up in seclusion, she did not know the difference between a captain and a corporal.

She only knew that she had heard of him as a dissipated young man, a desperate flirt and that she had herself seen him on one occasion intoxicated. That was enough for her, bred up in the strictest kind of Presbyterian education. It had been more than enough for her father, to whom no young man seemed good enough for his darling. In short, the young lady received him with cold reserve, and tried to freeze the audacious youth. But Custer was not the man to yield to repulses in love or in war.

He totally routed the young lady's dignity before they had been five minutes together by asserting that he had met her before, and that she had spoken to him first. A freezing suggestion that he "must be mistaken" was met by the bold response, "Oh no, I'm not. It was - let me see -seven, eight, nine years ago - you were swinging on a gate and you said to me, hello, you Custer boy."

What could an innocent young lady fresh from boarding school do but blush like fire at this brusque accusation, declare it was not possible, feel a guilty memory that it might have been so, feel half angry, half amused, half ashamed and wholly subdued by the audacity of this strange, abrupt, singular young man with the bright curls, the bold handsome face, and flashing blue eyes so full of fun!

Custer had evidently, even in those early days, laid to heart the advice of the experienced Byron, that master of affairs of the heart. To overcome a lady's indifference, says Byron, "first pique, then soothe, soon pleasure crowns thy hopes." Custer had already attracted attention. The lady did him the honor to think him "a very impudent young man," for he had been in the habit of sending her messages through one of her friends for some months before he was introduced to her.

Somehow or other though, the Judge never heard of these messages, which to veterans in these affairs is symptomatic. At all events, that meeting proved the beginning of a certain amount of interest felt in the strange young man, and as the winter wore on he laid such fierce and audacious siege to the heart of the little Puritan maiden that no woman could resist him, nor did she.

Obstacle the first was soon safely surmounted, but the second proved more formidable. It was the Judge. Now while the Judge was perfectly willing to take Captain Custer by the hand in public and recognize him in his military capacity to the fullest extent, this was a very different matter to receiving him as a son-in-law, as the husband of an only daughter. The Judge was a man of the most rigid principles, and apt to believe that it was impossible for the wicked to reform permanently. At all events, he did not believe in the thoroughness of Custer's change, and especially distrusted his firmness and stability of character. Under these circumstances, he positively forbade any engagement being entered into, and intimated that he should prefer the discontinuance of Captain Custer's visits.

It is under these circumstances that the real nobility of Custer's character first shines fully out. We have seen hitherto the virtues of courage, gratitude, fidelity, resolution to put down temptation; to these was now to be added that of the purest, most knightly and sensitive honor, exhibited under most trying circumstances. Nothing would have been easier than for the handsome, dashing, determined fellow to overcome the scruples of a tender, fond, trusting girl, and to have induced her to fly with him, or to marry him openly in defiance of her parents. Nine men out of ten, men in good repute in the world would have done so, treating the father's scruples as mere trifles, not to be regarded in the settlement of the question. Not so Custer, not so did he treat his future wife.

McCLELLAN'S REMOVAL

Without a complaint, without a murmur, the lovers, now devoted lovers really, acquiesced in the fiat of the Judge that the intimacy should be discontinued. So scrupulous were they on this point that they did not even correspond, although that had not been in terms forbidden. For the rest of the period during which Custer remained in Monroe (several weeks yet, for his wooing had been as short, sharp and decisive as his charges of cavalry), the lovers never conversed in public or in private, though frequently meeting at parties. Custer apparently devoted himself with great ardor to flirting with other young ladies, and the Judge was fully convinced that the danger was over, and much relieved thereby.

But with all of his scrupulous honesty of obedience, Custer had by no means given up the idea of his marriage. He was only biding his time, trusting to that and his own exertions to overcome the opposition of the Judge. There is something, to me, particularly touching and noble in the spectacle of this fiery, impatient, young man, used to swift success, and hitherto always chafing under the least delay, now submitting himself to the requirements of a long and weary probation, ready to serve for his Rachel as long and patiently as Jacob of old.

When we consider the ordinary morals of American society in the matter of filial obedience, and the ease with which marriage can be contracted by a pair of lovers desirous of evading parental injunctions, the contrast between the conduct of Custer and most young men is very marked. He was faithful to his love, and determined irrevocably that he would only receive his wife with the full approval of her father, if he had to wait ten years to gain that approval. He was too scrupulous to attempt in the faintest degree to shake the obedience of the Judge's daughter. He had learned from his own family experience the value of unhesitating filial obedience, of the overmastering claims of duty and honor and now, in the first serious trial of his life, his character stood the test.

Fortunately for his own happiness, he was saved from the prolonged torture which must have attended his residence in Monroe in this state of affairs. In the middle of January, he was summoned by letter to New Jersey to meet McClellan, and the rest of his period of absence from the army was passed in hard work with his chief, in the preparation of his voluminous report on the movements of the Army of the Potomac under his command.

Fredericksburg, 1863. The Battle of Fredericksburg was the only major engagement of the Army of the Potomac in which George A. Custer did not participate.

The preparation of McClellan's report occupied a long time during which Custer, very luckily for his peace of mind, was kept hard at work. All the work however could not blunt his feelings, nor dim the fervor of his love and his determination that the Judge's daughter and no one else should at last be his wife. He could not honorably write to her, but he kept up during the whole of that year a close correspondence with a mutual friend, which served to mitigate the severity of his banishment, as he heard in reply of the movements of the one woman he cared to hear about.

It was not until April that the report was finished, and at its close Custer was ordered to Washington, and finally to rejoin his company, then at the headquarters of Hooker's army near Falmouth, Virginia, opposite Fredericksburg. The order was one which put him back a step in rank. His staff position as captain lapsed and he became once more

McCLELLAN'S REMOVAL
plain Lieutenant Custer. In that capacity, he rejoined the army.

THE CAVALRY CORPS

THE winter of 1862-63 was a period of great gloom for the whole of the United States, and perhaps for none more than young Captain Custer, awaiting orders that did not come, and kept like his chiefs in forced retirement. At no period of the war were the national spirits so low, for the year had closed on the crowning disaster of Fredericksburg, where thousands of brave soldiers had been uselessly slaughtered. At that time too, the opposition party, in and out of Congress, was exceedingly strong, and this party at once took up McClellan as their representative, and exulted over every new disaster to the Army of the Potomac as an evidence that no one but its first leader could ever conduct it to victory.

Every city of the north was full of deserters, who at that time numbered over a hundred thousand, and a very large proportion of these were from the Army of the Potomac. Numbers of officers who belonged to the McClellan faction resigned their commissions in disgust and went home to spread dissatisfaction, so that when Hooker was finally appointed third commander of the much abused army, he found it a jarring mass of discontented bodies instead of the homogeneous whole it had once been under McClellan.

It was however, to the hard work and enthusiasm of this, its third commander, that the Army of the Potomac was yet to owe the first victory of a series that was never afterwards broken by positive disaster. Hooker reorganized it effectively. A very different army it was from that which triumphed at Antietam, and even the severe repulse at Chancellorsville failed to shake its spirit, for the reason that the meanest soldier could see that the battle was a perfectly barren victory for Lee, in which he lost more than he gained.

But the greatest change effected by Hooker was one which affected

THE CAVALRY CORPS

Custer himself. It was the reorganization of the cavalry. Under McClellan and Burnside, the Union cavalry had been scattered about at different headquarters assigned to the command of infantry generals, used in small forces for outpost duty and scouting, and seldom or never employed on the field of battle. The few exceptions to the rule had been signally disastrous.

Army of Potomac winter camp. The camps were organized much like small towns complete with criss-crossing lanes called company streets, plus churches and sutler shops. Cozy on the surface, these temporary towns lacked systems to provide clean water and to remove waste. Therefore, disease and even death both spread rather easily.

At Gaines Mills, a single regiment of cavalry, the Sixth Pennsylvania, then acting as McClellan's body guard, had been sent to charge a whole hostile army, and had of course effected nothing. One or two mounted charges with equally poor results had taken place in Pope's campaign, but as a rule the Federal cavalry was too green to be usefully employed. The only portion kept in mass was a brigade under Pleasonton, and this small force had been worked to death.

Hooker gathered together all the regiments, organized them into three divisions under Pleasonton, Gregg and Averill, and kept them together, where they remained ever after as the Cavalry Corps, Army of the Potomac.

FREDERICK WHITTAKER

After a long winter's rest in huts before Fredericksburg, the whole army commenced its move across the river at the end of April. The design of the campaign was generally good, but marred by one fault. The army was cut up into three parts. It was nearly twice as numerous as Lee's forces, but the division gave him the opportunity to strike and defeat each fraction in detail, which he subsequently did with much success. The only part that escaped serious damage was the cavalry corps, to which Custer had lately been attached as an aide on the staff of General Pleasonton.

Hooker retained with the main army, with which he fought the Battle of Chancellorsville only a single brigade of cavalry, that of Colonel Thomas C. Devin. With this brigade, General Pleasonton himself was present and, small as it was, it contributed materially to the repulse of Jackson's column at an early period of the fight when the Eleventh Corps had given way, and a general Bull Run panic seemed impending. The rest of the division was off under Buford, with the rest of the cavalry on Stoneman's raid.

It is not our intention here to dwell on the battle of Chancellorsville, and the events of Stoneman's raid were so unimportant compared to the means used that they deserve no more than a brief account. The combination of circumstances under which the raid was made was peculiarly favorable to success, owing to the foresight of Hooker. He had ascertained that most of Stuart's cavalry was absent in the back country, recruiting and procuring remounts. Only the brigade of Fitzhugh Lee was with the army, and that of W.H.F. Lee was at Brandy Station, some fifteen miles off.

On the 29th of April, Stoneman crossed the Rappahannock on the right of Hooker's army, at Kelly's Ford, with the divisions of Buford, Gregg and Averill, eight brigades in all. On the 30th, they marched from the Rappahannock to the Rapidan, taking matters very coolly. The force was there weeded of all poor horses and pack animals, and only the pick of it went forward.

Next day, May 1st, they crossed the Rapidan with no more difficulty than the Rappahannock, driving off the few Confederate skirmishers, Averill pushing on to Brandy Station in the direction of

THE CAVALRY CORPS

Culpepper, Buford turning towards Fredericksburg, Gregg moving on in the middle, straight for Columbia, on the James River. The only column that met with resistance was that of Averill, which found W.H.F. Lee's brigade at Brandy Station, fought him awhile and then retired. The rest of the force continued on to Louisa Court House, northwest of Richmond and half way between the Rapidan and James.

There, it was divided into a number of small columns and roamed all over the country, burning bridges, cutting the banks of the James River Canal, and destroying railroads, with perfect safety to itself and much discomfort to the enemy. The only force left in the whole country to oppose it was W.H.F. Lee's brigade of two regiments, which was utterly inadequate to resist effectively. The raid lasted until May 9th, the division of forces taking place May 3rd.

Union Army camp on the James River

Kilpatrick, then a colonel, took his regiment to the very border of Richmond, found part of the Twelfth Illinois there, found also that he had roused the Home Guards and that they were flocking out to catch him, and finally marched down the Peninsula, crossed the Pamunkey and came out at Gloucester Point opposite Yorktown, whence he was taken off by the Union gunboats, returning by way of Washington.

The rest of the cavalry returned as they came and recrossed the Rappahannock and Rapidan high up the river, finding Hooker's army after the defeat of Chancellorsville, back in its old quarters at Falmouth, watching Fredericksburg. The results of the raid were thus stated at the time by an enthusiastic newspaper correspondent:

General Stoneman moved about at will for nine days within the enemy's lines; cut every railroad and canal; stopped traffic on the highways; kept ten counties in a turmoil; destroyed twenty-two bridges, seven culverts, five ferries, seven railroads (in spots), seven supply trains, one hundred and twenty-two wagons, two hundred horses (carried off), one hundred and four mules (same), three canals (in spots), five canal boats, three trains of cars, two storehouses, four telegraph stations, five telegraph lines (cut), three depots, (burned). The cavalry visited twenty-five towns and liberated one hundred and fifty slaves, who followed the column.

All this was very nice, but amounted to nothing, for the railroads were soon after repaired. The real weakness of the whole raid was that it only exasperated, without terrifying the enemy, and gave color to the accusations that the Federal cavalry were merely mounted robbers. Had Stoneman destroyed W.H.F. Lee's brigade, which he might well have done, it would have been of far more value to the cause he represented than all the plunder and destruction that attended his path. As it was, it entirely failed to retrieve the disgrace of Chancellorsville, in public estimation at the time, and the fact that Stoneman never attacked Richmond, which he might easily have done as it was almost undefended, added to the unfavorable impression produced by his conduct of the raid.

He was shortly after relieved by Pleasonton, the First Division falling to General Buford, the senior brigadier; and on the staff of the former Captain Custer found himself in June, 1863, with the prospect of a career once more open to him. The success of the Stoneman raid, such as it was, had still a good effect on the cavalry of the army. It was the first success that had fallen on its banners since Antietam, and had fallen to the lot of the despised cavalry, which needed it.

THE CAVALRY CORPS

At that time and ever since the beginning of the war, a great jealousy existed between the horse and foot of the Army of the Potomac, and the former had been so badly handled that it had fallen into contempt with the infantry. Cut up into small detachments and placed under control of infantry generals who disliked it, the few unfortunate charges it had made confirmed the general impression that was trumpeted through the press that "the days of cavalry were over" as a fighting body, and that it was only to be used thereafter for picket and scouting duty, in other words to look at the enemy and run away.

Hooker himself, while in command of the army, was currently reported to have heaped contempt on his cavalry, by starting the ironical question as to "who ever saw a dead cavalryman?" The plodding infantry soldier, weary with his long march, naturally feels jealous of the horseman riding by him, and if he is taught to despise him as a fighter is only too glad so to do. Under these remarks, the cavalry officers, high and low, had long chafed and longed for an opportunity to prove that they could fight as well as the "dough-boys" and "mud-mashers," whom they could not retort upon as yet.

The time was however, coming for these sneers to be silenced, and the young staff captain who now followed Pleasonton was destined to be a mighty instrument to change public opinion. Chancellorsville had hurt the infantry badly, while the small cavalry brigade that had shared in that fight had stood firm in the midst of a cloud of demoralized foot soldiers, whom they were detailed to drive back with their sabres in some instances. For the next two months, the infantry hardly fired an angry shot, while the cavalry under Pleasonton covered itself with glory, beat back Stuart again and again, and finally won itself the fair right to be called the sword and shield of the Federal army.

The close of Stoneman's raid was followed by perfect inactivity in Hooker's army for a month. In the meantime, Lee was preparing for an offensive movement behind Fredericksburg. He had fought Chancellorsville with less than sixty thousand men to Hooker's one hundred thousand; but by the end of June, conditions were changed. Many of Hooker's regiments were broken, their time being out, and Lee had received reinforcements from all quarters. Stuart's cavalry, remounted and recruited, was now at least ten thousand strong, and the Confederate infantry was increased until his army equaled if it did not exceed Hooker's.

Screened behind the curtain of woods in the Wilderness, Lee prepared to start off up the valley to repeat his Maryland campaign and if possible raid into Pennsylvania. Hooker, deprived of all certain news, was still very uneasy, and at last did what he should have done earlier. He sent out his cavalry to the extreme right of the army to cross the Rappahannock high up. They started under the lead of Pleasonton, and crossed at several points, Buford and Averill at Beverly Ford, Gregg several miles up at Rappahannock Bridge.

Rappahannock Bridge. The bridge was destroyed early in the war and was not standing at the time of the Battle of Rappahannock Station.

Both columns met the enemy in heavy force and drove him back past Brandy Station towards Culpepper. There, reinforcements arrived and the fight remained stationary during most of the morning. Several charges and counter charges took place, and the enemy's force was found to consist of Stuart's cavalry, while country people reported that infantry had passed that way in heavy force towards Madison Court House a day or two before.

In the evening, Pleasonton returned across the Rappahannock, followed at a distance by the enemy, but without suffering loss. The cavalry had shown in their first general fight that they were capable of holding their own against the much dreaded "Stuart's Cavalry," that caused the Army of the Potomac so much alarm from the Peninsula to Maryland.

They had met and parted fairly, "broken a lance" as it were, found that all they needed was to put a bold face on matters; and so learned their first lesson under Pleasonton's command. In this fight, Custer was in attendance on his general most of the day, a great favorite of the latter. The time was coming and very near at hand, though he knew it not, for him to win his star and emerge from the inconspicuous position of a staff officer to one in which he could command public attention.

The personal history of Custer during the time that intervened between joining the army and winning his star comes out so well in his animated and picturesque correspondence that we are sure our readers will be glad to see some of his letters. He still kept up his communications with his sister, but the letters to her are filled out and completed by some to another person, to whom he commenced to write early in April.

From these letters, it appears that after the completion of the report he paid a short visit to Monroe, thence to New York City, where he met orders sending him to Washington. Here, he was put on nominal staff duty, which was really genteel idleness, and filled up his time by going to the theatres and trying to forget his discontent. He was evidently at the time, sore, dissatisfied, unsettled, but imbued with a strong notion that "Destiny" had something in store for him, which no power of his would be able to avert.

In his letters to this second person he speaks very earnestly on this subject, and also of the earnest and enduring nature of his feelings towards "one of the parties most interested," to whom he never refers by name. It seems that this "party" had predicted that absence and time would change his feelings, but he earnestly assures his correspondent that this can never be, and warns her that time will only strengthen and deepen them.

FREDERICK WHITTAKER

On his first arrival in camp, General Pleasonton requested him to join his staff, but Custer expresses himself as doubtful whether he will go or not. He seems to have regarded it as a sort of possible slur on his former general, whom he speaks of in his first letter as "the only man I ever loved," the words underscored. Writing after Chancellorsville, he is very bitter on Hooker and says vindictively, "The whole army are speaking against him and asking for McClellan." This letter is dated May 6th, but a week later he writes in better spirits from General Pleasonton's headquarters that he has accepted the position offered him, and finds it very comfortable.

The passion for dogs is already strong, "I have got another dog, a hound pulp about two months old. One of my men got it from an old Negro woman. I have named the handsomest of my two horses - the black - 'Harry' after Aut." (His nephew Henry Armstrong Reed, born while he was a cadet). He has picked up a little deserted waif of a boy called Johnny, who acts as his servant, and who always takes the pup to bed with him. Johnny was devoted to him. "I think he would rather starve than see me go hungry. I have dressed him in soldiers' clothes... he rides one of my horses on the march." Returning from a ride one day, "I found, Johnny with his sleeves rolled up. He had washed all my dirty clothes and hung them on the bushes to dry. He did them very well."

Later comes a letter to the other correspondent, describing a secret expedition full of romance, but unattended with fighting. This is too good to be lost:

HEADQUARTERS CAVALRY CORPS, ARMY OF THE POTOMAC
Tuesday, May 26th, 1863

DEAR FRIEND: In accordance with my promise and my inclinations, I now propose to hold a short and uninterrupted conversation with you. I will agree to do all the talking tonight. I was extremely glad to receive your letter, and through you to hear of "one of the parties, etc." I will tell you about my expedition into Dixie. With my little party of seventy-five men (cavalry), I embarked at Aquia Creek on board the steamers Caleca and Manhattan on the evening of the 21st, taking our departure down the Potomac as soon as it was dark. At 11 o'clock next day, we arrived at our landing on the banks of

THE CAVALRY CORPS

the Yocomico River about five miles from its mouth.

Aquia Creek Landing, Virginia. Aquia Landing was the terminus of the RF&P Railroad. During the war, it became a destination for many escaped slaves seeking refuge behind Union lines.

Mounting our horses, we made a rapid march of forty miles in but little over five hours, arriving in sight of the Rappahannock River near Urbana. To avoid discovery, our party remained concealed in the woods till next morning. Taking nine men and another officer in a small canoe, the only boat we could find, I started in pursuit of a small sailing vessel which was coming from the direction of Urbana. After a chase of ten miles down the river we compelled our game to run their boat aground on the south bank.

The crew jumped overboard and reached the shore. We captured the boat and passengers. The latter proved to be a portion of the party which we desired to capture. They had only left Richmond the previous morning, and had quite a large sum of Confederate money in their possession. Six of the party composed a Jewish family. Do you remember what I said in case I captured a stagecoach full of young ladies? There were two young ladies in the party, Jewesses, who with the rest of the party I was compelled to make prisoners of.

With four of my men, I made my way on shore, leaving the remainder of the party to guard the prisoners and boats. The river at that point is over four miles wide, and so shallow near the land as to render it impossible for us to approach within three hundred yards of the shore in our boats, so that no course was left but to wade.

After landing with the four men, we went to the nearest house, which proved to be a fine country mansion. While at some distance from it, I observed someone on the piazza lying down with a book in his hands; his back was toward us so that we were not seen. As we neared the house, I saw that whoever it was, he wore the Confederate uniform. At first, I thought we were in a trap; that others might be near, perhaps in the house, and with my little party of four men, I could not hope to contend against a very large force.

Cautiously approaching, I was within four feet of the Confederate before he noticed us; it was then too late for him to escape or resist. I told him that he was my prisoner and must come with us. He replied very coolly, "I suppose so." On interrogating him, he informed me there were no other rebel soldiers within six miles of us. He was at home on a short visit. The volume he was so intently reading was a copy of Shakespeare, and he had just read the first few lines of that well known soliloquy, *"To be or not to be."*

On our march back, he and I had many a hearty laugh over his literary habits. His sisters were in the house, but heard nothing of what occurred until I entered and informed them that it was my painful but imperative duty to take their brother away with me. They were very sorry, of course, but tried to assume a very independent air at first. I could not but feel sorry that they were to be made unhappy through any act of mine. I imagined myself in their brother's stead, and thought how sorry my own dear sister would be if I were taken away under similar circumstances.

Returning to our boats, we took our prisoners to the north bank, leaving them in charge of the main party. Then with twenty men in three small boats, I rowed over to Urbana on the opposite bank, where we burned two schooners and a bridge over Urbana Bay, after which we drove the rebel pickets out of the town. We then returned to the north bank, where after capturing twelve prisoners, thirty horses, two large boxes of Confederate boots and shoes and two barrels of whiskey which we destroyed, our party remounted our horses, and with our captures set out on our return to the Yocomico where the steamers were in waiting for us.

To carry our lady prisoners, I pressed into the service a family carriage, horses and driver. We marched until two o'clock that night to avoid pursuit and capture, then camped until morning; resumed the march, reached our boats about noon on Saturday and arrived here safely Sunday morning without having lost a man. Yesterday, General Hooker sent for me and complimented me very highly on the success of my expedition, and the manner in which I had executed his orders.

Now, I suppose I have wearied you with this long (interesting to me, but perhaps not to others) story. I will not apologize for it however, as that would be breaking a rule which I have always laid down - never to regret anything after it is done. Yesterday I spent in visiting a number of my friends throughout the army. I saw the 4th Michigan and the Monroe

THE CAVALRY CORPS

members of the regiment. I took dinner with Lieutenant Yates, who you remember was in Monroe last winter. By the way, I have induced General Pleasonton to appoint Lieutenant Yates on his staff, so that I will have him with me here-after. He was at our headquarters this evening, and will join us permanently in a few days.

ARMSTRONG

A little later, in a letter to his sister under the date of June 6th, he writes that they are going to cross the river to Culpepper, but there is no account of Beverly Ford fight. The last letter accessible at this period of his life is dated June 25th, four days before his elevation to the dignity of a brigade commander, and the place for that will be more proper in the next chapter. Events were now beginning to crowd so fast, and the campaign was opening so actively, that home correspondence was practically impossible. Love and the softer side of his life was to be hidden for a while behind the murky clouds of war, and not until after Gettysburg was there a lull in the incessant activity.

Custer was still, as appears from these letters, nothing more immediately ambitious in feeling than a staff officer. There are no idle aspirations after high command in his wishes, and he seems, as always before and after, intensely practical in his notions of life. He is satisfied to do his duty in whatever position he is placed, only taking care to perform that duty thoroughly and completely, and better than anyone else.

The letter we have quoted reveals the perfect officer of the staff, active and daring, on the watch for every little scrap of information, perfectly ready to hide and play the fox when the role of the lion is out of place, with that peculiar combination of qualities, very rarely found, which makes the model officer of *eclaireurs*.

These qualities are very rare, and no school can teach them. Even experience totally fails if natural genius is not found in the man. The most preeminent attribute of the perfect *eclaireur* is tact, and this Custer developed in a remarkable degree. The sudden and rapid decision, the intuitive sense of the exact thing to do at the moment, and the energy that seizes the fleeting moment, are all present, and it is no wonder that Pleasonton treated him as the most useful officer of his staff.

FREDERICK WHITTAKER

Custer could do what no one else could do. Nine men out of ten would have made a blunder of the secret expedition into the heart of the enemy's country, but Custer treats it almost as a joke, and never falters a moment. What a wonderful contrast between this expedition and the one he so naively describes as occurring when he was on Kearny's staff only eighteen months before. Truly, Custer had graduated in the school of war. He was no longer a pupil, but a master in the duties of a staff officer. Even Hooker, far from being well disposed to any member of McClellan's staff, could not help complimenting Custer, and truly he deserved every word of praise he received.

WINNING HIS STAR

THE spirited little fight at Beverly Ford, June 9, 1863, developed the intentions of the enemy. It showed that his cavalry was concentrated near Culpepper, and subsequent reports from signal officers and others showed that the concentration was only preparatory to a general movement of the Confederates around the Union right by way of the valley, up towards Maryland and Pennsylvania.

Hooker's army being then in front of Fredericksburg, two courses were open to it. One was to strike straight for Richmond, disregarding Lee, the other to fall back towards Washington, interposing before the enemy could do much damage. The first course was the boldest and would undoubtedly have ended in the recall of Lee, and the fighting of a desperate battle to the northwest of Richmond, but it would have been in the nature of a gambler's last throw. The Union communications must have been left completely exposed by the line of the Orange and Alexandria Railroad, and would have certainly been cut unless changed to the seacoast bases, in later times occupied by Grant.

On the other hand, falling back toward Washington, Hooker would retain the advantage of interior lines, and his communications were secure. The second course was the safest, if not the most brilliant. At all events it was determined on, and the Union infantry started on the march which was to culminate in Gettysburg. For the next few weeks, the legs of the infantry of both armies were to do all the work, for they did not come in serious contact until they met at Gettysburg.

The Beverly Ford fight checked Stuart in his first purpose, which was to cross the Rappahannock east of the mountains, followed by Lee, repeating the movements of 1862 and bringing on a third battle of Manassas. On the 6th of June, he held his review at Culpepper, preparatory to his advance. Three days after, he concluded to go west of the mountains, take a longer trip, and trust to his heels to get to Pennsylvania first.

The first week of the three that intervened between Beverly Ford and Gettysburg was passed by Hooker in feeling for the enemy with his cavalry, which scoured the country as far as the Blue Ridge. In the meantime, Lee's columns were pushing on up the valley, Ewell's corps capturing Winchester on the 13th of June. Lee's intentions being then fully developed, the Army of the Potomac started to catch him, and on the 14th was at Bull Run. On the 16th, Governor Curtin of Pennsylvania issued his proclamation, announcing the invasion of his state, and from thenceforward all was bustle and activity.

On the same day that Governor Curtin issued his proclamation was fought the Battle of Aldie in Virginia, in which battle Custer gained his star, and as it was the first cavalry action in which the Union forces met the enemy fairly and defeated him fairly, it is worthy of some special notice.

At the time, both armies were scattered over a considerable range of country. The head of Lee's column, preceded by Ewell and a small force of cavalry and mounted infantry, was in Pennsylvania, the rear still in Virginia. Stuart's cavalry was scattered along the flanks, and on the 16th a portion of it came through Snicker's Gap, hoping to take a short cut into Maryland and Pennsylvania.

They were met by part of Gregg's division, consisting of Kilpatrick's brigade and the First Maine Cavalry. With them was a young staff officer of Pleasonton, Captain George A. Custer. The rest of the Union cavalry was scattered through the country, the afterwards renowned Michigan Brigade was not yet fully organized, but some of its component parts were in Maryland, fighting Jenkins' Raiders. Everything was in more or less confusion, especially on Hooker's side, for Lee had undoubtedly stolen a march on him and got ahead.

On the 16th, General Gregg's advance reached Aldie, and found a Confederate brigade with which General Stuart was present. It seems that Gregg must have struck the extreme advance of the Confederate cavalry. Colonel Kilpatrick's brigade composed the Second and Fourth New York, First Massachusetts and Sixth Ohio. The Second New York had the advance.

They ran into the enemy's picket outside Aldie, drove them through the town, and found the Confederate line in position near Middleburg in front of the middle of Ashby's Gap. It seems that Stuart was advancing through Ashby's Gap, and this unexpected encounter checked him. When the exact position of the enemy was found by their fire, Kilpatrick deployed his regiments and put them in the fight in the order following; First Maine, Sixth Ohio, Second New York, Fourth New York, First Massachusetts.

The enemy had four guns on a hill, in the centre of their line. Their dismounted skirmishers held fences and ditches enfilading the Middleburg Road, of which the advance must be made, and the position was strong. In front of the line of battle were half a dozen haystacks which concealed the ditch and fence.

The Second New York was ordered to charge down the road and take the haystacks. One squadron made the charge and passed the stacks, only to find themselves heavily punished by the enemy in rear. The rest of the regiment galloped in on the left, followed soon after by the Sixth Ohio, and the result was that the Confederate line was broken, fences thrown down and the enemy were driven in confusion up the hill on their guns. They made a short stand at a rail fence, halfway up, when a squadron of the Fourth New York that had been supporting Kilpatrick's battery dashed in and drove them over the hill, Stuart's guns going to the rear full gallop.

The First Maine was then called in from the left and placed beside the First Massachusetts, in support of the troops already engaged, and the line advanced again. This time, Stuart was resolved on vengeance. His guns were in position farther to the rear, and he now charged down the road, driving before him the remains of the Second New York, disordered and blown by previous charges.

In a moment it seemed as if the tide were turned. Cavalry is always liable to sudden reverses of this sort, and Stuart's fresh reserves came yelling on, driving everything before them. Kilpatrick ordered in at once the Maine and Massachusetts regiments, as yet fresh, and that part of the Fourth New York which had not already charged.

WINNING HIS STAR

Coming into action as a reserve to check the tide of defeat is always the hardest task for young soldiers, and it must be remembered that this was the first serious action in which many of the Union regiments had been engaged. At all events, the reserves wavered and halted, confusion began to spread, horses were plunging and fighting, men turning pale and shrinking back from the moral effect of the yelling line of Confederate cavalry coming on wrapped in clouds of dust and preceded by the scattered fugitives of the Second New York.

Add to this the shrieking of the enemy's shells and the sharp crash of their explosions, the dead and wounded horses and men lying about, and the tremendous moral force at that day of the name of "Stuart's Cavalry," and it is not surprising that the green Northern men wavered, nor that their officers were yelling confusedly instead of commanding coolly.

For a moment, a rout seemed inevitable, when out of the press dashed Kilpatrick and Colonel Douty of the First Maine, the first shrieking out curses and wildly waving his sabre, the second beckoning his men to follow. So great was the turmoil that neither could be heard, when forth from the crowd rode a third figure, a young captain, wearing a broad plantation straw hat, from under which long bright curls flowed over his shoulder.

His uniform was careless and shabby, but his bright curls attracted attention wherever he went. Out he rode beside Kilpatrick and Douty, waved his long blade in the air, and pointed to the enemy, then turned his horse and galloped alone towards them. An electric shock seemed to silence the line. He looked back and beckoned with his sword. "Come on, boys," he shouted. The next moment, Kilpatrick and Douty were abreast of him, waving their swords and shouting "Come on." An involuntary yell burst from the men, and away they went. All fear and hesitation had vanished and the long line, broken by its own impetuosity into little clumps of horsemen, went racing down to charge the enemy.

They were met by a tremendous fire. As usual, the Confederate cavalry shrank from the sabre and relied on firearms to repel the assault, and as usual they were worsted. The sabre was freely used for the first time during the war, and the enemy was driven in utter confusion, the Maine and Massachusetts men cutting and slashing right and left, the enemy fleeing in the direction of Ashby's Gap.

In the foremost of the triumphant group was the young captain with the bright curls, and in all the confusion, the men followed him as a guiding star. Kilpatrick went down, his horse shot under him. Douty was stricken dead, but the young captain with the floating curls seemed to bear a charmed life.

Away with a thunder of cheers, a rapid rattling fusillade of shots, a cloud of dust, the clatter of innumerable horse shoes, the jingle of arms, bright flashes gleaming redly through the thin blue pall of smoke that hung over the field, the fierce hot smell of powder in the air, titillating the nostrils with a mad sense of intoxication, away went Custer and his men in that wild charge and pursuit! The faint hearts of a moment ago were turned to steel, and a frenzy of eager ferocity seized the mildest.

Were you ever in a charge, you who read this now by the winter fireside, long after the bones of the slain have turned to dust, when peace covers the land? If not, you have never known the fiercest pleasure of life. The chase is nothing to it; the most headlong hunt is tame in comparison. In the chase, the game flees and you shoot; here the game shoots back, and every leap of the charging steed is a peril escaped or dashed aside. The sense of power and audacity that possesses the cavalier, the unity with his steed, both are perfect. The horse is as wild as the man, with glaring eyeballs and red nostrils he rushes frantically forward at the very top of his speed, with huge bounds, as different from the rhythmic precision of the gallop as the sweep of the hurricane is from the rustle of the breeze. Horse and rider are drunk with excitement, feeling and seeing nothing but the cloud of dust, the scattered flying figures, conscious of only one mad desire, to reach them, to smite, smite, smite!

Far ahead of the Northern riders was the young captain with the floating curls. He rode his favorite black "Harry," named after the innocent child at home. In his hand gleamed the long straight blade he had captured from the Confederate one year before, when he shot him and took his horse, down in front of Richmond. Custer wore that

WINNING HIS STAR

sword all through the war, a long straight Toledo blade, with the Spanish inscription, "*No mi tires sin razon, No mi envaines sin honra.*" "*Draw me not without cause, sheathe me not without honor.*" Years after, men said that hardly an arm in the service could be found strong enough to wield that blade, save Custer's alone.

Far ahead of all his men he rode, outstripping the swiftest, and a moment later was in the midst of the enemy, and close to the left rear of one of their horsemen. The man heard him coming, turned in his saddle and fired his revolver at Custer, missing him. A moment later, the long Toledo flashed in the air, and his enemy fell from his horse, his left arm nearly cut off. A second man wheeled his horse and dashed at the daring officer, riding up alongside on the left, taking Custer at the same disadvantage he had taken the other man, and this fellow had a sabre.

Then the two raced away in the midst of the flying cloud of dust, one cutting away at his foeman, the other parrying the blows but unable to return them. The wild race lasted for several seconds, both horses at full speed, when they found themselves beyond all the fight and in the quiet rear, out of the dust. Then Custer suddenly checked "Harry," and his enemy shot past him. Before his antagonist could stop, Custer was almost up to him, and as he wheeled round they met fairly on the right front. The fight was short. Two or three mighty blows of the long sword and the Confederate cavalier's guard was beaten down and himself knocked off his horse with a cloven skull.

Then Custer turned and found himself all alone in the midst of the enemy, probably a good mile from the Union lines. He mentions this in a letter to his sister: "I was surrounded by rebels, and cut off from my own men, but I made my way out safely, and all owing to my hat, which is a large broad brim, exactly like that worn by the rebels. Everyone tells me that I look like a rebel more than our own men. The rebels at first thought I was one of their own men, and did not attack me, except one who rushed at me with his sabre, but I struck him across the face with my sabre, knocking him off his horse. I then put spurs to "Harry" and made my escape."

It was at this time that Mr. A.R. Waud of *Harper's Weekly* made a sketch of Custer, which is still in the possession of his sister, Mrs. Reed. It represents such a wild, careless, slouchy-looking figure, as the same artist has put in the illustration to the battle in the present book, "only a little more so." There are the long unkempt locks, the broad straw hat, a soldier's blouse and trousers and a pair of captured boots.

This picture accompanied the letter from which we quote, dated June 25th, 1863. We quote it especially for one reason. Only four days later, Custer was made a brigadier, and this letter would naturally be expected to show some inkling of knowledge on his part of his coming promotion. So far from this, it is evident that he is quite unconscious of his coming honors. In one place he says, "General Pleasonton has been promoted to be a major-general. This will make me a captain again." The fact of his staff rank being relative to the rank of his commander explains this passage, and shows that he had no higher aspirations at the time.

Confederate prisoners at Aldie. The Battle of Aldie sparked Custer's rise when, as the 1st Maine Cavalry charged, the regiment's commander fell dead. Custer took the lead in his place; and his success led to the promotion to Brigadier General at the end of the month.

Thus ended Custer's connection with the Battle of Aldie. After he cut down the last rider who tried to stop him, he got off in safety, and on his way back captured the first man whom he had cut. The poor fellow was glad to surrender and be taken in.

It turned out afterwards that the force with which Gregg's advance was thus engaged was the extreme advance of Stuart's cavalry, pushing away from the rear of Lee's army to cross the Blue Ridge. Stuart's column was spread out and scattered over a large expanse of country, as also was Pleasonton's, and it took both of them four days more to concentrate their forces for the second and more decisive fight in the same vicinity, which took place at Upperville, some five miles from Aldie.

At the time of the Battle of Aldie, Colonel Duffie, a French officer on a two years' leave, who then commanded the First Rhode Island Cavalry, threw himself with his regiment, two hundred and eighty strong, into the little town of Upperville, attacking the rear of the same brigade defeated by Kilpatrick and putting more confusion into it. Unluckily, he found himself in the midst of all Stuart's advancing forces, and yet determined to hold on to the town, trusting to Pleasonton's advance to relieve him. He was ultimately completely surrounded, and cut his way out with only twenty-seven men, thus terminating that haphazard scrambling fight termed the Battle of Aldie.

For his part in determining the principal success of the day, as well as for his past services, General Pleasonton sent in the name of Captain Custer, along with those of Colonel Kilpatrick, Captain Farnsworth and Captain Merritt to the President, for promotion to the rank of Brigadier General. Colonel Duffie was promoted at the same time.

The force with which Kilpatrick was engaged consisted of the First, Third, Fourth and Fifth Virginia Cavalry, with four guns. A hundred prisoners were taken and one flag. Custer's promotion sent him to Maryland, where he joined the Michigan Brigade he was soon to render so famous, at Hanover, Maryland.

From henceforth the young staff officer, so suddenly transformed into a general, instead of carrying others' orders, was to issue his own and to fight more or less independently, in that confused series of cavalry actions that preceded and followed the Battle of Gettysburg. Here begins that public career of Custer, which was so soon to eclipse that of all the other cavalry leaders of the army and which, by a combination of audacity, ability and good luck, was to carry him to Appomattox Court House.

We have previously said that Custer's promotion was entirely unexpected by himself; the way in which he received it, illustrates this. That he felt, from the very beginning of his career, a conviction that he should win distinction in the war and become a general officer is undoubted. His hopes and aspirations on this point were so well defined that he did not hesitate to speak of it to his brother officers in the course of their many firelight talks.

As was inevitable in those early days, he encountered a great deal of sarcasm and merciless ridicule on this point from his comrades, far more so than would have occurred later in the war when every man who stayed at the front was in grim earnest. In the enormous staffs fashionable at that period, there were always to be found a few officers who did all the work, and a large residue of genteel idlers whose highest ambition seemed to be to make the time pass pleasantly, and to do as little for their pay as they could.

The same class of men, a few grades farther down, goes by the name of "malingerers" and "coffee-coolers," and indulges when in camp in the same general line of sarcasm towards those comrades who do duty cheerfully and aspire to win promotion by good conduct. At that early period of the war, the regular routine of promotion had not become so rapid and certain as it afterwards became, and many advances were still due to favor. At all events, the incautious admission of Custer to some of his comrades that he was "determined to be a general before the war was over," was received by many with ill-natured sneers, and was frequently made the occasion of severely sarcastic bantering.

One evening, eleven days after Aldie, when Custer returned to headquarters after a long ride in which he had been posting the pickets of the entire corps for the night, he was greeted in the large tent where the staff was wont to gather at night, by the salutations, "Hal-o, general." "How are you, general?" "Gentlemen, General Custer." "Why, general, I congratulate you." "You're looking well, general."

WINNING HIS STAR

The greetings came from all quarters of the tent, where staff officers were lounging, smoking, chatting, laughing, telling stories. They impressed Custer as being merely a continuation of the usual ill-natured banter on the subject of his aspirations and further as being carried a little too far. However, he had always been noted for his remarkable control over a hot and hasty temper, and he was not going to allow his comrades to laugh him out of it on this occasion. Still, it was with some bitterness that he answered: "You may laugh, boys. Laugh as long as you please, but I will be a general yet, for all your chaff. You see if I don't, that's all."

He was greeted by a universal shout of laughter in answer. It seemed as if his tormentors were determined to irritate him into an explosion; and they nearly succeeded; for his blue eases began to flash, and he looked round as if seeking someone on whom to fix a quarrel. His old friend Yates,[*] whom he had been himself the means of putting on Pleasonton's staff, came to his relief with a few words; "Look on the table, old fellow. They're not chaffng." He pointed to the table in the tent, and there, in the midst, lay a large official envelope, and on it was written: "BRIGADIER GENERAL GEORGE A. CUSTER, U.S. VOLUNTEERS."

The reaction was instantaneous and the young fellow was completely overcome. A moment later, and all his old comrades were gathered round him in real earnest, congratulating and shaking hands, while Custer, too much overpowered to speak, could only smile faintly, turn very pale, find his eyes full of tears and sink down in a chair, feeling very much as if he was going to make a fool of himself and cry.

However, he regained his self control in a few moments and was able to thank his comrades, who were really in earnest this time, and after a while was permitted to read the orders which accompanied his commission, and which directed him to report to General Pleasonton for instructions.

---

[*] Afterwards brevet lieutenant colonel, and captain in the Seventh U.S. Cavalry, and one of the little band of heroes who fell with Custer. Yates was an old Monroe friend of Custer, and it was at Custer's request that Pleasonton appointed Yates on his staff, where he proved to be a valuable officer.

FREDERICK WHITTAKER

George Yates. After the Civil War, Yates became a captain in the 7th Cavalry, commanding F Company. He was killed during the Battle of the Little Bighorn, and believed to have fallen near Custer.

Of the interview between Pleasonton and himself it is unnecessary to speak. It was marked on the one side by great kindness and good sense. A few months later, Custer writes home about Pleasonton, "he has been more like a father to me than a general," and this was indeed the truth. There must however, have been something peculiarly magnetic about Custer to have attracted to himself as he did, the enthusiastic affection of three men of such very different characters as his three successive commanders.

McClellan, the polished scientific soldier, kind-hearted to a fault, slow, methodical and cautious; Pleasonton, acrid, sarcastic, exacting, an excellent cavalry chief, but generally failing to attract any affection from his subordinates, a martinet in his discipline; Sheridan, fiery, impetuous, untiring, remorseless in the amount of work he exacted from his troops; all these three men loved, admired and trusted Custer entirely; and it was nothing but the transcendent ability of his character that forced them to do so.

Had McClellan remained in command and promoted Custer, it might have been said that favoritism and luck presided over his elevation. That a man like Pleasonton, who was notoriously hard to please, should have evinced so much trust in the abilities of a simple lieutenant as to take the responsibility of urging his promotion to the command of a brigade, without even the intermediate experience of a colonelcy, was the proudest of tributes to Custer's real merit, for it must be remembered that he had not a single friend at court, and that his previous connection with McClellan's staff was at that time a positive disadvantage to him.

It was the greatest misfortune of General McClellan that after his removal he was taken up, petted, and made a martyr of, for political purposes, by the party which at that time was actively and passively in sympathy with the rebellion, and in the minority besides. This fact rendered all his friends objects of political and partisan dislike - of all dislikes the most bitter and unreasoning - to the members of the party in power. The very strength of the McClellan party made it the object of the more bitter animosity, the instincts of self-preservation being enlisted against it in the minds of all ardent Republicans. It became impossible to secure fair play for a known "McClellan man," however brave and capable. The bad example of some of the less capable of McClellan's partisans in high places had rendered the government suspicious of them down to their humblest ranks, and not without much reason.

Custer himself had experienced the evil effects of this feeling during the previous winter when at Monroe, awaiting orders. During that period, backed by the earnest help of Judge Christiancy, now United States Senator from Michigan and then a very influential member of the Union party, Custer applied to Governor Blair for the command of one of the cavalry regiments then being fitted out by the State of Michigan for the war. The last of these regiments, the Seventh Cavalry, was then only partly organized, two battalions leaving Grand Rapids, Michigan, in February, the rest in May.

It was for this special regiment that Custer applied without success, despite the influence of Judge Christiancy. The excuse made by Governor Blair was very plausible, and apparently convincing. It was that the commissions in the new regiments could only be given to those officers who were instrumental in raising them, and that it was not possible to depart from the rule, save in very exceptional cases. The governor promised however, to remember Captain Custer's application, "the first vacancy that occurred," and with this promise (Custer was obliged to be content, well aware that like all politicians' promises, it was a mere delusion, and that the real obstacle behind all was the fact of his being a "McClellan man."

George Armstrong Custer, 1864

This experience was one of those which occasioned the great bitterness of tone which marks his private letters about the time he first rejoined the Army of the Potomac. The man felt that he was unjustly treated, and that the holiest feelings of his nature, love and gratitude, had been made instrumental to his damage; and he felt outraged. Only the advance of the season of hard work, and the activity which he enjoyed under Pleasonton, caused these feelings to fade away. It is probable too that the creditable fight at Beverly Ford and the sharply fought action at Aldie, the latter culminating in victory, had aided to persuade him that there were as good generals left as McClellan, even if he would not admit it in public.

Now his sudden elevation contributed to eradicate the last remains of bitterness from his mind, and Pleasonton put the final touch to the picture of happiness when he announced that he had assigned the

WINNING HIS STAR

young general to the command of a brigade of troops from his adopted state, Michigan, comprising - *mirabile dictu* - the very regiment for the command of which Captain Custer had applied in vain three months before to Governor Blair. There let us leave him to join his command, all inexperienced and untried as he was.

It is rather curious in connection with what we have said before, that from the time of McClellan's fall to the end of his career, Custer always found himself directly opposed in politics to the party in power, he being a strong Democrat. He was even opposed to Pleasonton who then and since has always been identified with the Republicans, and it was solely on his military record, then and after, that he gained all his many honors.

He never received favors, only work. When any work was to do which no one else could do, Pleasonton first and Sheridan afterwards always set Custer to do it. Months after he gained the star, when he had won many battles and had had four or five horses shot under him in action, it became a question whether his commission should be confirmed in the Senate on account of his being a "McClellan man." Pleasonton got him his promotion with the rest, because he wanted someone to do the work, and no one could do it so well as these young energetic officers. So it was all through the war and after. It seemed to be fated that he should always be an anti-administration man, getting all the hard knocks and little reward. What reward he bad, he earned. The rest of his life will show how he earned it.

THE GETTYSBURG CAMPAIGN

THE first fight at Aldie on the 16th June was succeeded by four days of skirmishing and scouting, during which Pleasonton united his two divisions under Gregg and Buford and Stuart brought up such of his forces as he could get together. On the 19th, the brigade of Colonel Gregg, a brother of General Gregg, and that of Kilpatrick, had a second fight near Aldie in which they again drove the enemy, this time into Middleburg; and on the 21st, Pleasonton arriving, drove the enemy about eight miles further and took from them three guns and a lot of prisoners.

So far as can be found, the Confederate forces in this last battle were inferior in number to the National forces, but the results were none the less inspiriting to the cavalry. Three victories under any circumstances were comforting, still more so to men who were depressed in spirit from the long succession of disasters that had followed the Army of the Potomac.

In the meantime, the greater part of Stuart's forces were already over the border, and it became necessary to follow them. The battles at the gap had prevented Lee from crossing his army at Poolesville below Harper's Ferry, and he was compelled to cross above the latter place at Haggerstown. The Union army followed by way of Poolesville, and when it arrived at Frederick, Maryland, Hooker was replaced by Meade, and the two armies concentrated at Gettysburg.

The cavalry crossed the Potomac on the 25th June and arrived at Frederick City next day. Here, it was reorganized into the form in which it was afterwards to win such enduring fame, as the Cavalry Corps, Army of the Potomac. All the loose regiments were gathered up into brigades, forming the famous three divisions which remained unaltered to the following spring. The First was commanded by John

THE GETTYSBURG CAMPAIGN

Buford, the Second by Gregg, while the Third, composed of the loose ends, given to the just promoted hero of Aldie, General Kilpatrick. In his division appeared the Michigan Brigade, assigned to Custer, who joined it on the 29th June at Hanover, Pennsylvania, as it went into camp.

Troops in Gettysburg. Often left out of Gettysburg accountings is the east cavalry field fighting. There, J.E.B. Stuart's Confederate cavalry attempted to get into the Federal rear and exploit any success that Pickett's Charge may have gained. Instead, Union cavalry under General David Gregg and George Armstrong Custer repulsed the Confederate advances. Had Stuart succeeded, it may have impaired the Union repulse of Pickett, and possibly changed the result of the entire battle.

The next day, the Gettysburg campaign commenced in earnest, and the country was full of roaming bodies of Union and Confederate cavalry hunting for each other. On this day, Kilpatrick himself with Farnsworth's brigade was attacked by Stuart, with Wade Hampton's division in right and rear, and for some time was pretty roughly handled. Custer's brigade had marched to Abbottsville, but, hearing the firing returned and aided in repelling the enemy, who lost fifty men and a flag. Here, Custer made his first appearance on a battlefield as a general officer and surprised and captivated everyone by his peculiar and picturesque appearance, thereafter to be indelibly associated with his name.

Hanover Junction. The Hanover Branch Railroad carried Abraham Lincoln from Hanover Junction to Gettysburg on November 18, 1863, where on the next day Lincoln delivered his Gettysburg Address at the dedication of the Gettysburg National Cemetery.

When we remember the condition of the United States Army at that date with regard to uniform, it seems almost impossible to make out of such a dress anything handsome and showy. The fatigue uniform allowed was slouchy and untidy, the full regulation uniform the most hideous imaginable. The whole dress was the invention of John B. Floyd, a rebel general who before the war had been United States Secretary of War. Yet keeping within the regulations, Custer managed to produce one of the most brilliant and showy dresses out of this hideous uniform, and to fashion it so that no one could mistake his rank.

The regulation hat was a soft felt abomination, redolent of reminiscences of Praise God Barebones and the Rump Parliament. The crown cut down, the brim widened, it became on Custer's head the veritable headgear of Prince Rupert, a regular cavalier hat, exactly suited to the long fair curls of the wearer. The custom of the service allowed a cavalry officer to wear a tight jacket instead of a coat. Custer wore a loose one. Velveteen was growing not uncommon for trousers on account of its strength. Custer had both jacket and trousers made of it to give richness of effect.

Officers were permitted to wear on the sleeves of their overcoats certain stripes of black braid to indicate their rank when epaulettes and shoulder straps were hidden. Custer put the braids in gold lace on his jacket sleeves until they covered him nearly to the shoulder. A blue shirt with a broad falling collar bore on its corner the silver star of a brigadier, and high boots, into which the loose trousers were thrust, completed the costume. He looked as if he had just stepped out of one of Vandyke's pictures, the image of the seventeenth century.

Such an appearance was exactly calculated to attract attention and wonder, comment and sneer, or else the most enthusiastic admiration. The boy general looked so pretty and effeminate, so unlike the stern realities of war, that he was certain to be quizzed and ridiculed unmercifully unless he could compel the whole army to respect him. There was envy enough about his sudden elevation, as it was. There were men in the cavalry corps who had been colonels when he was only a second lieutenant, and who had commanded brigades when he was only a staff captain.

Jumped over the heads of all these men as he was, they cordially disliked him, and none would have been sorry to see him come to grief with his fine feathers. The very assumption of his peculiar and fantastic uniform was a challenge to all the world to notice him. He must do something brilliant to justify the freak. Imitating as he did the splendor of appearance of Murat, he must equal him in deeds if he did not wish to be set down for a carpet knight.

Long after, in private life, Custer used to describe his novel sensations, and those apparently controlling his regimental commanders when he first took command of the Michigan Brigade. He had not had time to go to Washington and procure the brilliant dress which he so soon assumed and rendered famous. He came to the brigade headquarters almost alone, and the first thing he had to do was to assume command and announce his staff. All he took with him was his personal baggage, his boy Johnny, and two buglers from his old regiment, the Fifth U.S. Cavalry.

He looked so young and boyish when he came in that it is no wonder if he felt awkward. He concealed all this feeling however, as effectually as did Napoleon sixty-two years before when taking command of the Army of Italy, almost as boyish and untried. He assumed an abrupt and distant manner at first, was curt and decided in his orders, and made himself felt as master from the first hour. But he was distinctly conscious all the time that his subordinates disliked, suspected and distrusted him.

Custer and General Pleasonton, Warrenton, VA. 1863

Grey-headed colonels came in to salute him with outward respect, but the stiff dignity of their manners convinced him that they were inwardly boiling over with disgust and anger at having this "boy," this "popinjay," this "affected dandy," with his "girl's hair," his "swagger" and "West Point conceit" put over "men, sir, men who had left their farms and business, men who could make their own living, sir, and asked no government a penny for their support, men old enough to be his father, and who knew as much about real fighting sir, as any epauletted government pensioner and West Point popinjay who was ever seen - too lazy to work for their living, and depending on government for support! Hired mercenaries, by heavens, good for nothing along side of the noble volunteers."

A good deal of this sort of thing was indulged in that night round the camp fires, and groups of irate officers poured forth their indignation in no measured terms. They were not aware that Pleasonton's recommendation of the three or four "boys" for high command was based on the fact that he found himself unable to get any sharp and effective work out of the elderly and over cautious colonels and generals in command of his divisions and brigades, in whom experience was the only military merit apparent to the eye, and who were so cautious and safe that there was no getting a hard fight out of them.

In recommending Custer, Merritt, and Farnsworth for high station, Pleasonton imperiled his own future. All these three were young and untried officers, only known to himself. Kilpatrick and Duffie were different, both having commanded regiments and brigades. Strange to say however, they were the very men who least justified their promotion in after days, both being excessively rash. Kilpatrick soon gained the unenviable sobriquet of "Kill cavalry," in spite of his really brilliant talents for getting out of scrapes as well as into them; and Duffie worked his division so hard and neglected its horses to such an extent that Sheridan was obliged to break it up and dismount the men the next year.

Custer, Merritt, and Farnsworth did nobly. The career of the last named was cut short within a week by death, but he left behind him the memory of a gallant and perfect cavalry general. What Custer did, we shall soon hear.

The first day, or rather night (for he joined the brigade in the evening), was passed in detailing a staff, which Custer did from the brigade itself, not going outside for a man. He selected old Monroe acquaintances, where he could find them, and at once set them to work.

He was compelled to be cold and distant in his manner to the colonels at first, as Napoleon was, and for the same reason, otherwise "I should soon have had them clapping me on the back and giving me advice." He could see that they envied him, and felt disposed to hate him, but he trusted confidently to the opportunity of the first battle to change all their opinions. That opportunity came very soon.

One thing that made the Michiganders dislike their boy general on his very first night was the excessive severity of discipline, as they thought it, which he at once inaugurated. They came from the loosest of schools, that of volunteer regiments, scattered over a peaceful country, officers without any of those traditions of the service that are second nature to a regular. All those little vexatious rules, apparently so trifling, which are enforced in a regular cavalry regiment as matters of habit, were unknown to them, and Custer enforced everyone from the first.

It was made a rigid rule from his first entrance that not a stable call should pass in a single company in the brigade without the attendance of a commissioned officer to superintend the cleaning of the horses, and there is nothing the average cavalry officer abominates so utterly as stable duty. The sergeants were no longer left alone in their glory at reveille roll call, but the officers had to turn out.

The baggage of regiments was curtailed, officers were brought up with a round turn for the slightest neglect of regulations, the salute was rigidly enforced, the new general went riding along from camp to camp, finding fault in his sharp quick way, and adding every moment to his unpopularity. All this on the very day after he assumed command and when the brigade was still lying in camp. How the angry officers and men cursed these "new-fangled West Point notions," and made up their minds to hate their boy general when they received orders to start next morning toward Gettysburg. That day, however, witnessed a change in their relations.

It was the first of July, 1863. The infantry was already hard at work at Gettysburg, fighting Lee. The Third Cavalry division, Kilpatrick's, was moving from Hanover toward Gettysburg, Custer's brigade in the advance. Custer had already been an hour on the road when Wade

THE GETTYSBURG CAMPAIGN

Hampton's rebel cavalry attacked Kilpatrick in the rear just as Farnsworth's brigade was moving out, and charged him ferociously. For some time, the fate of the battle was very doubtful until Custer, hearing the firing, halted his column, faced it about and trotted up, putting in his own men with such judgment that the Michiganders were compelled to own that the boy understood his business. There was however, no severe fighting that day after they arrived, and the grumblers were not yet silenced.

The next day, July 2nd, Kilpatrick moved on a place called Hunterstown, near Gettysburg, on the prolongation of Meade's position. The Battle of Gettysburg was now in still progress, and the cavalry on each side was feeling its way toward the flanks of its own army. The division arrived at Hunterstown at four in the afternoon, when the very fiercest battle was in progress a few miles off between Sickles and Longstreet. Kilpatrick ordered in Custer's and Farnsworth's brigades, the first on the left, the second on the right of the road leading to Gettysburg, to attack Stuart's cavalry, (again Wade Hampton's division) which barred the way.

Now was Custer's time. He ordered out Company A, Sixth Michigan, for a mounted charge, and deployed two more companies of the same regiment on foot in a wheat field at the side of the road so as to rake it with their fire. At the end of the road could be seen a party of the enemy, apparently a squadron. Captain Thompson commanded Company A. All was ready, and Thompson was preparing to charge when to everyone's surprise, the boy general flashed out his long Toledo blade, motioned his staff to keep back, and dashed out in front of Company A with the careless laughing remark, "I'll lead you this time, boys. Come on!"

Then away he went down the road at a gallop, his broad white hat on the back of his head, while the men raised a short yell of delight and followed him. Down the road in a perfect cloud of blinding dust went the boy general in front of that single company, and the next moment they were into the midst of the enemy, only to find they had struck a very superior force. They were received with a rattling fire of carbines, more efficacious than common, and the next moment down went the general, horse and all in the road, the animal shot stone dead.

Hunterstown. On the afternoon of July 2, 1863, General Wade Hampton's cavalry brigade was ordered to protect the Confederate Army's left flank at Hunterstown Road. However, Union cavalry under General George Armstrong Custer attacked Hampton's rear. The Federals retreated, and lured Hampton into an ambush. While Hampton fended off Custer, another brigade stepped in to cover the flank against the threat from other Union cavalry. Custer's action prevented 2,129 more Confederate infantry from fighting in that evening's battles for Culp's Hill and East Cemetery Hill at Gettysburg.

The enemy raised a yell and came rushing on. Thompson was shot down, mortally wounded, and a man rode at Custer, who was struggling up from his dead horse. The Michiganders were demoralized and turned, all but one boy named Churchill, who was near the general. He shot down Custer's assailant, took up the general on his horse and started back with him. They had not far to go, for the dismounted men were already nearly up to them, running and firing with the dash and energy peculiar to dismounted cavalry. Pennington's and Elder's batteries in the rear were both beginning to pitch shells into the rebels and the end of the affair was that the exulting enemy was repulsed.

But the Michiganders had learned one lesson; that their "popinjay," their "boy general," was not afraid to fight like a private soldier, and they began to feel a little more in the humor to follow him, which they did that very night to join the main army at Two Taverns on the right of Meade's position at Gettysburg.

General George Gordon Meade

At Two Taverns, Custer arrived with Kilpatrick on the morning of July 3rd; and from henceforth he shall tell his own story, as embodied in his report, made subsequent to the battle. Omitting the preamble, we come at once to the narrative, written in the same graphic and picturesque style which marks all his reports and orders and which makes them such interesting reading. As with his usual personal modesty, he omits mention of his own exploits. We shall supplement the report with the account of an eyewitness present at the time. In his report of the battle, General Custer says:

> At an early hour on the morning of the 3rd, I received an order through a staff officer of the Brigadier-General commanding the division to move at once my command, and follow the First Brigade on the road leading from Two Taverns to Gettysburg. Agreeably to the above instructions, my column was formed and moved out on the road designated, when a staff officer of Brigadier-General Gregg, commanding Second

Division, ordered me to take my command and place it in position on the pike leading from York to Gettysburg, which position formed the extreme right of our battle on that day.

Upon arriving at the point designated, I immediately placed my command in position, facing toward Gettysburg. At the same time, I caused reconnaissance to be made on my front, right and rear, but failed to discover any considerable force of the enemy. Everything remained quiet until 10 a.m., when the enemy appeared on my right flank and opened upon me with a battery of six guns.

Leaving two guns and a regiment to hold my first position and cover the road leading to Gettysburg, I shifted the remaining portion of my command, forming a new line of battle at right angles to my former line. The enemy had obtained correct range of my new position and were pouring solid shot and shell into my command with great accuracy. Placing two sections of Battery M, Second (regular) Artillery, in position, I ordered them to silence the enemy's battery, which order, notwithstanding the superiority of the enemy's position, was successfully accomplished in a very short space of time.

My line, as it then existed, was shaped like the letter L, the shorter branch formed of the section of Battery M, supported by four squadrons of the Sixth Michigan cavalry, faced toward Gettysburg, covering Gettysburg pike; the long branch composed of the remaining two sections of Battery M, Second Artillery, supported by a portion of the Sixth Michigan cavalry on the right, while the Seventh Michigan cavalry still further to the right and in advance, was held in readiness to repel any attack the enemy might make coming on the Oxford Road.

The Fifth Michigan cavalry was dismounted and ordered to take position in front of my centre and left. The First Michigan cavalry was held in column of squadrons to observe the movements of the enemy. I ordered fifty men to be sent one mile and a half on the Oxford Road, while a detachment of equal size was sent one mile and a half on the road leading from Gettysburg to York, both detachments being under the command of the gallant Major Webber, who from time to time kept me so well informed of the movements of the enemy that I was enabled to make my dispositions with complete success.

At 12 o'clock, an order was transmitted to me from the Brigadier-General commanding the division by one of his aids, directing me, upon being relieved by a brigade from the Second Division, to move with my command and form a junction with the First Brigade on the extreme left. On the arrival of the brigade of the Second Division, commanded by Colonel McIntosh, I prepared to execute the order. Before I had left my position, Brigadier-General Gregg, commanding the Second Division, arrived with his entire command. Learning the true condition of affairs on my front, and rightly conjecturing that the enemy was making his dispositions for attacking our position, Brigadier-General Gregg ordered me to remain in the position I then occupied.

Major Peter Webber

The enemy was soon after reported to be advancing on my front. The detachment of fifty men sent on the Oxford Road were driven in, and at the same time the enemy's line of skirmishers, consisting of dismounted cavalry, appeared on the crest of the ridge of hills on my front. The line extended beyond my left. To repel their advance, I ordered the Fifth Cavalry to a more advanced position with instructions to maintain their ground at all hazards. Colonel Alger, commanding the Fifth, assisted by Majors Trowbridge and Ferry, of the same regiment, made such admirable disposition of their men behind fences and other defenses as enabled them to successfully repel the repeated advances of a greatly superior force.

I attributed their success in a great measure to the fact that this regiment is armed with the Spencer repeating rifle, which in the hands of brave, determined men, like those composing the Fifth Michigan cavalry, is in my estimation the most effective firearm that our cavalry can adopt. Colonel Alger held his ground until his men had exhausted their ammunition, when he was compelled to fall back on the main body. The beginning of this movement was the signal for the enemy to charge, which they did with two regiments, mounted and dismounted.

FREDERICK WHITTAKER

Colonel Russell Alger

I at once ordered the Seventh Michigan Cavalry, Colonel Mann, to charge the advancing column of the enemy. The ground over which we had to pass was very unfavorable for the maneuvering of cavalry, but despite all obstacles this regiment advanced boldly to the assault, which was executed in splendid style, the enemy being driven from field to field, until our advance reached a high and unbroken fence behind which the enemy were strongly posted. Nothing daunted, Colonel Mann, followed by the main body of his regiment, bravely rode up to the fence and discharged their revolvers in the very face of the foe. No troops could have maintained this position; the Seventh was therefore compelled to retire, followed by twice the number of the enemy.

By this time, Colonel Alger of the Fifth Michigan Cavalry had succeeded in mounting a considerable portion of his regiment and gallantly advanced to the assistance of the Seventh, whose further pursuit by the enemy he checked. At the same time, an entire brigade of the enemy's cavalry, consisting of four regiments, appeared just over the crest in our front. They were formed in columns of regiments. To meet this overwhelming force, I had but one available regiment, the First Michigan Cavalry, and the fire of Battery M, Second Regular Artillery.

I at once ordered the First to charge, but learned at the same moment that similar orders had been given by Brigadier-General Gregg. As before stated, the First was formed in column of battalions. Upon receiving the order to charge, Colonel Town, placing himself at the head of his command, ordered the "trot" and sabres to be drawn. In this manner this gallant body of men advanced to the attack of a force outnumbering them five to one. In addition to this numerical superiority, the enemy had the advantage of position, and were exultant over the repulse of the Seventh Michigan

Cavalry.

THE GETTYSBURG CAMPAIGN

Colonel Charles Town

All these facts considered would seem to render success on the part of the First impossible. Not so, however. Arriving within a few yards of the enemy's column, the charge was ordered, and with a yell that spread terror before them, the First Michigan Cavalry, led by Colonel Town, rode upon the front rank of the enemy, sabring all who came within reach. For a moment, but only a moment, that long, heavy column stood its ground; then, unable to withstand the impetuosity of our attack, it gave way in a disorderly rout, leaving vast numbers of dead and wounded in our possession, while the First, being masters of the field, had the proud satisfaction of seeing the much vaunted chivalry, led by their favorite commander, seek safety in headlong flight.

I cannot find language to express my high appreciation of the gallantry and daring displayed by the officers and men of the First Michigan Cavalry. They advanced to the charge of a vastly superior force with as much order and precision as if going upon parade; and I challenge the annals of warfare to produce a more brilliant or successful charge of cavalry than the one just recounted. Nor must I forget to acknowledge the invaluable assistance rendered by Battery M, Second Regiment of Artillery, in this charge. Our success in driving the enemy from the field is due in a great measure to the highly efficient manner in which the battery was handled by Lieutenant A.C.M. Pennington, assisted by Lieutenants Clark, Woodruff, and Hamilton.

The enemy made but slight demonstrations against us during the remainder of the day, except in one instance he attempted to turn my left flank, which attempt was most gallantly met and successfully frustrated by

FREDERICK WHITTAKER

Second Lieutenant J.H. Kellogg with Company H, Sixth Michigan Cavalry. We held possession of the field until dark, during which time we collected our dead and wounded. At dark, I returned with my command to Two Taverns, where I encamped for the night.

Pennington's Battery near Fair Oaks, VA. From left: Lt. Robert Clarke, Capt. John C. Tidball, Lt. William N. Dennison, Capt. Alexander C.M. Pennington.

In this engagement, my command lost in killed, wounded and missing a total of five hundred and forty-two. Among the killed, I regret to record the name of Major N.H. Ferry of the Fifth Michigan Cavalry, who fell while heroically cheering on his men. It would be impossible for me to particularize those instances deserving especial mention; all, both men and officers, did their duty. There were many cases of personal heroism, but a list of their names would make my report too extended. To Colonel Town, commanding the First Michigan Cavalry, and to the officers and men of his regiment, for the gallant manner in which they drove the enemy from the field, great praise is due.

Colonel Mann of the Seventh Michigan Cavalry, and Colonel Alger of the Fifth Michigan Cavalry, as well as the officers of their commands, are entitled to much credit for their united efforts in repelling the advance of the enemy. The Sixth Michigan Cavalry rendered good service by guarding both my right and left flank; also by supporting Battery M, under a very hot fire from the enemy's battery. Colonel Gray, commanding the regiment, was constantly seen wherever his presence was most needed, and is deserving of special mention.

THE GETTYSBURG CAMPAIGN

Confederate dead at Gettysburg. Nearly one-third of the total forces fighting at Gettysburg became casualties. Of these, 7,058 were fatalities (3,155 Union, 3,903 Confederate). Another 33,264 were wounded (14,529 Union, 18,735 Confederate) and 10,790 were missing (5,365 Union, 5,425 Confederate).

    I desire to commend to your favorable notice Lieutenants Pennington, Clark, Woodruff and Hamilton of Battery M, Second Artillery, for the zeal and ability displayed by each on this occasion. My thanks are personally due to the following named members of my staff, who on many occasions exhibited remarkable gallantry in transmitting and executing my orders on the field: Captain G.A. Drew, Sixth Michigan Cavalry, Assistant Inspector General, First Lieutenant R. Baylis, Fifth Michigan Cavalry, Acting Assistant Adjutant-General, First Lieutenant William H. Wheeler, First Michigan Cavalry, A.D.C., First Lieutenant William Colerick, First Michigan Cavalry, A.D.C. I desire also to mention two of my buglers, Joseph Fought, Company D, Fifth U.S. Cavalry, and Peter Boehn, Company B, Fifth U.S. Cavalry; also Orderlies Norval Churchill, Company L, First Michigan Cavalry, George L. Foster, Company C, First Michigan Cavalry, and Benjamin H. Butler, Company M, First Michigan Cavalry.
    Respectfully submitted,
        G.A. CUSTER, Brigadier-General Commanding Second Brigade
            Jacob L. Greene, Assistant Adjutant-General

    The charge of the First Michigan at Gettysburg is described by an eyewitness as something magnificent, and yet the one thing that gave it weight is not mentioned in Custer's report. We have seen how the previous day the general had charged at the head of a single company, solely for the purpose of encouraging his men and to win their respect and affection. At Gettysburg, he completed his victory over the brigade by the manner in which he led the second charge in which he participated with his men.

Confederate General Wade Hampton. When Hampton's father died in 1858, he inherited a vast fortune, plantations, and one of the largest collections of slaves in the South. After the war, he returned to find his estate burned in Sherman's march, and his slaves freed.

When that single regiment, in column of squadrons, moved forward to the attack, every man knew that it was the last reserve and had started on an almost hopeless task. Nothing but the sight of the young general at their head, sharing their dangers, could have inspired them to such an effort, and it was the magnificent spectacle of his gallant and knightly figure, far in the van, that nerved every arm in that column. Hating him at Hanover, they began to respect him at Hunterstown; after Gettysburg they adored him.

The result of this attack was that Hampton's cavalry was driven back, the infantry ordered up to support it, the whole ammunition train of Lee threatened, and much of the vigor of the assault on the Union right paralyzed. Meanwhile Buford, on the other flank of the army, had prevented an equally dangerous turning movement in that direction, and the battle of Gettysburg had been won.

THE GETTYSBURG CAMPAIGN

AFTER GETTYSBURG

IN giving an account of the cavalry movements which followed the battle of Gettysburg, we are indebted largely to the spirited narrative of Mr. E.A. Paul, then correspondent of the New York Times, who accompanied Kilpatrick's division throughout the expedition. Those portions which relate to Custer are especially interesting. It must be remembered that the young general was then entirely unknown to the public, but these letters opened people's eyes. At the same time, they marked the brilliant commencement of that career which henceforth never knew a serious disaster. At Gettysburg, he began by charging whenever he had a ghost of a chance, and he continued in the same way.

Saturday morning, July 4th, according to Mr. Paul, it became known that the enemy was in full retreat, and General Kilpatrick moved on to destroy his train and harass his column. A heavy rain fell all day, and the travelling was anything but agreeable. The division arrived at Emmetsburg about midday during a severe storm. After a short halt, the column moved forward again, and at Fountaindale, just at dark, commenced ascending the mountain.

Imagine a long column of cavalry winding its way up a mountain, on a road dug out of the mountain side, which sloped at an angle of thirty degrees - just wide enough for four horses to walk abreast. On one side a deep abyss, and on the other an impassable barrier in the shape of a steep embankment; the hour 10 o'clock at night, a drizzling rain falling, the sky overcast and so dark as literally not to be able to see one's own hand if placed within a foot of the organs of vision.

The whole command, both men and animals, were worn out with fatigue and loss of sleep. Then imagine that, just as the head of this tired, hungry and sleepy column nears the crest of the mountain, a piece of cannon belches forth fire and smoke and destructive missiles directly in front. Imagine all this and a little more, and the reader can then form some idea of what occurred to General Kilpatrick's command on Saturday night, July 4th, 1863 as it ascended the mountain to the Monterey Gap, and so across to Waterloo on the western slope.

The column commenced to ascend at about dark, and arrived at the Monterey House, at the top, between nine and ten o'clock. The enemy had planted a piece of artillery near this spot so as to command the road, and also had sharpshooters on the flanks. It was intended to make a strong defense here, as one half-mile beyond Lee's train was crossing the mountain on the Gettysburg and Hagerstown pike. The Fifth Michigan Cavalry was in advance, and although on the lookout for just such an occurrence, it startled the whole column. A volley of musketry was fired by a concealed force at the same time at the head of the column; the first squadron of the Fifth broke, fell back upon the second and broke that, but there was no such thing as running back a great way on that road. It was jammed with men and horses. The broken squadron immediately rallied, skirmishers were posted on the most available points, the First Virginia, Major Copeland was ordered to the front, and upon arriving there was ordered to charge.

Charge they did at a rapid gait, down the mountain side into the inky darkness before them, accompanied by a detachment of the First Ohio, Captain Jones. As anticipated, the train was struck in rear of the centre at the crossing, just one half mile west of the Monterey House. A volley was fired just as the train was reached. "Do you surrender?" "Yes," was the response, and on the First Virginia dashed to Ringgold, ordering the cowed and frightened train guard to surrender, as they swept along for eight miles, when the head of the train was reached.

Here the two hundred men who started on the charge had been reduced to twenty-five, and seizing upon a good position, the rebels made a stand. As the force in front could not be seen, Major Copeland decided not to proceed further, but to await daylight and reinforcements. Both came, and the enemy fled. Arriving at Gettysburg pike, the Eighteenth Pennsylvania was placed here as a guard and a barricade was hastily thrown tip. No sooner was this done than cavalry was heard charging down the road. "Who comes there!" calls the officer in charge at the barricade. "Tenth Virginia Cavalry," was the reply. To - with your Tenth Virginia Cavalry and the squadron fire a volley into the darkness.

That was the last heard of the Tenth Virginia Cavalry that night, until numbers of the regiment came straggling in and gave themselves up, prisoners of war. Other rebel cavalry moved up and down the road upon which the train was standing, and some most amusing scenes occurred. The train belonged to Ewell's division, and had in it also a large number of private carriages and teams containing officers' baggage. Four regiments were doing guard duty, but as they judged of the future by the past, they supposed our army would rest two or three months after winning a battle, magnanimously permitting the defeated enemy to get away his stores and ordnance and have a little time to recruit.

Therefore, the attack was a complete surprise. A thunderstorm was prevailing at the time, and the attack was so entirely unexpected that there was a general panic among both guard and teamsters. The howling of the storm, the rushing of water down the mountainside, and the roaring of wind, altogether were certainly enough in that wild spot to test the nerves of the strongest. But when is added to this a volley of pistol and carbine shots occasionally, a slap on the back with the flat of a sword, and a hoarse voice giving the unfortunate fight the choice of surrendering or being shot, then add to this the fearful yells and imprecations of the men, wild with excitement, all made up a scene certainly never excelled before in the regions of fancy.

Two rebel captains, two hours after the train had been captured, came up to one of the reserve commands and wanted to know "what regiment that was" - supposing it belonged to their own column. They discovered their mistake when Lieutenant Whittaker, of General Kilpatrick's staff, presented a pistol and advised them to give up their arms. Several other officers who might easily have escaped came in voluntarily and gave themselves up.

Under so good subjection were the enemy that there was no necessity of making any change in teamsters or drivers, they voluntarily

AFTER GETTYSBURG

continuing right on in Uncle Sam's service as they had been in the Confederate service, until it was convenient to relieve them. At first, the prisoners were corralled near the Monterey House. When the number had got to be large, they were driven down the mountain toward Waterloo.

A gang started off in this direction about midnight. It was not prudent to wait until morning, for daylight might bring with it a retreating column of the enemy, and then all the prisoners would have been recaptured; finally, when near the Gettysburg road crossing, a band of straggling rebels happened to fire into the head of the party from a spur of the mountain overlooking the road. Here was another panic, which alike affected guards and prisoners. The rain was falling in torrents and the whole party, neither one knowing who this or the other was, rushed under the friendly shelter of a clump of trees. All of those prisoners might have at that time escaped. Hundreds did escape before daylight dawned.

The head of the column reached Ringgold at about daylight - the whole command, horses as well as men, tired, hungry, sleepy, wet and covered with mud. Men and animals yielded to the demands of exhausted nature, and the column had not been halted many minutes before all fell asleep where they stood. Under the friendly protection of the dripping eaves of a chapel, a gay and gallant brigadier could have been seen, enjoying in the mud one of those sound sleeps only obtained through fatigue, his long golden locks matted with the soil of Pennsylvania.

Near him in the mud lay a dandyish adjutant, equally oblivious of the toilet upon which he generally bestowed so much attention. Under a fence near at hand is reclining a well-got-up major, whose stylish appearance and regular features have turned the heads of many fair damsels on Chestnut street; here a chaplain, there a trooper, a Commanding General, aids, orderlies and servants, for the nonce, meet on a level. The faithful trooper lies by his horse, between whom and himself there seems to exist an indescribable community of feeling.

Two hours are thus passed in sleep - the provost-guard only on duty - when word is passed that "the column has all closed up," which is the signal to move on again. The indefatigable Estes shakes himself and proceeds to shake the Commanding General to let him know that the object for which the halt was made had been accomplished; that it is time to move.

Five minutes more, all are in the saddle again and marching for Smithsburg. A body of armed men, mailed in mud! What a picture. Smithsburg was reached by 9 o'clock a.m. The reception met with there made all forget the trials of the night - made them forget even their fatigue. It was Sunday. The sun shone forth brightly, young girls lined the street sides singing patriotic songs; the General was showered with flowers and the General and troops were cheered until reechoed by the mountain side; young ladies and matrons assailed the column with words of welcome and large plates heaped up with pyramids of white bread, spread with jelly and butter, inviting all to partake.

While the young sang, the old shed tears and wrung the hands of those nearest to them. The little town was overflowing with patriotism and thankfulness at the arrival of their preservers. While these things were detaining the column, the band struck up *"Hail Columbia,"* followed by the *"Star Spangled Banner."*

Many eyes, unused to tears, were wet then. The kind reception met with here did the command more good than a week's rest. Even the horses, faithful animals, seemed to be revived by the patriotic demonstration. No one who participated in the raid of Saturday night, July 4th, 1863, can ever forget the reception met with in Smithsburg. It was like an oasis in the desert - a green spot in the soldier's life.

Early on Monday, July 6th, General Kilpatrick, hearing that the enemy had a train near Hagerstown, moved upon that place. The enemy's pickets were met near the edge of the town. It was 4 o'clock p.m. when General Kilpatrick, with the main column, reached the crest of the hill overlooking Williamsport on the Boonsboro Pike. General Buford's command had been engaged with the enemy two or three miles to the left for two or more hours; Major Medill, of the Eighth Illinois, had already fallen mortally wounded. Two pieces of Pennington's battery were placed on the brow of the hill to the right of the pike, and the other pieces to the left. A squadron of Fifth

AFTER GETTYSBURG

Michiganders had previously charged down the pike, driving in the enemy's pickets and a battalion which occupied an advanced position.

1862 stereograph of Boonsboro Pike, with stone house on the eastern side of Antietam Bridge.

The First Michigan, Colonel Town, was deployed as skirmishers to the right and ordered to drive the enemy from a brick house a little in advance, and to the right of the artillery. Several unsuccessful attempts were made to obey this order; but before it could be done, the brisk firing of the rear guard warned the commanding general that his force occupied a dangerous position. Never was a command in a more critical situation; never before was a man cooler, or did one display more real generalship than General Kilpatrick on this occasion.

Tapping his boot with his whip and peering in the direction of the rapidly approaching rear guard, he saw it falling back, apparently in some disorder. Not a moment was to be lost; inaction or indecision would have proved fatal, and the moral effect of a successful campaign destroyed in an hour. Fortunately, General Kilpatrick was cool and defiant, and felt the responsibility resting upon him. This made him master of the situation, and by a dashing movement, saved the cavalry corps from disaster.

FREDERICK WHITTAKER

Seeing his rear guard falling back, he bethought himself of what force could be withdrawn from the front in safety. The enemy were pressing his front and rear - the crisis had arrived; he ordered the Second New York (Harris's Light) to charge upon the exultant foe, then coming like an avalanche upon his rear. Nobly did this band of heroes perform their task. They fell into the breach with a yell, and sword in hand drove back the enemy, relieving the exhausted rear guard and holding the enemy in check until the whole command was disposed of, so as to fall back, which they did in good order, fighting as they went.

For three miles, over one of the worst roads ever travelled by man, was this retreat conducted, when the enemy, dispirited at their want of success in surrounding and capturing the whole command, halted, and the cavalry corps went into camp, men and officers, exhausted from the labors of the day, falling asleep on the spot where they halted. Colonel Devin's brigade of General Buford's command had relieved the rear guard, and were harassed by the enemy all night.

Tuesday morning, July 7th, the cavalry force moved back to Boonsboro, the enemy following the rear guard, and at intervals there was brisk skirmishing between General Buford's command and the enemy. The same was true of the night. The Sixth Cavalry, (regulars) under Captain Chafiant, made a reconnaissance at night and had a brisk fight, in which they lost eight or nine men. Wednesday morning, there were indications that the enemy were present in large force, and by ten o'clock the "fandango" opened in real earnest, in which both Buford's and Kilpatrick's troops participated. The enemy were forced back to Antietam Creek. Thursday, the fight was renewed and again on Friday, when Funktown was occupied. Saturday, the enemy was again forced back, and on Saturday, General Kilpatrick's command again moved upon Hagerstown. After fighting for an hour, the town was fully occupied and the enemy fell back to the crest of the hill, one and a half miles west of the town.

The streets picketed by the enemy were barricaded, and the troops were disposed of outside the town so as to resist an attack. In clearing the outskirts of the town for skirmishers, the One Hundred and Fifty-seventh New York Infantry of General Ames's Brigade (Eleventh

Corps), rendered material assistance. Upon entering the town, the hearts of our troops were made glad by finding between thirty and forty Union soldiers who had been missing since the Monday before, a majority of whom were supposed to be dead. A few were wounded; all had been concealed by citizens and had been treated well. Captain Snyder, reported killed, was found wounded at the Franklin Hotel, carefully attended by a bevy of lovely damsels.

General Kilpatrick was much annoyed at the restraint he was under all day Monday and Tuesday; he desired to move on, believing that the enemy, while making a show of force, was crossing the river. This subsequently proved to be true. Had the army advanced on Tuesday morning, Lee's whole army would either have been captured or dispersed. When, on Wednesday morning, an advance was made without orders, the fact was ascertained that the enemy had commenced falling back when the attack was made the day before, the enemy believing that it was the initiatory movement of a general advance.

Such was the panic among the rebel troops, that they abandoned wagons, ammunition, tents, arms and even provisions. Hundreds of rebels, fearing Kilpatrick's men, fled to the right and left to avoid their charges, and subsequently surrendered themselves. One strapping fellow surrendered to a little bugler, who is attached to General Custer's brigade. As he passed down the line escorting his prisoner, a Colt's revolver in hand, he called out; "I say boys, what do you think of this fellow?" "This fellow" looked as if he felt very mean, and expected he would be shot by his captor every moment for feeling so. All along the road to Williamsport, prisoners were captured and their rear guard was fairly driven into the river.

The Fifth Michigan charged into the town and captured a large number of soldiers as they were attempting to ford the river. From thirty to fifty of the rebels were drowned while attempting to cross; twenty-five or thirty wagons and a large number of horses and mules were washed away. A regiment of cavalry was drawn up on the opposite bank, but a few of "Pennington's pills" caused them to skedaddle. They fired a few shells in return, but no harm was done.

Hearing that a force had marched toward Falling Waters, General

Kilpatrick ordered an advance to that place. Through some mistake only one brigade, that of General Custer, obeyed the order. When within less than a mile of Falling Waters, four brigades were found in line of battle in a very strong position, and behind half a dozen crescent-shaped earth walls.

General Kilpatrick was nicknamed "Kilcavalry" for using tactics in battle that were considered a reckless disregard for lives of soldiers under his command.

The Sixth Michigan Cavalry was in advance. They did not wait for orders, but a squadron, Companies D and C under Captain Royce (who was killed) and Captain Armstrong, were deployed as skirmishers, while companies B and F, led by Major Weaver (who was killed), made the charge. The line of skirmishers was forced back several times, but the men rallied promptly and finally drove the enemy behind the works. A charge was then made, the squadron passing between the earth works.

So sudden and spirited was the dash, and so demoralized were the enemy that the First Brigade surrendered without firing a shot. The charging squadron moved directly on and engaged the Second Brigade, when the brigade that had surrendered seized their guns, and then commenced a fearful struggle. Of the one hundred who made this charge, only thirty escaped uninjured. Seven of their horses lay dead

AFTER GETTYSBURG

within the enemy's works. Twelve hundred prisoners were here captured, and the ground was strewn with dead and wounded rebels. Among the killed was Major-General Pettigrew of South Carolina. A.P. Hill was seated, smoking a pipe, when the attack commenced; it came so suddenly that he threw the pipe away, mounted his horse and crossed the river as speedily as possible.

Three battle flags were captured, two of them covered with the names of battles in which the regiments owning them had been engaged. Prisoners were captured all along the road between Williamsport and Falling Waters, in which service the First Ohio squadron under Captain Jones, acting as bodyguard as usual, took an active part. Sergeant Gillespie of Company A, being in advance, overtook a body of men trying to get off with a Napoleon gun; the horses balked, and the Sergeant politely requested the men to surrender, which order they cheerfully obeyed.

Seven men and four horses were taken with the gun. The caissons were filled with ammunition, and Captain Hasbrouck of the General's staff at once placed it in position and used it upon the enemy - a whole brigade being then in sight. Another Napoleon gun was abandoned and taken in charge by the Eighteenth Pennsylvania Cavalry, Lieutenant-Colonel Brinton. Captain Royce of the Sixth Michigan was with the skirmishing party and was shot twice; the first time through the leg, the second ball through his head. Company C of the skirmishers lost fifteen men, ten of whom were wounded.

Just at the close of the fight, General Buford's command came up and pursued the flying foe to the river, capturing four hundred and fifty prisoners. The enemy succeeded in destroying their pontoon bridge however, and thus effectually prevented immediate pursuit.

This closed the Gettysburg campaign. It was the last time that Lee crossed the Potomac. From henceforth he was compelled to defend Virginia. A detachment under Early tried the same operation next year, but his force proved insufficient to detach Grant's hold on Richmond, and the advent of Sheridan introduced a new phase constant aggression and victories consummated with the Union programme.

During the rest of July and August, the cavalry had but little work to do. Meade was moved down to Virginia, and occupying the same line on which McClellan had moved the previous fall while Lee, behind the shelter of the Blue Ridge, was gathering up his forces, which he finally concentrated behind the Rapidan. The cavalry work did not begin until September.

Confederate prisoners at Fisher Hill

The operations immediately after Gettysburg, in the case of Custer's brigade, first show clearly, in the handling of the command, a high order of military talent in the young general. Just as when an aide-de-camp he had placed his whole ambition on being the best and most active officer of all Pleasonton's staff, so now as a brigade commander he became indisputably the best in the cavalry corps, and his single brigade seemed to do more work and attract more notice than any other.

This success was owing mainly to the same qualities conspicuous in the Urbana expedition tact. What had been tact in the lieutenant became *coup d'œil* in the general. The basis of the faculty is found in most brilliant men, and still more so in brilliant women. In the arena of politics, it makes the ready debater, in society the wit and the belle, in journalism the powerful writer whom everyone fears to oppose, in business the bold and successful operator. It consists in doing (or saying) the right thing at the right time, the power of rapid decision.

The Battle of Falling Waters illustrates this character in Custer, as also his superiority to the headlong rashness of Kilpatrick. Custer came up alone, saw his enemy wavering, and with the use of only four companies put in at the right moment captured a whole Confederate brigade. Then he stopped; he knew when audacity had been pushed far enough. A moment later, up comes Kilpatrick. Not satisfied with a single brigade, he must need attempt to take four with an inadequate force, and ordered the charge of the Sixth Michigan continued.

What was the result? Of the one hundred who made the charge, only thirty escaped uninjured. The surrendered brigade, thinking no quarter was to be shown, resumed the struggle and the victory, gained by Custer's tact was nearly lost by Kilpatrick's foolhardy assault. It was not the last time, as we shall see further on. With the possession of plenty of physical courage, Kilpatrick mingled so much of besotted rashness and vanity during his career as a division commander that his greatest successes were always marred by unnecessary slaughter, while he suffered more than one mortifying and humiliating defeat. In Custer was found that temper of discretion which made his courage tact. While under Kilpatrick, few believed he possessed it. His independent career demonstrated it long after.

In his handling of cavalry as a tactician, he seems always to have observed the just medium between exclusive charging work and that which degenerates into mere mounted infantry contests. No man knew better than he that the sole aggressive strength of cavalry is found in the charge, while dismounted skirmishers are the best weapon for defensive battles. This truth was very seldom observed by other brigade commanders who grew altogether too fond of dismounted work. Custer, at Gettysburg and after, always used both kinds of lines together, just as Caesar did at Pharsalia when opposing an enemy of superior force, but when his foes were equal or inferior, as invariably availed himself of the moral influence of the mounted charge as the most efficacious of all.

TO THE RAPIDAN AND BACK

AT the beginning of September, the Army of the Potomac had resumed on the upper Rappahannock with the same lazy attitude, much resembling that of a siege, which it had occupied before Richmond under McClellan, and before Petersburg under Burnside and Hooker. The different infantry corps were grouped at points near the bank of the river and comfortably settled in permanent camps, while the cavalry was drawn back on either wing, almost entirely out of danger, picketing the back country to prevent raids on Meade's line of supply, the Orange and Alexandria Railroad.

Orange and Alexandria Railroad Crossing. The O & A was the most fought over railroad in Virginia. In connection with the Virginia Central, it was the only rail transport between the capitals of Washington, D.C. and Richmond.

Lee's position was different, as his line of supply was different. His main force was drawn back to Gordonsville, at least forty miles off, and before him lay both the Rappahannock and Rapidan Rivers. The triangle of country between these streams was occupied by his cavalry, which served as a veil to his army, behind which it could move in perfect security. In a military point of view, the whole position was far better than that of Meade. Lee knew all the latter was doing, and Meade was ignorant of his enemy's exact position.

At last, on the 13th September, a move was made to dissipate the uncertainty. The cavalry was taken from its camps in the rear, moved down to the Rappahannock, and on that day crossed the river, Buford in the centre, Gregg on the right, Kilpatrick on the left, and advanced toward Culpepper, midway between the two rivers.

The advance was made on the line of the railroad which went straight to Culpepper, the country being quite open and level, with beautiful park like clumps of huge trees dotting the green sward around Brandy Station, the first house. From thence to Culpepper, the whole place was beautifully adapted to cavalry fighting, fences being all destroyed and ditches few. A fringe of coppice hid the movements of the cavalry near the Rappahannock while they were preparing for the advance.

In half an hour or so, all was ready. There were now nine brigades in the three divisions, and their method of fighting had become uniform. The advance on Culpepper will give a very good idea of its nature. Each brigade had an average of four regiments, with a regimental average of three hundred men. Thus, the whole force was nearly 12,000 strong. In front of each brigade was a full regiment, deployed as skirmishers, each man riding some twenty feet from his fellows, carbine in hand. Behind the right and left of this open line of men, at a distance of some two hundred yards, were two regiments with drawn sabres in line of battle, but moving at a walk. In rear of the centre, and retired some two or three hundred yards further, was the last regiment in column of march. Before this was the brigade commander, and in front of him was his battery. Each brigade thus occupied more than half a mile, and the whole line was between five and six miles in length.

FREDERICK WHITTAKER

At last, at a given signal, this great line started on its way and the word was passed to "trot on to Brandy Station." In a few minutes, the sharp crack of carbines along the line told that the enemy were found, and answering puffs told that they were resisting the advance. Then, from the summit of a gentle slope beyond Brandy Station came broad bright flashes and great clouds of white smoke as the enemy's batteries opened on the advancing cavalry.

Their efforts were perfectly useless, for the rapidly trotting and wavy line of skirmishers offered nothing to fire at, and the length of the line threatened to curl round the flanks of the defenders every moment. There was no serious fight. Ere five minutes were over, Brandy Station was reached, a picket post captured bodily, and the advance was resumed across the open country to Culpepper without a check. As the cavalry swept on, the enemy gathered thicker in the front and more guns came into action, but it was evident at all times that they were heavily overmatched, as they fell back from knoll to knoll, fighting all the time, but in vain.

Some idea of the rapid and dashing nature of the fight may be gathered from the time it occupied. The advance left Rappahannock Bridge about 10 o'clock, and by half past twelve the enemy were driven through Culpepper, nine miles off.

Custer had the extreme left of the line, covering the flank of Kilpatrick's division. It was a race, and a matter of emulation between all the components of that long line, to keep abreast of each other, "dressed" in perfect order. Of course, this was impossible sometimes on account of the different nature of the ground in front of different brigades; but whenever the line assumed a wavy appearance, one could hear the officers shouting to the men to "dress up," and the poor horses would be spurred on to a more rapid pace to make up for lost time. The whole advance resembled a fox hunt, animated and inspiriting to the highest degree, with just enough spice of danger to make it delightfully exciting.

At Culpepper, the enemy made a stand with all his artillery. General Stuart was there, getting ready to leave, fancying the whole of Meade's army was advancing. A locomotive and train of cars was ready, all steam up, when Custer's brigade came dashing on, only to find themselves stopped by a deep creek with a single ford. The enemy opened fire with three batteries, and Custer's guns tried to cripple the locomotive.

Train at Culpepper. Culpepper sat midway between Richmond and Washington, D.C., and railroads linked it to both national capitals. The Orange and Alexandria ran northward from the Culpeper Court House to Alexandria; the Virginia Central connected the county to Richmond via Gordonsville. Consequently, armies from both sides occupied the area back and forth during the war.

In the hurry and confusion at the ford, however, the train got away. Custer himself was far ahead of his own skirmishers, who were bothered by the swamps at the border of the creek below, and he rode on with the skirmishers of the next brigade on the right, which happened to be the Second New York (Harris' Light). With them and a few of his own men he galloped into Culpepper, cut off two of the enemy's guns and captured them. Ten minutes later, Culpepper was ours and the enemy hastily retreating towards the Rapidan.

The advance had been so rapid that a halt was necessary at Culpepper to gather up the loose ends, and it was not until two hours later that the march was resumed. It was unaccompanied by serious resistance and by the next morning the whole triangle of country between the Rapidan and Rappahannock was in full possession of Meade's army.

Now was the real time for Meade to advance in force. At the time of the fight at Culpepper, Lee was seriously weakened, having sent away the whole of Longstreet's strong corps to help Bragg at Chattanooga. Had Meade struck hard at that time when all the roads were dry, and at least two months active work was possible, the heroes of the war would have been differently named. But like all the commanders of the Army of the Potomac, he was paralyzed by the fear of Lee, and did not dare to undertake a rapid movement.

The rest of September was passed in camp around Culpepper, the cavalry picketing the fords of the Rapidan; and it was not till the beginning of October that he ventured, in a hesitating manner, to move. When he did, Lee, by a simple feint at his flank, frightened him so much that he abandoned all his ground in haste and fell back in confusion, without a battle, to Washington, leaving the cavalry to cover his retreat, alone and unassisted, in the face of the greater part of Lee's army.

Of this retreat of Meade's, no one has ever spoken a good word. The only feature of its origin pleasant to contemplate is in the light of a compliment to Lee. The latter, at the time he made his flank movement, possessed less than two-thirds of Meade's force, but Meade occupied the exact position occupied by Pope and Banks the previous year, when the disasters of Cedar Mountain and Manassas Second occurred. He was out at Culpepper, and Lee was moving round his flank by way of Thoroughfare Gap, threatening his communications, just as Jackson had done the year before.

True, he was in a very different position otherwise from Pope. Pope was numerically inferior to Lee, and depended for help on McClellan's army, which help came too late. Meade's force was all concentrated, his cavalry superior to that of his enemy, his men had the moral advantage of the recent victory of Gettysburg to inspirit them, and he had every reason to trust the issue to a desperate and decisive battle. Nevertheless, Lee's shadow scared him out of his wits.

On the ninth of October, Meade cautiously began his advance on

TO THE RAPIDAN AND BACK

Lee by sending his cavalry over the Rapidan and its upper tributaries, one of which was called Robertson's River. Buford occupied the extreme left, Kilpatrick the centre, Gregg the extreme right up at White Sulphur Springs. In narrating the part taken by Custer's Michiganders we shall quote the language of his report bodily.

On the night of October 9th, 1863, says Custer, my picket line, which extended along the north bank of Robertson River in the vicinity of James City, was attacked, and a portion of the line forced back upon the reserves; at the same time my scouts informed me that the enemy was moving in heavy column toward my right; this report was confirmed by deserters. In anticipation of an attack of the enemy at daybreak, I ordered my entire command to be saddled at 3 a.m. on the 10th. At daybreak, the enemy began by cautiously feeling my line; but seeing his inability to surprise us, he contented himself by obtaining possession of Cedar Mountain, which point he afterwards used as a signal station. At 1 p.m., I received orders from the General commanding the division, to report with my command at James City.

The head of my column arrived in the vicinity of that point at 3 p.m. The enemy had already obtained possession of the town, and had brought several guns to bear on the position I was ordered to take. Battery M, Second United States Artillery, under command of Lieutenant Pennington, was unlimbered, and succeeded in shelling the enemy out of the woods on the right of the town. At the same time, Colonel Alger of the Fifth Michigan Cavalry, who held the extreme left of my line, moved forward with one battalion of his regiment, under the gallant Major Clark, and charged the enemy's battery. The charge, although daring in the extreme, failed for want of sufficient support. It was successful so far, however, as to compel the enemy to shift the position of his battery to a more retired point.

Night setting in, prevented us from improving the advantages we had gained. Most of my command rested on their arms during the night. Early in the morning, I retired on the road leading to Culpepper, which point I reached without molestation from the enemy. It was not until the rear of my column was leaving the town that the enemy made his appearance and attempted, unsuccessfully, to harass my rear guard.

FREDERICK WHITTAKER

On the hills north of the town, I placed my command in position to receive an attack.

Culpepper. Robert E. Lee launched the Gettysburg Campaign from Culpeper. Lee returned following Gettysburg, and would have wintered there had not the Army of the Potomac pushed him out shortly after. Lee returned the favor a month later by ousting the Union troops, only to be expelled yet again in the Battle of Rappahannock Station.

The enemy not feeling disposed to accept the invitation, I retired on the road leading to Rappahannock Station. My column had scarcely begun to march before the officer commanding the rear guard, Colonel Mann of the Seventh Michigan Cavalry, reported the enemy to be pressing him closely. At the same time, a strong column was seen on my outer flank, evidently attempting to intercept our line of march to the river.

The vigorous attacks now being made upon my rear guard compelled me to place my battery at the head of the column and to employ my entire force to keep the enemy from my guns. My advance had reached the vicinity of Brandy Station when a courier hastened back with the information that a brigade of the enemy's cavalry was in position directly in my front, thus cutting us completely off from the river. Upon examination, I learned the correctness of the report. The heavy masses of Confederate cavalry could be seen covering the heights in front of my advance.

When it is remembered that my rear guard was hotly engaged with a superior force, a heavy column enveloping each flank, and my advance confronted by more than double my own numbers the perils of my situation can be estimated. Lieutenant Pennington at once placed his battery in position and opened a brisk fire, which was responded to by the guns of the enemy. The Major-General commanding the cavalry corps at this moment rode to the advance. To him I proposed, with my command, to cut through the force in my front and thus open the way for the entire command to the river. My proposition was approved, and I received orders to take my available force and push forward, leaving the Sixth and Seventh Michigan Cavalry to hold the force in rear in check.

I formed the Fifth Michigan Cavalry on my right, in column of battalions; on my left, I formed the First Michigan in column of squadrons. After ordering them to draw their sabres, I informed them that we were surrounded, and all we had to do was to open a way with our sabres. They showed their determination and purpose by giving three hearty cheers. At this moment, the band struck up the inspiring air, "Yankee Doodle," which excited the enthusiasm of the entire command to the highest pitch, and made each individual member feel as if he was a host in himself.

Simultaneously, both regiments moved forward to the attack. It required but a glance at the countenances of the men to enable me to read the settled determination with which they undertook the work before them. The enemy, without waiting to receive the onset, broke in disorder and fled. After a series of brilliant charges during which the enemy suffered heavily, we succeeded in reaching the river, which we crossed in good order.

So for Custer, but it seems necessary to explain how it was that he found himself thus surrounded. It all came of Meade's falling back. On the 8th, he had thrown his cavalry over the Rapidan to scout up and down the river. Had he merely followed them, he must have marched right into Lee's camp, for only Stuart's cavalry was left in that vicinity. But on the 8th, he heard that Lee's infantry was trying to get around his flank, and instead of cutting in on this flanking party, he fell back without any warning, leaving his three cavalry divisions spread out like a fan, each pressed by cavalry and infantry combined.

Buford, who had crossed at Germania Ford with the promise of the whole First Corps to support him, next day found himself driven back over Morton's Ford, and not an infantryman to be seen. He fell slowly back in the direction of Brandy Station, and as his road there was much shorter than that of Kilpatrick's division, found himself there before Kilpatrick. Custer's brigade was on the right of the Third Division, and Pleasonton was with Kilpatrick. Therefore, the position was now very curious.

At Brandy Station, with his back to the river, was Buford, a force of cavalry and infantry, with several batteries pressing all round him. Several mounted charges had been made to drive back the enemy, and in every instance they fell back. Suddenly, the heavy fire in Buford's front ceased, and then recommenced with tenfold fury, but not a shot came near Buford's men. It increased to a perfect roar, while the yells of charging men were plainly audible over the firing.

The next moment, out of the woods into the open field came tearing Kilpatrick's men, charging in column, dark masses of horsemen in considerable confusion, Pleasonton with the guns in the middle of the column, all looking pretty well used up. Had it not been for the firm attitude of Buford's division, whose flanks were safe, and who had kept the enemy all in tile front, Kilpatrick's men must have suffered as fearfully as they did a few days later at Buckland's Mills.

As it happened, Buford's stand gave them time to rest and get into decent order, and the rest of the afternoon the two divisions confronted the enemy without further disaster until nightfall. The most exasperating part of this battle at Brandy Station was however yet to come. It was when the cavalry, after dark, rode down to the fords to cross the Rappahannock and beheld the whole country on the further bank bright with the campfires of their own infantry, who had been compelled to lie idle all day, passive spectators of a fight which their presence could have determined. The sight was a fair specimen of the pusillanimous policy of General Meade in this celebrated retreat. It was a courting of disgrace.

To the cavalry, the battle at Brandy Station was creditable. It was a gallant struggle against fearful odds. The figure borne by Custer is evidenced in the following racy anecdote by a member of the Fifth Michigan:[*]

Army of the Potomac infantry at Brandy Station. The Battle of Brandy Station was the largest cavalry battle ever fought in North America. It was also the first battle of the Gettysburg campaign.

At Brandy Station, Virginia, during Meade's fall back, Custer and the cavalry brought up the rear, and all soldiers know it is the worst place on God's footstool to cover a retreat. To allow the infantry ample time to cross the Rappahannock, the cavalry kept fooling around with an average of 10,000 'Rebs' on all sides of them. Once, when a lull had seemed to come with an ominous stillness, someone remarked, "Helloa, look ahead," and sure enough about 5,000 Rebs were suddenly seen to be massed in our front and right in the path we must travel if we ever

---

[*] Mr. J. Allen Bigelow of Detroit, published in Detroit Evening News.

saw 'the girls we left behind us.'

Custer was sitting on his horse at the head of our regiment, the Fifth Cavalry. He took one look of about ten seconds, then snatched off his hat, raised up in his stirrups and yelled out, "Boys of Michigan, there are some people between us and home; I'm going home - who else goes?" Suffice it to say, we all went. General Alger, then colonel of our regiment, can vouch for our flying movements as we followed Custer, with his bare head and golden locks and long straight sabre, putting the very devil into the old Fifth Cavalry, until a clear track was before us. When out of the woods up came Kilpatrick, and sung out, "Custer, what ails you?" His reply was, "Oh nothing, only we want to cook coffee on the Yank side of the Rappahannock."

In narrating the further events of the campaign, Custer shall resume the story in his report, made at the time:

> From the eleventh to the fifteenth, my command was employed in picketing and guarding the flank and rear of the army. On the afternoon of the fifteenth, the brigade being posted on the Bull Run battle ground, I detailed Major Kidd with his regiment, the Sixth Michigan Cavalry, to reconnoiter the strength and position of the enemy in the vicinity of Gainsville. The reconnaissance was entirely satisfactory, and showed the enemy to be in considerable force at that point.
>
> Sunday, the 18th October, at 3 p.m., the entire division was ordered to move on the pike leading from Groveton to Warrenton. The First Brigade moved on the pike, the Second moved on a road to the left of, and parallel to the pike, but soon encountered the enemy, and drove him as far as Gainsville, where the entire command bivouacked for the night. The First Vermont Cavalry, under Colonel Sawyer, deserves great credit for the rapidity with which they forced the enemy to retire.
>
> At daybreak on the morning of the 19th, my brigade took the advance and skirmished with the enemy's cavalry from Gainsville to Buckland; at the latter point I found him strongly posted upon the south bank of Broad Run. The position for his artillery was well chosen. After a fruitless attempt to effect a crossing in his front, I succeeded in turning his left flank so completely as to force him from his position. Having driven him more than a mile from the stream, I threw out my pickets and ordered my men to prepare their dinner.
>
> From the inhabitants of Buckland, I learned that the forces of the enemy with whom we had been engaged were commanded by General J.E.B.

TO THE RAPIDAN AND BACK

Stuart in person, who at the time of our arrival at that point was seated at the dinner table eating; but owing to my successful advance, he was compelled to leave his dinner untouched - a circumstance not regretted by that portion of my command into whose hands it fell.

The First Brigade took the advance. At this point, I was preparing to follow when information reached me that the enemy was advancing on my left, from the direction of Greenwich. I had scarcely time to place my command in position to resist an attack from that direction before the enemy's skirmishers appeared. Pennington's battery opened upon them, while the Sixth Michigan cavalry, under Major Kidd, was thrown forward and deployed as skirmishers. One gun of Pennington's battery, supported by the First Vermont Cavalry, was placed on my extreme left.

The First Michigan cavalry, under Major Brewer, acted as a reserve, and as a support for the remaining five guns of the battery. The Fifth Michigan Cavalry, under Colonel Mann, were engaged in the woods on my right. At first, I was under the impression that the skirmishers were composed of dismounted cavalry, but later developments convinced me that it was a very superior force of infantry that now confronted me.

Major James H. Kidd

After completing his dispositions for an attack, the enemy advanced upon me. In doing so, he exposed a line of infantry of more than a mile in extent; at the same time he opened a heavy fire upon me from his artillery. Pennington's battery, aided by the Sixth Michigan Cavalry, poured a destructive fire upon the enemy as he advanced but failed to force him back. A desperate effort was made to capture my battery. Pennington continued to fire until the enemy was within twenty yards of his guns. He was then compelled to limber up and retire to the north bank of Broad Run.

The First Michigan Cavalry was entrusted with the duty of covering the movement - a task which was gallantly performed. My command being very much exhausted, I returned to the vicinity of Gainsville where I encamped for the night. Major Clarke, Fifth Michigan Cavalry, was detached from his regiment with one battalion. When the command retired to the north bank of Broad Run, he with a small portion of his battalion became separated from the rest of the command and was captured by the enemy. Computing my losses from the 9th October, I find them to be as follows:

	Officers	Men	Total
Killed	0	9	9
Wounded	2	41	43
Missing	8	154	16
Aggregate			214

Before closing my report, I desire to make honorable mention of the highly creditable manner in which both officers and men of my command have discharged their duty during the long and arduous marches, as well as the hard fought engagements of the past few days. Too much praise cannot be given to the officers and men of Battery M, Second Artillery, for the gallantry displayed on more than one occasion. For the untiring zeal and energy, added to the unflinching bravery displayed in transmitting and executing my orders upon the field, my acknowledgments are due to the following members of my staff: Captain R.F. Judson, A.D.C., Lieutenant R. Baylis, A.A.D.C., Lieutenant William Colerick, A.D.C., and to Lieutenant E.G. Granger, A.A.A.G. Lieutenant Granger, while leading a charge at Brandy Station, had his horse shot in two places. Surgeon Wooster of my staff, in addition to his professional duties, rendered me valuable assistance by aiding in transmitting my orders.

G.A. CUSTER,
Brig. Com. Second Brigade, Third Cavalry Corps

It will be noticed in both of Custer's reports, during this summer and fall, how much stress he lays upon the doings of Pennington's battery. The commander of this force seems always to have been a fast friend and favorite of Custer, and he was subsequently promoted to the command of a volunteer cavalry regiment, and became senior officer and commandant of a brigade in Custer's division, in which capacity he

TO THE RAPIDAN AND BACK

served all through the Valley Campaigns and up to Appomattox surrender.

After the fight at Buckland's Mills in which the division of Kilpatrick was so roughly handled, Meade's army resumed its advance and finally took up winter quarters at Brandy Station, the cavalry picketing the front and flanks out toward Madison Court House.

It is time, now that the summer and fall campaigns of 1863 are concluded, to advert to the private life of the young general during this interval. During the first period of his career as a commander, his occupations and cares seem to have been too engrossing to permit of any home correspondence, and after the Michigan Brigade entered Virginia he did not relax his work. Well as the brigade behaved at Gettysburg, it was far from satisfying Custer, who was determined to make it fully the equal of a regular cavalry command in drill and discipline.

With that object, no sooner did the cavalry get a week's rest than the indefatigable young general began to give them daily drills of great severity, and by constant inspections so harassed the souls of the honest volunteers that they began to hate him as badly as ever, or thought they did. Just as at Gettysburg however, the first battle compelled them to forego all their bad language, and made them sorry they had ever uttered a word against him. This first battle was the advance on Culpepper and in the action, it will be remembered, Custer was wounded.

A piece of shell killed his horse and inflicted a painful wound on the inside of the rider's thigh, which though not dangerous compelled Custer to retire from the field. Inasmuch as the rest of the month was passed in perfect quiet, the general experienced no difficulty in obtaining, on the strength of this wound, a leave of absence for twenty days. He took it, hastened to Washington, and one day later was travelling due northwest just as fast as the iron horse could carry him.

To those who remember the state of mind in which he left home in the spring, it will not be surprising to learn that he made his way to Monroe, Michigan with the utmost rapidity, nor that when there, he happened to meet "one of the parties most interested." He had, during the summer, many things to make him anxious and unhappy in regard to matters at Monroe, especially intimations that reached him that "one of the parties interested" was quite likely to meet someone else, while his own affair was still unsettled.

He realized very keenly that the objections of the Judge to his engagement were not based altogether on his want of fortune, but on an apprehension of the fickleness and instability of his disposition, and that his sudden success in life had not altogether removed this. Only a week before the time of his wound, he received a letter from his kind-hearted confidant, warning him that his persistence was "not for the best," and that a time must at last come when he "must give her up utterly and forever." To this he replies, sadly but bravely:

>That time may come, perhaps soon. When it does come, I hope it will find me the same soldier I now try to be, as capable of meeting the reverses of life as I am those of war. You no doubt know me well, perhaps better than any person in Monroe, except L., and yet you know little of my disposition. You, fearing that disappointment might render me unhappy, are doubtful as to whether it is best for me to cherish the remembrance of one who is now to me, all that she ever will be.
>
>I would think the same, were I the adviser instead of the person advised. Do not fear for me. What you have hinted as being probable in reference to L. may occur. My bosom friends may desert me; my own mother may disown me and turn me from my home; I may lose my position among men, and be thrown solitary and alone among strangers without the sympathy of a single friend; and yet, with all this, there is a strange, indescribable something in me, that would enable me to shape my course through life, cheerful, if not contented. Rest assured that whatever fortune may have in store for me will be borne cheerfully. Now that you know this, you need not hesitate in future to tell me all.

These are good brave words, but they are not quite brave enough to hide the sad heart beneath them, and when we remember the position of Custer at the time, we can see how strong must have been his feelings to force such a letter from the outwardly brilliant and successful general. No doubt he hailed with gratitude the piece of ragged iron that gave him the excuse, a week later, to return to Monroe, and see for himself how affairs stood.

He arrived there to find himself a lion. Captain Custer, the idle and discontented officer on waiting orders, sharing the sombre cloud which enshrouded his unfortunate chief, with the reputation of a reckless dissipated soldier in love with every fresh face, a desperate flirt, was a very different person from the "boy general with the golden locks," the pet of the papers, brilliant, successful, a rising man, a real live brigadier-general.

On his previous visit, Monroe had begun to think that there might possibly "be something in that young Custer." Now, Monroe had "always prophesied that young Custer would do something," and the only trouble was, who should be the first to welcome him, ask him to his house, be able to say to his friends, "Ah, by the by, I had General Custer to dinner today."

Mrs. Grundy was ready and anxious to go down on her knees to arrange a soft pillow, "under his poor wounded limb, you know, my dear," and Miss Grundy was amiably anxious to sing the pathetic ballad of "*When this cruel war is over*" to the listening general, ogling him all the time, and ending with a languishing gaze of perfect love at the line, "*Praying we may meet again*," as she slowly left the piano. To a man with any sense of humor, and Custer had his share of this quality, what a spectacle Mrs. Grundy and the charming Miss Grundy presented, especially when he remembered their neglect in former days. However, he kept his counsel and wore his honors meekly.

There was however, one man on whom the brilliant success of the young general had not yet operated as a complete blind. This man was Judge Bacon, stern, upright and honorable, who had not yet got beyond the point of thinking that there might be "something in that young Custer after all." The Judge knew a good deal more of the world than most Monrovians, and he had heard of the celebrated stone thrown by Orpheus C. Kerr, which struck so many brigadier-generals.

He knew moreover, that the commission was subject to confirmation by the Senate, which might be refused, a piece of knowledge not common to all Monroe. In a worldly point of view therefore, the Judge was quite right in being cautious as to receiving the brilliant young warrior as a conqueror. In a moral point of view, a matter which weighed far more with Judge Bacon, his objections to Custer remained unaltered, and were even strengthened. He was forever mentally referring to his intemperance, and especially distrusted his fickleness. The latter was Custer's own fault.

In order to calm the Judge's uneasiness the previous spring, Custer had entered into a violent flirtation with a young lady of the place, and the result had been to disgust the Judge. However objectionable as a suitor for your daughter a man may be, still you do not like to see him, as soon as rejected, off with the daughter of someone else as if nothing had happened. The rapid consolation is decidedly uncomplimentary to your own family, which is of course always the best in the country.

With all these objections, in a private capacity, to Custer, even coming back as a general, the Judge yet welcomed him cordially as a public character and permitted him to resume his visits at the house, ostensibly in the guise of ordinary friendship. He was apparently completely deceived as to the strength and duration of Custer's affection for his daughter, and imagined that the affair was safely over. On the contrary, it was only just really beginning, and Custer was already laying his plans to gain the consent of the father of his lady love as his leave progressed.

Whether absence might in time have caused him to be forgotten is uncertain, but certain it is that his second visit was just in time to settle the affair in his favor, and to secure a perfect understanding, conditional on the Judge's consent, it is true, but none the less an implied engagement. This was towards the close of Custer's visit, and he made up his mind to ask the Judge before he went.

In this instance, however, resolution and action were not the same with Custer. Days passed on, opportunities were rare and possibly courage was lacking. At all events, the time came for his departure, the lovers were compelled to leave each other and still the Judge had not been asked. Brave as Custer was, he actually seems to have trembled before the Judge, and it is no wonder when we reflect on what he was about to request from him - an only daughter.

He was finally compelled to leave Monroe and return to the front, with the question unasked, the matter to be finally decided by letter. The sensitive conscientiousness and strict honor of the two lovers is shown in the fact that they both still declined to avail themselves of a clandestine correspondence to evade the Judge's notice.

Nothing would have been easier than for this to have happened, and the fact of its still being steadfastly refused by both is an honor to both. They cannot be blamed for their love, that being a matter beyond the control of any human being. It comes and goes like the wind, and it is hard to assign a cause for it.

That Custer, young, brilliant, successful in everything else, knowing himself secure in the most vital point of all - the feelings of the "party most interested" - should have been willing to wait as he did, patiently and uncomplainingly, for the consent of one whom he knew to be prejudiced against him, shows a devotion to duty remarkable in these days, and especially in this country, where filial obedience is subject to so many drawbacks. The sequel proved that he did wisely, and duty met its reward.

To console himself for his self-enforced abstinence from correspondence with "the party most interested," Custer threw himself with fresh ardor into letters to his kind and sympathizing confidant. From this time forth, these letters are frequent; beginning even while on his journey to the east. The first is dated on board the lake steamer "Morning Star," October 6th, 1863, the very day of his departure. In its course he refers, as he frequently did in those days, to the motto which he had adopted and wore engraved on his seal ring, "*Per augusta ad augusta.*"

ON BOARD THE MORNING STAR
9 p.m. Monday, Oct. 6, 1863

KIND FRIEND: I feel so sad and lonely, so sick at heart, that to kill time and "drive dull care away," I have determined to occupy a few moments in writing to you. We are just getting under full headway, and will soon be bounding o'er the billows of Erie. I have been sitting on deck watching the motion of the vessel as it speeds through the crested waves, and while intently watching wave after wave, as they roll along in their ceaseless motion, I cannot but be reminded of the great ocean of life on whose stormy bosom each of us is engaged, steering our little barks over, each acting under a separate impulse, yet all tending to the same harbor. When I look back on the track passed over by mine, I cannot but feel unbounded gratitude to that power which thus far has carried me safely through so many storms.

Hour after hour have I seen wave after wave rolling down on my little bark, threatening to swallow it with all it contained, and yet that unseen power would interfere, and either avert the coming danger, or cause it to strike harmlessly. If I look around me now, I see evidences of danger in all directions, but buoyed up with hope and guided by duty, I trust for the best, confident that my motto "Through trials to triumphs" will still hold good.

How I wish I could be with my little girl tonight, and yet I cannot complain. I saw the Judge at the depot, who spoke very encouragingly of my prospects in my profession and of the bright future he pictured for me; said he would be disappointed if he did not hear such and such things of me soon. I had no opportunity to speak of that which was nearest my heart. I only said just before leaving that I had desired to speak to him, but being prevented from doing so, I would write to him, to which he replied, "Very well, Good bye."

ARMSTRONG

Only twenty-four hours later, and he writes from Baltimore as follows:

COLEMAN'S EUTAW HOUSE, BALTIMORE
Wed., Oct. 7th, 1863, 2.30 p.m.

DEAR FRIEND: Do not be alarmed. I am not going to write to you again today. I have taken a stroll and a drive around the Monumental City, and it is yet an hour till car time. I know of no more pleasant mode of occupying that time, than by writing to you. In every city I pass through, I see something to admire, something which gives rise to pleasant thoughts, and often I am struck with wonder at the extent to which man's art and ingenuity have improved what nature has already rendered beautiful. But after all, my heart turns longingly to one quiet little town far away on the banks of the Raisin, and I find infinitely more enjoyment, more real pleasure from the memories and associations of that unassuming little spot, than in contemplating all the world beside.

I need not tell you why this is so. I do not think a single half hour has passed since I bade adieu to Monroe, during which I did not think of the place, or more particularly perhaps of those whom it contains. I have also thought much of my intended letter to L's father. My mind has been alternating between hope and fear, hope that my letter will be well received; that now, when all else appears bright and encouraging, no obstacle will be interposed to darken or cloud our happiness. And yet I cannot rid myself of the fear that I may suffer from some unfounded prejudice. Oh, I wish some guardian angel would tell me what course to pursue, to insure her happiness and mine. I feel that her father, valuing her happiness and welfare as he does, will not refuse if he learns from her lips our real relation to each other.

I regret that I was unable to have a personal interview with him, and yet it may be better as it is; I will hope. I will write you tomorrow, or next day from camp. Tell my little girl I am so lonely without her. Kiss her for me, and tell her I have been real good since I left her.

Good bye,

ARMSTRONG

We have inserted these letters to show the state of anxiety and uneasiness that still oppressed Custer when he returned to his command, where he was received with the most rapturous demonstrations of delight:

HEADQUARTERS, SECOND BRIGADE, THIRD DIVISION
Oct. 9th, 1863, 8 p.m.

DEAR FRIEND: I promised to write you soon after my return to camp. I arrived here last evening about dusk, and was welcomed in a style that was both flattering and gratifying. I wish you could have seen how rejoiced my men seemed to be at my return. Whatever may be the real sentiments entertained by the world at large, I feel assured that here, surrounded by my noble little band of heroes, I am loved and respected. There is such a feeling of mutual trust and confidence existing between us, as renders our intercourse one of pleasure.

Often in my meditations, I think of the vast responsibility resting upon me; of the many, many lives entrusted to my keeping; and consequently, of the happiness of so many households depending upon my discretion and judgment. And to think that I am just leaving my boyhood makes the responsibility appear greater. And yet I have no fears, nor do I think that this latter fact is due to any self conceit or egotism on my part. I try to make no unjust pretensions. I assume nothing that I know not to be true. It requires no extensive knowledge to inform me what is my duty both to my country and to my command.

Knowing my duty, all that is then requisite to insure success, is honesty of purpose and fixed intentions, or to express the same meaning in different language, I have only to adopt the well-known motto, "First, be sure you're right, then go ahead." To this simple rule, framed though it be in humble language, I can attribute, more than to any other, my success in life. When deciding upon any course to pursue, I have asked myself, is it right? Satisfied that it is, I allow nothing to swerve me from my purpose.

Few persons have disregarded public opinion so much as I. Not but that I think a proper regard should be shown for that which the "world might say," but one who adopts public opinion as his guide cannot entertain one purpose long. He will find that what pleases one displeases another.

Why have I written all this? Surely, I do not know. You did not say it was not so. I have been very busily engaged all day. I found time, or rather stole time to write. I would have written that letter to her father today, but that I knew I should be interrupted, which I do not wish to be, when writing so important a document. I can scarcely realize its importance. How much depends upon the result it obtains. All my future destiny hangs on the answer my letter shall bring. I will not despond, nor will I take trouble before it is upon me, but I cannot but be anxious. I shall probably defer the writing of that letter until I have heard at least once from you and of her.

I had hoped to be left free and undisturbed this evening, and thus permitted to write you a long letter. But several applicants are waiting my pleasure, and I must defer my anticipated pleasure. Do write me soon. Tell me all about my little girl. Is she well, etc., etc? Kiss her for me, and tell her I had a dream last night concerning somebody in Monroe who I think very much of, "But I'll not tell you who."

Ever your friend,

ARMSTRONG

Please give these flowers to L. They were plucked in front of my headquarters, not far from the "Rapidan."

Luckily for Custer's peace of mind he was soon at work, for within forty-eight hours of his return he started on the expedition which ended in the Brandy Station fight, of which he gives, in a letter of October 12th, a short account, much the same as in his report. Three days later, he writes a hasty pencil scrawl from the Bull Run battlefield:

I dreamed of my little girl last night, and was so disappointed to wake and find it but a dream. How often I think of her. Last Sunday, while in front of my men, and just as we were about to charge the enemy, I unclasped my locket, and took what I thought might be my last look at her likeness. Even in the thickest of the fight, I can always find time to think of her.

TO THE RAPIDAN AND BACK

Five days later he writes, evidently under great mental depression, just after the disaster at Buckland's Mills, an interesting letter which shows that his was not the rashness which brought on that defeat. In its course, after telling of his first victory over Stuart, he tells of Kilpatrick coining up and congratulating him on his success, and adds:

> All would have been well had General K. been content to let well enough alone. My scouts had informed me of heavy columns of infantry moving around on both my flanks, their intention evidently being to cut me off. I informed General K. of this, and advised him to guard against it; but no - he did not believe it, and ordered me to halt till the First Brigade passed me and then to follow on the road to Warrenton. The First Brigade had scarcely passed, and I was preparing to follow, when the enemy made a vigorous attack from the direction I had prophesied they would. My consolation is that I am in no way responsible for the mishap, but on the contrary urged General K. not to take the step which brought it upon us, and the only success gained by us was gained by me.

He refers at the close of this letter to the one which he had written to Judge Bacon soon after Brandy Station fight, in which he formally asks the Judge for his child. That letter is a model in its way of quiet dignity and self respect, mingled with a modesty peculiarly touching from a man in Custer's position. Were it not for those private details which are too sacred for publication, it would be the pride of Custer's biographer to lay it before the world, exhibiting as it does in the truest and most unconscious manner the real nobility of the writer's character.

In making his request he refers, fully and frankly, to the objections to himself existing in the Judge's mind, especially those of dissipation and fickleness. In regard to the first he tells him how two years before he had made a solemn pledge to his sister Mrs. Reed, in the presence of Almighty God, never to taste another drop of intoxicating liquor, which promise he had strictly kept ever since. With regard to the second, he referred the Judge to his own daughter for an explanation of the apparent fickleness of his conduct. Of his success in life and his ability to maintain a wife he speaks briefly, with modest pride, and adverts to the fact that he had not ventured to correspond with the object of his love until he should obtain her father's consent.

The Judge's reply is exactly in character with the whole of this stately and quixotically honorable correspondence. He speaks of his intense love for his only child, left motherless so early, of his anxious fears for her future, and the care he must exercise over the character of the man to whom he can entrust her happiness. He owns that "it may be weeks, perhaps months, before he can make up his mind to give a decided answer," but expresses his intention of conversing with his daughter on the subject, the result of which interview "she is at full liberty to communicate to you."

It appeared, from the letter, that the Judge and his daughter had already had a full confidence with each other on the same evening on which poor Custer, gloomy and dispirited, had left Monroe. It was clear that the Judge had virtually yielded, though the fond idolizing father still hesitated to perform that irrevocable act of consent which would forever separate him from the child who had so long been the very core of his heart. Most young men think little of this feeling, but to Custer it seems to have been peculiarly sacred.

There is something touching in the correspondence between these two noble, high-minded men, both sensitive to a fault, both idolizing this one delicate girl in their different ways, both anxious only for her happiness, both respecting each other as highly as men could, and yet jealous and stiff at first. So punctilious was Custer that he refused in a second letter to take the implied permission to correspond contained in the expression "which she is at liberty to communicate to you," without a clear understanding and an explicit answer, one way or the other.

Pressed in this manner, and having learned from his daughter how much her happiness was really interested in Custer, the father yielded at last, and consented to the engagement, the consent reaching Custer late in November. During this interval, the punctuality and frequency of his correspondence with his kind-hearted confidant are alike exemplary, but that correspondence comes to an abrupt close December 4th, with the satisfactory information, "Your kind favor of the 26th was received last evening along with two from my little girl."

We cannot suppose that anyone would desire this love-making by proxy to continue any longer. We have brought our hero through his love troubles, as interesting as those of a novel hero, in safety. Henceforth, he was formally engaged. The close of this last letter, is however very symptomatic of the curious fact well known to ladies of all time that there is "no satisfying these men." A little while ago, his only aspiration was for an open engagement and permission to correspond; now that he has obtained both, his petition is changed to something else:

> I am glad you incline to my way of thinking, in regard to my little girl coming to the army this winter. Why shouldn't she? I have been pleading earnestly with her in my last letters to tell me when I can come for her. I can come whenever she bids me do so. Now don't you think she ought to tell me to come soon? You know if I don't come this winter, it is not probable that I shall be granted a leave before next winter. Cannot you threaten her, or use your influence to induce her to do as she ought. If I was there, how I would talk to her! She would be glad to say yes to get rid of me.

His petition was nearer to being granted than seemed possible a few months before. While the army lay quiet that winter, Custer's commission was confirmed in the Senate, and he obtained leave of absence to go to Monroe where he was formally married, February 9th, 1864, in the Presbyterian Church by the Reverend Mr. Boyd; pastor and schoolmaster to Elizabeth; only daughter of Judge Daniel S. Bacon.

What a wedding that was. Mrs. Grundy talks of it to this day; and all Monroe that could get inside the church crammed the pews and filled the aisles to suffocation. The Monroe papers were full of the wedding of "our distinguished townsman," and details of personal appearance of bride and bridegroom were plentiful.

Custer was attended by his staff, and wore, perhaps for the first time, his full uniform as a brigadier-general, sash and all. His hair had been cut, and he was no more the "boy general with the golden locks" of the reporters. How often he and his friends had laughed over that name when they read it!

The bride, with veil and orange blossoms, a white figure of timid purity, won all hearts as she came into church on her father's arm; the

FREDERICK WHITTAKER

Judge, tall, stalwart, with his grand old Webster head towering above the crowd, proud of his daughter, and now also of his son-in-law, yet had a hard struggle to choke down the desolate feeling which comes over a father giving up his only child forever.

Monroe, Presbyterian Church. Here, the Custer wedding took place at 8 p.m. February 9, 1864. On her wedding day, Libbie Custer wore a white silk long-sleeved dress with a long veil and a crown of orange blossoms. She carried a bouquet of red roses and wore a brooch with a lock of her deceased mother's hair.

It was a beautiful, a romantic wedding, such as seldom occurs in these humdrum days, and only one such could then occur, for there was only one Custer, only one knight of romance, brave and loving, famous and tender. No wonder Monroe was proud of him.

But what was the pride of Monroe to that of the brigade, a few days later, when Custer returned to camp, bringing with him his timid, child-like bride, with her innocent dark eyes, delighted and astonished at the novelty of everything. Ah, Custer was a wise man, and a patient one, to wait for his reward as he did, but it was worth all his trials at last, and proved the entrance for him to a life of perfect happiness thereafter.

The gentle, timid girl, so scrupulously obedient to her father, proved to Custer a jewel above all price when she became his wife. With a fidelity and devotion rarely paralleled, she followed him to the front and remained near there just so long as it was possible, in all his subsequent career. Only when the troops were in actual and fierce campaign and her presence might have proved an embarrassment to her husband did she consent to remain behind, and then she was always ready to hasten to the front as soon as there was the first sign of a long halt.

Reverend William Boyd

Her influence over the state of society at the headquarters of the Michigan Brigade, and subsequently in all the different commands to which Custer was assigned, was traceable in every instance in a refinement of tone, an absence of the usual roistering drinking scenes too common in the army, in a standard of morality such as prevailed nowhere else. Before Mrs. Custer's arrival at the headquarters of Custer's brigade, the presence of respectable women was almost unknown in the army. While Hooker lay at Falmouth, after Chancellorsville, Miss Harris, sister of Senator Harris of New York, with a few other noble disinterested women, had come out to take charge of the hospitals, within range of the enemy's shells, but these were the only exceptions, so far as I am aware.

When Mrs. Custer made her appearance, it was the prevalent belief that camp was no place for ladies, and many were the comments her visit created. It was only after observing the effect of her presence that the sneerers were compelled to admit that it was altogether pure and elevating, and to wish that a similar blessed influence might extend over their own camps.

Custer wrote: "Libbie Bacon is the fortunate or unfortunate person, whichever it will be, who will unite her destinies with mine."

Like a good angel, she came to the brigade at Stevensburg; like a good angel she remained with them until spring. All that Custer's already noble character needed of dignity and repose, of sweetness and patience, she gave him. Finding him good, she left him perfect, and her sweet and gracious influence can be traced on all his afterlife.

THE WILDERNESS AND THE VALLEY

THE spring of 1864 witnessed a great change in the Army of the Potomac, and especially in the Cavalry Corps. Hitherto, there had been a marked difference in success between the conduct of the war in the eastern and western departments. In the latter, beginning with the capture of Fort Donelson and the substantial repulse of the Confederates at Shiloh, the campaigns of the Union forces had resulted in carrying the war from the banks of the Ohio, where the Confederates once threatened Louisville down to the borders of Georgia at Chattanooga, a substantial advance of over two hundred miles.

The general success of the western generals had only been marred by the desperate and bloody battles of Shiloh, Murfreesboro and Chickamauga. In all these three battles, the Confederate generals, starting with decided strategic successes and beginning by driving the Union forces, had ended by retreating and losing the fruits of victory. In the case of Chickamauga alone, had Bragg held his own; and a few weeks later he was driven from his vantage ground in confusion by Grant.

Contrasted with this, the achievements of the Army of the Potomac were empty and barren of results. Beginning with the disastrous defeat of Bull Run, the eastern men gave their foes the advantage of morale at the start, and the flank movement of evasion made by McClellan, which terminated in the Peninsular Campaign, had only provoked further disaster. Lee had entered Maryland, and three times threatened the capital of the nation in as many years. Now, the experience of Meade's timidity, displayed in his October retreat and the equally unnecessary failure at Mine Run in November, showed plainly that he was not the man to whom an aggressive campaign could be committed. Excellent for defense, his aggressive ability was confessedly

THE WILDERNESS AND THE VALLEY

unequal to the task of driving Lee.

Under these circumstances, General Grant was called from the West, made Lieutenant General, placed in chief command of all the armies, and came himself to Virginia to direct operations personally. He did not assume the direct command of the Army of the Potomac. The memory of Gettysburg saved Meade from the humiliation of removal, and his cheerful, uncomplaining obedience to orders on all occasions, so different from the independent ways and constant complaints of McClellan and Hooker, pointed him out as just the man to execute Grant's orders, whatever they were.

At the same time that Grant came to the field, General Pleasonton was removed from the command of the cavalry corps, which was given to a western man of whom none in the Army of the Potomac had ever heard, an infantry division commander named Philip Henry Sheridan. Grant however, knew him as one of the very hardest fighters in the west, and his choice of men was never more abundantly justified.

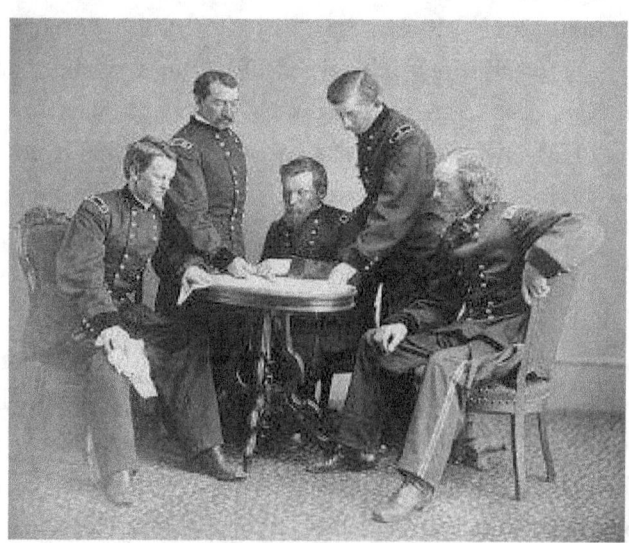

Wesley Merritt, Philip Henry Sheridan, George Crook, James William Forsyth, George Armstrong Custer

Other changes took place in the cavalry corps, no less radical. John Buford, the most capable of the division leaders, was dead, Kilpatrick was sent out west to join Sherman, and a young brigadier named Wilson was taken from staff duty and put in his place. Gregg was the only one left of the old set. Buford was replaced by Brigadier-General A.T.A. Torbert, who had for sometime commanded the Jersey brigade of infantry, once trained by Phil Kearny.

To Custer, the change was great. He was transferred with his "Michiganders" to the First Division, and found himself under an infantry general, side by side with Devin, an old, steady-going man, not given to dash, in a place where his enthusiasm must necessarily be cooled to conform to the slower movements of his comrades. That spring, which witnessed a change in his surroundings, witnessed also a change in his personal appearance. He cut his long locks away and began to grow side whiskers. The change was decidedly a disfigurement, and before the end of the summer he repented of it, for he allowed his hair to grow again and became the old Custer once more by October.

On the 3rd May, 1864, the anniversary of the disaster of Chancellorsville, the Army of the Potomac was once more over the Rapidan, a part of it on the very same ground which had witnessed that defeat. The main body of the army however, was higher up toward Orange Court House, and the fighting took place away from all houses in the midst of scrub woods, whence no view of the battle could be obtained. It was a haphazard sort of a fight, the heads of columns on the road feeling for each other; and it terminated only in a drawn battle; while Grant moved across Lee's front in the night, to get between him and Richmond.

In the Wilderness fight, the cavalry was on the left. Wilson, with the Third Division, had the lead, Gregg was next, Torbert third. Wilson ran into the enemy at Tod's Tavern and was driven back by Fitzhugh Lee in some confusion. All the fighting was dismounted, the woods being so thick that any other method was impossible.

The first serious fighting of Torbert's division was still further to the left at Spottsylvania Court House. It took place after the main battle of the Wilderness was over, and was the first indication to Lee that his enemy was working round on that flank. It was sulky, stubborn bull dog fighting, entirely opposed to the brilliant methods by which

THE WILDERNESS AND THE VALLEY

Custer had gained his reputation, dismounted lines of skirmishers pressing grimly forward through tangled woods, firing at each other like lines of infantry, holding on to hasty breastworks of rails and fallen trees and making but little progress.

One thing however was noticeable in all the battles. The Confederate cavalry were not fighting with the obstinacy a vigor which characterized them in 1863. They were in as strong force to all appearance, and would fight well in the morning, but the evening invariably showed a relaxation very different from their old ways. This feature was clearly noticeable in the Wilderness and after. The infantry fought as fiercely as ever, but the cavalry was beginning to lose its backbone.

Confederate dead at Spottsylvania. In May 1864, Confederate forces clashed with the advancing Union army in the Battle of Spotsylvania Court House. The battle cost 18,000 Union and 11,000 Confederate casualties and included nearly 20 hours of brutal hand-to-hand combat at the infamous "Bloody Angle."

It is not our intention to dwell long on this period of Custer's career as a brigade commander. It was marked by less individuality than during the previous summer, and for a simple reason. Torbert was a slow and steady chief, who always kept his division close together and never got it into scrapes; consequently Custer was generally alongside of someone else, and sharing the ordinary incidents of every fight, uninteresting save to professional readers. His only rival for dash was General Merritt, who had left West Point a year before Custer and therefore ranked him.

Merritt commanded the Regular Brigade of the same division and was always trying to be side by side with Custer. Something, however, he lacked. It is hard to say what it was, except beauty of person and that chivalrous romantic spirit which pervaded Custer's every look and action. Certain it is that Custer was idolized by his men, and could give by his personal presence weight to a charge of which Merritt could not boast, although as a general he was held in higher esteem by many, as not being thought so rash and reckless. There is little doubt that in this respect Custer had lost as much in reputation by his long association with Kilpatrick as he had gained in popular favor by being so frequently mentioned in the papers, however unjust the verdict of rashness.

The savage and determined fighting of the cavalry on the left of Grant's army lasted until the 7th of May, when the horsemen were relieved at Spottsylvania and withdrawn to prepare for Sheridan's first raid. In his final report, the general tells us his reasons for this step, and very good ones they were. Up to that time, save in the short Gettysburg campaign, the cavalry of the Army of the Potomac had been hampered by being always attached to the infantry, taking care of the latter, and engaged in indecisive actions in which the infantry never supported it. Sheridan's idea was that it should operate as an independent body, raid around the enemy's rear, and fight his cavalry only, until that should be destroyed, living off the country meantime.

Grant consented to allow him to try the experiment, and it succeeded so well that it was constantly repeated thereafter. The former raids of the cavalry under Stoneman had been made in detached bodies, liable to be crushed by superior force. Sheridan determined to act with his whole mass in unison, knowing it to be stronger than any cavalry force Stuart could bring against it.

On the 9th of May, 1864, accordingly, the whole cavalry corps, nearly twelve thousand strong, started out on its road to Richmond and

THE WILDERNESS AND THE VALLEY

was soon well on its way, Custer's brigade in the extreme advance. Before the evening, Custer reached the North Anna River at Beaver Dam Station, where the Richmond and Gordonsville railroad crosses the river. He at once charged right into the station, which was directly in the rear of Lee's centre, captured three long trains and two engines, and released four hundred Union prisoners going to Richmond. The cars were full of rations for Lee's army and were burned and the railroad was destroyed for miles.

To reach this point, the cavalry column had made a march of over thirty miles, and had completely got the start of Stuart. During the afternoon, the Confederate chief followed up the rear of the column, which was nearly ten miles long, and attacked it fiercely, but was easily beaten off. All that night, Stuart marched on to get ahead of the Union cavalry, with Fitzhugh Lee's and Wade Hampton's divisions of horse.

The next day, Sheridan started again and marched more leisurely to Ashland, about fifteen miles farther. He was quite safe from Lee's infantry, for Grant had all that fully employed at Spottsylvania, and he did not care much for the assaults of the cavalry. Ashland Depot was burned, with more cars, and more track was torn up here.

On the 11th of May, the whole cavalry corps was within four miles of Richmond, on the Brooks Pike, Custer once more in the advance. It was in this campaign that Sheridan or Torbert commenced the practice of giving Custer the advance whenever anything serious was to be done, and this day Custer fully justified it. Stuart had by this time got in front of Sheridan, and gallantly endeavored to stay his course. Custer in his report says:

The Second and Reserve Brigades were first engaged, afterwards my brigade was thrown in on the left of the Reserve Brigade, connecting on my left with the right of the Third division. The enemy was strongly posted on a bluff in rear of a thin skirt of woods, his battery being concealed from our view by the woods. The edge of the woods nearest my front was held by the enemy's dismounted men, who poured a heavy fire into my line.

The Fifth and Sixth Michigan were ordered to dismount and drive the enemy from the position, which they did in the most gallant manner. On reaching the woods, I ordered Colonel Alger to establish the Fifth and Sixth upon a line near the skirt of the woods, and hold his position until further orders. From a personal examination of the grounds, I discovered that a successful charge might be made upon the battery of the enemy by keeping well to the right. With this intention, I formed the First Michigan in column of squadrons under cover of the woods.

At the same time, I directed Colonel Alger and Major Kidd to move the Fifth and Sixth Michigan forward to occupy the attention of the enemy on the left, Heaton's battery to engage them in front, while the First charged the battery in the flank. As soon as the First Michigan moved from the cover of the woods, the enemy divined our intention and opened a brisk fire from his artillery. Before the battery could be reached, there were five fences to be opened and a bridge to cross over which it was impossible to pass more than three at one time. Yet notwithstanding these obstacles, the First Michigan advanced boldly to the charge, and when within two hundred yards of the battery charged it with a yell which spread terror before them. Two pieces of cannon, two limbers filled with ammunition and a number of prisoners were the fruits of this charge.

While this was going on in the First, Alger was at work with his Fifth Michigan, had driven the enemy through the woods into the open, and the order was given to cease firing, the enemy being worsted. Just at that instant, a Confederate officer, who afterwards proved to be General J.E.B. Stuart, rode up with his staff to within four hundred yards of the line, when a man of the Fifth fired at him. John A. Huff of Company A remarked; "Tom, you shot too low and to the left," and turning to Colonel Alger, who was near, said, "Colonel, I can fetch that man." "Try him," said Alger. Huff took a steady aim over a fence and fired. The officer fell. Huff turned to the colonel and coolly said; "There's a spread eagle for you." Huff had previously been in Berdan's Sharpshooters, and was an excellent shot. He was killed a month later at Cold Harbor.

After Stuart's, fall the enemy rallied desperately for awhile, but finally gave way in a complete rout, before a general charge led by Custer in which the First, Fifth, Sixth, and Seventh Michigan and the First Vermont all joined together. Thus once more, Custer had taken the brunt of the fighting for his whole division, and driven the enemy from the field.

Whitehouse Landing. White House Landing was a major Union Army supply base in 1862 during the Peninsula Campaign and again in 1864 during the Overland Campaign. There, the Richmond and York River Railroad, which was completed in 1861 between Richmond and West Point, crossed the Pamunkey River.

That evening, Sheridan was in a dilemma. He had beaten the enemy's cavalry and was in front of Richmond, but he could do no more without infantry and heavy guns. He had one chance of success, however. Butler, with twenty thousand men, was known to be on the James River, south bank near Richmond, and it was possible that he might advance, capture the city and join the cavalry.

The hope was vain, however. Butler was too far away. Nothing was heard of him, and every available Confederate infantry soldier was hurrying out of Richmond to attack Sheridan in front, while Fitzhugh Lee and Wade Hampton were pressing on his rear. Sheridan had two courses left open. One was to march back, crushing the cavalry in the way, and join Grant; the other to strike off to the east, down the Peninsula to Whitehouse Landing, and rest his command until Grant's advance reached the head of the Peninsula.

He chose the latter course for two reasons. First, he did not care to march back, with a certain fight, while he was out of forage, when a stubborn enemy could delay him sufficiently long to starve his command; second, having gone so far, it would hurt the morale of the whole campaign to recede. He marched down the old and now deserted Peninsula to Whitehouse Landing, where gunboats and supplies awaited him, and rested in peace after his first raid.

After a few days' repose, the cavalry corps marched up the Peninsula and found the Union army drawn up near Hanover Court House. On the 28th May, Sheridan, with a division of the Sixth Corps and the cavalry, started off on the next flank movement of Grant, which ended at Cold Harbor. By successive flanking movements, Grant's army had come in a slanting direction, all the way from Orange Court House, crossing successively the Rapidan, North Anna, South Anna and Pamunkey and now found itself just where McClellan was two years before, at Cold Harbor not twelve miles from the centre of Richmond.

The position of the two armies was however different from the days of McClellan. The latter's lines had been drawn east and west, his rear being open to Jackson's attack coming from the valley. Grant's lines were drawn north and south, across the head of the Peninsula, with his base indifferently at either Whitehouse on the Pamunkey, or Harrison's Landing on the James.

In this position, the Battle of Cold Harbor was fought. It began by the cavalry moving to the left, driving off Fitzhugh Lee and holding the enemy's infantry in breastworks. It ended as at Spottsylvania in the infantry coming up, relieving the cavalry, and making a savage attack on Lee's army heavily fortified along the whole line. The assault was repulsed with heavy loss, as all the others had been, but the Army of the Potomac retained the advantage, for the first time in its history, of having always attacked and never retreated.

The disadvantage to the Southern infantry of the defensive attitude was great. As long as they had things all their own way, as during 1862, no soldiers fought better and their attacks were heroic. The disaster at Gettysburg on the other hand, when they were obliged to defend

THE WILDERNESS AND THE VALLEY

themselves, developed the great weakness of the Confederate armies, a tendency to scatter, each man for himself and to surrender in small squads.

Cold Harbor. General Grant later expressed remorse for the egregious Union casualties at Cold Harbor, stating, "I have always regretted that the last assault at Cold Harbor was ever made... no advantage whatever was gained to compensate for the heavy loss we sustained."

The Union troops under similar disasters displayed an opposite tendency, to huddle together and look blindly to the Government for help. The disintegrating tendency of reverses during 1864 did more to strip the Southern army of strength than the material blows of Grant's troops. Only the very best soldiers, under the personal lead of Lee and Johnston, held together. When anyone else took them, as in the cases of Early and Hood, they broke all to pieces at the first serious defeat.

The close of the Battle of Cold Harbor was marked by Sheridan's second raid. His first had been around Lee's right and succeeded perfectly. Now he proposed to try the same experiment round his left. The army lay in front of Cold Harbor, sulkily watching Lee, and it is possible that the latter thought a second McClellan was about to begin a second siege. If so, on the 7th June he was undeceived, for on that day Sheridan, with the First and Second Divisions, started around his left flank and very soon was roaming over the country lately occupied by Lee's army.

He was compelled, after the first day, to march very slowly. The country was almost entirely bare of forage for his horses, and when the grain that his men carried with them was exhausted, they were obliged to subsist by grazing their animals to a large extent. Four days after starting, Sheridan reached Trevillian Station, about five miles from Gordonsville. He found Fitzhugh Lee there, drove him away, burned the station, and tore up the track.

It was his intention while there to have effected a junction with General Hunter, who was ordered to come down through the Shenandoah Valley to meet him. Hunter never got so far, for he met Breckinridge and was driven back. Sheridan, hearing that Breckinridge was close to him with a heavy force of infantry, judged that he could not afford to fight a battle. His supply of ammunition was not sufficient for more than one contest, his horses were in poor condition, and in the event of a defeat he would be in a bad plight. He therefore fell back in the night, marched to the Peninsula, and finally rejoined Grant's army, which had crossed the James at Petersburg on the 25th June.

In all these operations, Custer had no opportunity for the display of any of his peculiar talents for brilliant success, save at Beaver Dam, and in front of Richmond at Yellow Tavern. The rest was all grim hard work, weary march or straight ahead assaults on breastworks, with nothing but hard knocks and a few feet of ground to gain.

During the whole of July, the cavalry and Custer had little to do. The position at Petersburg, where the siege was now going on, rendered them useless. At the end of June, they tried, in conjunction with the Second Corps, to turn Lee's right flank by getting between Petersburg and Richmond at Deep Bottom, but the attempt was frustrated by fortifications.

During July however, Lee took the initiative into his own hands once more. He did not dare attack Grant, but he did dare attack

THE WILDERNESS AND THE VALLEY

Washington by way of the Valley. His lines at Petersburg were so strong that he could afford to send away considerable force to the Valley without compromising the safety of Richmond; he did so.

On the 3rd of July, Early marched up the Valley to Martinsburg, and soon after entered Maryland and Pennsylvania. The raid, though made at first by a small force, had the effect Lee intended it should have. It caused Grant to detach the Sixth Corps from Petersburg and finally two divisions of his cavalry (Torbert's and Wilson's) to the succor of Washington.

Early fought one battle; at Monocacy, against Lew Wallace, who had hastily gathered together a lot of militia and hundred days' men. He whipped Wallace and advanced to Washington, but the battle had detained him so long that it gave time for the Sixth Corps to arrive and man the defenses. Nearly at the same time, the Nineteenth Corps also began to arrive by sea from Louisiana where it had been serving; and Early retreated down the valley with his plunder.

The Sixth Corps was again ordered back to Petersburg, and had reached Washington when the news came that Early was again advancing, this time in heavier force. Lee had found his first experiment so successful that he hoped to better it. Early, with twelve thousand men, had called away Wright's corps; it was probable that another twelve thousand might call out still more, and weaken Grant sufficiently to enable Lee to even attack him. Lee reckoned without his host. Instead of another corps, Grant sent Sheridan, on the 2nd of August, 1864, and what is more, went himself.

NOTE: In the fight at Trevillian Station, mentioned shortly before, Custer's Brigade was at one time in great peril. It had been sent off to the left and had cut off a Confederate brigade from its led horses. On the right, Torbert and Wilson had driven back the force opposed to them, and as it happened, straight on to Custer's rear. The Michigan Brigade found itself surrounded, its guns in peril, and finally the enemy were so close on Custer's colors that his color-bearer was shot, and the general only saved the colors by tearing them from the staff and stuffing them into his breast.

We extract from Custer's and Sheridan's official reports of the operations of his brigade, the main incidents of this fight. His column moved on Trevillian Station by a different road from that of the rest of the division, followed at a respectful distance by Wickham's brigade of Confederate cavalry. Coming to the station, Fitzhugh Lee was found in front, and a wagon train was in sight. Custer ordered in that inevitable Fifth Michigan; with the equally inevitable Alger, and as usual Alger went in on the charge.

He captured a large number of wagons, ambulances and caissons, and some eight hundred men with 1500 led horses. These were the horses of the enemy engaging Merritt and Devin on the other road. Had Alger obeyed his orders to halt at the station, all was well; but he was so transported with ardor that he charged nearly a mile down the road. The enemy in front of Merritt and Devin came driving back on Custer's right, in great confusion. Wickham made a desperate assault on his rear, and a third force coming up to the support of Merritt's foes made its appearance on the left and front, between Custer and Alger.

Then the fight became lively for a while. Custer naively observes in his report that his lines were "very contracted" and "resembled very nearly a circle." He was only intent on holding on to his captures until Merritt and Devin came in, for he could hear their firing steadily advancing. All his plans were frustrated by a single coward. The quartermaster in charge of the trains and captures, demoralized by his unaccustomed position under fire, moved out his train without orders and ran right into the enemy. Everything was retaken with much of Custer's property, and the enemy broke into his lines.

It is very satisfactory to record that this quartermaster was cashiered for cowardice. It was at this juncture when everything was in confusion on both sides, that Sergeant Mitchell Belvir, First Michigan Cavalry, Custer's color-bearer, was killed, right in the advance of a charge. His death grip on the color-staff was so tenacious, and the danger at the moment so imminent, that Custer was compelled to wrench the flag from the staff to save it. A little later, Merritt and Devin came in and the enemy was driven in confusion. Alger cut his way back, but with heavy loss.

WINCHESTER

ON the 4th of August, 1863, Major Philip H. Sheridan reported in Washington to Halleck, Chief of Staff, for instructions. He was informed that he was assigned to the Army of the Shenandoah, and would receive further instructions from General Grant personally at Monocacy Junction in Maryland. He went there and received them, brief and to the point. He was to find the enemy, drive him up the Shenandoah Valley as soon as he could, and to destroy all forage and provisions in that valley so as to prevent the enemy from going that way again. Grant noticed that all Lee's raids went up this rich valley, not over the bare and desolated field of Bull Run, and he was resolved to strip the one as bare as the other.

The Army of the Shenandoah then consisted of the Sixth Corps, much reduced in numbers, one division of the Nineteenth Corps, two small divisions under Crook, a small division of cavalry one thousand strong under Averill, and Torbert's cavalry division. Averill was off after McCausland's cavalry, which had just burned Chambersburg, Pa., and Torbert's men had not yet all reached Washington. The losses of horses and men in the raids had reduced them in number so much that the total effective force of Sheridan when he started down the valley, within a week of his arrival, was only eighteen thousand infantry, and three thousand-five hundred horse.[*]

Opposed to these was Early, with a total force in the neighborhood of twenty-five thousand infantry, and five thousand horse scattered throughout the country. It is very difficult and almost impossible to verify Early's numbers, for the reason that his own final report, written after the war, avers that he had less men in his whole army, than were returned as prisoners by Sheridan's provost-marshal at the close of the

---

[*] Sheridan's Report.

campaign. Of this, we shall speak further on.

Torbert was at once appointed chief of cavalry for the Army of the Shenandoah, and Merritt was given the First Division, in which he was now senior brigadier. Sheridan gathered his forces so quickly that on the 10th of August, he was beyond Strasburg, driving Gordon's division before him, the First Union cavalry division in advance. All through the valley campaign, after this, whenever Sheridan wanted work done, he called on the remnants of his old cavalry corps, already "old" to him, though he had taken them for the first time in May, and it was now only August.

While at Strasburg however, he heard that a column of the enemy was moving over the old campaigning ground towards Front Royal on his left rear; and on the 13th, he dispatched Devin's brigade to Front Royal to find out what was the matter. The same day, he received a special message from Washington by an officer who rode all the way. The message was from Grant, who was already back at Petersburg, and informed him that Lee had certainly sent two divisions and at least twenty guns to join Early.

To meet these, another division of the Nineteenth Corps, and Wilson's division of his own old cavalry corps were coming to join Sheridan. He determined to fall back to the end of the valley while waiting for these and hold the line of Halltown in front of Harper's Ferry, which he did at once. The expected column of the enemy did come down on him at Front Royal, with Kershaw's infantry division and Fitzhugh Lee's cavalry division, but Merritt, who was there by this time with his single cavalry division, beat the enemy back, Devin's brigade taking the honors, two flags and some hundred prisoners. In this fight, Devin won his star at last.

From the date of Front Royal to the middle of September, the movements of the two armies around Halltown were very confusing. Sheridan, by careful inquiry and reconnaissance, ascertained at last exactly what troops had joined Early. They were only Kershaw's and Fitzhugh Lee's divisions, the first foot, the second horse. This made his force superior to Sheridan's by a few thousands, but when the latter was joined by his own reinforcements, they were about equal.

FREDERICK WHITTAKER

At Front Royal, brother fought brother as Confederate 1st Maryland attacked Federal 1st Maryland. The Battle of Front Royal was a rare example of urban combat during the Civil War.

The question now was what to do? Sheridan was obliged to be very cautious. There was nothing behind him if he got beaten, and Early was a hard fighter. He was placed there to keep Early from going into Maryland, and he did his duty well, but with a caution in great contrast to his previous and subsequent career. He kept on his shifty tactics so long, marching and countermarching, reconnoitring and falling back, that Grant began to fear he had mistaken his man.

It seemed as if "Sheridan the Bold" was paralyzed by the responsibility and growing into a nervous engineer, afraid to move. So strong was this impression that Grant actually left Petersburg, came to Washington, and travelled all the way to Harper's Ferry to find what was the matter. He arrived on the 18th September and found things so well settled that, as he says, he never again interfered with Sheridan. The cavalry chief knew his business.

It turned out that Sheridan had learned beyond question from his scouts that Kershaw's division of four brigades, at least five thousand men in all, was ordered back to Richmond, and he was patiently waiting, and had been for two weeks, for its departure. With all his usual impetuosity, he was yet willing to wait, so as not to throw away a single chance. Another remark in Sheridan's report is very significant. "Although the main force remained without change of position from September third to nineteenth, still the cavalry was employed every day in harassing the enemy, its opponents being principally infantry. In these skirmishes, the cavalry was becoming educated to attack infantry lines."

This was worth more than all the rest, as was made evident on the 19th of September. On the 15th, Sheridan heard that Kershaw's division was off, and he determined to strike. He allowed two days to pass over so that Kershaw might be well out of reach; then, on the next night he gathered his men, and on the morning of the 19th of September marched on Winchester.

The Battle of Winchester was perfectly simple in its nature, and was finally decided by the cavalry, the first instance in the Civil War in which such was the case. Sheridan outnumbered Early since the withdrawal of Kershaw, but Early had still four strong divisions of infantry and five brigades of cavalry. With these, he made a stand in front of Winchester, and his line was long enough to outflank Sheridan.

The Union cavalry under Torbet now consisted of Merritt's, Wilson's and Averill's divisions, numbering in all about seven thousand men. It began the action on Opequan Creek, nearly ten miles from Winchester, near Martinsburg, where it was met by Early's cavalry under Rosser, the "Savior of the Valley," as he was dubbed when he first came there. It was considerably inferior to the veterans of Sheridan, both in numbers and composition; and was driven, together with Breckinridge's corps of infantry found with it, steadily back along the pike to Winchester, and so on to Early's left flank.

During the day, until the arrival of the Union cavalry, the fight between Early's and Sheridan's infantry was very even. The Sixth Corps was the only force that Sheridan could thoroughly depend on to stand, for the two divisions of the Nineteenth Corps, coming from Louisiana where the enemy was very inferior both in numbers and discipline to Lee's army, was not yet used to the "stand up and take it" kind of fighting that had greeted the Army of the Potomac ever since its first campaign.

FREDERICK WHITTAKER

Knowing its weakness, Sheridan held Crook's little force, only about three thousand men, in reserve; and it was well he did so. The Sixth Corps stood well up to its work, but the Nineteenth broke under the tremendous fire of musketry, and Sheridan's centre was all giving way. Then it was that he himself, seeing the danger, dashed in and for the first time in his history in Virginia, treated the infantrymen to a taste of the tallest swearing they had ever heard.

No one in the cavalry corps had ever heard him vituperate in such a manner, the general impression there being that he was a kind, indulgent chief. The only time he was heard to swear in such fearfully profane style was when troops were breaking, as in this instance, and the line in danger. Then he seemed to be beside himself. Ordering up a reserve brigade, which charged very gallantly, he threw himself among the fugitives and fairly cursed them back into the lines, raving in such a manner that they feared him more than the enemy. The line was restored, and once more advanced; and Sheridan, finding his right flank in danger of being turned, put in Crook and by so doing extended his line so far as to turn his enemy's left.

The influx of fresh troops on the flanks so dismayed and disheartened the stubborn infantry of Early that they broke and fell back in confusion. At the edge of the town, they rallied desperately and seemed about to drive back their foes, when the clouds of dust and rattle of volleys, away to their left rear, announced the coming of Sheridan's cavalry, driving Rosser and Lomax before them. The crisis was come with the cavalry. How they came there, let Custer tell, as also what followed.

My command, he says, was in readiness to move from its encampment near Summit Point at 2 o'clock in the morning. It being the intention to reach Opequan, some five miles distant, before daylight, the march was begun soon after 2 a.m., and conducted by the most direct route across the country, independent of road. My brigade moved in advance of the division and reached the vicinity of the Opequan before daylight, unobserved by the enemy, whose pickets were posted along the opposite bank. Massing my command in rear of a belt of woods and opposite a ford, situated about three miles from the point at which the railroad crossed the stream, I awaited the arrival of the division commander and the remainder of the division.

At daylight, I received orders to move to a ford one mile and a half up the stream, and there attempt a crossing. This movement was also made beyond the view of the enemy, and my command was massed opposite the point designated in rear of a range of hills overlooking the Opequan. Owing to a reconnaissance made at this point by our forces a few days previous, the enemy were found on the alert, thereby destroying all hopes of securing possession of the ford by a surprise.

Two regiments, the Twenty-fifth New York and Seventh Michigan, both under command of that reliable soldier Lieutenant-Colonel Brewer of the Seventh Michigan, were selected to charge the ford and obtain possession of the rifle pits under the opposite bank. By request of the senior officer of the Twenty-fifth New York Cavalry, that regiment was placed in advance, and both regiments moved under cover of a hill, as near to the ford as possible without being exposed to the fire of the enemy. At the same time, the Sixth Michigan Cavalry, Colonel Kidd commanding, advanced, dismounted to the crest overlooking the ford, and engaged the enemy on the opposite bank. Everything promised success, and the order was given for the column of Colonel Brewer to charge.

Accordingly, both regiments moved rapidly toward the ford. The advance of the Twenty-fifth New York reached the water when the enemy, from a well covered rifle pit opposite the crossing, opened a heavy fire upon our advance, and succeeded in repulsing the head of the column, whose conduct induced this entire portion of the command to give way in considerable confusion. No responsibility for this repulse could be attached to Lieutenant-Colonel Brewer, who had left nothing undone to insure success. Giving him orders to reform his command under the cover of the ridge of hills before mentioned, and directing Colonel Kidd to engage the attention of the enemy as closely as possible, such a disposition of sharpshooters was made as to quiet that portion of the enemy lodged in the rifle pits covering the ford.

The First Michigan Cavalry, Colonel Stagg commanding, which had been held in reserve, was ordered to accomplish what two regiments had unsuccessfully attempted. No time was lost, but aided by the experience of the command which preceded it, the First Cavalry secured a good position near the ford.

Colonel Stagg, detaching two squadrons as an advance guard under Lieutenant-Colonel Maxwell, one of the most dashing and intrepid officers of the service, ordered the charge, and under cover of the heavy fire poured in by the Sixth Michigan, gained a footing on the opposite bank, capturing the rifle pits and a considerable number of prisoners. The enemy retired about one mile from the ford in the direction of Winchester and took a position behind a heavy line of earthworks protected in addition by a formidable *chevaux de frise*.

My entire command was moved to the south of the stream and placed in position along the ridge just vacated by the enemy. About this time, a battery of horse artillery under command of Lieutenant Taylor reported to me, and was immediately ordered into position within range of the enemy's works. Prisoners captured at the ford represented themselves as belonging to Breckinridge's Corps, and stated that their corps, with Breckinridge in command, was posted behind the works confronting us.

Deeming this information reliable, as the results of the day proved it to be, I contented myself with annoying the enemy with artillery and skirmishers until the other brigades of the division, having effected a crossing at a ford lower down, established connection with my left. Acting in conjunction with a portion of Colonel Lowell's brigade, an advance of the First and Seventh Michigan and Twenty-fifth New York was ordered to test the number and strength of the enemy.

This movement called forth from the enemy a heavy fire from his batteries. It failed however, to inflict serious damage. Lieutenant-Colonel Maxwell, who headed the charging column, as was his custom, succeeded in piercing the enemy's line of infantry and reaching to within a few feet of their artillery. Overwhelming numbers alone forced him to relinquish the intent of their capture and he retired, after inflicting a severe loss upon the enemy. This advance, while clearly developing the position and strength of the enemy, was not without loss on our part. Among those whose gallantry on this occasion was conspicuous was Lieutenant Jackson, of the First Michigan Cavalry, who while among the foremost in the charge, received a wound which carried away his arm and afterwards proved mortal. He was a young officer of great promise, and one whose loss was severely felt.

At this time, the engagement along the centre and left of our fine was being contested with the utmost energy upon both sides, as could be determined by the heavy firing both of artillery and small arms. While it was known to be impossible to carry the position in my front with the force at my disposal, it was deemed important to detain as large a force of the enemy in our own front as possible, and thus prevent reinforcements of other parts of their line. With this object in view, as great a display of our forces was kept up as circumstances would allow.

At the same time, skirmishing was continued, with little or no loss to either side. From the configuration of the ground, the enemy was enabled to move or mass troops in rear of his position, unseen by my command. Either divining our intentions of delaying him, or receiving orders to this effect, he abandoned the position in our front and withdrew towards our left. In the absence of instructions, I ordered a general advance, intending, if not opposed, to move beyond the enemy's left flank and strike him in reverse.

I directed my advance toward Stevenson's Depot, and met with no enemy until within two miles of that point when I encountered Lomax's division of cavalry, which at that time was engaged with Averill's division, advancing on my right on the Martinsburg Pike. Our appearance was unexpected, and produced such confusion upon the part of the enemy that, though charged repeatedly by inferior numbers, they at no time waited for us to approach within pistol range, but broke and fled.

Soon after, a junction was formed with General Averill on my right, which with the connection on my left made our line unbroken. At this time, five brigades of cavalry were moving on parallel lines. Most if not all of the brigades moved by brigade front, regiments being in parallel columns of squadrons. One continuous and heavy line of skirmishers covered the advance, using only the carbine, while the line of brigades, as they advanced across the open country, the bands playing the national airs, presented in the sunlight one moving mass of glistening sabres. This, combined with the various and bright colored banners and battle flags, intermingled here and there with the plain blue uniforms of the troops, furnished one of the most inspiring as well as imposing scenes of martial grandeur I ever witnessed upon a battlefield.

No encouragement was required to inspire either men or horses. Only the contrary it was necessary to check the ardor of both until the time for action should arrive. The enemy had effected a junction of his entire cavalry force, composed of the divisions of Lomax and Fitzhugh Lee. They were formed across the Martinsburg and Winchester pike, about three miles from the latter place. Concealed by an open pine forest, they awaited our approach.

No obstacles to the successful maneuvering of large bodies of cavalry were encountered. Even the forests were so open as to offer little or no hindrance to a charging column. Upon our left and in plain view could be seen the struggle now raging between the infantry lines of each army, while at various points the small columns of light-colored smoke showed that the artillery of neither side was idle.

At that moment, it seemed as if no perceptible advantage could be claimed by either, but the fortunes of the day might be decided by one of those incidents or accidents of the battlefield which, though insignificant in themselves, often go far towards deciding the fate of nations. Such must have been the impression of the officers and men composing the five brigades now advancing to the attack. The enemy wisely chose not to receive our attack at a halt, but advanced from the woods and charged our line of skirmishers. The cavalry were here so closely connected that a separate account of the operations of a single brigade or regiment is almost impossible. Our skirmishers were forced back, and a portion of my brigade was pushed forward to their support.

The enemy relied wholly upon the carbine and pistol; my men preferred the sabre. A short but closely contested struggle ensued, which resulted in the repulse of the enemy. Many prisoners were taken, and quite a number of both sides were left on the field. Driving the enemy through the woods in his rear, the pursuit was taken up with vigor, the enemy dividing his column from necessity, our forces did likewise. The division of General Averill moved on the right of the pike and gave its attention to a small force of the enemy which was directing its retreat towards the commanding heights west of the town.

My command, by agreement with General Averill, took charge of all forces of the enemy on the pike, and those in the immediate vicinity of the ground to its left. Other portions of the First Division made a detour still farther to my left, so that that which had lately been one unbroken line was now formed into several columns of pursuit, each with a special and select object in view. Within three-fourths of a mile from the point where the enemy had made his last stand, he rallied a portion of his force.

His line was formed beyond a small ditch, which he no doubt supposed would break if not wholly oppose an attacking column. Under most circumstances, such might have been the case, but with men inspired with a foretaste of victory, greater obstacles must be interposed. Without designating any particular regiments, the charge was sounded and portions of all the regiments composing my brigade joined in the attack. The volleys delivered by the enemy were not enough to check the attacking column, and again was the enemy driven before us, this time seeking safety in rear of his line of infantry.

Here, he reformed for his last attempt to check our advance. The batteries of the enemy were now enabled to reach us, an advantage they were not slow to improve. At this time, a battery of the enemy, with apparently little support, was being withdrawn. My command, owing to the repeated charges, had become badly broken, rendering it impossible for me to avail myself of the services of a single organized regiment. With detachments of each regiment, a charge was ordered upon the battery which, but for the extreme smallness of our numbers, would have proved successful.

Lieutenant Lonusbery, Fifth Michigan Cavalry, with great daring, advanced with a handful of men to within a few paces of the battery, and was only prevented from capturing it by an infantry support, hitherto concealed and outnumbering him. Sergeant Barber, Fifth Michigan Cavalry, clerk at headquarters distinguished himself in this charge as my color-bearer. He carried the colors in advance of the charging column, and was conspicuous throughout the engagement until severely wounded in the latter part of the day.

It being necessary to reform my regiment before attempting a further advance, advantage was taken of a slight ridge of ground within one thousand yards of the enemy's line of battle. Behind this ridge and protected from the enemy's fire, I formed as many of my men as could be hastily collected. Two guns, which had been annoying us on our right, were now charged and taken by the First and Second Regular Cavalry.

This gave us possession of a portion of the main line of the enemy's fortifications. At the same time our infantry on the centre and left had, after our successes on the right, been enabled to drive the enemy and were now forcing him towards the town. Still determined to contest our further advances, the enemy now contracted his lines. This gave me an opportunity to move my brigade to a small crest within five hundred yards of the enemy's position.

This movement was entirely unobserved by him, his attention being drawn toward the heavy lines of our infantry now advancing in open view far to our left. At this moment, I received an order from the division commander to charge the enemy with my entire brigade. Having personally examined the situation, and knowing that a heavy force of the enemy was lying down behind these works, facts of which I knew the division commander was ignorant, I respectfully requested that I might be allowed to select my own time for making the charge. My reasons for this course were that I was convinced that the advance of our infantry on the centre and left would compel the force in my front to shift its position to the rear, and the most favorable moment to strike it would be after this movement had commenced, not while they were awaiting us in rear of their works.

My opinions were verified. Watching the enemy until his force had arisen from behind their works and commenced their retrograde movement, I gave the command to charge. The order was obeyed with zeal and alacrity by all. The First, Fifth, Sixth and Seventh Michigan, with a portion of the Twenty-fifth New York, advanced in one line, using the sabre alone. Officers and men seemed to vie with each other as to who should lead. The enemy, upon our approach, turned and delivered a well directed volley of musketry, but before a second discharge could be given, my command was in their midst, sabring right and left and capturing prisoners more rapidly than they could be disposed of.

Further resistance on the part of those opposed to us was suspended. A few batteries posted on the heights near the town continued to fire into our midst, fortunately killing more of their own men than ours. Their fire was silenced however, as we advanced toward them. Nothing more remained but to collect the prisoners and other trophies of the victory. No further resistance was offered; the charge just made had decided the day, and the entire body of the enemy, not killed or captured, was in full retreat up the valley.

Many of the prisoners cut off by my command fell into the hands of the infantry, whose advance soon reached the ground. My command however, which entered the last charge about five hundred strong, including but thirty-six officers, captured over seven hundred prisoners, also fifty-two officers, seven battle flags, two caissons and a large number of small arms. Night put an end to the pursuit, and the brigade bivouacked on the left of the valley pike, three miles from the battlefield. Our loss was by no means trifling.

So closed the Battle of Winchester, the first decisive field victory won in the Civil War made decisive only by the proper use of cavalry. It must not be imagined that Custer's brigade was all alone in its glory, but it had a large share of it. How it appeared in the last charge to a neighboring brigade is told so well by a participant, who was taken prisoner, that we cannot forebear the transcription.[*]

While awaiting in suspense our next movement, the enemy's infantry was distinctly seen attempting to change front to meet our anticipated charge. Instantly, and while in the confusion incident to their maneuver, the Second Brigade burst upon them, the enemy's infantry breaking into complete rout and falling back a confused and

---

[*] From *"Everglade and Canon,"* a history of the Second U. S. Dragoons by General Rodenbough, used by permission of the author.

broken mass. General Merritt in his official report writes; "The brigade emerged from the fray with three stands of colors and over three hundred prisoners. This blow, struck by General Devin, was at the angle of the line caused by the enemy refusing his left to meet our attack. Soon, Colonel Lowell (Reserve Brigade, which formed to the left of the old position from which Devin charged) entered the lists. His heroic brigade - now reduced to about six hundred men - rode out fearlessly within five hundred yards of the enemy's line of battle, on the left of which, resting on an old earthwork, was a two gun battery. The order was given to charge the line and get the guns.

Colonel Charles Lowell

It was well toward four o'clock, and though the sun was warm, the air was cool and bracing. The ground to our front was open and level, in some places as smooth as a well cut lawn. Not an obstacle intervened between us and the enemy's line which was distinctly seen nervously awaiting our attack. The brigade was in column of squadrons, the Second United States Cavalry in front.

At the sound of the bugle, we took the trot, the gallop, and then the charge. As we neared their line, we were welcomed by a fearful musketry fire, which temporarily confused the leading squadron, and caused the entire brigade to oblique slightly to the right. Instantly, officers cried out, "Forward, forward!" The men raised their sabres and responded to the command with deafening cheers.

Within a hundred yards of the enemy's line, we struck a blind ditch, but crossed it without breaking our front. In a moment, we were face to face with the enemy. They stood as if awed by the heroism of the brigade, and in an instant broke in complete rout, our men sabring them as they vainly sought safety in flight. In this charge, the battery and many prisoners were captured. Our own loss was severe, and of the officers of the Second, Captain Rodenbough lost an arm and Lieutenant Harrison was taken prisoner.

It was the writer's misfortune to be captured, but not until six hundred yards beyond where the enemy were first struck, and when dismounted in front of their second line by his horse falling. Nor did he suffer the humiliation of a surrender of his sabre; for as he fell to the ground with stunning force, its point entered the sod several inches, well-nigh doubling the blade which in its recoil tore the knot from his wrist, flying many feet through the air.

Instantly, a crowd of cavalry and infantry officers and men surrounded him, vindictive and threatening in their actions but unable to repress such expressions as these; "Great God, what a fearful charge! How grandly you sailed in! What brigade? What regiment?" As the reply proudly came, "Reserve Brigade, Second United States Cavalry," they fairly tore his clothing off, taking his gold watch and chain, pocket book, cap and even spurs, and then turned him over to four infantrymen. What a translation - yea, transformation! The confusion, disorder and actual rout produced by the successive charges of Merritt's First Cavalry division would appear incredible, did not the writer actually witness them.

To the right, a battery, with guns disabled and caissons shattered, was trying to make to the rear, the men and horses impeded by broken regiments of cavalry and infantry. To the left, the dead and wounded, in confused masses around their field hospitals - many of the wounded in great excitement, seeking shelter in Winchester. Directly in front, an ambulance, the driver nervously clutching the reins while six men, in great alarm, were carrying to it the body of General Rhodes. Not being able to account for the bullets which kept whizzing past, the writer turned and faced our own lines to discover the cause and if possible, catch a last sight of the Stars and Stripes.

The sun was well down in the west, mellowing everything with that peculiar golden hue which is the charm of our autumn days. To the left, our cavalry were hurriedly forming for another and final charge. To the right front, our infantry, in unbroken line, in the face of the enemy's deadly musketry, with banners unfurled, now enveloped in smoke, now bathed in the golden glory of the setting sun, were seen slowly but steadily pressing forward. Suddenly, above the almost deafening din and tumult of the conflict, an exultant shout broke forth and simultaneously our cavalry and infantry line charged. As he stood on tiptoe to see the lines crash together, himself and guards were suddenly caught in the confused tide of a thoroughly beaten army - cavalry, artillery and infantry - broken, demoralized and routed, hurrying through Winchester.

The Battle of Winchester possessed some remarkable features, considered in a scientific point of view, especially when contrasted with those which had previously been fought during the American Civil War. It was the first which resembled in any degree one of those actions which, under Napoleon and Frederick, have become models for the military student; the first which displayed on the Federal side the possession of a real general, capable of planning and executing every movement of an engagement, and of personally handling all his troops.

Up to that time, the history of every American battle on both sides, with the exception of the valley campaign of Stonewall Jackson, had been the history of a number of nearly independent corps commanders. It has been said that Von Moltke once remarked about the American war that "the struggles of two armed mobs were of no service to a military student." Although the general has officially denied that he used such scornful language; there is a strong probability that he did, in private conversation, say something very like it.

There was much truth in the remark, whoever made it, even if it was severely expressed. A "mob" is a crowd without absolute chiefs. It follows different leaders from time to time with a certain degree of docility, but always requires persuasion, resists command and is subject to sudden changes. Instead of one impulse, it has fifty or more. While this latterly ceased to be true of the lower ranks of the American army, it remained to the very last among the general officers, especially the corps commanders.

Each had his own notion of what ought to be done, and each would do things in his own way. Meade could not control his corps generals, and their lack of quick obedience marred more than one battle in 1864, and nearly at one time spoiled the success of 1865. In the valley, Sheridan changed all this. He made his generals obey his orders without following opinions of their own, and his army consequently pulled together. Winchester was won, and what was more improved, because Sheridan was a man who would be obeyed.

General Philip Sheridan. In 1864, Sheridan defeated Confederate forces in the Shenandoah Valley and his destruction of the economic infrastructure of the Valley was one of the first uses of scorched earth tactics in the war.

WOODSTOCK RACES

ON the 26th September, 1864, Brigadier-General Custer was relieved from the command of the famous Michigan Brigade in the First Cavalry Division Army of the Potomac, and transferred to the head of the Second Division, West Virginia Cavalry, hitherto operating under General Averill. At the time of the transfer, the whole valley was in confusion. Early's army, scattered and demoralized after the crushing disasters of Winchester and Fisher's Hill, was slowly gathering itself together at the very head of the Valley, from Port Republic to Staunton, and the Union Cavalry, spread out fanlike, was operating by independent brigades, on the old Donnybrook Fair principle of hitting every head they could see.

Custer accordingly found himself separated from his new command, which had gone on up the pike towards Staunton and turned to the left in the direction of Piedmont. The country was full of guerillas and scattered parties of Confederate cavalry, and it was not so easy to open communication between the different divisions without proceeding bodily and in force, one toward the other.

All through the valley campaigns, from the days of Banks downwards, the same trouble was met by the Federals as soon as they neared Staunton. Their line of supply was so long and easily cut that it was impossible to go further in safety with a regularly organized army. The only solution of the problem was that afterwards adopted, of cutting loose from the infantry and trains and moving as an independent raiding column, living off the country. Even this was lot practicable for long, for the country was so much impoverished by the near neighborhood of Richmond that two or three days' subsistence for a cavalry corps was its utmost capacity.

Under these circumstances, Custer was doomed to several days of inaction before he could reach his command, and having left his beloved Michigan Brigade was obliged to remain with General Torbert at cavalry headquarters, until the Second Division was near enough to be reached. On the 26th, he entered Staunton with that General, accompanied by Wilson's Division (the third), and the Reserve Brigade (the regulars). At Staunton, fifty-seven prisoners were made, and a quantity of stores destroyed.

On the 27th, Custer, impatient to reach his command, started with a single regiment to reach it at Piedmont, but was compelled to return the next day with the news that Early had again massed his forces and was trying to cut off the cavalry from the rest of the army. It turned out that Early had been reinforced from Richmond by Kershaw's division, and was coming through the gaps to which he had retreated, resolved on revenge.

The main Union army was concentrated some miles back behind Harrisonburg, and each brigade of cavalry, as it successively struck the enemy, found him in such force that they could make no impression. It was exceedingly tantalizing, for the troopers had become so used to victory that when they saw the enemy's trains in plain sight, as they often did, blocked in the mountain roads, they would charge recklessly in only to find a heavy force of infantry in the woods, pouring in such volleys as showed that Early was yet far from being whipped.

On the 28th, the Confederates came down to Staunton and Port Republic and did their best to drive out the First and Third Cavalry Divisions, passing by the Second, which was out near Brown's Gap. The cavalry fought them until dark, holding on to their positions, but during the night, Torbert fell back toward Harrisonburg with Wilson's division, leaving Merritt and Powell, with the First and Second, out on the left still. On the 29th, the enemy fell back from Port Republic to the gaps of the Blue Mountains, and on the 30th, Sheridan's army was again concentrated, the infantry at and beyond Harrisonburg at the head of the valley pike, the cavalry spread out fanwise around the head of the column.

On this day occurred the second important change of Custer's life. General Wilson was relieved from the command of the Third Division, and sent to join Sherman in the west. Custer was at the same time transferred from the Second Division, which he had not yet been able to join and placed at the head of the same division in which he had first won his star. It was the same old Third, which under Kilpatrick had done such service in the Gettysburg campaign, always ready for hard knocks, dashing pell-mell into the enemy no matter what the odds, and trusting to the wonderful luck which never deserted it to get out of its scrapes.

Under Kilpatrick, this division had done more fighting, killed more horses, marched further and charged oftener, than perhaps any other in the army. The reckless valor and want of discretion of its first leader had both their bad and good sides. Had infantry been handled in the same way, the division would long before have been annihilated, but the traditions of the cavalry service are essentially different. Kilpatrick had acted from the first as if he thoroughly believed the maxim of Seidlitz, that under no conceivable circumstances can a mounted cavalry officer be justified in a surrender. Charging in and cutting out were the everyday experiences of the division under his orders and their losses had been proportionately heavy.

When Wilson took command of the division in the spring of 1864, he found it depleted by the loss of its crack brigade, Custer's "Michiganders," and the real secret of its previous high fighting reputation was shown in the summer campaigns. Custer, the lance-head of Kilpatrick, had become the lance-head of Torbert, and it was the First Division that was to do most of the fighting and charging while he was with it. As good as ever, the Third had still lost much of its old fiery fame under the more cautious lead of Wilson.

It was Custer and Merritt who were now in people's mouths when the cavalry was mentioned, as the previous year it had been Buford, Kilpatrick and Custer. There is something so fleeting and hard to grasp in this phenomenon of public favor and fame, that it is difficult to assign a reason for the fact, but it was none the less patent during the Shenandoah campaign and before. Torbert, the division commander of Custer and Merritt, was lost to public view in a large measure, through the lustre of his subordinates who engaged in a fierce rivalry with each other which resulted in splendid successes.

General Wesley Merritt

Now Custer and Merritt were again to engage in the same rivalry, but as division commanders, the latter having the additional advantage of retaining the brigade which Custer had made so famous. Custer was to take up the division which had so far, under Wilson's lead, only held its own with respectability, and was to transform it into the most brilliant single division in the whole Army of the Potomac, with more trophies to show than any, and so much impressed with the stamp of his individuality that every officer in the command was soon to be aping his eccentricities of dress, ready to adore his every motion and word.

The accession of Custer to the command of the Third Division took place at a time when a change in Sheridan's policy was impending. He had come to the Valley to clear out Early; he had done his work, and the question remained - what next? Concentrated at Harrisonburg, he was at the end of his tether. The whole valley is traversed by a single long turnpike, which forms a splendid avenue of communication, perfectly dry and hard in the muddiest winter. At Harrisonburg it ceases, and beyond it are dirt roads only. The enemy was waiting in the Blue Ridge gaps, prepared to dispute any further advance to Richmond. The course of action necessary is indicated by Sheridan himself in his subsequent report. He says:

The question that now presented itself was whether or not I should follow the enemy to Brown's Gap, drive him out, and advance to Charlottesville and Gordonsville. This movement I was opposed to for many reasons, first that it would have necessitated the opening of the Orange and Alexandria Railroad, and to protect this road against the numerous guerilla bands would have required a corps of infantry. Then, there was the additional reason of the uncertainty whether the army in front of Petersburg would be able to hold the entire force of General Lee there, and if not, a sufficient number might be detached and move rapidly by rail to overwhelm me, quickly returning.

I was also confident that my transportation could not supply me further than Harrisonburg, and therefore advised that the valley campaign should terminate at Harrisonburg, and that I return, carrying out my original instructions for the destruction of forage, grain, etc., give up the majority of the army I commanded, and order it to the Petersburg line, a line which I thought the Lieutenant General believed if a successful movement could be made on, would involve the capture of the Army of Northern Virginia.

I therefore, on the morning of the 6th of October, commenced moving back, stretching the cavalry across the valley from the Blue Ridge to the eastern slope of the Allegbanies.

On the way, the horsemen were directed to burn all the forage, but to spare the houses. These orders were obeyed to the letter as the infantry moved back towards Winchester. Merritt marched on the pike while Custer took the side road next the Blue Ridge. Of course, this was nearest the enemy, whose cavalry had not yet suffered very much. It consisted of Rosser's division (three brigades) and the extra brigades of Lomax and Bradley Johnson. Rosser had about thirty-five hundred, Johnson and Lomax about fifteen hundred together, a total of five thousand men.

It must be conceded to the Confederate forces in the last valley campaign, that they fought and were fought with the most obstinate heroism and skill by all concerned, and that they showed in these days of disaster, more conduct and skill against heavy odds than they had ever shown before. When Sheridan first arrived in the valley, Early considerably outnumbered him; but every day strengthened the former and weakened the latter. When finally Kershaw's division was withdrawn a few days before the battle of Winchester, the scale was turned, and as soon as Sheridan had certain intelligence of its departure, he gave battle with heavy odds in his favor, though by no means so great as Early insists.

At Fisher's Hill, despite its strong defensive position, the Confederate army of Jubal Early was defeated by the Union Army commanded by General Philip Sheridan. Four Union Army enlisted men and one officer received the Medal of Honor in the action there.

During the whole valley campaign, thirteen thousand prisoners were taken from Early, which added to the eleven thousand men he claims, gives about twenty four thousand. Added to these the sick, wounded, extra duty men, stragglers, etc., and it is probable that in real truth Early had at Winchester at least twenty-six thousand men, infantry, artillery and train, which with Rosser's cavalry gives a total of about thirty thousand men, outside of Kershaw's division, which was not engaged until Cedar Creek.

When this came, it was probably about enough to fill up the gaps of Winchester and Fisher's Hill. This is hardly the place to enter into a complete analysis of the figures on both sides, but reason and statistics seem to point after making all allowances to an effective total for Early about this time of at least twenty thousand infantry and five thousand horse.

Opposed to these, from the nearest figures attainable at present, it seems that Sheridan must have had about seven thousand cavalry in his three divisions, and twenty-five thousand infantry. These figures are derived from a comparison of his force in August, when with the First and Second

Cavalry Divisions, Sixth Corps, Nineteenth and Crook's force, he reported 18,000 infantry and 3,500 cavalry. He was afterwards joined by a division of the Nineteenth Corps and by the Third Cavalry Division, with such recruits as could be sent from Remount camp. In one of these detachments, the present writer arrived at Harper's Ferry, the evening of Winchester fight, and after scraping up every available man and horse, the result was less than three hundred men.

The odds in Sheridan's favor were heavy enough for practical purposes, though by no means enough to account for the succession of complete and crushing blows delivered on the devoted Early without admitting conduct and capacity of the highest kind to Sheridan and his officers, especially those heading the cavalry.

Rosser, overmatched in numbers as he was, on this occasion did his duty heroically. The feelings of himself and his men were excited to the highest pitch of fury at sight of the remorseless destruction meted out to the valley by the retreating foe. True, that foe was part of the terrible army that had punished them so fearfully ever since the 19th September, but the arrival of Kershaw's division had put new heart into them, and they followed the cavalry down the valley, constantly attacking them.

Lomax and Johnson followed Merritt at a respectful distance, but Rosser hung on Custer's skirts with vindictive tenacity. The first night of the retreat he fell on Custer's camp at Turkeytown, near Brooks Gap, but was repulsed. Next morning, as Custer moved on, Rosser was again after him, Custer proceeding leisurely towards Columbia Furnace. His rear guard was fighting Rosser all day long in the peculiar style developed by Virginian warfare. The main body, in column of fours, was in the road, detaching parties to right and left to burn every barn and haystack to be seen.

Confederate General Thomas Rosser. Thomas Rosser's roommate at the academy, George Armstrong Custer, was a close friend. Despite being on opposing sides, their friendship continued during and after the Civil War ended. Of Custer's death at the Little Bighorn, Rosser wrote: "As a soldier, I would sooner lie in the grave of General Custer and his gallant comrades alone in that distant wilderness, that when the last trumpet sounds, I could rise to judgment from my part of duty, than to live in the place of the survivors of the siege on the hills."

Ordinarily, the rear guard followed at a slow walk, the greater part deployed as skirmishers. When the enemy pressed too close, the men would halt and face about, a brisk fusillade lasting some minutes when the advancing grey coats would be repulsed. Then trotting on, the rear guard would halt at the edge of the next hill or belt of woods, to repeat the operation.

Not far from the Union rear guard could be seen a brilliant group of cavaliers, headed by the same bright debonair figure we remember at Aldie and Brandy Station. As usual, there are the bright brazen instruments of the band near him, the men not much of players perhaps, but what is better, capable of sticking to their posts under fire, and playing "*Yankee Doodle*" to the shrill accompaniment of whistling lead.

Whenever any trouble is anticipated, when Rosser becomes too bold, the flaming scarlet neckties of Custer and his staff are seen coming, and the bright-haired warrior comes trotting leisurely along the skirmish line, whistling a tune and tapping his boots with his riding whip, his blue eyes glancing keenly about, his short curls, just growing again, flung from side to side as he jerks his head in his peculiar nervous manner. There is no more trouble about standing the assault.

But this mode of fighting was peculiarly irksome to one of Custer's impatient temperament, and when he knew, as he soon did, that it was his old classmate Rosser who was following him so persistently, he was doubly disgusted. All that long day of the 7th October, he was compelled by his orders to retreat from the face of a foe he was only too anxious to fight, and even until dark his pickets were annoyed.

All this time, Merritt's column pursued its way without fighting, only observed by Lomax and Johnson. The reason was very simple. The two Union divisions each numbered about two thousand five hundred effective men, and Powell's Second Division about two thousand more. Powell was off to the right of Merritt following the Luray Valley, separated from the rest by hills and gaps. Consequently, the forces in the main valley of the Shenandoah were equal, and thus divided, roughly speaking. Custer's two thousand five hundred against Rosser's three thousand five hundred were falling back. Merritt's two thousand five hundred against Lomax's one thousand five hundred were also falling back, but quite unmolested.

The next day, 8th October, General Torbert, in command of the cavalry, thinking Custer had had about enough, halted Merritt in the afternoon, sent back one of his brigades about a mile on the pike, to develop Lomax, and the other two to relieve Custer, who all that day had been suffering even fiercer assaults than before. The experience of the three days had given the enemy confidence, and Custer had been retreating in the face of a superior force who fancied they were driving him. The arrival of Merritt's brigade checked Rosser, and the fighting ceased at dark when Merritt withdrew his men to his own camp.

The position on the night of the 8th was as follows; Merritt was in camp at Brook Creek, on the pike, at the foot of Round Top Hill. The pike runs up the middle of the valley. Custer camped at Tumbling Run, on the back road, some six miles off, to the left and retired. Powell was further off still, to the left and rear, having crossed behind the others to Front Royal. Rosser lay opposite Custer, Lomax and Johnson opposite Merritt. The back road so often mentioned is a dirt road, nearly parallel to the pike, between it and the Blue Ridge, and about three miles from the pike.

That night, "Little Phil" came up to the front to see how things were going on, and soon learned the exact posture of affairs. The enemy, grown bold through impunity, was becoming too troublesome. He must get a lesson. The story of the orders to Torbert for next day is thus told by both parties. Sheridan says, "On the night of the eighth, I ordered General Torbert to engage the enemy's cavalry at daybreak and notified him that I would halt the army until he defeated it." Torbert says, "I had received orders from Major-General Sheridan to start out at daylight and whip the rebel cavalry, or get whipped myself."

The difference in the literalness of the stories is in favor of Torbert, but there is no question as to the way in which the order was obeyed. When it was given, the cavalry was in front of Strasburg, where the infantry was concentrated. Merritt was ordered to move one brigade on the pike and two more to the left, to open communication with Custer.

At daybreak, the movement commenced, soon to become famous under the name of "Woodstock Races." The forces were not far from equal, the difference in favor of the Federal cavalry being but slight. In guns, they were about the same. Each division had a battery, and Rosser and Lomax were similarly equipped, six guns on the pike, six on the back road.

Now Custer was to avenge himself for his long suffering. His experience, it must be confessed, since he had taken command of the Third Division, was peculiarly mortifying. For the first time since Meade's retreat, he had been obliged to retrograde in face of the enemy, and to suffer severe punishment while doing it. As in the former however, nothing but orders had compelled him to do so, and now had come the far more congenial orders to advance.

Out swept, as at Winchester, side by side, Custer and Merritt were to attack Rosser and Lomax; and to Custer's share fell the greater part of the force of his old classmate Rosser. On the pike moved the steady old Reserve Brigade, the Regulars under Lowell. Next to them was Devin's Brigade, the Second, with "Old Tommy," or the "Old War Horse" as he was nicknamed, at its head. Then the Michiganders, Custer's old brigade, connected Merritt's line with that of their former division, under their own commander of a few days back, and the union of the line was perfect.

Old and new were only impatient to pay off the enemy. In front of each brigade stretched a regiment, deployed as skirmishers, then a second line of two regiments, deployed in double rank, behind each wing, finally a fourth regiment in close column, to the rear of the centre, with the brigade commander and staff in its front. Merritt rode in rear of the centre of his division, with his battery near him. Custer was up even with his skirmish line, his own guns following.

In this order, the two gallant looking divisions swept over the beautiful level surface of the valley. It was a magnificent place for a cavalry fight, and very different from the scrub woods of Central Virginia, where all the fighting had to be dismounted. There was room to deploy, smooth ground to ride on, all the rail fences had long ago vanished for soldiers' fires, and the field was clear.

Rosser and Lomax were met on the other side of Tom's Run, a rivulet too small to intercept the movement of either force, and both sides were drawn up and ready for the fray. That it was to be a severe and decisive fight, both knew. The Southerners had recovered from the demoralization of their first reverses; and their apparent successes of the last few days had further elated them. They were part of the same cavalry that once, under Stuart, had raided round the Army of the Potomac, and captured Pope's headquarters; and they were burning to avenge the destruction of their homes which they had lately witnessed.

Both sides deployed within plain view of each other, and the skirmishers opened with their carbines in the dashing and picturesque style that makes a cavalry fight so pretty a sight at its outset. Very little harm is done, but the long lines of horsemen go trotting on, waving to and fro as the individuals halt to take aim, fire their pieces and trot on, loading as they go.

At the first gentle knoll that presents itself on either side, the batteries gallop up and unlimber on the crest, opening fire and mingling their crashing reports with the sharp crack of the rifles. Not much smoke, the order is too open and the breeze strong, the bright sunlight and clear air of the autumn day aiding to inspire everyone to do his best. It is exciting, romantic, intoxicating. The little white puffs of smoke on the skirmish line, the dark bodies following in rear, all fringed with the steel of their drawn sabres, the little groups of general officers and their staffs at regular intervals in the three mile line, the white clouds round the four opposing batteries as points of peculiar interest.

Rosser's position for his main body was well chosen, and as his pickets fell back and revealed it, this became evident. He occupied a low but abrupt range of hills on the south bank of Tom's Run and had posted his dismounted men behind stone fences at the base of the ridge. A second line of barricades crowned the ridge, also defended by dismounted men. On the summit, he had six guns in position strongly supported, and he had the great advantage of being able to see all of Custer's movements.

And now occurred one of those little incidents that stamp the innate romance of Custer's character on his biography, like the echo of his famous last speech at the Academy, "Let's have a fair fight, boys." Here it was, fair and square and no favor, perhaps the first in the war. No infantry to bother the horse, numbers about equal, his first fight as a division commander, and Rosser in sight.

Out rode Custer from his staff, far in advance of the line, his glittering figure in plain view of both armies. Sweeping off his broad sombrero, be threw it down to his knee in a profound salute to his honorable foe. It was like the action of a knight in the lists. A fair fight and no malice.

On the ridge before him he had seen Rosser, his classmate at the academy with whom he had held many a wordy contest in days of old and who had been his great rival at "the Point." Rosser had but just come to the valley and was already hailed as its savior. He saw Custer and turned to his staff, pointing him out, "You see that officer down there," said he. "That's General Custer the Yanks are so proud of, and I intend to give him the best whipping today that he ever got. See if I don't." And he smiled triumphantly as he looked round at his gallant Southern cavaliers.

Then Custer lifted the hat and clapped it on his head, turned to his line of men, and the next moment the Third Division was sweeping on at a trot, the flaming scarlet necktie and bright curls of Custer before all, followed by his staff; all with swords out.

Now the pace quickens. Rosser's and Lomax's guns open furiously at shorter range, and the rattling of volleys rolls along the Confederate line. The bullets go pattering around, whistling overhead, knocking up the dirt, killing or wounding a few horses and men, but doing surprisingly little damage, all things considered. The trot has become a gallop, and as the pattering of bullets becomes heavier, a wild savage yell breaks from every throat in that long wave of cavalry, and away they go, the lines lost in confused clumps of horsemen with waving sabres, the horses crazy with excitement, leaping half out of their skins as they race for the Confederate batteries and lines of cavalry.

Custer's attack, arranged in full sight of Rosser, yet proved triumphantly successful. One brigade in front, another to the right, the third to the left, they swept on at a charge, not heeding the fire, curled round Rosser's flanks in a moment, and before he could tell what had happened, had him enclosed in a semi-circle of charging horse. Vain all his efforts when his flanks were threatened.

Had the attack been made on foot, he might have had time to think, but the sudden and impetuous rush of a whole mounted division completely demoralized the Confederates. Despite Rosser's efforts, away they went in the wildest confusion, driven back at a gallop for nearly two miles when one brigade, shamed by the frantic appeals of their leader, made a desperate stand, and the lately fugitive battery opened a furious fire which staggered Custer's advance and threw it into momentary confusion.

Rosser was not whipped yet. Seizing his moment, he charged with his remaining brigades and forced Custer's advance back half a mile, when Custer's battery of four guns made its appearance and checked

WOODSTOCK RACES

Rosser again. Now was Rosser's time to fight, and now was the time he missed it. Disappointed in his charge, he again trusted to defensive battle, while Custer reformed his three brigades for a second grand charge and once more advanced at the trot in a long sweeping line of steel.

Ill fared it with Rosser and his men then that they received the charge at a halt, and trusted to fire for their defense. Through the dust, turmoil and confusion of the Northern charge could be seen, far in advance, another cloud of dust, out of which the glittering horseshoes are shining, as the squadrons flee from the charge. The Confederates were thrown into immediate confusion, and behind them was nothing but an open field as far as Mount Jackson, twenty-six miles away.

Every gun opposite Custer is taken and only one of Lomax's escapes by being limbered up in desperate haste and taken off over the hill at full speed. It was no longer a fight. "Woodstock races" had begun. All the way to Woodstock, now at a gallop and at a trot, occasionally at a walk to breathe the reeking horses, the Union lines swept on with scarcely a pause, the Confederates fleeing before them like sheep.

Sheridan sums up the victory in a portion of a sentence, stating that "the enemy was defeated with the loss of all his artillery but once piece, and everything else which was carried on wheels. The rout was complete, and was followed up to Mount Jackson, a distance of some twenty-six miles."

Torbert says, "The First division (Brigadier-General Merritt) captured five pieces of artillery (all they had on the road except one), their ordnance, ambulance and wagon trains, and sixty prisoners. The Third division (Brigadier-General Custer) captured six pieces of artillery (all they had on the back road) all of their headquarter wagons, ordnance, ambulance and wagon trains. There could hardly have been a more complete victory and rout. The cavalry totally covered themselves with glory and added to their long list of victories the most brilliant one of them all, and the most decisive the country has ever witnessed. Brigadier-Generals Merritt and Custer, and Colonels Lowell and Pennington commanding brigades, particularly distinguished themselves. My losses in this engagement will not exceed sixty killed and wounded, which is astonishing when compared with the results. The First Division returned to Woodstock and camped for the night, the Third returned about six miles and camped for the night."

Thus ended "Woodstock Races," the first pitched battle in which the Third Division took part under Custer's command. As always, before and after, he and Merritt were in close rivalry as to distance and results, but Custer was just a little ahead. The completeness of the victory was owing to two things; the open ground and the vicious cavalry school in which Rosser and his command had been reared.

All through the Virginia campaign, the Confederate cavalry displayed the same taste for fire arms and the same distaste and contempt for the sabre as a weapon. In the West, the case was even worse, for the cavalry in that vicinity abandoned their sabres entirely and trusted to nothing but fire arms. Out in the woods, this method of warfare is possible, but on a plain suicidal. The only place in Virginia besides the Valley where open fields exist, adapted for mounted cavalry fighting, is around Brandy Station, where the sabre had always proved triumphant. Rosser, in common with most of the Confederate officers, distrusted the sabre, which was rarely used by the Confederate cavalry after Stuart's death, and not enough during his life.

Custer, on the other hand, was never more in his element than in a sabre charge, and the same thing was true of the whole of the First and Third divisions, especially the former. Custer's influence soon gave the same taste to the latter, and they became excessively fond of rapid mounted work, wherein pistol, carbine and sabre were used, one with the other, with the happiest effect. The moral impetus of that day of charges never left the Third Division.

Henceforth they became imbued with a certain contempt for the Confederate cavalry. They had found the certain way to drive it in confusion. It never afterwards gave them serious trouble. The time was coming and not far distant either, when the cavalry of the Shenandoah Army was to measure itself with a more stubborn foe, the infantry, and be the means of achieving the last and most glorious victory of all at Cedar Creek only ten days later. Meanwhile, let us leave

WOODSTOCK RACES
it to its hard earned repose, after "Woodstock Races."

CEDAR CREEK

FOR about ten days after "Woodstock Races," the cavalry and army in general enjoyed comparative quiet. Sheridan and Grant were in correspondence as to further movements, and it was almost determined by the latter that Sheridan should continue his advance and operate on Charlottesville and Gordonsville, through Manassas Gap. Sheridan on the other hand wished to send back the Sixth Corps to Grant; and on the 10th of October, it actually started and marched toward Front Royal on its way to Washington.

On the 12th, it was at Ashby's Gap; but the same day news came that Early had once more advanced to Fisher's Hill. The Federal army was encamped at Cedar Creek near Strasburg, and the Sixth Corps was recalled. On the 13th, Rosser, not yet discouraged, came down on the extreme right of the army and drove in Custer's pickets. He had three brigades of cavalry and one of infantry, but retired when Custer moved out of camp. From thence to the 18th, all was quiet.

Merritt and Custer sent frequent reconnoissances up the pike and the back road, but found no enemy nearer than Fisher's Hill. The Confederates cavalry was in the Luray Valley, and occasionally annoyed the extreme right of the army. Everything seemed to point in Wright's opinion to a quiet sulky enemy, with a possible attack on their right rear.

On the 16th, Sheridan was summoned to Washington to see Secretary Stanton. As he was at Manassas Gap, and about taking the train, he received a note from General Wright of the Sixth Corps, who was left in command of the army. It enclosed a dispatch which the signal officers had just read off the Confederate signal flags on Three Top Mountain, near Fisher's Hill. It ran thus:

CEDAR CREEK

To Lieutenant General Early: Be ready to move as soon as my forces join you, and we will crush Sheridan.

LONGSTREET, Lieutenant General

The Union cavalry was at this time moving toward Front Royal, preparatory to going through Manassas Gap on a raid towards Gordonsville. Wright asked that it might be recalled, as he expected an attack on his right. Sheridan was inclined to believe the dispatch a ruse, as it turned out afterward to be. He sent back the cavalry however, told Wright to be careful, and proceeded to Washington from whence he returned to Winchester on the night of the 18th October.

During the same night, Early, plucky and enterprising to the last, a general who fully deserved, if he did not attain, good fortune, left Fisher's Hill, crossed the Shenandoah and came down on Wright just where he was least expected, on the almost unguarded left of the Federal army. Powell, with the Second Cavalry Division, small as it was, should have been there. In Sheridan's last dispatch, dated the 16th, he had distinctly told Wright to "close in Colonel Powell," who was then at Front Royal. Powell was not closed in. One brigade of his skeleton force, commanded by Colonel Moore was moved near the infantry, the only cavalry on that side of the army.

Early attacked at dawn; nothing between him and Wright's camps but a line of infantry pickets only a few hundred yards out. He swept them away like chaff, fell on Crook's demoralized camps, drove his half-dressed men in utter rout, then falling on the Nineteenth Corps in front, drove that, and finally crushed the left of the Sixth Corps, next in line. In less than an hour, Wright's army was all driven in confusion, twenty-four guns taken, the camps in possession of the enemy, and the Confederate line, in an enveloping crescent of flame, was pressing on, driving the scattered remains in confusion toward Winchester.

The only force left untouched was the cavalry on the extreme right of the army, and the only infantry division not broken to pieces was Getty's of the Sixth Corps. Wright had been thus far completely deceived. Expecting an attack on one flank, he had received it on the other, and by 10 o'clock the battle was virtually over. Between 9 and 10,

Wright, seeing his first mistake, tried to remedy it by ordering the cavalry to the left of the army, against Torbert's opinion. The latter however, obeyed the order, but on his own responsibility detached three regiments on the flank he was leaving to protect it.

The enemy had been trying Custer's pickets on the extreme right since daylight, but without success, being evidently in small force there. When the Union cavalry left, he began to press harder, and the three regiments were put to their utmost efforts to keep Rosser from breaking in and capturing the streams of fugitives going to the rear from the infantry.

Meantime, Moore's little brigade, which he noticed as being the only cavalry on the left of the Union army, had been cut off from the rest in the first attack, and was confronted by Lomax's brigade, stronger than himself. In no wise daunted, the plucky Moore sent back his trains to Winchester, and boldly attacked the Confederate infantry in rear until Lomax attacked him in turn. Then he formed across the pike, and stubbornly contested every foot of ground all the way to Middletown, thus saving the trains and fugitives from being broken in upon by Lomax, just as the three regiments on the other flank were doing with Rosser.

Merritt and Custer, recalled from the right and put in on the left, flung themselves on the advancing infantry and stayed the course of Early's victory. Colonel Powell, with the rest of his division, had joined Moore by this time, and the strange spectacle was beheld of six or seven thousand cavalry, with a few batteries, holding in check and repulsing charge after charge from an army of nearly twenty thousand infantry flushed with victory, and acting as a shelter, behind which at several miles distance Wright's broken infantry was hastily reforming.

The only infantry on the line with Custer and Merritt was Getty's division of the Sixth Corps. On this line, the enemy was held until 12 o'clock, by which time Wright had restored a semblance of order in the rear, and it seemed as if the battle was turning. From that time until 2 o'clock, Early ceased to advance, and at 2, General Sheridan arrived on the ground, reformed his whole line and finally ordered the advance which culminated in that crushing defeat of Early, so famous in history.

CEDAR CREEK

In the meantime, let us see what Early had been doing. His first conception and execution of the battle had been masterly. He had completely surprised Wright, and practically annihilated all the Union infantry but a single division. This and the cavalry, ten thousand men at most, were all that was left to oppose Early's infantry, strengthened by Kershaw's arrival to at least eighteen thousand men, while the Confederate cavalry, still four or five thousand strong, was untouched.

Cedar Creek Battlefield. The battle was the final Confederate invasion of the North. The Confederacy was never again able to threaten Washington, D.C. through the Shenandoah Valley, and the Union victory aided the reelection of Abraham Lincoln.

Yet Early ceased to advance, and his men began to plunder the Union camps, giving his enemy time to recuperate and reorganize. For this conduct, the general offers the excuse that his men were uncontrollable, and that to their plundering solely the after disaster was attributable. A calm review of the battle points to another cause, Early's improper use of his horse. Had he concentrated it at first on his right, he could have swept away the feeble resistance of Moore's brigade and cut in on all the stragglers and trains that continued their flight quite unmolested. Had he done that, the two hours delay of his infantry would not have mattered. Infantry are not supposed to pursue a defeated foe.

As it was, the same stragglers that under a vigorous pursuit of cavalry would have surrendered by whole brigades were gathered up and reformed by Wright, and subsequently by Sheridan. When the latter arrived, the rout was over, and Wright was entitled to claim that he had retrieved his first misfortune, and was ready to advance once more.

Sheridan's arrival, and his immense enthusiasm, effected a wonderful change in the beaten army. Much of the work of reorganization was already effected, but there was little hope that an advance would be made. A stand and a stubborn defense of what was left was the utmost that could apparently be hoped for. It required the magic of Sheridan's name and genius to transform defeat into such a complete victory. The enemy was skirmishing without much vigor, but preparing for a new advance. Early had gathered up most of his plunderers.

Sheridan's first step was to send his cavalry to its true post, on the flanks. It had been holding the infantry long enough. Accordingly, Custer's division was called out and sent off to the extreme right, while the rest of the Sixth Corps moved up to fill the gap. Merritt was sent off to the extreme left, and the Nineteenth Corps moved up to take his place. There was but little left of Crook's two divisions, but what there was went in with the rest, and the stragglers began to pour in from the rear once more. From two until four they kept coming in and Getty's line was prolonged further and further, and hasty breastworks being thrown up.

About three, Early's troops, flushed with victory, resumed their advance. They assaulted the centre of the line, and were repulsed. Their line was longer than Sheridan's, especially on the right, showing that fresh troops must have come in there. No sooner was the assault repulsed and the battle again languishing than Sheridan ordered a general advance, at 4 p.m., October 19th, 1864. That order may be said to have sounded the death knell of the Southern Confederacy, for it was the signal for the almost instant and total destruction of its last aggressive army in Virginia. The only parallel to the utter ruin of Early is found in that of Hood's army, two months later, by Thomas at

CEDAR CREEK

Nashville.

It was moreover, as sudden as the rout of the cavalry of Rosser and Lomax at Woodstock Races, but with this difference; Rosser and Lomax saved most of their men alive, only losing their guns and wagons. Good horses and spurs saved the rest. At Cedar Creek, Early's infantry was not so lucky. It was scooped in by hundreds. Just what Early had failed to do at 9 o'clock in the morning, Sheridan did at 4 in the evening. He used his cavalry as it should be used, and completed his victory. The history of the last advance is thus told by Sheridan:

> The attack was brilliantly made, and, as the enemy was protected by rail breastworks and stone fences, his resistance was very determined. His line of battle overlapped the right of mine, and by turning with this portion of it on the flank of the Nineteenth Corps, caused a slight momentary confusion. This movement was checked, however, by a charge of McMillan's brigade on the reentering angle, and the enemy's flanking party cut off. It was at this stage of the battle that Custer was ordered to charge, with his whole division, but though the order was promptly obeyed, it was not in time to capture the whole of the force thus cut off, and many escaped across Cedar Creek. Simultaneously with this charge, a combined movement of the whole line drove the enemy in confusion to the creek, where owing to the difficulties of crossing, his army became routed.

Torbert's account explains more fully the part taken by the cavalry:

> In the general advance, Brigadier-General Custer, commanding Third Division, left three regiments to attend to the cavalry in his front, and started with the balance of his division to take part in the advance on the enemy's infantry. Thus the cavalry advanced on both flanks, side by side with the infantry, charging the enemy's lines with an impetuosity they could not stand. The rebel army was soon routed and driven across Cedar Creek in confusion. The cavalry, sweeping on both flanks, crossed Cedar Creek about the same time, charged and broke the last line the enemy attempted to form (it was now after dark) and put out at full speed for their artillery and trains.
>
> The captures were forty-five guns (twenty-four being Union guns, lost in the morning and now recaptured) besides weapons, horses, prisoners and battle flags. Only night saved the whole of Early's army from capture. From thenceforth it may be said to have ceased to exist as an organized body of

any importance, Lee ceased to make any more efforts to save it, and all that there was of any value in the troops composing it was recalled to the Army of Northern Virginia, especially Kershaw's division.

Cedar Creek looking south toward Massanuttin Mountain. Today, the Cedar Creek Foundation Visitor Center including the center, bookstore, and souvenir shop is located in the center of the battlefield across from the land of Belle Grove.

The Battle of Cedar Creek completed the noteworthy commencement of Custer's fame as a cavalry division leader. Woodstock Races and Cedar Creek showed his abilities to give weight to a charge, obstinacy to a defense. In all his valley experience, he and Merritt were in constant rivalry as to results, and a comparison of their losses and captures will show just how they stood. It comes from Torbert's report:

The First division lost, during the whole campaign, 186 killed, 778 wounded, 594 missing, total 1558. The Third division lost 67 killed, 385 wounded, 321 missing, total 773.*

The captures were as follows: First division: 29 guns 12 caissons, 36 wagons, 40 ambulances, etc., 306 horses and mules, and 14 battle flags.

Third division: 29 guns, 30 caissons, 44 wagons, 23 ambulances, etc., 602 horses and mules and 6 battle flags.

---

* The smaller proportion of loss was probably due to the more rapid style of fighting adopted in the Third Division, but largely also to the fact that in the early part of the campaign it generally operated as an unit, while the First was pretty often cut up in detachments, on one occasion losing nearly the whole of a single regiment, that was cut off and surrounded while guarding an ambulance train. The assailants were Mosby's guerillas and two regiments of Ransom's cavalry, and the regiment lost nearly 200 men, the rest cutting their way out.

CEDAR CREEK

During this winter, Custer received, for his brilliant services in the campaign, the brevet of Major-General. Merritt was similarly decorated, and Colonels Gibbs of the Regular Brigade and Devin of the Second Brigade, First division, were made brigadiers. Both were comparatively elderly men, and deserved their promotion. Colonel Devin had been the senior colonel of the cavalry corps and in command of his brigade as early as January, 1863. General Gibbs was an old regular cavalry officer of many years experience. At the close of the war, Devin was brevetted major-general in the regular army, and made lieutenant-colonel of the Eighth cavalry, at the same time that Custer and Merritt received the same rank in the Seventh and Tenth cavalry respectively. Merritt is now colonel of the Fifth Cavalry. He graduated from West Point the year before Custer. Devin's regiment was the Sixth New York Cavalry, to which he was promoted in November, 1861, having before been captain in the First New York Militia Cavalry.

NOTE: At the close of this campaign, the flags captured by the cavalry were sent to Washington in Custer's charge, carried by the different men who had taken them. Custer, on his arrival in Washington, where Mrs. Custer had been during the campaign, hurried away to find her. By a curious instance of cross purposes, Mrs. Custer went to the War Department on purpose to see him, hearing of his coming with the flags. She was kindly received by Mr. Stanton, but was dreadfully frightened when she found herself among strangers and that her husband was not there. To add to her confusion, in came the sergeants with the captured flags, and a great deal of speechifying followed, ending by Mr. Stanton publicly introducing her to the brave fellows as the wife of their beloved general. While much embarrassed, the dear little lady acquitted herself splendidly, and said something appropriate to each. During the winter, she was able to remain with the general at his headquarters near Winchester.

THE LAST RAID

DURING the fall and winter of 1864-65, after the Battle of Cedar Creek, nothing of importance occurred, the army of Sheridan being concentrated around Winchester. The Sixth Corps was sent away to join Grant, and Merritt's division was sent through Chester Gap to raid on the interior. He met the enemy near Gordonsville, took a couple of guns, destroyed the railroad, and returned.

Custer raided out to Harrisonburg and returned about the same time, the middle of December. Both columns suffered very much from the cold, and no more movements were made during January, the cavalry receiving recruits doing its best to feed up its horses and get ready for spring work.

On the 5th February, Lieutenant-Colonel Whittaker of the First Connecticut Cavalry, Custer's division, went out with Colonel Young, Sheridan's chief of scouts, and they succeeded in capturing the renowned Harry Gilmor, the most active and enterprising partisan chief of whom the Confederates could boast after Mosby. The latter had by this time ceased to be capable of serious mischief; and Gilmor's capture cleared Sheridan's rear.

He began to think it was time to advance, and called in all his cavalry from cantonments around Winchester, starting out on the 27th February, on the last raid to be made by Sheridan's cavalry. The chief took with him Merritt, now Brevet Major-general, as chief of cavalry. Brigadier-General Devin commanded the First division, 4,787 men, and Brevet Major- General George A. Custer commanded the Third, 4,600 men. Each division had one section of artillery, and the train consisted of three baggage wagons, eight ambulances, twenty ammunition wagons and about three miles of pack mules. The horses were ill good flesh, and each carried thirty pounds of grain, with five days' rations for the

THE LAST RAID

men and coffee and sugar for ten days. One extra wagon laden with coffee and sugar accompanied the force, and that was all the train, except eight pontoons.

As it turned out, all the lightness and strength of the column was needed. Its destination was no less a place than Lynchburg, and thereafter it was to march into North Carolina to join Sherman, who was then moving north. This part of the programme was afterwards altered, through the impossibility of crossing the James River, the bridges being destroyed. Failing Lynchburg, the orders were to destroy all that was left of the Virginia Central Railroad and the James River Canal, then to return to Winchester. These orders Sheridan took the liberty to exceed, by joining Grant, just as the latter needed him worst.

Wrecked train near Richmond

On the 27th February, 1865, the great raiding column, with a total strength, including teamsters and artillerymen, of nine thousand four hundred and eighty four men, started up the valley. Before it was the valley pike, a splendid hard road on which in one or two spots there was actually dust; on each side were broad fields, softened by the early spring thaw into quagmires in which the horses sunk over their fetlocks. This pike lasted to Harrisonburg and beyond, some seventy miles, followed dirt roads in red Virginia clay.

FREDERICK WHITTAKER

The first day's march was to Woodstock, thirty miles, and nothing of interest occurred. All day long the steady clatter of hoofs was almost uninterrupted, a bright sky overhead, the men talking and singing, everybody in high spirits. Occasionally, on the side roads, on either flank, a glimpse could be caught of small parties of horsemen in grey, keeping pace with the column and evidently watching its movements. Once, a few men left the column to chase the nearest of these gentry, who kept almost within carbine range, but the state of the fields prevented active pursuit and the enemy were left unmolested.

Kline's Mill, Vaucluse, Virginia, built in 1794.

They were a few of Mosby's guerillas, latterly joined by some of Rosser's cavalry, but no damage was done by or to them. Sheridan's policy to the guerillas in general was to leave them alone. They served, as he naively tells us in his reports, as "a very good provost guard for his army," and prevented straggling.

Next morning, at daybreak, the column moved on twenty-nine miles further to within nine miles of Harrisonburg. At daybreak of the 1st of March, the advance pressed on through Harrisonburg and Mount Crawford to Kline's Mills. The advance that day was given to Custer's division, and the march was long and wearisome, the mud beginning to be troublesome. Devin's rear did not get into camp until four in the morning. Next day, by right, he should have had the advance, but work was growing nearer now and Sheridan told Custer to press on.

Rosser's men had come out during the day, and tried to burn a bridge over one of the forks of the Shenandoah. Rosser had about three hundred men. Colonel Capehart's brigade, of Custer's division, came up in time, swam the river above the bridge, charged Rosser, sent him flying, saved the bridge and cleared the way for their comrades.

Kline's Mills are seven miles from Staunton, where Early had his headquarters; and he, poor fellow, seeing his rest so rudely disturbed, left Staunton and went to Waynesboro, ten miles further on, leaving word at Staunton that he was "coming back to fight." Now it was that a man of rapid decision and fiery energy like Custer was worth his weight in gold. A slower and more methodical man would have utterly failed in the task set him next day. It was to reach Waynesboro seventeen miles off, in the midst of a driving rainstorm, on a dirt road, mud up to the horses' knees everywhere, and up to their bellies in the mud holes, to cross a river of unknown depth, and to attack and whip Early, who had an unknown force.

He did it with the triumphant success that always marked his independent efforts. He had three brigades, each about 1,500 strong, commanded by Colonels Wells, Pennington and Capehart; and Devin was to follow with Gibbs, Fitzhugh's and Stagg's brigades, of Merritt's old division. Sheridan's record is brief and to the point:

> General Custer found General Early as he had promised, at Waynesboro, in a well chosen position, with two brigades of infantry and some cavalry under General Rosser, the infantry occupying breastworks.
>   Custer, without waiting for the enemy to get up courage over the delay of a careful reconnoissance, made his dispositions for attack at once, sending three regiments around the left flank of the enemy, which was somewhat exposed by being advanced from, instead of resting upon, the bank of the river in his immediate rear; he, with the other two brigades, partly mounted and partly dismounted, at a given signal boldly attacked and impetuously carried the enemy's works, while the Eighth New York and First Connecticut Cavalry, who were formed in columns of fours, charged over the breastworks and continued the charge through the streets of Waynesboro, sabring a few

men as they went along, and did not stop until they had crossed the South Fork of the Shenandoah, which was immediately in General Early's rear, where they formed as foragers, and with drawn sabres held the east bank of the stream.

The enemy threw down their arms and surrendered, with cheers at the suddenness with which they were captured. The general officers present at this engagement were Generals Early, Rosser, Long, Wharton, and Lilley; and it has always been a wonder to me how they escaped, unless they hid in obscure places in the houses of the town.

Custer pushed on after Early's trains, and did not halt until he got to the Blue Ridge. The results of this capture, made by Custer, single-handed, were eleven guns, complete with caissons, teams, etc., two hundred wagons, sixteen hundred prisoners, and seventeen battle flags. He had fully balanced his account of rivalry with the First Division, and passed it fairly. His loss was insignificant, owing entirely to the dash and rapidity of his fighting.

That night he crossed the Blue Ridge and encamped on the other side, in full view of that mysterious land which had been a sealed book for the Federal army, the country where lay Charlottesville, Gordonsville, Columbia, the upper James, never visited since the short and hasty raid of Stoneman at the time of Chancellorsville, and then only hastily skimmed in fear and trembling. Thanks to Custer, it was now open to our forces in every direction, with not an enemy nearer than Petersburg, and the end was coming fast.

Devin's division camped at Waynesboro that night, and the cavalry corps was divided. The horses had been suffering fearfully from grease-heel and scratches ever since they had left the pike and entered the mud roads. The great fatigue, the poor food and finally the change from oats to corn when they used up their first forage and lived off the country, was running them lame by fifties and hundreds. Only the toughest were able to march well enough to be trusted on a further raid through the mud of the low countries, and the next day's work to Charlottesville promised to be worse than the road to Waynesboro.

It was necessary to send back the Confederate prisoners and train to Winchester, and with that object a column of 1,500 men under

THE LAST RAID

Colonel Thompson, First New Hampshire Cavalry, was detached at Waynesboro, and ordered back to Winchester. Colonel Thompson went off, followed by Rosser, who made a fierce attack on him at Mount Jackson, thirty miles from Winchester, trying to rescue the prisoners. Rosser failed to do this; and lost instead some of his own men, whom Thompson took safely in with him.

The valley being tranquil, Sheridan resumed his march, Custer ahead as usual. The young general did not seem to like to give up the advance, rule or no rule, and Sheridan indulged him. Custer marched to Charlottesville, and was met outside the town by a polite deputation, headed by the Mayor, who brought him the keys of the public buildings. Here, the whole command rested two days until the train could be brought up, the roads being in horrible condition. The two divisions, now reduced to about eight thousand men all told, enjoyed themselves hugely at Charlottesville, forage and food being plentiful. Parties were sent out to destroy the railroads, and did so in the most effectual manner, but the necessary delay caused Sheridan to abandon all idea of reaching Lynchburg.

On the 4th of March, the real business of the raid began. Merritt took the First Division, went up the James River Canal to Scottsville, and returned to Columbia. Sheridan took Custer's division to Amherst Court House. Each column on its way destroyed every piece of public property likely to be of use to the enemy, blew up the locks of the canal, ruined it utterly, burned the flour mills and factories, and made a dash for the bridges at Dugaldsville and Hardwicksville. It was Sheridan's intention, had he saved the bridges, to have crossed the river, struck for Appomattox Court House, and so forced Lee to come out and probably surrender a month earlier than he afterwards did.

But the bridges were burned before he could get there, and he was left complete master of all the country north of the James. He could no longer get at the enemy, nor could the latter get at him either. When the columns united at New Market on the James River, Sheridan finally determined on his grand stroke of joining Grant. His plan involved marching down the north bank of the James, destroying the canal as he went.

FREDERICK WHITTAKER

Only one danger remained. The railroad from Richmond to Gordonsville remained open for some distance, and it was probable that Lee might send out a heavy force of infantry to crush Sheridan. Custer and Devin were ordered to spread out in different directions and cut this road as near Richmond as they could get. They accomplished the feat successfully, and Sheridan's scouts soon brought him news that showed him what he had escaped by not crossing the James. It turned out that Pickett's division of infantry and Fitzhugh Lee's cavalry were waiting for him on the Southside Railroad, but that no movement had been made from Richmond to the north.

When Custer struck the Gordonsville Railroad at Frederickshall, he came on some very agreeable intelligence in the telegraph office. It informed him that the irrepressible Early was not either dead or sleeping. The telegram was from Early to Lee, stating that he was following Sheridan with two hundred cavalry, and intended to strike him in rear about daylight. The news tickled Custer immensely. He at once dispatched a regiment after the unfortunate Early, caught and destroyed his party, and nearly took Early himself, the latter swimming the South Anna to escape, accompanied by a single orderly, after a campaign in which he lost all his army, every piece of artillery and all his trains.

Through the country to the north of Richmond, Custer and Merritt now roamed at will for more than a week. On the 14th March, Custer's scouting parties burned a railway within eleven miles of Richmond itself, while Merritt burned the bridges over the North and South Anna Rivers. By this time, Sheridan's scouts had reached Grant and returned with the welcome news that supplies awaited the cavalry at Whitehouse Landing on the Peninsula. The way there was open.

Lee was at Petersburg, on the other side of the James, and could not send much force through to the north of Richmond, but what he had he sent. Another telegram was captured, dated at Hanover Junction. It was from Longstreet, addressed to a Colonel Haskell, presumably a cavalry officer hovering round Sheridan. It directed Haskell to "follow the enemy if he goes east," and to observe whether he struck for the Rapidan or the Peninsula.

THE LAST RAID

Next day, Custer and Devin struck Ashland, to the northwest of Richmond, on the Gordonsville road. Prisoners taken reported Pickett's and Johnson's divisions of infantry, at least 12,000 men, with Fitzhugh Lee's cavalry division of 4,000 men, only four miles off, waiting to bag Sheridan, Longstreet in command. This was all Sheridan wanted to know. By his feints, he had drawn the slow moving infantry far away from Whitehouse Landing, which is on the Pamunkey River, on the north side of the Peninsula.

Burned railroad cars near Richmond

He pretended an attack with Pennington's brigade of Custer's division, and moved off towards the Whitehouse. Longstreet soon saw it was no use for him to follow with infantry, and Fitzhugh Lee did not dare, single handed, his force being so far inferior to Sheridan's. The latter took his time, reaching Whitehouse on the 19th March, to be welcomed by gunboats and supplies.

Longstreet returned to Lee. He knew how much he was wanted. The end was coming faster and faster. Sheridan rested at Whitehouse five days, feeding his horses on all the oats they could eat. Supplies were prodigal, and with reason. The government had saved nearly a month's subsistence for ten thousand men, and the Confederates had during the whole raid fed Sheridan's men on the fat of the land. On the 24th March, the refreshed column started, crossed the Peninsula, and reached the James, filed over the long pontoon bridge, and finally on the 26th, went into camp at the rear of Grant's army, which lay in front of Petersburg. The last raid was over, and Custer was coming to that brief and brilliant campaign which was to complete his glory and leave him a full major-general at twenty-six years of age.

Captain Alexander Pennington

FIVE FORKS

ON the 27th of March, the cavalry corps went into camp behind the extreme left of Grant's Army of the Potomac, at Hancock Station. This station was the terminus of the military railroad, which ran from flank to flank of the besiegers, occupying as they did a line of nearly fifteen miles in length. There they had lain in front of Lee's lines at Petersburg for some nine weary months, in the monotony of siege operations, wherein incessant picket firing and equally incessant artillery duels by day were alternated with pauses of sulky repose, after a more than common expenditure of ammunition.

The only reliefs to the monotony had been found in the occasional attempts of the Federals to extend their left wing and turn Lee's right. These attempts had taken place at various intervals, the most desperate and successful having been made by the Second Corps under the lead of Hancock. This cause led to the naming of the last station of the military railroad after that dashing corps commander.

So far, Lee had succeeded in maintaining his main position intact, in spite of the inferior numbers with which he confronted Grant. His skillful use of fortifications made his lines impregnable, and he was able to hold them one against ten with little difficulty or danger. Thus he could always spare for the threatened flank sufficient force to repel any assault and prevent the turning of his position. The country on that flank was for some distance much like the Wilderness he had found so favorable for defense - a desolate land of scrub woods, abandoned tobacco fields and dirt roads, where the defense and attack were alike depressing to the spirits, and where knowledge of the country was the one point of importance.

When Sheridan, with Custer's and Devin's divisions, went into camp at Hancock Station, he received an accession of force. The old

FIVE FORKS

Second Cavalry division; once Gregg's, was restored to its old comrades, this time under the command of General Crook. Poor Crook was, at the moment of joining, under a cloud. He had done very well in the Valley under Sheridan's command, until late in the winter. Then, owing to inexcusable negligence, he was one night snapped up in his headquarters by a party of guerillas, carried off and made a prisoner. At the close of the winter he was exchanged, and found himself at Petersburg, where he was given the command of this little division.

Robert E. Lee. Lee was married to Mary Anna Randolph Custis, great-granddaughter of Martha Washington by her first husband Daniel Parke Custis, and step-great-granddaughter of George Washington.

The curious and very unphilosophical grades of rank in the Federal army at that time, as contrasted with those of the Confederates, was illustrated by the number of major-generals in the cavalry corps. Sheridan, Crook, Merritt and Custer, were all major-generals, the last two being brevets assigned. Devin and Gibbs were brigadiers. The assignment to command of each was curious. Sheridan seemed to have a sort of roving commission to go where he pleased and Merritt was in the same interesting condition. Devin, Custer and Crook each had a division, though each held a different rank, the first a brigadier, the second a brevet major-general, the third a full major-general. Gibbs, although of the same rank as Devin, had only a brigade, and all the other brigade commanders under Custer and Devin were colonels. Crook's division was the only one that was properly and philosophically officered, having three brigadiers for the brigades, and a major-general for the division.

Apart from all these confusions of rank, the anomalous position of Merritt in the campaign, as well as that of Sheridan, was marked. Nominally, Merritt had been commander of Custer and Devin, but inasmuch as both seemed to be able to take care of themselves, he really became very much like the fifth wheel on a caisson, only useful in case of accidents. Actually, he was most of the time occupied as a sort of dry nurse for Devin, who was a slow and cautious officer, new to the control of a division, and in the mixed movements of the following campaign, very apt to get confused and miss opportunities.

Devin was one of those safe, steady men who always like to keep their enemy straight in front, and who lose their heads if they find themselves surrounded. For a stubborn defense or straight ahead movement, no one was better; but he always did best where he could see his whole battlefield. In the midst of such haphazard combinations as distinguished the campaign before Gettysburg, so long as Devin was united to the division to which his brigade was attached, he did splendidly; and under the fostering care of John Buford, who knew well how to develop his officers, the steady old colonel of volunteers, all guiltless of West Point as he was, became a first-rate brigade commander who could be trusted out alone on his own responsibility.

For such a series of movements as distinguished the Five Forks campaign to Appomattox, Devin was too slow, and when compared to the brilliant keen-witted Custer, appeared to singular disadvantage, save at the battle of Five Forks, where his division had nothing to do but straight bull-dog fighting. He utterly lacked that keen instinct, which seemed inborn in Custer, that told him where an enemy might be safely pushed and when the most reckless audacity would pay. While Devin was reconnoitring and getting ready to fight, Custer was already half through his battle; and before Devin was fairly engaged, on several

FIVE FORKS

occasions he found Custer had snatched away the prize from under his very nose, gaining glory, guns and flags, with little comparative danger, while Devin was wondering what it was all about, and when the enemy were going to charge.

The trouble was that Devin was old, and Custer young. The quick wit of the latter made him invincible; and Merritt, who was paralyzed by the divided nature of his command, appeared to the same disadvantage as Devin. The result of the whole campaign was that Custer was invariably triumphant. Everything he did succeeded, failure seemed unknown to him, and the surrender at Appomattox left him with the highest individual fame as a cavalry commander of any man except Sheridan.

His name and figure, when only a division commander, were better known all through the Union, and attracted more compliments from Confederates than those of any corps commander then in the Army of the Potomac, and we question much whether at that time there was not far more curiosity to see Custer than either Meade, Hancock, Burnside or Hooker, or indeed any one short of Grant, Sherman and Sheridan. Custer came right behind them in the popular favor and enthusiasm; and it was mainly owing to his series of brilliant successes in this, his last campaign against a civilized foe.

Of course this fact (popular favor) attracted much envy to Custer, and much detraction from him. Hardly a cavalry officer outside of his own commands but was intensely jealous of him, and detraction was ready to belittle all of his exploits. A great deal of this was due to the boasting and sarcastic remarks of his injudicious friends, who could not be satisfied with praising their own chief without depreciating others. This caused a good deal of bitter feeling at the time; and added to the fact that part of Custer's success in the last campaign was due to his perception of the demoralization of the enemy, gave rise to many sneers at Custer's captures, which were ascribed by his detractors to mere luck, without serious fighting.

A cool and candid examination of the evidence however, shows that "Custer's luck" was peculiar to Custer himself, and coming to other men would have been lost. It consisted mainly in the quickness with which he seized every opportunity as soon as it occurred, and this quickness was entirely owing to the difference of his method of directing a battle from that adopted by most general officers.

The prevalent custom among commanders, whether of companies, regiments, brigades, divisions, corps or armies, when their commands are in a battle, is to take post in rear of the centre of the line, whence they can see all or most of the line of battle of their own men, and be able to order in reserves to any threatened part of the line. For a defensive position this is well, and if an eminence can be secured for the commander, from which he can survey the field, so much the better. If the country is open and the enemy in plain sight from the commander's post, nothing better could be desired.

The ideally perfect position for such a general would be up in a balloon, from whence he could see both armies spread out as on a chess board, and direct the operations of his own by telegraph. Unfortunately, no means has yet been found by which a balloon can be anchored at a great elevation in any weather except a dead calm, and consequently the balloon plan has been abandoned, lofty hills being preferred.

Some commanders, like McClellan at Antietam, take the highest ground in the neighborhood, no matter how far back it is, and trust to their glasses to tell them of the movements. This again, is only possible in an open country. In a heavily wooded place, such as the Wilderness or the vicinity of Five Forks, no chief in rear of the centre of his line can learn anything of what is going on, save by listening to the firing and requiring constant reports to be sent in from the skirmish line.

There is however, another position which may be taken by a leader in any country and which offers special advantages in a closely wooded one. This position was the one habitually taken by Custer. It was up with the skirmish line itself, keeping in constant motion from end to end of the line. This position has many advantages over the rear centre post. The general sees more, and knows by experience over what ground his men are going. He sees as much as anyone can, for he is nearest to the enemy. If the latter falters or presses, he is on the spot and gives suitable orders, *viva voce*, not through an aide-de-camp.

FIVE FORKS

The only orders he needs to send are those which go to the reserves in rear. Moreover, his constant presence is a great encouragement to the soldiers, who value kind words exactly in proportion to the rank of the person from whom they come. The general who shares their dangers they are ready to adore, after one or two battles, as Custer always found.

The objections to this position for a general are two. First, it is fatiguing and uses up horses very fast. Second, the general may get shot. These risks Custer always took, along with Sheridan, Phil Kearny and one or two others in the army who followed the same plan. To be always in the advance, and always in rapid motion, was their secret. It showed them the opportunities the moment they occurred. This was the secret, the real secret, of Custer's wonderful success in Sheridan's last campaign, and the difference between him and Devin. While the latter was watching his own line, Custer was watching that of the enemy. Who shall deny that his laurels were fairly won?

It was a fine sight to see Custer and his staff on the field during that last campaign. The appearance of the leader had slightly changed since he was brevetted major-general. The old blue shirt, with its star in the corner remained, but the velvet jacket was replaced by a blue sack with major-general's shoulder straps, and his trousers were now of the regulation sky blue. The cavalier hat, long curls and flaunting red necktie were as conspicuous as ever, and every man in the division had apparently mounted the same insignia, with an attempt to imitate the careless grace of their leader. There were more shocks of long, shaggy, unkempt hair in the Third Division than anywhere else in the army. As for neckties, Custer's division could be recognized a mile off by its fluttering, scarlet handkerchiefs, and they were to be met with all over the country.

With his forces under this leadership, Sheridan left camp on the 29th of March, starting out to the extreme left of the army. It was Grant's first intention that the cavalry should only make a raid in Lee's rear, cut the Southside Railway and after ravaging the country, join Sherman's force. It was expected that this raid would be a long and weary one, and Sheridan weeded his force of all weak and broken down horses and dismounted men, who were left at Petersburg.

It will give some idea of how tremendously severe the last raid through the mud had been on Sheridan's horses, to note the numbers he now took with him. The First and Third divisions had started from Winchester, a month before, 9484 strong. They had been weeded of 1500 men at Waynesboro, leaving about 8000 men; and now all they could muster was 5700 men all told, fit for a march. To this, 5700 was added Crook's 3300 men, and at a later date McKenzie's skeleton cavalry division from the Army of the James, 1000 strong. This made Sheridan's total cavalry force 10,000 men, and to his command was subsequently added the Fifth Corps.

Sheridan was no longer attached to the Army of the Potomac. He took his orders direct from Grant, without the interposition of Meade, and the fact of his having been made a major-general in the regular army made him senior to everyone but Meade. Grant gave him a sort of general command over the left wing of the Army of the Potomac during the subsequent operations.

On the 29th March, the cavalry moved out of the lines, striking off to the southwest. The first night, they crossed Hatcher's Run, and moved on in the direction of Dinwiddie Court House, which was reached by Devin, who had the advance, about 5 o'clock. Devin and Crook went into camp there. Custer was left behind at Hatcher's Run (called Rowanty Creek there, having been joined by Gravelly Run). It had begun to rain, the roads were horrible, the creek was only bridged by pontoons, and it was supposed that Fitzhugh Lee's cavalry was off to the south, ready to pounce on Sheridan's trains if he saw an opportunity. It turned out that this was an error.

The Confederate cavalry was really to the north, inside of Lee's lines, on the very right of his army. Sheridan, by his rapid march, had left a gap of about ten miles between himself and the head of the Union column of infantry. This was composed of the Fifth Corps, near Custer, and the Second Corps next behind it.

On the morning of the 30th of March,* Sheridan sent Devin,

---

* During the night of the 29th March, Grant changed his mind as to Sheridan's ultimate disposition, and sent him word to that effect. He had passed the flank of

FIVE FORKS

together with Davies' brigade of Crook's force from Dinwiddie, due north to gain Five Forks on the White Oak Road. Sheridan himself remained behind to help out Custer and the trains, a job which was not over at dark of the 30th. Devin came to Five Forks, and found the enemy in such force that he could not dislodge him. It rained all day, and Devin's pickets were fighting all the time, but made no impression.

Dinwiddie Court House. The drawing depicts General Sheridan with his cavalry officers Custer, Merritt, Devin and Crook, leaving the court house on March 31st, 1865 to reconnoiter Five Forks.

The position on the morning of the 31st was this. (See map) Sheridan was at Dinwiddie, about seven miles from the head of the infantry, over roads so muddy that the distance must be doubled to give an idea of the time necessary for help to reach him. Grant's column was circling around Lee's left, but the latter saw an opportunity for a brilliant stroke. It was to send down a heavy force by the White Oak Road to Five Forks, smash Devin, roll him back on Sheridan, and crush the latter, separating him from Grant by entering the gap between them. To do this, Lee detached Pickett's division, part of Johnson's and all the

---

Lee's army. Instead of sending him off to ravage the country and join Sherman, Grant now ordered him to turn on Lee's right flank. This order was the one that sent Devin to Five Forks, and determined the issue of the campaign.

Confederate Cavalry. The whole force was about 11,000 men. The only trouble was, Lee did it too late. Had he struck Devin and Sheridan on the 30th, the Fifth Corps was still out of supporting distance. On the evening of the 31st, it was within five miles of Sheridan.

He tried it on the 31st, in the style in which Lee always delivered his attacks. It was carefully and secretly prepared, and executed about two in the afternoon. Striking Devin, whose total force did not exceed four thousand men, of which one-fourth were horse-holders, the fighting being dismounted, the Confederates drove him out of the woods into the road to Dinwiddie with crushing force. They formed a perfect horseshoe of fire around the little division, and resistance was useless. It was made however, with that savage obstinacy peculiar to dismounted cavalry covering the retreat of their horses. The men held on till the beasts were out of danger, rallied and charged again and again, and finally emerged in the fields, repulsed but not conquered, having saved every horse and gun, and without the loss of a prisoner.

This was the last brilliant move Lee's army, or any portion of it, ever made. This dashing corps of eleven thousand men, starting from the White Oak Road, first drove back the head of the Fifth Corps, then swung over and beat Devin, followed him down the road and charged Crook, and was only brought to a final halt in front of Dinwiddie Court House by the rest of the cavalry corps, deployed in the open fields, dismounted. Devin's division was separated from the rest. Custer brought up two brigades from the belated train and with three others managed to hold the victorious foe until night, when Pickett rested on his arms in front of Dinwiddie Court House.

Such was the position at nightfall of the 31st. Sheridan was isolated, and Pickett was in front of him, but a glance at the diagram will show that Pickett was also isolated from Lee and that Warren, with the Fifth Corps, was right behind Pickett. All Warren had to do was to move down the Boydton Plank Road to strike the enemy directly in the rear.

Sheridan saw this plainly enough, and sent another officer to Warren, telling him to "attack Pickett at daylight." It appears from General Warren's "Narrative," that Sheridan misconceived Warren's

FIVE FORKS

position; imagining that he was about two miles nearer to Five Forks than he really was. Actually, the bulk of the Fifth Corps was nearly six miles off, but Warren's headquarters were only four miles from Sheridan's, on the Boydton Plank Road. We have been careful to take, in regard to the subsequent battle, the exact statements of fact of General Warren as true, and it seems quite clear that the difficulty which ensued between the two generals was one of temperament wholly.

Warren was a cool, cautious, methodical man, whose training as an engineer had assisted to make him, like McClellan, careful and painstaking. He did his very best, but his temperament rendered it an absolute impossibility for Warren to do anything in a hurry. Sheridan, on the other hand, was rapid and impetuous, and his contact with such a totally dissimilar character as Warren was sure to bring difficulty, unless indeed the latter, like Devin, was willing to obey orders blindly, no matter what the consequences to himself.

This, however, was just what Warren's character again rendered him incapable of doing. Being a polished and perfectly educated soldier who had graduated high at West Point, he set a value on his own notion of how a thing should be done, and this is very evident in his "Narrative." When Sheridan asked him to hurry, he replied in effect that he was doing the best he could; he differed in opinion from Sheridan as to the proper place of a general on the battlefield; and whenever the opinions of the two came in conflict, as they did on almost every point of real importance, Warren stuck to his own opinion, and tacitly implied that he was going to do as he pleased. This fact develops itself in his subsequent "Narrative," in one very important point on which we have already touched in speaking of the difference between Custer and Devin.

Sheridan's idea of the proper place of a general was at the front, in rapid motion, where he could see for himself. Warren's idea was that of rear of the centre, and out of fire. He justifies it in the following sentence in his narrative. "While giving orders thus, I did not think it proper to leave my place in the open field, because it was one where my staff officers, sent to different parts of the command, could immediately find me on their return, and thus I could get information from all points at once, and utilize the many eyes of my staff and those of my subordinate commanders, instead of going to some special point myself, and neglecting all others."

This sentence shows the radical difference between the two men. It was a clash of wills, and Warren would not yield. Sheridan sent word to him, that night, where the cavalry was, and where the enemy was; also that he, Warren, was behind the enemy. He concluded, "I will hold on here. Possibly they may attack Custer at daylight; if so, attack instantly and in full force. Attack at daylight anyhow."

He pointed out that by so doing, Sheridan and Warren could bag the whole of Pickett's isolated force. The message reached Warren at 4:50 a.m., April 1st; too late for obedience. The Fifth Corps could not get to Sheridan by daylight, as the nearest brigade was four miles off, and the sun rose at six. It seems too, that although Sheridan knew Warren was under his orders, Warren did not. It was not until an hour and a half after receipt of Sheridan's order that Warren received one from Meade, the immediate commander of the Army of the Potomac, directing him "to report to Sheridan."

As it happened, no harm was done. Pickett was just as astute as Sheridan. He saw his danger, and quietly left in the morning, falling back to Five Forks where he held a line of breastworks to the north of the White Oak Road; and there the cavalry followed him. The position was some three miles to the north of Dinwiddie, and about three miles and a half to the west of Warren. The latter did not join Sheridan, under his orders, until eleven o'clock.

One can fancy how this must have irritated the impatient cavalry leader. His men had been out since six o'clock, pushing Pickett back to Five Forks, and here was Pickett before him, separated by a gap of about five miles from Lee's army while Warren, with 15,000 men, ready to occupy that gap, was letting the precious moments slip. It seemed almost impossible that Pickett could be fool enough to stay where he was, to be trapped; and it was much more reasonable to suppose, from his obstinate attitude, that Lee was bringing up more forces behind to serve Sheridan as he had served Devin. In such a case, an ugly and disheartening check to the Army of the Potomac, such as had happened so often before, was pretty certain.

When at last Warren was up, Sheridan did not hurry him unduly. McKenzie's little division reported to the general at the same time, coming down the White Oak Road, and brought the news that the country in that direction was clear, so that it was settled that the gap between Lee and Pickett really existed. Sheridan sent back McKenzie to Dinwiddie as a reserve, and to guard the trains while Custer and Devin, under Merritt's orders, proceeded to assault the works at Five Forks, threatening especially to turn the right flank of the enemy. Not until one o'clock did Sheridan deem the attack sufficiently serious to hold the enemy; then he sent word to Warren to bring up his infantry, which was lying about half a mile from the works. It was ordered to advance in the following order:

Ayres and Crawford's divisions in the first line, and Griffin's behind Crawford, were to strike the left of Pickett's line and sweep down behind the breastworks, while Custer and Devin were to charge home in front. Crook was not engaged. It must be remembered that Custer and Devin, with only 5,700 men, had been fighting and driving the enemy all the morning, and that the Fifth Corps had not yet struck a blow that day.

Imagine then, the impatience with which Sheridan saw Warren bringing up his corps of 15,000 men, the order given at one o'clock, and he not ready until four. Three whole hours consumed in putting a single corps, already massed, into line of battle, were more than enough, and we can see the sarcasm of the remark which Sheridan made to him, as Warren reports in the "Narrative." "General Sheridan expressed to me his apprehension that our cavalry, which continued to fire on the enemy, would use up all their ammunition before my troops would be ready. I informed him that they would not all be in position before four p.m."

Here, the difference of the two men was again manifest. Sheridan was all hurry, with no such word as "impossible;" Warren, with a constitutional inability to hurry, was finding so many things impossible.

At last however, Warren was ready, and advanced. After that, he had no more trouble. With a simultaneous charge, Pickett's men and Wise's brigade were swept out of existence as an organized body, and Five Forks was won. As soon as Warren entered the fight, Sheridan at once possessed twenty thousand men to Pickett's ten, and the surrender of the Confederate infantry was a foregone conclusion. When the Fifth Corps charged, Custer and Devin followed suit, swept over the breastworks, and captured all the guns and battle flags in the works. Pickett was no longer a division commander.

No sooner was the fight fairly over, than Sheridan sent a curt note to Warren. "Major-General Warren, commanding the Fifth Army Corps, is relieved from duty, and will report at once for orders to Lieutenant General Grant, commanding armies United States." It came like a thunderbolt to Warren. He had evidently not expected it. He, even in his "Narrative," seems to be seriously impressed with the idea that the victory at Five Forks was owing to his exertions, and that he had done his whole duty, for which he should have been praised. He complains in this "Narrative" of the peculiar hardship and injustice of relieving him at the very moment when he had done his work and was triumphantly successful.

After a careful examination and comparison of his account with that of Sheridan, the conduct of the latter is easy to explain. Sheridan was above all things a practical soldier, with little solicitude for anyone's feelings in a matter where success was involved. When he found, as he early did, that he and Warren could not pull together, there is little doubt that he determined to relieve him, as he had the power to do. But to have relieved Warren from command at the commencement of a movement like this – an assault in force - would have been very perilous. Had he been suddenly removed, it would have involved a change of leaders all through the corps, unfamiliar officers, and a prospect of failure, with a perfect certainty of delay even greater than Warren caused.

Through Sheridan's own activity in reaching Dinwiddie Court House in a single day, he had gained time on the enemy, and Lee's hesitation to abandon Petersburg had given him more. It was clear that the cavalry could hold Pickett stationary until night, and a single hour was time enough to consummate the victory of Five Forks, once the combined attack was made. Sheridan weighed his chances and calculated that he would have just about enough time, even if he gave Warren his own way, which he did.

Success attained, he had no further need to keep Warren, and every reason to get rid of him. In the further prosecution of the campaign, activity and hearty cooperation were absolutely necessary, and neither of these was to be looked for from Warren. Sheridan wanted a man who would obey orders, not dispute them, and Warren's weakness lay in the latter direction. By the sudden exercise of arbitrary power, there is no doubt that Sheridan made a bitter enemy of Warren, and excited much ill-feeling in the whole Fifth Corps, but the practical success of the future movements in pursuit justified him to the country.

Rightly considered, the relief of Warren was no discredit to that officer, as a soldier employed in scientific warfare. He was as good a commander as he had ever been, but in the pursuit of Lee, scientific warfare was not needed so much as unremitting activity. The enemy had little or no force left to fight in open country; the only difficulty was to catch him. Warren was an engineer, Sheridan a huntsman, and the latter needed more huntsmen, not engineers. The best proof that Warren's relief was not regarded by Grant as an indication of incapacity was afforded by Warren's almost immediate assignment to the command of the Department of the Mississippi. He was as good as ever for any purpose, except the one for which Sheridan needed him, that was all.

We have been somewhat lengthy in our account of the difficulty between Warren and Sheridan at Five Forks, because it is essential to the complete understanding of the campaign in which Custer bore so important a part. Another thing must be taken into account in estimating the subsequent operations, to explain the difference between the cavalry and infantry.

When Sheridan arrived at Petersburg, he came from a campaign in the open field, wherein entrenchments had played no part. He was used to activity, as were his cavalry. He found the Army of the Potomac enfeebled by a long siege, of which the effects are well known.

They disincline men to long marches and active exertions. What was a mere bagatelle to Sheridan's riders was a terribly long march to the infantry, fresh from winter quarters, out of condition and heavily loaded as they were. Infantry generals are so much used to being hampered by the exhaustion of their men, that they are apt to sink down and pronounce a long march "impossible," especially at the beginning of a campaign.

It needed all the fiery energy of Sheridan and the example of the cavalry to nerve the infantry up to their work. They would fight as well as ever, but had got out of the habit of marching; and it was marching that was now needed. Moreover, so used was the whole army to encountering a foe rendered formidable by fortifications, and always ready to fight, that it was not dreamed of by any until some days after that Lee was on his way to surrender. Besides Grant, Sheridan seems to have been the only man who had the idea, and it was he who suggested it to Grant, in his laconic dispatch, "I think, if things are pushed, Lee will surrender." The still more laconic reply of Grant is equally well known; "Push things." Sheridan did push them, and his right arm was Custer.

The present chapter, while part of the life of Custer, has unavoidably wandered away from him to the principal actors in the Battle of Five Forks. Custer's division had not had the advance on the march to Dinwiddie, and the difficulties with road and train had kept it back to Rowanty Creek, all of the thirteenth of March and until evening of the thirty-first. Even then, only two of Custer's brigades were able to get up to help Crook's two brigades and one of Devin's, and it was these five brigades that held Pickett's entire force that evening.

In the morning of the first of April, Custer and Devin did all the fighting in advance, Crook being held in reserve. Custer's division held the extreme left of the line, threatening Pickett's right. The fighting was dismounted and quite severe, the cavalry driving back the enemy from two lines of defense to the last breastwork at Five Forks. Here they stopped, a lull taking place in the fight at noon until one o'clock when the assault was resumed and seriously pressed.

The dismounted lines of skirmishers never dreamed but what it was their duty to carry the works unassisted, and with that notion, savage over the reverses of the day previous, they made two desperate charges over the tangled brushwood, piled in front of the works, right in the teeth of the rebel infantry. The heaviest fire fell on Devin, who occupied the centre, but Custer's men, by their audacity in trying to turn Pickett's flank, suffered nearly as heavily. It was their bitter and determined assaults that caused Sheridan's sarcastic remark to Warren about the ammunition. When at last the rolling volleys of the Fifth Corps, to the right of the enemy, showed they were really at work, the excitement of the cavalry rose once more.

Twice they had been repulsed before the fearful fire from the works, but now they rose again. Their eagerness was changed to a perfect frenzy a moment later when Sheridan himself, with his battle flag behind him, and all his staff, came galloping down the line through a storm of bullets, waving his sword and pointing onwards. In a moment, every brigade commander caught the impulse and dashed forward, while Custer, his red necktie and golden curls shining like a star, galloped out in front of his line and rode right at the breastwork. Such a yell was never heard as then burst from the whole line of men as they swept forward. The volleys of the enemy were answered by a perfect hell fire from the carbines, and the works were taken with a rush.

What a spectacle presented itself then! A crowd of fleeing men in grey, running wildly and confusedly together from side to side, while a long line of fire and smoke was coming through the woods from the right sweeping away the hapless Confederates. Only for a moment that sight was seen and the next the grey-coated crowds were throwing down their arms and waving their handkerchiefs, or anything white, in token of surrender.

The battle was over, the Confederate infantry annihilated. What was left of the cavalry made its escape to the left of Custer and struck off to the west, followed by McKenzie's and Custer's men for about six miles after dark. The last fight had been fought. The pursuit was now to begin, and Custer had the advance.

APPOMATTOX

THE night of the 1st of April was passed in serious work, and events were still in a doubtful condition. Lee's main army of unknown strength was still intact and Pickett's defeat was after all only the capture of a detachment. Sheridan was on Lee's flank with 25,000 men, including cavalry and Fifth Corps, but they were facing west, while Lee's main force was at Petersburg to the northeast, and probably not more than five miles off. Obviously, it was still possible for Lee to crush Sheridan in the morning, if he turned on him with all his force.

Sheridan perceived this so clearly that he at once sent back two divisions of the Fifth Corps to open connection with the Second, and to face toward Petersburg. They found the advance of the Second Corps before they had gone two miles on the White Oak Road. That night, the sound of heavy guns was incessant from Petersburg all night long, and at 4 a.m. increased to a tempest. At daybreak came the news that Wright, with the Sixth Corps, had assaulted Lee's lines in front, found them to be weakly guarded, that Petersburg was taken, and that Lee had evacuated all his positions and was moving away to the open country in the hope of joining Johnston for an offensive campaign.

On the morning of the 2nd of April, the pursuit began. The cavalry pushed on to the westward and reached Ford Station on the railroad from Petersburg to Lynchburg. In order to understand the further movements of the pursuit, a clear idea of the country is necessary.

Previous to the battle of Five Forks, Lee's lines were nearly north and south, running between Petersburg and Richmond, a distance of nearly twenty miles. His army was now concentrated and moving west. There were two railroads crossing the country he was in. One ran from Richmond, southwest to Danville, North Carolina, known as the

APPOMATTOX

"Danville Road." The other ran from Petersburg, nearly due west, to Lynchburg. These roads crossed each other at Burke's Station, some forty miles west of Petersburg.

Lee's first plan was to move on the Danville Road, so as to get to North Carolina and join Johnston. The way to block his game was for the cavalry and Fifth Corps to push for Burkesville, throw themselves in his way, entrench and fight, to give time for the rest of the army to come up and take Lee in rear. On the 2nd of April, Custer, in advance, reached Ford Station, about half way to Burke's Station on the Lynchburg road.

On the 3rd, the Union cavalry pursued its march. Nothing was met but Fitzhugh Lee's cavalry, which gave way wherever struck. Lee's main army was pressing on in a parallel line, some six or seven miles north toward Amelia Court House on the Danville road. This place is about ten miles northeast of Burke's; Custer and Devin pursued the road to Burke's, but Crook and McKenzie were sent out towards Amelia Court House along with the Fifth Corps, and soon found the enemy's infantry and trains.

Appomattox Station. Here, Custer captured and burned three trains loaded with provisions for Lee's army on April 8, 1865.

Lee was come to the turn of his fortune. He was encumbered by an enormous train, full of all that accumulation of rubbish that marks the exit of troops from winter quarters. He had been compelled to leave in such a hurry that this train was perfectly unmanageable, and entirely unfit to go on campaign. Grant was able to move out with only the pick of his troops and trains, leaving the rest in safety at his lines before Petersburg. Lee had to take everything, good and bad, or leave it to be captured.

The result was quickly visible to the cavalry and Fifth Corps. The enemy was completely demoralized. Prisoners dropped in by dozens, fifties and hundreds, giving themselves up without resistance, wagons were found abandoned and - surest sign of all - guns, limbers and caissons full of ammunition were found all along the road.

Custer pushed on, and by the evening of the fourth, cavalry and Fifth Corps had struck the Danville Road and interposed at a village called Jetersville, between Lee and Burke's Junction. Sheridan arrived at Jetersville at dusk, and learned without doubt that Lee was at Amelia Court House, hardly five miles off. The Second Corps was moving right in Lee's rear, and the Sixth Corps was coming up between the Fifth and Second.

That night was Lee's last chance. It was a desperate one at best; but the Lee of Chancellorsville, who had Stonewall Jackson to back him, would have seized it. The chance was to march down on Sheridan with all his force, and crush him out of the way; then go ahead to Danville. This, Lee feared to do. He was still encumbered with his long train, and the worst part of his position was that the train carried no rations. His army was already short of food. Sheridan that very night intercepted a dispatch from the sorely tried Confederate general to the commissaries at Danville and Lynchburg, ordering 200,000 rations to be sent to Burkesville. They never reached there. Next morning Lee, finding his road to Burkesville barred, stretched out for Lynchburg directly across country, hoping to strike the railroad at Appomattox Court House, forty miles from Amelia.

Sheridan had first curled around Lee's right at Five Forks, compelling him to fall back. Now he had again curled round, blocked his southern road, and left his only way open to the west. Very soon he was to bar even that way.

During the fifth of April, the cavalry and Fifth Corps lay quiet at Jetersville. Crook was sent out on the left to the northwest to find what the enemy was doing. Davies' brigade of his division struck a wagon train going west towards Appomattox, by way of Deatonsville. It was guarded by cavalry. Davies took the train and five guns. In the afternoon, Lee came down and attacked Jetersville, but without vigor. His old pluck was gone. He simply desired to gain time by the demonstrations to get his trains off. The road to the west was still free. Had Sheridan stayed at Jetersville, Lee might have got off yet.

That evening, the rest of the army came up from Petersburg and the Fifth Corps was taken from Sheridan to be replaced by the old Sixth, with which he had fought in the valley. This was done at Meade's request, as we are informed in Sheridan's report.

On the morning of the 6th of April, the Second, Fifth and Sixth Corps struck north towards Amelia Court House, only to find that Lee had gone and was already past Deatonsville, and near Farmville, on the road to Appomattox. Away went the cavalry after him, Crook leading, Custer and Devin following. It was only five miles to Deatonsville; and there, in the bright spring morning, the whole Confederate army was to be seen, its trains stretching for miles and miles trying to escape. Close to Deatonsville ran the little stream known as Sailor's Creek, which gave its name to the fight that followed.

Now was the time to catch Lee's trains and capture at least his rear guard. If the whole Confederate army stopped to fight, so much the better. The Union infantry was moving off towards Amelia Court House, but a dispatch reaching it, the direction of the columns was speedily changed, and it only remained for Sheridan's cavalry to hold Lee long enough for the infantry to catch up.

Sheridan's method of action was very simple, as he records it in his report. "Crook was at once ordered to attack the trains, and if the enemy was too strong, one of the divisions would pass him while he held fast and pressed the enemy, and attack at a point farther on, and this division was ordered to do the same, and so on, alternating, and this system of attack would enable us finally to strike some weak point.

FREDERICK WHITTAKER

This result was obtained just south of Sailor's Creek, and on the high ground over that stream. Custer took the road, and Crook and Devin coming up to his support, sixteen pieces of artillery were captured and about four hundred wagons were destroyed, while three divisions of the enemy's infantry were cut off from their line of retreat."

The description that follows of the part taken by Custer's division in this fight is taken from the account of one of Custer's staff officers. It is so picturesque and lifelike as to be worth full quotation:

> Early on the morning above mentioned, our command was watering and massing, when a staff officer from General Wesley Merritt, then commanding the cavalry corps, came with orders directing General Custer to move forward at once with his command and attack the enemy's wagon train at a certain point which he, the staff officer, would designate. General Custer, turning to his staff, selected me to convey the order to cease watering the command and direct the different brigade commanders to forward their commands at a trot.
>
> When I reached the road again, after having delivered the order, I found General Custer at the head of his column, returning. I learned from him afterward that he had gone forward as directed, but did not like the position designated as the attacking point, and seeing in the distance a position, in his opinion more desirable, he rode forward just in time to meet the Confederates placing a battery of nine guns in position. He immediately charged the battery, capturing the nine guns before they could be placed in position, and with the guns he took 800 prisoners.
>
> Still charging a mile beyond, he cut the enemy's wagon train, capturing and destroying nearly 1,000 wagons. Returning, he took up his position in a sort of a ravine. Here he reformed his command for the very active work that was to follow. Just over the brow of the hill, the enemy had thrown up earthworks behind which was stationed the Confederate General Kershaw, one of the best generals commanding the finest division of the Confederate army. All day, until dark, General Custer was charging these works, always retreating to and reforming his command in the ravine first selected. He knew they must give way sooner or later, as the Sixth Corps were doing excellent execution just beyond and would soon have their flank turned.
>
> About five o'clock in the afternoon, I rode out toward our battery, which had been in position all day shelling the enemy. My attention was attracted to a large batch of prisoners off to the left of our position, and my curiosity being somewhat excited, I rode out to the guard for the purpose of inquiring whether there were any distinguished officers among the captives.

APPOMATTOX

But a short distance from me, mounted on a thoroughbred mare, I saw what I at once knew to be a rebel officer of distinguished rank. In a moment his eye caught mine, and he beckoned me to come within the enclosure, as he desired to talk with me.

I did so, and the following conversation ensued; "Are you not one of General Custer's staff?" "I am, sir; a surgeon, however." "Sir, I desire to surrender my sword to General Custer. A non-commissioned officer is continually demanding it, but I consider that I have the right to request the privilege of surrendering it to a commissioned officer." "Whom have I the honor of addressing?" I asked. "My name," said he "is Kershaw - General Kershaw, sir." "General," I said, "I am glad to meet you. I assure you sir, we always had great respect for you and your command when you confronted us in the valley." "I look upon General Custer as one of the best cavalry officers that this or any other country ever produced. I shall indeed, consider it an honor to surrender my sword to him."

He continued, "Ever since the battle of Cedar Creek, when he and General Sheridan embraced each other after the battle, I have had a most perfect admiration for the man. I read a full account of it in the New York Herald some days after the engagement. All through today's battle, I directed my men to concentrate their fire upon his headquarters flag, knowing he was there always at the front. While I should have deprecated the idea of killing a man so brave, good and efficient, yet I knew it was my only hope."

"General," I said, you merely succeeded in killing his best horse. Now, if you will accompany me outside the guard, I will take you over to Woodruff's Battery, and leave you in charge of its commanding officer while I communicate your desires to General Custer." In company with two or three other rebel generals of minor importance, he followed me. As General Custer was then making another charge, I awaited the result. It was the last, and proved to be the grandest success of the day, as the balance of the enemy's command surrendered.

The capture of the day was upward of 7,000 prisoners, thirty-seven battle flags and a large number of guns. The Third Cavalry division at no time during the day had more than 600 engaged against the enemy. As General Custer was returning from the charge with his prisoners, battle flags, etc., I rode forward and met him. After congratulating him, I communicated the desires of General Kershaw.

The general seemed very much pleased, and rather accelerated his movement in direction of the battery. In presenting his sword, General Kershaw was exceedingly complimentary in his remarks. After the surrender, General Kershaw and friends, by invitation, spent the night with Custer and his staff, and in the morning they were sent to the rear with the rest of the prisoners.

This account gives a very fair idea of Sailor's Creek. Custer was its grandest figure. Crook struck the enemy first, and then Devin, but neither could make an impression, and did not demonstrate seriously. Custer passed Devin and took up the first real attack, charging again and again, mounted.*

All the while, the infantry was coming up. When Custer was hotly engaged, Devin was withdrawn and sent on still further, but only one of his brigades charged mounted. This was Stagg's Michiganders, Custer's old brigade. As Devin left, the Sixth Corps came up. Succor had been delayed a long time by Meade's withdrawal of the Fifth Corps. In the morning, the Second, Fifth and Sixth Corps had started to the north, the Second nearest Sheridan, the Fifth next, the Sixth furthest of all.

Instead of ordering in the Second to help Sheridan, Meade transferred the Sixth all the way over from right to left, thus losing valuable time, according to his own report. When it came into action however, as with the Fifth at Five Forks, it finished the battle in a very short time. Humphreys, with the Second Corps, also joined in at a further point to the north on his own responsibility. All through the campaign indeed, he seems to have acted with more energy, without orders, than any of the corps commanders.

When Humphreys came up, Lee's rear guard was surrounded. One of Stagg's Michigan men, in the last charge, went right over the Confederate breastworks and dashed through their whole line, reaching Sheridan, who was on the other side, hurrying up the infantry.

General Ewell and all his corps were taken bodily, and so ended

---

* It was in one of these desperate charges that Tom Custer, the general's brother, took with his own hand, his second flag within ten days. Tom had been a private soldier in an Ohio infantry regiment, in which he enlisted at the age of sixteen. The general procured him a commission in the Michigan Cavalry in the winter of 1864, and put Tom on his staff, where he was serving at Sailor's Creek. In the charge, Tom leaped the breastworks, seized the flag, and at the same moment was shot by the color-bearer, the bullet entering his cheek and going right through out of the back of his neck. Nothing daunted, Tom shot the color-bearer, took the flag and got back safely, when the doctor ordered him to the rear. His previous flag was taken at Namozin Church.

APPOMATTOX

the battle of Sailor's Creek. Sheridan says, "I have never ascertained exactly how many prisoners were taken in this battle. Most of them fell into the hands of the cavalry, but they are no more entitled to claim them than the Sixth Corps; to which command equal credit is due for the good results of this engagement."*

That night, nearly the whole of the old Army of the Valley encamped together by Sailor's Creek. Sheridan, Merritt, Custer, Devin, Crook and Wright were all there, and their old success had attended them.

Next morning, away went the cavalry again after Lee, Crook in advance. By this time, another corps had come up; Ord, with the little Army of the James, once Butler's command. Sheridan, still thinking Lee was as bold as ever, and knowing well that the Confederate leader's objective point must be Danville if he hoped to join Johnston, imagined that he would cross the Lynchburg railroad and move south through the open country.

In the morning of the 7th April therefore, he sent Custer and Devin off under Merritt's command to the southwest, away from the railroad to Prince Edward Court House. Crook was pushed directly after Lee, in the direction of Farmville, which lies due north of Prince Edward Court House, and some seven miles there from.

It turned out that Sheridan had overrated Lee's boldness, and still more his supplies. The Confederate leader was only intent on his western road to Appomattox where at last, provisions awaited him. Crook struck him at Farmville, and attacked him with his division, but it proved too weak to capture the whole rebel army, and was driven back, badly punished; General Gregg, one of the brigade commanders, being taken prisoner. As it happened, he was only held for a couple of days.

Devin and Custer arrived at Prince Edward Court House to find the country deserted. The part taken by Custer shall be told by Custer's surgeon, already quoted.

Nothing of importance in the way of an engagement occurred until the afternoon of the 8th. Among the prisoners captured was one who

---

* Sheridan's Report. This incident would seem almost incredible did not Sheridan personally vouch for it.

seemed to be well posted and desired to give information. From him, the general learned that the enemy were loading four trains of cars at Appomattox station with artillery, ammunition, etc. Just as we had learned these facts, a staff officer came from General Merritt directing General Custer to halt, mass his command and rest.

By the same staff officer, General Custer sent his compliments and requested him to state to General Merritt what he had heard from this prisoner, and say to General Merritt that "unless I get further orders from him, I shall continue my march and capture those trains of cars." Immediately after the departure of General Merritt's staff officer, General Custer dispatched two of his own staff officers to reconnoitre. They quickly returned, reporting everything as the prisoner had stated. We were now only two miles away from the station.

General Custer directed two regiments of the division to move forward at a trot as advance guard. The balance of the command followed at the same gait. The advance had orders to charge the station the moment they came in sight of it, and capture the trains. As we were nearing the station, and surely not a mile away, an exciting incident occurred which I must stop a moment to relate, as it helps to illustrate the noble character of the man of whom I am writing. Two young ladies came running, screaming, down the walk leading to the road, from a large and elegant mansion.

"They are robbing us! They are robbing and trying to murder us!" they screamed with all their might. General Custer, without saying a word, stopped short and quickly dismounting, ran up the walk just in time to catch a man in United States uniform running from the front door. With his fist he almost annihilated the miserable scalawag. Then, running through the house, he caught another making his exit from the rear door.

Catching up an axe, he threw it, hitting the brute in the back of his head, thus quickly disposing of the two wretches. In a moment, he was in his saddle again, and after hurriedly directing Captain Lee, the provost marshal, to place a guard on the premises, he charged down the road at terrific speed, capturing the four trains in less than five minutes after this event.

APPOMATTOX

Now commenced a brisk cannonading from some rebel guns near the station. General Custer, through colored prisoners, learned of their position and, although he was advised by one of his brigade commanders and other officers not to attempt their capture that night, he at once dismounted his command, as he was obliged to go through the woods and heavy undergrowth, and caught up his headquarters flag saying, "I go; who will follow," and the result was that after hard fighting, some thirty guns were brought in by hand that night.

The next morning General Lee surrendered. The flag of truce - a towel on a pole - was brought to the command of General George A. Custer, and to him the desire of General Lee to surrender was first communicated. The towel is still in possession of the family, along with many other relics of that noted event.[*]

This account is confirmed by Sheridan's report, and the action closes Custer's career during the war. The incidents of the surrender are too well known to need enlarging on. Once more, by his wide sweep, Sheridan had headed Lee, and the slower infantry, following directly, had come up in time to bag the game the cavalry had brought to bay. In all the pursuit, Custer had been the foremost and he was fairly entitled to wear his laurels, for by his audacity he had taken more trophies than any man in the army. We can hardly close this part of his life better than by a literal copy of his farewell order to the Third Division, written the same day. It rings like one of Napoleon's:

HEADQUARTERS, THIRD CAVALRY DIVISION
APPOMATTOX COURT HOUSE, VA., April 9, 1865

Soldiers of the Third Cavalry Division: With profound gratitude toward the God of battles, by whose blessings our enemies have been humbled and our arms rendered triumphant, your Commanding General avails himself of this, his first opportunity to express to you his admiration of the heroic manner in which you have passed through the series of battles which today resulted in

---

[*] This famous towel, the flag of truce which so suddenly terminated a bloody four years' war, is still in Mrs. Custer's possession, together with the little table on which the agreement was signed. Both are accompanied by letters of authentication, and were given to Custer by Sheridan, as the most proper person to possess them, he having been first in the pursuit all the time, and having received the first flag.

the surrender of the enemy's entire army.

The record established by your indomitable courage is unparalleled in the annals of war. Your prowess has won for you even the respect and admiration of your enemies. During the past six months, although in most instances confronted by superior numbers, you have captured from the enemy, in open battle, one hundred and eleven pieces of field artillery, sixty-five battle flags and upwards of ten thousand prisoners of war, including seven general officers. Within the past ten days, and included in the above, you have captured forty-six field-pieces of artillery and thirty-seven battle flags. You have never lost a gun, never lost a color and have never been defeated; and notwithstanding the numerous engagements in which you have borne a prominent part, including those memorable battles of the Shenandoah, you have captured every piece of artillery which the enemy has dared to open upon you.

Truce flag taken by Custer, now on display at the Smithsonian Museum in Washington DC.

The near approach of peace renders it improbable that you will again be called upon to undergo the fatigues of the toilsome march, or the exposure of the battlefield; but should the assistance of keen blades, wielded by your sturdy arms, be required to hasten the coming of that glorious peace for which we have been so long contending, the General commanding is firmly confident that, in the future as in the past, every demand will meet with a hearty and willing response.

Let us hope that our work is done, and that blessed with the comforts of peace, we may be permitted to enjoy the pleasures of home and friends.

APPOMATTOX

For our comrades who have fallen, let us ever cherish a grateful remembrance. To the wounded, and to those who languish in Southern prisons, let our heartfelt sympathy be tendered.

And now, speaking for myself alone, when the war is ended and the task of the historian begins when those deeds of daring which have rendered the name and fame of the Third Cavalry Division imperishable, are inscribed upon the bright pages of our country's history, I only ask that my name may be written as that of the Commander of the Third Cavalry Division.

                      G.A. CUSTER, Brevet Major General Commanding
                      OFFICIAL: L.W. BANHAUT, Captain and A.A.A.G.

Appomattox Court House. Today, the Appomattox Court House National Historical Park includes a visitor center in the old courthouse, a book store, the reconstructed McLean House where Lee and Grant met April 9, 1865, Lee's Headquarters, Grant's Headquarters, Clover Hill Tavern, Meeks Store, a Confederate Cemetery and a hiking trail.

Custer had his wish. It is as commander of the Third Cavalry Division that his name will be cherished as long as there are survivors of the war. When that memorable flag of truce came into his lines, it was an honor well deserved that he should be the first to receive it, and none more fitting than he to keep it, for as Sheridan said in his letter accompanying it, "I know no one whose efforts have contributed more

FREDERICK WHITTAKER
to this happy result than those of Custer."

THE GREAT PARADE

THE negotiations for surrender and the tedious operation of paroling Lee's army occupied several days, and then the cavalry started on their return to Petersburg, living on the country as they proceeded. So great had been the hurry of the last nine days that supplies were short, and the trains had not arrived with forage. They were met however, at Nottaway Court House, where also something else was met, in the shape of a dispatch which thrilled the whole country and army with horror and indignation.

It conveyed the news of the assassination of President Lincoln at a theatre in Washington, by John Wilkes Booth. At the same time came news that Sherman had been outwitted by Johnston in the latter's surrender, and that the capitulation was annulled. Then came fresh orders. The work of the cavalry was not quite over yet, and away they went again to the Roanoke, marching rapidly towards Johnston's army. The advance had actually reached the Roanoke and looked into North Carolina when the order was recalled. Johnston had surrendered on the same terms as Lee, and the war was over.

Once more, the cavalry corps took up its march for Petersburg, which was reached without special incident. There it remained a few days resting, and then parted forever from its beloved chief. Sheridan was called to Washington and ordered away to Texas. The work of the volunteer army was done, but that of the regulars was only just commencing. The last glimpse the volunteers caught of Sheridan was when he rode through their camps as they lay above Petersburg, just before his departure. Little did the men dream they would never see him again, or they would have been crazy with excitement.

As it was, the sight of "Little Phil" brought them out from their tents to look at him, but it was remarkable that little cheering greeted

THE GREAT PARADE

his progress. The men looked happy to see him, and he conversed freely as he passed along, but all the cheering business seemed to have died out of the cavalry corps except in action. None the less, their love and confidence in their leader was greater than any other chief had known since McClellan's removal, and Sheridan never encouraged cheers, rarely bowed in response, generally laughed at the men who cheered him, or made some good humored "chaffing" response.

After some days' rest at Petersburg,* the cavalry corps under the command of General Crook started on its homeward way by easy stages, passing through the long sought city of Richmond in parade style. How proud they all felt, few can realize but those who marched with them. Their toils were over and they were going home to be disbanded; that was in everyone's heart. Some regret at the loss of a life of excitement and adventure troubled a few, but as a rule everyone was thinking of home and civil life.

The column passed through Richmond, gazed at by curious crowds, and thence over the back country, where the men had raided and fought so often. They passed Trevillian Station, and found the ruined railroad just as they had left it a year before, crossed Rappahannock Bridge, the old battle grounds at Brandy Station, and camped on the Bull Run battlefield. Everywhere, the landscape was full of memories, sad and joyful, glorious or disastrous, but everywhere they were now sources of pleasure.

They visited all the old friends they had made at the different places where they had sojourned during four years of strife, these wandering, raiders, and congratulated each other that the "war was

---

*No one needed this rest more than Custer, whose work during the past campaign had been tremendous. It was one of his peculiarities that when under strong excitement he could do with very little sleep or food, but the last campaign had nearly worn even his iron frame out. His portrait, taken just after the surrender, shows the effect of the hard work in his gaunt, haggard appearance. Petersburg restored him, however. He was met by Mrs. Custer before he got there, the brave little woman being the first Northern woman who went out on the Southside Railroad after the surrender of Richmond. Together with Mrs. Pennington, wife of one of Custer's brigade commanders, Mrs. Custer made the whole of the march to Washington with the cavalry corps, the ladies riding on horseback at the head of the column, where the author first saw Mrs. Custer.

over." Then at last, they reached Alexandria and were dispersed all over the landscape, some in the very camps they had occupied in 1861 or 1862 when they were first mounted and sent to the front.

Ruins of Richmond. After a siege, Grant captured Richmond in early April, 1865. As the fall became imminent, Confederate President Jefferson Davis abandoned the city and fled south on the last open railroad line. The retreating soldiers set fire to bridges, the armory and warehouses as they left. The fire quickly spread out of control, and large parts of Richmond were destroyed.

For several days, the different regiments rested in their camps, and then they were ordered over the river to take ground near Washington. Clothing awaited them by the car load, provisions were plentiful; they drew everything needful to make a good appearance. For the first time in years, they began to experience the pleasant part of a soldier's life, the pomp and circumstance of war, with all its glitter and glory. Then, at last came the order for the Grand Parade at Washington. The whole Army of the Potomac, with Sheridan's cavalry at the head of the column, was to pass in review before the President through the streets of Washington, and Sherman's army was to follow next day in the same ceremonies.

THE GREAT PARADE

The Grand Review of the Armies took place on May 23 & 24, 1865. The Union Army paraded through the streets of Washington DC to receive accolades from civilians, politicians, officials, and prominent citizens, including President Andrew Johnson.

And what a review that was! The first, and it may be well hoped the last, of its kind in America, the passage of two armies of veterans, who had fought for four years, in such a series of battles as had not been seen in Europe for half a century. There was no sham about that parade. Every man was a veteran soldier. It might have been swelled to much larger proportions if need be, for every regiment had been joined, since it reached its safe camp, by crowds of recruits, malingerers, quartermaster's men and all those who had been left back at Remount Camp. But until the review, as a rule, only those who had shared in the last campaign took part; and the camps were left behind full of men.

There, you might see regiments reduced to a single squadron, tattered banners muffled in crape for the President's death, but every man a veteran. The uniforms were neat and quiet. Every man wore the undress uniform, blouse and fatigue cap, in which the army was arrayed for work. The only difference was that all were neat and clean, boots inside trowsers, sergeants' stripes fresh and new, bright brass letters and numbers on every cap, buttons brightly brushed up.

In the parade, as in the pursuit, Custer had the advance, and not to be behind his men, he had, for the first time, doffed his careless attire and wore a full-dress major-general's coat, over the collar of which his bright curls played merrily. The broad hat was the only remnant of his old careless yet dandified costume. He submitted to regulations otherwise.

The route of the column was from the east of Washington to the Capitol, where it turned to the right and swept straight up Pennsylvania Avenue. At this turning point, the regiments of cavalry successively drew their sabres as they passed, and here the crowd began.

Such a crowd as that was, will never be seen again. They seemed to be crazy with joy, and they shouted and hurrahed at every fresh regiment. There was a perfect jam on the sidewalks, and halfway into the road, and every window was crammed. Girls in white, in large bands, were singing sweet songs of welcome and throwing flowers and garlands to the soldiers.

The girls thought how gallant the soldiers looked; they little dreamed how nearly divine they appeared to the soldiers, who had not seen a pretty girl for so long. Still, it was these very floral angels that caused Custer's mishap at this place, a mishap which attracted more attention, admiration, and cheering to him than anything else could have done. It is thus described by one of the bystanders, who calls it "One glimpse of Custer," and the incident is correctly told in the main.[*]

One bright May morning in 1865, when the very sky seemed brighter and the air lighter and purer for the exultant sense of the fact that the war was over and that thousands had gathered under the shadow of the capitol's dome to welcome the nation's children - the dust stained, battle scarred veterans of the Union army – the writer caught a glimpse of the brave, yellow-haired chief, whose fate has so recently thrilled the hearts of all who admire true heroism and sublime courage. Never can the picture made by the gallant Custer that day be forgotten.

---

[*] Detroit Evening News

THE GREAT PARADE

Soon after the formal head of the line, Provost-Marshal General Patrick had ridden down the broad avenue, bearing his reins in his teeth and his sabre in his only hand, and had passed by a few rods, a cry was raised, "See him ride!" "That's Custer and his raiders," and like a flash came a gallant Arab* horse up the avenue, bearing in its headlong gallop a young officer, on whose shoulders shone the stars of a major-general, and as Custer dashed past the President's stand and the stand for the wounded soldiers, the latter caught up the shout, and such a scene as followed!

Grand Review president's stand. In the stand were President Andrew Johnson, General Grant and Johnson's Cabinet.

The gallant cripples staggered to their feet or crutches and hailed him with cheer after cheer, and then looked about for his gallant followers - but they were not there. The secret soon became plain. Soon after the column had set in toward Pennsylvania Avenue, a bevy of white-clad maidens stationed near the side of the street (there were 300 of them), had, as the brave fellow drew nigh, risen simultaneously and bursting into the song, *"Hail to the Chief,"* each threw a bouquet or wreath at him.

354

FREDERICK WHITTAKER

It was the first surprise he ever had, but instead of dodging the floral missiles, he began trying to catch them. The sudden rush, the pelting of bouquets and the peal of the 300 voices frightened his steed, and before he could gather up the reins, the excited animal had made the rush we saw from the other end of the Avenue.* As the gallant general flew past the President's stand, he bethought him to salute Johnson and General Grant, but in doing so, in the rush his sabre caught in hip wide hat, and sabre and head gear fell to the ground.

Then, with his long, yellow, curly hair floating out behind, he settled himself in the saddle as if he grew there, and by one of the most magnificent exhibitions of horsemanship he in a moment reined in the flying charger and returned to meet his troops. An orderly had picked up his hat and sword, and pulling the hat down over his eyes Custer dashed back past the assembled thousands, and soon reappeared at the head of his division.

Will those of us who saw that last grand review ever forget those two pictures - Custer conquering his runaway horse, and Custer at the head of the well dressed lines of the most gallant cavalry division of the age, as with the hot flush of victory yet visible on their bronzed faces, he led it through the capital at a gallop march. It was but a momentary vision, but one that has fixed itself upon at least one memory in indelible lines.

That very evening, Custer was going to fresh labors in the Southwest, while his old comrades were to disperse to their homes; the close of the review was also the close of his connection with the Third Cavalry division. As soon as the column left the front of the Grand Stand, it filed off toward its old encampment, and was drawn up on the familiar parade ground; then the officers of that proud little division

---

* Quite a history belongs to this horse. He was a thoroughbred "four mile racer," who had run thirty-three races, of which he had won twenty-six. Just before Appomattox surrender, Custer's scouts captured this horse, who was named "Don Juan," from the stable on the stud farm, and brought him to Custer. The horse was regularly appraised as captured property, contraband of war, and sold to Custer by the Quartermaster, Custer holding the receipt. The horse was a magnificent dark bay stallion of a most furious temper. Custer sent him home to Monroe, and had him exhibited at the State Fair, where Don Juan killed a groom. The horse finally dropped dead in his stall of heart-disease a year later.

THE GREAT PARADE

were summoned to the front to take their last leave of their beloved general.

The solemnity and mutual affection of that parting has been beautifully described by one of the participants; it was such a leave taking as comes to few in a lifetime, like the parting by death of near relatives, sad and solemn. When it was over, Custer rode slowly down the line and off the ground, while many of the rough men in the ranks could not cheer for the choking in their throats. He passed from their view as a beloved chief, and all felt, as we feel today, that never shall we look on his like again.

Grand Review. One of the goals of the review was to lift the mood of the capital, which was still in mourning following the assassination of Abraham Lincoln the month before at Ford's Theater.

THE VOLUNTEERS IN TEXAS

THE close of the war found the forces of the United States in a very curious and anomalous position. The sudden collapse of the rebellion, while it took everyone by surprise, still had its disadvantageous side. The armed occupation of the Southern States that followed the surrender of Lee, assumed the attitude not so much of a fair conquest as of a mere military progress. There was no more fighting to do. The same men who had been so stubborn up to the 9th of April, suddenly abandoned all hope and voluntarily dispersed to their homes, in apparent peace and quietness.

Then it was found that the real strain on the wheels of government was to begin. The United States was not a kingdom, but a republic; and a large party of the people held that just as soon as the population of the revolted States chose to cease armed opposition to the government, they were entitled to resume their old relations with the general body of the nation, with all rights unimpaired. To these views another party objected that self-preservation was the first law of nations, as well as of nature, and higher than any written constitution; and that it was manifest folly to invite men who had fought the general government until all hope was lost, to become legislators for their conquerors. Thus, the few months next after the surrender of Lee witnessed the two new parties taking shape. One was the "constitution party," headed by the President; the other was the "expediency party," which held the majority of Congress in both houses.

The uncertainty and excitement of the contest that ensued had its effect on the army, and especially on that portion of the volunteers that remained in the service. As long as the war lasted, these men had been to all intents and purposes regular troops. Their term of service, their pay, rations, dress and privileges were the same, and it was difficult to

THE VOLUNTEERS IN TEXAS

distinguish one from the other, in the case of old regiments. So long as the duration of the war was uncertain, the feelings and *esprit de corps* of the volunteer service were identical with those of the regulars. They were simply soldiers, and entirely different from militia, who are always looking forward to the termination of their brief terms of service as a release from irksome slavery.

The close of the war changed all this, as if by magic. At once it became the universal desire of the volunteers to go home. They were enlisted for three years or during the war, and the war was over; they ought to be disbanded forthwith and sent home. This was the universal logic of their reasoning, and it must be admitted that it was sound on the premises.

The only trouble was who should decide that the war was over. The President at one time undertook the job, and was formally rebuked by Congress, after which followed the long contest between the Executive and Legislative branches of the government, culminating in the President's impeachment and terminating in the election of General Grant. But in the meantime, the close of the year 1865 and the early part of 1866 were distinguished by uncertainty and disorder, which to a great extent affected the troops in the field.

After the surrenders of Lee and Johnston, there still remained a third army to the Confederacy, and towards this Jefferson Davis was making his way when he was captured. This army was commanded by Kirby Smith, the very man who had brought up the Confederate brigade which decided the Battle of Bull Run. His numbers were larger than those of either Lee or Johnston, his force well equipped, and - most favorable circumstance of all - the State of Texas in which he was stationed was entirely untouched by the war, and offered excellent strategic positions for a defensive fight.

There is little doubt that had Davis, with his indomitable pride and energy, succeeded in reaching Kirby Smith, the two might have continued the war for some time to come, with a fair prospect of making an independent slave state out of Texas. The capture of Davis, however, put an end to any such schemes, and Kirby Smith, in his turn, peaceably surrendered his army to General Sheridan.

FREDERICK WHITTAKER

On the events of the surrender and subsequent occupation of Texas we do not intend to dwell, save so far as they concern Custer and the volunteers, and especially the latter. In the state of uncertainty which still prevailed as to the ultimate state of affairs in the South, it was found necessary to retain a considerable force under arms to meet expected insurrections. It was fully anticipated that the ex-Confederates would resolve themselves into bands of guerillas and harass the country.

In order to guard against this possibility, considerable forces retained their army organization in brigades and divisions, and were stationed at railroad junctions and other strategic points instead of being scattered at small company posts through the country. These forces were largely composed of volunteers. Any other arrangement would have been an impossibility. The regular army, which had entered the war less than 16,000 strong, hardly mustered that number now, after all its' recruiting, and was totally unequal to the task of holding such an immense territory as now demanded military occupation.

But the volunteers, almost without exception, were clamorous to be discharged and sent home. The officers, who were receiving good pay and doing easy duty, were comparatively reconciled to their lot, but the men were sullen and discontented. The weakness of the volunteer organization, which had not revealed itself during the war, became plain now. It was only a temporary make-shift, after all, and the close of the war showed it. The same men who in campaign had been docile soldiers, in perfect discipline, became once more the same self-opinionated mob which had been beaten at Bull Run.

The men resumed their functions as citizens, began to think and to grumble, disputing orders, disobeying them and fast sinking into a state of demoralization that would appear incredible when compared with the experience of a few months back, were it not recorded. During the war, it seemed as if America had become a military nation. Peace revealed the fact that it had not done any such thing. Some million of citizens, under the pressure of national pride and self-preservation, had consented to play the part of soldiers while necessity existed. Now they had done their work, were heartily sick of the unnatural life, and wanted to return to a natural one.

THE VOLUNTEERS IN TEXAS

The disgust and anger of the volunteers who were retained in the service was further increased by the disbandment of so many of their comrades. Most of the eastern regiments were mustered out, and the Army of the Potomac entirely broken up, while the regiments retained in service were generally from the West. This was in consequence of their being nearer to the dangerous places in the southwest, and in no sense a discrimination against them, but they would not listen to explanations.

They heard of their friends who had gone home, who were now in business and prosperous, while they felt only too keenly that they were wasting their own time, that opportunities were slipping away and could never be replaced, and that by the time they got home all the avenues to employment might be filled, and they turned out to starve. All this grumbling and discontent increased daily among the volunteers, while among the regulars it was unknown.

A calm retrospect of the facts, at this late day ten years after the event, shows the cause to be very simple. The real trouble was that the volunteer organization, coming as it did from the individual States, was merely a temporary loan to the United States. New York, or New Jersey, or Michigan, or Illinois, as the case might be, had lent the government a regiment bodily, officers and all, for a certain purpose, and the men keenly realized that the purpose was accomplished. They enlisted to end the war, not to help in reconstruction. A new force was needed for this.

In a regular regiment, with different traditions, the case was different. The men enlisted to serve their time out individually. The organization was fixed and perennial. No matter if every man in the regiment was killed, something invisible - the United States regiment remained; all it needed was to be recruited. With the volunteers, it was different; they could not be recruited; the war was over, and there was no authority for them to recruit under.

As the men deserted, the regiments dwindled. Then consolidation was tried, but with even worse effect. The members of the old regiments had a bond of union, *esprit de corps*. It kept many a man from desertion, for fear of disgracing his old command that carried the name of so many battles on its flag. For the new regiment, the "provisional" organization, they cherished no feeling but dislike.

Even the officers hated it. They secretly sympathized with the men, and connived at disorder, or only checked it feebly. The new regiments dwindled away even more rapidly than the old. The only thing that kept most of the men in the service was the fact that the government owed them many months' pay, and that they did not care to forfeit that by desertion. At last the government was obliged to give up the attempt to make professional soldiers of the volunteers, and to do what it should have done at first, increase the regular army.

The last of the volunteers were not discharged, however, until the spring of 1866. During this time, Custer found his hands pretty full as far as discipline was concerned. He was first sent from Washington, after the great parade, to follow Sheridan to Texas. Mrs. Custer was able to travel with him, and his old staff accompanied him. At the time Custer left for the Southwest, he was very much pulled down by the tremendous labor which he had imposed on himself during the last campaign, and the relaxation of the present journey was very pleasant to him.

Before he had arrived at New Orleans, the news of Kirby Smith's surrender announced that all was safe, so that he was no longer obliged to hurry; and the trip was consequently delightful. For the first time in his life, Custer was tasting the sweets of a major-general's life; which he had not hitherto enjoyed. With a large staff, free transportation, plenty of horses, ample pay, his family with him, travelling luxurious, he began to enjoy life thoroughly.

The party went from Washington by railroad to Parkersburg on the upper Ohio, where they took one of the great luxurious western river boats and thence travelled down the Ohio and Mississippi, all the way to New Orleans. Of all methods of travel, this is perhaps the pleasantest, on account of the ample and commodious quarters, the beauty of the scenery passed through, and the length of time occupied in the passage, just sufficient to form pleasant acquaintances.

There is always ample room on the three or four different decks for all the exercise one needs, the dinner table is plentifully and well

THE VOLUNTEERS IN TEXAS

supplied, the evenings are enlivened by a band of music in the main saloon, while the passengers almost invariably get up a dance. It resembles life on an ocean steamer, without the formidable drawback of seasickness, and is altogether delightful. Custer and his little wife found it entirely so.

Riverboat Sultana. On April 27, 1865, the Sultana, carrying 2,300 just released Union prisoners of war plus crew and civilian passengers, exploded and sank seven miles north of Memphis, Tennessee, killing 1,700 people. It was the worst maritime disaster in U.S. history, even more costly than the sinking of the Titanic, where 1,517 people were lost.

Hitherto their life had been strange and peculiar. To Custer, with his earnest, impatient temperament, his different steps of promotion had brought little of luxury and enjoyment, but a great deal of hard work, which had at last completely worn him out. He owns as much in a letter written home to his sister from Petersburg, just after Appomattox surrender. He says that he feels completely exhausted, and needs rest badly. During the easy marches back to Washington, together with his little wife, he obtained some rest, and this long pleasant boat journey was another resting time. He enjoyed it with a perfect dreamy delight, such as he had never felt, and all the more because he could not help feeling that he had earned it.

Arriving at New Orleans, he stepped ashore a new man, fit for any amount of work and already tired of rest. He was sent up the river to Alexandria, Louisiana, there to take charge of a division of cavalry gathered from the Western States.

Steamboat landing, New Orleans

Here, his troubles commenced. Very few of these troops had been in action to any great extent. They were green regiments, and therefore all the harder to discipline. For all that, Custer set to work at them, as he had with his Michigan Brigade in old days, and established the most rigorous discipline from the first. The sort of success he had was not very gratifying, however; no one could have hoped that in those days. The trouble lay in the penny-wise, pound-foolish policy of Congress, which preferred the temporary employment of half a million of discontented volunteers to the authorization at once of a permanent standing army of a hundred thousand regulars, such as could then have been organized in three weeks.

To Custer, with his memories of the perfect adoration extended to him by his former commands, the present experience was very trying. The men under his orders all hated him furiously. He needed a battle to make them love him, and there were no more battles to be fought. His

THE VOLUNTEERS IN TEXAS

charging days were over.

What he could do, he did to get his troops into decent order, and accomplished a great deal, but nothing satisfactory to himself, when the division was finally ordered to Austin, Texas. The transfer was made by easy marches, and once on the road there was not so much trouble with the troops. They had something to do, and were not so full of discontent. The great difficulty then, as always after the war, was to keep the men from marauding. They were so used to living off the country in war time that it required a powerful provost-guard to patrol the flanks of the column to keep the stragglers from going off to plunder.

Apart from these troubles, the march was delightful. Mrs. Custer marched at the head of the column, riding on horseback nearly all the way. A large, roomy spring wagon, with a team of four matched greys belonging to the general, accompanied headquarters, and was so fitted up that it could be used as a tiring room or a sleeping apartment while on the march should the delicate little woman get tired out. She used it but little however, making the journey as well as any of the men.

At last they arrived at Austin, where their command, still called the Third Division, found itself with Merritt's, still known as the First. The state of affairs there was worse than at Alexandria, Merritt's division aggravating the troubles of Custer's.

A little extract will give an idea of the state of things. It is quoted from the correspondence of the New York Times, March, 1866. The correspondent gives an explanation of the unpopularity of General Custer with the enlisted men:

Everyone who glances at the heading of this paragraph will say, "Well, there's no discount on him." But there is though, in the estimation of some. The soldiers are down on him like a thousand of brick, and so are their friends. And why? I'll tell you. As a general thing, the Volunteers wanted to go home as soon as the war was over, and that portion of them who were sent out have acted badly, and were encouraged in such performance by their friends in the North, who wrote them letters, in which they told them to come home - that the war was over, and that it would not be desertion.

Austin. 200 East Sixth Street, 1866. The Missouri House, seen on right, was touted as Austin's first boarding house and was rumored to be a brothel.

General Custer, knowing that the trial for desertion was a farce, tried every humane way to save his army from going to pieces, but failed. He then tried a new way; and flogged several men and shaved their heads. This had the desired effect, but brought down the friends of these soldiers upon him, who charge him with being disloyal, inhuman and everything that is bad. Now, I leave it to everyone if Custer didn't do right. The Volunteers are not acting in a good spirit here, while nearly half of them have deserted. This state of things operates badly in the two regular cavalry regiments which are stationed in this section, nearly one-third of whom have deserted.

These deserters turn murderers and robbers and horse thieves, and are a terror to the traveling community. Scarcely a night passes but that some poor fellow is waylaid and killed. The great necessity of the increase of the Regular Army and the discharge of all the Volunteers - white and colored - must be apparent to all.

He also gives an account of the mutiny of the Third Michigan Cavalry, for the truth of which he vouches:

THE VOLUNTEERS IN TEXAS

It is pretty well known that this regiment has had the reputation of being one of the best bodies of cavalry in the service. For fighting, marching or drilling it is unequaled by any cavalry regiment in the United States. Like all of the Volunteers, the men composing this regiment wanted to go home. A few weeks ago, while upon parade, General Thompson complimented the regiment in eloquent terms, and stated to them that it was an honor to be kept in the service. Says the general; "To say nothing about your past services, no inspector in the army would permit such a well-organized, well-dressed and well-disciplined regiment to quit the service as long as any necessity exists for retaining the services of Volunteers."

It happened that the next day they were to be inspected by one of General Sheridan's staff officers, and they prepared themselves accordingly. Such a crowd never before appeared upon inspection, except the Ancients and Horribles. Some had on caps, some had on hats with the corners jammed out or stuck in, some had on boots and some had on shoes covered with oil and ashes; some had on coats, some had on jackets, and some were in their shirt sleeves; some had their breeches stuck into their boots, some had their belts and cartridge boxes on bottom side upward; and on the whole, presented a most wry appearance. All those men who were not dressed in this manner were ordered to arrest their "Horrible" companions, when they refused, and the whole regiment mutinied. Subsequently, the thing was fixed up and ninety of them are in confinement and are to be tried for mutiny.

As may be imagined, the trial for mutiny amounted to very little, and the regiment was at last disbanded, to its own relief and that of everyone else. In this matter, just as before and since the war, Custer and the regular army officers suffered in common with their comrades from the incompetency and stupidity of their management by Congress. During the war, this sapient body was confined to its true functions as regards the army. These were to legislate on general subjects, and to provide money; the executive arranged all the details.

Instead of many masters, the army had but one, Stanton, a harsh and severe ruler sometimes, but generally just and sensible. Good or bad, every man knew what to expect and as a whole, the army was managed by men who knew their business. Now all this was changed. The law, whether good or bad, had to be obeyed and expediency was no longer consulted. Troops were governed not according to necessity, but according to what Congress chose to order; and Congress, like all deliberative bodies, halted and hesitated and did nothing while discontent increased.

This state of things is peculiar to a republic, and especially to a federative government like the American. It is part of the price paid for personal liberty. To a king or emperor, the situation would have offered no difficulties, either at the beginning or close of the war. He would have levied his troops, used them and disbanded them as seemed fit to him; the increase or diminution of his army would not have affected its stability. President Lincoln could not raise a company; he was obliged to ask the States for regiments. President Johnson could only return the regiments lent him, and the fact of his needing many of them made no difference. He could only retain them by a legal fiction, for the rebellion had ceased.

Had Congress, on Kirby Smith's surrender, at once increased the regular force and authorized the change of volunteer regiments into regular regiments, leaving their formation to volunteering from the "natural soldiers" of the old regiments, and retaining the traditions of the war, the trouble would never have arisen. A change from temporary to permanent organization was needed, and it came too late to save the volunteers from unmerited reproach. Custer, among the rest, paid the penalty of doing his duty, in unpopularity among the men who had adored him. At last, Congress thought better of it and passed the Bill of 1866, "to increase and fix the military establishment of the United States."

THE REGULAR ARMY

IT is one of the consequences of republican institutions as affecting modern civilization that the standing army of a republic is pretty sure to be constantly abused. The fact is that republics and standing armies are incompatible, and always will be so. The one theory of government is predicated on the liberty of every man to go where he pleases, and do what he pleases, so long as he does not hurt his neighbors. The other is founded on the duty of every man to obey his superior officer without question, and to stir no step without permission.

The only footing on which standing armies have ever been tolerated in free republics has been as a police force, to control the criminal classes. As such, the regular army of the United States before the war acted. It was kept up solely to control the dangerous Indians, and to keep burglars out of the nearly deserted forts. The people at large saw but little of it; soldiers being rare spectacles in the *ante-bellum* days.

During the war, this little police force practically vanished from the struggle. A brigade of cavalry and a division of infantry in a single army, both mere skeletons, constituted all the regulars, except in the batteries of artillery and the headquarter escorts of a few generals. These, from the feebleness of their numbers, attracted little attention. It might have been and probably was expected that this small force, by its innate superiority, should fill to the volunteers the office of Napoleon's Old Guard to the rest of the French army, to be the last reserve, steady and invincible, capable of deciding every battle.

This expectation, if entertained, was disappointed. The regulars, after Bull Run, ceased to be distinguished for any special valor or constancy, and merely fought alongside of the rest of the army, neither better nor worse. The cause for this state of things was simple. At Bull

Run, the small force of regulars present was made up of veterans, and shone by contrast with the rest of the army. As time went on, the veterans grew less and less in number, and were replaced by green recruits.

Worse still, the regular officers, instead of remaining with their old commands, sought and easily obtained volunteer commands, far higher than any the regulars could offer. Lieutenants and captains were jumped to colonels, and field officers became generals of brigade and division, to the benefit of the volunteers and the detriment of the regulars. The vacancies thus created were either unsupplied, or filled by new appointments, and more than half of these latter were from civil life.

The civil appointments as a rule were perfectly green young gentlemen, precisely the same as those who entered the volunteers as officers and privates, but they happened to possess political influence, to know a senator or representative, and so they were commissioned. Thus it very soon resulted that, as a rule, only the poorest of the old officers remained with the regulars.

The energetic and ambitious had left for the volunteers; what remained may be divided into three classes. First were the lazy ones and plodders, who preferred the old groove; second were the few who looked down on the volunteers and fancied themselves of a superior class; third were the new officers, who needed training. To these must be added however, a fourth class of modest and capable officers, who had not sufficient influence to secure high volunteer commands, and who remained with their old regiments from necessity.

It was the influence of this last class that kept up the reputation of the little skeleton force of regulars and enabled them to hold their own with the volunteers. It is indeed surprising how strong was their influence over the new material from civil life. The same men who came in, raw un-licked cubs, proud of their political friends, and chiefly anxious for everyone to understand that they were regulars, at a time when their ignorance would have disgraced a squad of country militia, found their level in a very short time.

Within a year from their first entrance, it was hard to recognize, in the quiet and self-possessed officer, in command of his picket post or scouting party, the rude gawky bumpkin who had joined in 1861. The old hands had licked him into shape, while the veterans in the ranks had done the same kind office for the recruits below. In the old regiments, which dated from before the war, this change was very marked, in the few new regiments that had been authorized since the commencement of hostilities, much less so.

Even there, however, there was some difference, and it was noticeable at the very close of the war. It consisted chiefly in a different standard of discipline, a difference of condition between officers and men, which was most prominent in camp. At the close of hostilities, it made itself visible in the different behavior of regulars and volunteers.

On the march and in the battle, there was nothing to choose between the regulars and the old first class regiments of volunteers, especially where the latter had been commanded by a West Point graduate. On the drill ground, if anything, the volunteers were smarter, and they almost always attacked in battle with an energy slightly superior to that of the regulars. Their camps were often much handsomer than those of the regulars, and at permanent camps they always displayed far more taste in adorning their habitations, while in cleanliness there was little to choose between the two.

But between the officers and men of volunteers, there was always, even to the last, a kindly and cordial feeling, which was the perfection of ideal relations. It was very different from the loose style prevalent at the beginning of the war, when the men elected their officers, or the latter were appointed to exercise duties of which they were totally ignorant. That class had vanished. What remained of officers were men of experience who had either risen from the ranks, or from being subalterns had become field officers.

The men knew that in case of vacancies in the lower ranks, these would be filled from among themselves. The career was open to all, and while the war lasted was excellent. This bred between the two classes a certain mutual respect which was noticeable. The men were punctilious in saluting, neat in their dress and obeyed orders promptly. The officers were kind in their manner, and only maintained the due distance essential to discipline in public.

When an officer and a sergeant, formerly comrades and tent mates, were alone together with no one to see them, they talked like the old friends they were, while the presence of a third party, especially an enlisted man, would instantly freeze up the sergeant into haughtily profound respect. The secret of subordination was that every man respected the rank he hoped to attain himself. During winter quarters, there was little or no trouble in maintaining perfect discipline among the old volunteer regiments on this account.

In the regular regiments, a very different state of things prevailed. Officers and men were practically distinct classes with lines of demarcation irrevocably fixed. The distance between them was impassable. The youngest subaltern newly joined was entitled to the same respect shown to a general, and the marks of respect enforced were and still are decidedly slavish. A little instance will show the contrast:

A company of regulars is in barracks. Their captain is detailed on staff duty, the first lieutenant is on a court martial, the second lieutenant is in his quarters, smoking a pipe, when some citizen friends arrive to pay him a visit. After a cigar and a visit to the barroom, "for officers only," the young sub proposes to show his friends the barracks, and after seeing the parade ground, goes quietly to the door of the company room and opens it to take his friends in. Instantly, a voice is heard shouting "Attention!" and in a moment, every man in the room is standing at the foot of his bunk, bareheaded, cap in hand and stiff as a post.

The lieutenant touches one of his buttons with his forefinger and drops it in a careless way, (meant for the return of a salute) looks around the room, makes a few remarks on its condition to his friends, as if the men were insensible blocks who could not hear, and goes out. Thence he takes his friends to the guard house, full as it is of manacled men, resting from their sentences of labor; and the same scene is repeated. Every prisoner has to stand up and be inspected like a prize ox, while the little sub moves about as if he were a demigod amid slaves.

FREDERICK WHITTAKER

A visit to a volunteer barrack or the camp of a crack regiment at the close of the war was very, different. In the first place, the lieutenant would not have voluntarily taken his friends round to exhibit his men in their bedrooms, neither would he have taken them to the guard house. If his friends had asked to see the men, he would have gone with them, the men would have stood to attention and saluted, and afterwards the friends might have conversed with the soldiers, who would have received them politely, but as a rule the friends of an officer would have remained with him alone or viewed the men at such a distance as not to constrain the latter.

In the one case was a constant strain on the reins of discipline; making the men feel the curb all the while, in the other a constant endeavor on the part of the officers to carry a light hand, to make things easy, to insist only on the needful, and not to regard the men as private property. During the war, the second system worked well, and the men fought cheerfully for officers whom they loved. Even in the regular regiments, the old slavish system of discipline was much relaxed, and principally in consequence of the fact that during the war some promotions were made from the ranks.

Elizabeth B. and George A. Custer

THE REGULAR ARMY

At the close of hostilities, all was changed. It was no longer possible to get men to do duty cheerfully. The duty was disagreeable and irksome, devoid of excitement or glory, promotion had ceased, there was no campaigning, and instead of the cheerful volunteer, fighting for the cause he loved, the hired mercenary was to be the soldier of the future.

The change was great, and demanded different discipline. Instead of willing obedience and easy government, absolute servility and rigid authority were needed. The class of men that enlisted in the volunteers would not have entered the regulars for double pay. They had been trained from boyhood to look down on soldiers, as men too lazy to work, and only one remove above criminals. The same feeling exists in England, and in fact in every country where military service is wholly voluntary. It is only in countries where the conscription and the soldier are universal, that the latter is treated with respect by the citizen.

The feeling with which the regular soldier is regarded in England and America is a curious compound of contempt and fear. The hard working artisan, who maintains a family by his labor, looks down on the soldier because the latter is content to live on contemptibly small pay, and is unable comfortably to keep a wife and children; and the same sentiment is common to the clerk, salesman, shopkeeper and every man who makes a comfortable living above the degree of a common laborer. They all look on the soldier as a poor creature who cannot make a living.

At the same time, whenever they see him drunk, they give him a wide berth, and as a great many "hard cases" enlist in the army, and afterwards become prominent for disorder, the citizen learns to regard the rank and file of the regular army as being made up entirely of the scum of the population. The truth is that he only sees their worst side in the cities. The old soldiers, men who have served more than one enlistment without a desertion, are quiet and unobtrusive; he hardly ever sees them, and takes little notice of them when he does; the chronic deserters and re-enlisters, the drunkards, the malingerers, are always thick around the recruiting offices in the cities, and help to give tone to the current idea of the army private.

FREDERICK WHITTAKER

Were the army, as in France and Germany, constantly in sight among the people, the citizens would discover that soldiers are men the same as themselves, with all sorts of characters. As a class a little more inclined to be reticent and silent to strangers than workmen, the best of them have a certain deprecatory air when thrown into a crowd of citizens, dashed with a spice of defiance. They know there is a prejudice against them, and they feel that it is unjust, so they keep among themselves as much as possible and nourish regimental pride to console them for civil depreciation. All they need to make their position happier is to be better known.

Another cause of the depreciation is found in the nature of a soldier's duties. There is nothing which is more inexplicable to the ordinary civilian than the true military spirit, that glories in hardships, danger and death, and that despises fine uniforms. He cannot understand it. To be a militia man in a gorgeous uniform, and to march through the streets behind a splendid band is his idea of soldiering, and when he finds that his real soldier friend hates this and loves the excitement of a battle pure and simple, the civilian is puzzled.

In a conscriptional country where everyone is liable to service, the feeling of pity and sympathy for men who are forced against their will to endure the hardships of real military life extends to every member of the population in the country who has a relative in the army, and helps to make the army popular. During the war of the rebellion, when the overpowering necessity of the times operated instead of the conscription, the same feeling tended to make the volunteers popular. They went (according to the public idea) not because they loved a soldier's life, but because it was their duty.

The men in the regular army after the close of the war could plead no such excuse. They enlisted either because they loved military life, or because they were too indolent or unskillful to make a living at anything else. In either case, the average citizen disliked the motive and despised the man.

This state of public estimation reacted injuriously on the army. It was so unpopular a thing to enlist, that no one would do it, save as a last resort, if he had a character to lose. The very worst men of the old

THE REGULAR ARMY

volunteers - the bounty jumpers - enlisted by hundreds and practiced on the regular officers the tricks which they had learned for the purpose of duping provost-marshals in draft times. The percentage of desertions was larger than it had ever been before, and the few good and decent soldiers were lost in the scamps that made up the popular idea of the regular army.

It was in the midst of these influences that the Bill of 1866, "to increase and fix" the regular army, went into operation. Forty-five regiments of infantry, ten of cavalry, and five of artillery were announced as the basis of the future army. Half of the regiments of horse and foot were quite new, and others dated from the period of the war. To officer these regiments, about fifteen hundred new officers were required, and here, as in the case of the enlisted men, great difficulties lay in the way of procuring good material.

As with the men, so with the officers, the best and most energetic of the volunteer material had returned to civil life where it was pushing forward and prospering. There were not enough graduates of West Point to fill the bill. The old army of twelve thousand men had been compelled to rely for officers to a great degree on civil appointments; and out of that old army at least half of the graduates had passed away, some into the Confederate service, others by death, others on the retired list.

The four years of the war had produced about fifty graduates a year, and the coming years would furnish the same proportion. A large residue still remained, that must be filled up by civil appointments. In these latter, the preference was to be given to ex-volunteers, and for the next few years all the so called "civil appointments" came from the volunteer officers.

This might have been expected to produce a very good class of officers, but it was soon found that this was far from being the case, principally owing to the baneful influence of politics. Had it been possible for the pick of the old volunteer officers to have been recommended at the very close of hostilities by their superior officers, on a strictly military basis for military aptitude alone, the results might have been good. As it was, the lower appointments were made entirely through the influence of members of Congress or Senators, who recommended their friends; and only those volunteers possessed of such influence obtained commissions. In many cases, they were given to men who had tried civil life for a time, failed therein, and went into the army to make a living. Some actually purchased their commissions through claim agents, who for the price of about five hundred dollars, engaged to procure a Senator's influence and bring the candidate for a commission before the examining board.[*]

This last named body was composed of old regular officers, and was authorized to examine the candidates to see whether they were fit for commissions. The test was chiefly educational. Tactics and regulations had little to do with it. The officers were examined in the ordinary branches of English education, including algebra up to quadratic equations, with a little plane trigonometry, and that was about all. Like all examinations of whatever character, they failed to touch the real capacity of the applicant, who generally "crammed" for the test. If he failed to pass, and had influence, he secured a second trial, in some instances a third. Influence was sufficient to pull almost anyone through.

The consequence of this state of things was that instead of the best of the volunteer element, the army secured, in too many cases, only the worst, and the incompetency of the new officers to control the army became very painfully evident. Contrary to the general idea, the task of a regimental officer of the United States Army in time of peace is far more difficult than in time of war. Then, he is in the midst of comrades, in a brigade, part of a division, a corps, an army. All he has to do is to keep his men together on the march and in the battle and to obey orders. His superiors do the thinking.

In time of peace, all is changed. The officer is often, generally, thrown much on his own responsibility. The troops are scattered in small posts, always short-handed; and officers are constantly detailed on special duty. Moreover, the army is always in the midst of a population intensely hostile to its spirit and traditions, in active sympathy with all

---

[*] This statement is founded on facts in the knowledge of various gentlemen who shall be nameless, but is not made loosely or from general or hearsay evidence.

deserters, and exceedingly jealous of military authority. The officer is subject to a code of minute regulations, born of the jealousy of the civil authority, which are all the more vexatious that half the time he does not know what they are.

The case in 1866 was even worse than it is now. The old army regulations of 1861 had become obsolete. They were replaced by a host of new laws, new general orders, decisions of departments and what not, none of which were gathered together in an accessible form. The heads of departments and their clerks, who had been grinding away for years in the same mill, had all these laws at their finger-ends. The new officers, whose idea of military life was confined to handling troops in campaign, found that in time of peace they were also expected to be expert lawyers, and in this they failed dismally.

They were constantly receiving sharp reprimands from headquarters as to the improper phraseology of a report or return, the absence of red ink on an endorsement, the bungling manner in which they tied their red tape. In the matters of discipline, they were also constantly in trouble. They had an unruly lot of men to control, desertion to check and the evil required sharp measures. These they were not allowed to use, under the law. Corporal punishment was abolished, stocks, tying up, bucking and gagging, all those rudely effective methods which had been used among the hard cases of the volunteers.

They were compelled to manage their men wholly by moral suasion, or punish them by the slow process of court-martial. They generally preferred the latter, and revenged themselves for their impotence in other directions by excessive punishments in this. At the same time, they retained too much of the old free and easy, hard drinking habits which the war had induced in them, and found that in time of peace, drunken officers were not allowed. Thus the spectacle was presented of frequent court-martials of men and officers, for substantially the same offense, drunken excesses, and the manifest injustice of the different sentences was almost always visible.

A man would be dishonorably discharged and sent to a military prison at hard labor for two years for what in an officer would only entail a reprimand or suspension from command for a month or two. All these circumstances combined to render the regular army of 1866 a very different and far inferior body to that which fought in the Mexican War. The men were discontented and unruly, the officers not fully up to their work, and the amount of trouble that took place during that and the following year, had a great influence on the future of Custer.

Under these circumstances, the Seventh Cavalry was formed, and to it Custer was assigned as Lieutenant-Colonel. It might be supposed that his declension in rank from the proud position of a major-general would be accompanied by some compensation and that at all events the duty in his new rank would be easier. To a certain extent this is true, and yet in many respects the contrary is the case. It doubtless sounds paradoxical to a civilian, to be told that the command of a regiment is in anything harder than that of a division, while at the same time it is asserted that the position of a general officer demands far more military knowledge and capacity than that of a colonel; and yet both these propositions are held to be true, and have been acted on by the few great commanders whose actions have settled the principles of success in military science.

Napoleon, in particular, frequently expressed the opinion that generals ought to be young and colonels old, and always acted on it. By this opinion, he intended to convey two important lessons, which are elaborated in other maxims. A short analysis of the conditions of military success may make the reason clear to those who have not studied military history in a professional light.

War requires two elements for its prosecution; troops, and a general. A good general may handle poor troops, so as to beat a poor general with good troops. The troops are the tools, the general the workman. With perfect tools, the perfect workman makes perfect work, and the best general can work better if he has good troops than if he has poor ones. Troops are made by their sergeants, captains, and colonels, handled by their generals. To make them requires patience and experience, qualities in which the old excel the young; to handle them requires adroitness, quickness and magnetic ardor, qualities in which the young excel the old.

THE REGULAR ARMY

So far, Custer had been content to take his troops readymade, good or bad, and to use them as he best could; now he was to try his success at fashioning them out of the raw material. The rest of his life will show what measure of success he attained in his task; for from first to last, he commanded his regiment whenever it was assembled, and had more to do with its training than almost any other regimental commander with any other regiment of the army since the Civil War.

THE SEVENTH CAVALRY

AMONG all the anomalies at the close of the rebellion, none was greater than the position in which the officers of the regular army found themselves. Many field officers of the old army had become major-generals of volunteers, and during the war this office carried all the privileges of command. The sudden end of hostilities showed the real hollowness of the title, and one by one, all the general and other officers of the volunteers were mustered out and paid off.

To those who were originally civilians, this did not matter. They had returned to their former stations. The old army officers, however, found it very different. They beheld themselves stripped of the privileges of rank, but still remaining soldiers. In Custer's case, the drop was all the way from Major-General to plain captain of the Fifth Cavalry. This rank was all that really remained to him. He had been brevetted major in the regular army in July, 1863, but brevets amounted to nothing, any more than volunteer commissions.

The formation of the new regiments offered a salve in some respect for the wounded pride of those officers who felt the change too keenly, while the retired list provided for many more. The great chiefs of the war found themselves retained in their rank, and the minor chiefs were consoled by field positions and brevets of general officers in the regular army.

The most conspicuous of these were to be found in the new regiments of cavalry. Sheridan's division commanders in the last campaign, Custer and Devin, also Merritt who had been their nominal chief, were made lieutenant-colonels, and brevetted brigadier and major generals in the regular army, all at the same time on the recommendation of their chief. It marked the estimate which he placed on them all, apart from popular praise or censure.

THE SEVENTH CAVALRY

Modest, hard working old Devin, coming from the militia with little political influence and nothing but his own perseverance and faithful work to recommend him, was placed on the same plane as Custer and Merritt, who had started with all the advantages of a West Point education in their favor. The only difference between them was that of seniority. Merritt had been an officer a year before Custer, and Custer's army commission ranked him over Devin, otherwise all were equal. With Merritt and Devin, we have finished in this history. Their paths no longer run near Custer's. The latter was appointed Lieutenant-Colonel of the new Seventh Cavalry, and henceforward will appear identified with that regiment of which it would appear that a short sketch is here proper.

The Seventh U.S. Cavalry was called into existence as a regiment and its first officers commissioned July 28th, 1866. On that day, the skeleton of the regiment was as follows; Colonel A.J. Smith, Lieutenant-Colonel George A. Custer, Major Alfred Gibbs, all three West Pointers, and Brevet Major Generals U.S.A. Smith was quite an old soldier, having entered the service in 1838, and Gibbs dated from before the Mexican War. During the rebellion, Gibbs had latterly commanded the Regular Cavalry brigade in the First Division of the Cavalry Corps.

Major Alfred Gibbs. Gibbs died while on active duty in the 7th U.S. Cavalry at Fort Leavenworth, Kansas of congestion of the brain on December 26, 1868.

Eight captains were appointed at the same date, of whom not one was from the academy. All came from the volunteers or had risen from the ranks in the regular army during the war. Their names were William Thompson, Frederick W. Benteen, Myles W. Keogh, Edward Myers, Robert M. West, Louis M. Hamilton, Albert Barnitz, and Michael V. Sheridan. Of these, Thompson and West had been brigade commanders, Benteen a colonel, and the rest Lieutenant-Colonels by brevet or otherwise.

Six first-lieutenants were commissioned the same day, Samuel M. Robbins, Mathew Berry, Owen Hale, Myles Moylan, F.V. Commagere and Thomas W. Custer. Of these, Custer and Commagere had been Majors, the rest captains of volunteers. T.W. Custer was the brother of the General. He had entered the army on the 23rd February, 1866 as second-lieutenant of the First Infantry, an office which he was allowed to resign on the 27th July, being appointed next day in his brother's regiment.

These were the first officers of the Seventh Cavalry appointed just ten years ago. Today, hardly one of them is left. The Colonel was retired from service not long after his appointment, and Major Gibbs died at Fort Leavenworth, a year after the formation of the regiment, from the effects of an old lance wound received before 1860. Before going any further, it will be well to trace here Custer's official and private career during the time of the formation of the Seventh Cavalry until the opening of his first Indian campaign.

He was mustered out of service as a major-general of volunteers in March, 1866, in Houston, Texas. During the year then past, his position in the regular army had been that of a simple captain in the Fifth Cavalry, on leave of absence. His leave was granted him in April, 1865, and read "until further orders." His successes then, just after Sailor's Creek and Appomattox, were too public and brilliant to be ignored, and as yet he had not excited the envy which afterwards assailed him. In the volunteer service, he had only experienced this envy for a few weeks, at his first elevation, and there were so many prizes in those days that the envy was soon forgotten in hope. Besides this, his services had been so wonderfully successful that he had conquered envy by admiration, in almost all cases. No one therefore seemed to be disposed to shorten his enjoyment of hard earned leisure by intriguing to get him ordered back to his regiment as a captain.

During 1865 and the beginning of 1866, he enjoyed full major-general's pay and allowances, then about $8000 a year. While in Texas, his expenses for living were very small, as appears from many of his letters home, and he saved a great deal of money. Moreover, there were so many opportunities of making money that he was very sorely tempted at times to leave the service and settle down in Texas.

His muster out, while it sent him home to Monroe, left him in a very different position. He became a captain once more, with only about $2000 a year pay and a small allowance of quarters. It was a heavy fall in pecuniary circumstances, modified by his savings and by the fact that he was still on leave. He went therefore to New York, and while there, entered into negotiations with the Mexican government to become chief of cavalry for Juarez in his last struggle with Maximilian. The history of this application will bring out the esteem in which he was then held by General Grant, as evinced in the following letter of introduction.

We append this letter as of special interest, in view of the altered relations of the parties in after days. His letter was written to Senor Romero, the Mexican Minister to Washington. It shows Grant's opinion of Custer in the days when Grant was nothing but an honest soldier.

HEADQUARTERS ARMIES OF THE UNITED STATES
Washington DC, May 16, 1866

DEAR SIR: This will introduce to your acquaintance General Custer, who rendered such distinguished service as a cavalry officer during the war. There was no officer in that branch of the service who had the confidence of General Sheridan to a greater degree than General Custer, and there is no officer in whose judgment I have greater faith than in Sheridan's. Please understand then that I mean by this to endorse General Custer in a high degree.

General Custer proposes to apply for a leave of absence for one year, with permission to leave the country, and to take service while abroad. I propose to endorse his application favorably, and believe that he will get it.

FREDERICK WHITTAKER

Yours truly,

U. S. GRANT
To Sr. M. Romero, Minister

Sr. Romero was delighted with the application, as he well might be. Mexico was then in the worst possible state, and the Liberal cause in a desperate condition. The Juarez people had plenty of men; but neither arms, money nor equipments. Carvajal, the head of the Juarez military government, offered Custer the position of Adjutant General of Mexico with double the pay of an American Major General, in gold, if he could only come to Mexico with one or two thousand men, Americans; the Mexican Liberal government offering to assume any debt he might incur in raising this force.

After events proved that the expedition would have been perfectly feasible, for the hold of Maximilian on Mexico, never strong, was weakening daily, and the arrival of Custer, with his brilliant reputation and the men he could easily have raised, would have ended the war with a blaze of glory. Money and men were both forthcoming, and success was certain. All these bright prospects however, were destroyed by a simple formality; the American government refused to grant Custer the year's leave he asked for, and he was compelled to choose between the smaller certainty of a captaincy in the American army and the glorious uncertainties of a soldier of fortune. The native good sense and sturdy habits of mind inherited and taught him by family influence saved him from the role of the last, and the first was soon bettered for him by the increase of the army.

While his application was still pending however, he was recalled, together with his wife, to Monroe, by the news of the dangerous illness of Judge Bacon. They arrived there only just in time to witness the Judge's death, which took place May 17th, 1866, and was a heavy blow to both. Long before this time, the good old Judge who had been so careful and anxious about the future of his daughter, had learned to lay aside all fears in that direction, and to feel for her husband a respect and liking, all the stronger for his previous mistrust. He died in Custer's arms, resting on his strong breast, and blessing with his latest breath his two children, finding that instead of losing a daughter he had gained a son, as attentive and affectionate as any of his own could have been had he possessed one.

While the brilliant deeds of Custer had so far gained him the applause of the world at large, the victory in which he felt the greatest pride of any was that gained during the latter part of his life, over the reluctance and distrust of the Judge, and the conversion of those feelings into the warmest respect and esteem. He had reason to be proud of it, for it was no common victory. It was obtained by a single course of conduct. The Judge, who was the kindest and most idolizing of fathers, full of fears at the future of his daughter on her marriage, was quite overcome by the fact of her entire happiness, and by that alone. The real unselfishness of paternal love, as distinguished from that between lovers is illustrated by this; that the Judge not only forgave, but learned to love the man who had taken away his daughter.

Monroe, Michigan

The death of Judge Bacon made some difference in the prospects of the young couple, most of the Judge's property, which included the house in Monroe in which she now lives, going to his daughter, but as it was not large, it did not alter their ordinary style of living. They continued to reside at Monroe for the next month or two until in July,

FREDERICK WHITTAKER

Custer received his commission from President Johnson as lieutenant-colonel of the new Seventh Cavalry.

He was still anxious to obtain his year's leave, so as to be able to go to Mexico, and with that object set out for Buffalo in August to meet President Johnson, who was then engaged in that celebrated operation known as "swinging round the circle." Mrs. Custer went with him.

Inasmuch as the present book will fall into the hands of many too young to remember distinctly the meaning of the expression "swinging round the circle," it may be well to explain it here. President Johnson, originally a strong Southern Democrat, had been nominated for Vice-President during the war on the same ticket with Lincoln, as a "War Democrat" and as a sort of compromise, beating Seymour and McClellan. When the assassination of Lincoln placed Johnson in power, he soon returned to his old *ante-bellum* associations, the result of which was a furious contest between Congress and himself in which the former had the best of it, through holding the legislative power with a compact majority.

The strife was, at this time, August, 1866, at its very hottest. Congress had adjourned, and the President then indulged in a trip which took him all round the country and in which he was in the habit of stopping at every railway station to make a political speech to the crowd that gathered on the platform to see the presidential party. He took along with him his whole cabinet and General Grant, and the ludicrous nature of the tour was commemorated by the term "swinging round the circle."

When Custer met President Johnson at Buffalo, the young general was still, as far as civil affairs went, a frank, innocent boy. Of political lore he was perfectly guiltless, and an old politician like Johnson could wind him round his finger with his wily tricks. Johnson saw at once what a political and popular help Custer's presence would be to him and accordingly, instead of granting his request for leave, ordered him to accompany the party in its tour, on duty. And that is the way Custer came to join Johnson in "swinging round the circle."

To the young couple, the whole jaunt was a pleasure trip, which cost them nothing, where they had delightful times and nothing to do but enjoy themselves. Of the political aspect of the trip, Custer was at first unaware, and as his commission as lieutenant-colonel was already safe, he had no axe to grind, after his first visit, when the President told him he could not give him leave to go to Mexico. The party travelled by the Lake Shore Railroad to Cleveland, Toledo, then to Monroe, Detroit, Chicago and so to Springfield, Illinois, the late residence of the murdered President Lincoln.

The "swinging around the circle tour" was a speaking campaign undertaken by President Andrew Johnson between August 27 and September 15, 1866, in which he tried to gain support for his Reconstruction policies. The tour was a disaster, and by the time Johnson returned to Washington, he had even less support in the north than he started with.

Johnson had at the time a great idea that his political enemies would try to assassinate him on the road, and insisted on Custer's occupying the next room to his own at every hotel and keeping loaded revolvers by him to protect the Executive from murder, a danger which, however, existed chiefly in his own heated imagination. The ostensible cause of the tour was the inauguration of a monument to President Lincoln, which took place at Springfield, the nominal termination of the journey.

Political effect and the President's monomania for speeches on the constitution continued the journey to St. Louis, whence the party returned to Washington another way. Custer got tired of the trip at last when he found that it was entirely a political movement and one productive of ridicule to all the participants, and as soon as the last semblance of danger was removed by their return to the civilized Eastern States, he parted from the President, refusing an invitation to Washington. He refused also during this trip the full colonelcy of the Ninth Cavalry, a black regiment, which was offered him, preferring a lower step to a lower grade of service.

On leaving the President, he went to the Soldiers' and Sailors' Convention at Cleveland, and excited quite a commotion by introducing to the meeting the ex-rebel cavalry general Forrest, a rough hewn man, something of his own stamp for fiery energy, and who had been far the most dangerous cavalry commander possessed at any time by the Confederate cause.

Nothing hurt Custer's political and military future like the movements of this summer, all of which were owing to his generous impulsive way of doing things. Honest to the backbone himself, he could not imagine that others could be less so, and he fell, as it were, bound hand and foot, into the midst of a den of hungry political wolves who would have picked his bones clean had he stayed much longer. Like Juvenal refusing to go to Rome, he could reply, when he was asked the cause of his non success in politics, "*Nescio mentire.*" It tells the whole story. He and Sheridan were political failures for the same reason, on opposite sides. Kilpatrick, Slocum, Banning, Logan, Butler, Garfield and a host of others were successes for the opposite reason.

At last, he was saved from the consequences of his indiscreet utterance of the truth by receiving orders to report at Fort Riley, Kansas, and assume his command. Never was order more welcome. It found him at Monroe, longing for the plains and the new life which he was to lead there. He was already developing into the sportsman he afterwards became. During his Texan residence, he had accumulated a pack of some twenty fox hounds, and had invested in rifles, having become a fair shot. In his letters home from Texas, he frequently speaks of his hunting expeditions after deer, rabbits, coons, possums and other animals. In those days, to all appearance he was as innocent as a child about the relative dignity of game, and talks of going on a coon hunt with an old Negro, with all the zest of a veteran trapper after a grizzly. He seems to have felt like a regular big boy out of school, eager for anything in the way of game, and making no distinctions.

Fort Riley Custer House. The Custer House is the house that most closely represents the style of home that General Custer and Libbie lived in at Fort Riley. Custer's actual house burned due to a kitchen fire, and Quarters 24A (pictured) has been restored with time period furnishings.

The foxhound pack of Texas was broken up, except one or two of the finest dogs which he took to Monroe, but during the "swinging round the circle" trip, he became wonderfully interested in the Scotch deerhound, of which he saw one or two specimens. He ended by buying a pair, bred in Canada from imported dogs, and afterwards received a present of another, an imported dog. From these others were afterwards bred, so that in a few years he possessed quite a pack of these dogs, besides foxhounds, setters, spaniels and others. He had always managed to have dogs at all periods of his career, even when as a lieutenant he took old "Rose" to Washington with him, but as soon as he was able to indulge his fancy freely he perfectly reveled in the collection of animals, having as many and varied a pack as used to

FREDERICK WHITTAKER

attend Sir Walter Scott at Abbotsford in days gone by.

The General and Mrs. Custer started for Fort Riley, which they reached when it was yet the terminus of the Pacific Railroad. A year later, in spite of an Indian war, ninety miles more were finished. Fort Riley, when they came there, was a perfect sink of iniquity, as far as concerned the village outside the military post. During the winter and spring, this sink of iniquity was moved on to Fort Hays; cause - extension of the railroad. All the desperate characters of the frontier flocked to the terminus of the railroad; gamblers, thieves, murderers, outcasts of all kinds. In Fort Hays, one year old, were thirty-six graves, every grave that of a man who had died "with his boots on," that is to say killed in a brawl.

Boot Hill Cemetery, Hays City, Kansas. The cemetery was the first in the West to be called Boot Hill. At least seventy-nine outlaws were buried at the site.

The tedium of life inside the post was only relieved by the arrival from day to day of the new officers of the Seventh Cavalry come to report to Custer, in command. On the appointment of these officers, the next thing in order was to provide them a regiment to command, and with that object the rest of the year was occupied in recruiting. The original intention seems to have been to form a regiment of only eight companies, but the Seventh, in common with the other cavalry regiments, was subsequently raised to one of three battalions, each of four companies, necessitating two more majors and four additional captains, besides lieutenants. Major Joel H. Elliot was appointed March 7, 1867, from Indiana. He had been a colonel of volunteers. Major W.S. Abert followed on the 8th, June. He had been one of the old army officers, a civil appointment, since 1855, and during the war had been brevetted brigadier-general of volunteers.

The new captains were Thomas M. Dayton, Lee P. Gillette, George W. Yates and Thomas B. Weir, of whom three had been lieutenant-colonels. The new first-lieutenants were Henry H. Abell, Charles Brewster, James M. Bell, D.W. Wallingford, William W. Cook and Henry Jackson. All these entered the regiment in 1867.

In the same year, the regiment also received five second-lieutenants. Three of these, James T. Leavy, Bradford S. Bassett and William B. Clark came from the volunteers, where Bassett had been a captain. The other two, John M. Johnson and Edward S. Godfrey, had just graduated from the "Point." Such was the composition of the Seventh Cavalry when Custer assumed command of the regiment in 1867. Colonel A.J. Smith was the department chief, and therefore never saw his regiment, the whole responsibility falling on Custer.

The material of which the men were composed was decidedly bad, as was the case with all the regular regiments at the close of the war. Recruits came from the large towns, and included a great many of the rough classes, men who enlisted with the purpose of shirking as much duty as they could, and of deserting whenever they got tired. We shall see before long how much trouble they brought on Custer, and how he at last licked them into shape.

There is perhaps today no regiment in the army which bears so strongly on itself the imprint of its leader as the Seventh Cavalry. What it is, Custer's name and influence have made it. He found it a crowd of green recruits. He made it into a regiment of veterans and heroes. How he did it will appear in the course of his life on the plains. Suffice it here to say that he managed to make the regiment too hot for officers who indulged in drunkenness on duty, and either drove them out entirely, induced them to take the pledge or compelled them to reserve their excesses for places where it concerned themselves alone, and did the least possible injury to the service.

This trait of Custer's character had always been prominent during his volunteer service. He began with it in the Michigan Brigade, continued it in the Third Division, and now brought it into the Seventh Cavalry. He realized so strongly the dangers of excess in his own nature, that he always sympathized with and aided all whom he found in the same difficulties, trying to escape from evil influence. In all this, he was very far removed from those total abstinence fanatics who have brought so much discredit on the name of "temperance" by their intemperance.

He never interfered with the free will of those officers who possessed enough self-control to remain moderate drinkers, and never forced his views on others unless it became a question of the interest of the service and the career of the individual. He found that his own high-strung, nervous temperament was utterly unfitted to indulge in stimulants, and he totally abandoned the habit. He induced his brother Tom to take the pledge and abstain from liquors and tobacco, because he saw that their temperaments were very similar; and the result was that Tom Custer became an ornament to his profession, inspired by his brother's example.

Whenever Custer found a brave and otherwise capable officer caught in the toils of dipsomania, he always did his best to reform and save him. It was only those willful and habitual debauchees who gloried in tempting others on whom Custer was remorselessly severe; and there he had no compassion. To those who know to what an extent the inroads of intemperance have penetrated in the army, and who are frank enough to acknowledge, instead of denying the evil, his conduct needs no excuse. For the opinions of others, he never cared. As he began, so he followed to the last, the right way as it appeared to him, regardless of consequences.

THE HANCOCK EXPEDITION

THE Seventh Cavalry was first mounted, armed and sent to the plains in the spring of 1867, and as this was the opening of a fresh experience for Custer, it is peculiarly fortunate that we are able to present his impressions in his own words. It was the first time in his life, it must be remembered, that he officiated as the commander of a single regiment, and against Indians, and all his former experience was at fault. He had to learn everything anew, and the record of his first experiences is so fresh and interesting that we shall extract freely there from.

Of the many important expeditions, says he, organized to operate in the Indian country, none perhaps of late years has excited more general and unfriendly comment, considering the slight loss of life inflicted upon the Indians, than the expedition organized and led in person by Major-General Hancock in the spring of 1867. The clique generally known as the "Indian Ring" were particularly malevolent and bitter in their denunciations of General Hancock for precipitating, as they expressed it, an Indian war.

This expedition was quite formidable in appearance, being made up of eight troops of cavalry, seven companies of infantry and one battery of light artillery, numbering altogether about 1,400 men. As General Hancock at the time and since has been so often accused of causelessly bringing on an Indian war, a word in explanation (in Custer's words) may not be amiss:

Being in command of the cavalry connected with the expedition, I had ample and frequent opportunities for learning the true purposes and objects of the march into the heart of the Indian country.

It may be asked; what had the Indians done to make this incursion necessary? They had been guilty of numerous thefts and murders

THE HANCOCK EXPEDITION

during the preceding summer and fall, for none of which had they been called to account. They had attacked the stations of the overland mail route, killed the employees, burned the stations and captured the stock. Citizens had been murdered in their homes on the frontier of Kansas; murders had been committed on the Arkansas route. The principal perpetrators of these acts were the Cheyenne and Sioux.

The agent of the former, if not a party to the murder on the Arkansas, knew who the guilty persons were, yet took no steps to bring the murderers to punishment. Such a course would have interfered with his trade and profits. It was not to punish for these sins of the past that the expedition was set on foot, but rather by its imposing appearance and its early presence in the Indian country to check or intimidate the Indians from a repetition of their late conduct.

This was deemed particularly necessary from the fact that the various tribes from which we had greatest cause to anticipate trouble had during the winter, through their leading chiefs and warriors, threatened that as soon as the grass was up in spring a combined outbreak would take place along our entire frontier, and especially against the main routes of travel. To assemble the tribes for the desired council, word was sent early in March to the agents of those tribes whom it was desirable to meet. The agents sent runners to the villages, inviting them to meet us at some point near the Arkansas River.

General Hancock, with the artillery and six companies of infantry, reached Fort Riley, Kansas, from Fort Leavenworth, by rail, the last week in March; here he was joined by four companies of the Seventh Cavalry and an additional company of the Thirty-seventh Infantry. It was at this point that I joined the expedition.

From Fort Riley, we marched to Fort Harker, a distance of ninety miles, where our force was strengthened by the addition of two more troops of cavalry. Halting only long enough to replenish our supplies, we next directed our march toward Fort Larned, near the Arkansas, about seventy miles to the southeast. A march from the 3rd to the 7th of April brought us to Fort Larned. The agent for the Comanches and Kiowas accompanied us. At Fort Larned, we found the agent of the Cheyenne, Arapaho and Apaches; from the latter we learned that he had, as requested, sent runners to the chiefs of his agency inviting them to the council, and that they had agreed to assemble near Fort Larned on the 10th of the month, requesting that the expedition would remain there until that date. To this request, General Hancock acceded.

Fort Larned, Kansas. With nine historic buildings, the fort is one of the best preserved examples of Indian Wars period forts. Most of the buildings are furnished to their original appearance.

On the 9th of April while encamped awaiting the council, which was to be held the following day, a terrible snow storm occurred, lasting all day until late in the evening. It was our good fortune to be in camp rather than on the march; had it been otherwise, we could not well have escaped without loss of life from the severe cold and blinding snow. The cavalry horses suffered seriously, and were only preserved by doubling their ration of oats, while to prevent their being frozen during the intensely cold night which followed, the guards were instructed to keep passing along the picket lines with a whip and to keep the horses moving constantly.

The snow was eight inches in depth. The council, which was to take place the next day, had to be postponed until the return of good weather. Now began the display of a kind of diplomacy for which the Indian is peculiar. The Cheyenne and a band of the Sioux were encamped on Pawnee Fork, about thirty miles above Fort Larned.

THE HANCOCK EXPEDITION

They neither desired to move nearer to us nor have us approach nearer to them. On the morning of the 11th, they sent us word that they had started to visit us, but discovering a large herd of buffalo near their camp, they had stopped to procure a supply of meat. This message was not received with much confidence, nor was a buffalo hunt deemed of sufficient importance to justify the Indians in breaking their engagement. General Hancock decided, however, to delay another day, when if the Indians still failed to come in, he would move his command to the vicinity of their village and hold the conference there.

Orders were issued on the evening of the 12th for the march to be resumed on the following day.

Rightly concluding that the Indians did not intend to come to our camp, as they had at first agreed to, it was decided to move nearer to their village. Our entire force therefore marched from Fort Larned up Pawnee Fork in the direction of the main village, encamping the first night about twenty- one miles from the fort. Several parties of Indians were seen in our advance during the day, evidently watching our movements; while a heavy smoke, seen to rise in the direction of the Indian village, indicated that something more than usual was going on.

This smoke we afterward learned arose from the burning grass.* The Indians, thinking to prevent us from encamping in their vicinity, had set fire to and burned all the grass for miles in the direction from which they expected us. Before we arrived at our camping ground, we were met by several chiefs and warriors belonging to the Cheyenne and Sioux. Among the chiefs were Pawnee Killer of the Sioux and White Horse of the Cheyenne. It was arranged that these chiefs should accept our hospitality and remain with us during the night, and in the morning all the chiefs of the two tribes then in the village were to come to General Hancock's headquarters and hold a council.

---

* This was the dried grass of the previous year, always peculiarly easy to fire. The battles of Hooker's and Grant's troops in the Wilderness of Virginia, in the early spring, were almost always noted by similar fires, the dead grass catching first from the artillery flashes.

FREDERICK WHITTAKER

White Horse

On the morning of the 14th, Pawnee Killer left our camp at an early hour, for the purpose, as he said, of going to the village to bring in the other chiefs to the council. Nine o'clock had been agreed upon as the hour at which the council should assemble. The hour came, but the chiefs did not. Now, an Indian council is not only often an important, but always an interesting occasion. And, somewhat like a famous recipe for making a certain dish, the first thing necessary in holding an Indian council is to get the Indian. Half-past nine o'clock came, and still we were lacking this one important part of the council.

At this juncture, Bull Bear, an influential chief among the Cheyenne, came in and reported that the chiefs were on their way to our camp, but would not be able to reach it for some time. This was a mere artifice to secure delay. General Hancock informed Bull Bear that as the chiefs could not arrive for some time, he would move his forces up the stream nearer to the village, and the council could be held at our camp that night. To this proposition, Bull Bear gave his assent.

At 11 a.m., we resumed the march and had proceeded but a few miles when we witnessed one of the finest and most imposing military displays, prepared according to the Indian art of war, which it has ever been my lot to behold. It was nothing more nor less than an Indian line of battle drawn directly across our line of march; as if to say, thus far and no further. Most of the Indians were mounted; all were bedecked in their brightest colors, their heads crowned with the brilliant war-bonnet, their lances bearing the crimson pennant, bows strung and quivers full of barbed arrows.

Sioux war party

In addition to these weapons, which with the hunting knife and tomahawk are considered as forming the armament of the warrior, each one was supplied with either a breech-loading rifle or revolver, sometimes with both the latter obtained through the wise forethought and strong love of fair play which prevails in the Indian Department, which, seeing that its wards are determined to fight, is equally determined that there shall be no advantage taken, but that the two sides shall be armed alike; proving too in this manner the wonderful liberality of our government, which not only is able to furnish its soldiers with the latest improved style of breech-loaders to defend it and themselves, but is equally able and willing to give the same pattern of arms to their common foe.

The only difference is that the soldier, if he loses his weapon, is charged double price for it; while to avoid making any charge against the Indian, his weapons are given him without conditions attached. In the line of battle before us there were several hundred Indians, while further to the rear and at different distances were other organized bodies acting apparently as reserves. Still further were small detachments who seemed to perform the duty of couriers, and were held in readiness to convey messages to the village. The ground beyond was favorable for an extended view, allowing the eye to sweep the plain for several miles. As far as the eye could reach, small groups or individuals could be seen in the direction of the village; these were evidently parties of observation whose sole object was to learn the result of our meeting with the main body and hasten with the news to the village.

For a few moments, appearances seemed to foreshadow anything but a peaceful issue. The infantry was in the advance, followed closely by the artillery, while my command, the cavalry, was marching on the flank. General Hancock, who was riding with his staff at the head of the column, coming suddenly in view of the wild fantastic battle array, which extended far to our right and left and not more than half a mile in our front, hastily sent orders to the infantry, artillery, and cavalry to form line of battle, evidently determined that if war was intended, we should be prepared.

The cavalry, being the last to form on the right, came into line on a gallop, and without waiting to align the ranks carefully, the command was given to "draw sabre." As the bright blades flashed from their scabbards into the morning sunlight, and the infantry brought their muskets to a carry, a most beautiful and wonderfully interesting sight was spread out before and around us, presenting a contrast which, to a military eye, could but be striking.

Here in battle array, facing each other, were the representatives of civilized and barbarous warfare. The one, with but few modifications, stood clothed in the same rude style of dress, bearing the same patterned shield and weapon that his ancestors had borne centuries before; the other confronted him in the dress and supplied with the implements of war which the most advanced stage of civilization had

THE HANCOCK EXPEDITION

pronounced the most perfect. Was the comparative superiority of these two classes to be subjected to the rude test of war here?

Such seemed the prevailing impression on both sides. All was eager anxiety and expectation. Neither side seemed to comprehend the object or intentions of the other; each was waiting for the other to deliver the first blow. A more beautiful battleground could not have been chosen. Not a bush or even the slightest irregularity of ground intervened between the two lines which now stood frowning and facing each other. Chiefs could be seen riding along the line as if directing and exhorting their braves to deeds of heroism.

After a few moments of painful suspense, General Hancock, accompanied by General A.J. Smith and other officers, rode forward, and through an interpreter invited the chiefs to meet us midway for the purpose of an interview. In response to this invitation, Roman Nose, bearing a white flag, accompanied by Bull Bear, White Horse, Gray Beard and Medicine Wolf on the part of the Cheyenne, and Pawnee Killer, Bad Wound, Tall Bear that Walks under the Ground, Left Hand, Little Bear, and Little Bull on the part of the Sioux, rode forward to the middle of the open space between the two lines.

Here we shook hands with all of the chiefs, most of them exhibiting unmistakable signs of gratification at this apparently peaceful termination of our encounter. General Hancock very naturally inquired the object of the hostile attitude displayed before us, saying to the chiefs that if war was their object, we were ready then and there to participate. Their immediate answer was that they did not desire war, but were peacefully disposed. They were then told that we would continue our march toward the village and encamp near it, but would establish such regulations that none of the soldiers would be permitted to approach or disturb them.

An arrangement was then effected by which the chiefs were to assemble at General Hancock's headquarters as soon as our camp was pitched. The interview then terminated, and the Indians moved off in the direction of the village, we following leisurely in rear.

Custer then proceeds to tell at some length how the Indians managed to deceive them, and the whole affair is very characteristic of the difference between savage and civilized warfare. The preliminary councils, the threatening demonstrations, were all part of a scheme to gain time, and when the troops were safely encamped close to the village, it was found that all the women and children of the Indians had left the lodges and fled in anticipation of a massacre. The chiefs themselves announced this, at the same time that two of them volunteered to follow after the fugitives and bring them back if General Hancock would lend them two Government horses to ride on.

This was done, and they set off at seven in the evening. It was the last seen of them or the horses. Two hours later, one of Hancock's scouts, who had been into the Indian camp, reported that the chiefs themselves were saddling up to leave. This scout was a half-breed Cheyenne, and the result showed that he was in all probability playing a double game.

Custer was at once directed to mount his cavalry, to surround the Indian village and prevent the departure of its inhabitants. This was done, and the village was found all peaceful and quiet, as if everyone was asleep. When it was entered however, it was found that the birds had flown, that the camp was empty. The Indians had left all their goods and fled in the night. The suddenness of their departure and their abandonment of so much property gives color to their own plea, that they feared a repetition of the "Chivington Massacre," that had taken place only a year previous.

The next thing was to pursue the Indians. The scout who reported their approaching departure had in all probability seen them go before he came, and the long operation of stealthily surrounding the camp had consumed much valuable time. Custer's description of the affair and of his own cautious approach, reminds one strongly of his first scout after Confederates under Kearny.

The cavalry was now ordered to follow the Indians; and the time occupied in getting ready was another illustration of how perfectly green everyone then was in Indian warfare. It must be remembered that the Indians were off and marching, and that speed was absolutely needed to catch them. This was the sort of speed of which the Seventh Cavalry in those early days was capable.

THE HANCOCK EXPEDITION

Mess kits were overhauled, says Custer, and fresh supplies of coffee, sugar, flour and the other articles which go to supply the soldier's larder were laid in. Blankets were carefully rolled so as to occupy as little space as possible; every useless pound of luggage was discarded, for in making a rapid pursuit after Indians much of the success depends upon the lightness of the order of march. Saratoga trunks and their accompaniments are at a discount. Never was the old saying that in Rome one must do as Romans do more aptly illustrated than on an Indian campaign.

The Indian, knowing that his safety either on offensive or defensive movements depends in a great measure upon the speed and endurance of his horse, takes advantage of every circumstance which will favor either the one or the other. To this end, he divests himself of all superfluous dress and ornament when preparing for rapid movements. The white man, if he hopes for success, must adopt the same rule of action, and encumber his horse as little as possible. Something besides well-filled mess chests and carefully rolled blankets is necessary in preparing for an Indian campaign. Arms must be reexamined, cartridge boxes refilled, so that each man should carry about one hundred rounds of ammunition on his person, while each troop commander must see that in the company wagon there are placed a few boxes of reserve ammunition.

Then, when the equipment of the soldier has been attended to, his horse, without whose assistance he is helpless, must be looked after; loose shoes are tightened by the driving of an additional nail, and to accomplish this one may see the company blacksmith, a soldier, with the few simple tools of his kit on the ground beside him, hurriedly fastening the last shoe by the uncertain light of a candle held in the hands of the rider of the horse, their mutual labor being varied at times by queries as to "How long shall we be gone?" "I wonder if we will catch Mr. Lo?" "If we do, we'll make it lively for him." So energetic had everybody been that before daylight, everything was in readiness for the start.

Before daylight however, according to Custer's own account, all chance was over. The cavalry followed the trail, preceded by their company of plainsmen and friendly Indians, but they failed to catch the Indians. The cavalry pressed the latter so close that they compelled them to disperse into small parties to lose the trail, but finally the trackers were obliged to give it up as a bad job.

It was while on this march and before the Indians had dispersed, that Custer had his first buffalo adventure. He says that he felt satisfied that the Indians must be many miles ahead, and that the country was full of game. Therefore he called his dogs around him and galloped off after some antelope in the distance. He says:

> Although an ardent sportsman, I had never hunted the buffalo up to this time, consequently was exceedingly desirous of tasting of its excitement. I had several fine English greyhounds, whose speed I was anxious to test with that of the antelope, said to be - which I, believe - the fleetest of animals.
>
> I was mounted on a fine large thoroughbred horse. Taking with me but one man, the chief bugler, and calling my dogs around me, I galloped ahead of the column as soon as it was daylight. A stirring gallop of a few minutes brought me near enough to the antelope, of which there were a dozen or more, to enable the dogs to catch sight of them. Then the chase began, the antelope running in a direction which took us away from the command. By availing myself of the turns in the course, I was able to keep well in view of the exciting chase until it was evident that the antelope were in no danger of being caught by the dogs, which latter had become blown from want of proper exercise.
>
> I succeeded in calling them off, and was about to set out on my return to the column. The horse of the chief bugler, being a common-bred animal, failed early in the race, and his rider wisely concluded to regain the command, so that I was alone. How far I had travelled from the troops I was trying to determine when I discovered a large, dark looking animal grazing nearly a mile distant. As yet I had never seen a wild buffalo, but I at once recognized this as not only a buffalo, but a very large one. Here was my opportunity.
>
> A ravine nearby would enable me to approach unseen until almost within pistol range of my game. Calling my dogs to follow me, I slowly pursued the course of the ravine, giving my horse opportunity to gather himself for the second run. When I emerged from the ravine, I was still several hundred yards from the buffalo, which almost instantly discovered me and set off as fast as his legs could carry him. Had my horse been fresh, the race would have been a short one, but the preceding long run had not

THE HANCOCK EXPEDITION

been without effect.

How long or how fast we flew in pursuit, the intense excitement of the chase prevented me from knowing. I only knew that even the greyhounds were left behind until finally my good steed placed himself and me close alongside the game. It may be because this was the first I had seen, but surely of the hundreds of thousands of buffaloes which I have since seen, none have corresponded with him in size and lofty grandeur. My horse was above the average size, yet the buffalo towered even above him. I had carried my revolver in my hand from the moment the race began.

Repeatedly could I have placed the muzzle against the shaggy body of the huge beast, by whose side I fairly yelled with wild excitement and delight, yet each time would I withdraw the weapon, as if to prolong the enjoyment of the race. It was a race for life or death, yet how different the award from what could be imagined. Still we sped over the springy turf, the high breeding and mettle of my horse being plainly visible over that of the huge beast that struggled by his side. Mile after mile was traversed in this way, until the rate and distance began to tell perceptibly on the bison, whose protruding tongue and labored breathing plainly betrayed his distress.

Determined to end the chase and bring down my game, I again placed the muzzle of the revolver close to the body of the buffalo, when as if divining my intention and feeling his inability to escape by flight, he suddenly determined to fight, and at once wheeled, as only a buffalo can, to gore my horse. So sudden was this movement, and so sudden was the corresponding veering of my horse to avoid the attack, that to retain my control over him I hastily brought up my pistol hand to the assistance of the other. Unfortunately as I did so, my finger, in the excitement of the occasion, pressed the trigger, discharged the pistol and sent the fatal ball into the very brain of the noble animal I rode.

Running at full speed, he fell dead in the course of his leap. Quick as thought, I disengaged myself from the stirrups and found myself whirling through the air over and beyond the head of my horse. My only thought, as I was describing this trajectory and my first thought on reaching *terra firma*, was, "what will the buffalo do with me?" Although at first inclined to rush upon me, my strange procedure seemed to astonish him. Either that, or pity for the utter helplessness of my condition, inclined him to alter his course and leave me alone to my own bitter reflections.

Such was the close of Custer's first buffalo hunt. He remained by his dead horse a little while, decidedly crestfallen, and then started for his command, attended by his dogs only. Luckily, the course of his last chase unwittingly took him ahead of his own column, and he was found by them.

The pursuit having failed to catch the village, it was judged best that the column should push on for the Smoky Hill River stage route to warn the stations that the Indians were up and would soon be on the warpath. This was done, but too late for useful purposes. The Indians were already out, and war had begun. General Hancock had lost his opportunity when he first had the Indian village in his power and allowed it to escape. Henceforth, the Indians were more than his match. It was Custer's first introduction to Indian warfare, and the lesson he then received sunk deep into his heart. He made no more mistakes.

Hancock's Burning of the Village. The illustration portrays soldiers under the command of General Winfield S. Hancock burning a Cheyenne village on Pawnee Fork, thirty miles west of Fort Larned. The illustration was drawn by Theodore Davis and published in Harpers Weekly, April 19, 1867.

To be sure, he was not responsible for the blunders of the campaign, not holding chief command. Being a young officer, naturally modest, he did not pretend to be competent to advise measures in Indian warfare in which he had as yet no experience. Hancock was an old soldier, his experience dating back to 1844, and had served on the plains long before the rebellion. It was not for Custer to presume to offer an opinion that the Indians were fooling his commander, although such was the fact. All the remedy left to Hancock was to do what he actually did, burn up the abandoned village of the Cheyenne and Sioux. He did so, and war was formally opened, a war in which the Indians had decidedly the best of it.

Satanta. While imprisoned, Satanta killed himself on October 11, 1878, by jumping from a window of the prison hospital.

Having burned the village, the next thing in order was a council. Hancock called one of all the Indian chiefs, and it was held at Fort Dodge, Kansas. The result of this council is thus adverted to by Custer:

The most prominent chiefs in council were Satanta, Lone Wolf, and Kicking Bird of the Kiowa, and Little Raven and Yellow Bear of the Arapahoe. During the council, extravagant promises of future good conduct were made by these chiefs. So effective and convincing was the oratorical effort of Satanta that at the termination of his address, the department commander and staff presented him with the uniform coat, sash and hat of a major-general. In return for this compliment, Satanta, within a few weeks after, attacked the post at which the council was held, arrayed in his new uniform.

FREDERICK WHITTAKER

Custer, with the cavalry, had in the meantime marched down the stage route and finally camped at Fort Hays, where he was joined by Hancock with the rest of the expedition at the termination of the council. Hancock then left for Fort Leavenworth and as it soon appeared that the war was fairly opened, Custer started on the 1st of June, from Fort Hays, the spring grass being fairly started at last. His column consisted of three hundred and fifty men of the Seventh Cavalry, and twenty wagons, and his course was towards Fort McPherson on the Platte River, two hundred and twenty five miles off. It was his first Indian scout.

THE FIRST SCOUT

GENERAL CUSTER gives the object of his journey in the following words; it had been decided that my command should thoroughly scout the country from Fort Hays near the Smoky Hill River, to Fort McPherson on the Platte; thence describe a semicircle to the southward, touching the head waters of the Republican, and again reach the Platte at or near Fort Sedgwick, at which post we would replenish our supplies; then move directly south to Fort Wallace, on the Smoky Hill, and from there march down the overland route to our starting point at Fort Hays. This would involve a ride of upwards of one thousand miles.

In telling the story of this, his first Indian expedition, we shall in all cases adopt Custer's own words, where they are practicable. The column saw but one war party of Indians on the way to Fort McPherson, and they were off before they could be caught. The scouts learned from the trail that the Indians were mounted on stage horses, showing that they must have swept the stage routes clean by this time.

"At Fort McPherson," says Custer, "we refilled our wagons with supplies and forage. At the same time, in accordance with my instructions, I reported by telegraph my arrival to General Sherman, who was then further west on the line of the Union Pacific Road. He did not materially change my instructions, further than to direct me to remain near Fort McPherson until his arrival, which would be in the course of a few days."

The interval was diversified by another "council," this time with Pawnee Killer, a Sioux chief like all the other councils it amounted to nothing. Pawnee Killer came in to fool the white man, to find what he was doing and where he was going. The chief promised to bring in his band to encamp by the fort, and received from Custer presents of coffee and sugar and such finery as gratified his Indian fancy. Of course he lied, but Custer was in his first season, and learning Indian tactics. Pawnee Killer left the fort, and soon after General Sherman arrived.

Fort McPherson was located near the site of present day North Platte, Nebraska. It was originally called Cantonment McKean, and was also known as Fort Cottonwood.

The common sense of Sherman realized that Custer, like Hancock, had been duped, and he at first proposed to send after Pawnee Killer and his band, and to retain some of them as hostages. It was too late, so that Custer only learned a valuable lesson from the transaction. This was never to trust to the professions of an Indian in time of war, when it is his interest to deceive.

Failing in catching Pawnee Killer, Custer was ordered to move to the forks of the Republican River, a country full of Indians at all times, and there to try and find Pawnee Killer's village, and make that chief do as he had promised. In the coming war, it was important to discriminate between friends and enemies, not so much for the sake of the Indians as on account of the Indian agents and Congress, and still more for fear of the newspapers at home. Custer was also to look after the Cheyenne and Sioux whom Hancock had let slip. He thus describes his departure:

FREDERICK WHITTAKER

"Owing to the rough and broken character of the bluffs which bound the valley of the Platte on the south side, it was determined to march up the men about fifteen miles from the fort and strike south through an opening in the bluffs known as Jack Morrow's Canon. General Sherman rode with us as far as this point where, after commending the Cheyenne and Sioux to us in his expressive manner, he bade us good-bye and crossed the river to the railroad station on the north side. Thus far, we had had no real Indian warfare. We were soon to experience it, attended by all its frightful barbarities."

Nothing particular happened for the first few days; on the fourth, the column reached the forks of the river in the heart of the Indian country, and as the adventures of the next few days were affected by Custer's determination on reaching that spot, it is well to resume in his own words. It must be remembered that his force consisted of the Seventh Cavalry, (350 strong and 20 wagons), exclusive of scouts and guides. He thus proceeds:

When I parted from General Sherman the understanding was that after beating up the country thoroughly about the forks of the Republican River, I should march my command to Fort Sedgwick, and there I would either see General Sherman again or receive further instructions from him. Circumstances seemed to favor a modification of this plan, at least as to marching the entire command to Fort Sedgwick. It was therefore decided to send a trusty officer with a sufficient escort to Fort Sedgwick with my dispatch, and to receive the dispatches which might be intended for me.

My proposed change of programme contemplated a continuous march, which might be prolonged twenty days or more. To this end, additional supplies were necessary. The guides all agreed in the statement that we were then about equidistant from Fort Wallace on the south and Fort Sedgwick on the north, at either of which the required supplies could be obtained; but that while the country between our camp and the former was generally level and unbroken - favorable to the movement of our wagon train - that between us and Fort Sedgwick was almost impassable for heavily laden wagons.

THE FIRST SCOUT

The train then was to go to Fort Wallace under sufficient escort, be loaded with fresh supplies, and rejoin us in camp. At the same time, the officer selected for that mission could proceed to Fort Sedgwick, obtain his dispatch, and return.

Fort Wallace. Today, Fort Wallace is represented by a small museum nearby in the town of Wallace, Kansas, with relics from the fort as well as photos and literature covering the post's history and the settlement of the Great Plains.

Major Joel A. Elliot, a young officer of great courage and enterprise, was selected as bearer of dispatches to Fort Sedgwick. As the errand was one involving considerable danger, requiring for the round trip a ride of almost two hundred miles, through country which was not only almost unknown but infested by large numbers of hostile Indians, the Major was authorized to arrange the details in accordance with his own judgment.

Knowing that small detachments can move more rapidly than large ones, and that he was to depend upon celerity of movement rather than strength of numbers to evade the numerous war parties prowling in that vicinity, the Major limited the size of his escort to ten picked men and one of the guides, all mounted on fleet horses. To elude the watchful eyes of any parties that might be noting our movements, it was deemed advisable to set out from camp as soon as it was dark, and making a rapid night ride get beyond the circle of danger. In this way, the little party took its departure on the night of the 23rd of June.

On the same day, our train of wagons set out for Fort Wallace to obtain supplies. Colonel West,* with one full squadron of cavalry, was ordered to escort the train to Beaver Creek, about midway, and there halt with one of his companies while the train, under escort of one company commanded by Lieutenant Robbins, should proceed to the front and return - Colonel West to employ the interval in scouting up and down Beaver Creek. The train was under special management of Colonel Cook, who on this occasion was acting in the capacity of a staff officer.

After the departure of the two detachments, which left us in almost opposite directions, our camp settled down to the dull and unexciting monotony of waiting patiently for the time when we should welcome our comrades back again and listen to such items of news as they might bring to us.

It will be remembered that Custer set out to find Pawnee Killer's village. He thus relates how Pawnee Killer found him next morning:

It was just that uncertain period between darkness and daylight on the following morning, and I was living in my tent deep in the enjoyment of that perfect repose which only camp life offers, when the sharp, clear crack of a carbine nearby brought me to my feet. I knew in an instant that the shot came from the picket posted not far from the rear of my camp. At the same moment, my brother, Colonel Custer, who on that occasion was officer of the day and whose duties required him to be particularly on the alert, rushed past my tent, halting only long enough to show his face through the opening and shout, "They are here!"

Now I did not inquire who were referred to, or how many were included in the word "they," nor did my informant seem to think it necessary to explain. "They," referred to Indians, I knew full well. Had I doubted, the brisk fusillade which opened the next moment, and the

---

* The rank of the officers of the Seventh Cavalry, owing to the strange system of brevets and titles of courtesy in use in our army at the close of the war, is often very puzzling. It is the etiquette of the army to call a man by the highest title he has borne, brevet or volunteer, except on duty. West was really only a captain, Cook, subsequently mentioned, a lieutenant.

wild war whoop, were convincing evidences that in truth "they were here!"

My orderly, as was his custom, on my retiring had securely tied all the fastenings to my tent, and it was usually the work of several minutes to undo this unnecessary labor. I had no time to throw away in this manner. Leaping from my bed, I grasped my trusty Spencer, which was always at my side whether waking or sleeping, and with a single dash burst open the tent, and hatless as well as shoeless, ran to the point where the attack seemed to be concentrated.

It was sufficiently light to see our enemies and be seen. The first shot had brought every man of my command from his tent, armed and equipped for battle. The Indians, numbering hundreds, were all around the camp, evidently intending to surround us, while a party of about fifty of their best mounted warriors had, by taking advantage of a ravine, contrived to approach quite close before being discovered. It was the intention of this party to dash through our camp, stampede all our horses, which were to be caught up by the parties surrounding us, and then finish us at their leisure. The picket however, discovered the approach of this party and by firing gave timely warning, thus frustrating the plan of the Indians, who almost invariably base their hopes of success upon effecting a surprise.

My men opened on them such a brisk fire from their carbines that they were glad to withdraw beyond range. The picket who gave the alarm was shot down at his post by the Indians, the entire party galloping over his body, and being prevented from scalping him only by the fire from his comrades who dashed out and recovered him. He was found to be badly though not mortally wounded by a rifle ball through the body.

The Indians, seeing that their attempt to surprise us and to stampede our horses had failed, then withdrew to a point but little over a mile from us, where they congregated and seemed to hold a conference with each other. We did not fear any further attack at this time. They were satisfied with this attempt, and would wait another opportunity.

It was desirable however that we should learn if possible to what tribe our enemies belonged. I directed one of our interpreters to advance midway between our camp and the Indians, and make the signal for holding a parley, and in this way ascertain who were the principal chiefs.

The ordinary manner of opening communication with parties known or supposed to be hostile is to ride toward them in a zigzag manner or to ride in a circle. The interpreter gave the proper signal, and was soon answered by a small party, advancing from the main body of the Indians to within hailing distance. It was then agreed that I, with six of the officers, should come to the bank of the river, which was about equidistant from my camp and from the point where the Indians had congregated, and there be met by an equal number of the leading chiefs. To guard against treachery, I placed most of my command under arms, and arranged with the officer left in command that a blast from the bugle should bring assistance to me if required.

Custer then tells how they arrived at the bank of the river and were met by their old friend Pawnee Killer and his chiefs, taking matters very coolly. His presence was one more lesson for Custer on Indian treachery, and he soon had another. On the pretext of coming over to say "How," several other Indians waded the river, and finally it appeared as if an attempt at murder was to take place, could the white man's suspicions be allayed.

Custer then broke off the conference, which had served no purpose except to inform them who their enemy had been. The close of the conference was characteristic; Pawnee Killer, who seems to have imbibed a great contempt for the youth and inexperience of Custer, had the impudence to beg for coffee, sugar and ammunition. It is needless to say that he did not get them. Custer returned to his regiment and pursued the Sioux for some hours, but was unable to catch the fleet Indian ponies with the coarse heavy troop horses of his command. He finally returned to camp.

Soon after returning, more Indians, a very small party, were seen in the opposite direction, and Captain Hamilton's troop was sent after them. The Indians divided their party, hired Hamilton on for several miles, and finally turned on him as soon as he had divided his own party to pursue them. They fought Hamilton two to one for about an hour, but he kept them off and returned to camp unharmed, having shot two Indians dead and wounded two others. The Indians fought in the peculiar manner known as "circling," which will be fully described in the next chapter.

Pawnee Killer

Hamilton's affair occurred in the direction of Fort Sedgwick, whereas Pawnee Killer had retired toward Fort Wallace. It became clear therefore that the country was full of Indians, and it became a matter of doubt where they were thickest on the route taken by Major Elliot, or that pursued by Robbins and Cook with the wagon train. The party that attacked Hamilton numbered forty-three, whereas Pawnee Killer had several hundred, but the greatest anxiety was felt for Major Elliot's little band of eleven, which had gone in the other direction. Many or few, there were clearly enough Indians on the trail to overwhelm him. Major Elliot, however, proved to be a careful and skillful officer. In five days after, he rode into camp, having trusted to his guide, an old hunter. The party had hidden in ravines all day, and only travelled by night.

FREDERICK WHITTAKER
The fate of the wagon train falls naturally into another chapter.

THE WAGON TRAIN

THE story of the attack on the train and its results in connection with the expedition is thus told by Custer:

Now that the Major and his party had returned to us, our anxiety became centered in the fate of the larger party which had proceeded with the train to Fort Wallace for supplies. The fact that Major Elliot had made his trip unmolested by Indians proved that the latter were most likely assembled south of us, that is, between us and Fort Wallace. Wherever they were, their numbers were known to be large. It would be impossible for a considerable force, let alone a wagon train, to pass from our camp to Fort Wallace and not be seen by the Indian scouting parties.

They had probably observed the departure of the train and escort at the time and divining the object which occasioned the sending of the wagons, would permit them to go to the fort unmolested, but would waylay them on their return in hope of obtaining the supplies they contained. Under this supposition, the Indians had probably watched the train and escort during every mile of their progress; if so, they would not fail to discover that the larger portion of the escort halted at Beaver Creek, while the wagons proceeded to the fort guarded by only forty-eight men; in which case the Indians would combine their forces and attack the train at some point between Fort Wallace and Beaver Creek.

Looking at these probable events, I not only felt impelled to act promptly to secure the safety of the train and its escort, but a deeper and stronger motive stirred me to leave nothing undone to circumvent the Indians. My wife, who, in answer to my letter I believed was then at Fort Wallace, would place herself under the protection of the escort of

THE WAGON TRAIN

the train and attempt to rejoin me in camp. The mere thought of the danger to which she might be exposed spurred me to decisive action. One full squadron, well mounted and armed, under the command of Lieutenant-Colonel Myers, an officer of great experience in Indian affairs, left our camp at dark on the evening of the day that Captain Hamilton had had his engagement with the Indians, and set out in the direction of Fort Wallace.

His orders were to press forward as rapidly as practicable, following the trail made by the train. Written orders were sent in his care to Colonel West, who was in command of that portion of the escort which had halted at Beaver Creek, to join Colonel Myers's command with his own, and then to continue the march toward Fort Wallace until he should meet the returning train and escort. The Indians however, were not to be deprived of this opportunity to secure scalps and plunder.

From our camp to Beaver Creek was nearly fifty miles, Colonel Myers marched his command without halting until he joined Colonel West at Beaver Creek. Here, the two commands united, and under the direction of Colonel West, the senior officer of the party, proceeded toward Fort Wallace, following the trail left by the wagon train and escort. If the escort and Colonel West's forces could be united, they might confidently hope to repel any attack made upon them by Indians. Colonel West was an old Indian fighter, and too thoroughly accustomed to Indian tactics to permit his command to be surprised or defeated in any manner other than by a fair contest.

Let us leave them for a time and join the wagon train and its escort - the latter numbering, all told as before stated, forty-eight men under the immediate command of Lieutenant Robbins. Colonel Cook, whose special duty connected him with the train and its supplies, could also be relied upon for material assistance with the troops in case of actual conflict with the enemy. Comstock, the favorite scout, a host in himself, was sent to guide the party to and from Fort Wallace. In addition to these were the teamsters, who could not be expected to do more than control their teams should the train be attacked.

The march from camp to Beaver Creek was made without incident.

Here, the combined forces of Colonel West and Lieutenant Robbins encamped together during the night. Next morning at early dawn, Lieutenant Robbins's party, having the train in charge, continued the march toward Fort Wallace while Colonel West sent out scouting parties up and down the stream to search for Indians.

William Comstock. Comstock not only looked the part of a frontiersman but also had a catchy frontier nickname "Medicine Bill."

As yet none of their party were aware of the hostile attitude assumed by the Indians within the past few hours, and Colonel West's instructions contemplated a very friendly meeting between his forces and the Indians, should the latter be discovered. The march of the train and escort was made to Fort Wallace without interruption. The only incident worthy of remark was an observation of Comstock's, which proved how thoroughly he was familiar with the Indian and his customs.

The escort was moving over a beautifully level plateau. Not a mound or hillock disturbed the evenness of the surface for miles in either direction. To an unpracticed eye, there seemed no recess or obstruction in or behind which an enemy might be concealed, but everything appeared open to the view for miles and miles, look in what direction one might. Yet such was not the case. Ravines of greater or less extent, though not perceptible at a glance, might have been discovered if searched for, extending almost to the trail over which the party was moving.

These ravines, if followed, would be found to grow deeper and deeper, until after running their course for an indefinite extent, they would terminate in the valley of some running stream. These were the natural hiding places of Indian war parties, waiting their opportunities to dash upon unsuspecting victims. These ravines serve the same purpose to the Indians of the timberless plains that the ambush did to those Indians of the Eastern States accustomed to fighting in the forests and everglades. Comstock's keen eyes took in all at a glance, and he remarked to Colonel Cook and Lieutenant Robbins, as the three rode together at the head of the column, that "If the Injuns strike us at all, it will be just about the time we are comin' along back over this very spot. Now mind what I tell ye all." We shall see how correct Comstock's prophecy was.

Arriving at the fort, no time was lost in loading up the wagons with fresh supplies, obtaining the mail intended for the command, and preparing to set out on the return to camp the following day. On the following morning, Colonel Cook and Lieutenant Robbins began their return march. They had advanced one half the distance which separated them from Colonel West's camp without the slightest occurrence to disturb the monotony of their march, and had reached the point where, on passing before, Comstock had indulged in his prognostication regarding Indians; yet nothing had been seen to excite suspicion or alarm.

Comstock, always on the alert and with eyes as quick as those of an Indian, had been scanning the horizon in all directions. Suddenly he perceived, or thought he perceived, strange figures resembling human heads peering over the crest of a hill far away to the right. Hastily leveling his field glass, he pronounced the strange figures, which were scarcely perceptible, to be neither more nor less than Indians. The officers brought into requisition their glasses, and were soon convinced of the correctness of Comstock's report. It was some time before the

Indians perceived that they were discovered. Concealment then being no longer possible, they boldly rode to the crest and exposed themselves to full view. At first but twenty or thirty made their appearance; gradually their number became augmented until about a hundred warriors could be seen.

It may readily be imagined that the appearance of so considerable a body of Indians produced no little excitement and speculation in the minds of the people with the train. The speculation was as to the intentions of the Indians, whether hostile or friendly. Upon this subject, all doubts were soon dispelled. The Indians continued to receive accessions to their numbers, the reinforcements coming from beyond the crest of the hill on which their presence was first discovered.

Finally, seeming confident in their superior numbers, the warriors, all of whom were mounted, advanced leisurely down the slope leading in the direction of the train and its escort. By the aid of field glasses, Comstock and the two officers were able to determine fully the character of the party now approaching them. The last doubt was thus removed.

It was clearly to be seen that the Indians were arrayed in full war costume, their heads adorned by the brilliantly colored war bonnets, their faces, arms and bodies painted in various colors, rendering their naturally repulsive appearance even more hideous. As they approached nearer, they assumed a certain order in the manner of their advance. Some were to be seen carrying the long glistening lance with its pennant of bright colors; while upon the left arm hung the round shield, almost bullet-proof, and ornamented with paint and feathers according to the taste of the wearer. Nearly all were armed with carbines and one or two revolvers, while many in addition to these weapons carried the bow and arrow.

When the entire band had defiled down the inclined slope, Comstock and the officers were able to estimate roughly the full strength of the party. They were astonished to perceive that between six and seven hundred warriors were bearing down upon them, and in a few minutes would undoubtedly commence the attack. Against such

THE WAGON TRAIN

odds, and upon ground so favorable for the Indian mode of warfare, it seemed unreasonable to hope for a favorable result. Yet the entire escort, officers and men, entered upon their defense with a determination to sell their lives as dearly as possible.

Note the coups sticks. Counting coup was an act of bravery and war honor. Any blow struck against the enemy counted as a coup, but the most prestigious acts included touching an enemy warrior with the hand or with a coup stick.

As the coming engagement, so far as the cavalry was concerned, was to be purely a defensive one, Lieutenant Robbins at once set about preparing to receive his unwelcome visitors. Colonel Cook formed the train in two parallel columns, leaving ample space between for the horses of the cavalry. Lieutenant Robbins then dismounted his men and prepared to fight on foot. The led horses, under charge of the fourth trooper, were placed between the two columns of wagons, and were thus in a measure protected from the assaults which the officers had every reason to believe would be made for their capture.

The dismounted cavalrymen were thus formed in a regular circle enclosing the train and horses. Colonel Cook took command of one flank, Lieutenant Robbins of the other, while Comstock, who, as well as the two officers, remained mounted, galloped from point to point wherever his presence was most valuable. These dispositions being perfected, the march was resumed in this order, and the attack of the savages calmly awaited.

The Indians, who were interested spectators of these preparations for their reception, continued to approach, but seemed willing to delay their attack until the plain became a little more favorable for their operations. Finally, the desired moment seemed to have arrived. The Indians had approached to within easy range, yet not a shot had been fired, the cavalrymen having been instructed by their officers to reserve their fire for close quarters. Suddenly, with a wild ringing war whoop, the entire band of warriors bore down upon the train and its little party of defenders.

On came the savages, filling the air with their terrible yells. Their first object, evidently, was to stampede the horses and draught animals of the train; then, in the excitement and consternation which would follow, to massacre the escort and drivers. The wagon-master in immediate charge of the train had been ordered to keep his two columns of wagons constantly moving forward and well closed up. This last injunction was hardly necessary as the frightened teamsters, glancing at the approaching warriors and hearing their savage shouts, were sufficiently anxious to keep well closed upon their leaders.

The first onslaught of the Indians was made on the flank which was superintended by Colonel Cook. They rode boldly forward as if to dash over the mere handful of cavalrymen, who stood in skirmishing order in a circle about the train. Not a soldier faltered as the enemy came thundering upon them, but waiting until the Indians were within short rifle range of the train, the cavalrymen dropped upon their knees, and taking deliberate aim poured a volley from their Spencer carbines into the ranks of the savages, which seemed to put a sudden check upon the ardor of their movements and forced them to wheel off to the right. Several of the warriors were seen to reel in their saddles, while the ponies of others were brought down or wounded by the effectual fire of the cavalrymen.

Those of the savages who were shot from their saddles were scarcely permitted to fall to the ground before a score or more of their

THE WAGON TRAIN

comrades dashed to their rescue and bore their bodies beyond the possible reach of our men. This is in accordance with the Indian custom in battle. They will risk the lives of a dozen of their best warriors to prevent the body of any one of their number from falling into the white man's possession. The reason for this is the belief which generally prevails among all the tribes that if a warrior loses his scalp he forfeits his hope of ever reaching the happy hunting ground.

As the Indians were being driven back by the well directed volley of the cavalrymen, the latter, overjoyed at their first success, became reassured and sent up a cheer of exultation while Comstock, who had not been idle in the fight, called out to the retreating Indians in their native tongue, taunting them with their unsuccessful assault.

The Indians withdrew to a point beyond the range of our carbines, and there seemed to engage in a parley. Comstock, who had closely watched every movement, remarked that "There's no sich good look for us as to think them Injuns mean to give it up so. Six hundred red devils ain't agoin' to let fifty men stop them from getting at the coffee and sugar that is in these wagons. And they ain't agoin' to be satisfied until they get some of our scalps to pay for the bucks we popped out of their saddles a bit ago."

It was probable that the Indians were satisfied that they could not dash through the train and stampede the animals. Their recent attempt had convinced them that some other method of attack must be resorted to. Nothing but their great superiority in numbers had induced them to risk so much in a charge.

The officers passed along the line of skirmishers - for this in reality was all their line consisted of - and cautioned the men against wasting their ammunition. It was yet early in the afternoon, and should the conflict be prolonged until night, there was great danger of exhausting the supply of ammunition. The Indians seemed to have thought of this, and the change in their method of attack encouraged such a result.

But little time was spent at the parley. Again the entire band of warriors, except those already disabled, prepared to renew the attack, and advanced as before - this time however, with greater caution, evidently desiring to avoid a reception similar to the first. When sufficiently near to the troops, the Indians developed their new plan of attack. It was not to advance en masse as before, but fight as individuals, each warrior selecting his own time and method of attack.

This is the habitual manner of fighting among all the Indians of the Plains, and is termed "circling." First the chiefs led off, followed at regular intervals by the warriors, until the entire six or seven hundred were to be seen riding in single file as rapidly as their fleet footed ponies could carry them. Preserving this order, and keeping up their savage chorus of yells, war whoops and taunting epithets, this long line of mounted barbarians was guided in such manner as to envelope the train and escort, and make the latter appear like a small circle within a larger one.

The Indians gradually contracted their circle, although maintaining the full speed of their ponies, until sufficiently close to open fire upon the soldiers. At first, the shots were scattering and wide of their mark; but, emboldened by the silence of their few but determined opponents, they rode nearer and fought with greater impetuosity. Forced now to defend themselves to the uttermost, the cavalrymen opened fire from their carbines with most gratifying results. The Indians however, moving at such a rapid gait and in single file, presented a most uncertain target.

To add to this uncertainty, the savages availed themselves of their superior - almost marvelous - powers of horsemanship. Throwing themselves upon the sides of their well-trained ponies, they left no part of their persons exposed to the aim of the troopers except the head and one foot, and in this posture they were able to aim the weapons either over or under the necks of their ponies, thus using the bodies of the latter as an effective shield against the bullets of their adversaries.

At no time were the Indians able to force the train and its escort to come to a halt. The march was continued at an uninterrupted gait. This successful defense against the Indians was in a great measure due to the presence of the wagons which, arranged in the order described, formed a complete barrier to the charges and assaults of the savages; and as a last resort, the wagons could have been halted and used as a breastwork behind which the cavalry, dismounted, would have been

THE WAGON TRAIN

almost invincible against their more numerous enemies. There is nothing an Indian dislikes more in warfare than to attack a foe, however weak, behind breastworks of any kind. Any contrivance which is an obstacle to his pony is a most serious obstacle to the warrior.

The attack of the Indians, aggravated by their losses in warriors and ponies, as many of the latter had been shot down, was continued without cessation for three hours. The supply of ammunition of the cavalry was running low. The "fourth troopers," who had remained in charge of the led horses between the four columns of wagons, were now replaced from the skirmishers, and the former were added to the list of active combatants. If the Indians should maintain the fight much longer, there was serious ground for apprehension regarding the limited supply of ammunition.

If only night or reinforcements would come; was the prayerful hope of those who contended so gallantly against such heavy odds. Night was still too far off to promise much encouragement; while as to reinforcements, their coming would be purely accidental - at least so argued those most interested in their arrival. Yet reinforcements were at that moment striving to reach them. Comrades were in the saddle and spurring forward to their relief. The Indians, although apparently turning all their attention to the little band inside, had omitted no precaution to guard against interference from outside parties.

In this instance, perhaps, they were more than ordinarily watchful, and had posted some of their keen-eyed warriors on the high line of bluffs which ran almost parallel to the trail over which the combatants moved. From these bluffs, not only a good view of the fight could be obtained, but the country for miles in either direction was spread out beneath them, and enabled the scouts to discern the approach of any hostile party which might be advancing.

Fortunate for the savages that this precaution had not been neglected, or the contest in which they were engaged might have become one of more equal numbers. To the careless eye, nothing could have been seen to excite suspicion. But the warriors on the lookout were not long in discovering something which occasioned them no little anxiety. Dismounting from their ponies and concealing the latter in a ravine, they prepared to investigate more fully the cause of their alarm.

That which they saw was as yet but a faint dark line on the surface of the plain, almost against the horizon. So faint was it that no one but an Indian or practiced frontiersman would have observed it. It was fully ten miles from them and directly in their line of march. The ordinary observer would have pronounced it a break or irregularity in the ground, or perhaps the shadow of a cloud and its apparent permanency of location would have dispelled any fear as to its dangerous character.

But was it stationary? Apparently, yes. The Indians discovered otherwise. By close watching, the long faint line could be seen moving along, as if creeping stealthily upon an unconscious foe. Slowly it assumed a more definite shape, until what appeared to be a mere stationary dark line drawn upon the green surface of the plain developed itself to the searching eyes of the red man into a column of cavalry moving at a rapid gait toward the very point they were then occupying.

Convinced of this fact, one of the scouts leaped upon his pony and flew with almost the speed of the wind to impart this knowledge to the chiefs in command on the plain below. True, the approaching cavalry, being still several miles distant, could not arrive for nearly two hours; but the question to be considered by the Indians was whether it would be prudent for them to continue their attack on the train - their ponies already becoming exhausted by the three hours' hard riding given them - until the arrival of the fresh detachment of the enemy, whose horses might be in condition favorable to a rapid pursuit, and thereby enable them to overtake those of the Indians whose ponies were exhausted. Unwilling to incur this new risk, and seeing no prospect of overcoming their present adversaries by a sudden or combined dash, the chiefs decided to withdraw from the attack and make their escape while the advantage was yet in their favor.

The surprise of the cavalrymen may be imagined at seeing the Indians, after pouring a shower of bullets and arrows into the train, withdraw to the bluffs, and immediately after continue their retreat until lost to view. This victory for the troopers, although so unexpected, was none the less welcome. The Indians contrived to carry away with them their killed and wounded. Five of their bravest warriors were known to have been sent to the happy hunting ground, while the list of their wounded was much larger.

After the Indians had withdrawn and left the cavalrymen masters of the field, our wounded, of whom there were comparatively few, received every possible care and attention. Those of the detachment who had escaped unharmed were busily engaged in exchanging congratulations and relating incidents of the fight.

In this manner, nearly an hour had been whiled away, when far in the distance, in their immediate front, fresh cause for anxiety was discovered. At first, the general opinion was that it was the Indians again, determined to contest their progress. Field glasses were again called into requisition, and revealed not Indians, but the familiar blue blouses of the cavalry. Never was the sight more welcome. The next moment, Colonel Cook, with Comstock and a few troopers, applied spurs to their horses and were soon dashing forward to meet their comrades.

The approaching party was none other than Colonel West's detachment, hastening to the relief of the train and its gallant little escort. A few words explained all, and told the heroes of the recent fight how it happened that reinforcements were sent to their assistance; and then was explained why the Indians had so suddenly concluded to abandon their attack and seek safety in quietly withdrawing from the field.

THE KIDDER MASSACRE

SO far, Custer's first Indian campaign had progressed, on the whole, favorably. He had been duped by the Indians in common with General Hancock, but he had suffered no disaster, and all his parties, large or small, had succeeded in beating off the Indians. At that time, the American army in regard to the Indians was much in the attitude of the Romans towards the Gauls, as depicted by Sallust in the closing sentences of his "*War against Jugurtha.*" Sallust says; "The Romans had always been strongly of opinion, and now no less so, that all other nations must yield to them in bravery; but that when they fought with the Gauls, they were to aim only at the preservation of their state, and not at glory."

Much the same opinion prevailed among army officers in America, to judge from the cautious proceedings, until Custer came. In this campaign, as a beginner, he was feeling his way and learning pretty rapidly. The first disaster that was to befall any of his troops befell an officer sent on a similar errand to that of Major Elliot, before mentioned, but in the other direction.

"On the morning of the 28th," continues Custer, "the train returned to the camp on the Republican. All were proud of the conduct of those detachments of the command which had been brought into actual conflict with the Indians. The heroes of the late fights were congratulated heartily upon their good luck, while their comrades who had unavoidably remained in camp, consoled themselves with the hope that the next opportunity might be theirs.

"The dispatches brought by Major Elliot from General Sherman directed me to continue my march, as had been suggested, up the North Republican, then strike northward and reach the Platte again at some point west of Fort Sedgwick near Riverside Station. This programme

THE KIDDER MASSACRE

was carried out. Leaving our camp on the Republican, we marched us the north fork of that river about sixty miles, then turned nearly due north and marched for the valley of the Platte."

Telegraph Station. In 1860, there were about 157 Pony Express stations along the Pony Express route. At each station, the express rider would change to a fresh horse and pick up the next mail pouch.

At the Platte, the column arrived, after a march of sixty-five miles without water, and found itself near Riverside Telegraph Station, fifty miles west of Fort Sedgwick. They learned that the Indians had attacked the nearest stage station the night before they arrived, and had killed three men. This information was obtained by a detachment which reached the station. Custer then relates the incident of the Kidder Massacre as follows:

Believing that General Sherman must have sent later instructions for me to Fort Sedgwick than those last received from him, I sent a telegram to the officer in command at the fort, making inquiry to that effect. To my surprise, I received a dispatch saying that, the day after the departure of Major Elliot and his detachment from Fort Sedgwick with dispatches, of which mention has been previously made, a second detachment of equal strength, viz., ten troopers of the Second United States Cavalry under command of Lieutenant Kidder, and guided by a famous Sioux chief Red Bead, had left Fort Sedgwick with important dispatches for me from General Sherman, and that Lieutenant Kidder had been directed to proceed to my camp near the forks of the

Republican, and failing to find me there, he was to follow immediately on my trail until he should overtake my command.

I immediately telegraphed to Fort Sedgwick that nothing had been seen or heard of Lieutenant Kidder's detachment, and requested a copy of the dispatches borne by him to be sent me by telegraph. This was done; the instructions of General Sherman were for me to march my command, as was at first contemplated, across the country from the Platte to the Smoky Hill River, striking the latter at Fort Wallace. Owing to the low state of my supplies, I determined to set out for Fort Wallace at daylight next morning.

Great anxiety prevailed throughout the command concerning Lieutenant Kidder and his party. True, he had precisely the same number of men that composed Major Elliot's detachment when the latter went upon a like mission, but the circumstances which would govern in the one case had changed when applied to the other. Major Elliot, an officer of experience and good judgment, had fixed the strength of his escort, and performed the journey before it was positively known that the Indians in that section had entered upon the war path.

Had the attack on the commands of Hamilton, Robbins, and Cook been made prior to Elliot's departure, the latter would have taken not less than fifty troopers as escort. After an informal interchange of opinions between the officers of my command regarding the whereabouts of Lieutenant Kidder and party, we endeavored to satisfy ourselves with the following explanation.

Using the capital letter Y for illustration, let us locate Fort Sedgwick, from which post Lieutenant Kidder was sent with dispatches, at the right upper point of the letter. The camp of my command at the forks of the Republican would be at the junction of the three branches of the letter. Fort Wallace relatively would be at the lower termination, and the point on the Platte at which my command was located the morning referred to would be at the upper termination of the left branch of the letter.

Robbins and Cook, in going with the train to Wallace for supplies, had passed and returned over the lower branches. After their return

THE KIDDER MASSACRE

and that of Major Elliot and his party, my entire command resumed the march for the Platte. We moved for two or three miles out on the heavy wagon trail of Robbins and Cook, then suddenly changed our direction to the right.

It was supposed that Kidder and his party arrived at our deserted camp at the forks of the Republican about nightfall, but finding us gone had determined to avail themselves of the moonlight night and overtake us before we should break camp next morning. Riding rapidly in the dim light of evening, they had failed to observe the point at which we had diverged from the plainer trail of Robbins and Cook and instead of following our trail had continued on the former in the direction of Fort Wallace. Such seemed to be a plausible if not the only solution capable of being given.

Anxiety for the fate of Kidder and his party was one of the reasons impelling me to set out promptly on my return. From our camp at the forks of the Republican to Fort Wallace was about eighty miles - but eighty miles of the most dangerous country infested by Indians. Remembering the terrible contest in which the command of Robbins and Cook had been engaged on this very route within a few days, and knowing that the Indians would in all probability maintain a strict watch over the trail to surprise any small party which might venture over it, I felt in the highest degree solicitous for the safety of Lieutenant Kidder and party.

Even if he succeeded in reaching Fort Wallace unmolested, there was reason to apprehend that, impressed with the importance of delivering his dispatches promptly, he would set out on his return at once and endeavor to find my command.

The third night after leaving the Platte, my command encamped in the vicinity of our former camp near the forks of the Republican. So far, nothing had been learned which would enable us to form any conclusion regarding the route taken by Kidder. Comstock, the guide, was frequently appealed to for an opinion which, from his great experience on the plains, might give us some encouragement regarding Kidder's safety. But he was too cautious and careful a man, both in word and deed, to excite hopes which his reasoning could not justify.

When thus appealed to, he would usually give an ominous shake of the head and avoid a direct answer.

On the evening just referred to, the officers and Comstock were grouped near headquarters discussing the subject which was then uppermost in the mind of every one in camp. Comstock had been quietly listening to the various theories and surmises advanced by different members of the group, but was finally pressed to state his ideas as to Kidder's chances of escaping harm.

"Well, gentlemen," emphasizing the last syllable as was his manner, "before a man kin form any ijee as to how this thing is likely to end, thar are several things he ort to be acquainted with. For instance now, no man need tell me any p'ints about Injuns. Ef I know anything, it's Injuns. I know jest how they'll do anything and when they'll take to do it; but that don't settle the question, and I'll tell you why. Ef I knowed this young lootenint - I mean Lootenint Kidder - ef I knowed what for sort of a man he is, I could tell you mighty near to a sartainty all you want to know; for you see Injun huntin' and Injun fightin' is a trade all by itself, and like any other bizness a man has to know what he's about, or ef he don't he can't make a livin' at it. I have lots uv confidence in the fightin' sense of Red Bead the Sioux chief, who is guidin' the lootenint and his men, and ef that Injun kin have his own way thar is a fair show for his guidin' 'em through all right; but as I sed before, there lays the difficulty. Is this lootenint the kind of a man who is willin' to take advice, even ef it does cum from an Injun? My experience with you army folks has allus bin that the youngsters among ye think they know the most, and this is particularly true ef they hev just cum from West P'int. Ef some of them young fellers knowed half as much as they b'lieve they do, you couldn't tell them nothin'. As to rale book-larnin', why I s'pose they've got it all; but the fact uf the matter is, they couldn't tell the difference twixt the trail of a war party and one made by a huntin' party to save their necks. Half uv 'em when they first cum here can't tell a squaw from a buck, just because both ride straddle; but they soon larn. But that's neither here nor thar. I'm told that the lootenint we're talkin' about is a new-comrer, and that this is his first scout. Ef that be the case, it puts a mighty onsartain look on the whole thing, and

THE KIDDER MASSACRE

twixt you and me, gentlemen, he'll be mighty lucky ef he gits through all right. Tomorrow we'll strike the Wallace trail, and I kin mighty soon tell ef he has gone that way."

But little comfort was to be derived from these expressions. The morrow would undoubtedly enable us, as Comstock had predicted, to determine whether or not the lieutenant and his party had missed our trail and taken that leading to Fort Wallace.

At daylight, our column could have been seen stretching out in the direction of the Wallace trail. A march of a few miles brought us to the point of intersection. Comstock and the Delawares had galloped in advance, and were about concluding a thorough examination of the various tracks to be seen in the trail, when the head of the column overtook them. "Well, what do you find, Comstock?" was my first inquiry. "They've gone toward Fort Wallace, sure," was the reply; and in support of this opinion he added, "The trail shows that twelve American horses, shod all round, have passed at a walk, goin' in the direction of the fort; and when they went by this p'int they were all right, because their horses were movin' along easy, and there are no pony tracks behind 'em, as wouldn't be the case ef the Injuns had got an eye on 'em." He then remarked, as if in parenthesis, "It would be astonishin' ef that lootenint and his lay-outs gits into the fort without a scrimmage. He may; but ef he does, it will be a scratch ef ever there was one, and I'll lose my confidence in Injuns."

The opinion expressed by Comstock as to the chances of Lieutenant Kidder and party making their way to the fort across eighty miles of danger unmolested, was the concurrent opinion of all the officers. And now that we had discovered their trail, our interest and anxiety became immeasurably increased as to their fate. The latter could not remain in doubt much longer, as two days' marching would take us to the fort. Alas, we were to solve the mystery without waiting so long.

Pursuing our way along the plain, heavy trail made by Robbins and Cook, and directing Comstock and the Delawares to watch closely that we did not lose that of Kidder and his party, we patiently but hopefully awaited further developments. How many miles we had thus passed over without incident worthy of mention, I do not now recall. The sun was high in the heavens, showing that our day's march was about half completed, when those of us who were riding at the head of the column discovered a strange looking object lying directly in our path, and more than a mile distant. It was too large for a human being, yet in color and appearance, at that distance, resembled no animal frequenting the plains with which any of us were familiar. Eager to determine its character, a dozen or more of our party, including Comstock and the Delawares, galloped in front.

Before riding the full distance, the question was determined. The object seen was the body of a white horse. A closer examination showed that it had been shot within the past few days, while the brand, U.S., proved that it was a government animal. Major Elliot then remembered that while at Fort Sedgwick, he had seen one company of cavalry mounted upon white horses. These and other circumstances went far to convince us that this was one of the horses belonging to Lieutenant Kidder's party. In fact, there was no room to doubt that this was the case.

Almost the unanimous opinion of the command was that there had been a contest with Indians, and this only the first evidence we should have proving it. When the column reached the point where the slain horse lay, a halt was ordered to enable Comstock and the Indian scouts to thoroughly examine the surrounding ground to discover, if possible, any additional evidence such as empty cartridge shells, arrows or articles of Indian equipment, showing that a fight had taken place. All the horse equipments, saddle, bridle, etc., had been carried away, but whether by friend or foe could not then be determined.

While the preponderance of circumstances favored the belief that the horse had been killed by the Indians, there was still room to hope that he had been killed by Kidder's party and the equipments taken away by them; for it frequently happens on a march that a horse will be suddenly taken ill and be unable for the time being to proceed further. In such a case, rather than abandon him alive, with a prospect of his recovering and falling into the hands of the Indians to be employed against us, orders are given to kill him, and this might be the true way of

THE KIDDER MASSACRE

accounting for the one referred to.

The scouts being unable to throw any additional light upon the question, we continued our march, closely observing the ground as we passed along. Comstock noticed that instead of the trail showing that Kidder's party was moving in regular order, as when at first discovered, there were but two or three tracks to be seen in the beaten trail, the rest being found on the grass on either side.

We had marched two miles perhaps from the point where the body of the slain horse had been discovered when we came upon a second; this one, like the first, having been killed by a bullet, and all of his equipments taken away. Comstock's quick eyes were not long in detecting pony tracks in the vicinity, and we had no longer any but the one frightful solution to offer; Kidder and his party had been discovered by the Indians, probably the same powerful and bloodthirsty band which had been resisted so gallantly by the men under Robbins and Cook; and against such overwhelming odds the issue could not be doubtful.

We were then moving over a high and level plateau, unbroken either by ravines or divides, and just such a locality as would be usually chosen by the Indians for attacking a party of the strength of Kidder's. The Indians could here ride unobstructed and encircle their victims with a continuous line of armed and painted warriors, while the beleaguered party, from the even character of the surface of the plain, would be unable to find any break or depression from behind which they might make a successful defense. It was probably this relative condition of affairs which had induced Kidder and his doomed comrades to endeavor to push on in the hope of finding ground favorable to their making a stand against their barbarous foes.

The main trail no longer showed the footprints of Kidder's party, but instead Comstock discovered the tracks of shod horses on the grass, with here and there numerous tracks of ponies, all by their appearance proving that both horses and ponies had been moving at full speed. Kidder's party must have trusted their lives temporarily to the speed of their horses - a dangerous venture when contending with Indians. However, this fearful race for life must have been most gallantly contested, because we continued our march several miles further without discovering any evidence of the savages having gained any advantage.

How painfully, almost despairingly exciting must have been this ride for life! A mere handful of brave men struggling to escape the bloody clutches of the hundreds of red-visaged demons who, mounted on their well trained war ponies, were straining every nerve and muscle to steep their hands in the life blood of their victims. It was not death alone that threatened this little band. They were not riding simply to preserve life. They rode, and doubtless prayed as they rode, that they might escape the savage tortures, the worse than death which threatened them. Would that their prayer had been granted!

We began leaving the high plateau and to descend into a valley through which, at the distance of nearly two miles, meandered a small prairie stream known as Beaver Creek. The valley near the banks of this stream was covered with a dense growth of tall wild grass intermingled with clumps of osiers. At the point where the trail crossed the stream, we hoped to obtain more definite information regarding Kidder's party and their pursuers, but we were not required to wait so long. When within a mile of the stream, I observed several large buzzards floating lazily in circles through the air, and but a short distance to the left of our trail. This of itself might not have attracted my attention seriously, but for the rank stench which pervaded the atmosphere, reminding one of the horrible sensations experienced upon a battlefield when passing among the decaying bodies of the dead.

As if impelled by one thought, Comstock, the Delawares and half a dozen officers, detached themselves from the column and separating into squads of one or two, instituted a search for the cause of our horrible suspicions. After riding in all directions through the rushes and willows, when about to relinquish the search as fruitless, one of the Delawares uttered a shout which attracted the attention of the entire command; at the same time he was seen to leap from his horse and assume a stooping posture, as if critically examining some object of interest.

Hastening, in common with many others of the party to his side, a

THE KIDDER MASSACRE

sight met our gaze which even at this remote day makes my very blood curdle. Lying in irregular order, and within a very limited circle, were the mangled bodies of poor Kidder and his party, yet so brutally hacked and disfigured as to be beyond recognition save as human beings.

General George A. Custer and his men discover the bones of Lieutenant Kidder and other members of the Seventh Cavalry. Illustration published in Harper's Weekly, August 7th, 1867.

Every individual of the party had been scalped, and his skull broken - the latter done by some weapon, probably a tomahawk - except the Sioux chief Red Bead, whose scalp had simply been removed from his head and then thrown down by his side. This, Comstock informed us, was in accordance with a custom which prohibits an Indian from bearing off the scalp of one of his own tribe. This circumstance then told us who the perpetrators of the deed were. They could be none other than the Sioux, led in all probability by Pawnee Killer.

Red Bead, being less disfigured and mutilated than the others, was the only individual capable of being recognized. Even the clothes of all the party had been carried away; some of the bodies were lying in beds of ashes, with partly burned fragments of wood near them, showing that the savage had put some of them to death by the terrible tortures of fire. The sinews of the arms and legs had been cut away, the nose of every man hacked off, and the features otherwise defaced so that it would have been scarcely possible for even a relative to recognize a single one of the unfortunate victims.

We could not even distinguish the officer from his men. Each body was pierced by from twenty to fifty arrows, and the arrows were found as the savage demons had left them, bristling in the bodies. While the details of that fearful struggle will probably never be known, telling how long and gallantly this ill-fated little band contended for their lives, yet the surrounding circumstances of ground, empty cartridge shells and distance from where the attack began, satisfied us that Kidder and his men fought as only brave men fight when the watchword is victory or death.

As the officer, his men and his no less faithful Indian guide, had shared their final dangers together and met the same dreadful fate at the hands of the same merciless foe, it was but fitting that their remains should be consigned to one common grave. This was accordingly done. A single trench was dug near the spot where they had rendered up their lives upon the altar of duty. Silently, mournfully, their comrades of a brother regiment consigned their mangled remains to mother earth, there to rest undisturbed, as we supposed, until the great day of final review.

But this was not to be so; while the closest scrutiny on our part had been insufficient to enable us to detect the slightest evidence which would aid us or others in identifying the body of Lieutenant Kidder or any of his men, it will be seen hereafter how the marks of a mother's thoughtful affection were to be the means of finding the remains of her murdered son, even though months had elapsed after his untimely death.

This sequel to the story mentioned by Custer is told by him in narrating subsequent events. It seems that Mr. Kidder, father of the lieutenant, came west in search of the body of his son, and learned that only a single mark remained by which to identify any of the bodies except that of Red Bead. The incident occurred at Fort Leavenworth in the winter of 1867. Custer thus describes the interview:

THE KIDDER MASSACRE

Mr. Kidder, after introducing himself, announced the object of his visit; it was to ascertain the spot where the remains of his son lay buried and, after procuring suitable military escort to proceed to the grave and disinter his son's remains preparatory to transferring them to a resting place in Dakota, of which territory he was at that time one of the judiciary. It was a painful task I had to perform when I communicated to the father the details of the killing of his son and followers.

And equally harassing to the feelings was it to have to inform him that there was no possible chance for his being able to recognize his son's remains. "Was there not the faintest mark or fragment of his uniform by which he might be known?" inquired the anxious parent. "Not one," was the reluctant reply. "And yet, since I now recall the appearance of the mangled and disfigured remains, there was a mere trifle which attracted my attention, but it could not have been your son who wore it." "What was it?" eagerly inquired the father. "It was simply the collar band of one of those ordinary check-over shirts so commonly worn on the plains, the color being black and white; the remainder of the garment, as well as all other articles of dress, having been torn or burned from the body."

Mr. Kidder then requested me to repeat the description of the collar and material of which it was made; happily I had some cloth of very similar appearance, and upon exhibiting this to Mr. Kidder, to show the kind I meant, he declared that the body I referred to could be no other than that of his murdered son. He went on to tell how his son had received his appointment in the army but a few weeks before his lamentable death, he only having reported for duty with his company a few days before being sent on the scout which terminated his life; and how, before leaving his home to engage in the military service, his mother, with that thoughtful care and tenderness which only a mother can feel, prepared some articles of wearing apparel, among others a few shirts made from the checked material already described.

Mr. Kidder had been to Fort Sedgwick on the Platte, from which post his son had last departed, and there learned that on leaving the post he wore one of the checked shirts and put an extra one in his saddle pockets. Upon this trifling link of evidence, Mr. Kidder proceeded four hundred miles west to Fort Wallace, and there being furnished with military escort, visited the grave containing the bodies of the twelve massacred men. Upon disinterring the remains, a body was found as I had described it, bearing the simple checked collar band; the father recognized the remains of his son, and thus as was previously stated, was the evidence of a mother's love made the means by which her son's body was recognized and reclaimed, when all other had failed.

In closing this episode, which gives a realizing idea of the terrible nature of Indian warfare, it is interest the reader to know that the engraving which illustrates was executed under the personal supervision of General Custer himself, during his life, as well as that representing the attack on the train. They give a truthful idea of two representative scenes, one the Indian method of battle, the other the appearance of Indian victims. It will be noticed that the slain have their throats cut. This is one of the marks by which the scouts knew that the Sioux had done it. The Arapahoe mark their victims by slitting the right arm, others in other manners.

It has often excited enquiry as well as horror in white men to know the reason that the present Indians of the plains perpetrate these mutilations on the bodies of their slain; and the records seem to point to great exasperation of feeling for the principal cause. In the battles of the last century between the wood Indians and the whites, as well as those in the early part of the present cycle, between the prairie Indians and the hardy hunters of the Fur Companies, it is very rare to hear of these refinements of mutilation. The slain were scalped, and living prisoners were generally taken to the villages for tortures which, however cruel, possessed a certain nobility of cruelty and lacked those peculiarly debasing and disgusting features which mark the modern Indian of the plains.

Catlin, Bonneville, Kendall, Lewis and Clark; and all those early voyagers who crossed the plains, down to the days of Fremont, record no such atrocities in their few contests with Indians, and leave on the whole a decidedly favorable impression of the savage character. At the present day, there is no doubt that such things are common, and the

THE KIDDER MASSACRE

real reason is not far to seek, judging from the circumstances surrounding both periods.

I am very strongly inclined to ascribe these mutilations to a mixture of hatred and contempt, produced by the different nature of the present contests from those waged up to the year 1850. In the past century in the woods, and up to 1850 on the plains, the Indians were principally fought by frontiersmen and veteran regulars, men of physical strength generally superior to the Indians, better shots, nearly as good riders, and their superiors in hand to hand fights. Above all things, savages respect physical prowess and courage, and there are strong indications that they were so proud to take the scalp of a brave white man in the days when they respected him that they scorned to otherwise mutilate his body when dead.

Now the case is reversed. They know that, man to man, almost all the green recruits in the regular army fear them, and the frontiersmen they meet and mutilate are no longer brave hunters, but in their eyes, despicable tillers of the ground. Hating and despising these men as cowards and plodders, yet finding themselves, slowly but surely, yielding to these loathed creatures, they take the same satisfaction in hacking them to pieces that many white men and boys do in beating a snake. This view comes out plainly in the Kidder massacre. The warriors mutilated his party because it ran in the first place, and allowed them to conquer it in the second. The only man partially respected was the chief Red Bead, probably because he was the bravest there.

THE COURT MARTIAL

CUSTER, who had come from the east with much experience and more previous success as a cavalry general, had speedily discovered while on the plains the difference between fighting civilized foes and Indians. No doubt he had frequently been reminded of this difference, and of the experience of older officers, in his intercourse with his official superiors. He was now to experience the further difference between getting along with a regiment in time of war, formal and declared, and the same body in time of nominal and legal peace, but of actual hostilities. The occasion of his trouble was during the search for Lieutenant Kidder's remains, and is thus described by himself:

In a previous chapter, reference has been made to the state of dissatisfaction which had made its appearance among the enlisted men. This state of feeling had been principally super-induced by inferior and insufficient rations, a fault for which no one connected with the troops in the field was responsible, but which was chargeable to persons far removed from the theatre of our movements, persons connected with the supply departments of the army.

Added to this internal source of disquiet, we were then on the main line of overland travel to some of our most valuable and lately discovered mining regions. The opportunity to obtain marvelous wages as miners and the prospect of amassing sudden wealth proved a temptation sufficiently strong to make many of the men forget their sworn obligations to their government and their duty as soldiers. Forgetting for a moment that the command to which they belonged was actually engaged in war, and was in a country infested with armed bodies of the enemy, and that the legal penalty of desertion under such circumstances was death, many of the men formed a combination to

THE COURT MARTIAL

desert their colors and escape to the mines.

The first intimation received by any person in authority of the existence of this plot was on the morning fixed for our departure from the Platte. Orders had been issued the previous evening for the command to march at daylight. Upwards of forty men were reported as having deserted during the night. There was no time to send parties in pursuit, or the capture and return of a portion of them might have been effected.

The command marched southward at daylight. At noon, having marched fifteen miles, we halted to rest and graze the horses for one hour. The men believed that the halt was made for the remainder of the day, and here a plan was perfected among the disaffected by which upwards of one-third of the effective strength of the command was to seize their horses and arms during the night and escape to the mountains. Had the conspirators succeeded in putting this plan into execution, it would have been difficult to say how serious the consequence might be, or whether enough true men would remain to render the march to Fort Wallace practicable.

Fortunately, it was decided to continue the march some fifteen miles further before night. The necessary orders were given and everything was being repacked for the march, when attention was called to thirteen soldiers who were then to be seen rapidly leaving camp in the direction from which we had marched. Seven of these were mounted and were moving off at a rapid gallop; the remaining six were dismounted, not having been so fortunate as their fellows in procuring horses. The entire party were still within sound of the bugle, but no orders by bugle note or otherwise served to check or diminish their flight.

The boldness of this attempt at desertion took everyone by surprise. Such an occurrence as enlisted men deserting in broad daylight and under the immediate eyes of their officers had never been heard of. With the exception of the horses of the guard and a few belonging to the officers, all others were still grazing and unsaddled. The officer of the guard was directed to mount his command promptly, and if possible overtake the deserters. At the same time, those of the officers whose horses were in readiness were also directed to join the pursuit and leave no effort untried to prevent the escape of a single malcontent.

In giving each party sent in pursuit instructions, there was no limit fixed to the measures which they were authorized to adopt in executing their orders. This unfortunately, was an emergency which involved the safety of the entire command, and required treatment of the most summary character.

It was found impossible to overtake that portion of the party which was mounted, as it was afterward learned that they had selected seven of the fleetest horses in the command. Those on foot, when discovering themselves pursued, increased their speed, but a chase of a couple of miles brought the pursuers within hailing distance.

Major Elliot, the senior officer participating in the pursuit, called out to the deserters to halt and surrender. This command was several times repeated, but without effect. Finally, seeing the hopelessness of further flight, the deserters came to bay, and to Major Elliot's renewed demand to throw down their arms and surrender, the ringleader drew up his carbine to fire upon his pursuers. This was the signal for the latter to open fire, which they did successfully, bringing down three of the deserters, although two of them were worse frightened than hurt.

Rejoining the command with their six captive deserters, the pursuing party reported their inability to overtake those who had deserted on horseback. The march was resumed and continued until near nightfall, by which time we had placed thirty miles between us and our last camp on the Platte. While on the march during the day, a trusty sergeant, one who had served as a soldier long and faithfully, imparted the first information which could be relied upon as to the plot which had been formed by the malcontents to desert in a body. The following night had been selected as the time for making the attempt. The best horses and arms in the command were to be seized and taken away.

I believed that the summary action adopted during the day would intimidate any who might still be contemplating desertion, and was confident that another day's march would place us so far in a hostile and dangerous country, that the risk of encountering war parties of

THE COURT MARTIAL

Indians would of itself serve to deter any but large numbers from attempting to make their way back to the settlements. To bridge the following night in safety was the next problem.

While there was undoubtedly a large proportion of the men who could be fully relied upon to remain true to their obligations and to render any support to their officers which might be demanded, yet the great difficulty at this time, owing to the sudden development of the plot, was to determine who could be trusted.

The difficulty was solved by placing every officer in the command on guard during the night. The men were assembled as usual for roll call at tattoo, and then notified that every man must be in his tent at the signal "taps," which would be sounded half an hour later; that their company officers, fully armed, would walk the company streets during the entire night, and any man appearing outside the limits of his tent between the hours of taps and reveille would do so at the risk of being fired upon after being once hailed. The night passed without disturbance, and daylight found us in the saddle and pursuing our line of march toward Fort Wallace.

The lesson given by Custer as thus told by him was sufficient. No further attempt was made at desertion. After the finding of the bodies of Lieutenant Kidder's party, the column proceeded on its way. It will be remembered that the telegraphic orders of General Sherman from Fort Sedgwick had directed Custer to go to Fort Wallace.

His proceedings after reaching that point we note because, in connection with the shooting of the deserters, they constituted the ground of his second court martial. The humorous commencement and ending of the first, on Custer's graduation from West Point, will be remembered. Thoughtless violation of military rule got him into trouble then. A very different course of conduct took him into similar trouble now. He tells his own story as frankly as ever.

On the evening, says he, of the day following that upon which we had consigned the remains of Lieutenant Kidder's party to their humble resting place, the command reached Fort Wallace on the Smoky Hill route. From the occupants of the fort, we learned much that was interesting regarding events which had transpired during our isolation from all points of communication. The Indians had attacked the fort twice within the past few days, in both of which engagements men were killed on each side. The fighting on our side was principally under the command of Colonel Barnitz, whose forces were composed of detachments of the Seventh Cavalry.

Our arrival at Fort Wallace was most welcome as well as opportune. The Indians had become so active and numerous that all travel over the Smoky Hill route had ceased; stages had been taken off the route and many of the stage stations had been abandoned by the employees, the latter fearing a repetition of the Lookout Station massacre. No dispatches or mail had been received at the fort for a considerable period, so that the occupants might well have been considered as undergoing a state of siege.

Added to these embarrassments, which were partly unavoidable, an additional and under the circumstances, a more frightful danger stared the troops in the face. We were over two hundred miles from the terminus of the railroad over which our supplies were drawn, and a still greater distance from the main depots of supplies. It was found that the reserve of stores at the post was well-nigh exhausted, and the commanding officer reported that he knew of no fresh supplies being on the way.

I decided to select upward of a hundred of the best mounted men in my command, and with this force open a way through to Fort Harker, a distance of two hundred miles, where I expected to obtain abundant supplies; from which point the latter could be conducted, well protected against Indians by my detachment, back to Fort Wallace. Owing to the severe marching of the past few weeks, the horses of the command were generally in an unfit condition for further service without rest. So that after selecting upward of a hundred of the best, the remainder might for the time be regarded as unserviceable; such they were in fact.

There was no idea or probability that the portion of the command to remain in camp near Fort Wallace would be called upon to do anything but rest and recuperate from their late marches. It was

THE COURT MARTIAL

certainly not expected that they would be molested or called out by Indians; nor were they. Regarding the duties to be performed by the picked detachment as being by far the most important, I chose to accompany it.

Fort Harker, Kansas. Today, the Ellsworth County Historical Society maintains three of the original buildings of Fort Harker as a museum. These include the guardhouse, Commanding Officer's Quarters and Junior Officer's Quarters. The museum also features a train depot with salt mine and other 19th/early 20th Century exhibits.

The immediate command of the detachment was given to Captain Hamilton, of whom mention has been previously made. He was assisted by two other officers. My intention was to push through from Fort Wallace to Fort Hays, a distance of about one hundred and fifty miles, as rapidly as was practicable; then, being beyond the most dangerous portion of the route, to make the remainder of the march to Fort Harker with half a dozen troopers while Captain Hamilton with his command should follow leisurely. Under this arrangement, I hoped to have a train loaded with supplies at Harker, and in readiness to start for Fort Wallace by the time Captain Hamilton should arrive.

Leaving Fort Wallace about sunset on the evening of the 15th of July, we began our ride eastward, following the line of the overland stage route. At that date, the Kansas Pacific Railway was only completed as far westward as Fort Harker. Between Forts Wallace and Harker, we expected to find the stations of the Overland Stage Company at intervals of from ten to fifteen miles. In time of peace, these stations are generally occupied by half a dozen employees of the route, embracing the stablemen and relays of drivers. They were well supplied with firearms and ammunition and every facility for defending themselves against Indians.

Overland Express stage station. The 1,900-mile-long mail route followed the Oregon and California Trails to Fort Bridger in Wyoming, then the Mormon Trail to Salt Lake City. From there, it followed the Central Nevada Route to Carson City before passing over the Sierras into Sacramento.

The stables were also the quarters for the men. They were usually built of stone, and one would naturally think that against Indians no better defensive work would be required. Yet such was not the case. The hay and other combustible material usually contained in them enabled the savages, by shooting prepared arrows, to easily set them on fire and thus drive the occupants out to the open plain where their fate would soon be settled.

To guard against such an emergency, each station was ordinarily provided with what on the plains is termed a "dug-out." The name

THE COURT MARTIAL

implies the character and description of the work. The dug-out was commonly located but a few yards from one of the corners of the stable, and was prepared by excavating the earth so as to form an opening not unlike a cellar, which was usually about four feet in depth, and sufficiently roomy to accommodate at close quarters half a dozen persons. This opening was then covered with logs, and loop-holed on all sides at a height of a few inches above the original level of the ground. The earth was thrown on top until the dug-out resembled an ordinary mound of earth, some four of five feet in height.

To the outside observer, no means apparently were provided for egress or ingress; yet such was not the case. If the entrance had been made above ground, rendering it necessary for the defenders to pass from the stable unprotected to their citadel, the Indians would have posted themselves accordingly and picked them off one by one as they should emerge from the stable. To provide against this danger, an underground passage was constructed in each case, leading from the dug-out to the interior of the stable.

With these arrangements for defense, a few determined men could withstand the attacks of an entire tribe of savages. The recent depredations of the Indians had so demoralized the men at the various stations that many of the latter were found deserted, their former occupants having joined their forces with those of other stations. The Indians generally burned the deserted stations.

Almost at every station, we received intelligence of Indians having been seen in the vicinity within a few days of our arrival. We felt satisfied they were watching our movements, although we saw no fresh signs of Indians until we arrived near Downer's Station. Here, while stopping to rest our horses for a few minutes, a small party of our men, who had without authority halted some distance behind, came dashing into our midst and reported that twenty-five or thirty Indians had attacked them some five or six miles in rear and had killed two of their number.

As there was a detachment of infantry guarding the station, and as time was important, we pushed on toward our destination. The two men reported killed were left to be buried by the troops on duty at the station. Frequent halts and brief rests were made along our line of march; occasionally we would halt long enough to indulge in a few hours' sleep. About three o'clock on the morning of the 18th, we reached Fort Hays, having marched about one hundred and fifty miles in fifty-five hours, including all halts.

Some may regard this as a rapid rate of marching; in fact, a few officers of the army who themselves have made many and long marches (principally in ambulances and railroad cars) are of the same opinion. It was far above the usual rate of a leisurely made march, but during the same season with a larger command I marched sixty miles in fifteen hours. This was officially reported, but occasioned no remark. During the war, and at the time the enemy's cavalry under General J.E.B. Stuart made its famous raid around the Army of the Potomac in Maryland, a portion of our cavalry, accompanied by horse artillery, in attempting to overtake them, marched over ninety miles in twenty-four hours. A year subsequent to the events narrated in this chapter, I marched a small detachment eighty miles in seventeen hours, every horse accompanying the detachment completing the march in as fresh condition apparently as when the march began.

Leaving Hamilton and his command to rest one day at Hays and then to follow on leisurely to Fort Harker, I continued my ride to the latter post accompanied by Colonels Cook and Custer and two troopers. We reached Fort Harker at two o'clock that night, having made the ride of sixty miles without change of animals in less than twelve hours. As this was the first telegraph station, I immediately sent telegrams to headquarters and to Fort Sedgwick announcing the fate of Kidder and his party.

General A.J. Smith, who was in command of this military district, had his headquarters at Harker. I at once reported to him in person, and acquainted him with every incident worthy of mention which had occurred in connection with my command since leaving him weeks before. Arrangements were made for the arrival of Hamilton's party and for a train containing supplies to be sent back under their escort. Having made my report to General Smith as my next superior officer, and there being no occasion for my presence until the train and escort

THE COURT MARTIAL

should be in readiness to return, *I applied for and received authority to visit Fort Riley, about ninety miles east of Harker by rail, where my family was then located.*

Commanding Officer's Quarters, Fort Harker. In the fall of 1868, General Philip Sheridan moved his headquarters from Fort Leavenworth to Fort Harker, from where he commanded the campaigns against the Indians in the winter of 1868-1869.

So ends Custer's story. The civilian reader, who has perused the account, will think nothing very wicked was done. Yet, for the events narrated in this chapter, Custer was actually court-martialed, tried and sentenced to be suspended from rank and pay for a whole year. In the very last sentence of the above frank account, the part quoted in italics, the officers at the time set over him found the whole wickedness.

Charges were brought against him on two counts; first, for leaving Fort Wallace without permission, marching his men excessively, allowing two of them to be killed, and losing several United States horses - all in a journey on private business; second, for excessive cruelty and illegal conduct in putting down mutiny in the Seventh, by shooting the deserters.

The second charge was not, however, seriously pressed; it was the first on which his enemies relied, and on which they obtained the conviction and sentence. The one inexcusable sin which Custer had committed, in the estimation of the military authorities, was going to Fort Riley to see his wife, and the preparation of the charges was due to the ingenuity of one of his personal enemies, an officer who was soon after obliged to leave the service for drunkenness.

The court-martial now under notice, indeed, brings us to that part of Custer's life when he was first surrounded with those enemies who followed him ever after, and the course of his trial will well illustrate those future crosses which were to develop him into one of the noblest characters of modern time. Hitherto, Custer had enjoyed a life of constant success. His labors had been altogether external, and had included no misfortunes, nor serious setbacks. In the great Union Volunteer Army, where there were so many prizes, those which he gained had not excited that actively malignant envy which he afterwards experienced. Now, for the first time, he found the atmosphere changed, and also found the great and fundamental difference between the war service of a great army and the nominal peace service of a small one.

In the present regular army of the United States, the great trouble is found in the fact that its rewards are so few, its officers so numerous. The consequence is that this little army is the constant abiding place, to an extent of which civilians have little or no idea of the most intense jealousy and envy from the majority towards everyone who possesses any great military merit and has attained early distinction. The one fact and the only one which commands respect in the regular army is seniority, and officers are forever computing their place on the list of their rank and calculating how soon they will "gain a step."

Before and since the war, merit has no place in the promotions of the regular army, the rigid rule of seniority being inflexibly adhered to, no services, however brilliant, being allowed to confer a single step on the officer rendering them. The war changed all this for the time and promoted, for merit alone, a few talented officers, of whom the most conspicuous at that time were Sherman, Sheridan and Custer. As a matter of course, all three of these officers were then, and are today, hated most cordially by most other officers, especially by those who

THE COURT MARTIAL

graduated from West Point before them and found themselves at the close of the war junior to them.

The system was to blame for this as much as the men, and inevitably tended to breed the feeling. The tendency of the seniority rule is and always has been to enervate and destroy military spirit. It offers a premium to all the lazy ones, the skulkers, the cowards, to keep out of danger themselves, to do anything that promises to keep themselves alive and to kill off every senior in their rank so that they may "gain steps." Not an Indian fight comes off, not an attack of yellow fever visits a post, but every officer in the army falls to calculating how many "steps" he will gain by so many deaths.

Towards the regular "seniority seniors" as they may be called - men who have gained their present rank by living long enough, keeping up respectability the while - no animosity seems to exist among the juniors. The expectants are always looking for another death to give them "a step." It is the men of brilliant talent, the real born soldiers, the successful ones of the war that they hate, and how bitterly they hate them soon appears when a group of juniors get to drinking freely. Then the spite, envy and jealousy, restrained at other times by official reticence and *esprit de corps*, break out and it is rare, very rare, almost unknown, to hear from army officers a single word of frank generous praise of their seniors. They can talk as much ill-natured gossip as fashionable women at a society ball, and for the same reason, each and all, jealousy.

The close of the Indian campaign of 1867 was the first experience which came to Custer of the effects of this feeling, and from henceforth it dogged him all his life. In the present instance, the charges were presented by an officer of his own regiment whom he had been compelled to place in arrest for repeated drunkenness on duty, and who afterwards had to leave the service for similar offences. They were carefully and ingeniously drawn, and the acts of Custer himself gave them a color of reason. He had left Fort Wallace without direct orders, but governed by military necessity; he had made a tremendous march; and some of his men were killed; and all the main facts were as alleged.

The only doubt was as to the intention. Custer in his defense showed that he was acting under the last orders he had received - those from General Sherman - which were to move towards Fort Wallace to meet General Hancock, who would give him further orders. He showed that when he reached Fort Wallace, Hancock had already passed through, and that he thought it his duty to follow him personally to obtain his orders for the future prosecution of the campaign.

He showed that while his main command was temporarily quite unfit for active work, the picked detachment he took with him was quite equal to the march, and that he had acted for the best in his journey to save his men at Fort Wallace from threatened starvation. He showed how, when he arrived at Fort Harker, he found that General Hancock had actually closed the campaign and retired to Fort Leavenworth, and how all his labor had been useless.

He showed how he had received express permission from his district commander to go to Fort Riley. He showed in fact, in his written defense, that whatever the appearance of his actions, he had done all in the very spirit as well as letter of the last verbal orders he had received from General Sherman, and he asserted that he should certainly do the like again were he placed in a similar dilemma with similar orders. He pointed out how he might certainly have been charged with cowardice and inefficiency had he remained idly at Fort Wallace, letting his command rot away piecemeal.

All his defense was in vain. The Indian campaign of 1867 was a ridiculous failure, and every army officer in the department felt sore and angry. It was necessary to find a victim, a scapegoat, someone to court-martial, someone to hold up as the cause of failure. In this instance, Custer was the man selected. For very decency, the court could not find any criminality in his manner of treating the mutineers of the Seventh, but on the first charge and all its important specifications, they found him guilty of making the journey on private business, and therefore of a serious breach of discipline. Consequently, he was sentenced to be suspended from rank and pay for a whole year.

Either this sentence was too severe or too light. Had all the accusations been true, and had Custer really made the journey he did on private business, he ought to have been dismissed from the service, no

THE COURT MARTIAL

matter what his previous record. The lives of brave soldiers are too precious to be sacrificed for the private business of anyone, however distinguished. That such could have been his motive is contradicted alike by his earnest protest and his previous and subsequent record. He never had done such a thing before, and never did after. No man was ever found more thorough and devoted to his ideas of duty. True, he was given to exercising his own judgment and discretion as to the proper mode of executing an order, a privilege allowed to all general officers, especially those of the cavalry.

At Winchester and at Sailor's Creek, when receiving an order to charge at a wrong place or an unpropitious moment, he had assumed the responsibility of choosing his own time, and events had justified him fully. He had the example of the great Prussian cavalry chief, Seydlitz, as a precedent, and that of many another great cavalry officer. Seydlitz, waiting for his moment at Rossbach (1757), received an order from the king, Frederick the Great, to charge; and sent back word that he would prefer to choose his own moment if his majesty would permit him. His conduct was approved by the king, and has since been justified by the customs of war.

In Custer's present case, the worst that could be alleged of him on the evidence was an error of judgment, for it was obvious that he fully believed, all the while, that he was doing right and obeying orders. Such an error of judgment would have been amply covered by a reprimand; while a willful disobedience of orders, prompted only by private business, could not have been punished too severely. As it was, the court-martial, like all similar bodies, took a middle course. It was necessary to punish someone to silence public sneers, and Custer was the most convenient scapegoat; so they degraded him on a flimsy pretence, in 1867, as he was again degraded on a still more flimsy pretext nine years later by another person.

They found him guilty of the charges involving disobedience of orders, and gave him such an inadequate sentence for such a heinous offence that even General Grant, reviewing the sentence at a distance, was compelled to notice the fact, and announced that he presumed the court had been so merciful on account of the past services rendered by the accused.

So Custer was degraded, and his enemies were for a brief space triumphant. Every elderly respectability in the army, every fossil with the sole merit of long service, every senior who had enjoyed the sweets of bureau duty during the war, every envious drunkard in the army, crowed over the victory and hugged himself to think that this pushing Custer, this desperate marcher and fighter, this incarnation of restless activity, was out of the way at last, for a year at all events.

His absence then was a wonderful relief, as his death is now, to that numerous class of officers who "make a convenience of the service," who are always studying how little they can do with respectability, to whom such men as Custer are a constant silent reproach. How they chuckled over the disgrace of this "lucky fellow," this "favorite," this "pet." Truly their turn had come at last and for a while, they were happy.

After a few months however, things began to look a little less smooth for "convenience men." Unluckily for them, behind the army lies the great body of taxpayers who do not admire the "convenience men," and even apply to them such ignominious slang terms as "deadbeats" and "useless soldiers."

The great body of taxpayers began to growl through the medium of some impudent newspapers, and the criticisms on the management of the Indian campaign were the reverse of complimentary. The result was that General Sheridan was ordered to take command of this Indian country, and he arrived at Fort Leavenworth, where Custer was tried, just after the promulgation of the sentence. Sheridan, as we well know, had a pretty fair acquaintance with the merits of Custer, and was likely to understand his case. What he thought of it is evinced by a single circumstance, though etiquette closed his lips from criticism of trial or sentence.

When he arrived, he found Custer a disgraced man, out of the service for a year, with no right to quarters and no apparent resource but to go away to Monroe. Sheridan, as department commander, possessed a suite of apartments at Fort Leavenworth, and he insisted on Custer's occupation of these, just as long as he pleased; so that instead of being sent home in disgrace, the young culprit found himself just where he was before, with the sole exception that he was free from duty.

The Sheridan House at 611 Scott Avenue, Fort Leavenworth, Kansas.

Hardly could Sheridan have displayed in a more pointed manner, without speaking, his conviction of the injustice and malice of the action in Custer's case than he thus did, and the action is one of the bravest and most creditable of all the brave deeds of that frank, outspoken soldier whose motto, like Custer's, might well be "*Nescio mentire.*"

With Sheridan for his friend, possessing the active sympathy of every good officer in his own regiment, and finally seeing the remorse even of his reckless accuser, Custer could well afford to pass the winter at Leavenworth. It was not until the spring that he began to experience the real miseries of his position. When the Indian campaign came on, and he was compelled to see the regiment depart for active service while he stayed behind, then indeed he could no longer bear his position at the scene of action.

He broke up his household and returned to Monroe, which he reached in June. The time was coming, though he knew it not, for the greatest triumph of his life. Hitherto, the seniority element had had its own way. This summer was to prove whether seniority or merit is the best ally in fighting an active enemy.

THE WINTER CAMPAIGN

IT can hardly be said that Custer did penance for his misdeeds in leaving Fort Wallace, by indulgence in sackcloth and ashes to any great extent. He retained at this period of his life a great deal of the boy's nature with which he had started. He had gone into his troubles regardless of the consequences, and having encountered them, was bound to make the best of it. As he tells us, while his regiment, under command of General Sully, as part of a large expedition, was studying how to kill Indians, Custer himself was trying to kill time. He pursues with his usual naivette:

"My campaign was a decided success. I established my base of operations in a most beautiful little town on the western shores of Lake Erie, from which I projected various hunting, fishing and boating expeditions. With abundance of friends and companions, and ample success, time passed pleasantly enough; yet with all there was a constant longing to be with my comrades in arms in the far West, even while aware of the fact that their campaign was not resulting in any material advantage. I had no reason to believe that I would be permitted to rejoin them until the following winter."

During the time of Custer's enforced retirement, the Indian War languished. In the summer of 1868, General Sully, with the Seventh Cavalry and some infantry, marched against the combined Cheyenne, Arapahoe and Kiowa, whom he struck near the present site of Camp Supply. After quite an animated fight, General Sully gave up the attempt to proceed further and retired, substantially defeated. This was in the Indian Territory, not far from the northwestern border of Texas.

At the same time that Sully was operating down there, General "Sandy" Forsyth, with a company of scouts and plainsmen, enlisted for special purposes, was scouting to the north round the Forks of the

THE WINTER CAMPAIGN

Republican, the same country where Custer had met Pawnee Killer the previous year. After some successes, Forsyth's party was at last surrounded by the Sioux, and besieged in a little island where the scouts lost all their horses, six men killed, eight crippled for life, and twelve more wounded, out of a total of fifty-one men, the rest being only saved from total annihilation by the arrival of reinforcements.

General Alfred Sully

Altogether, the summer campaign against both Northern and Southern Indians had been a failure. The troops had lost men and prestige, the Indians had lost nothing but men killed in action. The fight with Forsyth took place the third week in September, and the fact of his being desperately wounded rendered it impossible to rely on him for any more work, while General Sully was getting too old for real active service against such foes as the Indians. It was on the 24th of September that Custer, who was then at Monroe, received the following telegram:

HEADQUARTERS, DEPARTMENT OF THE MISSOURI
IN THE FIELD, FORT HAYS, KANSAS, September 24, 1868

General G.A. CUSTER, Monroe, Michigan:

FREDERICK WHITTAKER

Generals Sherman, Sully, and myself, and nearly all the officers of your regiment, have asked for you, and I hope the application will be successful. Can you come at once? Eleven companies of your regiment will move about the 1st of October against the hostile Indians, from Medicine Lodge creek towards the Wichita Mountains.

> P.H. SHERIDAN, Major-General Commanding

It may surprise the reader to hear that Custer, if he obeyed this request, disobeyed the letter of the law just as much as when he left Fort Wallace without orders, a proceeding which cost him a year's retirement owing to the strictures of red tape. He had been by the War Department especially enjoined from taking command of his regiment; and his sentence had been approved by the President. No less authority could give him leave to go into the field.

However, he decided to take the risk of Sheridan's application being refused and accordingly started at once. It was almost worth a court-martial and a year's retirement to receive such a dispatch. Red tape and envy had sent him home, and tried to get along without him, but red tape and envy were found unequal to the tasks of war. Like law, red tape is all very nice while people choose to submit to it, but it depends on the consent of the governed. In the case of the Indians, as in the case of the Confederates, it proved useless, for both spurned it. A man was wanted, and they had to send for Custer.

He telegraphed to Sheridan that he was coining by the next train, and by the next train he went. He was overtaken at a way station by a telegram from the adjutant-general of the army, directing him to report to Sheridan so that for this once, red tape yielded gracefully and legalized his journey. The rest of his story we shall tell briefly and as much in his own words as possible.

"Arriving at Fort Hays," says Custer, "on the morning of the 30th, I found General Sheridan, who had transferred his headquarters temporarily from Fort Leavenworth to that point in order to be nearer the field of operations. My regiment was at that time on or near the Arkansas River, in the vicinity of Fort Dodge and about three easy

THE WINTER CAMPAIGN

marches from Fort Hays. After remaining at General Sheridan's headquarters one day and receiving his instructions, I set out with a small escort across the country to Fort Dodge to resume command of my regiment.

Custer House, Fort Dodge. On Nov. 12, 1868, Custer and his men left from near Fort Dodge to begin the march in bitter cold and deep snow to launch the dawn surprise attack at Washita.

Arriving at Fort Dodge without incident, I found General Sully, who at that time was in command of the district in which my regiment was serving. With the exception of a few detachments, the main body of the regiment was encamped on Bluff Creek, a small tributary of the Arkansas, the camp being some thirty miles southeast from Fort Dodge. Taking with me the detachment at the fort, I proceeded to the main camp, arriving there in the afternoon."

He found his regiment practically in a state of siege, the Indians having become so impudent that they fired into the pickets almost every afternoon, and made the vicinity of the camp decidedly dangerous.

His arrival changed matters materially. All that the troops needed was a man like Custer at their head, one who was not afraid of the enemy. The afternoon of his arrival was distinguished by a skirmish, and the very same night he inaugurated the first scout against the Indians in which the regiment had indulged since General Sully's repulse. Four squadrons were sent out in different directions, each accompanied by scouts, and it is on this occasion that we are first introduced to Custer's great subsequent ally and friend, California Joe, whom he here appointed chief of scouts. He thus describes the meeting, in which Joe received news of his promotion:

"After the official portion of the interview had been completed, it seemed proper to Joe's mind that a more intimate acquaintance between us should be cultivated, as we had never met before. His first interrogatory, addressed to me in furtherance of this idea, was frankly put as follows:"

'See hyar, Gineral, in order that we hev no misonderstandin', I'd jest like to ask ye a few questions.'

"Seeing that I had somewhat of a character to deal with, I signified my perfect willingness to be interviewed by him."

'Air you an ambulance man, ur a hoss man?'

"Pretending not to discover his meaning, I requested him to explain."

'I mean do you b'leve in catchin' Injuns in ambulances or on hossback?'

"Still assuming ignorance, I replied; Well, Joe, I believe in catching Indians wherever we can find them, whether they are found in ambulances or on horseback." This did not satisfy him.

'That ain't what I'm drivin' at. S'pose you're after Injuns and really want to hev a tussle with 'em, would ye start after 'em on hossback, or would ye climb into an ambulance and be hauled after 'em? That's the pint I'm headin' fur.'

I answered that "I would prefer the method on horseback, provided I really desired to catch the Indians; but if I wished them to catch me I would adopt the ambulance system of attack." This reply seemed to give him complete satisfaction.

'You've hit the nail squar on the hed. I've bin with 'em on the plains whar they started out after the Injuns on wheels, jist as ef they war goin' to a town funeral in the states, an' they stood 'bout as many

THE WINTER CAMPAIGN

chances uv catchin' Injuns az a six-mule team wud uv catchin' a pack of thievin' Ki-o-tees, jist as much. Why that sort uv work is only fun fur the Injuns; they don't want anything better. Ye ort to've seen how they peppered it to us, an' we a doin' nuthin' a' the time. Sum uv 'em wuz 'fraid the mules war goin' to stampede and run off with the train an' all our forage and grub, but that wuz impossible; fur besides the big loads uv corn an' bacon an' baggage the wagons hed in them, thar war from eight to a dozen infantry men piled into them besides. Ye ort to hev heard the quartermaster in charge uv the train tryin' to drive the infantry men out of the wagons and git them into the fight. I 'spect he wuz an Irishman by his talk, fur he sed to them, 'Git out uv thim wagons; Yez'll hev me tried fur disobadience uv ordhers fur marchin! tin min in a wagon whin I've ordhers but fur ait!'

Joe's career as a chief scout was cut short. He got drunk the very first night, and another man was put in his place, but as a scout, pure and simple, he remained with Custer the rest of the campaign and did good service.

California Joe was working for General George Crook's 5th U.S. Cavalry when on October 29, 1876, he was shot in the back by Thomas Newcomb, a man with whom he had quarreled.

The first night's expeditions found no Indians. They served

however, to accustom the regiment to taking the aggressive once more; and the Indians, finding the trails of the four parties, realized the fact that their enemies had ceased to fear them. The next move was to transfer the regiment from Bluff Creek to Medicine Lodge Creek, which was done the day after. The reason for the move was that the war parties that annoyed the camp were said to come from the direction of Medicine Lodge Creek, and it was always Custer's instinct to beat up his enemies in their own quarters.

As soon as he started out, the waiting Indians charged his wagon train, which was in the rear, and compelled him to detach two companies for a rear guard to repel their attacks. Having driven them off without halting, they abandoned the attempt to stop his march, and he established a temporary camp at Medicine Lodge Creek. After scouting a few days in that vicinity, he marched the regiment to Fort Dodge, on the Arkansas River, and put them into camp on the 21st of October, 1868, where they remained until November 12th, when they started on the soon-to-be-famous Washita campaign.

Custer made this halt in his movement for one purpose. He had found on his arrival in camp that the Seventh Cavalry was not what it used to be. So many of the old men had deserted, encouraged by the fact that their commander had been court-martialed for stopping desertion, and so many recruits had been put in that the regiment as a whole was greener than when it started. It was full enough as to numbers, but the men had not been drilled; they could not ride, they could not shoot, and they were to be pitted against "the best light cavalry in the world."

He saw plainly that if he wanted to get a regiment fit to fight the Indians, he must give it a little training. The three weeks' encampment at Fort Dodge was accordingly devoted to the individual instruction of the men in rifle shooting and riding; and to secure emulation, he organized a picked body of forty men to be called the sharpshooters, and to be selected from the men showing the best records of shooting in the command.

These were commanded by Colonel Cook, the same young officer who with Robbins had defended the train the previous year. The

THE WINTER CAMPAIGN

horses of the regiment were then divided off into squadrons, each of a single color, and the result of all the preparations was that on the 12th of November, 1868, Custer led out of camp a smart regiment of horse, able to give a good account of themselves. He had entirely remade the Seventh Cavalry, and he had laid the foundations of a regimental pride which was soon to be consolidated by the triumph of the Washita.

The question may now be asked, what was the object of moving out of camp into the Indian country at the very beginning of winter? Custer tells the reason in a few words. It was the policy of Sheridan, founded on rude common sense:

"We had crossed weapons with the Indians," says Custer, "time and again during the mild summer months, when the rich verdure of the valleys served as bountiful and inexhaustible granaries in supplying forage to their ponies, and the immense herds of buffalo and other variety of game roaming undisturbed all over the plains supplied all the food that was necessary to subsist the war parties, and at the same time to allow their villages to move freely from point to point; and the experience of both officers and men went to prove that in attempting to fight Indians in the summer season we were yielding to them the advantages of climate and supplies - we were meeting them on ground of their own selection, and at a time when every natural circumstance controlling the result of a campaign was wholly in their favor; and as a just consequence the troops, in nearly all these contests with the red men, had come off second best."

"During the fall, when the buffaloes are in the best condition to furnish food, and the hides are suitable to be dressed as robes or to furnish covering for the lodges, the grand annual hunts of the tribes take place, by which the supply of meat for the winter is procured. This being done, the chiefs determine upon the points at which the village shall be located; if the tribe is a large one, the village is often subdivided, one portion or band remaining at one point, other portions choosing localities within a circuit of thirty or forty miles."

"Even during a moderate winter season, it is barely possible for the Indians to obtain sufficient food for their ponies to keep the latter in anything above a starving condition. Many of the ponies actually die from want of forage, while the remaining ones become so weak and attenuated that it requires several weeks of good grazing in the spring to fit them for service - particularly such service as is required from the war ponies.

Guided by these facts, it was evident that if we chose to avail ourselves of the assistance of so exacting and terrible an ally as the frosts of winter - an ally who would be almost as uninviting to friends as to foes - we might deprive our enemy of his points of advantage, and force him to engage in a combat in which we should do for him what he had hitherto done for us; compel him to fight upon ground and under circumstances of our own selection.

To decide upon making a winter campaign against the Indians was certainly in accordance with that maxim in the art of war which directs one to do that which the enemy neither expects nor desires to be done. At the same time, it would dispel the old fogy idea, which was not without supporters in the army, and which was confidently relied on by the Indians themselves, that the winter season was an insurmountable barrier to the prosecution of a successful campaign."

This policy of a winter campaign was inaugurated by General Sheridan; and Custer, with his old eager assent to anything requiring action, cooperated with him heartily. The regiment being in good trim, thirteen of the Osage Indians, a semi-civilized tribe living on their reservations, were engaged as scouts and the expedition started from Fort Dodge, November 12th.

It was well planned for success. A train of four hundred wagons, with a guard of infantry, was to accompany the Seventh Cavalry to the edge of the Indian country, and then establish a depot of supplies from which the cavalry could move out on a three or four days' march, with a secure basis on which to fall back in "Camp Supply," as the new station was named. Custer was not in command of the whole expedition, but General Sully conducted the march in such a manner as to encounter the least possible danger from any Indians that should attack them while encumbered with this enormous supply train. Custer thus describes the arrangements:

The country over which we were to march was favorable to us, as we were able to move our trains in four parallel columns formed close together. This arrangement shortened our flanks and rendered them less exposed to attack. The following morning after reaching Mulberry Creek, the march was resumed soon after daylight, the usual order being; the four hundred wagons of the supply train and those belonging to the troops formed in four equal columns; in advance of the wagons at a proper distance rode the advance guard of cavalry; a corresponding cavalry force formed the rear guard.

The remainder of the cavalry was divided into three equal detachments; these six detachments were disposed of along the flanks of the column, three on a side, maintaining a distance between themselves and the train of from a quarter to a half mile, while each of them had flanking parties thrown out opposite the train, rendering it impossible for an enemy to appear in any direction without timely notice being received.

The infantry on beginning the march in the morning were distributed throughout the train in such manner that should the enemy attack, their services could be rendered most effective. Unaccustomed however to field service, particularly marching, the infantry apparently were only able to march for a few hours in the early part of the day, when becoming weary, they would straggle from their companions and climb into the covered wagons, from which there was no determined effort to rout them.

In the afternoon, there would be little evidence perceptible to the eye that infantry formed any portion of the expedition, save here and there the butt of a musket or point of a bayonet peeping out from under the canvas wagon covers, or perhaps an officer of infantry, "treading alone his native heath," or better still, mounted on an Indian pony - the result of some barter with the Indians when times were a little more peaceable and neither wars nor rumors of wars disturbed the monotony of garrison life.

Nothing of interest occurred however, until the command reached Camp Supply, where it lay some days, when General Sheridan arrived. His arrival was the signal for Custer's emancipation from the control of General Sully, whose age and extreme caution had served as a continual curb on the fiery young chief of horse; and he narrates it with evident glee:

Camp Supply. Today, the Oklahoma Historical Society operates a visitor center and is restoring five of the original structures. The buildings include the Ordnance Sergeant's Quarters and Civilian Employee Quarters, Commanding Officer's Quarters, the duplex Officers' Quarters and the Guard House. The site also features a replica of the stockade.

Hearing of his near approach, I mounted my horse and was soon galloping beyond the limits of camp to meet him. If there were any persons in the command who hitherto had been in doubt as to whether the proposed winter campaign was to be a reality or otherwise, such persons soon had cause to dispel all mistrust on this point. Selecting from the train a sufficient number of the best teams and wagons to transport our supplies of rations and forage, enough to subsist the command upon for a period of thirty days, our arrangements were soon completed, by which the cavalry, consisting of eleven companies and numbering between eight and nine hundred men, were ready to resume the march.

In addition, we were to be accompanied by a detachment of scouts, among the number being California Joe; also our Indian allies from the Osage tribe, headed by Little Beaver and Hard Rope. As the country in which we were to operate was beyond the limits of the district which constituted the command of General Sully, that officer was relieved from further duty with the troops composing the expedition, and in accordance with his instructions withdrew from Camp Supply and returned to his headquarters at Fort Harker, Kansas, accompanied by Colonel Keogh, Seventh Cavalry, then holding the position of staff officer at district headquarters.

After remaining at Camp Supply six days, nothing was required but the formal order directing the movement to commence. This came in the shape of a brief letter of instructions from Department Headquarters. Of course, as nothing was known positively as to the exact whereabouts of the Indian villages, the instructions had to be general in terms. In substance, I was to march my command in search of the winter hiding places of the hostile Indians, and wherever found, to administer such punishment for past depredations as my force was able to.

On the evening of November 22nd, orders were issued to be in readiness to move promptly at daylight the following morning. That night, in the midst of other final preparations for a long separation from all means of communication with absent friends, most of us found time to hastily pen a few parting lines, informing them of our proposed expedition, and the uncertainties with which it was surrounded, as none of us knew when or where we should be heard from again, once we bade adieu to the bleak hospitalities of Camp Supply.

It began snowing the evening of the 22nd, and continued all night, so that when the shrill notes of the bugle broke the stillness of the morning air at reveille on the 23rd, we awoke at four o'clock to find the ground covered with snow to a depth of over one foot, and the storm still raging in full force. Surely this was anything but an inviting prospect as we stepped from our frail canvas shelters and found ourselves standing in the constantly and rapidly increasing depth of snow which appeared in every direction."

'How will this do for a winter campaign?' was the half sarcastic query of the adjutant, as he came trudging back to the tent through a field of snow extending almost to the top of his tall troop boots, after having received the reports of the different companies at reveille. 'Just what we want,' was the reply. Little grooming did the shivering horses receive from the equally uncomfortable troopers that morning.

Breakfast was served and disposed of more as a matter of form and regulation than to satisfy the appetite. It still lacked some minutes of daylight when the various commanders reported their commands in readiness to move, save the final act of saddling the horses. While they were thus employed, I improved the time to gallop through the darkness across the narrow plain to the tents of General Sheridan, and say good-bye. I found the headquarter tents wrapped in silence, and at first imagined that no one was yet stirring except the sentinel in front of the General's tent, who kept up his lonely tread, apparently indifferent to the beating storm. But I had no sooner given the bridle rein to my orderly than the familiar tones of the General called out, letting me know that he was awake, and had been an attentive listener to our notes of preparation.

His first greeting was to ask what I thought about the snow and the storm. To which I replied that nothing could be more to our purpose. We could move and the Indian villages could not. With an earnest injunction from my chief to keep him informed, if possible, should anything important occur, and many hearty wishes for a successful issue to the campaign, I bade him adieu.

By the time I rejoined my men, they had saddled their horses and were in readiness for the march. 'To horse' was sounded, and each trooper stood at his horse's head. Then followed the commands 'Prepare to mount' and 'Mount,' when nothing but the signal 'Advance' was required to put the column in motion. The band took its place at the head of the column, preceded by the guides and scouts, and when the march began it was to the familiar notes of that famous old marching tune, *'The girl I left behind me'*.

The Washita campaign was begun.

BATTLE OF THE WASHITA

THE march of the Seventh Cavalry was begun in the face of the blinding snowstorm; and before they had gone many miles even the Indian guides owned that they had lost their way and could not recognize the country till the snow ceased. It had been intended to encamp at Wolf Creek, fifteen miles from Camp Supply, but the guides could not find it. Most men would have stopped in the face of such obstacles. Not so Custer.

He took his course by the pocket compass, became his own guide, and reached Wolf Creek in the afternoon. Next morning at dawn the column started, with eighteen inches of snow on the ground, but a clear sky overhead, with a cold north wind. The march was continued with little incident except the cold, through a country abounding in game, where they found plenty of buffalo.

At last they crossed the Canadian River. The crossing with the wagons occupied the best part of a day, and during that time Major Elliot, with three troops, was dispatched on a scout down the Canadian to hunt for Indian sign. So far, the column had met no Indians. Bad as the storm was for the soldiers, the Indians had found it still worse. It had made them hug their lodges.

The last wagon of the Seventh Cavalry had crossed the ford and was parked on the plains to the south when a courier from Major Elliot came dashing in to report to Custer that Elliot had found the fresh trail of a war party, 150 strong, leading nearly due south with a trifle of easting. It was evidently that of the last war party of the season, going home, disgusted with the cold weather; and the snow had given it into Custer's hands.

There was no more difficulty about finding the Indian village. Custer's perseverance and pluck in marching away in the midst of a blinding snow storm had been rewarded by "Custer's luck." A little earlier start and the war party would have probably found him, not he them. As it was, he had the advantage of a surprise; he was in the heart of the Indian country, and as yet unperceived; the snow had proved his salvation.

Major Joel Elliott

The pursuit was almost immediately taken up. Custer gave the regiment just twenty minutes to prepare; then, leaving eighty men with the poorest horses as a guard for the wagons, he started with the rest, provided only with what supplies could be carried on the horses, to intercept Major Elliot's party. The train was ordered to follow the trail of the regiment.

Custer struck off at an angle to intercept Elliot's supposed course. That officer, having started the Indian trail twelve miles down the river, and at right angles thereto, it was probable that if Custer moved off to the southeast, he would cut the line of march. Just about sunset he found it, but it was not until nine o'clock at night that the whole command overtook Elliot's party, in camp on the trail of the Indians. Then the whole regiment, 800 strong, was reunited at last. They remained an hour in camp, getting supper and feeding the horses; and at ten resumed the march. They were already in the valley of the

Washita River, and so close to their enemies that henceforth we must let Custer tell the story his own way. He says:

As soon as each troop was in readiness to resume the pursuit, the troop commander reported that fact at headquarters. Ten o'clock came and found us in our saddles. Silently, the command stretched out its long length as the troopers filed off four abreast. First came two of our Osage scouts on foot; these were to follow the trail and lead the command; they were our guides; and the panther, creeping upon its prey, could not have advanced more cautiously or quietly than did these friendly Indians as they seemed to glide rather than walk over the snow clad surface.

Osage scouts and Custer near Fort Dodge, prior to heading out on the Washita campaign.

To prevent the possibility of the command coming precipitately upon our enemies, the two scouts were directed to keep three or four hundred yards in advance of all others; then came, in single file, the remainder of our Osage guides and the white scouts - among the rest, California Joe. With these I rode, that I might be as near the advance guard as possible. The cavalry followed in rear at the distance of a quarter or half a mile; this precaution was necessary from the fact that the snow, which had thawed slightly during the day was then freezing, forming a crust which broken by the tread of so many hundreds of feet, produced a noise capable of being heard at a long distance.

Orders were given prohibiting even a word being uttered above a whisper. No one was permitted to strike a match or light a pipe - the latter a great deprivation to the soldier. In this silent manner we rode mile after mile. Occasionally, an officer would ride by my side and whisper some inquiry or suggestion, but aside from this our march was unbroken by sound or deed. At last, we discovered that our two guides in front had halted, and were awaiting my arrival.

Word was quietly sent to halt the column until inquiry in front could be made. Upon coming up with the two Osage, we were furnished an example of the wonderful and peculiar powers of the Indian. One of them could speak broken English, and in answer to my question as to "What is the matter?" he replied, "Me don't know, but me smell fire."

By this time, several of the officers had quietly ridden up, and upon being informed of the Osage's remark, each endeavored, by sniffing the air, to verify or disprove the report. All united in saying that our guide was mistaken. Some said he was probably frightened, but we were unable to shake the confidence of the Osage warrior in his first opinion. I then directed him and his companion to advance even more cautiously than before, and the column, keeping up the interval, resumed its march.

After proceeding about half a mile, perhaps further, again our guides halted, and upon coming up with them I was greeted with the remark, uttered in a whisper, "Me told you so;" and sure enough, looking in the direction indicated, were to be seen the embers of a wasted fire, scarcely a handful, yet enough to prove that our guide was right and to cause us to feel the greater confidence in him.

The discovery of these few coals of fire produced almost breathless excitement. The distance from where we stood was from seventy-five to a hundred yards, not in the line of our march, but directly to our left, in the edge of the timber. We knew at once that none but Indians, and they hostile, had built that fire. Where were they at that moment?

Perhaps sleeping in the vicinity of the fire.

It was almost certain to our minds that the Indians we had been pursuing were the builders of the fire. Were they still there and asleep? We were too near already to attempt to withdraw undiscovered. Our only course was to determine the facts at once, and be prepared for the worst. I called for a few volunteers to quietly approach the fire and discover whether there were Indians in the vicinity; if not, to gather such information as was obtainable as to their numbers and departure.

All the Osage and a few of the scouts quickly dismounted, and with rifles in readiness and fingers on the triggers, silently made their way to the nearest point of the timber; Little Beaver and Hard Rope leading the way. After they had disappeared in the timber, they still had to pass over more than half the distance before reaching the fire. These moments seemed like hours, and those of us who were left sitting on our horses, in the open moonlight and within easy range from the spot where the fire was located, felt anything but comfortable during this suspense.

If Indians, as then seemed highly probable, were sleeping around the fire, our scouts would arouse them and we would be in a fair way to be picked off without being in a position to defend ourselves. The matter was soon determined. Our scouts soon arrived at the fire and discovered it to be deserted. Again did the skill and knowledge of our Indian allies come in play. Had they not been with us, we should undoubtedly have assumed that the Indians who had had occasion to build the fire and those we were pursuing constituted one party.

From examining the fire and observing the great number of pony tracks in the snow, the Osage arrived at a different conclusion, and were convinced that we were then on the ground used by the Indians for grazing their herds of ponies. The fire had been kindled by the Indian boys who attend to the herding to warm themselves by, and in all probability we were then within two or three miles of the village. I will not endeavor to describe the renewed hope and excitement that sprang up. Again we set out, this time more cautiously if possible than before, the command and scouts moving at a greater distance in rear.

In order to judge of the situation more correctly, I this time

BATTLE OF THE WASHITA

accompanied the two Osage. Silently we advanced, I mounted, they on foot, keeping at the head of my horse. Upon nearing the crest of each hill, as is invariably the Indian custom, one of the guides would hasten a few steps in advance and peer cautiously over the hill. Accustomed to this, I was not struck by observing it until once, when the same one who had discovered the fire advanced cautiously to the crest and looked carefully into the valley beyond.

I saw him place his hand above his eyes as if looking intently at some object, then crouch down and come creeping back to where I waited for him. "What is it?" I inquired as soon as he reached my horse's side. "Heaps Injuns down there," pointing in the direction from which he had just come. Quickly dismounting and giving the reins to the other guide, I accompanied the Osage to the crest, both of us crouching low so as not to be seen in the moonlight against the horizon. Looking in the direction indicated, I could indistinctly recognize the presence of a large body of animals of some kind in the valley below, and at a distance which then seemed not more than half a mile.

I looked at them long and anxiously, the guide uttering not a word, but was unable to discover anything in their appearance different from what might be presented by a herd of buffalo under similar circumstances. Turning to the Osage, I inquired in a low tone why he thought there were Indians there. "Me heard dog bark," was the satisfactory reply. Indians are noted for the large number of dogs always found in their villages, but never accompanying their war parties. I waited quietly to be convinced; I was assured, but wanted to be doubly so. I was rewarded in a moment by hearing the barking of a dog in the heavy timber off to the right of the herd, and soon after I heard the tinkling of a small bell; this convinced me that it was really the Indian herd I then saw, the bell being one worn around the neck of some pony who was probably the leader of the herd.

I turned to retrace my steps when another sound was borne to my ear through the cold, clear atmosphere of the valley - it was the distant cry of an infant; and savages though they were, and justly outlawed by the number and atrocity of their recent murders and depredations on the helpless settlers of the frontier, I could but regret that in a war such as we were forced to engage in, the mode and circumstances of battle would possibly prevent discrimination.

Cheyenne village on Washita. Today, the Washita Battlefield National Historic Site Visitor Center is located just west of Cheyenne, Oklahoma on Highway 47A. The visitor center is home to the U. S. Forest Service's Black Kettle National Grasslands.

Leaving the two Osage to keep a careful lookout, I hastened back until I met the main party of the scouts and Osage. They were halted and a message sent back to halt the cavalry, enjoining complete silence and directing every officer to ride to the point we then occupied. The hour was past midnight. Soon they came, and after dismounting and collecting in a little circle, I informed them of what I had seen and heard; and in order that they might individually learn as much as possible of the character of the ground and the location of the village, I proposed that all should remove their sabres, that their clanking might make no noise, proceed gently to the crest and there obtain a view of the valley beyond.

This was done; not a word was spoken until we crouched together and cast our eyes in the direction of the herd and village. In whispers, I briefly pointed out everything that was to be seen, then motioned all to

BATTLE OF THE WASHITA

return to where we had left our sabres; then, standing in a group upon the ground or crust of snow, the plan of the attack was explained to all and each assigned his part.

The general plan was to employ the hours between then and daylight to completely surround the village, and at daybreak, or as soon as it was barely light enough for the purpose, to attack the Indians from all sides. The command, numbering as has been stated, about eight hundred mounted men, was divided into four nearly equal detachments. Two of them set out at once, as they had each to make a circuitous march of several miles in order to arrive at the points assigned them from which to make their attack. The third detachment moved to its position about an hour before day, and until that time remained with the main or fourth column. This last, whose movements I accompanied, was to make the attack from the point from which we had first discovered the herd and village.

Major Elliot commanded the column embracing G, H and M troops, Seventh Cavalry, which moved around from our left to a position almost in rear of the village; while Colonel Thompson commanded the one consisting of B and F troops, which moved in a corresponding manner from our right to a position which was to connect with that of Major Elliot. Colonel Myers commanded the third column, composed of E and I troops, which was to take position in the valley and timber a little less than a mile to my right. By this disposition it was hoped to prevent the escape of every inmate of the village.

That portion of the command which I proposed to accompany consisted of A, C, D, and K troops, Seventh Cavalry, the Osages and scouts, and Colonel Cook with his forty sharpshooters. Captain Hamilton commanded one of the squadrons, Colonel West the other.

After the first two columns had departed for their posts - it was still four hours before the hour of attack - the men of the other two columns were permitted to dismount, but much intense suffering was unavoidably sustained. The night grew extremely cold towards morning; no fires of course could be permitted, and the men were even ordered to desist from stamping their feet and walking back and forth to keep warm, as the crushing of the snow beneath produced so much noise that it might give the alarm to our wily enemies.

During all these long weary hours of this terribly cold and comfortless night each man sat, stood or lay on the snow by his horse, holding to the rein of the latter. The officers, buttoning their huge overcoats closely about them, collected in knots of four or five and seated or reclining upon the snow's hard crust, discussed the probabilities of the coming battle - for battle we knew it would be, and we could not hope to conquer or kill the warriors of an entire village without suffering in return more or less injury.

Some, wrapping their capes about their heads, spread themselves at full length upon the snow and were apparently soon wrapped in deep slumber. After being satisfied that all necessary arrangements were made for the attack, I imitated the example of some of my comrades, and gathering the cavalry cape of my great coat about my head, lay down and slept soundly for perhaps an hour. At the end of that time I awoke, and on consulting my watch found there remained nearly two hours before we would move to the attack.

Walking about among the horses and troopers, I found the latter generally huddled at the feet of the former in squads of three and four in the endeavor to keep warm. Occasionally, I would find a small group engaged in conversation, the muttered tones and voices strangely reminding me of those heard in the death chamber. The officers had disposed of themselves in similar but various ways; here at one place were several stretched out together upon the snow, the body of one being used by the others as a pillow. Nearly all were silent; conversation had ceased, and those who were prevented by the severe cold from obtaining sleep were no doubt fully occupied in their minds with thoughts upon the morrow and the fate that might be in store for them.

Seeing a small group collected under the low branches of a tree which stood a little distance from the ground occupied by the troops, I made my way there to find the Osage warriors, with their chiefs, Little Beaver and Hard Rope. They were wrapped up in their blankets, sitting in a circle and had evidently made no effort to sleep during the night. It was plain to be seen that they regarded the occasion as a momentous one, and that the coming battle had been the sole subject of their conference.

What the views expressed by them were, I did not learn until after the engagement was fought, when they told me what ideas they had entertained regarding the manner in which the white men would probably conduct and terminate the struggle next day. After the success of the day was decided, the Osages told me that, with the suspicion so natural and peculiar to the Indian nature, they had, in discussing the proposed attack upon the Indian village, concluded that we would be outnumbered by the occupants of the village, who of course would fight with the utmost desperation in defense of their lives and lodges, and to prevent a complete defeat of our forces or to secure a drawn battle, we might be induced to engage in a parley with the hostile tribe, and on coming to an agreement we would probably, to save ourselves, offer to yield up our Osage allies as a compromise measure between our enemies and ourselves.

They also mistrusted the ability of the whites to make a successful attack upon a hostile village, located - as this one was known to be - in heavy timber, and aided by the natural banks of the stream. Disaster seemed certain in the minds of the Osages to follow us if we attacked a force of unknown strength and numbers; and the question with them was to secure such a position in the attack as to be able promptly to detect any move disadvantageous to them. With this purpose, they came to the conclusion that the standard bearer was a very important personage, and neither he nor his standard would be carried into danger or exposed to the bullets of the enemy.

They determined therefore to take their station immediately behind my standard bearer when the lines became formed for attack to follow him during the action, and thus be able to watch our movements, and if we were successful over our foes to aid us; if the battle should go against us then they, being in a safe position, could take advantage of circumstances and save themselves as best they might.

Turning from our Osage friends who were unknown to us entertaining such doubtful opinions as to our fidelity to them, I joined another group nearby, consisting of most of the white scouts. Here were California Joe and several of his companions. One of the latter deserves a passing notice. He was a low, heavy set Mexican, with features resembling somewhat those of an Ethiopian - thick lips, depressed nose, and low forehead. He was quite a young man, probably not more than twenty-five years of age, but had passed the greater portion of his life with the Indians, had adopted their habits of life and modes of dress, and had married among them. Familiar with the language of the Cheyenne and other neighboring tribes, he was invaluable both as a scout and interpreter. His real name was Romero, but some of the officers of the command with whom he was a sort of favorite had dubbed him Romeo, and by this name he was always known, a sobriquet to which he responded as readily as if he had been christened under it; never protesting, like the original Romeo:

> Tut, I have lost myself; I am not here;
> This is not Romeo, he's some other where.

The scouts, like nearly all the other members of the command, had been interchanging opinions as to the result of the movements of the following day. Not sharing the mistrust and suspicion of the Osage guides, yet the present experience was in many respects new to them, and to some the issue seemed at least shrouded in uncertainty. Addressing the group, I began the conversation with the question as to what they thought of the prospect of our having a fight. "Fight," responded California Joe. "I havn't nary doubt concernin' that part uv the busness; what I've been tryin' to get through my topknot all night is whether we'll run aginst more than we bargain fur." "Then you do not think the Indians will run away, Joe?" "Run away! How in creation can Injuns or anybody else run away when we'll have 'em clean surrounded afore daylight?" "Well, suppose then that we succeed in surrounding the village, do you think we can hold our own against the Indians?" "That's the very pint that's been botherin' me ever since we planted ourselves down here, and the only conclusion I kin come at is that it's purty apt to be one thing or t'other; if we jump these Injuns at daylight, we're either goin' to make a spoon or spile a horn, an' that's my candid

BATTLE OF THE WASHITA

judgment, sure. One thing's sartin, ef them Injuns doesn't har anything uv us till we open on 'em at daylight, they'll be the most powerful 'stonished redskins that's been in these parts lately - they will, sure. An ef we git the bulge on 'em and keep puttin' it to 'em sort a lively like, we'll sweep the platter - thar won't be nary trick left for 'em. As the deal stands now, we hold the keerds and are holdin' over 'em; they've got to straddle our blind or throw up their hands. Howsonever, thar's a mighty sight in the draw."

The night passed in quiet. I anxiously watched the opening signs of dawn in order to put the column in motion. We were only a few hundred yards from the point from which we were to attack. The moon disappeared about two hours before dawn and left us enshrouded in thick and utter darkness, making the time seem to drag even slower than before.

At last, faint signs of approaching day were visible, and I proceeded to collect the officers, awakening those who slept. We were standing in a group near the head of the column when suddenly our attention was attracted by a remarkable sight, and for a time we felt that the Indians had discovered our presence. Directly beyond the crest of the hill which separated us from the village, and in a line with the supposed location of the latter, we saw rising slowly but perceptibly, as we thought, up from the village, and appearing in bold relief against the dark sky as a background, something which we could only compare to a signal rocket, except that its motion was slow and regular.

All eyes were turned to it in blank astonishment, and but one idea seemed to be entertained, and that was that one or both of the attacking columns under Elliot or Thompson had encountered a portion of the village, and this that we saw was the signal to other portions of the band near at hand. Slowly and majestically it continued to rise above the crest of the hill, first appearing as a small brilliant flaming globe of bright golden hue. As it ascended still higher it seemed to increase in size, to move more slowly, while its colors rapidly changed from one to the other, exhibiting in turn the most beautiful combinations of prismatic tints.

There seemed to be not the shadow of a doubt that we were

discovered. The strange apparition in the heavens maintained its steady course upward. One anxious spectator, observing it apparently at a standstill, exclaimed, "How long it hangs fire! Why don't it explode?" still keeping the idea of a signal rocket in mind. It had risen perhaps to the height of half a degree above the horizon as observed from our position when lo; the mystery was dispelled. Rising above the mystifying influences of the atmosphere, that which had appeared so suddenly before us and excited our greatest apprehensions, developed into the brightest and most beautiful of morning stars.

Often since that memorable morning have I heard officers remind each other of the strange appearance which had so excited our anxiety and alarm. In less perilous moments, we probably would have regarded it as a beautiful phenomenon of nature, of which so many are to be witnessed through the pure atmosphere of the plains.

All were ordered to get ready to advance; not a word to officer or men was spoken above undertone. It began growing lighter in the east, and we moved forward toward the crest of the hill. Up to this time, two of the officers and one of the Osage had remained on the hill overlooking the valley beyond, so as to detect any attempt at a movement on the part of the village below. These now rejoined the troops. Colonel West's squadron was formed in line on the right, Captain Hamilton's squadron in line on the left, while Colonel Cook with his forty sharpshooters was formed in advance of the left, dismounted.

Although the early morning air was freezingly cold, the men were directed to remove their overcoats and haversacks so as to render them free in their movements. Before advancing beyond the crest of the hill, strict orders were issued prohibiting the firing of a single shot until the signal to attack should be made. The other three detachments had been informed before setting out that the main column would attack promptly at daylight, without waiting to ascertain whether they were in position or not. In fact, it would be impracticable to communicate with either of the first two until the attack began.

The plan was for each party to approach as closely to the village as possible without being discovered, and there await the approach of daylight. The regimental band was to move with my detachment, and it was understood that the band should strike up the instant the attack opened. Colonel Myers, commanding the third party, was also directed to move one half of his detachment dismounted. In this order, we began to descend the slope leading down to the village.

Washita Battlefield Overlook and Trail are open daily from dawn to dusk. The walking trail down to the site of Chief Black Kettle's Cheyenne village begins at the overlook. This self-guided trail is approximately 1.5 miles long.

The distance to the timber in the valley proved greater than it had appeared to the eye in the darkness of the night. We soon reached the outskirts of the herd of ponies. The latter seemed to recognize us as hostile parties and moved quickly away. The light of day was each minute growing stronger, and we feared discovery before we could approach near enough to charge the village. The movement of our horses over the crusted snow produced considerable noise, and would doubtless have led to our detection but for the fact that the Indians, if they heard it at all, presumed it was occasioned by their herd of ponies.

I would have given much at that moment to know the whereabouts of the two columns first sent out. Had they reached their assigned positions, or had unseen and unknown obstacles delayed or misled them? These were questions which could not then be answered. We had now reached the level of the valley and began advancing in line toward the heavy timber in which, and close at hand, we knew the village was situated.

Immediately in rear of my horse came the band, all mounted, and each with his instrument in readiness to begin playing the moment their leader who rode at their head, and who kept his cornet to his lips, should receive the signal. I had previously told him to play "Garry Owen" as the opening piece. We had approached near enough to the village now to plainly catch a view here and there of the tall white lodges as they stood in irregular order among the trees. From the openings at the top of some of them we could perceive faint columns of smoke ascending, the occupants no doubt having kept up their feeble fires during the entire night.

We had approached so near the village that from the dead silence which reigned I feared the lodges were deserted, the Indians having fled before we advanced. I was about to turn in my saddle and direct the signal for attack to be given - still anxious as to where the other detachments were - when a single rifle shot rang sharp and clear on the far side of the village from where we were. Quickly turning to the band leader, I directed him to give us "Garry Owen." At once, the rollicking notes of that familiar marching and fighting air sounded forth through the valley, and in a moment were re-echoed back from the opposite sides by the loud and continued cheers of the men of the other detachments, who, true to their orders, were there and in readiness to pounce upon the Indians the moment the attack began.

In this manner, the Battle of the Washita commenced. The bugle sounded the charge, and the entire command dashed rapidly into the village. The Indians were caught napping; but realizing at once the dangers of their situation, they quickly overcame their first surprise, in an instant seized their rifles, bows and arrows, and sprang behind the nearest trees, while some leaped into the stream, nearly waist deep, and using the bank as a rifle pit, began a vigorous and determined defense.

Mingled with the exultant cheers of my men could be heard the defiant war whoop of the warriors, who from the first fought with a desperation and courage which no race of men could surpass. Actual possession of the village and its lodges was ours within a few moments after the charge was made, but this was an empty victory unless we could vanquish the late occupants, who were then pouring in a rapid and well directed fire from their stations behind trees and banks. At the first onset, a considerable number of the Indians rushed from the village in the direction from which Elliot's party had attacked. Some broke through the lines, while others came in contact with the mounted troopers and were killed or captured.

We had gained the centre of the village, and were in the midst of the lodges, while on all sides could be heard the sharp crack of the Indian rifles and the responses from the carbines of the troopers. After disposing of the smaller and scattering parties of warriors, who had attempted a movement down the valley, and in which some were successful, there was but little opportunity left for the successful employment of mounted troops.

As the Indians by this time had taken cover behind logs and trees, and under the banks of the stream which flowed through the centre of the village, from which stronghold it was impracticable to dislodge them by the use of mounted men, a large portion of the command was at once ordered to fight on foot, and the men were instructed to take advantage of the trees and other natural means of cover and fight the Indians in their own style.

Cook's sharpshooters had adopted this method from the first, and with telling effect. Slowly but steadily, the Indians were driven from behind the trees; and those who escaped the carbine bullets posted themselves with their companions who were already firing from the banks. One party of troopers came upon a squaw endeavoring to make her escape, leading by the hand a little white boy, a prisoner in the hands of the Indians, and who doubtless had been captured by some of their war parties during a raid upon the settlements.

Who or where his parents were, or whether still alive or murdered by the Indians, will never be known as the squaw, finding herself and prisoner about to be surrounded by the troops, and her escape cut off, determined with savage malignity that the triumph of the latter should not embrace the rescue of the white boy. Casting her eyes quickly in all directions to convince herself that escape was impossible, she drew from beneath her blanket a huge knife and plunged it into the almost naked body of her captive. The next moment retributive justice reached her in the shape of a well-directed bullet from one of the troopers' carbines. Before the men could reach them, life was extinct in the bodies of both the squaw and her unknown captive.

The desperation with which the Indians fought may be inferred from the following: Seventeen warriors had posted themselves in a depression in the ground, which enabled them to protect their bodies completely from the fire of our men, and it was only when the Indians raised their heads to fire that the troopers could aim with any prospect of success. All efforts to drive the warriors from this point proved abortive and resulted in severe loss to our side. They were only vanquished by our men securing position under cover and picking them off by sharpshooting as they exposed themselves to get a shot at the troopers. Finally, the last one was dispatched in this manner.

In a deep ravine near the suburbs of the village, the dead bodies of thirty-eight warriors were reported after the fight terminated. Many of the squaws and children had very prudently not attempted to leave the village when we attacked it, but remained concealed inside their lodges. All these escaped injury, although when surrounded by the din and wild excitement of the fight, and in close proximity to the contending parties, their fears overcame some of them and they gave vent to their despair by singing the death song, a combination of weird-like sounds which were suggestive of anything but musical tones.

As soon as we had driven the warriors from the village, and the fighting was pushed to the country outside, I directed Romeo, the interpreter, to go around to all the lodges and assure the squaws and children remaining in them that they would be unharmed and kindly cared for; at the same time he was to assemble them in the large lodges designated for that purpose, which were standing near the centre of the village. This was quite a delicate mission, as it was difficult to convince the squaws and children that they had anything but death to expect at our hands.

BATTLE OF THE WASHITA

Raphael Romero

It was perhaps ten o'clock in the forenoon, and the fight was still raging, when to our surprise we saw a small party of Indians collected on a knoll a little over a mile below the village, and in the direction taken by those Indians who had effected an escape through our lines at the commencement of the attack. Any surprise was not so great at first, as I imagined that the Indians we saw were those who had contrived to escape, and having procured their ponies from the herd, had mounted them and were then anxious spectators of the fight, which they felt themselves too weak in numbers to participate in.

In the meantime, the herds of ponies belonging to the village, on being alarmed by the firing and shouts of the contestants, had from a sense of imagined security or custom rushed into the village, where details of troopers were made to receive them. California Joe, who had been moving about in a promiscuous and independent manner, came galloping into the village and reported that a large herd of ponies was to be seen nearby, and requested authority and some men to bring them in.

The men were otherwise employed just then, but he was authorized to collect and drive in the herd if practicable. He departed on his errand, and I had forgotten all about him and the ponies when in the course of half an hour I saw a herd of nearly three hundred ponies coming on the gallop toward the village, driven by a couple of squaws who were mounted and had been concealed nearby no doubt; while bringing up the rear was California Joe, riding his favorite mule and whirling about his head a long lariat, using it as a whip in urging the herd forward.

He had captured the squaws while endeavoring to secure the ponies, and very wisely had employed his captives to assist in driving the herd. By this time, the group of Indians already discovered outside our lines had increased until it numbered upwards of a hundred. Examining them through my field glass, I could plainly perceive that they were all mounted warriors; not only that, but they were armed and caparisoned in full war costume, nearly all wearing the bright-colored war bonnets and floating their lance pennants.

Constant accessions to their numbers were to be seen arriving from beyond the hill on which they stood. All this seemed inexplicable. A few Indians might have escaped through our lines when the attack on the village began, but only a few, and even these must have gone with little or nothing in their possession save their rifles and perhaps a blanket. Who could these new parties be, and from whence came they?

To solve these troublesome questions, I sent for Romeo, and taking him with me to one of the lodges occupied by the squaws, I interrogated one of the latter as to who were the Indians to be seen assembling on the hill below the village. She informed ne, to a surprise on my part almost equal to that of the Indians at our sudden appearance at daylight, that just below the village we then occupied, and which was a part of the Cheyenne tribe, were located in succession the winter villages of all the hostile tribes of the southern plains with which we were at war, including the Arapahoe, Kiowa, the remaining band of Cheyenne, the Comanche and a portion of the Apache; that the nearest village was about two miles distant, and the others stretched along through the timbered valley to the one furthest off, which was not over ten miles.

What was to be done? For I needed no one to tell me that we were certain to be attacked, and that too, by greatly superior numbers, just as soon as the Indians below could make their arrangements to do so; and they had probably been busily employed at these arrangements ever since the sound of firing had reached them in the early morning, and been reported from village to village. Fortunately, affairs took a favorable turn in the combat in which we were then engaged, and the firing had almost died away. Only here and there, where some warrior still maintained his position, was the fight continued.

Leaving as few men as possible to look out for these, I hastily collected and reformed my command and posted them in readiness for the attack which we all felt was soon to be made; for already at different points and in more than one direction we could see more than enough warriors to outnumber us, and we knew they were only awaiting the arrival of the chiefs and warriors from the lower villages before making any move against us.

In the meanwhile, our temporary hospital had been established in the centre of the village, where the wounded were receiving such surgical care as circumstances would permit. Our losses had been severe; indeed we were not then aware how great they had been. Hamilton, who rode at my side as we entered the village, and whose soldierly tones I heard for the last time as he calmly cautioned his squadron, "Now, men, keep cool, fire low, and not too rapidly," was among the first victims of the opening charge, having been shot from his saddle by a bullet from an Indian rifle. He died instantly. His lifeless remains were tenderly carried by some of his troopers to the vicinity of the hospital.

Soon afterward, I saw four troopers coming from the front bearing between them, in a blanket, a wounded soldier; galloping to them, I discovered Colonel Barnitz, another troop commander, who was almost in a dying condition, having been shot by a rifle bullet directly through the body in the vicinity of the heart. Of Major Elliot, the officer second in rank, nothing had been seen since the attack at daylight when he rode with his detachment into the village. He too had evidently been killed, but as yet we knew not where or how he had fallen. Two other officers had received wounds, while the casualties among the enlisted men were also large.

The sergeant-major of the regiment, who was with me when the first shot was heard, had not been seen since that moment. We were not in as effective condition by far as when the attack was made, yet we were soon to be called upon to contend against a force immensely superior to the one with which we had been engaged during the early hours of the day. The captured herds of ponies were carefully collected inside our lines, and so guarded as to prevent their stampede or recapture by the Indians. Our wounded, and the immense amount of captured property in the way of ponies, lodges, etc., as well as our prisoners, were obstacles in the way of our attempting an offensive movement against the lower villages. To have done this would have compelled us to divide our forces, when it was far from certain that we could muster strength enough united to repel the attacks of the combined tribes.

Colonel Albert Barnitz

On all sides of us, the Indians could now be seen in considerable numbers, so that from being the surrounding party, as we had been in the morning, we now found ourselves surrounded and occupying the position of defenders of the village. Fortunately for us, as the men had been expending a great many rounds, Major Bell, the quartermaster, who with a small escort was endeavoring to reach us with a fresh supply of ammunition, had by constant exertion and hard marching succeeded in doing so, and now appeared on the ground with several thousand rounds of carbine ammunition, a reinforcement greatly needed.

He had no sooner arrived safely than the Indians attacked from the direction from which he came. How he had managed to elude their watchful eyes, I never could comprehend, unless their attention had been so completely absorbed in watching our movements inside as to prevent them from keeping an eye out to discover what might be transpiring elsewhere.

Issuing a fresh supply of ammunition to those most in want of it, the fight soon began generally at all points of the circle, for such in reality had our line of battle become a continuous and unbroken circle of which the village was about the centre. Notwithstanding the great superiority in numbers of the Indians, they fought with excessive prudence and a lack of that confident manner which they usually manifest when encountering greatly inferior numbers - a result due, no doubt, to the fate which had overwhelmed our first opponents. Besides, the timber and the configuration of the ground enabled us to keep our men concealed until their services were actually required.

It seemed to be the design and wish of our antagonists to draw us away from the village; but in this plan they were foiled. Seeing that they did not intend to press the attack just then, about two hundred of my men were ordered to pull down the lodges in the village and collect the captured property in huge piles preparatory to burning. This was done in the most effectual manner. When everything had been collected, the torch was applied, and all that was left of the village were a few heaps of blackened ashes.

Whether enraged at the sight of this destruction or from other cause, the attack soon became general along our entire line, and was pressed with so much vigor and audacity that every available trooper was required to aid in meeting these assaults. The Indians would push a party of well mounted warriors close up to our lines in the endeavor to find a weak point through which they might venture, but in every attempt were driven back. I now concluded, as the village was off our hands and our wounded had been collected, that offensive measures might be adopted.

To this end, several of the squadrons were mounted and ordered to advance and attack the enemy wherever force sufficient was exposed to be a proper object of attack, but at the same time to be cautious as to ambuscades. Colonel Weir, who had succeeded to the command of Hamilton's squadron, Colonels Benteen and Myers with their respective squadrons, all mounted, advanced and engaged the enemy.

The Indians resisted every step taken by the troops, while every charge made by the latter was met or followed by a charge from the Indians, who continued to appear in large numbers at unexpected times and places. The squadrons acting in support of each other, and the men in each being kept well in hand, were soon able to force the line held by the Indians to yield at any point assailed. This being followed up promptly, the Indians were driven at every point and forced to abandon the field to us.

Yet they would go no further than they were actually driven. It was now about three o'clock in the afternoon. I knew that the officer left in charge of the train and eighty men would push after us, follow our trail and endeavor to reach us at the earliest practicable moment. From the tops of some of the highest peaks or around hills in the vicinity of the village, I knew the Indians could reconnoitre the country for miles in all directions. I feared if we remained as we were then until the following day, the Indians might in this manner discover the approach of our train and detach a sufficient body of warriors to attack and capture it; and its loss to us, aside from that of its guard, would have proven most serious, leaving us in the heart of the enemy's country, in midwinter, totally out of supplies for both men and horses.

By actual count, we had in our possession eight hundred and seventy-five captured ponies, so wild and unused to white men that it was difficult to herd them. What we were to do with them was puzzling, as they could not have been led had we been possessed of the means of doing this; neither could we drive them as the Indians were accustomed to do. And even if we could take them with us, either the one way or the other, it was anything but wise and desirable on our part to do so, as such a large herd of ponies, constituting so much wealth in the eyes of the Indians, would have been too tempting a prize to the warriors who had been fighting us all the afternoon, and to effect their recapture they would have waylaid us day and night with every prospect of success, until we should have arrived at a place of safety.

Besides, we had upwards of sixty prisoners in our hands, to say nothing of our wounded, to embarrass our movements. We had achieved a great and important success over the hostile tribes; the problem now was how to retain our advantage and steer safely through the difficulties which seemed to surround our position. The Indians had suffered a telling defeat, involving great losses in life and valuable property. Could they succeed however, in depriving us of the train and supplies, and in doing this accomplish the killing or capture of the escort, it would go far to offset the damage we had been able to inflict upon them and to render our victory an empty one.

We did not need the ponies, while the Indians did. If we retained them, they might conclude that one object of our expedition against them was to secure plunder, an object thoroughly consistent with the red man's idea of war. Instead, it was our desire to impress upon their uncultured minds that our every act and purpose had been simply to inflict deserved punishment upon them for the many murders and other depredations committed by them in and around the homes of the defenseless settlers on the frontier.

Impelled by these motives, I decided neither to attempt to take the ponies with us nor to abandon them to the Indians, but to adopt the only measure left - to kill them. To accomplish this seemingly - like most measures of war — cruel but necessary act, four companies of cavalrymen were detailed dismounted as a firing party. Before they reluctantly engaged in this uninviting work, I took Romeo, the interpreter, and proceeded to the few lodges near the centre of the village which we had reserved from destruction, and in which were collected the prisoners, consisting of upward of sixty squaws and children.

Romeo was directed to assemble the prisoners in one body, as I desired to assure them of kind treatment at our hands, a subject about which they were greatly wrought up; also to tell them what we should expect of them, and to inform them of our intention to march probably all that night, directing them at the same time to proceed to the herd and select there from a suitable number of ponies to carry the prisoners on the march.

When Romeo had collected them in a single group, he, acting as interpreter, acquainted them with my purpose in calling them together, at the same time assuring them that they could rely confidently upon the fulfillment of any promises I made them, as I was the "big chief." The Indians refer to all officers of a command as "chiefs," while the officer in command is designated as the "big chief."

After I had concluded what I desired to say to them, they signified their approval and satisfaction by gathering around me and going through an extensive series of hand shaking. One of the middle aged squaws then informed Romeo that she wished to speak on behalf of herself and companions.

So far, we have followed Custer's direct narrative and now resume our own. This squaw last mentioned, turned out to be the sister of Black Kettle, chief of the band Custer had struck; she bemoaned the wickedness of Black Kettle, and told Custer how only that night the last war party returned with white scalps and plunder, and how they got so drunk that the white man was able to ride into their lodges next morning, before they woke up. She concluded by reminding him that it was his duty to help the helpless, and offered him a young girl in marriage.

As soon as the general found from the interpreter what she was doing, he declined the honor, though not until Mahwissa - the old squaw's name - had performed the whole of the Indian part of the ceremony, which consisted of placing the girl's hand in Custer's and invoking the Great Spirit on the union. The general asked Romeo the scout what could have been Mahwissa's object in this marriage, and received the following very plain reply:

"Well, I'll tell ye; ef you'd 'a married that squaw, then she'd 'a told

BATTLE OF THE WASHITA

ye that all the rest of 'em were her kinfolks, and as a nateral sort of a thing you'd 'a been expected to kind o' provide and take keer of your wife's relations. That's jist as I tell it to you - fur don't I know? Didn't I marry a young Cheyenne squaw, and give her old father two of my best ponies for her, and it wasn't a week till ever tarnal Injun in the village, old and young, came to my lodge, and my squaw tried to make me b'lieve they were all relations of hern, and that I ought to give 'em some grub; but I didn't do nothin' of the sort." "Well, how did you get out of it, Romeo?" "Get out of it? Why, I got out by jist takin' my ponies and traps, and the first good chance I lit out; that's how I got out. I was satisfied to marry one or two of 'em, but when it come to marryin' an intire tribe, 'scuse me."

Chief Black Kettle and his wife were killed at the Battle of Washita.

The end of the matter was that the squaws took their ponies from the herd, and that the rest of the animals were shot. Search was then made for the killed, wounded and missing of the command of which all, except Major Elliot and nineteen troopers, were found. These last were never heard of again until their bodies were discovered some weeks later. It seems that a party of Indians, at the beginning of the attack on the village, had escaped through a gap in the lines of the cavalry, that Elliot had pursued them, and run into the large force that was then hovering round Custer, fearing to attack him. Having fruitlessly searched for the major, it was rightly concluded that he and his party had been attacked and killed, and Custer prepared for his return march.

Placing his prisoners in the centre, he first deployed his forces and marched straight down the river at the threatening parties of Indians from the other villages, with colors displayed and band playing. His intention was to strike consternation into their hearts, and make them think he was about to serve them as he had served Black Kettle's band. The movement had all the effect he desired.

The Indians fled in confusion, leaving only a few warriors to hover around him and watch him. He did not start until within an hour of sunset, and his feint diverted Indian attention from his wagon train, which he knew must be pretty near him by this time. About an hour after dark, he reached the abandoned villages of the alarmed tribes, where he halted, and at ten o'clock retraced his steps, marching rapidly for the wagons. At two o'clock, he halted in the valley of the Washita, and went into bivouac, the men building huge fires to supply the loss of their overcoats, which the Indians had captured during the fight. They had been left in a heap on the ground.

Secrecy was no longer necessary now, and the men enjoyed themselves hugely. Next day, they reached the wagons and pushed on, encamping at night at the place where the regiment first struck Elliot's trail. From thence, California Joe and another scout were dispatched to Camp Supply to carry the news to General Sheridan. The two scouts made the journey in safety. The country was apparently denuded of Indians, the blow on the Washita having demoralized them. California Joe met Custer's column with a return dispatch before the regiment could reach Camp Supply. It was read at the head of the troops, and repaid them for all their hardships. It was as follows:

HEADQUARTERS, DEPARTMENT OF THE MISSOURI, IN THE FIELD, DEPOT ON THE NORTH CANADIAN, AT THE JUNCTION OF BEAVER CREEK, INDIAN TERRITORY
November 29, 1868

BATTLE OF THE WASHITA

GENERAL FIELD ORDERS No. 6: The Major-General commanding announces to this command the defeat by the Seventh regiment of cavalry, of a large force of Cheyenne Indians, under the celebrated chief Black Kettle, reenforced by the Arapahoe under Little Raven, and the Kiowa under Satanta, on the morning of the 27th instant, on the Washita River near the Antelope Hills, Indian Territory, resulting in a loss to the savages of one hundred and three warriors killed, including Black Kettle, the capture of fifty-three squaws and children, eight hundred and seventy-five ponies, eleven hundred and twenty-three buffalo robes and skins, five hundred and thirty-five pounds of powder, one thousand and fifty pounds of lead, four thousand arrows, seven hundred pounds of tobacco, besides rifles, pistols, saddles, bows, lariats, and immense quantities of dried meat and other winter provisions, the complete destruction of their village, and almost total annihilation of this Indian band.

The loss to the Seventh Cavalry was two officers killed, Major Joel H. Elliot and Captain Louis McL. Hamilton, and nineteen enlisted men; three officers wounded, Brevet Lieutenant-Colonel Albert Barnitz (badly), Brevet Lieutenant-Colonel T.W. Custer, and Second Lieutenant T.Z. March (slightly), and eleven enlisted men.

The energy and rapidity shown during one of the heaviest snow storms that has visited this section of the country, with the temperature below freezing point, and the gallantry and bravery displayed, resulting in such signal success, reflect the highest credit upon both the officers and men of the Seventh Cavalry; and the Major-General commanding, while regretting the loss of such gallant officers as Major Elliot and Captain Hamilton, who fell while gallantly leading their men, desires to express his thanks to the officers and men engaged in the Battle of the Washita, and his special congratulations are tendered to their distinguished commander, Brevet Major-General George A. Caster, for the efficient and gallant services rendered, which have characterized the opening of the campaign against hostile Indians south of the Arkansas.

By command of Major-General P.H. SHERIDAN
J. SCHUYLER CROSBY, Brevet Lieutenant-Colonel, A.D.C., A.A.A. General

We cannot terminate the campaign better than by the description in Custer's own words of the review which closed it. General Sheridan was so much pleased with the success of the expedition that he personally honored the regiment by reviewing it, a great condescension, in military etiquette, from a major-general to a single regiment. Custer describes it thus:

"In many respects, the column we formed was unique in appearance. First rode our Osage guides and trailers, dressed and painted in the extremest fashions of war, according to their rude customs and ideas. As we advanced, these warriors chanted their war songs, fired their guns in triumph, and at intervals gave utterance to their shrill war whoops. Next came the scouts riding abreast, with California Joe astride his faithful mule bringing up the right, but unable, even during this ceremonious and formal occasion, to dispense with his pipe. Immediately in rear of the scouts rode the Indian prisoners under guard, all mounted on Indian ponies, and in their dress, conspicuous by its bright colors, many of them wearing the scarlet blanket so popular with the wild tribes, presenting quite a contrast to the dull and motley colors worn by the scouts.

Wild Cat - Osage Scout

Some little distance in the rear came the troops formed in column of platoons, the leading platoon preceded by the band playing "Garry Owen," being composed of the sharpshooters under Colonel Cook, followed in succession by the squadrons in the regular order of march.

BATTLE OF THE WASHITA

In this order and arrangement, we marched proudly in front of our chief who, as the officers rode by giving him the military salute with the sabre, returned their formal courtesy by a graceful lifting of his cap and a pleased look of recognition from his eye, which spoke his approbation in language far more powerful than studied words could have done.

In speaking of the review afterwards, General Sheridan said the appearance of the troops, with the bright rays of the sun reflected from their burnished arms and equipments, as they advanced in beautiful order and precision down the slope, the band playing, and the blue of the soldiers' uniforms slightly relieved by the gaudy colors of the Indians, both captives and Osage, the strangely fantastic part played by the Osage guides, their shouts, chanting their war songs and firing their guns in air, all combined to render the scene one of the most beautiful and highly interesting he remembered ever having witnessed."

So closed the Washita campaign, December 2nd, 1868. It will be observed however, that General Sheridan's congratulatory order calls the battle only "the opening of the campaign against the hostile Indians south of the Arkansas." Such it was meant to be. Five days later, December 7th, the regiment, with thirty days' rations in the wagons, started for the Washita once more, accompanied by General Sheridan and staff. Along with Sheridan were the Nineteenth Kansas Volunteer cavalry, a special force, just raised for Indian hostilities, and the whole expedition numbered about fifteen hundred men.

CLOSING OPERATIONS

THE Seventh Cavalry reached their old battle ground in safety without adventure. What California Joe thought of the renewed winter campaign is characteristic.

"I'd jist like to see the streaked count'nances of Satanta, Medicine Arrow, Lone Wolf, and a few others o 'em, when they ketch the fust glimpse of the outfit. They'll think we're comim to spend an evenin' with 'em sure, and hev brought our knittin' with us. One look'll satisfy 'em. Thar'll be sum of the durndest kickin' out over these plains that ever war heern tell uv. One good thing, it's goin' to cum as nigh killin' uv 'em to start 'em out this time uv year as ef we hed an out an out scrummage with 'em. The way I looks at it, they hev jist this preference; them as don't like bein' shot to deth kin take ther chances at freezin."

After a careful search around the battleground, they came on the bodies of Major Elliot's party, all horribly mutilated in a manner similar to that which is recorded of the Kidder party. The bodies were tenderly buried. The position of affairs in the neighborhood is thus described by Custer:

The forest along the banks of the Washita, from the battleground a distance of twelve miles, was found to have been one continuous Indian village. Black Kettle's band of Cheyenne was above; then came other hostile tribes camped in the following order; Arapahoe under Little Raven; Kiowa under Satanta and Lone Wolf; the remaining bands of Cheyenne, Comanche, and Apaches.

Nothing could exceed the disorder and haste with which the tribes had fled from their camping grounds. They had abandoned thousands of lodge poles, some of which were still standing as when last used.

CLOSING OPERATIONS

Immense numbers of camp kettles, cooking utensils, coffee mills, axes and several hundred buffalo robes were found in the abandoned camps adjacent to Black Kettle's village, but which had not been visited before by our troops.

By actual examination, it was computed that over six hundred lodges had been standing along the Washita during the battle, and within five miles of the battleground, and it was from these villages, and others still lower down the stream that the immense number of warriors came who, after our rout and destruction of Black Kettle and his band, surrounded my command and fought until defeated by the Seventh Cavalry.

The ground having been examined, the campaign was resumed as follows, according to Custer's account:

At daylight on the following morning, the entire command started on the trail of the Indian villages, nearly all of which had moved down the Washita toward Fort Cobb, where they had good reason to believe they would receive protection. The Arapahoe and remaining band of Cheyenne left the Washita valley and moved across in the direction of Red River. After following the trail of the Kiowa and other hostile Indians for seven days over an almost impassable country, where it was necessary to keep two or three hundred men almost constantly at work with picks, axes and spades before being able to advance with our immense train, my Osage scouts came galloping back on the morning of the 17th of December and reported a party of Indians in our front beating a flag of truce.

The party turned out to be the Kiowa, under Satanta and Lone Wolf. They were accompanied by a scout who said that he came from Fort Cobb, Indian Territory, a station on the Washita one hundred miles below the battleground. At this fort was stationed General Hazen, who had been placed by General Sherman in control of the Kiowa and Comanche. The scout bore the following note:

FREDERICK WHITTAKER

CLOSING OPERATIONS, HEADQUARTERS SOUTHERN INDIAN DISTRICT, FORT COBB
9 p.m., December 16, 1868

To the officer, commanding troops in the Field: Indians have just brought in word that our troops today reached the Washita some twenty miles above here. I send this to say that all the camps this side of the point reported to have been reached are friendly, and have not been on the warpath this season. If this reaches you, it would be well to communicate at once with Satanta or Black Eagle, chiefs of the Kiowa, near where you now are, who will readily inform you of the position of the Cheyenne and Arapaho, also of my camp.

Respectfully,

W.B. Hazen, Brevet Major-General

"This scout," says Custer, "at the same time informed me that a large party of the Kiowa warriors, under Lone Wolf, Satanta and other leading chiefs, were within less than a mile of my advance, and notwithstanding the above certificate regarding their friendly character, they had seized a scout who accompanied the bearer of the dispatch, disarmed him, and held him a prisoner of war. Taking a small party with me, I proceeded beyond our lines to meet the flag of truce. I was met by several of the leading chiefs of the Kiowa, including those above named.

Large parties of their warriors could be seen posted in the neighboring ravines and upon the surrounding hilltops. All were painted and plumed for war, and nearly all were armed with one rifle, two revolvers, bow and arrow, some of their bows being strung, and their whole appearance and conduct plainly indicating that they had come for war."

Very unwillingly, Custer was restrained from attacking the Kiowa, but the presence of Sheridan compelled him to submit to the assurance of Hazen's note and refrain from war.

"After meeting the chiefs, who with their bands had approached our advance under flag of truce, and compelling the release of the scout whom they had seized and held prisoner, we continued our march

CLOSING OPERATIONS

toward Fort Cobb, the chiefs agreeing to ride with us and accompany my command to that place. Every assurance was given me that the villages to which these various chiefs belonged would at once move to Fort Cobb and there encamp, thus separating themselves from the hostile tribes, or those who preferred to decline this proposition of peace and to continue to wage war; and as an evidence of the sincerity of their purpose, some eighteen or twenty of the most prominent chiefs, generally Kiowa, voluntarily proposed to accompany us during the march of the day and the next, by which time it was expected that the command would reach Fort Cobb. The chiefs only requested that they might send one of their numbers mounted on a fleet pony to the villages in order to hasten their movement to Fort Cobb."

Custer consented to this cheerfully, but as he was exceedingly suspicious of the Indians, watched them closely. On the next day's march, the chiefs, on one pretext or another, began to drop out of the column, and Custer became convinced that they were fooling him to gain time to send their villages away from, not towards Fort Cobb. Feeling sure of this, he waited until the inferior chiefs had departed, leaving only Satanta and Lone Wolf, when the officers at the head of the column drew their revolvers, and the two chiefs were informed they were prisoners, and hostages. Custer did not need two lessons in Indian diplomacy. Pawnee Killer had fooled him once, but Satanta and Lone Wolf were not equal to repeating the trick.

Here, it is necessary to notice a dispute which arose at the time between Custer and General Hazen, which turned on the identity of the Indians engaged in the late battle. Custer, relying on the statements of Mahwissa and the other squaws of Black Kettle's band, was convinced that he had been fighting the Kiowas of Satanta and Lone Wolf. Mahwissa even pointed out Satanta's camp, close to that of Black Kettle.

General Hazen, on the other hand, was convinced that Satanta and Lone Wolf were not in the battle, that the major part of the Kiowa were in camp at Fort Cobb, a hundred miles from the battlefield, and that only a small band of either Kiowa or Comanche, who had not come in, could possibly have been in the battle.

FREDERICK WHITTAKER

Not for six years was the difficulty cleared up. It was then settled by the production of various affidavits from the disbursing officers and agents at Fort Cobb, which proved conclusively that Satanta and Lone Wolf visited and slept at the officers' quarters in Fort Cobb on the 27th November, the same night that Custer fought Black Kettle a hundred miles away, and that rations were issued to nine-tenths of the Kiowa on the 26th of November at the same place.

General Hazen's statement was published in brief in the Army and Navy Journal of March 30, 1874, and settles the question. It seems however, that the Kiowa, knowing that a small band of their friends had been in the battle, were naturally frightened to death when they heard of Custer's return a fortnight later. They at once scattered and left Fort Cobb, fearing to be punished for past misdeeds; and the embassy of Lone Wolf and Satanta probably had just the intention which Custer divined, that of giving the lodges time to get away safe.

At all events, the capture of the two chiefs as hostages had the happiest effect. The column continued its march to Fort Cobb. On the way, they were met by Satanta's son, who was allowed to come and go within the lines as a medium of communication between the whites and the Kiowa. For a long time, the Indians tried to procrastinate and avoid yielding to Custer's demands. These were simple; that the Indians should come in and settle once more on their reservations by the fort, in the power of the troops.

At last, General Sheridan's rapid decision cut the knots of diplomacy in a very effectual manner. He told Custer, through whom he conducted all the negotiations, to assure Lone Wolf and Satanta that if their bands were not in camp before sunset of the following day, both chiefs would be hung at that hour, and troops sent after the Kiowa. This settled the question very quickly. Satanta's son was sent off full speed to the tribes, and long before the said sunset, the Kiowa were quietly settled under the guns of Fort Cobb.

The next tribe that needed subduing was the Arapahoe. The Cheyenne had been humbled, the Kiowa pacified without bloodshed, thanks to Custer's seizure of Satanta, the Arapahoe must also be brought on their reservations. To do this required either hard fighting and marching, or the exercise of finesse. General Sheridan, who had so far left the fighting and negotiation entirely to Custer, continued to do so.

The young lieutenant-colonel found him a very different chief, sympathetic and appreciative to the others by whom he had been commanded since the war. Sheridan continued to let him have his own way, and it was crowned with the same triumphant success which had marked it hitherto. Briefly, Custer succeeded in bringing the Arapahoe as he had the Kiowa, but by a different method.

First, a friendly chief of the Apache named Iron Shirt, who volunteered for the office, was selected as an ambassador in the cause of peace to both Cheyenne and Arapahoe. With him was dispatched Mahwissa, the sister of Black Kettle, and both were well supplied with presents. Their instructions were to go to the Cheyenne and Arapahoe, see the chiefs, tell them that if they chose to come in and settle on their reservations they should be well treated, and to remind them that if they did not come in, they might get the same treatment as Black Kettle.

The departure of the envoys made an end of all hope of a winter campaign for which, no doubt, the officers of the Seventh Cavalry were not sorry. It was late in January before Iron Shirt returned, without Mahwissa. He brought the news that the distance was too great and the ponies too thin for the tribes to move, and that the Cheyenne had detained Mahwissa from returning. He reported however that Little Robe, chief of the Cheyenne, and Yellow Bear, second chief of the Arapahoe, were both very anxious to accept the government's proposition, and would themselves visit the camp shortly.

A few days after, sure enough Little Robe and Yellow Bear arrived and were handsomely received. The latter was about the least cruel and most sensible of the chiefs on the plains, a great contrast to the peculiarly savage and insolent Satanta. He was the one good Indian whom Custer appears to have met. The sequel to the visit is thus told by Custer:

They reported that their villages had had under consideration the question of accepting our invitation to come in and live at peace in the future, and that many of their people were strongly in favor of adopting this course, but for the present it was uncertain whether or not the two tribes would come in. The two tribes would probably act in concert, and if they intended coming, would make their determination known by dispatching couriers to us in a few days.

In spite of the sincerity of the motives of Little Robe and Yellow Bear, whom I have always regarded as two of the most upright and peaceably inclined Indians I have ever known, and who have since that time paid a visit to the President at Washington, it was evident that the Cheyenne and Arapahoe, while endeavoring to occupy us with promises and pretences, were only interested in delaying our movements until the return of spring when the young grass would enable them to recruit the strength of their winter famished ponies and move when and where they pleased.

Yellow Bear

After waiting many long weary days for the arrival of the promised couriers from the two tribes, until even Little Robe and Yellow Bear were forced to acknowledge that there was no longer any reason to expect their coming, it occurred to me that there was but one expedient yet untried which furnished even a doubtful chance of averting war. This could only be resorted to with the approval of General Sheridan, whose tent had been pitched in our midst during the entire winter, and who evidently proposed to remain on the ground until the Indian question in that locality should be disposed of. My plan was as follows:

After weighing the matter carefully in my own mind, I decided that with General Sheridan's approval, I would select from my command forty men, two officers and a medical officer and, accompanied by the two chiefs, Little Robe and Yellow Bear, who regarded my proposition with favor, I would set out in search of the hostile camp, there being but little doubt that with the assistance of the chiefs, I would have little difficulty in discovering the whereabouts of the villages; while the smallness of my party would prevent unnecessary alarm or suspicion as to our intentions.

From my tent to General Sheridan's was only a few steps, and I soon submitted my proposition to the General, who from the first was inclined to lend his approval to my project. After discussing it fully, he gave his consent by saying that the character of the proposed expedition was such that he would not order me to proceed upon it, but if I volunteered to go, he would give me the full sanction of his authority and every possible assistance to render the mission a successful one; in conclusion urging me to exercise the greatest caution against the stratagems or treachery of the Indians, who no doubt would be but too glad to massacre my party in revenge for their recent well merited chastisement.

Returning to my tent, I at once set about making preparations for my journey, the extent or result of which now became interesting subjects for deliberation. The first thing necessary was to make up the party which was to accompany me. As the number of men was to be limited to forty, too much care could not be exercised in their selection. I chose the great majority of them from the sharpshooters, men who, in addition to being cool and brave, were experienced and skillful marksmen.

My standard bearer, a well-tried sergeant, was selected as the senior noncommissioned officer of the party. The officers who were to accompany me were my brother Colonel Custer, Captain Robbins, and Dr. Renick, Acting Assistant Surgeon U. S. Army. As guide I had Neva, a Blackfoot Indian, who had accompanied General Fremont in his explorations, and who could speak a little English. Little Robe and Yellow Bear were also to be relied upon as guides, while Romeo accompanied us as interpreter.

Little Robe

All were well armed and well mounted. We were to take no wagons or tents; our extra supplies were to be transported on pack mules. We were to start on the evening of the second day, the intervening time being necessary to complete our preparations. It was decided that our first march should be a short one, sufficient merely to enable us to reach a village of friendly Apache, located a few miles from our camp, where we would spend the first night and be joined by Little Robe and Yellow Bear, who at that time were guests of the Apache. I need not say that in the opinion of many of our comrades, our mission was regarded as closely bordering on the imprudent, to qualify it by no stronger term.

So confident did one of the most prudent officers of my command

CLOSING OPERATIONS

feel in regard to our annihilation by the Indians that in bidding me good-bye, he contrived to slip into my hand a small pocket Derringer pistol, loaded, with the simple remark, "You had better take it, general; it may prove useful to you." As I was amply provided with arms, both revolvers and rifle, and as a pocket Derringer may not impress the reader as being a very formidable weapon to use in Indian warfare, the purpose of my friend in giving me the small pocket weapon may not seem clear.

It was given me under the firm conviction that the Indians would overwhelm and massacre my entire party; and to prevent my being captured, disarmed and reserved for torture, that little pistol was given me in order that at the last moment I might become my own executioner - an office I was not seeking, nor did I share in my friend's opinion. Everything being ready for our departure, we swung into our saddles, waved our adieus to the comrades who were to remain in camp, and the next moment we turned our horses' heads westward.

We do not intend to enlarge on the incidents of the journey which ensued, which are fully recorded in *"Life on the Plains,"* to which the reader is referred. Suffice it to say that it was successful, that Custer reached the Arapahoe camp in safety, and that the expedition ended in the quiet location of the whole tribe under the guns of the fort on their reservation. The Cheyenne however, were not so tractable. The destruction of Black Kettle's band had only exasperated, not cowed them, and they needed another lesson. It was soon given them by Custer.

General Sheridan departed for Camp Supply as soon as the Kiowa and Arapahoe were settled, while Custer, taking with him the Seventh Cavalry and Nineteenth Kansas, started on the 2nd of March, 1869, on the search after the Cheyenne. The story of his march is so well and succinctly told in his official report, that we give it nearly entire:

On the morning of the 2nd March, my command, composed of eleven troops of the Seventh U.S. Cavalry and ten troops of the Nineteenth Kansas Cavalry, left its camp on Medicine Bluff Creek, about thirty miles due south from Fort Cobb. My course was via Camp Radziminski, mouth of Elk Creek, to a point on the North Fork of Red River, a few miles above the mouth of Salt Creek.

Here, I divided my command into two columns. Selecting about eight hundred of the most effective men from both regiments, I directed Brevet Lieutenant-Colonel Myers, Seventh Cavalry, to proceed in command of the remainder and surplus train up the North Fork, and across to a point on the Washita, near the late battleground; and there await further orders.

With that portion of the command selected for the purpose, I left our camp on the North Fork on the morning of the 6th instant and marched due west, striking the Salt Fork after a few hours' march. About noon, we struck a fresh trail of a single lodge and fourteen animals heading up the Salt Fork. Taking up the pursuit, we followed the trail three days and one night, and on the afternoon of the third day surprised the party we were pursuing, while seeking shelter from an approaching storm, capturing their lodge, cooking utensils, provisions and eleven of their ponies, the party, which consisted of nine Cheyenne, barely making their escape into one of the many ravines nearby.

This was one of the small parties which the Cheyenne had sent to the vicinity of our camps on Medicine Bluff Creek to observe and report our movements, and was then on its way to the main village to report that we were again on the move. The point at which the capture was made was in Texas, on a small fresh water tributary of Salt Fork.

On the morning of the 9th, we moved in a westerly direction, marched all day, but were unable to find water, and were forced to make a dry camp on the prairie. Before daylight next morning, we resumed the march, changing our course to the south, and by noon reached camp on Middle Fork, a stream which, on some maps, is designated as Gypsum Creek.

On the following morning, we moved toward the southwest, crossing Mulberry Creek. Our march was continued until we came in sight of the banks of the main Red River. Here, we discovered the trail of one lodge leading northwest. The trail was nearly one month old, but with the hope that it would lead to others, we took it up, and before

CLOSING OPERATIONS

pursuing many miles had the satisfaction of seeing the trail increased by that of eleven lodges, all about the same time.

That night, we encamped on the headwaters of Mulberry Creek, occupying the ground selected for the same purpose by the Indians. From this point, the trail led northward. Notwithstanding the trail was very old, I felt confident that with due precautions, and knowing the lazy manner in which Indians moved when not pursued, we could overhaul them, or at least get very near them before our proximity was discovered. Thanks to their superior geographical knowledge, I was not troubled by routes, water or camping grounds. The trail led us by easy marches to good water, plenty of timber and the best camping grounds that could be selected.

On the morning of the 12th, the pursuit was resumed. Early in the day, the trail was found to be enlarged by the addition of forty-two lodges, and before night about as many more joined, making the trail one of over a hundred lodges and so plain we could follow it at a gallop, could our horses have kept up the gait. That night, we encamped on Middle Fork.

The morning of the 13th, we observed fresher signs of Indians than we had yet seen, indicating that they had left the Middle Fork not more than a week previous. This will be understood when it is known that in the ordinary manner of moving the village remains from three days to a week in each camp, and then moves but about ten miles before making another camp.

We moved without delay, and one of our marches equaled two or three made by the Indians. As the trail grew warmer, it became necessary to adopt additional precautions to insure success. No bugle calls or discharges of firearms were permitted. Fires were lighted after dark and covered with earth before daylight. Tents were burned, and all blankets in excess of one per man, and all clothing shared the same fate.

Daily the pursuit was continued until the morning of the 15th, when we reached a camp ground on the North Fork which had been abandoned only two days before. Encouraged by the prospect, we pressed forward, and by noon the advance had made twenty miles.

Hard Rope, the war chief of the Osages, and who at this moment was running the trail, discovered about one mile in advance a herd of forty or fifty ponies, grazing and herded by two Indians. The latter discovered us at the same time, and drove the herd rapidly in the direction of a timber stream which could be seen some two or three miles beyond. I at once sent orders back to the column, which was still a considerable distance in the rear, to close up at a rapid gait.

The deep sand and the exhausted condition of horses and men prevented this being done promptly. I was uncertain as to whether the village was in our front, or whether the herd seen driven off was merely on the move. If the latter, desiring to effect its capture, I advanced with the few men then in front in the direction taken by the herd. After proceeding about two miles, Indians could be seen in front, partially concealed behind the sand hills, and watching our movements.

Taking my orderly with me, I advanced to learn their character and intentions. After considerable signaling and parleying, eight Indians came forward to meet me. From them, I learned that the entire Cheyenne tribe, numbering two hundred and sixty lodges, was encamped at different points within ten or fifteen miles from where we then were.

A few moments afterward, thirty or forty Indians rode up to us, including Medicine Arrow, the head chief of the Cheyenne, and several other noted chiefs of the same tribe. From the latter, I learned that over two hundred lodges were encamped on the stream directly in our front, the remainder, under Little Robe, being some ten or fifteen miles lower down. Included in the two hundred lodges were nearly all the lodges belonging to the Dog Soldiers, the most mischievous, bloodthirsty and barbarous band of Indians that infest the Plains.

Here then was the opportunity we had been seeking, to administer a well merited punishment to the worst of all Indians. My intentions were formed accordingly, and as I rode with Medicine Arrow in the direction of the village, I made my plans for surrounding the village and attacking as soon as the troops came up. I did not pursue this course however, and for the following reasons; On my way to the village, I learned that the two white women captured in Kansas last autumn - one Mrs. Morgan, on the Solomon; the other, Miss White, on the

CLOSING OPERATIONS

Republican - were then held captive in the Cheyenne village.

It was then out of the question to assume a hostile attitude, at least until every peaceable means for their recovery had been exhausted. The opening of our attack would have been the signal for their murder by their captors, as we very well knew. I therefore determined to encamp my command, as soon as it arrived, near the village. In the meantime, I accompanied Medicine Arrow to his lodge in the centre of his village, where all the principal chiefs and the medicine man of the tribe soon assembled.

Before entering the village, I observed the greatest excitement prevailed; the entire herd was collected; the squaws had everything except their lodges packed, and their ponies were saddled ready for a precipitate flight. So that had my intention to attack been carried out, it is doubtful whether, with the timely warning they had received, and considering the jaded condition of my animals, we could at that time have inflicted any very serious injury beyond the capture of their lodges.

The recovery of the captive white women was now my first object. The squaws and children remained seated upon their ponies until the troops approached the village, when their fears, coupled with the remembrance of the crimes of the tribe and their deserved punishment, got the better of them, and like a herd of frightened sheep, old and young squaws, papooses, ponies and mules, started in the direction of Little Robe's village, abandoning to us their lodges and poles, and immense numbers of camp kettles, robes, shields and ponies.

I ordered my men not to fire upon the fugitives, but caused four of their principal men, two of them noted chiefs of the Dog Soldiers - Big Head and Dull Knife - to be seized and held under guard, intending through them to compel the release of the two white women. At the same time, to prevent the Cheyenne from breaking up into small parties and renewing hostilities, I sent word to them to return and take their lodges with them, adding that if they would all agree to encamp near Little Robe and his band, I would not permit their abandoned village to be disturbed until the lodges had been removed.

This proposition was generally accepted. I then sent a runner to Little Robe, who was well known to me, and whose influence with his tribe was great, to come and see me, promising him safe passport back to his village. He accepted my invitation, came to my camp, and after a long talk promised to use his influence for the best. No promise to deliver up the captives into our hands without the payment of a large ransom could be obtained. I was determined to secure their release, and that unconditionally, and thereby discourage the custom of ransoming captives from Indians, which is really nothing more or less than offering the latter a premium upon every captive.

Cheyenne chiefs captured by Custer. From left to right; Curly Head, Fat Bear, Dull Knife.

To obtain a better camp, and at the same time accomplish my purpose, I told Little Robe I would change my camp the following day, moving in the direction of his village, but that I had no desire to approach its immediate vicinity, and that after my arrival in camp, if he and the other chiefs would visit me, I would talk with them.

On the evening of the second day, a chief who had accompanied Little Robe the first day came to my camp to learn what I had to say and to procure, if possible, the release of the chiefs and warriors held by me. No satisfactory statement could be gotten from him regarding the return of the white women or the intentions of the chiefs. I therefore determined not to be put off any longer, and told him we had then

CLOSING OPERATIONS

waited three days for them to give us the white women, and had obtained no satisfactory response; that I should wait one day longer, but if by sunset the following day the white women were not delivered up, I would hang to a tree, which was there designated, three of the men held captive by me (the fourth one having been sent as a runner to Little Robe), and that the following day I would follow and attack the village.

With this message, the chief departed. The next day was one of no little anxiety to all, and to none more than to the three captive Cheyenne whom I certainly intended to hang if their people failed to accede to our demands. The ropes were ready, and the limb selected when, about three o'clock p.m., a small party of Indian warriors were seen approaching camp. They halted on a knoll about one mile distant, while one of their number came forward with the welcome intelligence that the women were with them and would be given up; but this was coupled with the proposition that I should exchange the three men, or two of them, for the women.

This was refused, and the return of the women demanded at once and unconditionally. A reluctant assent to this was given. The Indians however, feared to come inside of our lines. Lieutenant-Colonel Moore and Majors Jones and Jenkins were therefore detailed to go out and receive them.

The matter ended by the release of the women, and their restoration to their friends, and the sequel of the story is thus told by Custer:

After the momentary excitement consequent upon the arrival of the girls in camp had subsided, officers, particularly of the Kansas volunteers, came to me with the remark that when we first overtook the Cheyenne village, and I failed to order an attack when all the chances were in our favor, they mentally condemned my decision as a mistake; but with the results accomplished afterward they found ample reason to amend their first judgment, and frankly and cordially admit that the release of the two captives was far more gratifying than any victory over the Indians could have been if purchased by the sacrifice of their lives.

With this happy termination of this much of our negotiations with the Indians, I determined to march in the morning for Camp Supply, Indian Territory, satisfied that with the three chiefs in our possession, and the squaws and children captured at the Washita, still held as prisoners at Fort Hays, Kansas, we could compel the Cheyenne to abandon the warpath and return to their reservation. The three chiefs begged to be released upon the ground that their people had delivered up the two girls; but this I told them was but one of the two conditions imposed; the other required the tribe to return to their reservation, and until this was done, they need not hope for freedom; but in the meanwhile I assured them of kind treatment at our hands.

Before dark, a delegation of chiefs from the village visited camp to likewise urge the release of the three chiefs. My reply to them was the same that I had given to the captives. I assured them however, that upon complying with their treaty obligations and returning to their reservation, the three chiefs would be restored to their people, and we would return to them also the women and children captured at the Washita. Seeing that no modification of these terms could be obtained, they finally promised to accede to them, saying that their ponies, as I knew to be the fact, were in no condition to travel, but as soon as practicable they would surely proceed with their entire village to Camp Supply and abandon the warpath forever; a promise which, as a tribe, they have adhered to from that day to this, with strict faith, so far as my knowledge extends.

The settlement of the Cheyenne closed Custer's services on the southern plains. His command proceeded to Camp Supply and thence to Fort Hays, where the Nineteenth Kansas was mustered out. From and after the Washita campaign, the frontiers of Kansas were untroubled by any considerable depredations. Pawnee Killer, and the single campaign of 1867, had taught Custer all he needed to know of Indian fighting. In 1868-69, he showed the fruits of his lesson in the first thoroughly successful campaign that had yet been prosecuted against the Indians of the plains.

As many of our readers may feel an interest in the various characters introduced in these southern campaigns of Custer, a short

CLOSING OPERATIONS

summary of the fate of his best scouts may not be uninteresting. It seems that Romeo, true to his amorous name, and not deterred by his previous experience in Indian marriages, took to himself one more Cheyenne wife, when the tribe came in on their reservation, and that he became and is an Indian trader.

California Joe disappeared for several years, until in 1874, when Custer was in command at Fort Lincoln, he sent the general this letter:

GENERAL GEORGE A. CUSTER
SIERRE NEVADE MOUNTAINS, CALEFORNIA, March 16, 1874

Dear General: after my respets to you and Lady i thought that i tell you that i am still on top of land yit i hev been in the
rockey mountain the most of the time sence last I seen you but I got on the railroad and started west and the first thing I knew I landed in San Francisco so I could not go any further except goin by water and salt water at that so i turned back and headed for the mountains once more resolved never to go railroading no more i drifted up with the tide to Sacramento city and i landed my boat so i took up through town they say thar is 20 thousand people living thar but it looks to me like to be 100 thousand counting chinaman and all i cant describe my wolfish feeling but i think that i look just like i did when we was chasing Buffalo on the cimarone so i struck up through town and i come to a large fine building crowded with people so i bulged in to see what was going on and when i got in to the counsil house i took a look around at the crowd and i seen the most of them had bald heads so i thought to myself i struck it now that they are indian peace commissioners so i look to see if i would know any of them but not one - so after while the smartess lookin one got up and said gentleman i introduce a bill to have speckle mountain trout and fish eggs imported to California to be put in the american Bear and yuba rivers - those rivers is so muddy that a tadpole could not live in them caused by mining - did any body ever hear of speckle trout living in muddy water and the next thing was the game law and that was very near as bad as the Fish for they aint no game in the country as big as mawking bird i heard some fellow behind me ask how long is the legislators been in session then i dropt on myself it wuzent Indian commissioners after all so i slid out took across to Chinatown and they smelt like a kiowa camp in August with plenty buffalo meat around - it was gettin late so no place to go not got a red cent so i happen to think of an old friend back of town that i knowed 25 years ago so i lit out and sure enough he was thar just as i left him 25 years ago baching [leading the life of bachelor - G.A.C.] so i got a few seads i going to plant in a

FREDERICK WHITTAKER
few days give my respects to the 7th calvery and except the same yoursly

CALIFORNIA JOE

Joe subsequently turned up again as a miner in the Black Hills, where he probably is today. He still smokes.

LOUISVILLE TO THE YELLOWSTONE

THE final submission of the Cheyenne completed the work of Custer in the southwest, and set on him the stamp of complete success. He had done what no other officer in the American army had yet succeeded in doing, beaten tribe after tribe of Indians, completely and decisively; and his exploits had justly earned the reputation for him of being the best Indian fighter on the plains. For a time, his bitterest enemies were silent. They could not alter the facts by their sneers, and their animnus was too palpable when they tried to belittle his exploits. The facts were Custer's best eulogy.

A hostile and prejudiced court had sentenced him to disgrace on a frivolous pretext, and his enemies had tried their best to get along without him. They had all the United States army to pick from, and yet they had done nothing all the summer but get into trouble and fail. The stage routes were deserted, travel stopped, and only the line of the railway, as far as built, was safe. At last, Custer's worst enemies were compelled to acquiesce silently in the request of Sherman and Sheridan to be given back Custer himself as the only hope of success.

Every officer of the Seventh, enemies and all, joined in the request. A few months' experience of being made ridiculous under another leader brought them to that. Custer might be severe on drunkards, he might be a hard marcher, but he never made a fool of the regiment, and his worst enemies in that regiment had been conscious that he was unjustly treated in his court-martial.

They knew that the principal instigator of the charges against him had since been compelled to leave the army on account of habitual drunkenness and that all the really good and valuable officers who had ever served under Custer were unanimous in his praise. They joined in that request, the like of which had never been known before. A whole department formally asked for the return to command of an officer whom a year before the powers had tried their utmost to disgrace. He came, and what was the result?

Before the winter had fairly turned into spring, Custer had ended the whole war and placed the frontier in peace, alone and unassisted; just because he was given his own way. In seven months, he had closed the campaign which commenced in 1867 when Hancock let the Cheyenne slip from between his fingers, and when Custer saw his first Indian chief. He learned the mysteries of Indian warfare pretty quickly after that.

The close of this seven months' campaign gave Custer a long and well-earned rest during the summer of 1869. During the whole winter campaign, he had been separated from his wife, who had remained at Fort Leavenworth; but now that hostilities were closed, she rejoined him. The Seventh Cavalry was encamped during the whole summer in the neighborhood of Fort Hays, at Big Creek, where the very perfection of prairie life was the portion of all.

This period and the next year may be called one of the very happiest of Custer's life, wherein he enjoyed himself as much as when in Texas after the close of the war. His whole military life seems to have been passed in a series of these changes, from periods of the hardest, most protracted and vigorous labor to periods of rest and pleasure, enjoyed with the keenest zest by himself and wife.

The summer of 1869 was a perfect round of pleasurable excitement, hunting excursions taking place almost every week, parties of tourists from the east or from Europe coming to visit the camp, attracted by the fame of Custer the successful Indian fighter, and anxious to see him. Every week or so, a single squadron would be sent off on a scout through southern Kansas to look after any small parties of Indians that might sneak out of the agencies on a cattle lifting raid; but there was no fighting or danger.

The main body of Indians was really and truly at peace, cowed by Custer's successes. The campaign had made them respect him, and they all held him in deep reverence. Already showing the thoroughness of his character, he had mastered the Indian sign language and was able to converse with Indians from any tribe on the plains by this universal medium of communication.

The summer being passed in entertaining eastern visitors, private and public, camp was struck in October, and the winter passed in Fort Leavenworth, where Custer began to write his War Memoirs in a slightly different form from that in which they afterwards appeared, but he gave them up when they had reached no further than the Battle of Williamsburg in the Peninsular Campaign. He was always very diffident as to his literary abilities, being keenly sensible of the deficiencies of a West Point education in that direction, and it was this diffidence which probably caused him to give up the War Memoirs so early.

People had accused him so often of vanity that he had become painfully sensitive on the subject of mentioning himself; and strove hard to keep his own name out of the War Memoirs, as well as later in the *Life on the Plains*. This is, in fact, the gravest literary fault possessed by either. Almost all the interest they possess is that which appertains to Custer personally, as the most romantic figure of the war, and instead of this he thought himself obliged to give us historical sketches of others not possessing half the same charm.

His literary labors at Fort Leavenworth were varied, late in the winter, by a leave of absence, spent in a trip to New York with the little wife still as fresh and childish in mind and heart as ever, a matter in which she and Custer were exactly alike. All the summer, they would be saving up their money for the eastern trip in the winter and when the time came, they started off like two happy children, determined to have a good time, seeing all the sights, going to all the theatres, laughing at Dundreary and weeping over the simulated sorrows of Clara Morris, enjoying themselves to the very utmost. From that time thereafter, every winter saw the same little trip, and every spring saw them returning to the rough frontier life, having spent all their spare cash, but having had a splendid trip full of enjoyment.

The spring and summer of 1870 were merely a repetition of those of 1869, with more visitors. By this time, Custer's fame as a cavalry general was completely overshadowed by his more recent triumphs as an Indian fighter, and his still more recent exploits as a mighty hunter.

LOUISVILLE TO THE YELLOWSTONE

His Scotch deerhounds had increased in number until he owned quite a large pack, his rifles were growing numerous, his sporting letters to the *Turf, Field and Farm* had made him a friend of every hunter in the United States, and the English noble and gentle tourists, out for a buffalo hunt, always stopped at Fort Hays and brought letters to General Custer, who was supposed to know everything about the plains and buffalo.

Fort Leavenworth. Today, the Frontier Army Museum at Fort Leavenworth highlights the efforts of the Frontier Army in exploration, expansion and protection of the Trans-Mississippi West from the Lewis and Clark Expedition to the Punitive Expedition involving General John Pershing, and the importance of Fort Leavenworth's role in the exploration and expansion of the nation throughout the nineteenth century. The museum is located at 100 Reynolds Avenue, Fort Leavenworth, Kansas.

Even the great humbug Barnum came out west to have a buffalo hunt, and was indulged with a run. It was of course a good deal of trouble entertaining all these greenhorns, and especially taking care of them in a buffalo hunt. It was necessary to send out a mounted orderly with each, to see he did not get lost, and as soon as the chase separated the hunters, the orderly used to kill the buffalo for his particular tourist, while the latter fired off all the barrels of his revolver into the carcass and then cut off the tail and claimed the beast as his own spoil.

The orderlies found it a paying business to sell silence, while the amateurs took home their buffalo tails in triumph and hung them up in their studies. There are a good many such trophies in the Eastern States today, which might not be such a cause of pride to their owners were the true story to leak out.

October, 1870, again took Custer to Fort Leavenworth, where the whole regiment was reunited under the command of General Sturgis, its new colonel. General A.J. Smith had gone on the retired list, and Sturgis had succeeded him, as being the senior lieutenant-colonel of the army. It was now determined, in view of the peculiar exigencies of the U.S. regular army, that the Seventh Cavalry should be broken up and moved elsewhere while another regiment relieved it in the West.

Custer was thus likely to find himself, like many another officer, put in garrison at some one or two company post in the States, and he wished to avoid this, as he was beginning to love his wild life on the plains. He therefore made a formal application to headquarters, requesting to be assigned to duty at Fort Hays or else at headquarters of his regiment. The endorsement on this communication will show what at that time was General Sturgis' opinion on Custer's merits as an Indian fighter, which he has since so strenuously denied. It runs thus:

HEADQUARTERS SEVENTH CAVALRY, CAMP NEAR FORT HAYS, KANSAS
August 13th, 1869

In forwarding this communication approved, I would respectfully ask for it that favorable consideration to which it would appear to be entitled, not only in view of General Custer's worth and former services, but also of the arduous and important services rendered by him against the Indians of this department, while in command of the Seventh Cavalry. There is perhaps no other officer of equal rank on this line who has worked more faithfully against the Indians, or who has acquired the same degree of knowledge of the country and of the Indian character. If however, it should be deemed impracticable to give him the command he desires, I would respectfully recommend that he be permitted to accompany the Headquarters of the Regiment.

S.D. STURGIS, Col. Seventh Cavalry
Bvt. Maj. Gen. U.S.A. Comd. Regt.

This was Sturgis's free and unbiased opinion on Custer, fresh from the experience of his Indian warfare. It reads well today, since he has tried to change his opinion now that Custer is dead. The application was unsuccessful. There was no longer an urgent necessity for a first class Indian fighter at Fort Hays, and any old seniority fossil would do. Custer had done his work very well no doubt, better than any other man who had been put out there, but that was a year before. It was necessary to give some other regiment a chance at the plains, so the Seventh was ordered away into the States and broken up into detachments at small posts.

Under these circumstances, the position of the field officers of a regiment, if they are inclined to be lazy, is very pleasant. There is really nothing for them to do. They become mere ornamental appendages tacked on to a post to sign their names to requisitions and reports. It was so far pleasant to Custer that he got all the leaves he wanted and was able to go to Monroe early in 1871, while his extended leave finally took him to New York on private business.

In March, the Seventh was ordered partly to Kentucky, partly to South Carolina, Custer being assigned to a two company post at Elizabethtown, Kentucky, a small place some forty miles south of Louisville. Here, the husband and wife settled down in June for the next two years to a monotonous existence, especially irksome to Custer. Nine officers out of ten of the common pattern, which aims at earning its money easily, would have been delighted with this snug billet, but to Custer it was the reverse of pleasant. All that saved him from unhappiness was his literary work, in writing for the Galaxy the papers entitled *"My Life on the Plains,"* which were begun and finished during his Kentucky residence.

Part of the time, he was detailed in Louisville on a board for buying horses for the regiment, which naturally brought him in contact with all the smart horse dealers of the "horsey" state. This horse purchasing business also took him out to the Blue Grass country at times, and while there he invested much of his private funds in race horses, on which he expected to realize handsomely.

Just as his luck in war had been good however, just so was his luck in horse buying during peace time decidedly bad. No sooner had he paid his money for a valuable mare than the mare would be kicked by another and get a leg broken, or fall sick or die; and in this way his horse ventures all came to grief, and he lost some ten thousand dollars in a few years.

Custer Home, Elizabethtown. Known as the Brown Pusey House, General George Armstrong Custer and wife Elizabeth lived here while on assignment in Elizabethtown to combat the influence of the Ku Klux Klan and the illegal distilleries.

    The fact was, Custer was too honest and frank, too much of a knight of romance, he loved his horses too well, to succeed in trade with them. To be a successful horse trader, a man must be thoroughly callous, and regard his horses as mere objects of trade, which Custer never would do. Only one of his purchases now remains alive, and that one has been nearly ruined by the carelessness of the person in whose care it was left.

    During his Louisville residence, Custer only caught one glimpse of his beloved plains - in the winter of 1872. During that year, the Russian Grand Duke Alexis came to the United States on a tour, and it was judged civil to show him a buffalo hunt. General Sheridan, still in command of the great western division and now moreover a lieutenant-general, was getting rather too stout for that kind of thing himself, and

LOUISVILLE TO THE YELLOWSTONE

yet it was necessary to find some officer of high rank and national reputation to escort the Grand Duke, and to show him the honors as well as the buffalo.

Custer and Grand Duke Alexis. In October 1871, the Grand Duke Alexis, fourth son of Czar Alexander II of Russia, arrived in New York City to begin a goodwill tour of the United States at the request of his father. President Grant asked General Sheridan to arrange a buffalo hunt to be held for the Duke the following January, in which Custer also served as host.

No one was judged so fit for the purpose as Custer, and accordingly he received a telegraphic order to report at Omaha in January, 1872, where he joined Alexis, the renowned scout William Cody (Buffalo Bill) being also ordered there. The Grand Duke was delighted with his hunt and with Custer, whom he saw for the first time in the picturesque buckskin hunting shirt which the General always wore on the plains. The hunt over, the duke insisted that Custer must accompany him on his further trip through the west, which the latter did, returning with Alexis to Louisville.

Here they were joined by Mrs. Custer, and the party visited Mammoth Cave, and finally started on a regular trip through the south which terminated March, 1872 at New Orleans, where Alexis took ship for Russia. Nothing of note transpired during the summer of 1872, during which the *Life on the Plains* was fairly begun and nearly completed during the rest of the year. In March 1873, the Seventh Cavalry was once more ordered to the Plains, this time up in Dakota.

This order perfectly delighted Custer. He was getting heartily sick of the useless life he had been leading, and he knew that work was coining, real work. When the whole Seventh Cavalry was ordered out in a body, it meant business. Once before they had been ordered out, and had ended in conquering the southwest. Now it was necessary to overrun the northwest.

When Custer pacified the Kiowa, Arapahoe, and Cheyenne by force, physical and moral, the Sioux of the northwest had fared very differently. They had frightened the Government into a treaty, the Treaty of 1868, by which the United States had promised to give up to them forever a large expanse of country and not to trespass thereon.

The Great Royal Buffalo Hunt by Louis Maurer, 1895.

Now that the danger was over, and the Pacific Railroad safely completed to the south, thanks to Custer, the treaty with the Northern Indians became irksome. It was all well enough to promise a lot of naked savages to give them up so much land, but it could not be expected that such a promise should be kept a moment longer than was necessary to secure a quiet building of the railroad. It was now time to break the treaty.

A northern Pacific road had become necessary, and its route was to lie right through the very midst of the territory solemnly promised the Indians by the Treaty of 1868. As a practical measure to provoke an Indian war, there is nothing so certain as the commencement of a railroad. With the power to run it through however, a different state of things ensues, as Custer himself forcibly illustrates in narrating the events of the Yellowstone Expedition, the last in which we are able to follow his words.

"The experience of the past," says Custer, "particularly that of recent years, has shown too that no one measure so quickly and effectually frees a country from the horrors and devastations of Indian wars and Indian depredations generally as the building and successful operation of a railroad through the region overrun." Nothing can be truer than this, when once the railroad is completed, but the trouble is that while it is being built, the war has to be paid for at the same time, for the Indians, recognizing that the railroad will be their ruin, do all they can to hinder it.

Knowing this, the Seventh Cavalry was ordered to Dakota in March, 1873. Custer, overjoyed, left Louisville with his two companies, and was joined at Memphis by the rest of the regiment, all delighted to be together. There was Tom Custer, who had been down in South Carolina hunting whiskey distillers, and was heartily sick of the nauseous business; there were Cook, Yates, Calhoun, Smith and all the fellows, glad to see each other and anxious for work.

What with friends and relatives, the little group of officers nearest to Custer seemed like one family. There was Calhoun, the young boyish looking Apollo of the regiment, who had married Maggie Custer a year before, and who was now acting as adjutant. There was Tom Custer, who had risen from the ranks of the volunteers, as Calhoun did from those of the regulars, and whose only privilege as the general's brother was to get put in arrest for the little breaches of discipline oftener than any officer in the regiment. There was "Queen's Own" Cook, with his high-bred face and long Dundreary whiskers, and sturdy business-like Yates, who kept the "band-box troop" of the regiment. How glad all the boys were to see each other, and how they delighted in the prospect of work!

The regiment was taken by boat to Yankton on the Missouri, where it was put ashore and remained a week or so, being finally organized again April 10th, 1873. Then, the whole Seventh Cavalry, in regular old style, took up their march along the banks of the Missouri all the way to Fort Rice, 600 miles off, which they reached in six weeks. In regular old style, Mrs. Custer rode on her horse at the head of the column, and this time she had the company of more than one lady. Mrs. Calhoun, Mrs. Yates, Mrs. Smith and several other of the officers' wives went with her, and all accomplished the journey in safety. They passed through the Cheyenne, Brule, Yanktonnais and Standing Rock Agencies, seeing for the first time the Northern Indians; and finally went into camp at Fort Rice late in May.

Fort Rice. Between 1871 and 1873, Fort Rice served as the base for the First, Second, and Third Yellowstone expeditions. Four companies of the Fort Rice contingent of the 7th U.S. Cavalry accompanied George A. Custer on the Black Hills expedition in 1874. Two companies from Fort Rice fought in the Battle of the Little Bighorn.

There however, the ladies found themselves very unwillingly compelled to turn back. The regiment was ordered to accompany the Yellowstone Expedition. Mrs. Custer and her friends returned to

LOUISVILLE TO THE YELLOWSTONE

Monroe, while Custer proceeded on that expedition which he shall henceforth tell in his own words:

In the early spring of '73, the officials of the Northern Pacific Railroad applied to the Government authorities at Washington for military protection for a surveying party to be sent out the ensuing summer to explore and mark out the uncompleted portion of the road extending from the Missouri River in Dakota to the interior of Montana, west of the Yellowstone.

To extend encouragement and aid to the projectors and builders of the Northern Pacific road, the Government granted the application of the road for a military escort and gave authority for the organization of what was afterward designated as the Yellowstone expedition. The troops composing the expedition numbered about seventeen hundred men, consisting of cavalry, infantry, an improvised battery of artillery and a detachment of Indian scouts, the whole under command of Brevet Major-General D.S. Stanley. Fort Rice, Dakota, on the Missouri River, was selected as the point of rendezvous and departure of the expedition.

It was not until July that the Yellowstone Expedition assumed definite shape and began its westward movement from Fort Rice. The engineers and surveyors of the Northern Pacific Railroad were under the direction and management of General Thomas L. Rosser. He and I had been cadets together at the Military Academy at West Point, occupying adjoining rooms, and being members of the same company, often marching side by side in the performance of our various military duties while at the Academy.

When the storms of secession broke upon the country in '61, Rosser, in common with the majority of the cadets from the Southern States, resigned his warrant, and hastened to unite his personal fortunes with those of his state - Texas. He soon won distinction in the Confederate army under Lee, and finally rose to the rank and command of major-general of cavalry.

When the war was ended, Rosser, like many of his comrades from the South who had staked their all upon the issue of the war, at once cast about him for an opportunity to begin anew the battle, not of war, but of life. Possessing youth, health, many and large abilities, added to indomitable pluck, he decided to trust his fortunes amidst his late enemies, and repaired to Minnesota, where he sought employment in one of the many surveying parties acting under the auspices of the Northern Pacific road. Upon applying to the officer of the road for a position as civil engineer, he was informed that no vacancy existed to which he could be appointed.

Nothing daunted, he persisted, and finally accepted a position among the axe men, willing to work, and proved to his employers not only his industry but his fitness for promotion. He at once attracted the attention of his superiors, who were not slow to recognize his merit. Rosser was advanced rapidly from one important position to another, until in a few months he became the chief engineer of the surveying party accompanying the expedition. In this capacity I met him on the plains of Dakota in 1873; nearly ten years after the date when in peaceful scabbards we sheathed the swords which on more than one previous occasion we had drawn against each other.

Omitting the incidents of the march from our starting point, Fort Rice, on the Missouri, we come to the time when we found ourselves encamped on the east bank of the beautiful and swift flowing Yellowstone, about a hundred miles from its mouth. At this point, the expedition was met by a steamer, sent for that purpose up the Missouri, hundreds of miles above Fort Rice, then up the Yellowstone to the point of junction. From it fresh supplies of forage and subsistence stores were obtained.

This being done, the entire expedition, save a small detachment left at this point to guard our surplus stores intended for our return march, was ferried by the steamer across the Yellowstone River. Our course for several days carried us up that stream; our tents at night being usually pitched on or near the river bank. The country to be surveyed however, soon became so rough and broken in places that we encountered serious delays at times in finding a practicable route for our long and heavily laden wagon trains, over rocks and through canons hitherto unexplored by white men.

LOUISVILLE TO THE YELLOWSTONE

Yellowstone Expedition. The Yellowstone Expedition of 1873 was an expedition to survey routes for the Northern Pacific Railroad along the Yellowstone River. The expedition was under the overall command of Colonel David S. Stanley, with Lieutenant Colonel George A. Custer second in command.

So serious did these embarrassments become, and so much time was lost in accomplishing our daily marches, that I suggested to General Stanley that I should take with me each day a couple of companies of cavalry and a few of the Indian scouts, and seek out and prepare a practicable road in advance, thereby preventing detention of the main command.

This proposition being acceded to, it was my custom thereafter to push rapidly forward in the early morning, gaining an advance of several miles upon the main expedition, and by locating the route relieving the troops and trains in rear of a great amount of fatigue and many tedious detentions. One result of this system was that I and my little party, who were acting as pioneers, usually arrived at the termination of our day's march, our camp ground for the night, at an early hour in the day, several hours in advance of the main portion of the expedition.

On the morning of August 4th, with two companies of the Seventh Cavalry commanded by Captain Moylan and Colonel Custer - who, with my adjutant, Lieutenant Calhoun, and Lieutenant Varnum, composed the officers of the party, and guided by my favorite scout, Bloody Knife, a young Arickaree warrior, the entire party numbering eighty-six men and five officers, I left camp at five o'clock in the morning and set out as usual to explore the country and find a practicable route for the main column. Soon after we left camp, Bloody Knife's watchful eyes discovered fresh signs of Indians. Halting long enough to allow him to examine the trail, Bloody Knife was soon able to gather all the information attainable. A party of Indians had been prowling about our camp the previous night, and had gone away, travelling in the direction in which we were then marching.

Custer (seated), with Bloody Knife on the left. At the battle of the Little Bighorn, Bloody Knife was standing next to Reno when he was shot in the head. Reno, his face smeared from Bloody Knife's wound, panicked. From that point on, the Reno theater of battle was "every man for himself."

This intelligence occasioned no particular surprise, as we had been expecting to discover the presence of Indians for several days. Bloody Knife's information produced no change in our plans. The hostile party of whose presence we had become aware numbered nineteen; our party numbered over ninety.

LOUISVILLE TO THE YELLOWSTONE

Over rock-ribbed hills, down timbered dells and across open, grassy plains, we wended our way without unusual interest, except at intervals of a few miles to discover the trail of the nineteen prowling visitors of the previous night, showing that our course, which was intended to lead us again to the Yellowstone, was in the same direction as theirs. Bloody Knife interpreted this as indicating that the village from which the nineteen had probably been sent to reconnoitre and report our movements, was located somewhere above us in the Yellowstone valley.

About ten o'clock, we reached the crest of the high line of bluffs bordering the Yellowstone valley, from which we obtained a fine view of the river and valley extending above and beyond us as far as the eye could reach. After halting upon the crest of the bluffs long enough to take in the pleasures of the scene and admire the beautiful valley spread out like an exquisite carpet at our feet, we descended to the valley and directed our horses' heads toward a particularly attractive and inviting cluster of shade trees standing on the river bank, and distant from the crest of the bluffs nearly two miles. First allowing our thirsty horses to drink from the clear, crystal water of the Yellowstone, which ran murmuringly by in its long tortuous course to the Missouri, we then picketed them out to graze.

Precautionary and necessary measures having been attended to, looking to the security of our horses, the next important and equally necessary step was to post half a dozen pickets on the open plain beyond to give timely warning in the event of the approach of hostile Indians. This being done, the remainder of our party busied themselves in arranging each for his individual comfort, disposing themselves on the grass beneath the shade of the wide spreading branches of the cottonwoods that grew close to the river bank. For myself, so oblivious was I to the prospect of immediate danger, that after selecting a most inviting spot for my noonday nap, and arranging my saddle and buckskin coat in the form of a comfortable pillow, I removed my boots, untied my cravat and opened my collar, prepared to enjoy to the fullest extent, the delight of the outdoor siesta.

I did not omit, however, to place my trusty Remington rifle within easy grasp - more from habit, it must be confessed, than from anticipation of danger. Near me, and stretched on the ground sheltered by the shade of the same tree, was my brother, the colonel, divested of his hat, coat and boots; while close at hand, wrapped in deep slumber, lay the other three officers, Moylan, Calhoun, and Varnum.

Sleep had taken possession of us all - officers and men - excepting of course the watchful pickets into whose keeping the safety, the lives, of our little detachment was for the time entrusted. How long we slept I scarcely know - perhaps an hour, when the cry of "Indians, Indians!" quickly followed by the sharp ringing crack of the pickets' carbines, aroused and brought us - officers, men, and horses - to our feet.

There was neither time nor occasion for questions to be asked or answered. Catching up my rifle, and without waiting to don hat or boots, I glanced through the grove of trees to the open plain or valley beyond, and saw a small party of Indians bearing down toward us as fast as their ponies could carry them. "Run to your horses, men! Run to your horses!" I fairly yelled as I saw that the first move of the Indians was intended to stampede our animals and leave us to be attended to afterward.

At the same time, the pickets opened fire upon our disturbers, who had already emptied their rifles at us as they advanced as if boldly intending to ride us down. As yet we could see but half a dozen warriors, but those who were familiar with stratagems knew full well that so small a party of savages unsupported would not venture to disturb in open day a force the size of ours. Quicker than I could pen the description, each trooper, with rifle in hand, rushed to secure his horse, and men and horses were soon withdrawn from the open plain and concealed behind the clump of trees beneath whose shade we were but a few moments before quietly sleeping. The firing of the pickets, the latter having been reinforced by a score of their comrades, checked the advance of the Indians and enabled us to saddle our horses and be prepared for whatever might be in store for us.

A few moments found us in our saddles and sallying forth from the timber to try conclusions with the daring intruders. We could only see half a dozen Sioux warriors galloping up and down in our front, boldly challenging us by their manner to attempt their capture or death. Of course it was an easy matter to drive them away, but as we advanced it became noticeable that they retired, and when we halted or diminished our speed, they did likewise.

It was apparent from the first that the Indians were resorting to stratagem to accomplish that which they could not do by an open, direct attack. Taking twenty troopers with me headed by Colonels Custer and Calhoun, and directing Moylan to keep within supporting distance with the remainder, I followed the retreating Sioux up the valley, but with no prospect of overtaking them, as they were mounted upon the fleetest of ponies. Thinking to tempt them within our grasp, I being mounted on a Kentucky thoroughbred in whose speed and endurance I had confidence, directed Colonel Custer to allow me to approach the Indians, accompanied only by my orderly, who was also well mounted; at the same time to follow us cautiously at a distance of a couple of hundred yards.

The wily redskins were not to be caught by any such artifice. They were perfectly willing that my orderly and myself should approach them, but at the same time they carefully watched the advance of the cavalry following me, and permitted no advantage. We had by this time almost arrived abreast of an immense tract of timber growing in the valley and extending to the water's edge, but distant from our resting place, from which we had been so rudely aroused, about two miles.

The route taken by the Indians and which they evidently intended us to follow led past this timber, but not through it. When we had arrived almost opposite the nearest point, I signaled to the cavalry to halt, which was no sooner done than the Indians also came to a halt. I then made the sign to the latter for a parley, which was done simply by riding my horse in a circle. To this, the savages only responded by looking on in silence for a few moments, then turning their ponies and moving off slowly as if to say, "Catch us if you can."

My suspicions were more than ever aroused, and I sent my orderly back to tell Colonel Custer to keep a sharp eye upon the heavy bushes on our left and scarcely three hundred yards distant from where I sat on my horse. The orderly had delivered his message and had almost rejoined me, when judging from our halt that we intended to pursue no further, the real design and purpose of the savages was made evident. The small party in front had faced toward us, and were advancing as if to attack.

I could scarcely credit the evidence of my eyes, but my astonishment had only begun when turning to the wood on my left I beheld bursting from their concealment between three and four hundred Sioux warriors mounted and caparisoned with all the flaming adornments of paint and feathers which go to make up the Indian war costume. When I first obtained a glimpse of them - and a single glance was sufficient - they were dashing from the timber at full speed, yelling and whooping as only Indians can. At the same time, they moved in perfect line, and with as seeming good order and alignment as the best drilled cavalry.

To understand our relative positions, the reader has only to imagine a triangle whose sides are almost equal; their length in this particular instance being from three to four hundred yards, the three angles being occupied by Colonel Custer and his detachment, the Indians, and myself. Whatever advantage there was in length of sides fell to my lot, and I lost no time in availing myself of it. Wheeling my horse suddenly around, and driving the spurs into his sides, I rode as only a man rides whose life is the prize to reach Colonel Custer and his men, not only in advance of the Indians, but before any of them could cut me off.

Moylan with his reserve was still too far in the rear to render their assistance available in repelling the shock of the Indians' first attack. Realizing the great superiority of our enemies, not only in numbers, but in their ability to handle their arms and horses in a fight, and fearing they might dash through and disperse Colonel Custer's small party of twenty men, and having once broken the formation of the latter, dispatch them in detail, I shouted to Colonel Custer at almost each bound of my horse, "Dismount your men! Dismount your men!" but the distance which separated us and the excitement of the occasion prevented him from hearing me.

Fortunately however, this was not the first time he had been called upon to contend against the sudden and unforeseen onslaught of savages, and although failing to hear my suggestion, he realized instantly that the safety of his little band of troopers depended upon the adoption of prompt means of defense.

Scarcely had the long line of splendidly mounted warriors rushed from their hiding place before Colonel Custer's voice rang out sharp and clear, "Prepare to fight on foot." This order required three out of four troopers to leap from their saddles and take their position on the ground, where by more deliberate aim, and being freed from the management of their horses, a more effective resistance could be opposed to the rapidly approaching warriors. The fourth trooper in each group of "fours" remained on his horse, holding the reins of the horses of his three comrades.

Quicker than words can describe, the fifteen cavalrymen, now on foot and acting as infantry, rushed forward a few paces in advance of the horses, deployed into open order, and dropping on one or both knees in the low grass, waited with loaded carbines - with finger gently pressing the trigger - the approach of the Sioux, who rode boldly down as if apparently unconscious that the small group of troopers were on their front. "Don't fire, men, until I give the word, and when you do fire, aim low," was the quiet injunction given his men by their young commander as he sat on his horse intently watching the advancing foe.

Swiftly over the grassy plain leaped my noble steed, each bound bearing me nearer to both friends and foes. Had the race been confined to the Indians and myself, the closeness of the result would have satisfied an admirer even of the Derby. Nearer and nearer our paths approached each other, making it appear almost as if I were one of the line of warriors as the latter bore down to accomplish the destruction of the little group of troopers in front. Swifter seem to fly our mettled steeds, the one to save, the other to destroy, until the common goal has almost been reached - a few more bounds, and friends and foes will be united - will form one contending mass.

The victory was almost within the grasp of the redskins. It seemed that but a moment more, and they would be trampling the kneeling troopers beneath the feet of their fleet limbed ponies when, "Now men, let them have it!" was the signal for a well-directed volley, as fifteen cavalry carbines poured their contents into the ranks of the shrieking savages. Before the latter could recover from the surprise and confusion which followed, the carbines - thanks to the invention of breechloaders - were almost instantly loaded, and a second carefully aimed discharge went whistling on its deadly errand.

Several warriors were seen to reel in their saddles, and were only saved from falling by the quickly extended arms of their fellows. Ponies were tumbled over like butchered bullocks, their riders glad to find themselves escaping with less serious injuries. The effect of the rapid firing of the troopers, and the firm, determined stand, showing that they thought neither of flight nor surrender, was to compel the savages first to slacken their speed, then to lose their daring and confidence in their ability to trample down the little group of defenders in the front.

Death to many of their number stared them in the face. Besides, if the small party of troopers in the front was able to oppose such plucky and destructive resistance to their attacks, what might not be expected should the main party under Moylan, now swiftly approaching to the rescue, also take part in the struggle? But more quickly than my sluggish pen has been able to record the description of the scene, the battle line of the warriors exhibited signs of faltering, which soon degenerated into an absolute repulse.

In a moment, their attack was transformed into flight in which each seemed only anxious to secure his individual safety. A triumphant cheer from the cavalrymen as they sent a third installment of leaden messengers whistling about the ears of the fleeing redskins served to spur both pony and rider to their utmost speed. Moylan by this time had reached the ground and had united the entire force. The Indians in the mean time had plunged out of sight into the recesses of the jungle from which they first made their attack. We knew too well that their absence would be brief, and that they would resume the attack, but not in the manner of the first.

We knew that we had inflicted no little loss upon them - dead and wounded ponies could be seen on the ground passed over by the Indians. The latter would not be satisfied without determined efforts to get revenge. Of this we were well aware.

A moment's hurried consultation between the officers and myself, and we decided that as we would be forced to act entirely upon the defensive against a vastly superior force, it would be better if we relieved ourselves as far as possible of the care of our horses and take our chances in the fight which was yet to come on foot. At the same time, we were then so far out on the open plain and from the river bank that the Indians could surround us.

We must get nearer to the river, conceal our horses or shelter them from fire, then with every available man form a line or semicircle, with our backs to the river, and defend ourselves until the arrival of the main body of the expedition, an event we could not expect for several hours. As if divining our intentions and desiring to prevent their execution, the Indians now began their demonstrations looking to a renewal of the fight.

Of course, it was easy to see what had been the original plan by which the Indians hoped to kill or capture our entire party. Stratagem of course was to play a prominent part in the quarrel. The few young warriors first sent to arouse us from our midday slumber came as a decoy to tempt us to pursue them beyond the ambush in which lay concealed the main body of the savages; the latter were to dash from their hiding place, intercept our retreat, and dispose of us after the most approved manner of barbarous warfare.

The next move on our part was to fight our way back to the little clump of bushes from which we had been so rudely startled. To do this, Captain Moylan, having united his force to that of Colonel Custer, gave the order "Prepare to fight on foot." This was quickly obeyed. Three-fourths of the fighting force were now on foot armed with the carbines only. These were deployed in somewhat of a circular skirmish line, of which the horses formed the centre; the circle having a diameter of several hundred yards. In this order, we made our way back to the timber; the Indians whooping, yelling and firing their rifles as they dashed madly by on their fleet war ponies.

That the fire of their rifles should be effective under these circumstances could scarcely be expected. Neither could the most careful aim of the cavalrymen produce much better results. It forced the savages to keep at a respectful distance however, and enabled us to make our retrograde movement. A few of our horses were shot by the Indians in this irregular skirmish; none fatally, however.

As we were falling back, contesting each foot of ground passed over, I heard a sudden sharp cry of pain from one of the men in charge of our horses; the next moment I saw his arm hanging helplessly at his side, while a crimson current flowing near his shoulder told that the aim of the Indians had not been entirely in vain. The gallant fellow kept his seat in his saddle however, and conducted the horses under his charge safely with the rest to the timber.

Once concealed by the trees and no longer requiring the horses to be moved, the number of horse holders was reduced so as to allow but one trooper to eight horses; the entire remainder being required on the skirmish line. The redskins had followed us closely, step by step, to the timber, tempted in part by their great desire to obtain possession of our horses. If successful in this, they believed no doubt that, flight on our part being no longer possible, we must be either killed or captured.

Taking advantage of a natural terrace or embankment extending almost like a semicircle in front of the little grove in which we had taken refuge, and at a distance of but a few hundred yards from the latter, I determined by driving the Indians beyond to adopt it as our breastwork or line of defense. This was soon accomplished, and we found ourselves deployed behind a natural parapet or bulwark from which the troopers could deliver a carefully directed fire upon their enemies, and at the same time be protected largely from the bullets of the latter. The Indians made repeated and desperate efforts to dislodge us and force us to the level plateau. Every effort of this kind proved unavailing.

Rather a remarkable instance of rifle shooting occurred in the early part of the contest. I was standing in a group of troopers, and with them was busily engaged firing at such of our enemies as exposed themselves. Bloody Knife was with us, his handsome face lighted up by the fire of battle and the desire to avenge the many wrongs suffered by his people at the hands of the ruthless Sioux. All of us had had our attention drawn more than once to a Sioux warrior who, seeming more bold than his fellows, dashed repeatedly along the front of our lines, scarcely two hundred yards distant, and although the troopers had singled him out, he had thus far escaped untouched by their bullets.

Encouraged by his success perhaps, he concluded to taunt us again, and at the same time exhibit his own daring by riding along the lines at full speed, but nearer than before. We saw him coming. Bloody Knife, with his Henry rifle poised gracefully in his hands, watched his coming, saying he intended to make this his enemy's last ride. He would send him to the happy hunting ground. I told the interpreter to tell Bloody Knife that at the a moment the warrior reached a designated point directly opposite to us, he, Bloody Knife, should fire at the rider and I at the same instant would fire at the pony.

A smile of approval passed over the swarthy features of the friendly scout as he nodded assent. I held in my hand my well tried Remington. Resting on one knee and glancing along the barrel, at the same time seeing that Bloody Knife was also squatting low in the deep grass with rifle leveled, I awaited the approach of the warrior to the designated point. On he came, brandishing his weapons and flaunting his shield in our faces, defying us by his taunts to come out and fight like men.

Swiftly sped the gallant little steed that bore him, scarcely needing the guiding rein. Nearer and nearer both horse and rider approached the fatal spot, when sharp and clear, and so simultaneous as to sound as one, rang forth the reports of the two rifles. The distance was less than two hundred yards. The Indian was seen to throw up his arms and reel in his saddle, while the pony made one final leap, and both fell to the earth. A shout rose from the group of troopers in which Bloody Knife and I joined. The next moment, a few of the comrades of the fallen warrior rushed to his rescue, and without dismounting from their ponies, scarcely pulling rein, clutched up the body, and the next moment disappeared from view.

Foiled in their repeated attempts to dislodge us, the Indians withdrew to a point beyond the range of our rifles for the apparent purpose of devising a new plan of attack. Of this, we soon became convinced. Hastily returning to a renewal of the struggle, we saw our adversaries arrange themselves in groups along our entire front. They were seen to dismount, and the quick eyes of Bloody Knife detected them making their way toward us by crawling through the grass. We were at a loss to comprehend their designs, as we could not believe they intended to attempt to storm our position on foot. We were not left long in doubt. Suddenly, and almost as if by magic, we beheld numerous small columns of smoke shooting up all along our front.

Calling Bloody Knife and the interpreter to my side, I inquired the meaning of what we saw. "They are setting fire to the long grass, and intend to burn us out," was the scout's reply, at the same time keeping his eyes intently bent on the constantly increasing columns of smoke. His features wore a most solemn look; anxiety was plainly depicted there. Looking to him for suggestions and advice in this new phase of our danger, I saw his face gradually unbend and a scornful smile part his lips. "The Great Spirit will not help our enemies," was his muttered reply to my question. "See," he continued; "the grass refuses to burn." Casting my eyes along the line formed by the columns of smoke, I saw that Bloody Knife had spoken truly when he said, "The grass refuses to burn."

This was easily accounted for. It was early in the month of August; the grass had not ripened or matured sufficiently to burn readily. A month later, and the flames would have swept us back to the river as if we had been surrounded by a growth of tinder. In a few moments, the anxiety caused by the threatening of this new and terrible danger was dispelled. While the greatest activity was maintained in our front by our enemies, my attention was called to a single warrior who, mounted on his pony, had deliberately, and as I thought rashly, passed around our left flank - our diminished numbers preventing us from extending our line close to the river - and was then in rear of our skirmishers, riding slowly along the crest of the low river bank with as apparent unconcern as if in the midst of his friends instead of being almost in the power of his enemies.

I imagined that his object was to get nearer to the grove in which our horses were concealed, and toward which lie was moving slowly, to reconnoitre and ascertain how much force we held in reserve. At the same time, as I never can see an Indian engaged in an unexplained act without conceiving treachery or stratagem to be at the bottom of it, I called to Lieutenant Varnum, who commanded on the left, to take a few men and endeavor to cut the wily interloper off.

This might have been accomplished but for the excessive zeal of some of Varnum's men, who acted with lack of caution, and enabled the Indian to discover their approach and make his escape by a hurried gallop up the river. The men were at a loss even then to comprehend his strange maneuver, but after the fight had ended, and we obtained an opportunity to ride over and examine the ground, all was made clear, and we learned how narrowly we had escaped a most serious if not fatal disaster.

The river bank in our rear was from twenty to thirty feet high. At its base and along the water's edge ran a narrow pebbly beach. The redskins had hit upon a novel, but to us most dangerous scheme for capturing our horses, and at the same time throwing a large force of warriors directly on our rear. They had found a pathway beyond our rear, leading from the large tract of timber in which they were first concealed through a cut or ravine in the river bank. By this, they were enabled to reach the water's edge, from which point they could move down the river following the pebbly beach referred to, the height of the river bank protecting them perfectly from our observation.

Thus, they would have placed themselves almost in the midst of our horses before we could have become aware of their designs. Had they been willing, as white men would have been, to assume greater risks, their success would have been assured. But they feared that we might discover their movements and catch them while strung out along the narrow beach, with no opportunity to escape. A few men on the bank could have shot down a vastly superior force. In this case, the Indians had sent on this errand about one hundred warriors.

After the discovery of this attack and its failure, the battle languished for awhile, and we were surprised to notice, not very long after, a general withdrawal from in front of our right and a concentration of their forces opposite our left. The reason for this was soon made clear to us. Looking far to the right and over the crest of the hills already described, we could see an immense cloud of dust rising and rapidly approaching. We could not be mistaken; we could not see the cause producing this dust; but there was not one of us who did not say to himself, "Relief is at hand."

A few moments later, a shout arose from the men. All eyes were turned to the bluffs in the distance, and there were to be seen, coming almost with the speed of the wind, four separate squadrons of Uncle Sam's best cavalry, with banners flying, horses' manes and tails floating on the breeze, and comrades spurring forward in generous emulation as to which squadron should land its colors first in the fight. It was a grand and welcome sight, but we waited not to enjoy it.

Confident of support and wearied from fighting on the defensive, now was our time to mount our steeds and force our enemies to seek safety in flight, or to battle on more even terms. In a moment, we were in our saddles and dashing after them. The only satisfaction we had was to drive at full speed for several miles a force outnumbering us five to one.

In this pursuit, we picked up a few ponies which the Indians were compelled to abandon on account of wounds or exhaustion. Their wounded, of whom there were quite a number, and their killed, as afterwards acknowledged by them when they returned to the agency to receive the provisions and fresh supplies of ammunition which a sentimental government, manipulated and directed by corrupt combinations insists upon distributing annually, were sent to the rear before the flight of the main body. The number of Indians and ponies killed and wounded in this engagement, as shown by their subsequent admission, almost equaled that of half our entire force engaged.

That night, the forces of the expedition encamped on the battleground, which was nearly opposite the mouth of Tongue River. My tent was pitched under the hill from which I had been so unceremoniously disturbed at the commencement of the fight; while under the wide spreading branches of a neighboring cottonwood, guarded and watched over by sorrowing comrades who kept up their lonely vigils through the night, lay the mangled bodies of two of our companions of the march, who although not present nor participating in the fight, had fallen victims to the cruelty of our foes.

Thus closes Custer's account of this, his first fight with the Northern Indians. In it will be noticed the same coolness and deliberately studied recklessness which made him so successful an Indian fighter. This was the first intimation that the Sioux were on the warpath against the whites, and their first opposition to the running of the railroad.

In the last sentence of Custer's account of this action, which closes his published articles on the plains, he mentions two victims of Indian cruelty. It is necessary to explain the allusion, because these two men were remotely the cause of Custer's own death, three years later.

They were both unarmed men, the veterinary surgeon and the sutler of the Seventh Cavalry. Dr. Houzinger, the first, was a corpulent old man of the quietest and most inoffensive habits, a great favorite with the regiment. Mr. Baliran, the sutler, was also an elderly man and a great friend of Dr. Houzinger. The two were in the habit of straying off from the main body of the command, picking up natural curiosities, and so far had experienced no trouble. On the day of Custer's fight, these two quiet old men were somewhere about two miles behind his party, and ahead of the main body.

Their bodies were found by the advance of the main expedition, where they had been swooped upon and killed by Indians, some outlying members of the main party. Dr. Houzinger's skull was fractured as with some blunt instrument, but neither body was mutilated. Who had killed them was of course not known then. It came to light in a very strange manner, two years after as we shall see in its place.

Another man, a soldier of Company F, Seventh Cavalry, was also found killed, where he had been surprised at a spring, and it was the discovery of these bodies, together with the reports of scouts and stragglers that the Indians were up, that had induced General Stanley to send on help to Custer, arriving in time as it did. Stanley mentions this fight in very handsome terms in his report.

For the next three days after the fight, Indians were to be seen hovering round the column, and on the 8th of August, the appearance was explained. A lodge pole trail, evidently belonging to a very large village, was found leading up the Yellowstone, and Custer was sent out with all the cavalry and scouts to pursue it, starting at nine that night. The trail was followed for thirty-six hours, and on the 10th August, it was found that the Indians had crossed the Yellowstone in "bull boats," the old trapper name for the wicker coracle, covered with a bull's hide, which is the transport of the plains Indians.

Custer tried all day to cross after them, but in vain; the American horses would not swim the river. Next morning, he was attacked by the Indians, who had been watching his discomfiture. Some came down and fired at him across the river, while another body, probably from a second village, came down behind him, firing from the rear. The place where they now were was on the north bank of the Yellowstone, three miles below the mouth of the Big Horn. Then as now, the valley of the Upper Yellowstone, especially the southern bank, was the headquarters of the hostile Indians, and then as now, Sitting Bull seems to have been their leader.

Such at least was the impression of men in the ranks at the time, as I learn from extracts from the diary of an old soldier, then of the Twenty-second infantry, and now in the marines. His name is Patrick Bresland, and he seems to have been a regular old warrior all over the world, having served in the English army in the Crimea and Indian Mutiny, and several enlistments in different corps of the United States Army.

This brave fellow it seems, kept a diary, meagre and bare enough, but still recording the main facts during the Yellowstone Expedition, and his entry of the fight of the 4th August is that it was "between the Sioux under Sitting Bull and Companies A and B, Seventh Cavalry." He says further, "the Indians retreated, followed by the Seventh Cavalry, Twenty-second infantry and the rest of the expedition under General Stanley. On the 10th, August, we struck their trail at the Yellowstone crossing. We lay in camp all night, or until 3 o'clock next morning, when the Indians, 1500 strong, who bad re-crossed to our side of the river, commenced an attack at a distance."

LOUISVILLE TO THE YELLOWSTONE

"General Custer ordered out two companies of his regiment as skirmishers, and they were joined by Companies C, I, F, and K of the Twenty-second infantry. We were ordered by Custer to charge in a body. I was present on this occasion, and followed the Indians nine or ten miles, when they reached the hills and scattered. From here, we went to Mussel Shell River, which is the extreme point of the survey on the Northern Pacific Railroad. We remained here several days, when we returned to the Yellowstone, where we had several engagements with the Indians."

Sitting Bull said: *"It was up there, where the last fight took place, where the last stand was made, the Long Hair stood like a sheaf of corn with all ears fallen around him. He killed a man when he fell. He laughed; he had fired his last shot. He rose up on his hands and tried another shot, but his pistol would not go off. One man was kneeling, that was all. But he died before Long Hair."*

Bresland's account mentions the killing of Dr. Houzinger, Mr. Baliran, and Ball of the Seventh Cavalry, and is valuable as coming from an independent and unofficial source, confirming the main facts. General Stanley's report mentions that artillery was used in the fight, which caused a complete stampede of the Indians, they being very much afraid of shells. He also mentions that the soldiers found on the field citizens' clothing, coffee, sugar, bacon, two Winchester rifles and plenty of shells of patent ammunition, showing that the Indians must have been at the agencies recently, as those are the only places where Indians can get these articles.

The station where the expedition left the Yellowstone and crossed the divide to the Mussel Shell was named "Pompey's Pillar." This is a knoll on the south side of the Yellowstone, thirty miles from the Big Horn. It stands alone, separated by the water from the other bluffs, with perpendicular sides one hundred and fifty feet high, with a top of grass sod, an acre in extent. In fact, says Stanley, it looks like anything but a pillar; however, such it was named, and such it remains on the map to the present day.

Pompey's Pillar. During his trip back to St. Louis, William Clark of the Lewis and Clark Expedition climbed the Pillar and carved his signature and the date in the sandstone.

At this place, several Indians came out and fired a volley into a number of soldiers belonging to the expedition who were bathing, causing a great scattering of naked men. No further serious trouble was experienced, and Custer returned at the close of the trip to Fort Rice late in September. From thence, he was ordered to Chicago to report to General Sheridan, with whom he went to Toledo to the reunion of the Army of the Tennessee, and thence to Monroe, where he again met

LOUISVILLE TO THE YELLOWSTONE

his little wife.

He was now granted a leave, part of which was spent at Chicago during which time the eldest son of President Grant, an officer on Sheridan's staff, was married to Miss Honore, a wedding duly reported by the Jenkinses of that date. At the close of his leave, Custer was ordered to assume command of the post at which he spent the remaining years of his life, Fort Abraham Lincoln, on the right bank of the Missouri River, opposite to the little town of Bismarck, which is the present terminus of the Northern Pacific Railroad. He started, with Mrs. Custer and all his belongings, and went through to Bismarck on the very last train that ran that year. The next day, down came the first snow, and thenceforth Custer and his little post were practically cut off from the rest of the world, until the spring opened the country once more.

THE BLACK HILLS

THE close of the Yellowstone expedition left Custer in quiet for the winter, and it was not until the year 1874 that he was called on for active service. This time, it was in connection with the Black Hills expedition, an enterprise that was to prove the cause of much trouble and ultimate war, while its first inception was founded in injustice and cupidity.

The Black Hills, from the time of the first overland travel down to the establishment of the Pacific Railroad, had been an unknown land to the whites. The region that passed by that name lay only some sixty or seventy miles to the north of Fort Laramie, which was the oldest fort on the plains, but it was out of the regular line of travel; and had never been visited by white men so as to be thoroughly explored. The Indians, when questioned about it, were very mysterious and refused to give definite information, and the few trappers who professed to have visited it reported it as a land of wonders.

Little dependence could be placed on their stories, however. Trappers are, like sailors, given to spinning long yarns, and it was seriously doubted whether any of them had ever been near the hills, as it was known that the Indians guarded the place with great jealousy.

In 1857 a small exploring party, led by Lieutenant Warren of the Engineers - the same who afterwards, as General Warren, had trouble with Sheridan at Five Forks - started from Fort Laramie to explore the Black Hills. Warren's party found the travelling very bad, but succeeded in reaching the western verge of the hills, near a lofty mountain which the Indians named *Inyan Kara*.

Here, the party was met by a number of Sioux chiefs, then at peace with the government, and warned that it could not proceed further into the hills, which the Indians regarded as sacred property. Warren, who states in his report that he believed the Indians to be justified in their demands, obeyed them and turned back. He went off to the south, and then turned to the east, keeping the hills in view all the time and skirting them till he came to the other side, where another lofty hill was found and marked Bear Butte. Warren's expedition and a previous one from another quarter, led by Captain, afterwards General Reynolds, determined the general figure of the unknown region, but left its interior as mysterious as ever.

Bear Butte. Mato Paha or "Bear Mountain" is the Lakota name given to the site. To the Cheyenne, it is "Noahvose." The mountain is sacred to many Native Americans, who make pilgrimages to leave prayer cloths and tobacco bundles tied to the branches of the trees along the mountain's flanks.

The Black Hills region was found to be a great oval, with the long axis running nearly north and south, about a hundred miles by fifty. It served as a watershed to divide the South Fork and the Belle Fourche or North Fork of the Cheyenne River. So far as it could be seen from the plains around, it seemed to be a nest of hills covered with dark pines, whence its name.

From the time of Warren to the running of the Pacific Railroad, no further efforts were made to penetrate the Black Hills. By the Treaty of 1868 (already referred to) with the Sioux Indians, that region, in common with others, was declared an inviolable part of Indian reservations, not to be trespassed on by white men, and such it remained for many years. At last, some Indians, coming to a trading post, brought in some gold dust and nuggets, which they admitted came from the Black Hills. The story, like that of the gold dust in Sutter's mill race in California, spread like wildfire, and the government was importuned to sanction trespasses on the Indians' land.

Parties of miners began to organize for the Black Hills, and the gold excitement waxed high in the west. Under these circumstances it was that the government ordered the Custer expedition of 1874. It was determined to send a strong column to explore the hills and ascertain whether there was any gold to be found there. Accordingly, on the first day of July, 1874, the village of Bismarck in Dakota Territory, in the vicinity of Fort Lincoln, was all alive with troops as the expedition started under command of Custer himself.

The column consisted of ten companies of the Seventh Cavalry, Company I, Twentieth Infantry, and Company G, Seventeenth Infantry, with sixty Indian scouts and four Gatling guns. General "Sandy" Forsyth was with the column, and the President's son, Lieutenant Fred Grant of the Second Cavalry, accompanied Custer on the staff. The whole force was over 1200 strong, and accompanied by a huge wagon train full of provisions.

It was to move southwest from Fort Lincoln, nearly two hundred miles, striking the Black Hills from the north. There was little or no danger to the powerful column, either real or apprehended. It started on a romantic and mysterious expedition as if for a picnic, and as such it found the whole journey. The progress of the expedition is best told by a few extracts from Custer's reports. He writes from Prospect Valley, a few miles to the north of the Belle Fourche, on the 15th July, 1874:

This expedition reached this point yesterday, having marched since leaving Fort Lincoln 227 miles. We are now 170 miles in a direct line from Lincoln within five miles of the Little Missouri River, and within about twelve miles from the Montana boundary, our bearing from Fort Lincoln being south 620 west. After the second day from Lincoln, we marched over a beautiful country; the grazing was excellent and abundant, wood sufficient for our wants, and water in great abundance every ten miles.

When we struck the tributaries of Grand River, we entered a less desirable portion of the country; nearly all the streams flowing into Grand River being more or less impregnated with alkali, rendering the crossings difficult. We found a plentiful supply of grass, wood and water however, even along this portion of our route. Upon leaving the headwaters of the Grand River, we ascended the plateau separating the watershed of the Little Missouri from that running into the Missouri, and found a country of surpassing beauty and richness of soil. The pasturage could not be finer, timber is abundant and water both good and plentiful.

Our march thus far has been made without molestation upon the part of the Indians. We discovered no signs indicating the recent presence of Indians until day before yesterday, when Captain McDougall, Seventh Cavalry, who was on the flank, discovered a small party of about twenty Indians watching our movements; the Indians scampered off as soon as discovered. Yesterday, the same or a similar sized party made its appearance along our line of march, and was seen by Captain Moylan, Seventh Cavalry, who was in command of the rear guard. Soon after, several signals of smoke were sent up, which our Indian guides interpret as carrying information to the main body of our presence and movements.

At the time that the expedition started, there were strong indications that the Sioux contemplated opening a general war of small parties, such as had greeted Custer in 1867 when he first went on the plains; but the presence of his column and the uncertainty of the Indians as to its destination served one good purpose; It kept the greater part of the Sioux forces busy watching Custer until he entered the Black Hills, and the knowledge of its presence deterred the Indians from overt war that year.

Once in the hills, the Sioux seem to have been reassured, for he was watched no further, and seems to have quite taken the denizens of the hills, such few as there were, by surprise. A second dispatch, dated August 2nd, gives the result of two weeks further progress. It seems to have been a regular picnic still. Having taken up his march from Prospect Valley, he pursues:

After leaving that point, this expedition moved in a south-westerly direction until it reached the valley of the Little Missouri River, up which we moved twenty-one miles. Finding this valley almost destitute of grazing along our line of march, I ordered the water kegs filled and a supply of wood placed on the wagons, and left the valley in search of a better camp ground.

During our passage up the valley of the Little Missouri, we had entered and were about to leave the Territory of Montana. Our course was near due south. After a further march of nine miles, we arrived before sundown at a point capable of furnishing us good grazing and water for our animals, having marched over thirty miles since breaking camp in the morning. From this point to the valley of the Belle Fourche on the 18th of July, we encamped where good grass, wood and water were abundant, at a point just west of the line separating Dakota from Wyoming.

The following day was spent in camp. On the 20th, we crossed the Belle Fourche and began, as it were, skirmishing with the Black Hills. We began by feeling our way carefully along the outlying ranges of the hills, seeking a weak point through which we might make our way to the interior. We continued from the time we ascended from the valley of the Belle Fourche to move through a very superior country covered with the best of grazing and abundance of timber, principally pine, poplar and several varieties of oak. As we advanced, the country skirting the Black Hills to the southwest became each day more beautiful.

On the evening of the 22nd, we halted and encamped east of and within four miles of the base of Inyan Kara. Desiring to ascend that peak the following day, it being the highest in the western range of the Black Hills, I did not move camp the following day, but taking a small party with me, proceeded to the highest point of this prominent landmark, whose height is given as 6,600 feet. The day was not favorable for obtaining distant views, but I decided on the following morning to move due east and attempt the passage of the hills.

Black Hills Expedition. The expedition set up a camp at the site of the future town of Custer; while Custer and the military units searched for a suitable location for a fort and geologists searched for gold. The expedition was photographed by William H. Illingworth, an English photographer.

We experienced considerable delay from fallen timber which lay in our pathway. With this exception, and a very little digging rendered necessary in descending into a valley, the pioneers prepared the way for the train and we reached camp by two o'clock, having marched eleven miles. We here found grass, water and wood of best quality and in great abundance. On the following day, we resumed our march up this valley, which I had explored several miles the preceding evening, and which led us by an easy ascent almost southeast.

After marching nearly twelve miles, we encamped at an early hour in the same valley. This valley in one respect presented the most wonderful as well as beautiful aspect. Its equal I have never seen, and such too, was the testimony of all who beheld it. In no public or private park have I ever seen such a profuse display of flowers. Every step of our march that day was amidst flowers of the most exquisite colors and perfume. So luxuriant in growth were they that men plucked them without dismounting from the saddle. Some belonged to new or unclassified species. It was a strange sight to glance back at the advancing column of cavalry, and behold the men with beautiful bouquets in their hands, while the head gear of their horses was decorated with wreaths of flowers fit to crown a queen of May. Deeming it a most fitting appellation, I named this Floral Valley.

General Forsyth, at one of our halting places, chosen at random, plucked seventeen beautiful flowers belonging to different species, and within a space of twenty feet square. The same evening, while seated at the mess table, one of the officers called attention to the carpet of flowers strewn under our feet, and it was suggested that it be determined how many different flowers could be plucked without leaving our seats at the dinner table. Seventeen beautiful varieties were thus gathered.

Professor Donaldson, the botanist of the expedition, estimated the number of flowers in bloom in Floral Valley at fifty, while an equal number of varieties had bloomed or were yet to bloom. The number of trees, shrubs and grasses was twenty-five, making the total flora of the valley embrace 125 species.

Through this beautiful valley meanders a stream of crystal water so cold as to render ice undesirable even at noonday. The temperature of two of the many springs found flowing into it was taken and ascertained to be 44 and 44 ½ degree respectively.

The next morning, although loath to leave so enchanting a locality, we continued to ascend this valley until gradually, almost imperceptibly, we discovered that we were on the crest of the western ridge of the Black Hills; and instead of being among barren, rocky peaks as might be supposed, we found ourselves wending our way through a little park, whose natural beauty may well bear comparison with the loveliest portions of Central Park. Favored as we had been in having Floral Valley for our roadway to the west of the Black Hills, we were scarcely less fortunate in the valley which seemed to me to meet us on the interior slope.

The rippling stream of clear cold water, the counterpart of that we had ascended the day before, flowed at our feet and pointed out the way before us, while along its banks grew beautiful flowers, surpassed but little in beauty and profusion by their sisters who had greeted us the day before. After advancing down this valley about fourteen miles, our course being almost southeast, we encamped in the midst of grazing, whose only fault, if any, was its great luxuriance.

Having preceded the main column as usual, with our escort of two companies of Cavalry E and C, and Lieutenant Wallace's detachment of scouts, I came upon an Indian campfire still burning, and which with other indications showed that a small party of Indians had encamped there the previous night, and had evidently left that morning in ignorance of our close proximity. Believing they would not move far, and that a collision might take place at any time unless a friendly understanding was arrived at, I sent my head scout, Bloody Knife and twenty of his braves to advance a few miles and reconnoitre the valley.

The party had been gone but a few minutes when two of Bloody Knife's young men came galloping back and informed me that they had discovered five Indian lodges a few miles down the valley, and that Bloody Knife, as directed, had concealed his party in a wooded ravine, where they awaited further orders. Taking E Company with me, which was afterward reinforced by the remainder of the scouts and Colonel Hart's company, I proceeded to the ravine where Bloody Knife and his party lay concealed, and from the crest beyond obtained a full view of the five Indian lodges, about which a considerable number of ponies were grazing. I was enabled to place my command still nearer to the lodges undiscovered.

I then dispatched Agard, the interpreter, with a flag of truce, accompanied by two of our Sioux scouts, to acquaint the occupants of the lodges that we were friendly disposed and desired to communicate with them. To prevent either treachery or flight on their part, I galloped the remaining portion of my advance and surrounded the lodges. This was accomplished almost before they were aware of our presence. I then entered the little village and shook hands with its occupants, assuring them through the interpreter that they had no cause to fear, as we were not there to molest them.

I invited them to visit our camp, and promised presents of flour, sugar and coffee to all who would accept. This invitation was accepted. At the same time, I entered into an agreement with the leading men that they should encamp with us a few days and give us such information concerning the country as we might desire, in return for which service I was to reward them with rations. With this understanding, I left them.

The entire party numbered twenty-seven. Later in the afternoon, four of the men, including the chief, "One Stab," visited our camp and desired the promised rations, saying their entire party would move up and join us the following morning as agreed upon. I ordered presents of sugar, coffee and bacon to be given them; and to relieve their pretended anxiety for the safety of their village during the night, I ordered a party of fifteen of my command to return with them and protect them during the night. But from their great disinclination to wait a few minutes until the party could saddle up, and from the fact that two of the four had already slipped away, I was of the opinion that they were not acting in good faith.

In this, I was confirmed when the two remaining ones set off at a gallop in the direction of the village. I sent a party of our scouts to overtake them and request their return; not complying with the request I sent a second party with orders to repeat the request, and if not complied with to take hold of the bridles of their ponies and lead them back, but to offer no violence.

When overtaken by our scouts, one of the two Indians seized the musket of one of the scouts and endeavored to wrest it from him. Failing in this, he released his hold after the scout became dismounted in the struggle, and set off as fast as his pony could carry him but not before the musket of the scout was discharged. From blood discovered afterward, it was evident that either the Indian or his pony was wounded.

One Stab, the chief, was brought back to camp. The scouts galloped down the valley to the site of the village, when it was discovered that the entire party had packed up their lodges and fled, and the visit of the four Indians to our camp was not only to obtain the rations promised them in return for future services but to cover the flight of their lodges. I have effected arrangements by which the chief One Stab remains with us as guide three days longer, when he will take his departure and rejoin his band.

THE BLACK HILLS

From this point, the march through the hills was continued without opposition or further incident. The small party of Indians seems to have found the white man's method of offering friendship not to its taste, for which we can hardly blame the poor savages. The major part of the dispatch is taken up with a description of the country, which Custer found delightful.

It was not until September that he returned, further explorations having confirmed his first glowing impression of the beauties and advantages of the country, and made his final report, which was mainly an enlargement of the passages already quoted. Then the fever of excitement commenced, as also a fever of controversy, Custer's statements being stigmatized by some officers who had not been with him as baseless and exaggerated.

Especially there arose between him and General Hazen a warm dispute as to the value of the Northwest, which was carried on with some acrimony in the western papers. There seemed to be a fate that was always bringing Hazen and Custer into collision, whenever they came near each other. It began at West Point, when Hazen's inopportune presence cost Custer a court-martial. After that, they did not meet for seven years more. When they did, it was to get into a dispute about Satanta and the Kiowa, in which each insisted that the other was wrong, and which was not decided for six years more.

Now, in a second seven years, they came into violent collision on another question of fact, Hazen insisting that the greater portion of the Northwest along the line of the Rocky Mountains was a barren waste, utterly unfit for human habitation and incapable of permanent amelioration, Custer insisting that it was the very garden of America, only needing cultivation to develop into a Paradise. As usual in such cases, the truth lies between the two. The majority of the seasons in Hazen's "Barren Belt" appear to be dry, but when a wet season comes, as it does every few years, the fertility of the land seems to be amazing.

A more serious dispute arose as to the mining value of the Black Hills, which the geologists who accompanied Custer reported in an unsatisfactory manner. To settle the dispute, a second expedition under Professor Jenney, with a military escort under Lieutenant Colonel

Dodge, Ninth Infantry, was sent from Fort Laramie the following year. This expedition, after trying in vain to enter from the southwest, finally effected an entrance near the point where Custer went in, and spent some time in the hills.

Arriving a month earlier than Custer, the expedition found Floral Valley in a miserable state, the snow hardly melted, the buds hardly started, not a flower to be seen, but a violent storm of sleet in progress. By the time the expedition was over however, the Black Hills revealed themselves as a perfect garden, and the gold region was carefully explored, turning out to be not as rich as expected, but enough so to attract miners.

Several camps of these enterprising individuals were found, one of twenty-two people having passed the whole of the previous winter there, untroubled by Indians. The two expeditions revealed one fact, that the Indians rarely visited the interior of the Black Hills, which they regard with superstitious feelings. Game was not very plentiful, but it was very tame. The soil was as fertile as Custer represented it, but the extreme shortness of the summer season made it improbable that the country could ever become valuable for arable purposes, though as a stock farm country it offered every inducement to settlers. Such was the final report on the subject of the Black Hills, and by that time it was full of miners who came there in defiance of treaties.

Dodge's expedition and the troops under General Crook made several trips into the Black Hills during the summer of 1875 to maintain the faith of the government, and half compelled, half persuaded, the miners to leave, escorting them to the military post where they were delivered over to the civil authority - the territorial government of Dakota - to be punished for disobedience to the law. In every case, the miners seem to have willingly complied with the injunctions of the military authority, though themselves far superior in numbers to the small force of troops, and well armed besides.

Just as soon however, as the civil authority took them in hand, the whole proceeding turned out to be a farce. The miners were invariably released, without even the formality of bail, and as invariably went straight back to the Black Hills. In August, there were over six hundred men there who had started a city which they called "Custer City," laid it out in lots, and staked out their claims as if the land belonged to them. They were removed and others took their places, so that today the Black Hills are fuller than last year.

Black Hills Expedition supply train. The expedition included 1200 men, 110 wagons and numerous horses and cattle of the U.S. 7th Cavalry, along with artillery and two months food supply.

In all this, the rights of the Indians to retain their property and the obligation of the United States to keep its word have been wantonly violated, as a natural and inevitable consequence of the expedition of 1874. Had it not been for the rumors of the presence of gold in that region, the expedition would never have started. As long as the Black Hills were regarded as worthless, the Indians were allowed to retain them. As soon as it was discovered that gold was there, all restraints of treaties were thrown aside and Custer was ordered on the Black Hills expedition.

FREDERICK WHITTAKER

That was the first wrong act, and from it flowed all the rest. Afterwards, when the miners began to crowd in, the government tried to keep its word by putting them out, but the first interlopers, the men who made the first trouble, were the troopers of Custer's column who started from Fort Lincoln July 1, 1874 in obedience to the orders of the United States Government.

It is a sad and humiliating confession to be made, but the irresistible logic of truth compels it, that all the subsequent trouble of the Sioux war really sprang from the deliberate violation by the United States Government of its own freely plighted faith when Custer was ordered to lead his column from Fort Lincoln to the Black Hills. The avowed purpose of the journey was to find out whether gold existed there, a matter which concerned no one but the owners. All the subsequent efforts of the government were mere palliations of its own first fault, and perfectly useless. Strange, but an illustration of poetic justice, that the very man, who in obeying his orders became the instrument of injustice towards the Indians, should fall a victim in the contest which ensued.

Strange but true! Yet we cannot blame Custer as we approach the tragic close of so bright and hopeful a career. He was a soldier, bound to obey orders, and a mere instrument in the hand of power. He was ordered to explore the Black Hills, and he went there. He was ordered on the trail of the Sioux, and he went. Nonetheless, the pleasant seeming and roseate hues of that long picnic party called the Black Hills Expedition close the brightness of his career. From thenceforth, clouds began to gather, and the time was swiftly coming when his sun should set in death.

The close of the Black Hills Expedition sent Custer back to Fort Lincoln, where he remained during the whole of the winter, his usual eastern leave being enjoyed before the snow closed in, and in New York as usual.

Happily ignorant of the coming storm, the last years of Custer's life were happy ones, so long as he was untrammeled by official difficulties or enmities. The reader will remember that he had always possessed a disposition remarkably cheerful, and a tendency to make the best of

THE BLACK HILLS

things; this tendency seemed to become more and more confirmed as he grew older, in spite of all surrounding difficulties, sobered as it was by the earnest Christianity which had marked his private character ever since the period of his marriage engagement.

To many men, Custer's lot and that of his little wife seemed hard at the best, but they seemed to enjoy it to the full. Where others would have been complaining of the isolation of a frontier post, of the lack of society, of the privation of luxuries, Custer and his wife seemed perfectly happy. A fire came and burned down their house, so that they lost everything save what was on the lower story, which the men helped to carry out, including, fortunately, most of the General's papers. Custer and the little wife made light of the misfortune, and passed the bitter cold winter of the Northwest in slight temporary quarters, laughing at their discomforts. Nothing seemed to ruffle either, and they even made the accident a source of subsequent congratulation when the new quarters were put up.

If their life was pleasant, if they were happy, it was their own sunny temperaments that made them so. They were happy where others would have been miserable. An air of luxury and good taste pervaded the General's room, where he wrote and received his visitors. What gave it that air? The furniture was of the plainest, and much of it old and worn.

But over every old chair or sofa, covering all deficiencies, were beautiful furs and skins that money could hardly have purchased, the spoils of Custer's rifle, and all around the walls hung grand heads of buffalo, of ahsata or big horn, graceful antelope heads. Prepared by Custer himself, the fierce faces of wolf, bear or panther, giving a wild and peculiar grace to the lofty room, lit up by the glow from yonder ample fireplace, with its blazing logs. There Custer was perfectly happy. Often, he would say to his wife, when all alone with her; "How happy we are, and how God has blessed us! It seems to me we have everything so good. Our horses are the best, our dogs are the best, our regiment is the best, our home is the best in all the lands God be thanked for his goodness."

In all this was no boasting. The man seemed to feel to the very core of his heart that his lot in life left him nothing to wish for; he was perfectly happy and devoutly grateful. And yet, had he known it, the end was coming, and the very happiest years of his life at Fort Lincoln were to bring him forth one more enemy, the man who finally slew him. Who he was, the next chapter will show.

Seventh U.S. Cavalry, Black Hills Expedition

RAIN-IN-THE-FACE

IT will be remembered that in a previous chapter we recorded the murder of two inoffensive old men, Dr. Honzinger and Mr. Baliran, on the Yellowstone expedition. They were killed; it was supposed, by "hostiles," but the discovery of agency property on the field of battle subsequently revealed that among these hostiles were some so called "good Indians" who drew rations at the agencies and received property from the government. No hope was felt that the names of the Indians who killed the two unarmed old men would be found out. During the winter of 1875 however, their identity came out in a very strange manner.

Charley Reynolds, one of Custer's scouts, who afterwards was killed at the Little Horn battle, happened to be at Standing Rock Agency, a place some seventy miles below Fort Lincoln where the Indians were drawing rations. As usual at their rejoicings, they were having "a dance." The Indians appear to signalize every great event by a dance, and this dance is always made the occasion of boasting about all the valiant deeds they ever have done.

In the course of this dance, Charley Reynolds heard one of the Indians boasting how he had killed two men at a time, white men too, and then the savage went on with his pantomime dance and described how he did it, how one of them was a fat old man, and how he fell from his horse, how he, the Indian, finished him off by smashing his skull with a big stone, and then shot the other white man and took all they had. Then, he proudly exhibited articles that Charley knew belonged to Dr. Honzinger, and the scout knew that he had found the murderer. That Indian was named "Rain-in-the-Face."

The rest of his story was written at the time, January, 1875, by Mrs. Custer, and she shall tell it to the reader in her own words:

RAIN-IN-THE-FACE

I have been so much interested in the capture and present imprisonment of an Indian murderer; I cannot but think that the story might entertain others. Since so many of the "ready writers" of the present day make up their histories of Indian life and incidents, thousands of miles from the actual scene, I do not wonder that the true impression of the real wild Indian is confined mostly to those who live either with or near them.

I must go back for a moment to the Yellowstone Expedition under General Stanley in the summer of 1873. Attached to the cavalry accompanying the expedition were two civilians who rode a great part of the time together. They were not obliged to submit to the regulation that compels soldiers to keep the ranks, and so they daily guided their horses where they chose.

One day, they stopped to water their steeds, and the main column was scarcely out of sight, hidden by a divide, before the two were surrounded and instantly murdered by Indians. A portion of the cavalry, under General Custer, had at the same time been surrounded and were fighting but unable of course to go to the relief of the two poor victims. Dr. Honzinger was an honest, kind-hearted old man who had followed the fortunes of the Seventh Cavalry for some years, as its veterinary surgeon. Mr. Baliran was the sutler for the cavalry. Both were favorites with the command and were much regretted. Both left families poorly provided for.

It is now over a year and a half since their death. A few weeks since, reliable information came from the Indian agency below here on the river that the murderer of Dr. Honzinger and Mr. Baliran was at the agency drawing his rations, blankets, ammunition, etc., from government, and boasting of his foul deed of the two summers preceding. This piece of news at once created the most intense excitement in our garrison, largely composed as it is of members of the Yellowstone expedition and friends of the slaughtered men.

It really seemed too aggravating to endure the knowledge of the fact that the government should feed, clothe and equip Indians, to go out and fight and kill soldiers and others who were working to protect the frontier. So after the excitement had somewhat lulled, a detachment was quickly prepared to march to the agency. No one knew the object of their trip. Most persons supposed it was to capture another Indian murderer, belonging to the agency, who had killed a citizen on Red River of the North last summer.

Four officers and a hundred men left this post, one cold windy day, under sealed orders. The orders directed them to capture and bring back an Uncpapa Indian called Rain-in-the-Face, the assassin of Dr. Honzinger and Mr. Baliran. Our next post is twenty miles distant, and had the orders not been sealed, General Custer knew that the Sioux scouts employed by government at Fort Rice, as soon as the troops arrived there and told their errand, would send out a runner to the agency below and inform the Indians of the intended arrest, giving time for the murderer to escape.

So the orders were not opened until Rice was left behind twenty miles. As the troops neared the agency, it was found necessary to observe the greatest care to prevent the Indians from finding out the object of the visit. It was the day for our red brethren to draw beef from their generous Uncle Sam. Hundreds of them were there at the agency, of course armed to the teeth, as they always are.

Indian scouts at Fort Rice, Dakota Territory

In the face of hundreds of fully armed Indians, though on the reservation, still most of them full of hate toward the white man, it seemed a very venturesome deed to appear in their midst and claim one of their number. The reservation Indians are constantly told that they will be fed, clothed and armed if they will consent never to make war on the white man, but if they do they must submit to the penalties of the law.

But in the instance of this murderer, he dared everything to prove his courage. He had been frequently to the agency, boasting of his base deed. One party of troops had been down to capture him earlier in the winter, but he had hidden and escaped them. So Captain Yates, who had charge of the troops, sent one of the lieutenants, with forty men, to the Indian camp ten miles below, to make inquiries for three Indians who had murdered citizens on Red River last summer.

This ruse succeeded in deceiving the Indians as to the real object of their presence among them. As the trader's store is the great place of resort for the Indians, it was presumed that in the course of the day Rain-in-the-Face would be there. Colonel Custer (brother of the general) was directed to take five picked men and go to the store and capture the murderer, should the latter put in an appearance. He remained in the store for several hours.

The day was cold and the Indians kept their blankets drawn about their heads, thus rendering it almost impossible to distinguish one from the other. At last, one of them loosened his blanket and Colonel Custer identified him as Rain-in-the-Face. Coming suddenly behind him, he threw his arms around him and seized the Winchester rifle that the Indian attempted in an instant to cock. The murderer was taken entirely by surprise.

Stolid as their faces usually are, his, in this moment of amaze, was a study. No fear to be seen, but other emotions showed themselves with lightning rapidity on his countenance. Surprise, hate, revenge, then the final determination that he would show his brother warriors he was not afraid to die. He had been considered brave beyond precedent, to even enter the agency store and encounter this risk of arrest.

As soon as Rain-in-the-Face was actually captured and his hands tied, an old Indian orator of the tribe began exhorting the Indians, who had assembled in the store to the number of thirty or more to recapture their comrade. He spoke in the key assumed by the Indian warriors, high and loud, but with no rising or falling inflections. The most intense excitement prevailed among the braves.

Thomas Ward Custer was a two time recipient of the Medal of Honor for bravery during the Civil War. He is buried at Fort Leavenworth, Kansas.

The instant Rain-in-the-Face was arrested, Captain Yates, who had remained outside a close observer of affairs, gave the signal and rallied his entire force in the immediate vicinity of the trader's store, prepared to repel any attempt to rescue the prisoner. These precautions were adopted none too quickly, for no sooner had news of the capture of Rain-in-the-Face been conveyed to the numerous groups of Indians to be seen in the vicinity of the agency, than a mass of armed warriors, estimated at over five hundred in number, rushed to the trader's store, and in loud, threatening and excited tones, demanded the instant release of their comrade.

The occasion was one requiring the exercise of the utmost prudence as well as the most determined courage upon the part of the little group of officers and men who stood with weapons in their hands about the prisoner. Determined to resist to the very death any attempt

RAIN-IN-THE-FACE

at a rescue, Captain Yates, presenting a bold front to the Indians, enraged as they were, prevented the immediate recapture of his prisoner. By means of an interpreter, he then briefly explained to the Indians the cause of the arrest, and announced the determination of himself and men to maintain their hold over their captive. He at the same time urged the chiefs to withdraw with their followers, and thus avoid a collision that would only result in loss of life on both sides without accomplishing any purpose.

Standing Rock Agency. Today, it is the sixth largest reservation in land area in the United States. It comprises all of Sioux County, North Dakota, and all of Corson County, South Dakota, plus slivers of northern Dewey and Ziebach counties in South Dakota, along their northern county lines at Highway 20.

Seeing they could not carry out their end by intimidation or the display of greatly superior numbers, the Indians then resorted to parley and offers of compromise. They offered through an interpreter to sacrifice two Indians of the tribe if Rain-in-the-Face could be released. He is a great warrior among them. He has five brothers at the agency, one of whom, Iron Horn, is a chief of influential standing in the tribe. It was not expected that Indians of any notoriety or rank would be offered as a sacrifice; only some who had not distinguished themselves in any way and the selections were to be made by the great moguls of the tribe.

These offers were of course refused, and Rain-in-the-Face was taken to the camp of the Cavalry. In an incredibly short time, not an

Indian was to be seen at the agency. All went to their camp, ten miles below. Later in the day, a party of fifty mounted Indians dashed by the agency on the road to be taken by our troops on the return. Of course, our officers expected to be attacked by this party the next morning, but they were unmolested and reached here after a march of three days, through cold and snow and winds such as only Dakota can furnish.

It was explained to us afterward that the party of fifty seen passing the agency were on their way to the camp of the chief "Two Bears" to try and induce him to urge his young braves to combine with them in the release of Rain-in-the-Face. But Two Bears is an old chief, and he opposed the attack. He has been a friend of the whites for a long time, but his age would induce one to think the motive of his friendship was policy.

After the officers had reported, General Custer sent for Rain-in-the-Face to interview him. He is a young man with an impenetrable countenance. This is as we saw him, but in a subsequent interview, when General Custer locked himself alone in a room with him, he showed some signs of agitation. After a time, when they had talked by signs as far as it was possible, the interpreter was admitted, and for hours General Custer attempted by every clever question he could invent, to induce Rain-in-the-Face to confess his crime. At last he succeeded in getting his account of the murder, and the next day in the presence of a number of the officers, Rain-in-the-Face made a full confession of his crime.

He called Dr. Honzinger "the old man," and says he shot him, but he rode some distance before falling from his horse. Mr. Baliran he described as being among some trees, and signaling to them by holding up his hand as an overture of peace. He says that Baliran gave them his hat when they reached him, but they shot him at once, first with a gun, then with arrows. One of the arrows entered his back and he tried to pull it through, but failed.

They did not scalp their victims. Dr. Honzinger was bald, and Mr. Baliran had his hair closely cut. Neither of these gentlemen were armed when attacked by the Indians. This short but cruel story made our blood boil when we afterwards learned what Rain-in-the-Face had confessed.

Rain-in-the-Face. At the Battle of Little Bighorn on June 25, 1876, Rain-in-the-Face is alleged to have cut the heart out of Thomas Custer in an act of revenge.

The brother of the prisoner, Iron Horn, and one other Indian, had followed the cavalry up from the agency and asked to see the captive before they went home. General Custer sent for Rain-in-the-Face, and he met his brother and had council with him. They expected it was a farewell interview, as the Indians all believed Rain-in-the-Face would be hung.

During the council, which was very solemn, Iron Horn took off his beautiful beaded blanket and put it on his brother, taking his common one in place of it. He also exchanged pipes with him, giving his highly ornamented one to Rain-in-the-Face, to present to General Custer. He charged his brother most solemnly not to try to escape, that should he get back to the reservation he would be recaptured, and he believed he would be kindly treated while a captive. He hoped the Great Father would not hang him, and perhaps General Custer would intercede in his favor. The Great Father rarely hung Indians. Asking him not to lose his spirits, they took a farewell smoke and he departed.

FREDERICK WHITTAKER

In about ten days he returned, bringing a party of Indians with him. Another interview with General Custer was obtained. After all the guests were seated, Rain-in-the- Face came over from the guard house and entered, having been sent for at the request of the Indians. He came into the room, trying not to show his pleasure at seeing his friends, nor his grief at his imprisonment and his evidently expected death; but these emotions passed over his face in quick succession, and then came the look of settled indifference that the Indian constantly tries to wear.

His brother rose at once and went to Rain-in-the-Face, and to the intense amazement of the few privileged spectators General Custer had allowed to enter, he kissed him. An Indian kiss, to be sure; the lips were laid quietly on his cheek, with no sound or motion; but it is a solemn caress, and one never seen before, with one single exception, by the oldest Indian fighter here.

Several of the ranking Indians stepped solemnly to the prisoner and gave him the same dignified salute. Then one of the old men of the tribe walked in front of him, and lifting his hand above his head and raising his eyes, said a few words in prayer to the Great Spirit for this unfortunate brother. Rain-in-the-Face hung his head low on his breast to hide the emotion that he thought would ill become a warrior as brave as he really is.

After a long speech by Iron Horn, delivered in the usual high monotonous key, the next in rank rose, and so on, until half a dozen had spoken. Iron Horn thanked General Custer for his care of Rain-in-the-Face, asked permission to visit him again, begged him to write again to the Great Father and intercede for the life of their brother, and then, taking off the buckskin shirt he wore, he presented the highly ornamented garment to the General.

Then came such a singular request. It was the story of Damon and Pythias among uncivilized warriors. Two shy young braves, sitting near the end of the circle among the untitled, asked through Iron Horn the privilege of sharing the captivity of Rain-in-the-Face. Not many murderers or felons in the States find friends who in the hour of arrest or capture ask to share the prison with them. Consent was given to this request, if the friends would be willing to be locked in the prison until the hour came for them to go home.

They rested in the guard house with their friend for a day and night, and then returned to the agency. The imprisonment of Rain-in-the-Face continued for several months, until a circumstance occurred that gave him his liberty.

So far, Mrs. Custer's narrative; written at the time. The circumstance she speaks of introduces another story which will give an excellent idea of another phase of Custer's character, besides completing the record. We are indebted for this story to the kindness of Mrs. Yates, widow of the brave captain whose party took the Indian. She entitles it the "Story of the Grain Thieves:"

It seems strange that any one at all acquainted with the working and planning of Custer's mind, could accuse him of rashness; there is the most wonderful denial of this imputation in every engagement which he entered during the war, in the planning of the Washita campaign, and last but not least, to many minds, the following up and final arrest of the grain thieves at Fort Abraham Lincoln, a matter which some might deem of unimportance, but which should be considered of value in showing the patient energy and tenacity of purpose as exemplified in his character. It is of importance also, because it established him in the eyes of the lawless frontiersmen of Bismarck and its vicinity, as one whom it would be as well to respect, one who was quick to pursue and sure to overtake.

During the spring of 1875, the grain from the several forage buildings at Fort Lincoln had been steadily disappearing. The river being still frozen, intercourse between the post and the town of Bismarck was fully established, and it became a difficult matter to trace the stolen grain to any particular parties, as well as a problem what to do with the parties in the event of finding it. Law and order had not resolved itself from the chaos of the newly put together town.

The General was also hampered by being forbidden by order to make arrests outside of the military reservation, all exterior justice being meted out by the good in mayor of Bismarck; who, slow to anger and plenteous in mercy, the General feared might not prove as powerful a coadjutor as he could desire. With all these discouraging facts to dampen his ardor, he quietly went to work, early and late, gathering in his proofs in which he was greatly assisted by Lieutenant Carland of the Sixth Infantry, formerly a lawyer. Ever watchful of the slightest opportunity, nothing escaped him. Believing with Pope that the proper study of mankind is man, he studied man as he found him in Bismarck.

Once he arose in the night, and himself inspected the grain on the landing to see that it was all right, questioning and examining the guard, and only retiring when fully satisfied that no robbery would be attempted that night. Months before the denouement, he knew where each of the dramatis personae was, could have arrested any one of them, or even a half a dozen, if he had been rash; but being patient, he waited until he possessed the required proofs to arrest everyone who had been in the least connected with the disappearance of the grain, knowing well that in arresting only a part of the number, he gave the rest warning to escape.

So when one bright day, just before the breaking up of the river in the spring, he issued orders for the regiment to be in readiness to start at the call of the trumpet for Bismarck, not an officer of his command but was as astonished, and knew as little of what was expected of them, as did the citizens of Bismarck, when they saw the cavalry, fully armed and equipped, come riding into their little town.

The Seventh Cavalry rode to the different places indicated by the General, and found the grain at every place pointed out by him, to the surprise and indignation of the honest citizens of Bismarck, who being in ignorance of the localities the thieves had chosen to secrete it, were naturally indignant at the slur cast upon their reputations. For a while, loud talking ensued and a riot of no mean pretensions was threatened.

Finally, upon the General insisting, doors were thrown open to him, and the stolen grain in every instance was exposed to view, the soldiers turning the bags over and showing the government brand. In the Mayor's own warehouse (he being also a prominent merchant at the time), a number were discovered. You can imagine the good mayor's surprise at this last selection of a repository for these stolen goods.

A number of arrests were made, the mayor now concurring heartily with the military, and for temporary safe keeping the corn thieves were escorted by the cavalry back to Fort Abraham Lincoln and lodged in the guard house.

Their trial, which took place at Fargo, Minnesota, occupied many months and employed numbers of witnesses, the leading actors in the scene shortly afterwards finding their way into the penitentiary. There is one amusing occurrence connected with the above arrest, and following upon the order received by General Custer to arrest all those implicated in the robbery that could be found upon the military reservation of Fort Lincoln.

Off this reservation, as before mentioned, such arrests devolved upon the mayor. The General one day became aware that two of the principal members of the gang were at that time in a shanty almost half a mile from the post. Not knowing the men, nor having any description of their appearance, his order to the officer of the day was merely, "go to shanty and arrest immediately two citizens who you will find there - put them in the guard house." The officer of the day started off and the General proceeded to make a call upon a certain family in the garrison. Seating himself near the window where he could command a view of the road in front of the officer's quarters, laughing and conversing meanwhile, his eye scarcely left the window.

Presently, a wagon drove by containing two inoffensive looking personages in citizen's attire; there was nothing at all suspicious in their appearance, nor was it unusual for citizens to have business in, and drive through the post. Only, one of the men looked back anxiously over his shoulder. This act aroused the General's interest, but he allowed them to drive around - which they did slowly - until they were almost in front of the guard house, when he rose abruptly, excused himself to the lady, and stepping upon the porch, placed both hands to his mouth shouting "Guard, arrest those men!"

The wondering guard obeyed, the men were assisted to alight, having driven up to their destination themselves. So it became evident what had occasioned the anxious looks over their shoulders. In a lumbering wagon drawn by four mules stood the officer of the day, jabbing the mules with his sabre and the while ejaculating in profound English.

He had obeyed orders, had searched the shanty, but finding no one there, was about to return home without making the arrest, when he observed the men in the wagon. At first thinking they were honest hay cutters, he allowed them to make considerable headway from him. On second thought, he concluded to overtake them, but finding that at this rate they would soon be off the reservation, and no arrest could then be made, he seized the nearest vehicle, which was a heavy water wagon, ordering the soldiers to jump out. Clutching the reins with one hand and punching the wheelers with his sabre in the other, he came upon the scene just as the general had made the arrest in person.

The arrests were made after Rain-in-the-Face had been several months in the guard house, and amongst others there were two particularly hard cases who had been caught driving wagons loaded with hay off the ground.

"The guard house," says Mrs. Custer, concluding her story, "was only a poorly built, wooden building, quite insecure, and these citizens had in one night cut a hole in the side of the rear wall, large enough to creep through. Two crept safely out, and Rain-in-the-Face, seeing the opening after they had gone, quickly made his escape. We found afterwards that he went at once to the hostile camp, and last spring he sent word by agency Indians that he had joined Sitting Bull and was awaiting his revenge for his imprisonment."

That he took it, all the world now knows, and they can see in his portrait taken from an excellent photograph, what sort of a man this desperado is. Truly, he looks soft enough and as innocent as a lamb, but for all that he is well known as one of the bravest men of his nation. The tribe were particularly proud of him for one thing, his extraordinary fortitude against physical pain. He was said to have hung for four hours in the "Sun Dance." *

---

* The Sun Dance, says Mrs. Yates, to whom we are already indebted, is a test of nerve and endurance of the Indian; in other words, it is the Military Academy from which he graduates a well-informed soldier. Here he is taught to be wily, hardy, stoical and

RAIN-IN-THE-FACE

The escape of Rain-in-the-Face to the hostiles was made in the spring of 1875, and during that summer these hostiles clustered around the headwaters of the Yellowstone, began to send their war parties out near the settlements, while the agency Indians were perpetually slipping off to join them. Dodge's Black Hills Expedition further contributed to unsettle the Indians, and when the miners moved in numbers into that region, it became evident that a general war with the Northern Sioux

---

cruel. It is held in the middle of summer, when the sun's rays are nearly vertical, and its heat therefore, the most intense. One of its features is the exposure, upon platforms erected for the purpose, of the nude forms of the Indian braves, to the direct and burning rays of the sun. Lying on their backs, with eyes distended, their gaze is fixed upon the solar king, until tears stream from their tortured and maltreated organs. Numerous tests are too horrible to mention, and would require as much nerve to witness and describe, as to participate in them. Visitors frequently faint away in the presence of such sickening details.

For these young Indian cadets to fail in the slightest detail is certain disgrace; to exceed what is demanded by competent judges, calls forth applause, admiration, and gifts. Many a chief goes back to the Sun Dance for the beginning of his record. His bravery and endurance there is never forgotten, and serves him in good stead ever after.

Not long since, an excellent engraving of a Sun Dance appeared in Harper's Weekly. In this picture, Indians could be seen undergoing the suspension test. This is done by cutting a gash under some of the sinews of the back, immediately under the shoulder blades, passing thongs of buffalo hide through the gashes, and by these thongs suspending the Indian to the roof of a large tepee. Here he hangs until his own weight or motion causes the thongs to cut through the sinews, when he falls to the ground, and has successfully passed the trial.

The summer before General Custer's expedition to the Black Hills, a grand Sun Dance was held at Standing Rock, Dakota. The tests were unusually severe; the judges exacting. A Sioux, nick-named "Pete," could not endure the suspension test, but fainted away, and upon coming to, begged to be taken down. He was released, but henceforth was irretrievably disgraced, compelled to dress as a squaw and forever debarred the privileges of a brave. The squaws held him in derision, and poor Pete's lot was a gloomy one indeed. Pete accompanied the General on the Black Hills expedition; he bore his disgrace with equanimity, and had always an amiable smile for everybody. The Indian scouts obliged Pete to cook and do all their other menial labor.

At this same dance, Rain-in-the-Face so distinguished himself as to win the popularity of several tribes. In the suspension test he was gashed so deep that he could not by his own weight cut through the sinews. He hung in mid air for several hours, blood streaming from his wounds, and going through the motion of dancing the while. He became faint from loss of blood, and the judges decided to cut him down. Rain-in-the-Face objected however to this, and so was allowed to swing in this manner for four hours - when the flesh at last gave way and let him down.

was impending. The short summer was the only salvation of the settlers, and when 1876 came, it was clear that the fight could no longer be averted.

Remains of the original Fort Abraham Lincoln Guard House.

Under these circumstances, the government resolved for the first time to make war on the hostiles.

SITTING BULL

WHILE the Treaty of 1868 had pacified most of the Sioux, and especially the great chiefs Red Cloud and Spotted Tail, with their bands, there was a small portion of the Sioux Nation which remained implacable in its enmity to the whites and kept to its original habits of life, out in the wilderness. This portion was generally known by the title of "the hostiles," and the most powerful chief of the different bands was and is known by the title of Sitting Bull. To explain to the general reader the meaning of the words "nation," "tribe" and "band," a short sketch of Indian polity is here necessary.

The Indian tribes of the plains bear a strong likeness in their modes of government to the Arabs and Tartars. Abstractly, it may be termed patriarchal, but actually it is nearly a pure republic. Every member of a band does just about what he pleases, and obeys his chief when it pleases him, subject always to the verdict of popular opinion and the physical ability of the chief to thrash him.

While the dignity of chieftainship appears to be hereditary, it is subject to so many checks, and depends so much on personal ability to persuade one's followers to pursue a certain line of conduct, that it may be called a mere delusion in the hands of any but a great warrior; and prowess in war is the only sure road to real power among Indians.

While the Indians as a mass are thus independent of all but persuasive influences, the patriarchal element so far prevails that the family is the basis of the organization for war and peace. The members of a family, in all its ramifications of brothers and cousins, uncles and nephews, generally travel together, hunt together and fight together, agglomerating in time, with their connections by marriage, into a band varying from two to twenty or thirty lodges.

SITTING BULL

These bands have a remoter connection by blood ties with other bands, and constitute together a tribe, which may number from two to thirty or forty bands. These tribes again have a still more remote blood connection with other tribes, constituting a nation, such as the Sioux Nation, which comprises the Yankton, Brule, Teton, Uncpapa and several other tribes, each tribe in its turn embracing several bands.

Sitting Bull. After the Battle of the Little Bighorn, Sitting Bull led his band across the border into Canada. He remained in exile for four years near Wood Mountain. Hunger and desperation eventually forced him to return to the United States and surrender on July 19, 1881.

The hostiles, so called, are formed of bands differently composed. The patriarchal ties noticeable in other bands are replaced here by a mere alliance of convenience. Every Indian who feels discontented at the agencies joins the "hostiles" and attaches himself to the band of Sitting Bull or Crazy Horse, the only two great chiefs who were, at the time we write of, avowedly hostile. Thus their bands, originally numbering perhaps twenty lodges apiece, with a fighting force of a hundred warriors to each band, were swelled by the arrival of discontented families to many more.

The village of Crazy Horse, at the close of the winter of 1875, was found to contain one hundred and five lodges, which at the ordinary rate of five or six warriors to a lodge or tepee furnished a force of about 560 warriors. Sitting Bull's band probably then numbered at least 150 lodges, he being a more famous chief than Crazy Horse.

During the summer time, the forces of both received constant additions from the agency Indians, who came out for a summer's hunt, provided with plenty of breech loading and magazine guns and ammunition. An inspection of the map at the end of this chapter will show the singular advantages which the agencies offered for this. The position of the hostiles was very well selected, near the head of the Yellowstone, in a country surrounded by badlands which prevented the whites from near approach, except on great and protracted expeditions, like that led by Stanley.

To form an idea of the badlands, the eastern reader can use a familiar illustration. You have all no doubt seen a clay field after a long and hot drought in summer, how it is seamed over with innumerable cracks, perfectly perpendicular, leaving miniature chasms between. Such, magnified by a hundred, are the badlands of the northwest. They are patches of clay soil, baked by the long and intense droughts of that climate into chasms four or five feet wide and perhaps twenty feet deep, absolutely impassable for wagons where they occur, quagmires in the early spring freshets, a labyrinth of ravines in the summer. These badlands surrounded the country of the hostiles in 1873, and surround them now.

So much for the natural advantages of Sitting Bull's position, considered in a defensive point of view, but a greater advantage accrues to him from the strategic lines of the country and the existence of the Indian agencies. A second look at the map will reveal how the agencies affect the strategic position.

Observe that the Missouri River, beginning in the northwest corner of the map, describes nearly a perfect circle around the country of the hostiles, and remember that all the Indian agencies are on this river, and you will begin to realize what is meant by the "strategic advantages" of

SITTING BULL

Sitting Bull. Beginning at the mouth of the Cheyenne River, there are Cheyenne Agency, Brule Agency, Grand River Agency, Standing Rock Agency, Fort Berthold and Fort Peck and several other places, all full of friendly Indians, supported by Government and ready to join the hostiles in the summer, bringing arms and ammunition with them.

To give an idea of the supplies of the latter, let us take what went through in the spring of 1876 alone, for distribution to Indians. Our evidence is contained in the private letter of an officer on the spot. This officer has investigated the matter, and finds that the following shipments were made by river steamer to these agencies and to Forts Benton, McLoud and Claggett (also agencies), on the 21st May, 20th June, 6th and 30th July, 1876; while the war was actually raging. No less than 56 cases of arms, or 1120 Winchester and Remington rifles and 413,000 rounds of patent ammunition went there on these steamers, besides large quantities of loose powder, lead and primers.

These shipments were all for issue to Indians through the Indian agents, or for sale through Indian traders. The country to which they were sent contains only Indians, soldiers and Indian traders or agents. These shipments moreover were as nothing to those of previous years, and especially those of the summer of 1875, when more than a million rounds of ammunition and several thousand "stand of arms" were sent through.

Now perhaps Sitting Bull's chief advantage can be seen, as first shown in the Yellowstone Expedition of 1873. This expedition started from Fort Rice in the summer of 1873 and moved off at a leisurely pace, due west. Indian runners at the same time started off, up and down the Missouri, to carry the news. Many of them travelled luxuriously by the steamers the government was kind enough to supply, to carry stores to the agencies for the use of the Indians.

By the time Stanley had reached the Little Missouri, (see map) every agency all along the line of the river was informed of his movements, and parties of warriors on their war ponies, with no burdens save arms, ammunition and food, were starting from the circumference of the quarter circle to find Sitting Bull and have a little fun.

FREDERICK WHITTAKER

All those from the upper agencies had a shorter distance to travel than Stanley, and knew the country better. No wonder they arrived before him. The trail which Stanley struck on the Yellowstone was in all probability that of the real acknowledged hostiles, the village of Sitting Bull, with a force of some 800 braves, but the reinforcements which afterwards swelled his numbers to 1500 in the fight near Pompey's Pillar must have come from the northern agencies, and Stanley says so in his report, specifying Fort Peck as "the centre of all the villainy of the Indian Department."

Thus, in carrying on war with the United States War Department, Sitting Bull had great and peculiar advantages from the nature of his position, and these advantages it was which had made him constantly triumphant. It may have seemed strange to many that Custer should have been able, alone, to have beaten the Indians of the Southern Plains, while the Sioux of the North had overcome all successive combinations against them, compelling the government to pacify them by giving them up all they asked in the Treaty of 1868.

The War Department had made a gallant struggle to hold this country, but Sitting Bull and the hostiles had beaten them. Look again on the map at the sites of old Fort Reno and old Fort Phil Kearny. The last is right at the edge of Sitting Bull's stronghold. It was the scene of the fearful massacre of 1868, when almost the whole garrison was annihilated.

It was difficult to keep this fort supplied. Everything had to come by wagon train from Fort Fetterman on the south, while Sitting Bull drew all his supplies of ammunition from Fort Peck and a dozen other places, and lived on the buffalo by which he was surrounded. The white men could not starve him, but he could harass them constantly, and he did so. Finally, the Department was compelled to abandon Fort Reno and Kearny, and gave up the country to Sitting Bull by the Treaty of 1868.

Five years later, in 1873, it was judged expedient to break that treaty and try a new line of operations, this time up the valley of the Yellowstone. This line possessed one and only one advantage; while the Yellowstone was navigable, supplies and even an expedition could be sent up by steamer, comparatively safe from the Indians. A fleet of light draught steamers with bullet-proof guards and a few Gatlings, may yet be found the true solution of the Sitting Bull difficulty; as such boats can ascend the Big Horn River to within sight of the Indian stronghold.

By land, as Stanley went, the Yellowstone route was as bad as the rest, except for provisions. It was very long, and did not stop the supplies of Sitting Bull. The only reason Stanley escaped serious disaster was that he kept near the river and was able to use his artillery, while Sitting Bull was not as yet joined by any very formidable force of Agency Indians.

In the War of 1876, all this was to be changed, and Sitting Bull was to find himself in a perfect position, occupying interior lines, able to strike at his enemies wherever he pleased and beat them in detail, and all the while able to draw his supplies and reinforcements from a number of concentrating lines, none of which his enemies were able to cut. Indians kept streaming in to his help from all the quarter circle of agencies, informing him of every step taken by his enemies, and bringing ammunition, guns, ponies and men by hundreds.

Of Sitting Bull personally, not very much is known. It is many years since he attended a council, and he has been so long secluded from the whites that no portrait of him is existent. From the description of Agency Indians and others, he is said to be a heavily built Indian, with a large massive head, and (strange to say) brown hair, unlike most Indians. He is heavily marked with the small pox.
The events of his life have been recorded by himself, and fell into the hands of the whites by an accident soon after the Phil Kearny massacre.

A scout brought into one of the forts an old roster book, once belonging to the Thirteenth U.S. Infantry, which Sitting Bull had captured, and in this was found a series of over a hundred little Indian pictures describing the various exploits of the artist. In the first, he is shown as a young warrior, naked and unadorned, taking his first scalp by charging a Crow Indian mounted. From the mouth of the young warrior goes a line which joins him to his "totem" or symbol, a buffalo bull sitting upon its haunches, which identified the book as the diary of Sitting Bull. This totem is found in all the pictures.

FREDERICK WHITTAKER

Almost every picture represents the killing of a man or woman or both, some Indians, some whites. A few represent Sitting Bull carrying off herds of horses. These pictures are in regular Indian style, such as a clever child without teaching might draw. There is no attempt at art, but there is no mistake as to what is meant. There are the men, the horses, the women, the Indian war bonnets, the white man's stovepipe hat, in the true spirit of caricature, the salient features seized and fixed. Facsimiles of many of these pictures were published in the New York Herald, and subsequently in Harper's Weekly, in the latter case accompanied by an article from Colonel Strother, better known as "*Port Crayon.*" We have hardly judged them worth insertion here, however.

It was stated at one time that Sitting Bull, while hating the white Americans and disdaining to speak their language, was yet very fond of the French Canadians, that he talked French, and that he had been converted to Christianity by a French Jesuit named Father DeSmet. How true this may be is uncertain, but probably there is some foundation for it. The French Jesuits have always been noted for their wonderful success in winning the affections of the Indians, as well as for the transitory nature of their conversions, and it is very possible that Father DeSmet may have not only baptized Sitting Bull at some time, but induced him and his braves to attend mass, as performed by himself in the wilderness. The benefits of the conversion seem however to have been only skin deep, as far as preventing cruelty in war is concerned.

One thing about Sitting Bull is certain; he is an Indian of unusual powers of mind, and a warrior whose talent amounts to genius, while his stubborn heroism in defense of the last of his race is undeniable. Cruel he may be; that is from the instincts of his race; a general of the first natural order he must be, to have set the United States at defiance as he has for the last ten years. That he has been able to do this so long is owing to his skilful use of two advantages, a central position surrounded by badlands, and the quarter circle of agencies from which he draws supplies and allies every campaign.

In the face of these advantages and of Sitting Bull's talents as a warrior, the government gave up the fight in 1868. In 1876, it was determined to try one more campaign against Sitting Bull. We shall see how it succeeded.

In the meantime, the people of America will not fail to remark that Sitting Bull's truest and most persistent allies are the Indian Department and the Indian traders who supply him with Winchester rifles and patent ammunition so that his men are better armed than the troops of the War Department.

Better soldiers individually they always were, for every man is a perfect rider and good shot, while the regular cavalry is mainly composed of green recruits, so unreliable that even a chief like Custer did not dare to fight them mounted, but had to turn his men into mounted infantry. But the inferior troops have discipline, and had they as good or superior weapons, could beat the Indians as they used to before 1861. There is still an easy way to stop all these slaughters, which is to stop the supplies of ammunition from going to the Indians.

To accomplish this, only one course can succeed. Congress in both branches must be compelled by public opinion to abolish the Indian Department forever. Everyone admits the necessity of the step, but the corruption fund of this department is so great that public opinion has not yet succeeded in killing the abuse. Politicians of both parties are interested in the money, and nothing else holds the Indian Department together.

The cost of the Indians to the government has risen in ten years from less than a million to twenty millions annually, and Indian agents and traders grow rich on the stealings of supplies used by Indians to kill soldiers, while the residue of the stealings goes into election funds. The events of the Indian War of 1876 have however, opened the eyes of the people to much of this abuse. God grant that it may end in the final destruction of the "Indian Ring."

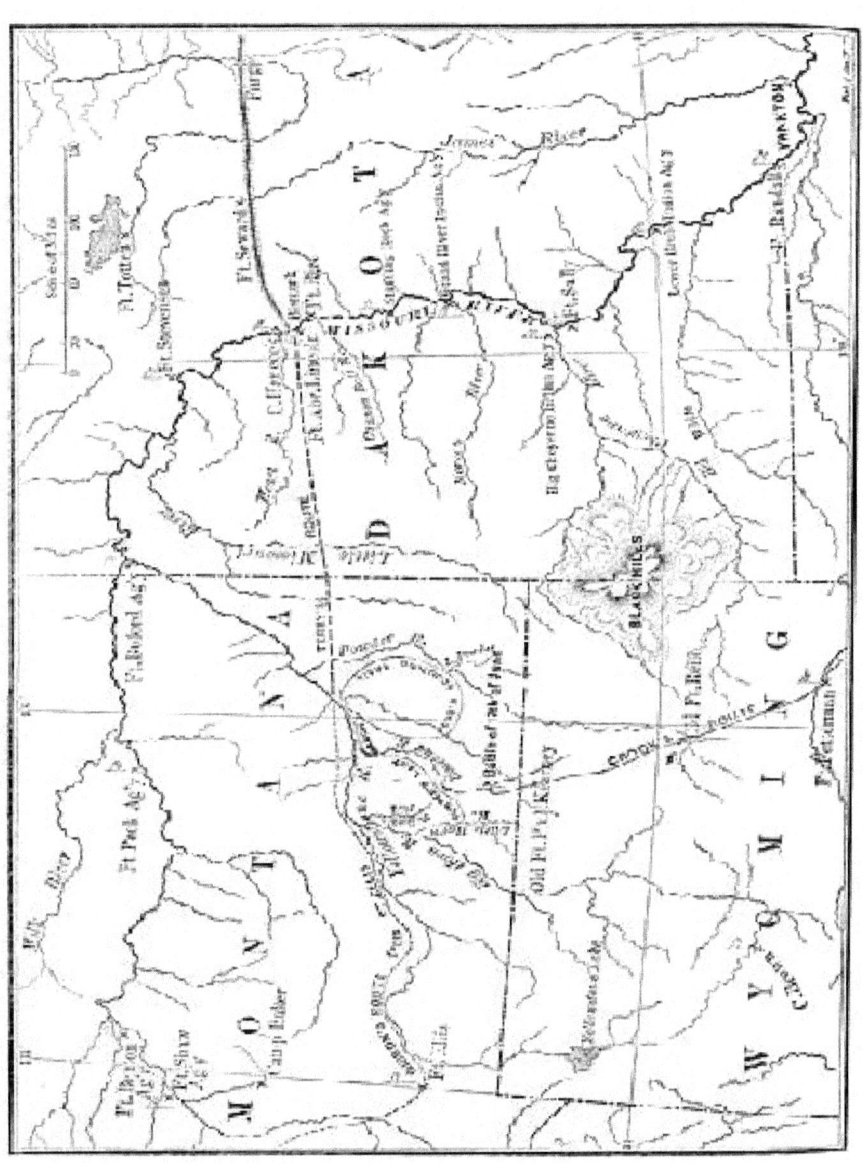

CRAZY HORSE

WAR having been once determined on against the Sioux, the only questions were who should begin it and where? It was finally resolved that three expeditions should start, one from the north, one from the south, and one from the east; and that the three should all strike for the country near the headwaters of the Yellowstone where Forts Reno and Phil Kearny had formerly been established.

The three columns could not be, or at all events were not, dispatched simultaneously. They were to start from two distinct departments, commanded by Generals Terry and Crook, whose headquarters were several hundred miles apart and in the midst of different climates. Terry, whose northern column must start from Fort Lincoln, up near the borders of the British Territory, could not move as early as Crook, who was far to the south. The latter started his column on the 1st of March, 1876, from Fort Fetterman, and struck off to the north for the Powder River.

The column consisted of ten companies of the Second and Third Cavalry and two companies of infantry, with a strength of 700 men and 40 days supplies on pack mules and in wagons. The whole was commanded by Colonel Reynolds, Third Cavalry, brevet Major-General, and was accompanied by Brigadier-General Crook, the department commander. This column started with fine weather in its favor, and every indication of opening spring. There were sixty wagons and 400 pack mules in the train, making, with the cavalry horses, 1,500 animals for which forage had to be carried. Nothing was heard of this expedition until March 26, when the following telegram was received by General Sheridan from Crook:

CRAZY HORSE

FORT RENO, March 22

We cut loose from the wagon train on the 17th inst., and scouted the Tongue and Rosebud Rivers until satisfied that there were no Indians upon them; then struck across the country toward Powder River. General Reynolds, with part of the command, was pushed forward on a trail leading to the village of Crazy Horse, near the mouth of Little Powder River. This, he attacked and destroyed on the 17th inst., finding it a perfect magazine of ammunition, war material, and general supplies. Crazy Horse had with him the Northern Cheyenne and some of the Minneconjou, probably in all one-half of the Indians off the reservation. Every evidence was found to prove these Indians in co-partnership with those at the Red Cloud and Spotted Tail Agencies,* and that the proceeds of their raids upon the settlements had been taken to those agencies, and supplies brought out in return. In this connection, I would again urgently recommend the immediate transfer of the Indians of those agencies to the Missouri River. I am satisfied that if Sitting Bull is on this side of the Yellowstone, that he is camped at the mouth of Powder River. We experienced severe weather during our absence from the wagon train, snow falling every day but one, and the mercurial thermometer on several occasions failing to register.

GEORGE CROOK, Brigadier-General

Such was the first brief intimation of the facts of the Powder River fight. After a while, the history was amplified by the reports of the newspaper correspondents. From their accounts and the subsequent full report of Crook, the whole story came out. After leaving Fort Fetterman, nothing happened for some days. The expedition left Crazy Woman's Fork with ten companies of cavalry on the night of March 7, with fifteen days' rations on pack mules. The infantry and wagon train were sent back to the rear.

The command marched down Tongue River nearly to the Yellowstone, scouting the Rosebud and adjacent streams. No Indians were found in this entire region. The expedition then moved to the head of Otter Creek, where General Reynolds was sent forward with six companies, and by a rapid night march reached Powder River early on

---

* These agencies are to the south, not on the map in this work.

the morning of the 17th, where he surprised and attacked Crazy Horse's village of 105 lodges. He captured the village, and after an engagement lasting five hours, entirely destroyed it.

So far, the expedition very closely resembled that of Custer on the Washita. A trail in the snow had been found and followed, and the Indian village had been surprised. There, the resemblance ended.

Custer's victory on the Washita had been complete and overwhelming, and he had brought away all his prisoners, besides destroying the most indispensable part of an Indian's property - the horses - in the face of a superior force of over-awed enemies. Reynolds had no such history. He found the village of the Indian chief all alone, and was free from other enemies. The contrast of his movements was great. It will be remembered how Custer, having found the enemy's village in the night, employed the time until morning in surrounding it. The correspondents with Reynolds tell a different story. From the account of the New York Tribune writer, (an officer of the expedition), which we shall in the main follow, the difference of leaders will be seen. This officer says:

At 4:20 a.m., we had marched thirty miles, and were, as near as we could tell, near the Powder River breaks. A halt was called here, and the column took shelter in a ravine. No fires were allowed to be kindled, nor even a match lighted. The cold was more intense than we had yet felt, and seemed to be at least 30f below zero. The command remained here until about 6 o'clock, doing their utmost to keep from freezing, the scouts meantime going out to reconnoitre.

At this hour they returned, reporting a larger and fresher trail leading down to the river, which was about four miles distant. The column immediately started on this trail. The approach to the river seemed almost impracticable. Before reaching the final precipices which overlooked the river-bed, the scouts discovered that a village of about 100 lodges lay in the valley at the foot of the bluffs. It was now 8 o'clock. The sun shone brightly through the cold, frosty air.

The column halted, and Noyes's battalion, Second Cavalry, was ordered up to the front. It consisted of Company I, Second Cavalry,

Captain Noyes, and Company K, Second Cavalry, Captain Egan. This battalion was ordered to descend to the valley, and while Captain Egan charged the camp, Captain Noyes was to cut out the herd of horses feeding close by and drive it up the river. Captain Moore's battalion, consisting of Company F, Third Cavalry and Company E, Second Cavalry, was ordered to dismount and proceed along the edge of the ridge to a position covering the eastern side of the village, opposite that from which Captain Egan was to charge.

Captain Mills's battalion was ordered to follow Egan, dismounted, and support him in the engagement which might follow the charge. These columns began the descent of the mountain through gorges which were almost perpendicular, and it seemed almost impossible that horses could be taken through them. Nearly two hours were occupied in getting the horses of the charging column down these rough sides of the mountain and even there, when a point was reached where the men could mount their horses and proceed toward the village in the narrow valley beneath, Moore's battalion had not been able to gain its position on the eastern side, after clambering along the edges of the mountain.

A few Indians could be seen with the herd, driving them to the edge of the river, but nothing indicated that they knew of our approach. Just at 9 o'clock, Captain Egan turned the point of the mountain nearest the river, and first in a walk and then in a rapid trot started for the village. The company went first in column of twos, but when within 200 yards of the village the command "Left front into line" was given, and with a yell they rushed into the encampment. Captain Noyes had in the mean time wheeled to the right and started the herd up the river.

With the yell of the charging column, the Indians sprang up as if by magic, and poured in a rapid fire from all sides. Egan charged through and through the village before Moore's and Mills' battalions got within supporting distance, and finding things getting very hot, formed his line in some high willows on the south side of the camp from which point he poured in rapid volleys upon the Indians.

Up to this time, the Indians supposed that one company was all they had to contend with, but when the other battalions appeared, rapidly advancing, deployed as skirmishers, and pouring in a galling fire of musketry, they broke on all sides and took refuge in the rocks along the side of the mountain.

The camp, consisting of 110 lodges with immense quantities of robes, fresh meat and plunder of all kinds, with over 700 head of horses, was in our possession. The work of burning began immediately, and soon the whole encampment was in flames. While the work of demolition was going on under the direction of General Reynolds, the Indians poured in a well-directed fire from the sides of the mountain and from every available hiding place. Not satisfied with this, they made a determined attack on the troops about noon, with a view to regaining possession of the camp.

Captain Mills, who had charge of the skirmish line, perceived their movement and asked for additional men. These were sent in promptly, and the attack was quickly and handsomely repulsed, the Indians retiring in disorder. After the work of destruction had been completed, the withdrawal of the troops began and the whole command moved rapidly up the river, twenty miles, to the mouth of Lodgepole Creek, where it went into camp after two days and one night of constant marching.

So far, so good. It will be observed that the troops, instead of surrounding the Indians, had been surrounded by them, and finally fell back. Now mark the sequel:

After the fight was over, the troops marched rapidly up the river to the mouth of Lodgepole Creek. This point was reached at nightfall by all except Moore's battalion and Captain Egan's company. Company E, Second Cavalry, was the rear guard, and assisted Major Stanton and the scouts in bringing up the herd of horses. Many of these were shot on the road, and the remainder reached camp about 9 p.m. These troops had been in the saddle for 36 hours, with the exception of five hours during which they were fighting, and all, officers and men, were much exhausted.

The horses had had no grazing, and began to show signs of

complete exhaustion. Upon arriving at Lodgepole, it was found that General Crook and the other four companies and pack train had not arrived, so that everybody was supperless and without a blanket. The night therefore, was not a cheerful one, but not a murmur was heard. The wounded men lay upon the snow or leaned against a tree, and slept as best they could on so cold a night.

Owing to some misunderstanding, our four dead men were left on the field to be mutilated by the Indians. These men could have been removed easily, and that they were not caused a great deal of dissatisfaction among the troops. Saturday at noon, General Crook and the remainder of the command arrived. In the mean time, a portion of the herd of ponies had straggled into the ravines and fallen into the hands of the Indians.

This is very unlike the sequel to Custer's triumph, and shows forcibly the lack of an energetic leader and officers imbued with the same enthusiasm. The correspondent closes with the following paragraphs of unconscious severity:

It is hardly proper to close this sketch of the engagement without referring more particularly to those causes which prevented its complete success. First among these was the failure of Captain Moore's battalion to reach the position assigned it in the rear of the village, or a point covering the rear, before the charge was made by Captain Egan. This failure allowed the Indians to make good their escape to the rocky fastnesses of the mountains overlooking the valley, from which they subsequently poured in a galling fire upon our troops.

Moore's battalion was a strong one in number, and needed only to be led to the front where it could be effective to do good service. When it was discovered that the battalion would not be at the place assigned it, and that its commander did not apparently intend to put it there, Major Stanton and Lieut. Sibley, with five men, left it and went on, taking up the position which the battalion should have occupied, and gave the flying savages the best enfilading fire they could. But they were too few to prevent the escape of the Indians.

FREDERICK WHITTAKER

This was the first serious blunder. The next was that after the herd of ponies, numbering over 700, had been captured, driven twenty miles from the scene of action, and turned over to General Reynolds, commanding the troops, he failed to place a guard around them, so that the greater portion of them strayed off during the night and were picked up by the Indians. Furthermore, there were large quantities of buffalo meat and venison in the village, which General Crook had directed in case of capture to be brought out for the use of the troops, who were on half rations of fresh meat. This was not done and as a result, the soldiers have had no fresh meat except ponies since that time.

In short, it became clear, when full news of the expedition leaked out, that the Powder River fight was an example of an opportunity thrown away, in which almost everyone was to blame for only one thing - want of energy. Capt. Noyes actually allowed his men to unsaddle and rest, after he had first driven away the Indian herd, and while the fighting was going on, and for this he was afterwards court-martialed and reprimanded in general orders.

But the real trouble seems to have been simple enough - a want of heart, an excessive caution in everyone, especially the leader. When Custer went after Indians, he himself was always in the advance and looking out for his enemy. At the Washita, we have found him with the advanced scouts on all occasions, and watching his enemy himself. Here, on the other hand, we see neither Crook nor Reynolds out in front, the night wasted in idle waiting and the battle commenced at 9 o'clock, with the result of everybody falling just a little short of his work.

The Powder River fight, which under Custer would probably have ended in the complete destruction of the band of Crazy Horse, ended in merely burning some of his property and exasperating him, while leaving him all his weapons and men and almost all his horses. It was an ominous commencement for a campaign of disaster.

After that time, the curtain was hardly ever lifted till the commencement of the winter of 1876, and even then not in the form of a victory over hostile Indians, but the more questionable success of a movement of far less danger, that should have been made long ago. This movement was the surrounding and forcible disarmament of the Sioux at the principal agencies, taking from them their ponies, and compelling them to live peaceably; and the army is fain to be proud of this, lacking other subjects of congratulation.

Recognizing fully the difficulties which surround army operations against the Indians, we must still admit the worst to be the low character of the regular troops. In the infantry, this is marked by apparent inability to execute severe marches on foot, in the cavalry by an almost total incapacity to fight mounted against the Indians. Infantry and cavalry advance well enough in the common skirmish line on foot, but there are so many recruits, so few veterans in the ranks, that the issue of a single combat between an Indian and a dragoon is, almost as a matter of course, the death of the dragoon.

Compelled as they are by the inferiority of their men, to fight dismounted, too many of our cavalry officers have fallen into the pernicious habit which spoiled the Confederate cavalry during the civil war, which ruined all European cavalry from the invention of firearms until the days when Gustavus Adolphus once more introduced the charge sword-in-hand, and which again ruined them in the interval between his days and those of Frederick the Great. This habit is the distrust of the sabre, and the consequent timidity evinced by all concerned, when a hand-to-hand fight is necessary.

The Indians, with all their improved firearms, universally retain the lance with their other weapons. The drilled soldier, possessing a sabre, uses it only as an ornament on dress parade, and leaves it in quarters when he goes out to fight - first, on the ground that its clattering may be heard by Indians, second on the singular plea, put forth by Colonel Brackett, in his "*History of the U.S. Cavalry,*" that "if the soldier gets near enough to an Indian to use his sabre, it is an even chance which goes under."

Can it be wondered at that Indians beat men who are so ignorant of the art of attack and defense, and who despise all the teachings of military history? If it be true that the chances are now even, or in favor of the Indian, there is a simple remedy. It is to teach the men how to use their sabres until they trust to them. When officers and men do that, the Indians will fear them, not they the Indians.

CUSTER AND GRANT

IT is now time to turn to that part of the campaign under General Terry's orders. When Sheridan and Sherman planned the destruction of Sitting Bull, it was ordered that Custer should be assigned to the command of the Dakota column. It was organized at his post, was mainly composed of his regiment, and was repeatedly denominated in orders "Custer's column." The reasons for giving him this post were perfectly simple. Custer had never yet met with a single disaster while in command of an important expedition, and he had been blessed with more complete success in his Indian expeditions than any other officer in the regular army.

His only rival as an Indian fighter was Crook, and Crook had gained his reputation by a pursuit and extermination of small scattered bands of Apaches in Arizona, who were not blessed with a semi-circle of Indian agencies in their rear to supply them with Winchester rifles and patent ammunition. Besides this, Crook was getting older, and having been made a brigadier, was not so likely to work as Custer, who was still only a lieutenant-colonel thanks to the seniority rule.

Brigadier General Terry, the department commander, had never been in the field as an Indian fighter, and felt quite content to leave the Indian laurels to Custer. Terry was a brigadier who owed his sudden elevation to his present rank to the capture of Fort Fisher. Having been a volunteer only, and before that a lawyer, not a West Pointer, Terry found himself in a peculiar position in the army. Had he been a nervously energetic officer like Custer, the enmity he would have excited among the old seniority officers, especially the graduates, would have been much greater. As it was, while they hated him passively, they had not the same opportunity to spite him, Terry being two steps higher than Custer. Only his great sweetness of temper and modesty preserved him from active enmity. Terry trusted Custer implicitly, and admired him greatly, and it was all settled; that Custer should lead the Dakota column.

Then came a sudden interruption to all these plans, a chain of incidents which ended in a disaster to the nation and in the temporary triumph of Custer's enemies. The facts of this business are so important to the vindication of Custer's character from the attacks of these enemies that the nation of which he was the pride will not deem wasted the space which brings them clearly to light.

While Custer was hard at work preparing for his part of the Sioux Expedition, eager for work and foreseeing a further triumph, he received a telegram from Mr. Hiester Clymer, Chairman of a certain Congressional Committee, requiring his presence in Washington to give testimony as to some alleged abuses in the War Department.

At the time, Mr. Belknap, who had lately resigned the office of Secretary of War, was under investigation in regard to an alleged sale by him of a post tradership[*] to a person called Marsh. The committee had stumbled on the evidence of this sale by accident, and the Secretary, overwhelmed with shame at the discovery of his apparent venality, had resigned his office under charges, and was at once impeached by the House of Representatives.

The defense of the delinquent secretary, so far as it appeared, was that his first wife had, unknown to him, sold her influence with him for the office, that his second wife, sister of the first, had continued the bargain with Marsh after the death of her sister, and that he, Belknap, was perfectly ignorant of the whole matter until shortly before the examination of Marsh, when the shame and misery experienced by him

---

[*] Post traders now supply the place of the old sutlers, whose office was abolished a few years since. They have the exclusive privilege of trading at the post to which they are appointed, and where the garrison is large the privilege is exceedingly valuable, as much of the pay of soldiers and officers is generally spent in the post trader's store, for little luxuries. The post tradership given to Marsh was at Fort Sill, Indian Territory, where ten companies of cavalry were generally stationed, aggregating about 600 men and forty officers, including staff, etc. The pay of the garrison amounted to about $160,000 a year, and at the ordinary sutler's rates, it was pretty certain that at least $100,000 would be spent at the store, with a profit to the post trader, at 100 per cent., of at least $50,000 per annum.

at the exposure of the delinquencies of his two wives was so great as to lead to his giving up the fight in advance.

William Belknap. After being accused of accepting illicit kickbacks in exchange for post tradership appointments, Belknap resigned his position as Secretary of War in an attempt to avoid impeachment. He was tried by the Senate during the summer of 1876, where his new role as a private citizen successfully shielded him from the impeachment.

Although this is not the place to enter into the merits or demerits of the Belknap case, which has since been legally settled in his favor, it may be stated that this explanation was believed to be the truth by all those who were personally intimate with the ex-secretary's career. One of these was President Grant, on whose staff the Secretary had served as General Belknap during the war, and who remained his firm friend in his trouble.

The Congressional committee was determined, however, to investigate every act of Belknap's career in regard to frontier posts, and began to call witnesses from all quarters, groping blindly after the facts. The vaguest hearsay evidence was snatched at, and at last someone suggested that General Custer knew something about corruption on the part of the ex-secretary; he had been heard by someone to say that he had heard something on the subject, and so forth. On this vague information, the sapient Chairman telegraphed a summons to Custer to come to Washington, and so started a train of circumstances which was to end in the untimely death of the best cavalry chief on the American continent.

Custer was much disturbed. He telegraphed at once to Terry to know what he should do, stating that his own information was only hearsay and devoid of value to the case, and asking whether an order was not necessary. He made these inquiries of Terry, knowing that his general had been bred a lawyer. At the same time, showing his scrupulous sense of justice, he asked whether he was not bound to go and tell what little he knew and how he knew it.

In the same telegram, showing his peculiarly sensitive honor, he asks for a court of inquiry on himself in regard to his own conduct towards a discontented officer of his regiment, concerning a transfer from one company to another, in which the officer complained that injustice had been done him. Terry's answer to this telegram was as follows:

HDQRS. DEPT. OF DAKOTA, ST. PAUL, MIN., March 16, 1876

To Lieut. Col. Custer, Port Lincoln, Dakota:

Dispatch received. You need no order beyond the summons of the committee. I am sorry to have you go, for I fear it will delay our movements. I should suppose that if your testimony is not as to the facts themselves, and will only point out the witnesses from whom the committee can get the facts, your information might be communicated by letter or telegraph, and that being done, you might ask to be relieved from personal attention without exposing yourself to misconstruction. However, you must use your own judgment.

In regard to the other matter, I don't think that you need a court of inquiry. Your statement to me vindicated you in my eyes: a repetition to General Sheridan would doubtless vindicate you in his. A court could not be convened until after the summer campaign is over. Your services are indispensable, and no thought of a transfer can be entertained.

TERRY, Comd'g. Dept.

Custer took Terry's advice and telegraphed to Clymer as follows:

FREDERICK WHITTAKER
FORT LINCOLN, DAKOTA, March 16, 1876

Honorable Hiester Clymer:

While I hold myself in readiness to obey the summons of your committee, I telegraph to state that I am engaged upon an important expedition, intended to operate against the hostile Indians, and I expect to take the field early in April. My presence here is deemed very necessary. In view of this, would it not be satisfactory for you to forward to me such questions as may be necessary, allowing me to return my replies by mail?

GEORGE. A. CUSTER

Clymer, proud of his power to see through a millstone much further than anyone else, would not be denied, and made Custer come on, besides putting him through a cross-examination that lasted two days, and compelling him to tell not only all he knew, but all he did not know, into the bargain. After a month's torture of Custer, he finally found out that the latter had written him an honest letter, and that the committee might better have left him in Fort Lincoln.

To only one fact was Custer able to testify of his own knowledge. This was that, on one occasion, the contractor at Fort Lincoln had turned him over a large quantity of grain, in sacks which had borne the Indian brand, and which he suspected had been stolen from the Indian Department as part of the gigantic system of fraud by which the Indian Ring played into the hands of army contractors.

At the time this grain was issued to Custer, he refused to receive it and telegraphed to Department Headquarters on the subject, expressing his suspicions. In due time, his communication having been forwarded through regular channels, he received a positive order to take the grain. This order, he stated to the committee, he believed to have come down from the Secretary of War.

This evidence, while avowedly only on information and belief, was regarded by Clymer as implicating the Secretary in some fresh fraud, and on the face of things there was ample ground for Custer's honest suspicions of the whole business. It turned out afterwards that Custer was mistaken as to the origin of the peremptory order. It really came from Terry alone, on the latter's responsibility. We shall see later how perfectly frank Custer was in the matter, and how ready publicly to retract his error.

Much has been said by strong political partisans as to this last public action of Custer. By those who were ardent supporters of the ex-secretary, and especially of his avowed friend, President Grant, the indirect and hearsay testimony which was all that Custer could give, was contrasted with the previous parade of its promised value made by the committee, and especially by the partisan newspapers on the side of the committee. Custer was called a "swift witness," a "retailer of gossip" and accused of intriguing for his summons in order to escape frontier duty. Much of this abuse might be now passed over on the score of partisan excitement were it not that the writer of Custer's biography feels himself bound by a sense of duty to probe the truth to the very bottom.

As regards the Belknap case, it is certain that Custer's evidence was wholly immaterial. His only item of personal knowledge adverse to the secretary was founded on an honest mistake, which he was swift to acknowledge when it was pointed out to him. As a witness of the prosecution, he should never have been called. Who called him?

Hiester Clymer and that ingenious committee which so studiously mismanaged the Belknap case were the real parties to blame. Custer had telegraphed to Clymer, begging to be excused from attendance at Washington, as an important expedition was about to take the field in which his presence was necessary. He earnestly begged to be left at his post, but his request was denied.

Clymer was bound to have him in Washington for political effect, just as Johnson in old times had been determined to have Custer's name associated with his, in "swinging round the circle." In both cases, the only party injured was the honest unsuspecting soldier. The more Clymer questioned him, the more ludicrous was his failure to extract anything but the truth. For this truth, Custer has been blamed by his enemies, when the real party to blame was the officious chairman who persisted in calling him.

On Clymer's shoulders, moreover, rests the responsibility of deferring Custer's departure after Sitting Bull a whole month. Had he gone in April, before the Indians had gathered in force, Custer might be alive now.

One person in the United States, however, would not believe in Custer's unwillingness to testify. Instead of this, he took Custer's presence and testimony in Washington as a personal affront to himself. This person was President Grant.

President Grant was once General Grant. As General Grant, he was chiefly distinguished for one virtue, an indomitable resolution and obstinacy in following whatever plan he had resolved on, an iron determination to pursue it at whatever cost. This quality of determination in war had finally conducted him to success, because as a general his power was absolute.

As the executive of a republic, it brought him hatred and ill will, for the successful head of a republic must be an eloquent and persuasive man who can win others to his side by flattery, and who knows how to yield outwardly while gaining his ends by craft and subtlety.

Another virtue possessed by General Grant was that of faithfulness to his friends, and this virtue also tended to his success in war, while in peace it operated in exactly the opposite direction. Had it been accompanied by good judgment in the choice of friends, it might not have been so disastrous, but unluckily, Grant seems from the first to have fallen into the hands of very questionable friends who would have fleeced him had he been a rich man, who were accused of fleecing the nation under his protection, he being a high officer.

The efforts of the Clymer committee and the House during the Belknap investigation had undoubtedly been directed towards the injury of Grant and his friends, who formed what was known under the general term of "the Administration;" and the animus of the whole attack was so evident, the persistency of the efforts to find something on which to hang more impeachments so untiring, that they had excited the bitterest indignation in Grant himself. His very virtues; pride, firmness, faithful friendship, conviction of honesty, tended to embitter his animosity against all connected with the attack on his administration.

CUSTER AND GRANT

He looked on them as mortal enemies and never forgave them. Amongst these, he now counted Custer. He never paused to inquire whether the latter was a willing witness, whether his testimony was dragged out of him or not; he made up his mind that Custer had turned against him in his period of trial, and he became bitterly and inexorably incensed against him personally. Custer heard of this through private sources, and knew that the President's impression as to his own testimony was quite unfounded.

As soon therefore, as he was released from his attendance at the committee, he called at the White House to pay his respects to the President, hoping by a frank personal statement to disabuse his mind of the mistake. For the first time in his life, Custer found himself treated with ignominy, compelled to wait in the ante-room for hours, to see other persons getting audiences before him, while he himself was left perfectly unnoticed, although his card was sent in from the first.

Three times he called at the White House, and on neither occasion was he even noticed. These visits were made at various times during his sojourn at Washington, while he was daily expecting his release and return to Dakota. He had left the fort, expecting to be gone ten days at furthest; he had now been detained at Washington for over a month, unable to go anywhere, uncertain of his movements from day to day.

He was only able to take one hurried trip to New York on one occasion, to have a little business talk with his publishers about his War Memoirs, which he had commenced during the past winter at Fort Lincoln. This hurried visit was the occasion of the last glimpse of Custer caught by the writer of this biography, while in the editorial rooms of the Galaxy.

Custer looked worn and thin, and somewhat worried, his hair cut short, a great change from the debonair cavalier of the Waynesboro fight. His manner conveyed the impression of a nervous man with his nerves all on edge, in a state of constant repressed impatience. He had left his wife behind at Fort Lincoln, and knew that every day brought the season of active operations nearer while he was away. No wonder he looked worried.

At last he was released from his attendance, May 1st, and went to the White House with a last, almost despairing effort to get an audience from Grant and to explain his action. Once more, he was compelled to submit to the slight of being kept waiting in the ante-room among the President's lackeys. Time was going on; his detention by the official summons was over, and he knew that his duty imperatively called him back to Fort Lincoln that very day. He sat down and wrote the following note, which he sent in:

To His Excellency the President:

> Today, for the third time I have sought an interview with the President - not to solicit a favor, except to be granted a brief hearing - but to remove from his mind certain unjust impressions concerning myself, which I have reason to believe are entertained against me. I desire this opportunity simply as a matter of justice, and I regret that the President has declined to give me an opportunity to submit to him a brief statement, which justice to him, as well as to me, demanded.
>
> Respectfully submitted,
> G.A. CUSTER, Lt. Col. Seventh Cavalry, Bvt. Maj. Genl. U. S. Army

This letter was sent in to, and read by, the President. During the last visit, as we are credibly informed, General Ingalls, then acting quartermaster-general, found Custer in the ante-room and went in to see the President. Ingalls was a good and just man, and a friend of both. He asked the President if he knew that Custer was outside, waiting. The President did - he did not wish to see him. Then, Ingalls urged, he should at least spare Custer the indignity of waiting outside and send him a message to save his time - that so much was due to Custer's past services at least.

Then the President sent out word that he refused to see Colonel Custer, and Custer sat down and wrote his quiet, manly letter, honest and proud, sad and dignified, like himself in every word. It was useless. Grant refused to see him. Custer had no longer any pretext for staying in Washington. He had already been to call on the General of the Army, and found that Sherman was away in New York, but was expected back in the evening.

CUSTER AND GRANT

He went off and secured his passage on the night train, calling on Inspector-General Marcy and Adjutant-General Townsend on the way. Adjutant-General Marcy had wished Custer, on the way back to Dakota, to perform some duty in Detroit which would delay him, but hearing from Custer of the urgency of his haste, on account of the lateness of the season and of the necessity of his immediate presence at Fort Lincoln, gave him the following letter:

WAR DEPARTMENT, INSPECTOR-GENERAL'S OFFICE
Washington, D.C., May 1st, 1876

Lieut. Col. G.A. Custer, U.S. Army
COLONEL: Understanding that the General of the Army desires you to proceed directly to your station, the service which I recommended you to perform in Detroit, Michigan, can be executed by another officer. And in the absence of the general, you have my consent to omit stopping at Detroit for the purpose specified in the Adjutant-General's letter to you.

Very respectfully, your obedient servant,

R.B. MARCY, Inspector General

Custer made a last call at Sherman's office. The General was not back from New York, and his length of stay was still uncertain. Custer took the train, and was soon whirling away toward Chicago. The next day, May 2nd, General Sheridan was awakened from his slumbers by the following extraordinary telegram:

WASHINGTON, D.C., May 2nd, 1876
General P.H. Sheridan, Chicago, Illinois

I am this moment advised that General Custer started last night for Saint Paul and Fort Abraham Lincoln. He was not justified in leaving without seeing the President or myself. Please intercept him at Chicago or Saint Paul, and order him to halt and await further orders. Meanwhile, let the Expedition from Fort Lincoln proceed without him.

W.T. SHERMAN, General

It was the hand of Sherman, but the head of Grant. The grim

implacable animosity of the President was aroused. Custer's testimony had made him the President's foe. Right or wrong, Grant was determined to punish him, and there was but one way to do it - deprive him of the command of the expedition, and so humiliate him. No one knew better than Grant that if Custer went in command of the Dakota column, he was certain to return victorious, with fresh laurels. That pill was too bitter for the President to swallow. All that Sheridan could do, in the face of such a positive order, was to obey it. An officer was sent to the station, and Custer was stopped on the 4th of May by the following letter:

HEADQUARTERS MILITARY DIV. OF THE MISSOURI
Chicago, Ill., May 4th, 1876

Lieutenant-Col. G.A. Custer, Seventh U.S. Cavalry, Chicago, Ill.
SIR: Agreeably to instructions contained in the enclosed copy of a telegraphic dispatch from the General of the Army, of the 2nd instant, the Lieutenant-General commanding the division directs you to remain in Chicago until the receipt of further orders from superior authority, to be furnished you through these headquarters.

Very respectfully your obedient servant,
R.C. DRUM, Assistant Adjutant-General

There was nothing for it but to obey. Custer drove in haste to Sheridan's headquarters and found him as friendly as ever. Sheridan knew no more of the cause of the order than did Custer himself, and told him so. He had no objection to Custer's telegraphing direct to Sherman for an explanation, and the astonished officer at once sent off the following dispatch:

CHICAGO, ILL.

General W.T. Sherman, Washington, D.C.
I have seen your dispatch to General Sheridan directing me to await orders here, and am at a loss to understand that portion referring to my departure from Washington without seeing you or the President, as I called at the White House at ten o'clock a.m. Monday, sent my card to the President,

and with the exception of a few minutes absence at the War Department, I remained at the White House waiting an audience with the President until three p.m., when he sent me word that he would not see me.

I called at your office about two p.m., but was informed by Colonel McCook you had not returned from New York, but were expected in the evening. I called at your hotel at four p.m. and about six p.m., but was informed by the clerk that you had not returned from New York. I then requested Colonel McCook to inform you of the substance of the above dispatch, and also that I was to leave at seven that evening to report to my command.

While at the War Department that day, I also reported the fact of my proposed departure to the Adjutant-General and to the Inspector-General of the army, and obtained from them written and verbal authority to proceed to my command without visiting Detroit, as previously ordered to do. At my last interview with you, I informed you that I would leave Washington Monday night to join my command, and you, in conversation replied that "that was the best thing I could do." Besides, you frequently, during my stay in Washington, called my attention to the necessity for my leaving as soon as possible. I telegraph you direct, with the permission of the Lieutenant-General.

G.A. CUSTER, Brevet Major-General

Later in the day he sent this further telegram:

CHICAGO, May 4, 1876, 2:30 p.m.

Gen. W.T. Sherman, Washington, D.C.

I desire to further call your attention to your statement to me, in your office, that I should go in command of my regiment. Also to your reply when I inquired if the President or other parties had any charges to make against me. In leaving Washington, I had every reason to believe I was acting in strict accordance with your suggestions and wishes. I ask you as General of the Army to do me justice in this matter.

G.A. CUSTER

No answer came to these dispatches, and Custer well knew the reason. It was not Sherman who was thus putting him to torture, but someone behind Sherman who was able to command him. Grant was resolved to humiliate Custer, no matter at what cost. He was stolidly determined to have his own way. As a last resort, Custer telegraphed a third time in the evening:

General W.T. Sherman, Washington, D.C.

After you read my dispatch of today, I would be glad if my detention could be authorized at Fort Lincoln, where my family is, instead of at this point.

G.A. CUSTER, Bvt. Major General

Not a word in answer to all this. Custer had committed no crime; there were no charges against him. He had done nothing but obey orders all through, but it was necessary he should be punished, as the President could punish no one else. In this, Grant showed great knowledge of human nature. No doubt he would have liked immediately to punish every officer who had testified against his administration, but he had no means by which to do it. No one else of the witnesses was in command of an expedition, no one was a successful Indian fighter, no one else was a high strung nervous cavalier, sensitive to a slight. Custer was the only man.

It was so easy to punish him by the simplest means; the reason assigned was so plausible. Grant knew that the torture lay in the first humiliation, the minor details were of little consequence. After all, the President, while a bitter foe, was not a cruel one. He had no objection to letting Custer see his family. So it appears by the following dispatch:

CHICAGO, May 5th

Brigadier General A.H. Terry, St. Paul, Minn.
The Lieutenant General directs me to transmit for your information and guidance the following telegram from the General of the Army:
"Have received your dispatch of today, announcing General Custer's arrival. Have just come from the President, who orders that General Custer be allowed to rejoin his post, to remain there on duty, but not to accompany the expedition supposed to be on the point of starting against the hostile Indians, under General Terry.

W.T. SHERMAN, General

CUSTER AND GRANT

Please acknowledge receipt.
R.C. DRUM, A.A.G., HDQRS. DEPT. OF DAKOTA, ST. PAUL, MAY 8th, 1876

Official copy respectfully furnished for the information of Lieutenant-Colonel Custer.
GEO. RUGGLES, Ass. Adj. Gen.

It appears clearly from the next message that Sherman was not inimical to Custer, for he telegraphed to him kindly enough. Immediately following Sherman's telegram will be found one from Custer, illustrating the frankness and completeness with which he always acknowledged his errors. It is the one we have before referred to, as connected with the matter of the grain frauds. Sheridan's telegram is as follows:

Gen. G.A. Custer, Chicago,
WASHINGTON, D.C.

Before receipt of yours, had sent orders to General Sheridan to permit you to go to Abe Lincoln on duty, but the President adheres to his conclusion that you are not to go on the expedition.

W.T. SHERMAN, General

The other telegram is as follows:

SAINT PAUL, May 6th, 1876

To Hon. Hiester Clymer, Washington, D.C.
General Terry, commanding the Department of Dakota, informs me that the report I forwarded from Fort Lincoln, regarding certain corn delivered at that post for the use of the army, in Indian sacks, was received at his headquarters in the city, and after due investigation, was acted upon finally by his authority and that it was he and not the late Secretary of War who sent the order to Fort Lincoln, directing that, under certain instructions intended to protect the government, the corn in question should be received. The receipt of the order was reported to me, and at the same time I derived the impression that the order emanated from the War Department. As I would

FREDERICK WHITTAKER

not knowingly do injustice to any individual, I ask that this telegram may be appended to, and made part of my testimony before your Committee.

G.A. CUSTER

Then Custer found himself, May 6th, in St. Paul, and condemned by the President's order to remain behind and see his comrades go to war. How bitterly it must have recalled to him his equally unjust detention, eight years before, at Fort Leavenworth, and the disasters to the nation which had followed his punishment.

That punishment led to the Phil Kearny massacre and Forsyth's disastrous siege on the island. It shows how free from vulgar ambition and how pure was Custer's patriotism, that he, the proud soldier, publicly insulted and humiliated without the pretence of a fault on his part, should have written such a letter as this, which follows. The last words we commend to the nation that loves him. We also commend Terry's letter of transmittal:

HEADQUARTERS DEPARTMENT OF DAKOTA,
SAINT PAUL, MINN., May 6th, 1876

Adjutant General, Division of Missouri, Chicago
I forward the following to HIS EXCELLENCY THE PRESIDENT, through Military Channels,
I have seen your order, transmitted through the General of the Army, directing that I be not permitted to accompany the expedition about to move against hostile Indians. As my entire regiment forms a part of the proposed expedition, and as I am the senior officer of the regiment on duty in this Department, I respectfully but most earnestly request that while not allowed to go in command of the expedition, I may be permitted to serve with my regiment in the field. I appeal to you as a soldier to spare me the humiliation of seeing my regiment march to meet the enemy and I not to share its dangers.

G.A. CUSTER, Bvt. Maj. Genl. U.S. Army

In forwarding the above, I wish to say expressly, that I have no desire whatever to question the orders of the President, or of my military superiors. Whether Lieut. Col. Custer shall be permitted to accompany my column or not, I shall go in command of it. I do not know the reasons upon which the orders already given rest; but if those reasons do not forbid it, Lieut. Col. Custer's services would be very valuable with his command.

TERRY, Commanding Department

It will be seen that Terry is cautious as to expressing an opinion, being restrained from speaking out by official reticence. He could not say to his superior officer, whether he thought it or not; "Look here; this is a scandalous shame. Custer has done nothing wrong, he has only obeyed the law and told the truth; and the President is taking a mean and cowardly advantage of his power to punish Custer indirectly, because he dare not do it directly." The old adroitness of the lawyer appears in all of Terry's conduct. He makes no enemies; even the old West Pointers over whose heads Fort Fisher had jumped him could not find it in their hearts to hate him.

But the opposition papers were not so mealy mouthed. All over the land, they teemed with double-leaded articles on "Grant's tyranny" and "Custer's degradation," and took the quarrel up, not because they cared for Custer, but because they could make political capital out of it. All the foul vultures of politics flocked to see the battle, expecting a feast at its conclusion. The administration papers were thus in a manner forced into the fight, and into an attitude of antagonism to Custer which has pursued him beyond his grave.

This was unfortunate enough, and it is to be hoped that it will go no further. I have written in this chapter a plain statement of facts, and introduced copies of the original documents, on purpose to show that Custer's action in the whole of this matter was entirely unpolitical, and in the earnest hope that it may prevent his memory from being made the subject of a partisan fight. No man was ever more thoroughly an honest soldier and less of a politician than Custer, and no man has suffered more from the efforts of those vampires of life, the politicians, to make use of him in their quarrels.

Two men were to blame for all the trouble; meddling, officious Hiester Clymer, who insisted on making Custer come to Washington; obstinate, implacable Grant - the man, not the President - who would not listen to a word, and who was actually willing to imperil the whole fate of the Sioux campaign and to permit hundreds of lives to be lost to gain his revenge on Custer.

The question has nothing to do with one party or the other, but the responsibility of all that follows rests personally on these two men - the busy body and the implacable tyrant. One was willing to imperil a nation to serve his faction, the other was ready to forget his office, to prostitute his position, to sacrifice a hecatomb of innocent lives, to gratify his private revenge. From the consequences of that act he cannot escape.

Grant was satisfied with his first disgrace of Custer, or dared not face the criticism which would have greeted the announcement of the fact that the President of the United States was willing to imperil the success of an important expedition to gratify his private revenge. That was going a step too far; so Grant yielded to Custer's petition so far as to let him go as a subordinate in the expedition which Grant well knew in his heart that Custer alone was fit to command.

The papers said this openly, both opposition and independents, whereupon the administration papers felt themselves compelled to print alleged utterances of General Sherman to the effect that there were "plenty of officers in the army just as capable as Custer." Here again the officious meddling of Custer's injudicious friends only embittered his single real enemy, Grant, and compelled Sherman, as an official person, to appear hostile to Custer.

Possibly the General of the Army did say there were plenty of officers fit to take Custer's place, but he knew well enough that there was not one, for it was now May 7th, and the operations of every other officer had so far been marked by want of energy all through, especially in the fiasco of the Powder River fight. The fact was, and Sherman, Grant, and Sheridan knew it none better, that no one could replace Custer's peculiar qualities. "Custer," said Sheridan at Fort Leavenworth seven years before, "You are the only man that never failed me."

Write those words in gold on his monument. None could wish a prouder epitaph.

CUSTER AND GRANT

NOTE: Since this chapter was printed and stereotyped, the author has received information from the publishers of the *Galaxy* that tends further to disprove the accusation that Custer was willing to go to Washington before the committee. In conversation with members of the firm, while on his way to Washington, Custer distinctly stated that he knew nothing of his own knowledge as to the Belknap or other cases that could be of the slightest value to the committee. He displayed the greatest anxiety to be back at his post, and the peremptory summons of the committee was a great disappointment to him. As he expressed it, he had "begged of the committee to allow him to remain at Fort Lincoln, where he was so busy preparing the expedition of which he had been promised the command."

Mrs. Custer, who of all persons is most capable of judging of her husband's wishes, has also most positively assured the author that it was with the greatest unwillingness that Custer departed from Fort Lincoln, and with the fear before his eyes that it would end in disaster to the expedition.

THE GREAT EXPEDITION

THE slight and partial success of the Powder River fight was productive of one very serious result, as it turned out. General Crook virtually agreed, and the authorities agreed with him as to the substantial truth of the following statement, made by a writer present with the expedition. He said: Instead of 15,000 or 20,000 hostile Indians in this country, the expedition has demonstrated that there are probably not 2,000 all told. The Tribune correspondent in his report also said:

It does not seem probable that there are half as many hostile Indians in this northern country as the War Department has supposed. For nearly two weeks, this command has been marching through the best part of the whole unceded Sioux lands, and it has not seen 1,000 Indians in all. I doubt if there are 3,000 hostile people south of the Missouri and east of the Big Horn Mountains. Other military expeditions will soon follow this one, and in the end all these tribes will be glad to take agency rations, poor and insufficient as they generally are, for the rest of their days.

These sentiments were echoed by others, and formed the basis of the calculation on which the expeditions to come were composed. The strength of the columns was as follows; Crook had ten companies of the Third Cavalry, five of the Second Cavalry, with six companies from the Fourth and Ninth Infantry, an aggregate strength of 1,300 men. His route was north from Fort Fetterman (See map).

Gibbon, whose route was due east from Fort Ellis, Montana, had four companies of the Second Cavalry and two companies of the Seventh Infantry, a total force of some four hundred men, including

THE GREAT EXPEDITION

train, etc.

The Terry column moving west from Fort Lincoln consisted of the whole of the Seventh Cavalry - twelve companies – under Custer, and three companies of the Sixth and Seventeenth Infantry, with four Gatling guns and a detachment of Indian scouts. Official returns show that this force comprised twenty-eight officers and seven hundred and forty-seven men of the Seventh Cavalry, eight officers and one hundred and thirty-five men of the Sixth and Seventeenth Infantry, two officers and thirty-two men in charge of the Gatling battery, and forty-five enlisted Indian scouts. The wagon train contained one hundred and fourteen six-mule teams, thirty-seven two-horse teams, and seventy other vehicles, ambulances, etc., with eighty-five pack mules, and employed one hundred and seventy-nine civilian drivers.

Thus there was a total force of twenty-seven hundred armed men seeking for the Sioux, divided into three columns, respectively of the strength of four hundred, one thousand and one thousand three hundred. These three columns were to start from the circumference of a circle with a radius of some three hundred miles to concentrate somewhere in the country where Reynolds had struck Crazy Horse and his band.

Crook did not leave Fort Fetterman until May 29th. His column reached old Fort Reno, June 3rd. In this vicinity, the expedition rested while a party of scouts were detached to the encampments of the Crow and Shoshone, tribes of Indians inimical to the Sioux, to obtain their assistance as scouts and light troops.

On the 7th of June, the column was on the head of the Tongue River, near old Fort Phil Kearny, where on the 8th a war party of Sioux came down and tried to stampede the American horses, bringing on a skirmish which resulted in the repulse of the Indians. On the 14th, the column was joined by a number of Crow, Shoshone and Nez Peirce whom the scouts had brought back, and on the 16th the whole party started to find the bands of Sitting Bull and Crazy Horse, reported to be on the Rosebud River to the north.

The Crow who came in reported that they had seen Gibbon's camp on the other side of the Sioux, on the Tongue River, and that the

FREDERICK WHITTAKER

United States forces had already been attacked by Sitting Bull's people, who had taken some horses from them.

Thus it will be seen that up to the 16th June, the United States programme was carried out as fairly as could be expected, and that two of the converging columns had already arrived within striking distance of Sitting Bull and his friends. It was now that its faults were to be glaringly exposed. The regular force near the enemy amounted to 1700 men, whereof 400 were separated from the other 1300 by a rough mountainous country of some hundred miles, and between the two lay Sitting Bull and his braves in a compact body.

On the 16th, Crook advanced his force early in the morning. Each man carried four days' rations, the infantry were mounted on mules, and the train was left behind them. The destination of the column was Sitting Bull's village on the Rosebud River, sixty miles north. By the evening of the 16th, the column had marched forty miles, and went into camp for the night.

The Tribune correspondent says very justly, "This was the first mistake." Crook should have marched all night and attacked at daybreak, but just as in the case of the Powder River fight, the time was wasted. The mistake is claimed by the correspondent to be the fault of the Indian allies, who had been out hunting buffalo that day, and who gorged themselves with meat at night and refused to advance. A poor excuse is better than none.

The next morning, Sitting Bull turned the tables on Crook by attacking him, and the story told by the correspondent is instructive. It shows what a tissue of blunders and cross purposes a battle may become under the command of the oldest of generals, in Indian warfare, when all are not animated by the same spirit. The Crows and other scouts had been sent forward to find the Sioux village, and the correspondent proceeds:

June 17th, having marched seven miles, being in camp unsaddled, successive shots were distinctly heard, and the advance of the Sioux confirmed by our scouts pouring over the hills. Our present position, being surrounded by bluffs, was an untenable one, and one well chosen by the Sioux for their attack. The advance was sounded, and the line of battle then formed, with Noyes' battalion right, Mills right centre, Chambers centre, Indian allies left centre, Royall (with Henry's battalion and one company of Mills) left.

Mills' and Noyes' battalion were pushed forward, charging the enemy in gallant style. The rest of the line did not advance. Mills and Noyes were ordered to march on the village, which order fortunately for them was revoked. Royall's right was separated from the main command by about a quarter of a mile. He occupied a very important and dangerous position; one which if held by the enemy would have rendered Crook's line on the bluff untenable unless he had advanced.

Having occupied this place under a heavy fire from the commencement of the fight (8 a.m.) until 2 p.m., Captain Nickerson of General Crook's staff brought, attended with great personal danger (as the Indians seemed to divine his mission), orders for Colonel Royall to retire or connect his line with General Crook's. This was effected, instead of by a forward movement, by a sort of left about wheel, or retreat.

The Indians seized this favorable opportunity by advancing and occupying the place vacated by ourselves and pouring upon us a galling fire from three different directions, charging upon our lines and trying to capture our led horses, our men being dismounted as skirmishers. Royall, by maintaining successive lines of retreat, aided by the great gallantry of his men and officers, succeeded, with loss, in joining Crook's command.

This loss was diminished by the charge made by our allies and two infantry companies from Crook's left upon the advancing Sioux. This charge should have been made when we first commenced our retreat movement. It was in what may be called "Death Hollow" during the retreat, while superintending the movements of his battalion, that Colonel Henry was severely wounded in the face, the ball entering near the left temple and coming out the right side of the face.

The order now was for all the troops to advance upon the village, supposed to be some six miles off. This order was twice given and twice changed, the latter owing to ammunition becoming short, and upon the representation of the guide, who had lived with the Sioux, that it would be impossible to pass through a difficult canon and secure the village without immense loss to our troops. These reasons, besides caring for his wounded, decided General Crook to go into camp on the battlefield of the day, which he did. The next two succeeding days, without further molestation, we returned to our permanent camp.

It will be seen that the correspondent puts the very best face on the battle that could be put there, but nonetheless it is impossible to hide the fact that Crook was taken by surprise. "Being in camp unsaddled" is the commencement of the fight, while on a march to surprise an active foe. In the course of the battle, Crook's left is driven in with serious loss, and only saved from annihilation by the charges of the Indian allies and the infantry. The Herald correspondent puts on a still better face by claiming a substantial victory, but even he cannot hide the fact of real defeat. He says:

The object of the scout which was so unsuccessful and yet not without an encouraging result, was to discover and destroy the village of the Sioux, which the guides, white, half-breed and Indian, agreed in declaring to be on the Yellowstone River, between the mouths of the Rosebud and the Tongue. It proved to be nearer the base of the expedition than was believed, and General Crook's ignorance of its proximity, due to the negligence and inactivity of the Crow allies who were entrusted with the work of scouting, is the cause of failure of the movement.

The Sioux were certainly repulsed in their bold onset, and lost many of their bravest warriors, but when they fled, could not be pursued without great danger in the rough country through which their way lay. Had his scouts proved faithful, so that he could have been prepared to occupy the commanding positions with infantry in advance of the main column, he would have had warning of the concentration of the enemy to impede his course, and could have driven him back into the village and ended the campaign by destroying it.

It will be seen that the blame of the miscarriage of the scout

THE GREAT EXPEDITION

belongs to the Crows, whose instinct, vigilance and knowledge of their own country was relied upon to render every move of the force intelligent. On the contrary, their undisciplined frenzy and failure to discover the lodgment of the enemy in time to frustrate their meditated attack precipitated a battle which began with a stupendous advantage on his side and in a spot of his own choice naturally suitable to the success of their method of warfare.

The Sioux strength was masked, except when emboldened by the disastrous withdrawal of the left wing of the cavalry, they made a dash from both ends of a deep hollow which lay in its way and exposed it to a murderous fire, and suddenly swarmed on the front, left and rear. Then it was that the timely fire of the infantry upon their main body, the charge of the Snakes into the hollow and a rapid pursuit of them for three miles, dismayed them utterly and they fell back and disappeared.

Had it not been for their occupation, unperceived by the General, of positions from which they could pour an enfilading fire upon both flanks of the body of cavalry on the left, they would not have stood in the face of the troops a moment after their first charge.

The last sentence, "had it not been" etc., is decidedly good. It shows that Crook was outgeneraled by Sitting Bull, and that the latter had troops not accustomed to the direct charge, and that is all. The Indians fought in their own way, and did all they wanted. They drove Crook back to his camp. Meanwhile, what were Terry and Gibbon doing? Reports show the following state of things:

Generals Terry and Gibbon communicated with each other, June 1st near the junction of the Tongue and Yellowstone Rivers, and learned that a heavy force of Indians had concentrated on the opposite bank of the Yellowstone, but about eighteen miles distant. For fourteen days, the Indian pickets had confronted Gibbon's videttes.

General Gibbon reported to General Terry that the cavalry had thoroughly scouted the Yellowstone as far as the mouth of the Big Horn, and no Indians had crossed it. It was now certain that they were not prepared for them, and on the Powder, Tongue, Rosebud, Little Horn, or Big Horn rivers General Terry at once commenced feeling for them.

General John Gibbon

Major Reno of the Seventh Cavalry, with six companies of that regiment, was sent up Powder River 150 miles to the mouth of Little Powder to look for the Indians, and if possible, to communicate with General Crook. He reached the mouth of the Little Powder in five days, but saw no Indians and could hear nothing of Crook. As he returned, he found on the Rosebud a very large Indian trail, about nine days old, and followed it a short distance, when he turned about up Tongue River and reported to General Terry what he had seen. It was now known no Indians were on Tongue River or Powder River, and the net had narrowed down to Rosebud, Little Horn and Big Horn Rivers.

General Terry, who had been waiting with Custer and the steamer Far West at the mouth of Tongue River for Reno's report, as soon as he heard it ordered Custer to march up the south bank to a point opposite General Gibbon, who was encamped on the north bank of the Yellowstone. Terry, on board the steamer Far West, pushed up the Yellowstone, keeping abreast of General Custer's column.

General Gibbon was found in camp, quietly awaiting developments. A consultation was had with Generals Gibbon and

THE GREAT EXPEDITION

Custer, and then General Terry definitely fixed upon the plan of action. It was believed the Indians were on the head of the Rosebud or over on the Little Horn, a divide of ridge only fifteen miles wide separating the two streams. It was announced by General Terry that General Custer's column would strike the blow.

Far West Steamboat. On June 21, 1876, the *Far West* was moored on the Yellowstone at the mouth of Rosebud Creek. There, it was the site of the fateful meeting of officers after which Custer and the 7th Cavalry were dispatched up the Rosebud seeking the Indian encampment. The 7th Cavalry suffered its disastrous defeat at the Battle of the Little Bighorn on June 25, 1876.

In order to understand the position of affairs, it will now be necessary to lay before the reader an outline sketch of the lines of the campaign so far, and show the position of the contending parties at this time (See map). This sketch indicates with sufficient accuracy for the reader the progress of the campaign. It shows the routes of the three columns up to the juncture when Custer was sent after the Indians, and the lines of march.

It will be seen that after Gibbon's and Terry's junction, the two were about a hundred miles from Crook, and that the Sioux were between them. Crook, after his defeat, fell back to the head of the Tongue River. The Powder, Tongue, Rosebud and Big Horn Rivers all run north into the Yellowstone, and Sitting Bull was between the headwaters of the Rosebud and Big Horn, the main tributary of the latter being known as the Little Big Horn. Thus stood matters when Terry sent off the following dispatch to Sheridan from his camp at the mouth of the Rosebud River; he writes:

No Indians have been met with as yet, but traces of large and recent camp have been discovered twenty or thirty miles up the Rosebud. Gibbon's column will move this morning on the north side of the Yellowstone for the mouth of the Big Horn, where it will be ferried across by the supply steamer, and whence it will proceed to the mouth of the Little Horn, and so on. Custer will go up the Rosebud tomorrow with his whole regiment, and thence to the headwaters of the Little Horn, thence down the Little Horn.

THE LAST BATTLE

BEFORE entering on the consideration of Custer's last march and battle, it is necessary to correct a mistaken impression set afloat by those same insincere friends and real enemies who had already done their best to embroil and embitter the close of his life. This impression is that Custer, during the whole of the last campaign, was suffering from depression of spirits, that he felt his disgrace keenly, that he was slighted by General Terry, and that these stings induced him to act rashly. The facts are exactly the reverse.

General Terry, from the very commencement of the expedition, trusted Custer implicitly, and the very best feeling existed between them. No one was more modest than Terry, nor more willing to defer to the experience of Custer; and inasmuch as the route followed by the Terry column was the very same as that followed three years before by the Stanley expedition, General Terry was only too glad to avail himself of Custer's help to pilot the column, just as Stanley had in his time.

It became Custer's regular duty to ride ahead of the main body with a battalion of the Seventh Cavalry, and to mark out the day's march for the wagons by leaving a broad trail. An officer present during the whole campaign, whose name we at present withhold, says:

As he seemed to me first, so he was to the last, the incarnation of energy. How often I watched him in our march to the Powder River, like the thoroughbred he rode, champing the bit and chafing to be off, longing for action. Our last day's march before reaching Powder River was through the worst and roughest country that I have ever seen a train taken over in campaign.

Early in the day, the guides and scouts were baffled by the labyrinth of ravines and confusion of badlands. Custer took the lead and took us through. I heard General Terry express his satisfaction that evening in these words; "No one but General Custer could have brought us through. He is the best guide I ever saw."

General Alfred Terry

Notwithstanding his manifestation of a little restiveness during this march, I was glad to know that he was steadily revealing his fine qualities to General Terry, and winning his way to the position which drew from his commanding officer the carte blanche under which he marched up the Rosebud on the 22nd June. It will not do for anyone to say that he disobeyed orders on that occasion. He did as everyone capable of comprehending him and his orders knew that he would do, and by those orders I am willing that he shall be judged, not by documents or explanations outside of them.

The reader will now very naturally ask to see these orders and find what they were. Fortunately they exist, and are as follows:

Lieut. Col. Custer, Seventh Cavalry:
COLONEL: The Brigadier-General Commanding directs that as soon as your regiment can be made ready for the march you proceed up the Rosebud in pursuit of the Indians whose trail was discovered by Major Reno a few days since. It is, of course, impossible to give any definite instructions in

regard to this movement, and were it not impossible to do so, the Department Commander places too much confidence in your zeal, energy and ability to wish to impose upon you precise orders which might hamper your action when nearly in contact with the enemy.

He will however, indicate to you his own views of what your action should be, and he desires that you should conform to them unless you shall see sufficient reason for departing from them. He thinks that you should proceed up the Rosebud until you ascertain definitely the direction in which the trail above spoken of leads. Should it be found, as it appears to be almost certain that it will be found, to turn toward the Little Big Horn, he thinks that you should still proceed southward, perhaps as far as the headwaters of the Tongue, and then turn toward the Little Big Horn, feeling constantly however to your left so as to preclude the possibility of the escape of the Indians to the south or southeast by passing around your left flank.

The column of Col. Gibbon is now in motion for the mouth of the Big Horn. As soon as it reaches that point, it will cross the Yellowstone and move up at least as far as the parks of the Big and Little Big Horn. Of course, its future movements must be controlled by circumstances as they arise; but it is hoped that the Indians, if upon the Little Big Horn, may be so nearly enclosed by two columns that their escape will be impossible. The Department Commander desires that on your way up the Rosebud, you should thoroughly examine the upper part of Tulloch's Creek, and that you should endeavor to send a scout through to Col. Gibbon's column with information of the result of your examination.

The lower part of this creek will be examined by a detachment from Col. Gibbon's command. The supply steamer will be pushed up the Big Horn as far as the forks of the river are found to be navigable for that space, and the Department Commander, who will accompany the column of Col. Gibbon, desires you to report to him there not later than the expiration of the time for which your troops are rationed, unless in the meantime you receive further orders.

Respectfully, etc.,

E.W. SMITH, Captain 18th Infantry,
Acting Assistant Adjutant-General

These orders are quite clear and explicit on one subject. Custer was sent out to find the Indians by following their trail up the Rosebud, and Gibbon was to hunt them from another direction, first up the Yellowstone, then up the Big Horn River. This would bring two columns together on the Big Horn somewhere to the south of the place where the battle finally occurred, if both moved at the same rate, for their trails would then be each round two sides of a rectangle, from corner to corner.

The first corner was the junction of the Rosebud and Yellowstone, the opposite one Sitting Bull's village on the Big Horn. Nothing however, was said in the order about rates of marching, and Custer was left entirely to his own discretion as to what he should do if he struck the enemy first. The only limit placed to his time is the period for which his troops are rationed. That period was fifteen days. The only expression of opinion on future movements is found in the sentence "it is hoped that the Indians, if upon the Little Big Horn, may be so nearly enclosed by the two columns that escape may be impossible."

The only fear of Terry seems to be that the Indians will escape. On Custer's way up the Rosebud, he is directed to examine the upper part of Tulloch's Creek. This creek runs into the Big Horn near its mouth. Its upper part was some ten miles to the right of Custer's actual trail, which followed that of the Indian village previously found by Reno.

Custer was to "endeavor to send through a scout to Colonel Gibbon's column." If he found that the trail turned (as it did) to the right, Terry "thinks you should still proceed southward" to the head waters of the Tongue before turning after the Indians. All these instructions, it will be noticed, are entirely advisory and permissory, not peremptory.

Terry expresses his conviction of the impossibility of giving any precise orders "which might hamper your action when nearly in contact with the enemy," and only desires Custer to conform to his views "unless you shall see sufficient reason for departing from them." It is quite clear on the face of these orders that Custer cannot be held legally or morally responsible for any departure from Terry's advice. The whole matter is left entirely in his discretion, the general placing "too much confidence in your zeal, energy and ability" to give any orders beyond one to report in fifteen days.

On his discretion solely he must be judged. In following him through the course of this his last march, we shall embody so much of the official report of his second in command, Major Reno, made at the close of the operations, as covers the period to Custer's death, illustrating it by the evidence of other persons taken since that time. This report is valuable on account of its presumed reliability as to dates, times and places. It was first published in the *Army and Navy Journal of New York City*, the official Army paper, and is addressed according to military etiquette, to the chief of Terry's staff for the time being. It commences as follows:

HEADQUARTERS, SEVENTH CAVALRY,
CAMP ON YELLOWSTONE RIVER, July 5, 1876

Captain E.W. Smith, A.D.C. and A.A.A.G.:

The command of the Regiment having devolved upon me, as the senior surviving officer from the battle of June 25th and 26th between the Seventh Cavalry and Sitting Bull's band of hostile Sioux on the Little Big Horn River, I have the honor to submit the following report of its operations from the time of leaving the main column until the command was united in the vicinity of the Indian village.

The regiment left the camp at the mouth of Rosebud River after passing in review before the Department Commander, under command of Brevet Major-General G.A. Custer, lieutenant-colonel, on the afternoon of the 22nd of June, and marched up the Rosebud twelve miles, and encamped, 23rd. Marched up the Rosebud, passing many old Indian camps and following a very large lodge pole trail, but not fresh, making thirty-three miles, 24th. The march was continued up the Rosebud, the trail and signs freshening with every mile until we had made twenty-eight miles, and we then encamped and waited for information from the scouts.

At 9:25 p.m., Custer called the officers together and informed us that beyond a doubt, the village was in the valley of the Little Big Horn, and that to reach it, it was necessary to cross the divide between Rosebud and Little Big Horn, and it would be impossible to do so in the daytime without discovering our march to the Indians; that we would prepare to move at 11 p.m. This was done, the line of march turning from the Rosebud to the right, up one of its branches, which headed near the summit of the divide.

About 2 a.m. of the 25th, the scouts told him that he could not cross the divide before daylight. We then made coffee and rested for three hours, at the expiration of which time the march was resumed, the divide crossed, and about 8 a.m. the command was in the valley of one of the branches of the Little Big Horn. By this time, Indians had been seen and it was certain that we could not surprise them, and it was determined to move at once to

THE LAST BATTLE

the attack.

Previous to this, no division of the regiment had been made since the order was issued on the Yellowstone annulling wing and battalion organizations. General Custer informed me he would assign commands on the march. I was ordered by Lieutenant W.W. Cook, adjutant, to assume command of Companies M, A and G; Captain Benteen, of Companies H, D and K; Custer retaining C, E, F, I and L under his immediate command, and Company B, Captain McDougall, in rear of the pack train.

I assumed command of the companies assigned to me, and without any definite orders moved forward with the rest of the column, and well to its left. I saw Benteen moving further to the left, and as they passed, he told me he had orders to move well to the left and sweep everything before him; I did not see him again until about 2:30 p.m.

The command moved down the creek towards the Little Big Horn valley; Custer, with five companies on the right bank; myself and three companies on the left bank; and Benteen farther to the left and out of sight.

Captain Frederick Benteen. Benteen's failure to come to Custer's assistance remains one of the most controversial aspects of the Battle of the Little Bighorn, which resulted in the death of Custer and the complete annihilation of the five companies of cavalry which comprised Custer's detachment.

Here, we must pause awhile. Major Reno, Brevet-colonel Benteen and President Grant have made the pause necessary by official accusations of Custer's action up to this point. Major Reno, near the close of his report, accuses Custer in these words:

FREDERICK WHITTAKER

I think (after the great number of Indians there were in the village) that the following reasons obtained for the misfortune; his rapid marching for two days and one night before the fight, attacking in the daytime at 12 a.m., and when they were on the *qui vive*, instead of early in the morning and lastly, his unfortunate division of the regiment into three commands.

General Terry, in a subsequent dispatch to Sheridan, quoting Benteen, accuses Custer of the same fault, and states that Custer had told him that his marches "would be at the rate of thirty miles a day."

Custer, according to Reno's report, left Terry at noon, 22nd June, and struck Sitting Bull on the morning of June 25th, having made one night march only. On the face of Reno's report, the night march was only from 11 p.m. to 2 a.m., or three hours. Then came a rest of three hours, with feed for man and horse, the march resumed at 5 a.m., the Indians seen at 8 a.m., finally struck at 12:30.

This gives a period of three whole days in all, at 30 miles a day, making 90 miles. The actual distance, measured on the best accessible map, makes the length of Custer's trail just 90 miles; and we can afford to allow 10 more for windings. According to Reno's report, the distance marched to the evening of the 24th June was 73 miles (12+33+28), leaving only 27 miles for the distance covered during the following night and day march.

In Terry's dispatch of self-justification above referred to, he says, "I learned from Captain Benteen that on the 22nd, the cavalry marched 12 miles; on the 23rd, 25 miles; from 5 a.m. until 8 p.m. of the 24th, 45 miles, and then after night 10 miles further, resting but without unsaddling, 23 miles to the battlefield." This account adds just 15 miles to the actual distance. It also subtracts 8 miles from Reno's report of the march of the 23rd June, and puts on 17 miles to Reno's account of the march of the 24th. Where Reno says 33, Terry, quoting Benteen, says 25; where Reno says 28, Terry, quoting Benteen, says 45.

President Grant, who hated Custer, as he had reason to, having injured him, distorts the facts still more in his published interview with a Herald correspondent months after.

We give this part of the interview entire, question and answer:

THE LAST BATTLE

CORRESPONDENT: Was not Custer's massacre a disgraceful defeat of our troops?

The PRESIDENT: (with an expression of manifest and keenly felt regret) I regard Custer's massacre as a sacrifice of troops, brought on by Custer himself; that was wholly unnecessary - wholly unnecessary.

CORRESPONDENT: How so, Mr. President?

The PRESIDENT: He was not to have made the attack before effecting a junction with Terry and Gibbon. He was notified to meet them on the 26th, but instead of marching slowly, as his orders required, in order to effect the junction on the 26th, he enters upon a forced march of eighty-three miles in twenty-four hours, and thus had to meet the Indians alone on the 25th.

Thus Reno, who, whatever his faults, is apparently an honorable man who labors to tell the truth, makes the whole march of the 24th and 25th June only 55 miles (28 + 27) agreeing with the map; Terry, quoting Benteen, makes it 78 miles (45 + 10 + 23); Grant, the President, in his eagerness to bury a dead man out of sight, makes it 83 miles.

On the face of Reno's report, and compared with the actual distance, judging Custer as we have a right to, solely on his "zeal, energy and ability," not on supposed orders, which Terry's written instructions prove he never received, it appears that so far he had done everything that a cool and wary Indian fighter could have done. At all events, the Indians had not escaped. Let us see now what followed, still quoting Reno. His report proceeds thus:

As we approached a deserted village, in which was standing one tepee, about 11 a.m., Custer motioned me to cross to him, which I did, and moved nearer to his column, until about 12:30 a.m., when Lieutenant Cook, adjutant, came to me and said the village was only two miles ahead and running away. To "move forward at as rapid gait as I thought prudent and to charge afterwards, and the whole outfit would support me;" I think those were his exact words.

I at once took a fast trot and moved down about two miles, when I came to a ford of the river. I crossed immediately, and halted about ten minutes or less to gather the battalion, sending word to Custer that I had everything in front of me, and that they were strong.

I deployed, and with the Ree scouts on my left, charged down the

FREDERICK WHITTAKER

valley, driving the Indians with great ease for about 21 miles. I however, soon saw that I was being drawn into some trap, as they certainly would fight harder, and especially as we were nearing their village, which was still standing; besides, I could not see Custer[*] or any other support, and at the same time the very earth seemed to grow Indians, and they were running towards me in swarms and from all directions. I saw I must defend myself, and give up the attack mounted. This I did, taking possession of a point of woods, and which furnished, near its edge, a shelter for the horses; dismounted, and fought them on foot, making headway through the wood.

I soon found myself in the near vicinity of the village, saw that I was fighting odds of at least five to one, and that my only hope was to get out of the wood, where I would soon have been surrounded, and gain some high ground.

Reno's charge. The Little Bighorn River can be seen at the upper right corner. Reno's charge crossed the river, rode through the timber on the opposite side and charged the lower end of the massive Indian village, where Sitting Bull and his Hunkpapa Sioux band were camped.

---

[*] This fact, of not seeing Custer, evidently frightened Reno excessively, and his story shows how unfit he was to take part in any operation requiring combined efforts. Had he gone on, as he was ordered, he would have found Custer supporting him in the most effective manner possible, by attacking the enemy in the rear.

THE LAST BATTLE

I accomplished this by mounting and charging the Indians between me and the bluffs, on the opposite side of the river. In this charge, First Lieutenant Donald McIntosh, Second Lieutenant Ben H. Hodgson, Seventh Cavalry, and A.A. Surg. J.M. De Wolf were killed. I succeeded in reaching the top of the bluff, with a loss of three officers and twenty-nine enlisted men killed, and seven men wounded.

Almost at the same time I reached the top, mounted men were seen to be coming towards us, and it proved to be Colonel Benteen's battalion, companies H, D and K; we joined forces, and in a short time, the pack train came up. As senior, my command was then companies A, B, D, G, H, K and M, about 380 men, and the following officers; Captains Benteen, Weir, French and McDougall; First Lieutenants Godfrey, Mathey and Gibson; Second Lieutenants Edgerly, Wallace, Varnum and Hare; A.A. Surg. Porter. First Lieutenant De Rudio was in the dismounted fight in the woods, but having some trouble with his horse, did not join the command in the charge out, and hiding himself in the woods, joined the command after nightfall of the 26th.

Still hearing nothing of Custer, and with this reinforcement, I moved down the river in the direction of the village, keeping on the bluffs. We had heard firing in that direction, and knew it could only be Custer. I moved to the summit of the highest bluff, but seeing and hearing nothing, sent Captain Weir with his company to open communication with the other command. He soon sent back word, by Lieutenant Hare, that he could go no farther, and that the Indians were getting around him; at this time he was keeping up a heavy fire from his skirmish line.

I at once turned everything back to the first position I had taken on the bluff, and which seemed to me the best. I dismounted the men, had the horses and mules of the pack train driven together in a depression, put the men on the crests of the hills making the depression, and had hardly done so when I was furiously attacked; this was about 6 p.m.; we held our ground with the loss of eighteen enlisted men killed and forty-six wounded until the attack ceased about 9 p.m.

A perusal of the first part of this account will show that whatever the length of the previous marches, the horses in Reno's column were not so fagged out but what they could take "a fast trot" for two miles to the ford, and then drive the Indians two and a half miles further. This makes nearly five miles at a fast pace in column or in ranks, with packed saddles and exhausted horses could not have done that.

The next point to be considered is that of dividing the regiment into three commands. Here, Custer is again blamed by Reno at the close of his report, as well as in a letter which the author lately received from him, totally unsolicited, and in which he tries to justify his conduct. In the report, he calls it "his unfortunate division of the regiment into three commands;" in the letter he says "The division of the regiment into three separate and independent commands he was responsible for, and must always be held so."

It will be here observed by those who have read this history through, that Custer's invariable method of attack on an enemy was the same which he adopted on the Big Horn, an attack on front and flank at all events, both flanks and front if possible, from all sides at once if he had time to execute it. In every battle in the Civil War when he was in an independent position, he always worked his command by fractions, so as to attack an enemy on several points at once, and always succeeded, because he was always heartily seconded by men who adored him.

He counted much on the moral effect to be produced on an enemy by combined attacks and a cross-fire, and always found his calculations correct. In fact, only one thing could vitiate them. This was cowardice or disobedience in the leader of any of the fractions which were to work simultaneously; and this misfortune Custer had never hitherto suffered. His subordinates were used to being put into tight places, where everything at first seemed hopeless, trusting implicitly to their leader's combinations to get them out.

Next, were these commands independent? We can hardly see that any more than regimental commanders are independent in a brigade. No general can do anything if his colonels will not support him, no colonel can fight a cavalry regiment under Upton's tactics if his battalion commanders slight, disobey, or even misunderstand his orders. Custer was a peculiar man. He fought in a peculiar way, and

THE LAST BATTLE

needed to have men under him used to his rapid energetic style, and who understood him. Did Reno understand him, and was he used to him? The official record says not. He had never served under Custer in the field, nor seen an Indian fight since the Civil War.

Let us see whether he supported Custer. He says he "charged down the valley, driving the Indians with great ease for about 21 miles." Then, he suddenly stops. Why? He says he "saw he was being drawn into some trap." An officer present with the expedition, who examined the ground, but whose name we prefer to withhold for the present, writes as follows:

He [Reno] marched until he came to the village, dismounted and occupied a timber bottom, which completely sheltered him and his horses. Girard (the interpreter) says, corroborated by Herndon, a scout, not many Indians in sight at this time, and firing at 500 and 600 yards. So long was the range that Charley Reynolds, another scout, said, "No use firing at this range; we will have a better chance by and by."

An officer present says that Reno mounted and dismounted, and then mounted again in hot haste and made what figures in his report as a "charge." He is the only person I have heard call it by that name. The surgeon present says there was only one man wounded before Reno abandoned the timber, and his loss began when he was making the charge, men and horses shot from behind.

Think of the charge they must have made across the Little Horn, and were checked in their flight by Benteen running into them. I say running into them, because it was mere accident. But where was Custer? He moved down to the lower end of the village from three to four miles. How long did Reno engage the Sioux village? Not over thirty minutes. What is the conclusion? That Reno was in and out of the fight before Custer was engaged. If further proof is wanting, it is found in the fact that Reno says in his report he heard Custer's firing from the top of the hill to which he had retreated.

Besides the letter from which this extract is taken, the author has received a letter from another officer present with Major Reno, in response to one asking several detailed and specific questions as to the fight in the bottom, the subsequent halt on the hill and the possibility of cooperation with Custer on the part of Reno and Benteen. This letter is especially valuable, because written with Major Reno's sanction and knowledge, and representing his side of the question as fully as could be desired.

In the expression of opinion on probabilities, this officer coincides with Reno, but his facts corroborate those stated by the other officer, whose opinions are exactly opposite. The facts furnished by Major Reno's friend are as follows:

At the time Reno ceased his forward movement, no man had been killed or wounded, but the cloud of dust denoted an immense number of Indians a short way off, and several times that number between us and that cloud, which was over the village, advancing in their peculiar manner and passing to our left and rear. The command was dismounted, the horses placed in a wood and the men deployed on foot across the plain.

The number of Indians continued to increase and to surround us. Colonel Reno ordered us to prepare to mount, which of course took everyone to the wood. We were mounted as though to charge, and in an instant afterward dismounted, and I supposed we were to fight it out there, when a fire opened from the rear through the brush.

We were ordered to mount. I was by the side of Colonel Reno, going out of the wood, and asked if we were to charge through. He said yes, and the command moved, Colonel Reno leading. I was here separated from the command for a time, and on turning towards it, saw it moving towards the ford that led to the hill. The column was fighting at close range from all sides.

I rejoined with difficulty and followed close along the rear to the ford, and here the confusion began. Previously the men had kept in column, using their pistols. When the ford was reached, it was each man for himself. In passing up the hill, beyond the river, horses and men were joined together and some of the hindmost suffered necessarily.

So far, as to the facts of the fight in the bottom, Reno's friend even exceeds the testimony of Reno's harshest critics as to his incapacity and

THE LAST BATTLE

utter demoralization during the attack of the Indians. We have italicized the places of most importance, as they tell the real story. "Advancing in their peculiar manner;" what does this mean in plain English? That the Indians were all at full speed, crouching over the necks of their fleet little ponies, flogging away with their short whips, and all the time yelling out their "Hi-yip-yip-yip-yip-hi-yah!" firing random bullets in the air.

These sights and sounds seem to have deprived Reno of all presence of mind. This he shows clearly by his repeated changes of policy, mounting and dismounting four times in as many minutes, and finally charging out in column, firing pistols, said column speedily becoming a huddled mass of frightened fugitives.

As to the halt on the hill, this officer differs materially with Reno and Benteen in point of time. He admits hearing shots down the stream, but no heavy firing, and states that it was an hour before Benteen arrived, and half an hour more before the packs came up, whereas Benteen and Reno both agree that they came together almost immediately after Reno's action.

In this matter, it is pretty clear that the recollection of Major Reno's friend must deceive him, as he places Weir's advance almost immediately after the junction, and it is clear from Reno's report that Weir must have started out after five o'clock, for it was only fifteen minutes from his return to the beginning of the siege on the hill (at 6 p.m.) on Reno's showing.

This officer, like Benteen, thinks that Custer had been destroyed by the time Benteen arrived on the hill, whereas Kill Eagle's evidence, subsequently mentioned, shows that this was not the case until sunset. He makes one curious assertion in giving his estimate of the Indian warriors, which he places at 3,500. It is this; in a village, standing, squaws, old men and boys are as effective as the ordinary recruit. Endorsing such opinions, is it any wonder Reno's battalion was beaten when they are ready to succumb to squaws, old men and boys?

Now let us return to Reno's report and try it by the test of time and place. He says that Adjutant Cook told him to attack at 12:30; that he advanced altogether 4 1/2 miles, crossed a river, halted ten minutes, had his fight, and came back, meeting Benteen. When did he meet Benteen? Look back to the report. He there says of Benteen, "I did not see him again until about 2:30 p.m." That gives two hours for his advance of 42 miles, fording the river twice, driving the enemy 2 miles, and the dismounted fight.

Our period of thirty minutes for the fight in the bottom seems to tally with Reno's report. It is clear that it was a short fight, and Reno confesses his over caution in the words "I saw that I was being drawn into some trap."

The next question is, how long did Reno remain on the hill with his seven companies, in safety and unassailed? Here again his report helps us. He met Benteen at 2:30 p.m.; he was "furiously attacked;" this was about 6 p.m. The time is thus complete. Three hours and a half of waiting on the hill listening to Custer's volleys; and not a step taken to renew the attack.

Another piece of evidence is found in the narrative of Herndon, the scout, who was with Reno. When the major "charged" out, Herndon's horse fell and threw him, then ran away, leaving him in the bush where he was joined by thirteen soldiers, three of them wounded and left behind. His story was published in all the papers, but I quote from the *Army and Navy Journal* of July 15, 1876, as a semi-official paper, and the one chosen by Reno for publication of his report. Statements in that paper on army subjects are apt to be more reliable than elsewhere, as being the only professional paper in the country, all army officers watch its columns and correct every mistake.

Herndon says of the "charge" which he saw from the timber, "Little resistance was offered, and it was a complete rout to the ford. I did not see the men at the ford, and do not know what took place, further than a good many were killed when the command left the timber." Herndon and his thirteen comrades remained in the timber unmolested for nearly three hours after Reno's flight, hearing firing down the river about two miles while nearly all the Indians in their front left and went down the valley.

Then the little party got out and went to Reno, meeting only a roving group of five Indians, whom they beat off, then crossed the river

THE LAST BATTLE

to Reno. In fifteen minutes after, the siege on the hill cointnenced.*

What should Reno have done? His only real safety was to hug the timber and defend himself, surrounded or not. Custer had done so on the Yellowstone in 1873, ninety against three hundred; Robbins had done even better in defending his wagons in 1867, forty against six hundred. In both these cases, there was no apparent hope of succor coming, and yet Robbins and Custer found the reward of their tenacity, help coming when it was least expected and victory following.

On Reno's own statement, he had one hundred and forty-five men, who in a circle, lining the edge of the wood, could have held it for hours. The Indians were fighting mounted, and could never have stormed the wood, and help was coming. Custer had promised to come. If Reno could get no further, he could at least defend himself, die in his tracks if need be, like a soldier.

Instead of this, he tried to escape by running away from an enemy who had the advantage in speed, and who could ride alongside of the demoralized cavalry, pouring in perfect streams of bullets from their Winchester rifles. By his inexperience in Indian warfare, Major Reno thus gave himself up, helpless to the favorite style of fighting of his enemies, wherein their superior horsemanship and superior arms had a full chance to assert themselves. Looking for personal security, he took the course least adapted to secure it.

The major indeed seems, from his hesitating movements in the fight, mounting and dismounting, to have been quite overwhelmed from the first by the novelty of his position, cowed by the fierce yells and rapid charge of the Indians, and finally to have completely lost his head. For all this, we wish it distinctly understood that we do not deem Reno so blamable, as for subsequent events. It was his first Indian fight, and many a man has done badly in his first fight who has afterwards succeeded.

---

* Lieutenant de Rudio, mentioned in Reno's report, was also left behind, and remained in the wood together with Mr. Girard, (the interpreter), Private O'Neill and a half breed scout. All these four got off, some that night, some next night. De Rudio's account shows a general careless haphazard state of things among the Indians, entirely opposed to any deliberate trap or generalship.

FREDERICK WHITTAKER

Reno's retreat. The Reno retreat began beyond the timber and continued across the river (pictured) to the heights of the east side, where Reno linked with Benteen. Custer's fight was in progress 2-3 miles up the river.

We should not have occasion to dissect his conduct in the affair, were it not for that unjust sentence in his official report in which he throws the blame of a disaster, brought on by his own incapacity, on the shoulders of his dead chief. The facts shown by himself in the same report, illustrated by eyewitnesses, pass a different verdict on his actions.

But now, where was Benteen all the time of this fight? His own statement, published in the New York Herald, gives his movements. It seems that when he was sent out on the left bank of the stream with orders to sweep everything, he found no Indians, and that he re-crossed the stream, and rejoined the main trail. He says, "the whole time occupied in this march was about an hour and a half," to the main trail, about three miles from the point where Reno came back over the ford.

From Major Reno's statement in the same paper, in reply to a letter of General Rosser, we learn that the division into battalions which sent Benteen off to the left was made at half past ten a.m. An hour and a half brings us to noon, and Benteen within three miles of the battlefield. At 12:30, Reno was ordered by Cook, the adjutant, to attack, and

THE LAST BATTLE

trotted off. At this time, Benteen says:

> About three miles from the point where Reno crossed the ford, I met a sergeant bringing orders to the commanding officer of the rear guard, Captain McDougall, Company B, to hurry up the pack trains. A mile further, I was met by my trumpeter, bringing a written order from Lieutenant Cook, the adjutant of the regiment, to this effect; "Benteen, come on; big village; be quick; bring packs." And a postscript saying, "Bring packs."
>
> A mile or a mile and a half further on, I first came in sight of the valley and Little Big Horn. About twelve or fifteen dismounted men were fighting on the plain with Indians, charging and recharging them. This body [the Indians] numbered about 900 at this time. Colonel Reno's mounted party were retiring across the river to the bluffs.
>
> I did not recognize until later what part of the command this was, but was clear that they had been beaten. I then marched my command in line to their succor. On reaching the bluff, I reported to Colonel Reno, and first learned that the command had been separated, and that Custer was not in that part of the field, and no one of Reno's command was able to inform me of the whereabouts of General Custer.

Reno's report states that he met Benteen at 2:30 p.m. It seems thus, that it took Benteen two hours and a half to cover a distance of three miles. What was he doing all this time? One incident, furnished us by an officer who was present, shows.

With Custer on this campaign was his brother, Boston Custer, who was the civilian forage master of the column. It seems that Boston Custer came to the rear during this period, went to the pack train in rear of Benteen, got a fresh horse, and passed Benteen on his way back, speaking to some of the officers. Benteen was then watering his horses. Where did he water?

He could only have done it at one place, where he crossed the river that is; three miles above the ford where he met Reno. Boston Custer had time to get back to the general and be killed in the fight. Benteen kept on at a slow pace. Did he obey the order "Benteen, come on; big village; be quick; bring packs?" What did this order direct from Custer mean; what could it mean, but that Custer wanted every man in his fight? He had sent in Reno, and he needed Benteen's battalion and the company guarding the packs with himself. That this was his intention is proved by Reno, in his letter to Rosser, by these words:

Trumpeter Martin of Company H, and who the last time of any living person heard and saw General Custer, and who brought the last order his Adjutant, Colonel Cook, ever penciled, says he left the general at the summit of the highest bluff on that side, and which overlooked the village and my first battlefield, and as he turned, General Custer raised his hat and gave a yell, saying they were asleep in their tepees and surprised, and to charge. Cook's order, [Custer's order, through his adjutant] sent to Benteen, and which I afterwards saw and read, said, "Big village; big thing* bring up the packs."

Thus Benteen and Reno both unite in ascribing the same plan to Custer; that of charging with all his force from two points. Both admit by their testimony that they disobeyed orders. Reno was ordered to "charge;" he obeyed by opening a hesitating skirmish and then running away. Benteen was ordered to "come on; be quick." He obeyed by advancing three miles in two hours, and joining Reno in a three hours halt.

The order to "come on" was from Custer, not Reno. Benteen made, on his own statement, no effort to obey it. He might have known where Custer was. Reno lets that much out. Benteen could have questioned Trumpeter Martin, who brought the order. No, he stopped, and let his chief perish.

Looking at all the testimony impartially from this distance of time, the conduct of Benteen is far worse than that of Reno. The major did his best in his fight, and it was nothing but want of experience in command and in Indian warfare that caused his defeat. Benteen's case

---

* There is a great difference between the words "big thing" and "be quick," and I am inclined to believe that the expression "big thing" is an afterthought of Major Reno's, as tending to confirm the notion which he inculcates all through his report and evidence, that Custer ran into a trap and was full of rash eagerness. Benteen got the order and he says it was "be quick," and that "bring packs" was repeated.

THE LAST BATTLE

is different. He was an old Indian fighter, a man of remarkable personal courage, as he proved in the subsequent battle, had often fought under Custer, and knew his business perfectly.

That he should have, as his own testimony confesses, deliberately disobeyed the peremptory order of Custer to "come on," argues either a desire to sacrifice Custer or an ignorance of which his past career renders him incapable.

Custer told him to "come on" and he "reported to Colonel Reno." Well then, it may be said, what did Benteen do afterwards? The rest of his testimony shows what he did. He says:

While the command was awaiting the arrival of the pack mules, a company was sent forward in the direction supposed to have been taken by Custer. After proceeding about a mile, they were attacked and driven back. During this time I heard no heavy firing, and there was nothing to indicate that a heavy fight was going on, and I believe that at this time Custer's immediate command had been annihilated.

The rest of the story you must get from Colonel Reno, as he took command and knows more than anyone else. It is curious in Benteen's evidence how his only estimate of time comes in before the battle. Afterwards, there is not a word about time. Who would think that this brief paragraph covered from 2:30 to 6 p.m.? If the one company was sent forward, why was it not supported by the whole outfit? Why was Custer left alone with his battalion while the other battalions were out of danger? The answer to the questions is given by Reno and Benteen in their evidence, almost unassisted by others. The reasons were Reno's incapacity and Benteen's disobedience.

We have now examined Reno and Benteen; it is time to go to Custer. Where was Custer during all this time, from 12:30 to 6 p.m.? Let Reno, Terry and the trail answer; assisted by Trumpeter Martin, the last white man who saw Custer alive; Curly, the Upsaroka scout, the last living being of his column; and Kill Eagle, an Indian chief who was in Sitting Bull's camp who has since come into Standing Rock agency to surrender, and has given evidence.

FREDERICK WHITTAKER

Reno, in his letter, says that Custer, after leaving him, "moved rapidly down the river to the ford, at which he attempted to cross." Curly, the Crow scout, calls it about four miles, and such the trail shows it, on account of the winding of the ravines. Reno's advance was about 2 1/2 miles in a diagonal line. Consequently, his skirmish line at the edge of the woods was not over two miles from the ford which Custer tried to cross. The Indian village was 3 1/2 miles long, and Custer struck it about the middle. When did he strike it?

We get this from the examination of Kill Eagle, published in the New York Herald of October 6th, 1876. The deposition was taken by Captain Johnston, First Infantry, acting Indian agent. We extract all that concerns the fight:

The troops struck our trail on the tributary, followed it down, swam their horses over the Greasy Grass Creek and struck the camp at the upper end where there was a clump of timber. On the southwest end of the camp, they dismounted and tied their horses in the timber and opened the fight. When the firing commenced, the Indians rushed to the scene of action.

I and my men were lower down, about the middle of the camp. The Indians drove the soldiers back out of the timber, and they crossed the Greasy Grass Creek below the mouth of the tributary, taking their position on the high hills, bare without any grass. There they were reinforced by the soldiers who had not crossed the creek (Colonel Benteen and Captain McDougall).

Before retreating across the creek, the soldiers (Colonel Reno) got into the camp and set fire to some of the lodges. On retreating across the creek to take position on the hill, they left their dead behind them. Another party appeared on top of a long hill moving toward the south.

After quitting the party on the knolls, word came that soldiers were on the left across the creek and there was great excitement in the camp, the Indian warriors rushing to the left to meet the troops. The Indians crossed the creek and then the firing commenced. It was very fast at times, then slower until it died away. (He describes the firing as follows: he claps the palms of his hands together very fast for several minutes, stopping suddenly, which denotes the sound of the firing when they (Custer) first began. After a few seconds elapse, he repeats the same as above and continues, but all the time lessens the quickness of the patting and sound until it gradually dies out.) The United States troops were all killed on the east side; none crossed the stream.

I got the following information from Sitting Bull himself: After crossing the creek with his warriors, he met his troops (Custer) about 600 yards east of the river. He drove the soldiers back up the hill. He then made a circuit to the right around the hill and drove off and captured most of the horses. The troops made a stand at the lower end of the hill, and there they were all killed. In going around the hill the Cheyenne Indians killed a warrior, thinking he was a scout who left this agency; but he was not, he was a hostile.

Q: How long did the fight last on the right?
A: It was about noon when they [Reno] struck the camp, and it only lasted a few minutes. The fight at the lower end (under Custer) was not finished till near sunset.
Q: Did all the warriors leave the right and go to the left?
A: They did; the whole thing left.
Q: When Reno was driven across the creek, where was Sitting Bull?
A: I don't know.
Q: What were the families doing when the fighting was going on the hill?
A: The women fled to the lower end of the camp and left everything.
Q: What did they do when they heard the firing on the left by Custer?
A: The upper end of the camp was at this time all deserted, and at the lower end of the camp they took down and packed the lodges ready for flight.
Q: I have heard that after the Custer fight, the Indians went back to the other end and attacked there again. How is it?
A: That is correct; the Indian soldiers went back and attacked the troops (Reno) on the hill again.
Q: Did you hear the firing?
A: Yes, I heard the firing while moving away.

It must be explained that Kill Eagle took the opportunity of the confusion to steal away from Sitting Bull's camp. His evidence shows that there was no design or trap on the part of the Indians, that they were really surprised that Custer's attack was a second surprise, and that they were in the wildest confusion; this too, when Reno's hesitating assault had convinced them that there was nothing to be feared from him.

Now for Custer's fight. The trail shows that he came down to the ford, and was there driven back, leaving dead men and horses. The rest of the description is thus given by an officer of the general staff who examined the ground, and refers to the map which we annex.

From this point, he was driven back to make successive stands on the higher ground. His line of retreat stretches from the river to the spot indicated on the map as that where he fell. On the line of retreat, Calhoun's company seems to have been thrown across it to check the Indians. At a distance of about three-quarters of a mile from the river, the whole of Calhoun's company lay dead, in an irregular line, Calhoun and Crittenden in place in the rear.

About a mile beyond this, on the ridge parallel to the stream, still following the line of retreat indicated on the map, Keogh's company was slaughtered in position, his right resting on the hill where Custer fell, and which seems to have been held by Yates' company.

On the most prominent point of this ridge, Custer made his last desperate stand. Here, with Captain Yates, Colonel Cook, Captain Custer, Lieutenant Riley and others, and thirty-two men of Yates' command, he went down, fighting heroically to the last against the tremendous odds which assailed them on all sides. It is believed by some that, finding the situation a desperate one, they killed their horses for a barricade.

From the point where Custer fell, the line of retreat again doubles back toward the river through a ravine, and along this line in the ravine, twenty-three bodies of Smith's company were found. Where this line terminates near the river are found the dead men and horses of Captain Custer's company commingled with Smith's, and the situation of the dead indicates that some desperate attempt was made to make a stand near the river or to gain the woods.

There we have the short and simple history of the fight which was going on within two miles of Benteen and Reno, for three long weary hours. It is dry and simple in its words, but what a wealth of heroism that simple story reveals. This little band was made of Custer's men,

THE LAST BATTLE

under Custer's best officers, Custer's little knot of chosen friends. All we can do is to fill out its details.

On this line, Calhoun's company was thrown across to check the Indians. The men lay dead in an irregalar line, Calhoun and Crittenden in place in rear. This is the order of the tactics, the officers watching and moving along their line, within a few feet. There they fell, every man in his place. They were ordered to stay and be killed, to save the day, and they obeyed orders. Who then was Calhoun that he was the first ordered to die?

Lieutenant James Calhoun of the Seventh Cavalry was the husband of Custer's only sister; he was Custer's dearest of all friends on earth; he was the bravest and gentlest of men, with the face and form of an Apollo, bright fair hair and dark eyes, a man whom a lady who knew him well describes as the "handsomest man I ever saw."

He was a gentleman's son, with all the education of a gentleman, and the most refined literary taste who yet had not hesitated to enlist as a private soldier in the regular army, and had actually worked his way up, refined and sensitive as he was, in the midst of all the discomforts, hardships and degradations which surrounded the life of a private soldier at the close of the war, to a well earned commission.

He married Maggie E. Custer in Monroe, Michigan, March 7th, 1872, and acted as Custer's post-adjutant during the time the regiment was divided. He was remarkably quiet and reserved in demeanor, but hid beneath his calm dignity of outward seeming the most lofty aspirations. Too young to have gained distinction in the Civil War, he hoped yet to gain it by unwavering fidelity to his duty. Duty was his one watchword, and by it he hoped to attain success. Such was the bright, brave youth whom Custer told to stay behind and be killed that so the day might be saved. Did Calhoun murmur - did he question the order? Why did Custer leave him there to die?

Not a murmur came from the one, and the other showed by this his first sacrifice that he placed the country above all his earthly loves. "The country needs; I give her a man who will do his duty to the death; I give them my first brother. I leave my best loved sister a widow, that so the day may be saved. Farewell."

Well did Calhoun redeem that trust. Every man in his place, no faltering, no going back, Calhoun's company kept on firing until the last cartridge was gone, and one by one dropped dead in his tracks under the fire of the swarms of Indians that kept dashing to and fro before them, firing volley after volley. Down they went, one after another, cheered up by this grand figure of DUTY, young Calhoun encouraging them to the last.

With him, young Crittenden of the Twelfth Infantry, a mere boy, only appointed the previous fall, and temporarily with the cavalry in his first and last battle, as cool as his chief, cheered and steadied by the calm princely dignity of courage that inspired that glorious stand. So they stood until the last man was down, and Crittenden was killed, and then came the friendly bullet that sent the soul of James Calhoun to an eternity of glory.

Let no man say such a life was thrown away. The spectacle of so much courage must have nerved the whole command to the heroic resistance it made. Calhoun's men would never have died where they did, in line, had Calhoun not been there to cheer them. They would have been found in scattered groups, fleeing or huddled together, not fallen in their ranks, every man in his place, to the very last. Calhoun, with his forty men, had done on an open field what Reno, with a hundred and forty, could not do defending a wood. He had died like a hero, and America will remember him, while she remembers heroes.

Let us go on with the tale. About a mile beyond, Keogh's company was slaughtered in position, his right resting on the hill where Custer fell. Custer had chosen the best ground to be found, and was determined to retreat no farther. By this time, he must have realized that Reno had been beaten, but he trusted at least to Benteen to come and help him. The Indians were all around him, but a vigorous attack by Benteen on their rear would beat them, could Custer only hold them long enough.

Keogh was an older soldier than any there. He had been an officer in the Papal service in the days when Garibaldi made war upon the Holy Father, and he had served on the staffs of Buford and Stoneman during the war. The sight of Calhoun's men, dying as they did, had

THE LAST BATTLE

nerved Keogh's men to the same pitch of sublime heroism. Every man realized that it was his last fight, and was resolved to die game. Down they went, slaughtered in position, man after man dropping in his place, the survivors contracting their line to close the gaps.

Myles Keogh served in the armies of the Papal States during a rebellion in Italy and was recruited into the Union Army during the Civil War. After the war, Keogh remained in the regular United States Army as commander of Company I in the 7th Cavalry Regiment under George Armstrong Custer, until he was killed along with Custer at the Battle of the Little Bighorn in 1876.

We read of such things in history, and call them exaggerations. The silent witness of those dead bodies of heroes in that mountain pass cannot lie. It tells plainer than words how they died, the Indians all around them, first pressing them from the river, then curling round Calhoun, now around Keogh, until the last stand on the hill by Custer with three companies.

How that fight went, Curly the Upsaroka scout tells us, he the only man who escaped alive, and who got away to the steamer Far West lying at the mouth of the river. His testimony was taken by the officers of Terry's staff, through an interpreter. It is plain and prosaic in its simplicity, but it tells the tale.

He says he went down with two other Crows and went into action with Custer. The General, he says, kept down the river on the north bank four miles, after Reno had crossed to the south side above. He thought Reno would drive down the valley, so that they could attack the village on two sides, he believing Reno would take it at the upper end, while he (Custer) would go in at the lower end.

Scene of Keogh fight. Keogh's bloody gauntlet and the guidon of his Company I were recovered three months after the Battle of the Little Bighorn at the Battle of Slim Buttes.

Custer had to go farther down the river and farther away from Reno than he wished on account of the steep bank along the north side; but at last he found a ford and dashed for it. The Indians met him and poured in a heavy fire from across the narrow river. Custer dismounted to fight on foot, but could not get his skirmishers over the stream. Meantime, hundreds of Indians, on foot and on ponies, poured over the river, which was only about three feet deep, and filled the ravine on each side of Custer's men.

Custer then fell back to some high ground behind him and seized the ravines in his immediate vicinity. The Indians completely surrounded Custer and poured in a terrible fire on all sides. They charged Custer on foot in vast numbers, but were again and again driven back. The fight began about 2 o'clock, and lasted, Curly says,

THE LAST BATTLE

almost until the sun went down over the hills.

The men fought desperately; and after the ammunition in their belts was exhausted went to their saddlebags, got more and continued the fight. He also says the big chief, (Custer) lived until nearly all his men had been killed or wounded, and went about encouraging his soldiers to fight on. Curly says when he saw Custer was hopelessly surrounded, he watched his opportunity, got a Sioux blanket, put it on, and worked up a ravine, and when the Sioux charged he got among them, and they did not know him from one of their own men. There were some mounted Sioux, and seeing one fall, Curly ran to him, mounted his pony and galloped down as if going towards the white men, but went up a ravine and got away.

Custer scout, Curly. At the Battle of the Little Bighorn, Curly separated from Custer's command and he watched the battle from a distance. His accounting of the battle is arguably the most accurate available, and was heavily relied upon at the subsequent army inquiry.

When questioned closely by one of the officers,* he mentioned one little fact about his escape that is pregnant with light on Custer's fate.

---

* This officer told the story personally to Mrs. Custer afterwards.

FREDERICK WHITTAKER

When he saw that the party with the General was to be overwhelmed, he went to the General and begged him to let him show him a way to escape. General Custer dropped his head on his breast in thought for a moment, in a way he had of doing. There was a lull in the fight after a charge, the encircling Indians gathering for a fresh attack.

In that moment, Custer looked at Curly, waved him away and rode back to the little group of men to die with them. How many thoughts must have crossed that noble soul in that brief moment. There was no hope of victory if he stayed; nothing but certain death.

With the scout, he was nearly certain to escape. His horse was a thoroughbred and his way sure. He might have balanced the value of a leader's life against those of his men, and sought his safety. Why did he go back to certain death? Because he felt that such a death as that which that little band of heroes was about to die, was worth the lives of all the general officers in the world.

Thanks to the story of the Crow scout, we know that he had the chance to live alone, and that he deliberately accepted death with his men as the worthier. He weighed, in that brief moment of reflection, all the consequences to America of the lesson of life and the lesson of heroic death, and he chose death. The Indian hovered around the fight, still watching; in the confusion he was not noticed, for taken for a Sioux. He had washed off his Upsaroka paint and let down his hair like a Sioux. Let us see what he saw.

Curly did not leave Custer until the battle was nearly over; and he describes it as desperate in the extreme. He is quite sure the Indians had more killed than Custer had white men with him.

There was the little group of men on the hill, the Indians hovering round them like hounds baying a lion, dashing up close and receding, the bullets flying like swarms of bees, the men in the little group dropping one by one. At last, the charm of Custer's charmed life was broken.

He got a shot in the left side and sat down, with his pistol in his hand. Another shot struck Custer and he fell over. The last officer killed was a man who rode a white horse (believed to be Lieut. Cook, Adjutant of the Seventh, as Lieuts. Cook and Calhoun were the only

THE LAST BATTLE

officers who rode white horses, and Lieut. Calhoun was found dead on the skirmish line, near the ford, and probably fell early in the action). At last they were all gone, every officer of the group. Custer fallen and Cook killed, the remaining men broke. Then, the scout fled too.

He says as he rode off he saw, when nearly a mile from the battlefield, a dozen or more soldiers in a ravine, fighting with Sioux all around them. He thinks all were killed, as they were outnumbered five to one, and apparently dismounted. These were no doubt part of the thirty-five missing men reported in the official dispatches of General Terry. Curly says he saw one cavalry soldier who had got away. He was well mounted, but shot through both hips, and Curly thinks he died of his wounds, starved to death in the badlands, or more likely his trail was followed and he killed by the Sioux.

Thirty-two men of Yates' company fell with their chief and the other officers on the hill, the rest of them, with Captain Custer's and Captain Smith's men, tried to cut their way to the river and all fell in the ravine, as marked on the map. Then, says Kill Eagle, the Indian wounded came streaming back into Sitting Bull's camp, saying; "We have killed them all; put up your lodges where they are."

From the account of some Indians who went across the line into British America to trade with the Manitoba Indians, we gain more particulars of the last fight than Curly could see. The scout was so utterly broken down with fear and agony of mind when he reached the steamer that he could not for a long time give a connected account, but his exultant enemies have filled the gap with their boasts.

From these, it appears that when only a few of the officers were left alive, the Indians made a hand to hand charge in which Custer fought like a tiger with his sabre when his last shot was gone, that he killed or wounded three Indians with the sabre, and that as he ran the last man through, Rain-in-the-Face kept his oath and shot Custer.

While this account disagrees with that of Curly, I am inclined to believe it for several reasons. Curly was some way off, the confusion was great, and the two brothers Custer were dressed alike and resembled each other closely in figure. I am inclined to believe that it was Colonel Tom Custer whom Curly saw fall as he described it. On the other hand, several Indians who were in the fight have told the same story about the sabre, and have given Big Rain or Rain-in-the-Face as the man who shot the General.

We know Custer to have been a man of great strength and activity, one who had used the sabre freely in the Civil War; and in his last struggle such a man would have been as able to kill three Indians, as was Shaw the famous English guardsman at Waterloo, who was seen to kill nine French cuirassiers with his sword before he was shot.

A last reason that is convincing is this; it is well known that the Indians did not mutilate Custer's body, it being the only one in that group entirely spared. The only reason for such a respect could have been a reverence for his valor. It is also well known that the Indians regard the striking of a living enemy with a hand weapon as the highest proof of valor possible, placing a very different estimate on shooting an enemy.

All the reports of the Indians who reached the British Possessions (Canada) were unanimous in saying that they dreaded the sabre more than anything, and this is easily understood when their superstition as to hand weapons is considered. It seems certain that they would never have reverenced Custer's body as they did had he not struck down their best men in that grim hand-to-hand fight wherein, among all the brave and strong, he was the bravest and best swordsman of all, the other officers having had but little teaching in the use of the sabre.

Be that as it may, it is known that he must have died under circumstances of peculiar heroism to win such respect, and that he was only killed by the bravest Indian of the whole northwest, a man whose unflinching fortitude had enabled him to hang in the air for four hours in the Sun Dance.

So fell Custer, the brave cavalier, the Christian soldier, surrounded by foes, but dying in harness amid the men he loved. Who fell with him?

There by his side lay his brother Tom, brave Colonel Custer, a double of the General, who had enlisted as a private soldier at sixteen, was an officer at nineteen, who wore what no other officer in the army could boast of, two medals, each for a flag taken from an enemy in

THE LAST BATTLE

battle. Brave and gentle, courteous and tender, a model officer of cavalry, God be with gallant Tom Custer until the last day. He died like all the Custers, with his face to the sky and his feet to the foe.

Not far off, close together, lay two more of the same family, poor young Boston Custer and little Autie Reed, Custer's nephew, son of that good gentle Christian woman who had saved Custer himself from a reckless career, whose prayers had helped to make him the Christian knight he became. Brave boys, nearly boys both, no sworn soldier of the state could die more nobly than they, who would not abandon a brother and kinsman. They could do little for him, but they could die with him.

Autie was fresh from school a few weeks before, and wild to see the plains with "Uncle Autie." To take him along, it was necessary to give him some official employment, and Custer, knowing that the rough hard life would make a man of the boy, had him and another schoolmate appointed herders, to help drive the great herd of cattle with the column. Rough as the lot was, the lad never complained. He was seeing wild life, which was all he wanted, and had obtained leave to go on this scout with the General.

Boston Custer's official position was that of forage master to the Seventh Cavalry, which he had held some time. He had been for years of a consumptive tendency, and his only chance for life was the open air existence of the plains. How far better for him the wild heroic death he died, under the blue sky, fighting like a true Custer, to the slow lingering failing end of a consumptive, which was his certain portion had he lived.

So closed the lives of the three Custers and their young nephew, fallen on that stricken field. It is time to turn to the comrades that fell with them. There is something remarkable in the power which Custer apparently possessed of attracting to his side and intimate companionship the noblest and best of the men with whom the army brought him in contact; and the facts of his death bring out this power in a conspicuous manner. It is clear that when he made the division of the regiment into battalions in the morning, Custer knew that heavy work was coming, and intended to take the heaviest work into his own hands, as he always did.

Into his own battalion, he seems to have gathered all of his own familiar friends, including his three brothers, as knowing he could depend on them to the death. His confidence was well repaid, and we may say today, without fear of contradiction, that Custer and Custer's friends were the flower of the Seventh Cavalry. The battalion that fell with Custer held them nearly all.

Boston Custer. Like his brothers George and Tom and nephew Autie, Boston was killed at Last Stand Hill. A marble marker commemorates the approximate place where his body was found.

There was the Adjutant, Brevet-Colonel Wm. W. Cook, the last officer left living, and whose final fall broke the hearts of his men and ended the battle. Cook was a model of manly beauty, in a very different style from that of Calhoun. Fully as tall (both were over six feet) and as powerfully framed, Cook was the image of a typical English Life Guardsman, with his highbred aristocratic features and long wavy black moustache and whiskers.

Like Keogh, he was a foreigner, having been born in Canada, whence he entered the American service in the Twenty-fourth New

THE LAST BATTLE

York Cavalry, rising to its colonelcy. The reader has seen his name frequently during Custer's life on the plains. One proud sentence will be his best epitaph. In choosing an officer to command the sharpshooters of the Seventh Cavalry in the Washita campaign, the question was not, says Custer, "to choose a good one, but among many good, to choose the best." He chose Cook. Let it be written; "Custer said he was his best officer."

By his side was gallant Yates, captain and brevet colonel, tender and true, a man like Calhoun, of old family and gentle blood, who had not hesitated to enter the ranks as a soldier in the war, had enlisted as a boy of sixteen and worked his way up to a captaincy in the Regular Army. Yates was a true, sterling fellow, a soldier to the backbone, with the crack company of the Seventh.

They used to call his troop the "band-box troop," so neat were they always, with an affectation of military dandyism. It was a tradition in that company that every man who died from it, "died with his boots on," the homely western phrase that tells such a story of unflinching courage. There fell brave old Yates, game to the last, with every man of the little band-box troop in his place round their leader, who fell with a smile on his lips. He and they had done their duty, and died like men. God will help the widow and fatherless.

The last company commander of all fell near Yates, Lieutenant and Brevet Captain Algernon E. Smith, one more member of that little circle of refined quiet gentlemen who had shared Custer's friendship at Fort Lincoln. Captain Smith was one of the bravest and most modest of men. One little incident will illustrate his character better than a volume of description. During the Civil War, while a captain of volunteers, Captain Smith was detailed on the staff of General Terry, at that desperate storming of Fort Fisher which gave Terry his star in the Regular Army. During the storming, a regiment faltered under the tremendous fire, having lost two color-bearers and all its field officers. Smith seized the colors, led on the regiment, sprang on the parapet, and was among the first in the works, where he fell severely wounded, his left shoulder smashed by a musket ball.

For this, he was brevetted major of volunteers. The wound healed, but in such a manner that he could never after lift his left arm above the shoulder. He was appointed to the Seventh Cavalry in 1867 and served in every campaign, in familiar intercourse with his brother officers; yet very few in the regiment even knew he had served in the Civil War, and none of the ladies would have known that he had been wounded, but for an accidental remark by his wife in 1875, from which it came out that he could not put on his uniform without assistance, on account of his crippled left arm.

Algernon Smith died as he had lived, a simple, modest soldier, in front of his men; while behind him lay the twenty-three bodies of the poor disheartened remnant that tried to cut their way out, when all was over and their beloved officer killed.

And now we come to the last of all, the youngest of that little band, Lieutenant William Van W. Reily. His portrait lies before me as these words are written, and it is hard to keep the cold composure of the impartial chronicler as I think of his peculiarly touching history. His father, a gallant officer of the U.S. Navy, went down in his ship in the Indian Ocean, and not a soul came back to tell the tale, before Reily was born. That father sailed away from a bride of a few months never to return, and his boy left the mother who idolized him, to meet a similar fate, amid foes as pitiless as the ocean waves.

Willie Reily fell next to Custer, and his fair young body was found lying at the feet of his commander. A good, noble-looking face he had, with a certain wistful musing expression, prophetic of his early fate. He had been ill for some time before the expedition started, and the surgeon wished to order him on some post duty, but he refused to stay and was eager to share the fate of his regiment, whatever it might be.

He had his dearest wish; he died like his brave father, at his post doing his duty. Let no man say such an end was sad; it was heroic. We must all die some time, but not all like him. To him and all such, America says, "God bless our brave dead."

I have told the facts of Custer's last battle as closely as the means at hand will permit the truth to be ascertained. Beginning my task with a strong impression, produced by the official reports that Custer had been rash and imprudent, and that the conduct of Reno and Benteen

THE LAST BATTLE

had been that of prudent and brave soldiers, a careful examination of all the accessible evidence has left me no other course than to tell the whole story to vindicate the reputation of a noble man from unjust aspersions. I leave the facts to the world to judge whether I am not right in these conclusions:

1. Had Reno fought as Custer fought, and had Benteen obeyed Custer's orders, the Battle of the Little Big Horn might have proved Custer's last and greatest Indian victory.

It may be objected to this conclusion that the numbers of the Indians were too great to admit it; but a careful examination of the conflicting statements leads to the belief that these numbers have been exaggerated by Reno in his report to cover his own conduct. He estimates the Indians at 3,500 "at the least," and the popular impression has since increased this estimate anywhere up to ten thousand.

Herndon, the scout, a much cooler person, puts them at only 2,000 or 2,500; and Benteen thinks they were only 900. One means of approximate computation is unwittingly offered by Reno. Near the close of his report, he mentions the whole village as defiling away before his eyes and says, "the length of the column was fully equal to that of a large division of the cavalry corps of the Army of the Potomac, as I have seen it on the march."

The divisions of the Cavalry Corps, at their strongest, were about 4,000 men; and they had no women and children with them. Making the very smallest allowance for led horses, pack horses, squaws and children, it is clear that at least one-half of the column must be taken away to leave the true number of warriors. This would give us 2,000, and if we allow 500 for the losses in fighting Reno and Custer, we come to Herndon's estimate.

These numbers were four to one of Custer's, but he had fought such odds before, at the Washita, and come out triumphant. The obstinacy of his attack shows that he expected to conquer. He could have run like Reno had he wished, and Reno says in the report he thought Custer had done so. It is clear, in the light of Custer's previous character, that he held on to the last, expecting to be supported, as he had a right to expect. It was only when he clearly saw he had been betrayed that he resolved to die game, as it was then too late to retreat.

2. Had not President Grant, moved by private revenge, displaced Custer from command of the Fort Lincoln column, Custer would be alive today and the Indian war settled.

The Dakota column would have been confided to the best Indian fighter of the army; Reno and Benteen would never have dreamed of disobeying their chief, had they not known he was out of favor at court; Custer and Gibbon would have cooperated, as men both familiar with Indian warfare; and cross-purposes would have been avoided.

The action of a Court of Inquiry, which will be able to call forth the testimony of officers whose names the author withholds from the public at present, will settle whether these conclusions are correct or not. Many witnesses have been deterred from speaking by fear of those superiors whom their evidence will impeach; and these witnesses will be able to swear in public to what they have hitherto only dared to say and write in private. The nation demands such a court to vindicate the name of a dead hero from the pitiless malignity, which first slew him and then pursued him beyond the grave.

CUSTER, THE SOLDIER

THE popular idea of Custer as a soldier is that of a brave, reckless, dashing trooper, always ready to charge any odds, without knowing or caring what was the strength of his enemy, and trusting to luck to get out of his scrapes. In the public mind, he has always been associated, even by his admirers, with Murat and Prince Rupert as a type of mere impetuosity.

A great deal of this impression among civilians has been the effect, partly of the frequency of his dashing personal exploits, but very largely also to a combination of the sneers of professional soldiers envious of his fame, and of the anxiety of the war correspondents to write home a "picturesque" letter. During the Civil War, the so called war correspondents seldom knew much of military life, and had rarely been soldiers before that war. As a consequence, they wrote home a great many ridiculous stories about Custer, the product of camp gossip. He was accused of putting his hair up in papers, of wearing stays, using curling tongs, etc., and the ingenious correspondent of one New York paper set the seal on the whole by a stilted account of the runaway of Don Juan and Custer at the last parade. He thus became, to a large part of the public, a perfectly ideal personage, as unlike the real Custer as Tom Moore's poetry was unlike the real quiet, domestic Tom Moore.

The real Custer was as far from being the reckless harum-scarum cavalier of public fancy as possible. He was a remarkably quiet, thoughtful man when any work was on hand, one who never became flurried and excited in the hottest battle and who, on a campaign, was a model of wary watchfulness; a man who was never surprised during his whole career, and who was equal to any emergency of whatever kind.

Three times during Custer's service as a brigade commander did he find himself surrounded by enemies and compelled to cut his way

CUSTER, THE SOLDIER

through; and on none of those three occasions could the slightest blame attach to him for the dilemma. The first time was at Brandy Station; and there the fault was that of Meade or Pleasonton, who had divided their cavalry forces so that when the separate units came together, the enemy was between them.

The second time was at Buckland's Mills, where the disaster was due entirely to Kilpatrick's headlong rashness, after he had been warned of his danger by the wary Custer. The third time was at Trevillian Station, in 1864. There, his danger was due to the accidental direction of a force of the enemy, driven in by Custer's friends from another direction. It was, in fact, Brandy Station reversed.

As a division commander, having no one else to trouble him, being responsible for his own actions, he was never in the slightest difficulty, and this is true of his whole after career. Put Custer in chief command and he never made a mistake; put him under anyone else except Sheridan - as perfect a soldier as himself - and he was always suffering for the blunders, mistakes, or faintheartedness of others, either his superiors or coadjutors.

The consequence was to both Custer and Sheridan, the envy and detraction of all those who could not understand their peculiar quality of instant and correct decision under fire, as to the right thing to do. This faculty is given to very few indeed. In the Army of the Potomac,

Custer and Sheridan were its only possessors, in the highest degree, the degree possessed only by such men as Napoleon, Cromwell, Gustavus, Adolphus, Caesar and Hannibal. It made them both supreme as "battle commanders," whatever their merits as strategists. Their detractors, who could not understand this faculty, tried to belittle it by setting down Sheridan as a "mere trooper," Custer as a reckless rider and fighter, a harum-scarum light dragoon.

In Custer's case, the prejudices of those who did not know him invariably preceded his entrance on any new command, as invariably to be replaced by a feeling akin to adoration, from all who served under him, if they possessed any nobility and generosity of character. To dislike him was the infallible result either of want of personal knowledge, which was innocent, or of some meanness of character, with which Custer's impulsive generosity clashed. Of his first appearance in the Third Cavalry Division, General (then colonel) A.B. Nettleton, commander of the "Fighting Second Ohio," thus speaks:

I had never seen General Custer, prior to his promotion to the command of our division, but he was well known to us by repute. Some of us were at first disposed to regard him as an adventurer, a disposition which a sight of his peculiar dress and long locks tended to confirm. One engagement with the enemy under Custer's leadership dissipated all these impressions, and gave our new commander his proper place. Once under fire, we found that a master hand was at the helm; that beneath the golden curls and broad-brimmed hat was a cool brain and a level head.

One thing that characterized Custer was this; having measured as accurately as possible the strength and morale of his enemy, and having made his own disposition of troops carefully and personally, he went into every fight with complete confidence in the ability of his division to do the work marked out for it. Custer's conduct in battle was characteristic. He never ordered his men to go where he would not lead, and he never led where he did not expect his men to follow. He probably shared with the private soldier the danger of the skirmish line oftener than any officer of his rank, not from wantonness of courage,

CUSTER, THE SOLDIER

but with a well-defined purpose on each occasion. He knew that the moral effect of his personal presence at a critical moment was equal to a reinforcement of troops, when a reinforcement could not be found.

A large part of Custer's success was due to the fact that he was a good pursuer. Unlike many equally brave and skilful officers, he was rarely content to hold a position or drive his enemy; he always gathered the fruit, as well as shook the tree of battle. He regarded his real work as only beginning when the enemy was broken and flying.

Although his special forte was the command of cavalry in the field, he was not deficient in camp. He was a good disciplinarian, without being a martinet; particularly thorough in maintaining an effective picket line or outpost service on which depends the safety of an army in quarters. By unexpected visits to the outposts by day and night, he personally tested the faithfulness and alertness of officers and men on picket duty.

On more than one occasion, I have known him take the trouble to write a letter of commendation to the commander of the regiment on the picket line, praising the manner in which the duty was performed. There was nothing of the military scold in his nature. By timely praise, oftener than by harsh criticism, he stimulated his subordinates to fidelity, watchfulness and gallantry.

General Nettleton is quite competent to give an opinion of Custer, for he served under him with the most distinguished gallantry; and his regiment, the Second Ohio Cavalry, won this official praise from their division commander in a letter to Governor Brough of Ohio "I assure your Excellency that in my entire division of twelve regiments, from various States, there is not one on which I rely more implicitly than on the gallant Second. I have known it repeatedly to hold its place against terrible odds, when almost any other regiment would have felt warranted in retiring."

Of Nettleton himself he says; "I regard him as one of the most valuable officers in the service, and do not know his superior in the army, as regards the qualities needed in a good cavalry commander."

We quote these words to show that in Nettleton a perfectly

competent critic is found, as well as one possessing personal knowledge of Custer. His testimony is merely the echo of that of every officer of capacity who ever served under that general.

Some may think that in all this, too much is claimed for our hero; but this verdict can only be given by those who have not examined the evidence on which the estimate is founded. As an army commander like Sheridan, as a corps commander, there are no means of estimating his powers, for he never had an opportunity of exhibiting them. As a cavalry officer, pure and simple, the most carping criticism can find no flaw in Custer's career, from the day he led the Michigan Brigade into the Battle of Gettysburg to that in which he fell, fighting like a lion bayed by the hunters, deserted by his supporting detachments. He was, in fact, as nearly perfect as a cavalry commander can be.

Viewed from the standpoint of Seydlitz and the Great Frederick, and that at present prevailing in Europe, the actions of Custer are faultless as far as he himself is concerned. The only wrong feature pervading them is one which was the fault of the system in which American cavalry has always been trained, and which even Custer could not remedy entirely, though he did his utmost towards checking it. This was the undue dependence of the men and officers on their firearms, and their reluctance to use the sabre.

This fault Custer constantly strove against, and during his valley campaigns succeeded in forcing his men by personal example into charging with the sabre, with invariable success whenever it was employed. We must however, for the truth's sake, undeceive the civilian reader who imagines that the sabre was the exclusive weapon used in any of the so called "sabre charges," either of Custer's or any other cavalry command during the war. A rattling irregular fusillade of pistol and carbine shots almost invariably accompanied the charge and as a rule, the men were very poor swordsmen, solely from want of fencing practice.

Since the war, the case has been still worse, the use of the sabre having been practically abolished; and the diminished power of Custer, reduced as he was from a general to a field officer, added to the fact that he found the sense of his brother officers generally against him on this point, prevented his giving the queen of cavalry weapons that attention which it deserves.

But as a cavalry leader, Custer displayed more genius and natural talent than any officer in the American army; genius, moreover of a kind that would have raised him to eminence in any service. Had Custer, with the same natural talent, served in the Franco-Prussian War as an officer of uhlans, there is little or no doubt that he would have risen to higher command than he attained in our own service. The well known personal supervision of Von Moltke, which has made the Prussian army what it is by promotions for merit alone, would never have passed by Custer, with his wonderful faculty of seizing the moment and its fleeting opportunity.

The best cavalry leader America has ever produced is the only truthful verdict that experience can pass on him; a great cavalry leader for any time or country, history will finally pronounce him; worthy to stand beside Hannibal's "thunderbolt" Mago; Saladin, the leader of those "hurricanes of horse" that swept the Crusaders from Palestine; Cromwell, Seydlitz or Zieten; a perfect general of horse.

CUSTER, THE INDIAN FIGHTER

IF we devote a separate chapter to the consideration of Custer as an Indian campaigner, it is not because we deem that any different grade of talent is required for fighting Indians other than that which obtains in a contest with a civilized foe, but rather as a concession to the popular idea that such is the case. This idea is partly due to the natural propensity of "old Indian fighters" to magnify their own office, but also to the equally common tendency of mankind in general to ignore talent and special genius as a possible factor of success in any pursuit, making experience and age the only tests of competency.

A comparison of results obtained in both kinds of warfare will give strong reason to believe that Indian fighting, the same as Arab fighting in Algeria, is by no means as difficult to master as the art of fighting a properly equipped, civilized foe. Many an officer who has attained considerable success as an Indian fighter has turned out but a poor general in campaign against a regular enemy, whereas generals of remarkable talent in civilized warfare - real generals, not mere "scientific soldiers," so miscalled - have never failed to give a good account of a barbarian foe, be it Indian, Arab, African or Tartar.

The natural tendency above referred to, has however, produced in the American army a very exaggerated estimate of the necessity of long experience in Indian fighting to produce a perfect officer, and a fashion of depreciating every officer, no matter what his talent elsewhere, if his Indian experience be brief. When Custer first went on the plains, he found this feeling in full force, and was constantly confronted with the express or implied statement that Indian fighting was so totally different from other warfare that his previous experience was valueless, and that he would have to sit humbly and learn at the feet of this or that officer,

CUSTER, THE INDIAN FIGHTER

because the latter was "an old Indian fighter."

Very early in his Indian career however, Custer seems to have discovered that few army officers were able to supply him with much valuable information on the Indian subject; and his keen perception showed him at the same time who could do it. He saw that the officers, especially the oldest of them, were too slow for him, just as they had been during the war, and he also saw that the rough and ready scouts who lived in the same style as the Indians would be his best masters.

From them, he seems from the first to have taken lessons, readily and humbly enough, as he tells us in his recorded experiences on the plains. His first master was Comstock, the scout who rode with him in his first campaign against Pawnee Killer; and Pawnee Killer himself, with Romeo and California Joe, gave him excellent lessons.

When we consider that Custer made his first appearance on the plains the beginning of April, 1867, perfectly green as the old Indian fighters thought, that the whole of his experience was limited to the months of April, May, June and a few days of July in that year, that front that time until September, 1868, he was under arrest and suspended from field service, it will appear that he must have used his time well to have called forth from his superior officers the request that

FREDERICK WHITTAKER

met him in Monroe in 1868.

His Indian fighting experience was then limited to less than four months; there was a whole army to choose from; the officers of the Seventh Cavalry had all been out on the plains a whole year; General Sully, an Indian fighter then possessing a high reputation, was in command; yet, such was the confidence in Custer's ability, produced by his record of three months and a half, that Sherman,
Sheridan, Sully and all the officers of the regiment, old and new, joined in a request to have Custer back for the command of the field expedition.

He came, and what was the result? In six months, he had pacified the whole of the southwestern tribes, first by a battle, then by diplomacy, exhibiting throughout the campaign a combination of boldness and dexterity, of tact and shrewdness that was crowned with complete success, and that stamped him as the best Indian fighter in the service. Measured by his deeds and comparing them with those of any Indian fighter in the service, no matter what his reputation, this claim is by no means extravagant.

The exploits of those officers who fought Indians before the Civil War were not attended with the same difficulties which surrounded Custer and the Indian fighters of the present day. In those days, the troops were better armed than the Indians; now the Indians are better armed than the troops; then there was no Indian Department to feed the Indians and supply them with patent ammunition; now this business has become recognized as the regular employment of an Indian agent.

In the old times, the army was left alone to manage the Indians, to fight them if necessary, and Indian wars were easily settled on the plains; now the army officer has to fight the Indians first and the Indian Department afterwards. All these things made Custer's task a much harder one than those of the officers who engaged in an occasional Indian skirmish before the Civil War.

With the services of any recent Indian campaigner, no matter who or what he may be, Custer's record need fear no comparison. The results of his campaign of 1868-69, when he was in full and unrestricted command, were superior to those gained by any other officer in the service since 1866, and nothing but prejudice can gainsay the undoubted facts.

What was it then, that gave Custer his remarkable success as an Indian fighter, after such a brief experience, and what were the qualities which, so early in his career, gained him the implicit confidence not of Sheridan, which was his already but of Sherman, who had only met him a few times, of Sully, who had not seen him at all in service? It was his remarkable tact, shrewdness, and quickness to learn, the ardor with which he applied himself to the study of the Indian character, and the safety which had accompanied his most apparently audacious operations against the enemy in his three months' service.

Besides this, when under arrest and suspension, Custer had not been idle. He had made up his mind to master the problem of Indian character, and he devoted his enforced leisure to the task. Where another man would have been brooding, Custer was working, and he devoted his winter of disgrace at Fort Leavenworth - to what, think you? To learning the Indian sign language; which passed current among all the tribes, and serves as a medium of communication between Indians speaking every variety of language. This he studied to such good purpose, then and after, that he was able to converse, without an interpreter, with Indians of any tribe as far as the sign language carries any of them.

That old Indian fighters in those days appreciated his knowledge of Indian character is evinced by the words of General Sturgis, himself an old *ante-bellum* Indian fighter of considerable reputation, which words we have quoted elsewhere. Custer, quick to learn Indian tactics, was equally quick to learn the habits and natures, peaceful and warlike, of the Indians themselves. An amusing anecdote, whose authenticity is vouched for, will show the tact and shrewdness with which he played on every point in Indian character.

While in camp on the Black Hills Expedition in 1873, being then in the zenith of his reputation as an Indian fighter, Custer retained a great many of his Indian scouts near headquarters, under command of Bloody Knife. One day, as Custer was writing in his tent, one of these Indian scouts came in, a good deal the worse for liquor, and began with some maundering complaint of something that had offended him. Custer looked up, saw the man was drunk and ordered him out of the tent. Like all Indians in liquor, this one was insolent, and squaring himself before the general, became louder in his complaints and boasts of his own importance.

Without another word, Custer sprang up with the peculiar catlike agility he possessed, and quick as lightning struck the Indian two blows, in regular professional style, sending him to grass with an ugly lump under the eye and a nose badly punished. The Indian was knocked half out of the tent door, and as Custer made a step towards him as if to renew the assault, the red man picked himself up with surprising humility and ran like a deer to the scouts' quarters, howling all the way.

Custer returned to his writing as if nothing had happened. Very few men possessed the physique to have punished a powerful Indian so quickly, but Custer's knuckles were very bony, and from a lad he had been the strongest of his playmates. So far, he had done nothing but what any powerful man of quick decision would have done. It is the sequel of the story which shows his tact.

In a few minutes after, there was a great commotion in the Indian quarters, and the voices of the warriors could be heard all together in the high monotonous scream of the excited Indian, trying to lash himself and fellows to fury. It brought out the guard in some alarm, and the other soldiers began to tumble out of their tents to see the fun. Custer, of course, heard the disturbance and knew the cause, but he continued tranquilly writing as if deafness had suddenly afflicted him.

The noise increased, and he could hear the stern tones of the officer of the day in the wrangle, but even that dreaded official's authority did not appear to cow the Indians, for their fierce chattering grew shriller every moment. He heard in the hubbub the English words; "Guard house, guard house, big chief, guard house!" and a smile gathered over his face as he went on writing.

Presently a sudden hush came on the tumult. He heard steps approaching, and a knock on the tent door, followed by the entrance of the officer of the day, who wore a countenance of some anxiety.

It appeared from the officer's report that the Indians were insisting

CUSTER, THE INDIAN FIGHTER

that the same measure of justice should be meted to Custer as to other offenders. They had been accustomed to see every man found fighting in camp put in the guard house. The big chief had hurt their comrade badly; therefore the big chief ought to go to the guard house. While we cannot help smiling at the idea, it must be admitted that the rude sense of justice of the Indians was perfectly correct. The officer of the day further stated that he had pacified them by coming to see the big chief, but that they were very firm in their demands.

It may be imagined by some that there was no great difficulty in this case, but the contrary is the fact. If Custer had allowed the first Indian to be drunk and insolent, he would have lost control over his capricious allies, who would have despised him. If he now refused them justice, they all would leave him, probably to join the hostiles. Custer's decision was instantly taken, though not in words.

As soon as the officer had concluded his report, the General walked out of the tent and found his Indian allies in a group, quite silent now, watching the tent. "Tell the chief to come here," said Custer to the officer of the day. In a few moments, Bloody Knife approached in a very lordly manner. As he left his comrades, he waved them back with the grand air of a "big Injun" full of his own importance.

Custer approached the chief several steps to meet him, took off his hat, and swept a low and ceremonious salute. Then shaking Bloody Knife's hand cordially, he and the Indian mutually ejaculated "How, how!" Still retaining the chief's hand, he led him into his own tent and seated him in his own chair, an honor that gratified Bloody Knife still more.

Then the general took up an Indian pipe, filled it, lighted it, took a few whiffs and handed it to the chief, the two sitting opposite to each other in solemn silence all the while. By this time, the Indian was swelling with importance, and evidently imagined that the white chief was about to apologize and offer presents to pay for the wrong he had done. He behaved however, with the strictest decorum as an Indian generally does at a council.

After several mutual whiffs, Custer gravely asked what had procured him the honor of this visit. Thus exhorted, Bloody Knife, in broken English, uttered his complaint with ceremonious gravity. "Big chief hurt Injun heap bad - near kill um - cut face open - Injun much heap mad - say big chief must go guard house." And the chief grunted and relapsed into silence, smoking vigorously.

"Is your man badly hurt?" asked Custer, after the usual pause of ceremony. "Much heap bad - face all blood - maybe die - Injuns put um in bed - tink he die - say big chief must go guard house." And he grunted a second time, feeling that he had made a point; then ceremoniously handed the pipe to Custer. The fact probably was, he was waiting to be bribed. After a minute's pause, Custer spoke very gravely. "Listen. I am the big chief here. All these soldiers are under me, and all their chiefs too. You see that?"

The chief bowed gravely, and grunted. "You are the chief of the scouts. All the Indians are under you, because you are a great warrior. You see?" A more decided grunt of approbation and gratified vanity. "Whenever any of my soldiers has a complaint, he goes to his chief, and his chief comes to me. You see?" A sort of doubtful grunt. The Indian began to see that something else was coming.

"No one ever enters this tent but chiefs and great warriors. Them, I am always glad to see. You, I am glad to see. You are a chief, and a great warrior. You see?" The grunt this time was one of unmixed satisfaction. "When a man comes into my tent without first going to his chief," pursued Custer slowly, watching his auditor closely, "he dishonors his chief - you see? Makes a squaw of his chief - you see? Throws dirt in his chief's face - you see? Says 'You are no chief - you are a squaw -a dog.' "Do you see?"

In his turn, Custer resumed the puffing of his pipe, which he had interrupted to speak. For fully a minute, there was a dead silence. Then the chief rose, and Custer laid aside the pipe and followed suit. Not being a smoker, he was only too glad to do it. The chief shook his hand ceremoniously.

"How, How!" said he. Then, suddenly dropping his dignity, he shot out of the tent toward the Indian quarters, and a moment later, Custer heard his voice raised in a perfect frenzy of rage, yelling out an impassioned appeal to his followers to avenge him on the man who had made a squaw of such great a chief as Bloody Knife, the Arickaree.

A few moments later, all the Indians rushed to the quarters, where the poor sufferer was in bed, nursed by his friends, pulled him out, and commenced lashing him with their heavy buffalo whips, the chief being the heaviest in his blows. The innate sense of the necessity of subordination in military society was aroused. Even the wild savage could see the force of Custer's lucid argument, though delivered in a strange language, and with some words only half understood.[*]

Custer had no more trouble with his Indian scouts, and he showed the same knowledge of Indian character throughout his career. The story of Rain-in-the-Face partly illustrates it, but there are enough anecdotes of the kind to fill a book much larger than this, which cannot now be told. In the southwest and northwest alike, when the outside world deemed that Custer was merely; stagnating in ordinary army style, he was carrying on his study of Indian character, and acquiring ascendency and reputation among the tribes.

In his visits to New York, he took occasion to learn a good many feats of conjuring, sleight-of-hand, etc., which he used in various adroit ways to increase this ascendency; so that, at the time of his death, he had the reputation among the Indians of being a great magician or "medicine man," which increased the awe with which they regarded him.

That, and his super-human courage, which Indians of all men are the first to respect, procured him the last honor which they could pay to his mortal remains. They dared to kill him from afar with bullets - that was merely the crooking of a finger - but something in that dead body struck even Rain-in-the-Face with a sense of awe, and the bravest Sioux of the northwest did not dare to lift his hand to strike dead Custer.

Will any be found to take his place and do as well as he has done? It is hard to say. So far, the American army has produced but one Custer, and it is doubtful whether the peculiar combination of qualities which made him what he was will ever be duplicated. If one be found

---

[*] A partial version of this anecdote first appeared in the Chicago *InterOcean*, and subsequent investigation by the author has resulted in the above facts. Poor Bloody Knife fell with Custer at the Little Horn.

to lead men to success as he has done, he must be looked for among the younger officers of the army, the men whose careers are yet to culminate, who show symptoms of life amid the too general stagnation of frontier service.

Two at least of this class, the hope of the army of the future have developed talents of the same nature as those of Custer, and which may in time equal them in degree. To them, the country looks to give it a successor to Custer the Indian fighter, in quickness of resolution, impetuosity of attack, sagacity of plan. One of them, since the greater part of these pages were written, has gained the only success of a disastrous campaign, by meeting Sitting Bull on open ground and aided by artillery, repulsing his attack with severe loss; the other, by his now nearly forgotten raid over the Mexican border, showed the possession of just such boldness and enterprise as were conspicuous in Custer; and to Miles and Mackenzie, the army looks to give them another successful Indian fighter, a man not afraid of the Indians, but fighting as if he expected a victory.

But, as we have before this insisted on, the greatest reform necessary in the present regular cavalry, to make it uniformly effective against Indians, is in the instruction of the rank and file, and especially in the cultivation of that neglected weapon, the sabre, to raise the morale of the force. As it is, it takes more than ordinary bravery and conduct in any officer to achieve success with the half-trained recruits that form the main body of the frontier army; and the disuse of the sabre has turned the once brave American dragoon into a timid skirmisher who shrinks from the shock of the leveled lance, and seeks safety in infantry tactics.

CUSTER, THE MAN

IF the readers of this book have not by this time formed some idea of the character of Custer as a man, the labors of the author have been spent in vain, and it would be useless to write further. Still, inasmuch as the beautiful family and social life of our hero has not been fully treated of elsewhere, we have judged it best to say here a few words on the subject to complete the picture.

Of General Custer's personal appearance at various times of his life, the portraits and illustrations of this book will give a good idea. They were, most of them, made by an artist who knew Custer well when he was a young officer, and whose war experience has enabled him to give truthful pictures. The face and figure of our hero varied much at different times of his life, his face as a cadet being smooth and beardless, and by no means as handsome as it afterwards became.

In the portrait on wood, with the broad hat and open collar, we have Custer at Appomattox, haggard and gaunt after his tremendous labors; in the steel portrait which heads the book, we have him in later life, with the strong impress of mature thought, and an earnestness of expression that tells of his single-minded nobility of purpose. It gives very truly his habitual expression during the long periods of deep musing into which he was wont to fall, when he would sit for hours totally silent.

In society, apart from these occasional moody intervals, he was exceedingly light-hearted, with a boyish tendency to frolic and playfulness that seemed common to all the Custer boys. In Fort Lincoln, where he was thrown almost alone during the winter into a very small circle of intimate friends, he and his brothers, Tom and Boston, were the life of the place, while the refining influence of the society of the few ladies that clustered round Mrs. Custer made the circle extremely delightful.

No man valued more highly than Custer the influence of women to ameliorate men, and no man had more reason. The little group of ladies, Mrs. Custer, Mrs. Calhoun, Mrs. Yates, Mrs. Smith and the one or two young ladies from Monroe who were always visiting Mrs. Custer, made the home circle at the fort a perfect haven of rest to the officers fortunate enough to possess Custer's friendship.

The general was always very fond of children. One of his Eastern friends, whom he frequently visited, tells how he would often leave a circle of fashionable people, with whom he was very shy and reserved, to sit in a corner with two children who begged him for Indian stories. Although very reticent to others about his deeds, he always unbent to these children, and so won their hearts that today they always protest that General Custer was the kindest and nicest gentleman that ever visited their father's house. I set a high value on this fact. Children, especially girls, are unerring readers of character, and there must have been something singularly pure and frank in Custer's character to have attracted the love of these children.

Agnus Bates and Custer play the roles of a Sioux Chief and his bride at a Fort Lincoln play, sometime in 1874.

FREDERICK WHITTAKER

Another point in Custer was his perfect nobility of forgiveness. We have seen how his court-martial in 1867 was caused by an officer, brave and capable enough, but who hated him. Only a year later, this same officer, then out of the service, applied to Custer for a position as trader or sutler in an expedition commanded by him, expressing his sorrow for the past. Custer at once gave him the place, which was in his gift. Yet his critics have called him "a good friend and a bitter enemy."

Never was a falser saying. The man seemed incapable of private malice. Even under the unjust persecution of Grant, he was cheerful, and always said to those who spoke bitterly of the President, "Never mind, it will all come right at last. The President is mistaken; but it will all come right at last if I do my duty." He was never known to return an injury.

In his devotion to duty and honesty, to fair dealing and justice, he was almost fanatical. There indeed he was stern, and his indignation at the robbery and rapacity of the Indian Ring and the post traders' ring was frequent and outspoken. It caused all his subsequent trouble. He saw the poor agency Indians robbed while the agents grew rich, and his anger, which could not find vent through official channels, was heard in the press, and given to the world in his *My Life on the Plains*. Can we blame him for that?

Custer knew, as every officer in the army knows, that the Indian Department is a perfect mine of wealth to the men of politics, and that were it not for the supplies of arms furnished to the Indians by that department, there would be no Indian wars. He and his men were finally shot to death with bullets loaded into Winchester metallic ammunition at New Haven and Bridgeport, Connecticut, and furnished to the Indians by the Indian Bureau.

He knew that in every fight he had with Indians, they confronted him with weapons sold them by traders under the protection of the agencies. He knew that every attempt by honest men in Congress to abolish this grand corruption mine had been defeated by the vote of a purchased majority. He knew that the reason for this vote was the enormous amount of power given by the use of such a huge corruption

CUSTER, THE MAN

fund for political purposes.

He knew that the very arms sold to hostile Indians were made a means of cheating them, so that a single Winchester rifle, worth thirty dollars, sold for two hundred buffalo robes at Fort Peck. He saw all these soulless cheats around him bartering away the lives of the frontier settlers by the hundred for their gain, and he groaned in spirit, and spoke out again and again in fiery anger against such monstrous wrongs. Can we blame him?

His one fault, to the sense of cool selfish men of the world, was his outspoken frankness, his anger at wrong, his want of concealment. Make the most of that, and it is a noble fault. It brought him his death. Truth and sincerity, honor and bravery, tenderness and sympathy, unassuming piety and temperance, were the mainspring of Custer, the man. As a soldier there is no spot on his armor, as a man no taint on his honor.

We have followed him through all his life, and passed in review boy, cadet, lieutenant, captain, general and Indian fighter, without finding one deed to bring shame on soldier or man. People of the land he loved; my task is ended. Would it had been committed to worthier hands. Four simple lines, written by an unknown poet, form his best epitaph.

> Who early thus upon the field of glory
> Like thee doth fall and die, needs for his fame
> Naught but the simple telling of his story,
> The naming of his name.

PERSONAL RECOLLECTIONS OF GENERAL CUSTER BY LAWRENCE BARRETT, THE GREAT TRAGEDIAN

CONTRIBUTED AT THE JOINT REQUEST OF MRS. CUSTER, THE AUTHOR, AND THE PUBLISHERS

GEORGE ARMSTRONG CUSTER was of that great industrial class from which so many of our original men are springing. With no marked advantages of education, no influence to push forward his fortunes or wealth to command situation, he yet passed through such a career, was so rapid in growth and development, that he was ripe in honors when the bullet of the Indian warrior pierced his heart.

Advancement so swift, a career so brilliant that his deeds have become household words in the land, indicate the possession of more than ordinary qualities in the subject of this memoir. Leaving, at barely his majority, the military academy where his original address and marked demeanor had placed him, without the usual influence which people's our national training schools, he was thrust at once into a command at the outbreak of the war.

Having barely reached a man's estate, unused to the world, unacquainted with men, untrained in active warfare, he was suddenly to be called upon for the exhibition of the qualities which lead and govern armies. The sword of the cadet was to be unsheathed by youthful hands amidst the din of a civil strife, unexampled in history for the fierceness of its character and for the importance of its results.

Out of this trial, our hero was to emerge covered with the glory of a veteran, decorated, after five years of service at the age of twenty-six with the stars of a Major-General, and renowned from one end of the country to the other - throughout the world indeed - as an original and brilliant fighter, a bold and dashing soldier, a successful commander.

PERSONAL RECOLLECTIONS OF LAWRENCE BARRETT

The greater part of his career, so sadly terminated, was passed where the fight raged hottest, where death and carnage reigned supreme; and finally, at the age of thirty-seven, an age when the careers of most men are beginning, he was snatched away, covered with glory, the mourned darling of a nation. We must look into the records of heroic ages for a parallel to this career, through which our biographer has so lovingly followed him.

The incidents of that extraordinary military history can be followed and proven in the annals of the war. Dates and official records will amply note and verify the conspicuous part borne by General Custer. His place among the heroes of our country will be gratefully allowed so long as patriotism endures; his chivalrous deeds will be immortalized by bard, and perpetuated by historian. The chapter of great warriors will hereafter be incomplete, which does not record the exploits of Custer and his gallant riders, from Bull Run to the Appomattox.

It is the misfortune of men in high public station that the brilliancy of their professional careers obscures the private character of the individual. They are seen through a misty veil and by their position shut out from the close observation of their fellows. It was my happiness to have known intimately, and to have enjoyed for many years the society of General Custer, and it may therefore be allowed me to record my impression of him as divested of the pomp of war, and mingling in the pursuits of social life.

Abler hands may collect and engross the various incidents of this heroic life, compiling a suitable biography for his countrymen's instruction, and these reminiscences should be accepted simply as a tribute of affection to a dearly beloved friend. No one had followed General Custer's military career with more enthusiasm than the writer. The successive battles in which he bore so conspicuous and gallant a part were studied with ardor by his then unknown friend, who was thus prepared, should the moment ever arrive, to meet with interest and embrace with affection the hero whose deeds had already won ardent admiration.

The stirring incidents of the war had developed two men whose exploits had made them objects of the writer's sincere attachment.

FREDERICK WHITTAKER

Both young, their rapidity of promotion alike extraordinary and acquired by absolute merit, it was my happiness to claim their friendship and at last bring them together. In the war they had fought side by side, each unacquainted with the other, except in their achievements. At my fireside, they came together in friendly meeting and cemented in private the attachment which sympathy of character always creates. One now lies ill among the Berkshire hills, his youthful form scarred with wounds received in his country's service; the other, dead at thirty-seven, sleeps where no stone may mark his resting place, beneath the blood-stained sod of the cold and cheerless plains.

In the fall of 1866, while fulfilling an engagement at St. Louis, I met the General for the first time, and under such peculiar circumstances that they may bear narration. The play was over, the curtain fallen, and while still preparing to return to my hotel after my night's entertainment, a knock was heard at my dressing room door. Obedient to the answering summons entered a tall, fair haired, blue eyed, smiling gentleman, clad in military undress. Apologizing for the intrusion, he gave his name as General Custer. No such introduction was necessary.

By those well known features, I recognized at once the young cavalry leader. He had been sent to bring me to the hotel where he was temporarily residing while en route to his command at Fort Leavenworth. I was to go with him to meet Mrs. Custer and other members of his party. Excuses were set aside. He pleaded "orders" which must be obeyed, and refusal was impossible. A happy hour in his society was passed; and thus began an acquaintance, ripening within the next ten years into the most genuine friendship, in which I learned to esteem the qualities of the man as sincerely as I bad admired the achievements of the soldier.

At that early time, General Custer had not outgrown the habits of the camp. He still wore the long hair which is so familiar in his early pictures, his face was bronzed and sun-burned by outdoor exposure, his bearing a mixture of the student and the soldier. No pen portrait of General Custer would be complete which did not give the simple, boyish side of his character, seemingly more marked from the daring, adventurous spirit which the war had made us familiar with.

St. Louis circa 1862-1872. View of Fourth Street looking north from Market Street.

His voice was earnest, soft, tender and appealing, with a quickness of the utterance which became at times choked by the rapid flow of ideas, arid a nervous hesitancy of speech, betraying intensity of thought. There was a searching expression of the eye which riveted the speaker as if each word was being measured mercilessly by the listener. Peculiarly nervous, he yet seemed able to control himself at will. His fond of humor was betrayed by a chuckle of a laugh, such as those who have ever known Artemus Ward will remember - a laugh which became infectious and seemed to gurgle up from the depths of the full and joyous heart of the sunny, affectionate Custer.

In the years which passed on following our first meeting, duty separated, vacations reunited us. Custer's appointment to duty in Kentucky afforded me several weeks of his society, during which we were rarely apart. At that time, he ran over his remembrances of the war to me, speaking of himself with modesty, of others with enthusiasm, until it became a delight to listen. Thus I had the description of the winter campaign against the Indians on the Washita before it was in print, told in his graphic, fervent style, and acted over until it seemed as if I were a participant in the strife.

At this time, he began those sketches in the *Galaxy* which were at once received with favor. Again separated, we were next to meet during the tour of the Grand Duke Alexis, in whose suite he had been placed by the government. Here, his truly American characteristics gained him a friend, whose quick eye discerned the depths of that genuine nature and valued it. The friendship which arose between the Russian Grand Duke and General Custer from their association on this tour was very honorable to both.

The polished courtier discerned in the young Democrat those sterling qualities of manhood which maintained their individuality in the midst of ceremonies and flatteries, and the correspondence which passed between them upon the return of the Grand Duke to Russia was highly gratifying to Custer. Enjoying his vacation as keenly as a school boy, General Custer was always apparently "awaiting orders," and when they came, his whole manner changed; he seemed to put on the soldier with the uniform.

He often said that his duties on the plains were the happiest events of his life - not that he loved war for war's sake, but that he loved to feel that he was on duty. The freedom of the plains, the constant companionship of his idolized wife - now sitting in the shadow of her last and greatest bereavement - his horses and his gun his regiment and its beloved officers, amply replaced the allurements of civil life.

It was impossible for Custer to appear otherwise than himself. He had none of that affectation of manner or bearing which arises from egotism or timidity. Reticent among strangers, even to a fault, his enemies, if he had any, must have recognized his perfect integrity of character. Indeed, this reticence often caused him to be misunderstood, and he himself frequently complained that he could not be all things to all men.

It was only in the companionship of his intimates and close friends that the real joyousness of his nature shone forth. Then he was all confidence, his eye would brighten, his face light up and his whole heart seemed to expand. He had something of the Frenchman in his gayety, much of the German in a certain tenacity of purpose. Utterly fearless of danger, he seemed in private to become as gentle as a woman.

Some have thought that Custer's courage was of the bulldog kind; that he knew no danger and feared none. Nothing can be further from the truth. He said to the writer that the first few battles he was in, he was almost overcome with fear; he also intimates this very clearly in his War Memoirs. His courage was purely a triumph of mind over physical fear. Toward the close of the war, he became convinced that he would not be killed. The truth doubtless is that he was fully conscious that he possessed the ability to rise in his profession, and he had determined to do so at all hazard.

He chose the post of danger at the head of his column simply because he was aware that it was the place to obtain success. He knew that thus, and thus only, he could inspire his men with confidence, and make of each a hero. All this was the result of a deliberate plan. He had counted the cost of success and was fully prepared to pay it. He wanted honor and distinction among his fellow men, or death on the field. He put this spirit into his division by his example, and they were invincible.[*] In the society of ladies, with whom his deeds had made him a favorite, he manifested none of the gallantries which arise from vanity.

When ordered to Fort Lincoln, General Custer was lost to me for several months, but our correspondence was constant. He was eager that I should visit him, and it was only by a pressure of professional duties at the time that I was denied the pleasure of being his companion upon the first expedition to the Black Hills. The succeeding fall, he made his vacation with me, and for two happy weeks we were constantly together. This was in Chicago. If an engagement to dinner took him away, he would hasten at its conclusion to my dressing room at the theatre; and thence, arm-in-arm, we would return home together.

Thus I have seen him in the midst of social temptations sufficient to overcome ordinary men, maintain the strict sobriety of his habits. He never touched wine, nor used tobacco in any form, and I never

---

[*] Remarks by another intimate friend of General Custer.

heard a profane word from his lips. His obstinate valor as a soldier made him courteous and forgiving to a defeated enemy, and he became a Democrat in his opinions, regarding the manner in which the South should be treated after the close of the rebellion. This made him unpopular at headquarters, and perhaps influenced his promotion and hindered his career.

Century Club. The Century Club resulted from the merger of two earlier private clubs for men "of similar social standing or shared interests." Its original membership primarily consisted of merchants, businessmen, lawyers and doctors.

Surrounded He loved his profession and was jealous of its fame, tenacious of the honor of his cloth, and intolerant of the abuses which the army suffered by that pernicious system wherein politics were the means by which many unworthy men entered the service. He had that love of military display which distinguishes the Frenchman, and his uniform was the badge of his glory. A fondness for theatrical representations he shared in common with the members of his profession, and a more enthusiastic auditor I never saw.

The last winter of Custer's life now approaches. He had obtained leave of absence for two months, intending to spend his time in New

PERSONAL RECOLLECTIONS OF LAWRENCE BARRETT

York; and that he might leave behind him. A record of his career, and also that he might eke out his slender income, his sketches in the *Galaxy* were resumed. It was during this vacation, extended to five months in all, that the happiest hours of my association with him were passed.

Being myself for the winter in New York, we made all our engagements mutual, going into company together, meeting at my own fireside always on Sundays; and each evening during the run of *"Julius Caesar,"* the place of honor in my dressing room at Booth's was filled by my dear friend. Those were indeed happy hours. I recall especially one passed at the Century Club, where he was the recipient of great attentions. How bright and joyous he was, and how eager that his friend should know and enjoy the friendship of those whom he himself esteemed.

by the followers of literature, science and art, and their cultured patrons, the young soldier, whose whole life and education were of the camp, attracted the attention and won the respect of all who met him. With that rare facility given but to few, he drew from the artist and the historian the best fruits of their labors and as warmly listened as he could warmly speak. His love for art was no affected dilettanteism. Appreciating the glories of nature with an enthusiast's soul, he learned to trace her likeness in the works of her copyists.

The studio of Bierstadt was a happy resting place for him. Here, while the great painter labored, the young soldier would lovingly follow the master hand, identifying the exactness of the picture by his own knowledge of the scenery or groupings so vividly reproduced. It has been said that "military experience so exhausts the body by daily and for the most part useless exercises, that it renders it difficult to cultivate one's mind," but this was not true of General Custer. Not having received in his youth the advantages of a college education, he betrayed the keenest desire for knowledge and cultivation.

General Custer was a great reader, and his taste ran almost entirely in the line of the best literature. His pleasure seemed to be to constantly add to his stock of information. He spent a large share of his time during the winter seasons in reading such works as *"Napier's Peninsular War,"* *"Napoleon's Campaigns,"* and works of this class which would perfect him in his profession. Often he would spend a whole day and a large part of the night over a few pages of these works; having a large map before him, he was determined to fully understand each movement and campaign made by these great masters of the art of war.

Perfection in his chosen profession seemed to be the mainspring of all his actions. He was ready to make any and all sacrifices which would contribute to this end. He seemed thoroughly to have adopted the motto that "nothing is done while anything remains to be accomplished." His powers of mental work were fully equal to his physical endurance; six hours of sleep seemed to be all he required, and his great mental activity rendered it almost impossible for him to be idle an hour.

A distinguished gentleman, whose Friday evenings at his home on Fifth Avenue were regarded as happy privileges for the best minds of the metropolis, extended to the General hospitality and advantages which were eagerly accepted and as earnestly enjoyed. Here, where the flame of thought was of the loftiest character, Custer would sit, an attentive and admiring listener, drinking from the rich fountain of instruction.

After an evening thus passed, and upon emerging into the silent avenue, the impressions of the recent conversation still upon us, excited by the interchange of friendly converse, he would take my arm, and against my entreaty become my escort home, alleging as a reason his want of exercise, although I knew that in his loving care he feared some danger might befall his friend, and thus went far out of his way to see me safely housed.

Such acts as these, trivial though they seem in narration, are those which make that fearful day in June so terrible to me, making it seem impossible that I am never again to clasp that hand so true and tried, never again to look into that face so dearly loved.

The winter passed only too quickly. His original leave of two months had been granted by his immediate superior, General Terry, his friend as well as commander, and his extended leave came from General Sheridan, no less friendly. But another extension, earned by him surely through his months of labor at Fort Lincoln, was refused as soon as asked, and he was at once ordered to rejoin his regiment by General Belknap, then Secretary of War. For some unexplained reason, General Custer believed the secretary to be his enemy, and dreaded the final appeal for that extension of leave which his affairs so much demanded.

When refusal came, although it disappointed him, it did not the less find him prepared for obedience to orders. His literary work for the *Galaxy* had been undertaken, as has been stated, to eke out his income and more generously support the expenses of his family, and he had formed another plan by which he hoped to still more liberally provide for the future of all those dependent upon him.

The agent of the Literary Bureau, Mr. Redpath of Boston, having made him a liberal offer to deliver a number of lectures during the next winter; he was, at the moment the Secretary's orders came, perfecting his plans to that end. After the summer's campaign, he was again to visit New York, his lecture in the meantime to be written, and we were to rehearse his appearance before the public passed judgment upon him. This project was left incomplete as to details, but he looked forward to its accomplishment as a happy means of increasing his income and meeting face to face his admirers, the public.

Custer went one March day upon his journey. No forebodings of evil embittered the parting; we were to meet again. He had not yet fallen under the public accusation which was afterwards hurled upon him. Although he left so many pleasant associations and gave up so many personal enjoyments, he was going to his duty, and that sufficed. A winter trip across the Dakota plains had no terrors for him, nor for her who never left his side while it was her privilege to remain there.

After many hardships, they at last reached Fort Lincoln, and then began his preparations for the fatal expedition. Loving friends, unacquainted with the details of warfare and jealous only of his reputation will always, perhaps unjustly, believe that had all gone forward as it began, under his own personal control, the disaster and annihilation which followed would never have occurred. No reflection upon the capacity of General Custer's superiors is here intended, but it may be justly claimed that the complications which followed as the result of the appearance before the investigating committee at Washington arose, in a great measure, from the disorders of a change of command almost in the enemy's front; that suspicion on the one side, and crippled powers, laboring under ungenerous and undeserved imputations upon the other, created a confusion which could not but be detrimental.

The belief will always prevail among the friends of General Custer that familiarity with the Indian mode of warfare, a certain subtlety in his preparations for attack or resistance, and the dash which has never been denied him, well fitted him to organize and conduct such a campaign. He who had so often challenged the bravest of the red warriors and wrung from them the title of the "Big Yellow Chief," was fully able not only to lead his own "gallant Seventh," but also to organize the campaign and overlook the plan. This was denied him. At the supreme moment of his fortunes, he was summoned to Washington.

The appearance of General Custer before the Investigating Committee at Washington and the effect of his testimony upon the public mind are already familiar to the reader. The fact came upon his most intimate friends unannounced, and the unfavorable comments of the party press upon his evidence and his character caused the greatest surprise to those who knew him best.

The most reserved and reticent of men had suddenly become politically conspicuous, and calumny was linked with that hitherto spotless name. The political temper of the time had undoubtedly much to do with the effect produced by his testimony. The strife of party, and the bitterness with which men of opposite opinions assailed each other; the influence upon the approaching election of the investigation then going forward; the reputation for truth and candor never denied to General Custer; combined to make the attacks upon him unusually severe.

He had never obtruded his political sentiments, but they were known to his friends and were never disowned. He could not have sought the unenviable position in which he found himself; he had endeavored by every honorable means to escape from it, but in vain.

PERSONAL RECOLLECTIONS OF LAWRENCE BARRETT

The effect upon his nature of the abuse suddenly heaped upon him may be measured by the desire he had always evinced to escape public observation, except in the line of his duty; and this was, undoubtedly, one of the saddest eras of his life.

The esteem of his countrymen, earned by years of hard service and dearly prized, seemed in an instant to be taken from him. His report upon the evils of the post trading system had been forwarded to the head of his department long before; his acquaintance with those evils was known to many; not to have answered frankly the questions of the committee would have exposed him to self-contempt.

How easily could he have trimmed his sail to the popular breeze and floated into the smooth waters of political favor. The promotion which his valor had earned; which was due to his merit; which had been bestowed upon his inferiors; lay within his grasp; but the sacrifice was one from which his proud soul revolted. The perfect integrity of his character should never be sullied, to purchase that preferment which had been denied to his public services, and which was in every way due him.

He could honestly exclaim, "It is better to be right than to hold the most exalted rank." That he was wounded, none who knew him can doubt. In the midst of those exposures which tarnished the reputation of so many brother officers, he had happily escaped. At his post upon the distant frontier, occupied with the duties which he loved, surrounded by a small band who regarded their young commander with veneration, he might well feel happy in his escape from that political whirlpool which engulfed so many of his friends, and which swallowed up reputations gained in hard-fought fields.

Now, against his will, called peremptorily from the organization of his command, he found himself helplessly drawn into the current, publicly condemned for speaking that which he knew to be true, commented upon by enemies in the coarsest terms, the target of political rancor. The depth of his humiliation was reached when, upon leaving the capital, he waited for hours at the door of the President, and was at last turned away with studied contempt.

The effect of these slights upon his proud and sensitive heart may be imagined. Upheld as he was by the conscience which whispered that he had done his duty, he must still have suffered much in concealing his sorrow from the world; though he scorned to complain, as he would have scorned to bend before the calumny of his enemies.

Our last meeting, which took place at the close of his first visit to Washington, was yet full of happiness. Rallied upon his political relations, he sunnily threw aside his chagrin, and seemed indifferent to all but the approaching separation, anxious only that our plan for the next winter should not fail. No premonition of danger clouded our parting. The thought that he was going into action, into certain peril, did not make me fearful. He was so associated with success, had escaped from so many dangers, his long future career was so hopeful, that he seemed invincible. He predicted a severe campaign, but was not doubtful of the result. His plans were well laid, his command efficient; and he joyfully obeyed the summons to return to his duty, happy to escape from the scene where truth was repaid with calumny.

The delay in Chicago; the deprivation of command which overtook him there by order of the President; all these anxious days passed while awaiting the orders of his superiors, were undeserved cruelties. The influences which at length ended his suspense, and gave him a subordinate place in the expedition planned by himself, have been explained elsewhere. The disgrace of being supplanted by an inferior in rank or an envious rival was averted, and thus much of the bitterness of his position softened.

If he could have chosen his successor, he could not have been better pleased than with the appointment of General Terry. Under him, he declared he would go with the command, if obliged to serve as a common soldier. By the tender consideration and courtesy of that gallant officer, Custer was permitted to recover that confidence in himself of which his unmerited trials must have well nigh robbed him. With the delicacy of a gentleman, the appreciation of a kindred soul, Terry restored him to the command which was his due, in fact if not in appearance, and brought to his aid the advice and experience of the young cavalier whose counsel would be invaluable, whose valor and foresight would be a support, and to whose sword the service would so soon be indebted for its defense.

Those who knew General Custer best can well understand how he valued such a privilege. To have been left behind would have been worse than death, when his gallant Seventh and so many of his old comrades were in the field. As he rode out of Fort Lincoln for the last time, he was as full of glee as a child; his duty lay before him, his glory, of which no enemy could rob him.

That the wishes of the nation, which followed that gallant band and looked hopefully forward to its movements as a final solution of the Indian question, dwelt with the greatest confidence upon the frontier experience of General Custer, will scarcely be denied. In every campaign, he had been victorious, and the wiles and stratagems of the foe were familiar to him. Calumny and envy must be silent before the intrepid heroism of that immortal band as they rode into the jaws of death, where perished not only the noble Custer and his adoring followers, but also the hope of a nation, the shield of a devoted family.

Glancing back over these pages, how poor and unworthy seems the picture I would paint. Compared with the image engraved upon the heart, this transcript is cold and artificial. When the smoke of the battle has passed away, when envy and cowardice have been consigned to their merited oblivion, some truer likeness shall be made of him who was the bravest of the brave.

His career may be thus briefly given; He was born in obscurity; he rose to eminence; denied social advantages in his youth, his untiring industry supplied them; the obstacles to his advancement became the stepping stones to his fortunes, free to choose for good or evil, he chose rightly; truth was his striking characteristic; he was fitted to command, for he had learned to obey; his acts found their severest critic in his own breast; he was a good son, a good brother, a good and affectionate husband, a Christian soldier, a steadfast friend.

Entering the army, a cadet in early youth, he became a general while still on the threshold of manhood; with ability undenied, with valor proved on many a hard fought field, he acquired the affection of the nation; and he died in action at the age of thirty-seven; died as he would have wished to die; no lingering disease preying upon that iron frame. At the head of his command, the messenger of death awaited him; from the field of battle where he had so often directed the storm, his gallant spirit took its flight.

Cut off from aid; abandoned in the midst of incredible odds; waving aloft the sabre which had won him victory so often; the pride and glory of his comrades, the noble Custer fell; bequeathing to the nation his sword; to his comrades an example; to his friends a memory; and to his beloved one a hero's name.

THE END

ILLUSTRATION CREDITS

COVER: Ruins of Richmond, Library of Congress; Richmond State Capital Building, Travel Bug/Shutterstock

EARLY LIFE: Custer's birthplace, Ohio Historical Society; Nevin Custer, Little Bighorn Battlefield National Monument/National Park Service; Boyd's Seminary, Dr. James DeVries Collection, Monroe County Historical Museum Archives, Monroe, Michigan; Hopedale Normal School, Puskarich Public Library; John Bingham, Library of Congress

PLEBE CUSTER: West Point South Wharf, Library of Congress; West Point Barracks, National Archives; West Point Mess Hall, National Archives; Benny Havens, Courtesy of Highland Falks Town Hall; West Point Chapel, National Archives; General Hazen, National Park Service; General Reynolds death spot, Library of Congress; Libbie Custer, Little Bighorn Battlefield National Monument

LIEUTENANT CUSTER, SECOND CAVALRY: Ebbitt House, Washington Old and New, 1914; James P. Parker, John Sickles Collection; General Winfield Scott and staff, National Archives; Major Innes Palmer, Library of Congress; Washington DC Livery, Library of Congress; Long Bridge, Library of Congress; Major James Wadsworth, Library of Congress

THE BATTLE OF BULL RUN: Union Mills, VA, Library of Congress; Blackburn's Ford, National Archives; Sudley Springs, Library of Congress; Warrenton Pike, Library of Congress; Bull Run Stone Bridge, Library of Congress; Centreville, New York Historical Society

ORGANIZING AN ARMY: Cub Run, Library of Congress; General McClellan and staff, Library of Congress; General Philip Kearny, Library of Congress; Bacon Family, Monroe County Library Digital Collection; Bacon House, State Historical Society of North Dakota;

ILLUSTRATION CREDITS

Monroe, Dr. James DeVries Collection, Monroe County Historical Museum Archives, Monroe, Michigan

THE PENINSULAR CAMPAIGN: Fairfax Court House, Library of Congress; Catlett's Station, Library of Congress; Federal Battery at Cedar Run, Library of Congress; Fort Monroe Sally port, Library of Congress; Bridge over Chickahominy River, Library of Congress; Confederate fortifications at the Siege of Yorktown, Library of Congress

WINNING THE BARS: Federal gunboat Mendota, Library of Congress; Custer, Library of Congress; Williamsburg, Library of Congress; Grant's headquarters at Coal Harbor, Library of Congress; Army of the Potomac, Library of Congress

FROM RICHMOND TO MALVERN HILL: Supplies at James River Landing, National Archives; Ruins of Gaines Mill, Library of Congress; Globe Tavern at Malvern Hill, Library of Congress

McCLELLAN'S REMOVAL: Harper's Ferry, Maryland Heights, National Archives; Custer, 1864, Dr. James DeVries Collection, Monroe County Historical Museum Archives, Monroe, Michigan; Baltimore B & O Railroad Station, Courtesy of Jennifer A. Ferretti, former Curator of photographs, MDHS; Antietam, Library of Congress; Monroe, Dr. James DeVries Collection, Monroe County Historical Museum Archives, Monroe, Michigan; Fredericksburg, Library of Congress

THE CAVALRY CORPS: Army of Potomac winter camp, National Archives; Army camp on James River, National Archives; Rappahannock Bridge, New York Historical Society; Aquia Creek Landing, Library of Congress

WINNING HIS STAR: Custer and soldiers, Library of Congress; Confederate prisoners at Aldie, Library of Congress; George Yates, Monroe County Historical Museum; Custer, Library of Congress

THE GETTYSBURG CAMPAIGN: Troops in Gettysburg, Library of Congress; Hanover Junction, Library of Congress; Custer and Pleasonton, Library of Congress; Hunterstown, as it appears on 50th Anniversary, 1913 in "The Story of the Battle of Gettysburg;" General Meade, National Archives; Major Peter Webber, Personal

FREDERICK WHITTAKER Recollections of a Cavalryman with Custer's Michigan Cavalry Brigade, J.H. Kidd, 1908; Colonel Russell Alger, Personal Recollections of a Cavalryman with Custer's Michigan Cavalry Brigade, J.H. Kidd, 1908; Colonel Charles Town, Personal Recollections of a Cavalryman with Custer's Michigan Cavalry Brigade, J.H. Kidd, 1908; Pennington Battery, Library of Congress; Confederate dead at Gettysburg, Library of Congress; Wade Hampton, Library of Congress

AFTER GETTYSBURG: Bridge on the Boonsboro Pike, Library of Congress; General Kilpatrick, Library of Congress; Confederate prisoners at Fisher Hill, Library of Congress

TO THE RAPIDAN AND BACK: Orange and Alexandria Railroad Crossing, Library of Congress; Train at Culpepper, Library of Congress; Culpepper, Library of Congress; Army of the Potomac infantry at Brandy Station, Library of Congress; Courtesy of Leon Reed; Major Kidd, Personal Recollections of a Cavalryman with Custer's Michigan Cavalry Brigade, J.H. Kidd, 1908; Brandy Station, Library of Congress; Monroe, Presbyterian Church, Courtesy of Danielle Brooks; Reverend William Boyd, Dr. James DeVries Collection, Monroe County Historical Museum Archives, Monroe, Michigan; Custer wedding photo, Library of Congress

THE WILDERNESS AND THE VALLEY: Custer and officers, Smithsonian; Confederate dead at Spottsylvania, Library of Congress; Wrecked railroad, National Archives; Whitehouse Landing, Library of Congress; Cold Harbor, Library of Congress

WINCHESTER: Front Royal, National Archives; Opequan Creek Crossing, DeGolyer Library, Southern Methodist University; Colonel Charles Lowell, Personal Recollections of a Cavalryman with Custer's Michigan Cavalry Brigade, J.H. Kidd, 1908; Sheridan, National Archives

WOODSTOCK RACES: General Wesley Merritt, Library of Congress; Fisher's Hill, DeGolyer Library, Southern Methodist University; General Thomas Rosser, The Photography History of the Civil War, 1911

CEDAR CREEK: Cedar Creek Battlefield, DeGolyer Library, Southern Methodist University, Cedar Creek looking south toward Massanuttin Mountain, DeGolyer Library, Southern Methodist

ILLUSTRATION CREDITS

University

THE LAST RAID: Wrecked train near Richmond, Library of Congress; Kline's Mill, published by R.A. Kline prior to 1923; Burned railroad cars near Richmond, Library of Congress; Captain Alexander Pennington, Library of Congress

FIVE FORKS: Robert E. Lee, National Archives; Dinwiddie Court House from National Museum of American History published in 1865; Ruins of bridge at White Oak Swamp, National Archives

APPOMATTOX: Truce flag, Smithsonian; Appomattox Station, DeGolyer Library, Southern Methodist University; Appomattox Court House, National Park Service

THE GREAT PARADE: Ruins of Richmond, Library of Congress; Grand Review, Library of Congress; Grand Review president's stand, National Archives; Grand Review cavalry, Library of Congress; Grand Review, Library of Congress

THE VOLUNTEERS IN TEXAS: Riverboat Sultana, Library of Congress; Steamboat landing, New Orleans, New Orleans Public Library; Austin, Austin History Center, Austin Public Library

THE REGULAR ARMY: Custer and Libbie, Kansas Historical Society

THE SEVENTH CAVALRY: Major Alfred Gibbs, Library of Congress; Monroe, Dr. James DeVries Collection, Monroe County Historical Museum Archives, Monroe, Michigan; Swinging around the circle tour, Library of Congress; Fort Riley Custer House, Courtesy of John Cirignani; Boot Hill Cemetery, Kansas Historical Society

THE HANCOCK EXPEDITION: General Winfield Scott Hancock, Library of Congress; Fort Larned, Courtesy of John Cirignani; White Horse, University Of Oklahoma Library; Sioux war party, Denver Public Library; Hancock's burning of the village, published in Harper's Weekly, 1867; Satanta, Kansas Historical Society

THE FIRST SCOUT: Fort McPherson, National Archives; Fort Wallace, Fort Wallace Museum; Indians, from The Vanishing Race, Joseph K. Dixon, 1914; Pawnee Killer, Smithsonian

THE WAGON TRAIN: William Comstock, Kansas Historical Society; Indians, Denver Public Library; Wagon Train attack, Kansas

FREDERICK WHITTAKER

Historical Society

THE KIDDER MASSACRE: Telegraph Station, Edmund Historical Society Museum; Kidder Massacre, published in Harper's Weekly, 1867

THE COURT MARTIAL: Fort Harker, Kansas Historical Society; Overland Express stage station, Kansas Historical Society; Commanding Officer's Quarters, Fort Harker, Courtesy of John Cirignani; Sheridan's suites, Fort Leavenworth, Courtesy of John Cirignani

THE WINTER CAMPAIGN: General Sully, State Historical Society of North Dakota; Custer House, Fort Dodge, Courtesy of John Cirignani; California Joe, National Park Service; Camp Supply by William S. Soule, 1836-1908

BATTLE OF THE WASHITA: Major Joel Elliott, National Park Service; Osage scouts, Oklahoma Historical Society; Cheyenne village on Washita, Kansas Historical Society; Washita Battlefield, Courtesy of John Cirignani; Raphael Romero, Fort Supply Historic Site; Colonel Albert Barnitz, National Park Service; Black Kettle, Oklahoma Historical Society; Wild Cat, National Anthropological Archives

CLOSING OPERATIONS: Yellow Bear, Kansas Historical Society; Little Robe, National Park Service; Cheyenne prisoners, Oklahoma Historical Society

LOUISVILLE TO THE YELLOWSTONE: Fort Leavenworth, Kansas Historical Society; Custer Home, Elizabethtown, taken 07/16/2011by Nyttend and release to public domain vie Wikipedia; Custer and Grand Duke Alexis, Harvard College Library; Custer and Grand Duke portrait "The Great Royal Buffalo Hunt" by Louis Maurer, 1895; Fort Rice, State Historical Society of North Dakota; Yellowstone Expedition, National Archives; Custer and Bloody Knife, Library of Congress; Sitting Bull, State Historical Society of North Dakota; Pompey's Pillar, MHS Photograph Archives, Helena

THE BLACK HILLS: Bear Butte, Courtesy of John Cirignani; Black Hills Expo, National Archives; Black Hills Expo Supply train, Denver Public Library; Seventh Cavalry, Black Hills Expo, DeGolyer Library, Southern Methodist University

RAIN-IN-THE-FACE: Indian scouts at Fort Rice, State Historical

ILLUSTRATION CREDITS

Society of North Dakota; Tom Custer, Library of Congress; Standing Rock Agency, State Historical Society of North Dakota; Rain-in-the-Face, Montana State University Library; Fort Lincoln guard house, Courtesy of Scott Nelson

SITTING BULL: Sitting Bull, Little Bighorn Battlefield National Monument

CUSTER AND GRANT: William Belknap, Library of Congress

THE GREAT EXPEDITION: General John Gibbon, Library of Congress; Far West, State Historical Society of North Dakota

THE LAST BATTLE: General Terry, National Archives; Captain Benteen, National Archives; Reno's charge; Courtesy of John Cirignani; Reno's retreat, Courtesy of John Cirignani; Myles Keogh, Library of Congress; Keogh fight, Courtesy of John Cirignani; Curly, National Anthropological Archives; Medicine Tail, Courtesy of John Cirignani; Boston Custer, Library of Congress

CUSTER, THE SOLDIER: Custer, Personal Recollections of a Cavalryman with Custer's Michigan Cavalry Brigade, J.H. Kidd, 1908

CUSTER, THE INDIAN FIGHTER: Custer, National Archives

CUSTER, THE MAN: Custer in play, Custer Battlefield Museum; St. Louis, www.collections.mohistory.org; Century Club, New York Public Library; Custer and Libbie, Kansas Historical Society

A preview into *History in Words and Pictures Series,*

Book Seven

LIFE AND ADVENTURES OF JESSE AND FRANK JAMES

The Noted Western Outlaws

By

Honorable J.A. Dacus, PH. D.

CHAPTER 1 – THE JAMES FAMILY

THE Reverend Robert James, the father of Frank and Jesse, was a native of Kentucky. His parents were quiet, respectable people, belonging to the middle class of society. Their desire was to raise up their children in the nurture and admonition of the Lord. Being themselves persons of intelligence and culture, far above the average of their neighbors in those days, the parents of Reverend Robert James resolved to give him as good an education as the facilities accessible to them would permit. Accordingly, Robert was early placed in a neighboring school, and made such progress as to gladden the hearts of his parents and call forth auguries of future distinction from the friends and neighbors of the family.

Robert James was a moral, studious youth, much given to reflection on subjects of a religious character. Before he had attained his eighteenth year, he had made an open profession of faith in the Christian religion, and united himself with a Baptist church, of which his parents were members. After passing through the various grades of an academic course, young James entered as a student of Georgetown College, Kentucky. Resolving to follow the profession of a minister, he commenced the study of Theology, was licensed to preach, and began his ministry in his twentieth year. Even then, he was regarded as a youth of decided culture and more than ordinary ability.

While yet a young man, Reverend Mr. James decided to remove to the then new State of Missouri. He settled on a farm in Clay County and commenced in earnest the onerous duties of a pioneer preacher. His labors were not unrewarded. He soon had the satisfaction of garnering the harvest of his sowing.

A congregation was gathered and a church organized in Clay County, called New Hope, which is still in existence. For some years, the Reverend Mr. James ministered to the people who had been gathered by his exertions, with great acceptance. Nor were his labors confined to the spiritual welfare of the people of New Hope. He visited many distant churches and preached with great acceptance in many places.

Old citizens of Clay County still entertain pleasant recollections of the earnest, God-fearing pastor, who went about only to do good by cheering the despondent, consoling the sorrowful, assisting the needy, upholding the weak, confirming the hesitating, and pointing the way of salvation to the penitent. Everywhere in that region of country, he was held in the very highest esteem. So the years of his early manhood passed away while he was engaged in the commendable effort to better the condition, by purifying the moral nature of his friends and neighbors.

In 1850, following in the footsteps of hundreds of others, Reverend Robert James bade adieu to his family, friends and neighbors and set out for the golden land of California on a prospecting tour. We do not know what motives actuated him in making this move, nor is it pertinent to this relation. He went away, and was destined to return no more.

Not long after his arrival in California, whither he had been preceded by a brother, Reverend Mr. James was stricken by a mortal disease which terminated his life in a short time. Far away from home, where the tall sequoias rear their lofty branches above the plain, on a gentle slope which catches the last beams of the setting sun, they laid the minister to rest in a soil unhallowed by the dust of kinsmen, in a grave unbedewed by the tears of loved ones left behind.

When yet a young man, Reverend Mr. James was united in marriage to Miss Zerelda Cole, a native of Scott County, Kentucky. Mrs. James is a lady of great determination of mind, and a masculine force of character. Those who knew the couple in the old days seem to think that the minister and his wife were an ill-assorted pair. He was gentle and amiable while on the contrary, his wife was strong in passion and of a very bitter, unrelenting temper -- traits of character prominently developed in her sons, Frank and Jesse.

It is said that the home life of the minister was not as smooth as it might have been, had he been united with a companion of a less passionate and exacting temper. With his domestic life however, we have nothing to do, except insofar as the home influences thrown around his children gave direction to their character and tinged their mental disposition. Whatever home cares he might have had, the public has little cause to inquire now. He went down to death with a stainless name long years before his sons entered upon a career of crime, and made their names a terror to those who care to obey the dictates of justice, love and mercy.

Mrs. Zerelda James was left a widow, having the responsible charge of a family of four small children. She was not left unprovided for, as

Mr. James was a prudent, careful man of business, and had already established a comfortable home. With that courage and determination which is so prominently manifested in her character, Mrs. James commenced the battle of life as the head of the family. With all the favoring circumstances, the task assumed by her was not a light one. But she was equal to the performance of any required service.

Continued in *History in Words and Pictures Series,*

Book Seven:

LIFE AND ADVENTURES OF JESSE AND FRANK JAMES
The Noted Western Outlaws
By
Honorable J.A. Dacus, PH. D.

www.ingramcontent.com/pod-product-compliance
Lightning Source LLC
Chambersburg PA
CBHW051122230426
43670CB00007B/645